Y TO TRIESTE
TAKEN BY ITALY

z Falls to Hammering oi
Latins Guns.

ʳARDED FOR FIVE MONTHS

Officers from Front Report That
an Offensive Is More Important
n Gen. Cadorna Has Given Out
wo Railroads to Trieste—Adri
22 Miles Away.

E — Goritz, the key to
tire campaign on the Isonzo
llen before the combined artil
d infantry attacks of the Ital
ccording to news brought to
by staff officers who have just
d from field headquarters.

e officers further report that
ults of the Italian offensive be-
veral days ago on the entire
rom the Alps to the sea are
nore important than has been
ced in the official reports from
Cadorna, chief of staff, which
en given out by the war office

GENERAL CADORNA

Commander of Italians Who
Led the Assault on Goritz.

BRITISH TO O
ᵀᴱ CRUISER

Ship of Prinz Adalbert Type Is
Sent to Bottom.

ACTION OCCURS NEAR LIBAU

FLEET TO SHELL
PORTS OF GREECE

Allies Decide On Drastic Meas-
ures With Constantine.

COMPLETE BLOCKADE PLANNED

Unfavorable Reply by Greek Ruler to
Demands of Kitchener Will Bring
Attack—Troops of Allies Continue
to Land at Saloniki—Destructive
Submarine Identified.

---

ost Money
For
CREAM
Try
ʲOLD BROS. for a
ᵁQUARE DEAL
At
ᴴIGAN PRODUCE CO.
CLARE.

CLARE COURIEʳ
Every Friday Afternoon in th
Block Rear Room, 2nd Floor.
ᴮELL 'PHONE 34.

. CANFIELD, EDITOR.

CLARE COUNTY IN
FINANCIAL STRAITS!

MICHIGAN'S HEARTLAND 1900-1918

MICHIGAN'S HEARTLAND
1900-1918

by

Forrest B. Meek

Published by Edgewood Press
2865 East Rock Road
Clare, MI 48617
1979

12-6-79
c. 75

*This history is dedicated to
Jay Bellinger.*

Table of Contents

Acknowledgements

The first two decades of the Twentieth Century were critical to this country for several reasons, not the least was the advent of the automobile in a rather robust fashion. Our adjustment to it and the continued migration to the Pacific coast states by our mobile citizens influenced our responses to an evolving society.

Clare county was just emerging from its frontier stage in 1900. As those who were its pioneers either died or adjusted to the challenges, we find an entirely new set of circumstances prevailing. Restless adults and surplus youths moved on. In their wake came the farmers and merchants assisted by the emerging service castes of our society. It is this group which dominated the heartland of Michigan during the Great War and their descendants, cut out of the same pattern, continue to dominate today.

As the region's population churned, some wrote letters back to those who remained behind. Their insights and overviews immensely aided this history of the mid-Michigan region. Just as our nation is made up of the several states, so is our state made up of the several geographical communities within it. Contained in a community are the myriad groups which constitute the whole. If one can closely analyze their microcosm during a limited period of time, insights so uncovered can be most beneficial to an analysis of the whole.

Woman Suffrage, Temperance, Prohibition, Roads, Politics, Electricity, Telephones, Agriculture and the Great War itself are the focal points of this era. Clare county in many respects is the ideal region to study American history. Individuals who lived here were leaders at the state and national level, but their influence is more easily traced at the county meetings and in county affairs. How these leaders reacted to those strong forces is really our history. The hundreds of characters who carried out their role on the stage set in Clare county can be duplicated in all of the other communities of this nation without much fundmental change. Whether they lived, acted and died in Clare county isn't what is so important to America's history, but the fact that they responded to the challenges of their times so perfectly in harmony with the national mood and tempo makes it easier to understand the scenario.

It is possible now to begin identifying the broad outlines of local forces which coalesced with other similar forces all across this great nation and crafted our responses to the momentous challenges of the War and the Great Depression which soon followed.

Because large numbers of our citizens and former residents left so many clear trails to follow, it has been possible to collect their impressions and their records for this in-depth history. The following have greatly facilitated this project and their contributions are herewith acknowledged. May this token of my thanks in some way convey my appreciation for their generous assistance. In most instances they went above and beyond the call of duty.

Mr. and Mrs. Melvin Allen
Erma Arnold
R. D. Benchley
J. Stuart Bicknell
James and Doris Bicknell
John Bicknell
Mark Bicknell
Alfred Bransdorfer
Peter Brown
Elvin and Doris Budd
Benjamin Burdo
Bernice Wells Carlson
Fred Cimmerer
Robert and Gayle Cimmerer
Arthur Clute
Irene Clute
Robert Clute
Sue Collom
Christy Cooper
Anna Crawford
Mrs. Alfred Doherty
A. J. Doherty
Donald Dunlop, M.D.
Donald J. Dunlop
Bert Douglas
Homer Douglas
Leon Dull, Jr.
Larry Everts
Robert Folkert
Lou and Monce Gee
Eugene Gillaspy, Ed. D.
Arlene Grove
James Grove
Verne and Muriel Hains
Albert and Lucille Haley
Lester Halstead
Kuno Hammerberg, M.D.
John Hartman
Leonard Hawks
Donald and Nettie Holbrook
Donald E. Holbrook
Mr. and Mrs. Arlie Iutzie
Joseph Johnston
Fred Jones

Jeannette Kleiner
Paul Koch
Willard Koch
A. J. Lacy Estate
Frank La Goe
Franklin Littlefield
Robert McDaniel
Warren McGuire
Dennis McNerney
Kenneth Martz
Holly Maxwell
Charles B. Meek
Jean G. Meek
Nancy L. Meek
Robert B. Meek
Sally K. Meek
Leanne Meyers
Paul Nass
Verl Newman
Thomas Nyquist
Peter Oman
Joanne Otto
Veryl Palmer
Patricia Pears
Merel Perry
Rod Raymond
Patricia Renner
Donald and Virginia Richardson
Emma Sager
Mr. and Mrs. Ronald Schunk
Wava T. Schwartz
Carl Wilson Signor
Carl and Virginia Stephenson
Joan Stoeker
John and Alice Stough
Percy Stough
M. D. Thompson
Margaret Verette
Ruth Wade
Margaret Wherly
Mrs. Edward White
Lyle Williams
Gerald Witbeck
Lorraine Wright

The following businesses and institutions have been of immense help in providing basic information and photographs. Without their generous and friendly assistance, this story could not have been told.

Bentley Historical Library
Buick Motor Division
Burton Historical Library
Chevrolet Motors
Clare County Archives
Clarke Historical Library
Detroit Public Library
Ford Motor Company
Garfield Memorial Library
Greenfield Village and
  Henry Ford Museum

Michigan History Division Archives
Michigan State Library
Mid-Michigan Community College
Oldsmobile Division of General Motors
Pontiac Motor Division
Sloan Auto Museum
Village of Farwell
United States National Archives
  and Records

Public Roads

A footpath connecting one location with another is sufficiently capable of meeting the needs of a pedestrian if he is not in any hurry to breech the distances involved, or if he is only concerned with a close observation of the countryside. Land-lookers in the nineteenth century traveled all over the northern part of Michigan, either on foot or horseback, but they were in no hurry to reach a distant point. A trail or an Indian trace was most adequate for their needs.

As the trees came down, stumps became the most obvious features of the land. They were in great profusion, dotting the landscape. Even after a few years, second growths of deciduous trees failed to screen the observer from their ubiquity. Their numbers and random densities frustrated and challenged the early settlers, sometimes beyond endurance, but the greatest hindrances were reserved for the farmers and the traveler.

THE BASIC ROAD PATTERN

Michigan's survey system demanded that section and township boundaries be run in straight lines and at right angles to each other. Swamps, hills, lakes, rivers and peat bogs were formidable obstacles to roads which generally paralleled these boundaries, but to a property owner, they were taken into consideration, usually when a purchase price for the land was negotiated. Until a sufficient volume of traffic demanded accommodation, these hazards to a roadway could be ignored, and generally were. Later, when pressures began to build for "terri-torial roads" criss-crossing the north, bridges, land-cuts and fills would be designed by pathmasters, who would "remedy" the problem as quickly and cheaply as possible, yet attempting to place roads either on the survey lines or as close to them as feasible.

Most counties in northern Michigan had the bulk of their population scattered along the railroads which were built through the dense forests. Local conditions determined where hamlets and villages would flourish, but a key factor was rail transportation.

As farmers replaced the lumbering crowd, the county's population tended to settle with less regard for railroad locations. Country trading stores would be erected among the concentrated populations, and these in turn would be connected to the larger markets by overland routes which a horse-drawn wagon could negotiate. Lap-pouch mail service would be provided to the country store, and neighbors would come in regularly for their shopping needs, but most importantly, for their mail.

Families living in isolation needed some type of communication with the outside world, and this was provided by newspapers, magazines, catalogs and personal letters. The U.S. Postal Service was placed in the central role of connecting the farmer to his larger world. As long as the rhythm of a nation stayed low-keyed, intermittant contact with it was acceptable to the citizen, but as that rhythm became more frenzied, better and more frequent contact with the outside world was demanded.

This is where we find the farm settlements in northern Michigan at the turn of the

1

century. The quickening tempo of international affairs which was soon to bring on the building of the Panama Canal, wars in Greece and North Africa, and finally, the World War of 1914, was energizing state and local governments. Footpaths, traces and wagon roads were now totally inadequate.

THE PRESSURE FOR RURAL FREE DELIVERY

Rural Free Delivery of mail was introduced into West Virginia on October 1, 1896. Michigan wasn't to reap its benefits until a bit later, but Calhoun County began hosting a twenty-eight mile route on March 13, 1900. Soon other counties began clamoring for this service. Patrons in Ingham County at Mason circulated petitions, as did those in Caro and St. Johns during the spring of 1900. Service out of Clare City didn't begin until February 1, 1904, and then only to those farm patrons who had an approved box located four feet off the ground. Carriers were not required to cross ditches or climb hills, but other than that, almost anything was permitted. For a mere two cents, a farmer was now in one-to-one contact with the big world out there. Of course, not all of Clare County's rural families were serviced by the R. F. D. routes in 1904. Grant, Sheridan and Arthur Townships were favored earliest, and they were covered from Clare.

As the new rural routes were established, the country-store post offices were phased out. Farmers no longer congregated at the store as before, and the storekeepers noticed a sharp reduction in their net revenues. When these stores began closing their doors, staples, clothing and other consumer goods could only be obtained in the larger centers such as Gladwin, Beaverton, Harrison, Farwell, Temple or Clare. As the distances became greater for the farm family, old Dobbin spent longer hours on the trail, and sometimes even longer hours hitched to the rail or in the village feed-barns.

In 1908, all fourth class post offices were placed under Civil Service, and names such as Temple, Farwell, Crooked Lake, Har-

rison, Leota, Hatton, Lake George, Clarence and Clare began replacing the more colorful names which identified the rural communities. Names familiar to the early twentieth century residents began to be used less and less. Floodwood, Berryville, Pleasant Valley, Colonville, Slab Town, Pig-Toe Avenue, Tough Street, Fordsville, Podunk, Brush College, Hardwood, Redner, Pennock, Nester Dam, Maple Grove, North Chicago, Wall Street, Cherry Hill, Brown's Corners, Tonkin, Alwood, Balsley, Riverside, Smith's Cross Roads, Delaney's Corners, Hoodoo Valley, Hermansdale, Summit, Lamont's Hill, Pratt, Herrick, Eagle, Brinton, Mud Lake, Silver Lake, Lochabar, Andersonville and Rinckey all were beginning to fade from the conversations of people. Some of them were the colloquial names for one-room school-house districts; others were the county trading centers, and still others identified a portion of a township which many called home.

In early 1909, the county rural mail carriers were numerous enough to form their own "Clare County Rural Carriers Association". Al Bryan of Crooked Lake was elected president, Will Bowler of Clare claimed the vice-presidency and E. B. Williams of Clare recorded the minutes. Their main interest was of a fraternal nature with some promotion of their job on the side. The momentum of R. F. D. service was sweeping the rural districts around Lake into the twentieth century.

Rural carriers hazarded all kinds of

George Palmer and his 1912 Ford. He delivered RFD mail for over thirty-five years.
Photo from the Palmer Collection

weather conditions and traveled over the most obscure roadways, sometimes in torrential rains which cruelly tortured the horses as they struggled to drag their mail wagons, hub-deep in clay, sand and mud. During the winter months, the horses pulled sleighs, but their flanks were exposed to the biting frigid blasts from out of the north, and their lungs were filled with searing cold. Most men constructed some type of shelter on their vehicles, but many a mail carrier returned to the post office with frost-bitten feet. Nevertheless, the farm families expected their mail to be delivered regularly.

The day when the farmer went for the mail was gone. "It's a thing of the past in our neighborhood — gone with the scythe, and the dinner horn all but forgotten." Everywhere the tin boxes reached out into the roads, nailed perhaps to the telephone pole, stuck on posts, now and then elaborately clamped on a piece of timber which had been cut in the woods, peeled of its bark, and by reason of its shape, curved over so as to make it easy for the postman to reach out of his buggy and open the box. There were various kinds of boxes used, but one made of tin or galvanized iron was popular. Round and oblong objects which were clumsy to open and shut were a common type. Soon ornate affairs appeared on the scene. Boxes which resembled little cottages, complete with a sloping roof, but with a regulation target attached, which indicated out-going mail, were showing up along the routes.

The rural carriers accepted most problems without major complaint, but the common practice of placing two pennies in the mail box was the limit! There was a general fumbling around, shifting the stacked mail within the wagon, then an attempt made to lift the small metal coins off the flat floor of the mail box, which caused many blue words to cascade, especially in frigid weather. The fingers of the postman were rarely

J. W. Glass' General Store in Dover, 1900.
Photo from the Lucille Haley Collection

Mr. and Mrs. Wes Glass

Miles Darling in his red RFD mail sleigh.

This country store in Hamilton Township became obsolete when Henry Ford put the farmers on the road.

warm, and cold fingers are never very nimble. In 1910, regulations came down prohibiting this problem, but before then . . . Oh, life's little vexations!

The mail wagons were all supposed to have been red, but each carrier fixed up his own vehicle, and they varied according to what was available for a cab's construction. If a can of green paint was handy, the mail wagon was green. In 1913, Postmaster General Hitchcock had seen enough green, gray and black paint. He issued orders in no uncertain terms, saying, "Postal regulations call for those mail wagons to be red. I want them red, and I mean Red with a capital 'R'." Gone overnight were the off-color contrivances.

So by 1913, R. F. D. red mail wagons were making their daily rounds in every township in Clare County, but the roads were still a "throwback" to the Dark Ages.

TOWNSHIPS TACKLE THE ROAD PROBLEMS

At a meeting in Harrison in April of 1903, the Clare County Board of Supervisors authorized $2,000 to be used on the county's roads. Close observers of the elected officials questioned this action, claiming it was at variance with the law. They claimed that existing laws and regulations were unclear as to how the money would be spread over the equalized valuation of the several townships and wards. They were equally critical of a plan the Supervisors proposed with

which to apportion those taxes. Should the money be distributed back to the townships according to its equalized valuation, or did the Board have the authority to award the entire sum to one local road project?

If a two thousand dollar road fund was going to bring out such legal opposition, how and under what conditions would it finally be resolved? A. R. Canfield said, "The vote indicated that the people are willing to do everything in reason for the improvement of highways, but it is equally clear that in the near future, some plan must be adopted whereby monies can be provided for a more rapid improvement of the roads than can be had under the township and city system."

CLARE CITY'S EFFORTS

In the meantime, until that great day arrived, the street marshals of the towns and cities and the pathmasters of the townships would have to make do with inadequate resources. So Clare City appointed William Ross, Jacob Mason and Freeman McGary to clay the portion of North McEwan Street from Goodman Hill (Wheaton Street) to the Tobacco River. They called for a road bee in June, and several men brought their teams and wagons and began to improve the sand trail. A few men were assigned the task of hauling dirt from the Vernon Hill section to the low spots on McEwan between the railroad tracks and Fifth Street.

The bridge in Winterfield over the Muskegon River had been constructed of wood several years earlier by John Fleming, but decay had been progressing rapidly, though unnoticed. During the huckleberry season of 1903, William Conn and his wife were returning home with several bushels of the little berries. As the team approached midspan, the bridge swayed and then collapsed, throwing the buggy and the Conns into eight feet of water. The buggy was wrecked, the horses nearly drowned, several bushels of huckleberries were lost and Mrs. Conn was badly shaken up.

Many men who were charged with the responsibility for maintaining roads shook their heads, but what could they do? The

These thin-tired vehicles continually cut into the sand trails which Clare County called roads. This photo shows Josiah Littlefield and his son-in-law in Surrey Township, 1905.

Photo from the Littlefield Collection

road system only allowed $200 or so to bridge a fair to mid-size stream, and even that would only last between seven and eight years. The Clare City Council discussed this matter in detail, and finally Mayor A. J. Lacy proposed that no more wooden bridges were to be built after October 1, 1903. It carried!

CAMPAIGN FOR GOOD ROADS

Isabella County had several R. F. D. routes in 1903, and they had the same type of inferior roadways. So Charles T. Russell, a Mt. Pleasant attorney collected a group of citizens who were interested in improving the transportation picture. He said, "The liberality of the government in delivering mail to the door should be sufficiently appreciated to warrant at least one day's work from each patron." He continued further, reasoning that each route had two hundred patrons. If each patron would take their team and spend one day hauling gravel in front of their respective homes, "the improvement would immediately be noticeable."

It would be nice to think that this little speech would have been rousingly supported, but that isn't the way farmers thought back in 1903. They thought improved roads would be expensive to build, more expensive to maintain, and besides, who needed good roads? If surplus farm goods were to be sold, they could be hauled to market sometime during the year, but if the taxes went up, he'd have to raise more crops just to pay them. "No, indeed! We don't want those city folks doing us any favors."

A $2,000 BRIDGE

Meantime, Winterfield needed a new bridge, and the Board of Supervisors had authorized $2,000 for highways back in early 1903. William Hales spoke up and moved that the money be used for a steel bridge across the Muskegon, replacing the wooden one which had collapsed. It was hotly discussed, but finally supported. Grubbing operations began east of the river, and a foundation was set for a heavy duty steel bridge.

Another bridge over the Muskegon was needed where it intersected the northwest corner of Section 36. A favorable vote was taken on this and the northwestern part of Clare County was in the twentieth century, but it was scheduled for 1904.

Surrey Township's highway commissioner, Ichabod Johnson, was busy looking after the low spots where the buggies' thin wheels cut deep into the trail. He would cut a few logs and throw them into the spongiest sections near Deadman's Swamp, but they were soon punched down below a level of service.

The spring of 1904 was very wet, and the roads were in a terrible condition. All over the county, people who had lived in isolation were now expecting more service from their government. The mail carriers, faithfully fulfilling their obligations fed these increasing expectations, but their thin-wheeled buggies were hard on the roads as they rolled, or were dragged, through the miserable potholes six times a week.

Even in Clare City, the portion of road from McEwan to the Cherry Grove Cemetery was so wet that school children waded in water on their way to and from school. Children sitting in classrooms all day with wet feet might be tolerated but when teams were forced to stop and rest several times in the area, this was "... a fact not conducive to the large amount of traffic that comes to Clare from the northeast." The city council had to take another look at the problem, which wasn't going away by itself. "The

A rural county bridge badly in need of replacement. This one is in Winterfield Township.

The Salt River near Shepherd had this steel bridge in 1905.

A country bridge in Winterfield Township. Notice the reinforcing beams on top.

main road which leads to the business district demands attention,'' shouted the CLARE SENTINEL in June of 1904.

So in August of 1905, that portion of the road received a three-inch coating of gravel. Five hundred wagonloads of gravel were taken from the pit just north of the river and spread. Furthermore, to show that the city council really meant business, they installed a new hitching rail on McEwan.

Moving gravel was a major problem in 1905. First of all, the soil overburden had to be removed. Charlie Galley put two men on this project, then twelve teams were moved in to be loaded by the six shovelers.

Finally, three men were employed on the roadbed itself, leveling the gravel, which was of a high quality. What Clare would have done if that rich nine-foot vein of gravel hadn't been discovered isn't known, but it is probable that much more time would have elapsed before Clare's horrendous roads were improved. As it was, each team hauled 360 cubic feet a day in loads of 30 cubic feet per load. Costs were computed at 41¢ per load plus 10¢ royalty for the gravel.

THE AUTO'S INFLUENCE

France had 1,672 horseless carriages in 1899. One year later, thanks to a large, rich, leisure class and a network of excellent country roads, 5,286 automobiles were on the roads. The number increased to 9,000 in 1901.

The United States, meanwhile, had a much slower growth in the automobile industry. There were fewer wealthy people at leisure here and good roads were strictly confined to the cities. Nevertheless, by 1902 a small number of autos began to cough and wheeze down the streets. Battle Creek, which had the highest percentage of bicycles to population, boasted in 1904 that it also had the largest number of automobiles per capita in the nation. Needless to say, roads which were favorable to the bicycles were also favorable to the pneumatic tires of the auto.

The leisure class might have taken to the automobile because of its novelty and snob appeal, but the average American responded

to its blandishments because it was swift, and offered personalized conveniences. By 1902 a wave of excitement had swept through the large cities, and it was overflowing into the rural districts via the daily newspapers and the monthly magazines, which were soon being delivered by the R. F. D. system all over the county.

FIGURING THE COST

Congressman Zenor of Indiana cited the high cost of moving agricultural products to market at 25¢ per ton per mile. The gross cost for shipping farm products was $1 billion. He further stated that ''. . . gross receipts by all railroads was $700 million.'' Thus the farmer paid 300 million dollars more than the total railroad bill, but ''he had to haul it all on worse roads than all other shippers combined.'' If farmers could save 10¢ to 12.5¢ per mile, they would form savings of $450 million per year.

Another strong voice was to be heard in the rural districts. Governor Fred M. Warner began speaking forcibly on the relationship between the prosperity of Michigan and good roads. ''The most efficacious and economical methods of serving them have by no means yet been found out . . . More and more, the people are becoming awake to the needs of the advent of the automobile, and the rural mail carriers are greatly adding to the urgency of this problem, for the auto is soon to be the beast of burden on the highways, instead of a plaything.''

The limitations of the law inhibited even such a far-sighted man as the governor, but he had a trick or two up his sleeve. He proposed that a three-mile experimental highway be built from the state capitol to the Agricultural College. He said, ''Our constitution does not permit the state to appropriate money for roads, but it is hoped (that we can) secure this road as an educational measure, and thus soon remove that restriction on the adoption of other measures for securing needed improvements.''

Being a man of his word, he had three amendments to the state constitution ready for the electorate in the 1905 spring election. Among other provisions was one which would permit the state to engage in improving roads if it desired. Senator Ely of Gratiot County introduced corresponding legislation to the Senate which also provided for a board of County Auditors who would supervise the monies locally.

Congress in 1904 had appropriated $27 million to be distributed to the states, but Michigan's constitution prohibited its being received or distributed without an amendment. All townships would need a road system would thus replace the old Pathmaster system. Clare County would receive approximately $1,000 if the changes were made.

The necessary changes were approved in the election of 1905, and the legislature began considering a new highway organization. Spear-heading this movement was the ex-senator from Detroit, Horatio S. Earle. Senator Ely introduced a bill which would provide $10,000 per year for administration and $170,000 for township aid, providing that the townships would share 50% of the cost and would build no more than six miles per year.

Meanwhile, hundreds of automobile owners clamored for a special license number for their vehicles. The Holmes auto bill of April, 1905, was introduced to systematically license the autos, and thereby give the owners their own numbers.

Big things were going on in Michigan in the spring of 1905, but in Clare, disagreement over the cost of fixing McEwan Street almost defeated the water bonding proposal Mayor Lacy wanted so badly. The Republicans had been given a minority role in the city council, but they were seriously contesting every move Lacy, Jackson, Jennings and Ward favored. So factious were their antics that it sickened even the most ribald hard-moneyed man. The voters decided to go with the Democrats, and they did at the next election — all the way.

Meanwhile, William Haley figured the cost of a six-inch gravel base road to be $175 per block. These computations came from his own expenditures on the ten lineal rods in front of his house on North McEwan. He had spent $70 on the grading and graveling of the public roadway. So years later, the city fathers were finally able to make the big

decision: "Yes, let's gravel one block of McEwan."

MICHIGAN'S STATE HIGHWAY DEPARTMENT

The new State Highway Department was organized in conformance with the law creating it. There was a commissioner, one deputy commissioner and a clerk. An office was opened in the Speaker's Room adjoining the Hall of Representatives at the capitol.

Commissioner Horatio S. Earle from Detroit made his first official inspection in Kalkaska County on a one-mile stretch that was completed as a Reward Road, but Dickenson County had the honor of completing the first mile under the new law. Another job in Macomb County, under the supervision of Warren Township, was the largest construction project in 1905. It was for two miles.

An observer of Earle noted as he followed him around the state, "Commissioner Earle has much ginger in his make-up, but no starch." Indeed, Earle was a human dynamo, strongly promoting modern roads for Michi-

Horatio S. Earle—The father of Michigan's highway system. This is a 1901 photo.
Photo: Michigan Department of State Archives

gan, serving as Commissioner from 1905-1909.

THE GOOD ROADS SPECIFICATIONS

The 1905 legislation called for "the road bed to be well graded with good and sufficient ditches to carry off the surface water, and the road bed to be not less than eighteen feet between the ditches, and to have a wagon track not less than nine feet wide, made in two courses; the bottom course to be of clay and sand not less than five inches thick after being rolled. The road and shoulders are to be rounded, so as to shed water to the ditches quickly and a five inch layer of gravel on top, rolled uniform." Such a road received from the state a reward of $250. A similar road, except that it had eight inches of sand and clay and eight inches of gravel carried a reward of $500 for each mile.

A road built with the same specifications, except that it have a minimum of four inches of sand and clay, four inches of gravel and a top layer of crushed stone not less than three inches uniformly distributed, netted $750 per mile. A road built under the same conditions, except that a top layer of six inches of a macadam put in two layers entitled the road district to a thousand dollars.

MORE PROJECTS

Mayor Lacy wanted to put in a more modern water tank and a better sewer system, but some prominent men were holding out for improvements on the main streets of town. John Jackson broke the impasse by compromising on the projects. "Let's fix both," he said. And so it began! Of course, very soon large expenditures would be made and an accounting would

A Ryssnorter tractor is pulling the grader during the widening of Grand River Avenue prior to the placement of the concrete. 1916.

Photo: Michigan Department of State Archives

have to be given to the city council, but that could be handled some way or other. Here, then, is the basis for the serious financial problems the city of Clare faced when the Democrats left office in 1909 when Dr. Mulder defeated candidate J. A. Jackson.

In 1904, the Clare Board of Supervisors spread $3,050 among twenty road projects. For an example, the city of Clare received $200 for a bridge over the Little Tobacco in the 1st Ward. The road near Windover Lake in Freeman was allocated $50, and Summerfield had $75 to repair and maintain its roads. Greenwood received $150 to repair two stretches of road between Sections 4 and 5, and also between 24 and 25.

The Clare County Treasurer, Thomas S. Dorsey, reported that $10,000 was, or would be collected in 1905, so the Board of Supervisors spread $2,250 among eleven townships, with Grant receiving $350 and Hayes securing $300. Townships such as Garfield, Lincoln or Summerfield received $100 or less. Surrey, Clare city, Franklin, Redding and Sheridan benefited by $200. Another $1,000 was allocated for five bridges in Hamilton, Winterfield, Sheridan, Arthur and Clare.

If we begin in 1903, when the Board began seriously considering highway needs with a $2,000 appropriation, we notice that the 1904 allocation was increased 152.5% or $3,050. 1905 wasn't a banner year, so only a modest increase to $3,250 was authorized. The Poor Farm's problems were a painful ulcer with which the Supervisors wrestled for several meetings before $2,500 was agreed upon, but 57.5% of the county's budget was now ear-marked.

THE ROAD BEES

Under the Pathmaster system, taxes could be paid by working them out on the public roads. In 1906, after the clamor for better roads began to rise, road bees became quite common. Townships were able to take the $75 from the county treasury and spread a lot of gravel. Communities in the townships rapidly adopted the "bees" and the R. F. D. routes began to take on a firmer base.

Again, townships were enabled to use other revenues for roads if they so desired.

Supervisor L. D. Sillaway of Garfield took $1,200 which the State of Michigan gave them for tax land sales and put it into roads. Sheridan's George Vandewarker spent about $1,000 opening up a road on the one-eighth section line which was to replace the section line road. Two bridges were needed, and he thought a more permanent solution was to cut a road east and west on the south side of the Tobacco. Of course, in this matter the voters would have the final word, but he was thinking all the time about ways to improve the roads.

Grant Township spent $1,070 of its funds on roads and an equal amount on statute labor, or the road bees of common usage. Redding Township bonded itself for $3,000 so that the main roads could be vastly improved. Lincoln and Greenwood also improved their main roads. Temple called for a work bee, and the men with teams responded, hauling clay and gravel.

In July of 1908, Sheridan Township Highway Commissioner Albert Allen was petitioned by fifty-five residents to open the new road on the one-eighth line just south of the river. He had been about to open it when Judge Dodds quashed it in the fall of 1907. The Judge furthermore refused to hear any new arguments in the case, but the fifty-plus petitioners re-opened the matter that was so hotly contested by a few farmers on the south side of the river in '07. This struggle see-sawed back and forth until 1910, when a $6,000 bonding for roads was defeated.

Vernon Township in Isabella County began an improvement two miles north of the town hall to the county line during the winter of 1907. Supervisor Henry Wild found the money and Township Highway Commissioner John Asline organized twenty farmers with teams. They hauled their gravel from the Clare city gravel pit north of the Tobacco River in their heavy-duty sleighs. The state re-imbursed Vernon $1,000 a mile as they met the highest "Good-Road" specifications.

Supervisors Wild said, "No township has anything on Vernon when (our) roads and drains are brought up to a reasonable state

A road crew of the Lake Huron Good Roads Work Bee, 1913.

of efficiency. He who travels over those heavy clay roads each spring and fall will certainly rejoice in the advent of gravel roads.''

Perhaps Grant Township couldn't exceed Vernon, but they were certainly going to try and equal her. One mile of roadway was let on Schaeffer Hill for $1,390 to a road-contracting firm from Owosso calling themselves Tyler and Geeck. They promised to meet state specifications which demanded eight inches of gravel on top of a sand base. Furthermore, they agreed to reduce the hill to a 5% grade.

CLARE'S GOOD ROAD MOVEMENT

Improved roads were the order of the day in Michigan. In the fall of 1907, Kent County hired the first county road engineer on a permanent basis. Within sixty days, Clare County took a giant step when it organized its Clare County Good Roads Institute. They invited State Highway Commissioner H. S. Earle, who promised to meet with all township highway commissioners in Clare on January 18, 1908. He added a further inducement of one full day's pay and mileage for every official in attendance. It was well attended, and should have been, for much important material was on the agenda.

In 1908, the Legislature was changing the road laws. Previously, the townships had a Pathmaster who was responsible for all roads in the township. He was normally appointed by the township officers, but he carried a great deal of authority. He could order the repair of a road by a farmer and know that it would be done. He also could authorize the taxpayers to work their annual taxes off on road maintenance, or he could compel a citizen to cut noxious weeds along the roadway. In spite of the inherent power vested in this position, the pathmaster system worked rather inadequately. First, no neighbor relished the idea of ordering his friends

Townships held road bees where some gravel was spread and the sand was re-arranged by this wheeled grader.
Photo from the Pioneer Collection

Grading Grand River Avenue for concrete.
Photo: Michigan Department of State Archives

around. Secondly, many farmers didn't have road repairing equipment, and so many taxes were paid by having "used" laundry water poured onto the public road in the summer time. The system was considered almost a joke.

Under the new law, each township was organized into one road district. There were some exceptions such as in Clare County, where Freeman and Lincoln Townships were combined. Each spring election, a township highway commissioner would be elected, and also a road overseer. The commissioner received between $2.90 and $3.00 a day. The overseer was paid $1.50 to $2.50 each day.

A road tax was authorized upon all property outside a village. It was levied at the rate of 50¢ per $100 equalized valuation. The commissioner then would submit written reports of all road and bridge projects and an accounting of how the money was actually spent. He had the power to spend the money only with the approval of the township board, but road repairs were levied also on the property adjacent to the specific problem. Finally, all work had to be pre-surveyed and profile drawings were made and kept on file with the township clerk.

It was this last provision which kept Arthur D. Johnson so busy during the next few years. According to the records, he must have engineered 80% of the roads in Clare County between 1908 and 1915.

Another permissive act had profound impact upon the countryside, that being the proviso which permitted a 25% reduction of one's annual taxes if he planted shade trees adjacent to the roadway. Their value was computed at 25¢ each. This benefit to the farmer was authorized by Section 2, Chapter X of Public Acts 242, 1881, but until the township system was improved, not much utilization of it was made.

The 1908 law was better than the old one, but many were convinced that it wasn't the

Some of the heavy machinery used on Grand River Avenue in 1916.
Photo: Michigan Department of State Archives

Road conditions such as this were an important factor in the growth of the automobile clubs. Their efforts helped change the face of American highways.

Photo: Michigan Department of State Archives

complete answer to Michigan's road problems. In 1906, a proposed Constitutional Convention was voted upon and Clare County approved it by a 734 yes to 467 no vote. Convening on October 22, 1907, the Con-Con delegates began the struggle over a new document. On March 3, 1908, they concluded that the latest version was the best one obtainable, so they adjourned and submitted it for the people's decision. It came on November 3rd, with a rousing 244,705 to 130,783 majority. Clare's support amounted to 81% of its electorate. Soon a better county highway system would be adopted— or at least everyone thought so.

THE 1908 CONSTITUTION

Article VIII, Section 26, permitted the state to lay out, construct, improve and maintain roads, bridges and culverts. It also permitted the counties, townships and road districts to operate a road system. The Boards of Supervisors were given authority to abolish the township highway commissioners and overseers, providing of course, that the county's electorate was favorably inclined. So the selling job began.

Wm. C. Cornwell fired the first gun when he wrote a letter to the CLARE SENTINEL on March 26, 1909. He maintained that expenditures on township roads were not well advised. Rather, "a county road system will be a better method of promoting permanent main roads," he said. Several other points were made about safe-guards being built into a county road committee's authority to levy two mills and a reference was made to the desire of the people to do the proper thing.

In early April, the people marched to the polls and by a vote of 704-814 decided that the old township system was pretty good, even in these days. Needless to say, Cornwell was stunned. His connections to the city way of thinking had caused him to mis-judge the mysterious thinking process of his farmer neighbors. But he shouldn't have been surprised. Many of his new neighbors in Arthur, Hatton and Sheridan were immigrating from Ohio and Indiana where the turnpike taxes were thought to be onerous.

F. A. Carncross summed it up quite clearly: "Good roads require good drainage. Drains cost money. Public money means taxes, and who pays the taxes? The farmers do! Twenty percent of Clare's taxpayers are able to pay their assessments without difficulty, but the other eighty percent have trouble. Do you think we left Ohio so we can raise our taxes in Sheridan?"

There it was, all clear and simple! The farmers were having no part of the county road system, and wouldn't until 1915, when Henry Ford began selling his Model T's in the county as if they were hot cakes. The advantages of good roads to the automobile would then be appreciated, but until that day, the best that could be expected from the horney-handed farmer was a grim toleration of those politicians in Clare and Harrison.

COUNTY ROAD SYSTEMS DEFEATED

Other counties in Michigan were having the same difficulty moving into the twentieth century. Voters in Livingston, St. Joseph, Ionia, Presque Isle, Gratiot and Gladwin leaned in the same direction as all of Clare's townships, except Hatton. Hatton favored the county system, or any system which would build the roads. If the county wouldn't do the job, then another way would be found.

Wm. C. Cornwell wanted a road between Section 30 in Arthur and Section 25 of Hatton. He agreed to financially assist in a one-mile road if it were built to State Reward Road specifications. A $1,250 contract was let to Thomas McGiven with the provision that he could finish it when the weather permitted. Hatton expected to pick up $500 from the state, and the balance would be split between the township and Cornwell.

Redding Township needed good roads more than some of the other townships, and

so Supervisor William A. Fry, Township Overseer Wesley M. Cross and Highway Commissioner Robert Nixon organized the Redding Good Roads Committee in the fall of 1909. They engineered a successful $3,000 road bond referendum, and began three road projects almost immediately. One mile of reward road was extended toward Greenwood, another went south and the last mile headed out of Temple in a westerly direction. Overseer Cross said the gravel they were using had about 10% clay. "It's just the thing for graveling a sandy road," he said.

PARTISAN POLITICS AGAIN

Within the county, most townships sent Republicans to the Board of Supervisors on a regular basis, but the cities of Harrison and Clare sent three Democrats each in the years just prior to 1909. Those six solid votes plus those of the supervisors from Franklin, Winterfield, Summerfield, Sheridan, Hatton and Lincoln generally made things go in the

Mr. and Mrs. W. C. Cornwell, along with J. S. Bicknell and his wife. This photo was taken in Havana, Cuba.

Photo from the Bicknell Family Collection

"easy money" direction. William Jennings Bryan was still hung up on his "Cross of Gold", and a lot of Clare people were hanging with him politically. However, in 1909, the Republicans were back in control of Clare city affairs, and also in most of the townships. This was the time to return a few insults to the enemy, and road money was the most handy tool. Not surprisingly then, some townships received not one dime for bridges, roads or culverts.

It didn't help Louis G. Sly in his campaign for more county money to be spent on Franklin roads, to be a Democrat, but the town's isolation from the hub of activity hurt also.

John Gordon, the ex-supervisor from Hatton, tried to clean up his political act by switching to the Republican side, but the voters overlooked his dedication to good roads and sent Herman Ross to Harrison to represent them. Ross had been a Republican for a longer time, and this was a Republican year in Clare County. As a result, Hatton was able to reach into the county treasury for a few dollars.

In Washington, the Public Roads Division of the U.S. Department of Agriculture looked over Clare County and appointed A. R. Canfield its correspondent. Upon its urging, Canfield asked Townsend A. Ely (1909-13), the new Michigan State Highway Commissioner to meet with local citizens and the township highway commissioners. The strategy was to begin convincing many of the township officials who would lose their jobs that good roads were more important than their own personal kingdoms.

A meeting was set for the Good Roads Institute of Clare County in the Doherty Opera House, February 23, 1910. All township highway commissioners were asked to be there so that the road laws could be reviewed. Since many of those who would be attending thought the old pathmaster system was better for the outlying townships, this was one of the topics certain to be tackled.

Deputy State Highway Commissioner (and later to be State Highway Commissioner), Frank F. Rogers was the main speaker. J. R. Herrick of Sheridan spoke on "The Possibilities of Correct Road Building", and Rogers spoke on "The New Highway Law and the County Road System". John A. Jackson took the topic "Is the Present Plan of County Aid in Clare County Advisable?" But, alas! This Democratic project was extremely poorly received. There was "a small turnout for the meeting," said Canfield.

Some citizens in Sheridan wanted a $6,000 bond issue voted on, so that stone roads, bridges and ditches could be made operational. This sounded like a good idea, so the question was placed on the ballot. It lost by a margin of 12 yes and 114 no votes. The Republican philosophy was still intact.

NO MICHIGAN CHAIN GANGS

Someone else suggested using the men locked up in the prisons for the construction of roads, but Highway Commissioner T. A. Ely replied that the prisoners would be difficult to guard effectively, and besides, they wouldn't work efficiently. "No," he said, "I'm against using the prisoners." He went on to say that he wasn't opposed to using the tramps and vagrants who were in the jails, because they weren't dangerous.

John Gordon, the red-hot advocate of better roads in the townships said, "In other words, he favors letting the petty criminals do the road work and dangerous men can break the stones where there is no danger of them running amok."

"Good Roads" men in the county were becoming very frustrated in 1910. One fact was clear to them and to the farmers, and that was simply that Clare wasn't getting very many State Reward dollars. "If we can't get state money now, how will we be in any better position to receive it under a county system?" wondered F. A. Carncross.

S. C. Kirkbride, the postmaster of Clare and the former Republican County Chairman for many years, had a farm in Sheridan, ten miles from town. He had seen cars on the streets of Clare from time to time, and he had heard of the car which passed through western Freeman during July in 1909. Now he began to wonder, "should the Republican party start promoting township roads?" It would make things easier when he went out to the farm in Elm Grove, but it would also cause taxes to go up. It was always a problem to know how fast to move in these matters. After all, the Republicans had survived during the Democratic years by reconciling the opposing forces, but they weren't sure about the strength of the Good Roads Committee.

In the end, Kirkbride's forces settled for a one-mile improvement east of Pratt's Corners, which took the gravel as far as Colonville.

Up in Hatton, the big sheep ranch was operating. The Johnson Ranch had been sold to the Klemans in 1906, and every year thousands of sheep were moved in and out of Hatton. Families were arriving from Chicago in June of each year and were hankering for a more convenient means of transportation. Cornwell was raising beef, and he had long expressed an interest in better roads. Perry D. Brown, J. R. Goodman, Joe Hudson and L. Burch were speculating on land along the Harrison Branch railroad, hoping that the Hatton Improvement Company would be successful. Fred Hamlin moved his family to his holdings, and he wanted a stone road, too.

The transition from an uncleared wilderness of cut-over lands to a modern rural community was on in many communities during the 1908-1910 era. The telephone had been extended east all the way to Franklin and northern Hamilton from Harrison, and broadened horizons were beckoning the rural citizens, but progress in modern terms was slow in arriving.

Still, some progress went on in the townships. A bridge went over the Doc and Tom River in western Freeman, and another was built on the Middle Branch near the dam.

Winterfield was busy with some internal affairs. During the 1908 fall election campaign, Edmond Cutler had been a candidate for Highway Commissioner. Supervisor A. M. Howard said that Cutler had been on the county relief roles three times, and as a result, the election was unfavorable to him. So Cutler hired John Quinn and his son, who was now in a law practice in Harrison, to pursue a libel suit. George Cummins and A. J. Lacy were retained by Howard, and the battle was on. Meanwhile, no roads were being built and no bridges were constructed. Cutler wasn't any more successful than was the road system.

PRIVATE REWARD ROADS

Wexford County had a unique situation during 1910. W. W. Mitchell, a man who had gathered a fortune in lumbering, offered a bonus of $300 a mile for every road constructed to state specifications during the next three years. This generous subsidy practically made a gift of the roads to the townships if they would only avail themselves of the opportunity.

Mitchell said, "Do men of large means, desiring of leaving a memorial to themselves, appreciate that few forms of memorials are more permanent and confer greater benefits upon those who come after them than a thoroughfare constructed after the most approved methods of road making?"

Unfortunately, the citizens in Wexford's townships weren't very anxious to leave many memorials to Mitchell, and so they continued to run their thin-tired buggies over the sand trails.

A NUDGE FROM LANSING

Incoming Governor Osborn suggested to the Legislature in January of 1911 that Michigan ought to inaugurate a policy to connect every county seat with a good permanent road. Among other things, he also said, "There are 70,000 miles of public highways in Michigan now . . . The question of proper aid for these roads will always be

discussed until the state assumes entirely the work of road building, which in my opinion, would bring about the best results and be the most satisfactory.''

So much for the Governor's thoughts! The Legislature was composed of many Republicans who viewed the concept of a dynamic state highway building program with a distinct disdain, and there was no public clamor for state roads being run into every district of Michigan — or was there?

Detroit was gearing up for the mass production of the automobile, and 1911 was a landmark year. During 1910, 18,355 automobiles were registered. The following year, 1911, 27,796 cars were rolled out onto Michigan's streets and highways. In Clare, L. E. Davy, Drs. F. R. Gray and Clute, J. W. and C. W. Calkins and Clark Sutherland purchased autos, and A. J. Doherty had been motoring in and out of Clare since 1908. There were more influential forces at work behind the scenes now demanding better roads. The R. F. D. carriers were gaining some powerful allies. Things were beginning to roll.

THE NATIONAL GOOD ROADS ASSOCIATION

Moving about the countryside were the big steam farm traction engines, going from job to job, traveling over the graveled or clay roads and wooden bridges. One of these was moving north out of Vernon from the LaMont place, coming down Maple Street in Clare toward a threshing job west of town, but it never cleared the wooden bridge, and pitching into the Little Tobacco, it splashed to a halt! A month later, new concrete piers had been poured, and steel stringers were laid spanning the water, and a permanent road bed of concrete was brought level with the street grade. This had been the last wooden bridge in the city of Clare, and it too was gone in 1911.

During the 1912 Good Roads Institute held in Clare during January, it was disclosed that the county now had 850 miles of roadway completed, and another 650 miles under construction. Graveled roads were the most popular, there being 514

miles in this category. 313 miles of road were macadam.

During February, the Barry County school kids were invited to write essays in the Good Roads sponsored contest, with a $10 and $5 prize awaiting the winners. Contestants had to be rural Barry County children only. We can see that a public education campaign was on in another troubled county. Maybe there was a connection between the essay contest and the fact that the president of Michigan's State Good Roads Association was P. T. Colgrove, who lived in Hastings, the county seat.

A LOUD CANNON FIRES

More information began coming from the pen of Howard H. Gross, who spoke through the National Good Roads Association. He began to go after the trouble makers — the farmers and their wagons. ''A wagon carrying a two-ton load having tires 1¾ '' wide will do more damage to a road than a wagon carrying four tons, but having a 3 '' wide iron tire,'' he stated.

People everywhere, including the farmers, were clamoring for the popular narrow tires, but ''They cut up the roads as fast as they are repaired,'' he insisted. ''Untold millions of dollars of damage is done each year by the narrow wheels.'' But he also realized that the wide tire was handicapped because it created too much drag.

Gross proposed that all wagons should be licensed just as the autos were. His fee schedule called for an annual charge of $7.50 for each wagon having tires 0 ''-1¾ '' wide. Wagons having tires 1⅞ ''-2¼ '' would pay $4.50; vehicles with tires 2⅜ ''-3 '' would be assessed $3.00 and farmers having a wagon with tires wider than 3 '' would be charged only $1.00.

Chicago adopted this 3 '' tire rule, and how the teamsters howled! Wagonmakers said it would take two years to make enough wide wheels to comply with the law, but the city officials held firm, and the conversion job was done in a matter of weeks. They simply added blocks on both sides of the felloes and slipped a 3 '' heavy duty tire over the old wheels. Shortly the teamsters forgot all about the injustice of it all, and the roads in Cook County improved rapidly.

The farmers, though, were having none of this! Again Gross took to the newspapers in Michigan and said, "In no community has a rural population gone for good roads without a truculent majority being won over. The strongest opposition sets in when good roads are brought up."

He was certainly correct as far as Clare County was concerned. Few questions were receiving more attention in 1912 than good roads, but fewer farmers believed that "good roads help farm values". Nevertheless, Gross kept holding their feet to the fire. "If a man spends money on wind-mills, barns, sheds, machinery, trees and fencing, he ought to spend some on the roads leading to them. Every community that has built good roads after a reluctant beginning has continued to build these roads as a matter of course. It makes life more bearable socially, and economically . . . worth living. Children are more willing to stay on the farms because they can take advantage of the market, rather than the market taking advantage of them . . . Good roads increase the value of crops 2-3¢ a bushel, . . . 10-30¢ a hundredweight on cattle and hogs," he concluded.

In many states (Texas, Tennessee and Kentucky), distances were now being measured by the time spent in reaching one point from another. Gross suggested that good roads prompted this local habit. "Communities ought to begin building good roads on a regular basis and spread the costs over a few years. It's the best investment they can make," he said, "and it will reduce your time spent on the road."

As if on cue, New York State passed a bond proposal for fifty million dollars, to be spread over ten years. "Scores of other states are doing the same thing on a lesser scale," Gross continued. "There is no reason the present generation should carry the whole burden of bettering the roads. They will last for generations."

$90,000,000 WASTED

Imagine the farmer's reaction when he saw the next headline staring at him.

"Twenty Years of Road Money Wasted." But Gross moved rapidly into supporting the claim. He said, "The hit-or-miss methods of the past twenty years have resulted in a $90,000,000 waste." He continued, "Consider the working-out tax! The farmer plows or scrapes the road, fills the center with sod and then when the heavy rains come, the road is all torn up by the first wagon that travels down it. Never mind the stunts of wrestling, jumping around, and athletic games that are played on the work day as normal hi-jinks. This working-out tax predates the Civil War, and it must be replaced by a road building program of larger units than the townships," he claimed. "The road district must hire an engineer who will supervise three or four gangs of road builders. Then we'll get proper drainage and good roads . . . The day will come, mark my word, when all roads will either be hard, smooth stone or brick."

A week later, in the April 19th edition of the 1912 CLARE SENTINEL, he flat-out stated, "Three-quarters of the township highway commissioners don't know what they are doing with roads." Then he ticked off their shortcomings:

1. They do the wrong things to the roads.
2. If they do it at all, they do it at the wrong time of the year (i.e. the fall).
3. They don't put tiles in the proper places, and the ditches don't drain.
4. Iron culverts should be used under the roadways, but they use clay.
5. Weeds are permitted to grow on the roadway.
6. They don't use wheeled scrapers to move dirt for distances under 600 feet.
7. They don't use wagons for moving dirt over distances which exceed 600 feet.
8. Finally, they don't keep the fill from becoming water-soaked.

If this wasn't condemnation enough, he then metioned the commonly accepted practice of windrowing the gravel and letting the traffic spread it. Normally the drivers avoided the windrows, but when it rained, they were forced up onto it, belatedly spreading the gravel into the tracks. "Use a field harrow

Curing the concrete on Grand River Avenue, 1916.
Photo: Michigan Department of State Archives

if it is nine feet wide,'' he chided. ''This puts the particles closer together.''

THE EUROPEAN ROAD SYSTEM

Paris hosted the International Association of Road Builders in 1908. There the superior techniques with which the Europeans had built their excellent roads were shared with the Americans. They indicated also that a full-time man maintained each road. A question from an American, ''How soon after building a road do you begin making repairs?'' brought the answer, ''The next day!''

Michigan had a delegation there, and a copy of the European system was printed by the state later that year, but the highway overseers had to write the Highway Commission in Lansing to receive a copy.

A GOOD ROAD IS AVAILABLE 365 DAYS A YEAR

By 1912, the Good Roads Campaign was in full stride, but its major thrust was education, both of the general public and also of the township highway officials. First, they attempted to show how the old way was ineffective. They stated, ''The old way provides the following:

1. A burst of good road activity.
2. One or two miles agreed as the limit.
3. An argument ensues over how to raise the funds.
4. Those not on the proposed road don't contribute.
5. The feed dealers and bankers are asked to contribute.
6. Farmers contribute sporadic labor.
7. A party is held at the town hall with all proceeds applied to the road fund.
8. Letters go out to the editors.
9. Everyone pats each other on the back and says 'We're getting things done.'

"This activity is all fine, but it doesn't get the roads built." They further contended, "The township may levy $1,000 a year and then build a mile or so of reward road, but usually under this plan, the road built receives no maintenance and it soon falls apart. Then, too, nineteen out of twenty overseers don't know how to wisely spend road dollars, so when they are finished with each project, it is usually half as good as it should be and has cost twice as much as it normally would.

"The proper way is for the township board to bond for a 15-20 mile stretch, hire an engineer to oversee the construction crew and build it right the first time."

Ignoring the sage advice of the state Good Roads group, Hatton built a mile of reward road between itself and Arthur. Thomas McGivern brought his horses and equipment up to Brown's Corners and started north one mile. He was keeping in mind the ideal grade which a heavily-traveled road should have, but this road would only be locally used, so it could be left at 6%.

A horse pulling a 1,000 pound load on the level can only pull 810 pounds on a rise of one foot in fifty. If the rise is one in ten, the maximum load can only be 250 pounds. Therefore, the road overseers sought to keep the grades at 3% and no more than 6% if possible.

THE MICHIGAN STATE FAIR ASSOCIATION

A. J. Doherty had served in the Michigan Senate during the early days of Governor Warner's administration. He was an effective leader and worked closely with the governor on his road projects. When he took over as secretary of the State Fair Board, it was only natural that roads would be accentuated. In 1910, 1911 and again in 1912, road exhibits were prominent. A road had actually been built in 1910 on the fair site, and it was very well attended. Many rural citizens were thus exposed to the latest techniques as well as the Good Roads' blandishments.

A MECHANICAL DIRT MOVER

North of Clare at the Grant-Hatton town-

A heavy-duty bridge for M-54.

ship boundary line was a hill of glacial deposits, mostly consisting of terminal moraine sand and boulders. So formidable was its elevation and gradient that teamsters usually by-passed it one mile to the east. During 1912, however, Hatton Township was making great efforts toward becoming a thriving farm community. An elevator was projected adjacent to the railroad siding, and the Hatton Farmer's Club had some very energetic members. Perry Brown, St. Clair and Fred Hamlin, Austin Trumble, Charles Heber, Holmes Kennedy, A. E. Haines, J. A. Hileman and others were really stirring things around.

It was too time consuming to detour through Dover when they wanted to make connections with Clare City. After thinking about the problem a bit, Fred and St. Clair Hamlin rigged a gasoline engine to a long cable ånd two scrapers. Mounting it on top of the hill, they were able to have one hauling a load while the other was returning. It was set up so it was self-loading and self-dumping. One man stood on the bank for signalling in case an obstruction got in the way of the scrapers, and that was the only help required.

The mechanical dirt mover made eleven cycles every five minutes and did the equivalent work in one hour that would normally have required four teams working a ten-hour day. It operated between the Redner School and James' Hill.

THE STATE HIGHWAY NETWORK

More assistance began coming from the Post Office Department. They offered to give Michigan $10,000 if the state would contribute $20,000 toward improving one fifty-mile post road. They suggested that a road traveled by several postal employees be set aside for this project. Governor Osborn favored this project, but he let incoming Governor Ferris sign the agreement.

By January 1913, the State Highway Department was thinking in terms of an annual $1,000,000 road construction fund. To gather this much money, Governor Ferris wanted to earmark the auto license money.

That was all right with the Grange, because the farmers wouldn't be saddled with a huge tax. They suggested that all cars be taxed at the rate of 50¢ per horse power.

Some of this fund would be used to build a highway from the Indiana-Michigan state line to Mackinac. It would stretch through fourteen Michigan counties and would connect South Bend, Niles, Dowagiac, Kalamazoo, Grand Rapids, Plainwell, Big Rapids, Reed City, Cadillac, Traverse City, Bellaire, Charlevoix, Petoskey and Mackinac City.

Another route was projected between Detroit and Mackinac, but no schedule was announced. Meanwhile, the townships kept nibbling away at the road problem.

During 1913, Clare County built twelve miles; in Grant (5.75 miles), in Hatton (3.25 miles), Greenwood (2 miles) and Arthur (1 mile).

The Allswede Bill of 1913 called for a highway on the Meridian Line north to the Straits. Not many communities favored this proposed location for a highway, as there weren't many towns along that route. A coalition of highway supporters from Alma, Shepherd, Mt. Pleasant, Clare, Harrison, Houghton Lake, Grayling and Gaylord suggested that the route could use their present gravel roads already now in place. "Most of the bridges are already in," they said.

During 1912, hundreds of tourists came by auto to Clare. William H. Caple, the local promoter of real estate and business opportunities during this era, began to boom a trunkline through his home base. He was a front-man, but people such as A. J. Doherty, A. R. Canfield, Dennis Alward, W. C. Cornwell and the Kleman interests gave a solid foundation for his lobbying efforts.

Slowly, but surely, the concept of state and national highways was maturing. Many of the senators and representatives in Congress were of the opinion that the building of a highway network had become the most important issue facing the American people. A few years before, road bills were given a short-shrift. The number of road proposals in Congress during March of 1913 was in excess of one hundred.

The big concrete mixer at work on Grand River Avenue, 1916.
Photo: Michigan Department of State Archives

Critics said, "The Good Roads concept may be deserving of some support, but they are all going in different directions." In Michigan, they started right. A state-wide survey began in June for the entire network, but the construction phase was to be delayed.

HATTON BEGINS TO DECLINE

The enthusiasm for roads and highways led the Hatton Improvement Company to spearhead a $12,000 bonding proposal for township roads. Six and one-half miles of prime roads were projected. The leaders said, "Here's what we think, but now it's up to you fellow citizens."

In March, they went to the polls and cast their "no" votes. As soon as the polls closed and the votes were tallied, Fred Hamlin said, "Well, there's more than one way to live on a good road," so he moved. He wasn't the last one to shake the sand out of his trousers' cuffs.

LAKE HURON GOOD ROADS ASSOCIATION

The eastern shore of Michigan north of Bay City was "long the dread of travelers", but boomers in the district were dreaming immensely proportioned dreams. They sought to organize enough work crews to build 260 miles of highway in one day. For weeks, area newspapers promoted the idea, and then at 4:00 a.m., June 9th, 1913, the ladies packed dinners for 5,000 men. By noon, the counties of Bay, Arenac, Alcona, Ogemaw, Iosco, Alpena, Presque Isle and Cheboygan knew they had a winning campaign underway. Before nightfall, "what were mostly impossible sand roads (were) all covered with clay."

Enoch Andrus, publisher of the CLARE SENTINEL, said, "If such is an example of what can be accomplished, it might be well if we have some more 'bees' around the state."

On June 20th, the automobile traffic

began heading north over this new roadway.

HARRISON-HOUGHTON LAKE ROAD BEE

C. W. Perry, the attorney from Clare thought Andrus' suggestion had some real merit. So he, J. F. Tatman and Don Canfield put together a "good roads" meeting in Clare for July 29, 1913. The city park was selected for a site, and Highway Commissioner Frank F. Rogers (1913-1929) was invited to speak. He explained the latest legislation concerning trunklines. If a township built three miles of roadway at a time, the state would pay half, plus the cost of the plans, bridges, etc.

James F. Tatman suggested that a permanent Clare County Good Roads Association be organized, and the crowd agreed. Perry was elected president, Tatman was given the pencil and paper and Canfield was given charge over the money. Before they adjourned, everyone agreed upon September 15th as the day a good highway between Harrison and Houghton Lake should be built.

The men around Clare agreed to work on the stretch of road between Harrison and James' Hill. Those who lived in Harrison and Hayes would work north toward Houghton Lake. A third crew would start in Roscommon County and work their way toward the Harrison bee.

L. W. Sunday of Arthur, E. E. Delling from Freeman, B. S. Alley of Garfield, Fred Hamlin, John Quinn and Otto Pietch from Hatton, Hayes and Lincoln, Ike Hampton, D. W. Rowe and William H. Caple all agreed to head up a work gang and would take a section of their assignment and complete it by nightfall.

This bee went so well that another, larger bee was drummed for June in 1914. Yet, the major hold-up was the township system.

After John A. Jackson came back from a Michigan Good Roads Congress, held in Detroit from September 29th to October 4th, 1913, he suggested that a county road system again be placed on the ballot in the spring. William H. Caple and A. J. Doherty had attended the National Good Roads Associa-

tion at Washington D. C. earlier, and they agreed that it was time to try again.

Cornwell again wrote his letters to the editors, extolling the virtues of a larger construction and maintenance unit. He also indicated that the local farmers were paying state taxes and other districts were using those taxes and building their roads with them. "Local townships have not taken advantage of the township highway system and built the necessary roads," he wrote.

Once again the men went to the polling booths, and once again they turned down that so-called superior road district. Hatton, of all the townships, favored the county district. The other fifteen townships favored their own system of highway construction.

Each township took on a mile or so of road work each year, and Surrey's Highway Commissioner McAninch opened his annual bid September 9th. Vernon let a bid for a mile between its Sections 2 and 3 and Grant Township's 34 and 35. Hatton agreed to a bid from Howard Grow for the Redner fill, but he couldn't move enough dirt in that fall season, so the Hudson brothers completed the job fifteen months later.

A state road inspector came onto the Redner cut and watched the Hudsons work. He was so impressed with them that he suggested that they become state-wide road builders, and they did. This job had been the deepest fill-job in the county.

James Davison, in Farwell, had constructed a heavy-duty gravel screen, and he began taking road contracts on a bid basis. One of his first jobs was the mile of gravel placed between Sections 14 and 23.

W. R. Hamlin took a one-mile stretch west of the Redner School in Section 28. Alec McNeil bid successfully on the mile of Hatton Road in Section 27.

In 1914, after Mitchell's generous offer had expired by one year, Wexford County was appropriating $15,000 for their share of the reward roads.

INFERIOR PRODUCTS USED

Initial costs had kept road construction down during the preceeding years. The hiring of a good engineer, even for extensive building projects was another problem. So a large number of faultily engineered roads were built during the 1910-1914 era.

Bricks were used in some districts where heavy vehicular traffic concentrated, but again, many inferior clays were used, and the roads oftentimes were less than minimal.

THE 1914 STATE ROAD BEE

The spectacular success of the Lake Huron Shore Roads Association during 1913 prompted many imitators. P. T. Colgrove, president of the Michigan State Good Roads Association, asked Governor Ferris to designate two days in early June for a state-wide road bee. The West Michigan Pike Association and the Lake Huron Good Roads Association agreed, and June 4th and 5th were set.

Clare took as its project the mile of road that headed west toward Farwell. A bee cleared the under-base, and Armstrong Allen, with Arthur Bradley, laid in the gravel. " 'Tis the finest road in our area,'' agreed observers. A by-stander looking at the smooth roadway said, "It will be a rare pleasure to start off on a motor trip to some distant city or town and be able to travel on roads such as this one.''

THE LINCOLN HIGHWAY ASSOCIATION

Henry B. Joy, President of the Lincoln Highway Association, had benefited financially from the Michigan Central Railroad, among other ventures, but he was a leading advocate for a first-class highway system which would connect the two oceans. He wanted the proposed trans-continental trunk-line to cut across the bottom tier of Michigan counties.

Joy also saw the vision of motorists riding in their automobiles to distant cities and towns, but he saw the horizon stretching into other states as well. He led a petition drive to force the State of Michigan to set the national example in roadway construction. He said, "Michigan is the manufacturing center for the automobiles of this country, yet her roads are a disgrace . . . No wonder her sister states look upon them with disgust.''

Governor Woodbridge N. Ferris appointed a committee to coordinate the project with the Lincoln Highway Association, but as we all know, nothing came from it.

A NATIONAL ROADS CONGRESS

The fifth Annual American Good Roads Congress met at the Union Stockyards in the International Amphitheatre December 14th-18th, 1914. There were 10,000 automobilists, farmers, highway officials and businessmen in attendance. Every year this convention grew more sophisticated, but in 1914 it reached into the very bowels of the rural regions, and the tillers of the soil wanted to see what was going on in this road business.

The state had its representatives in the Associated Road Organization of Michigan. A large photo exhibit depicting street-paving work in Detroit was featured. Machinery manufacturers had a live demonstration of an actual roadway being constructed, and there were seminars by the dozens, giving short courses to any and all who showed up.

The federal exhibit showed road-building techniques from Caesar's time until the present. It was a beauty!

Since 1901, Michigan had spent a gross amount of $49,940,804. The townships contributed $40,135,897 of that amount, the counties appropriated $7,854,907 and the state dibbled in $1,950,000. It surely wasn't much of a leadership role that the state played during those thirteen years, and it didn't bode well for the next few years either. True, there were trunklines planned for connecting the far corners of Michigan, but the pieces weren't falling into place very rapidly.

The Lincoln Highway had moved into high gear and was projected through twelve states, connecting New York City and San Francisco. True, the 3,384 miles wouldn't be completely hard surfaced for a few years yet, but a third of it was done in 1915, and Michigan was left out.

DIXIE HIGHWAY

A major highway connecting Chicago to Miami was scheduled to be completed in 1916, traversing five states and the Cumberland Mountains. A national pride was being touched in this, the second year of the Great War. "Americans are building roads today for the wheels of peace and commerce, but old Rome built her roads for the spread of war and misery," observed the January 3th, 1916 issue of COLLIER Magazine. The article went on:

"The south depended upon the oceans for her trade and commerce, while the north had an inland waterway, canals and railroads . . . Thus grew up the north. By the nature of its roadways, it was isolated from the south . . . They produced separate cultures and peoples and finally a war.

"The Dixie Highway transcends this isolation."

A spur to the Dixie was run up through Michigan to the Straits, thus connecting the Lake State to the south. Changes were profoundly affecting the future in ways no one could foresee exactly, but most observers were aware that something important was going on.

By the end of 1916, Michigan had completed 4,200 miles of State Reward Roads. Of this total, only eighteen were constructed in 1906. Genessee County was the heaviest consumer of Reward funds, having 190 miles completed by 1916. Saginaw (173), Gratiot (143), Clare (30), Clinton (16), Roscommon (4) and Gladwin (1) were also taking advantage of the State Aid Act of 1905. Counties such as Otsego, Baraga, Alpena, Chippewa, Montmorency, Oscoda and Mackinac constructed exactly zero miles of Reward Roads.

During 1916, the road between Detroit and Lansing and from Lansing to Grand Rapids and Muskegon were contracted out for a concrete surfacing. A grand total of $1,466,985.38 was spent by the state, $1,111.47 of which was sent to Clare. Isabella received $4,628.05 during the same period.

A road between Saginaw and Mt. Pleasant was boosted by William Reardon, William H. Caple and W. S. Linton from Midland, Clare and Saginaw, respectively. Members of the Mt. Pleasant Board of Trade drove over the proposed route in July. They wanted to check its routing before they got behind it.

NORTHERN MICHIGAN AGRICULTURAL AND GOOD ROADS CONGRESS

A meeting of a farm boosters' Good Roads Association met at Mackinac City during July of 1916 also. Mayor David Ward from Clare and W. Holmes Kennedy, the Agricultural Extension Agent from Hatton attended. During the course of the Congress, a monument to the Dixie Highway was unveiled, and also one to the conjunction of the East and West Michigan Pikes.

By mid-summer of 1916, the trunkline through Hatton Township had reached the southern border of Hayes. Slowly, yet surely, the road connecting Clare and Harrison was reaching the Good Roads specifications.

FEDERAL AID ROAD ACT OF 1916

Back in 1904, the Federal role in road construction was limited to $2,000,000 expended through the states. Prior to 1912, its chief role was in research and the testing of methods to build suitable highways. The Department of Agriculture gave $500,000 for R. F. D. road improvements, but only twenty-nine states were approaching a professional standard for their highway departments.

Congress changed all of that in 1916 when it passed the Federal Aid Road Act. Five million dollars were appropriated for highway construction in 1917. Michigan's share, based on a formula which allowed for number of acres, population and the mileage of Star Routes was $145,783.72. During fiscal year 1917, $10,000,000 was ear-marked, and every year thereafter, an additional $5,000,000 was added to the preceeding year's allotment. During the 1920 fiscal year, therefore, $25,000,000 was to made available. Another million dollars was channeled through the National Forests for fire roads.

The 1916 Road Aid Act did several important things: first, it authorized the Secretary of Agriculture to co-operate with the respective state highway departments; second, it limited federal dollars to the Post Roads (formerly the Territorial Roads); third, it called for a federal inspection of construction; fourth, it limited a passing on to the federal level, a maximum of 50% of construction costs.

During the five years covered by this act, a total of $180,000,000 worth of new road construction was promoted. Under the old system, Clare County had built 73 miles of State Reward Roads and trunklines.

Considering the total number of miles of highways needed in a modern county, at least 2,200 miles would have been required in Clare. That only 3.3% of that total had been eked out in thirteen years of the modern road-building era testifies to the tremendous problems facing those citizens.

One of those problems is north of Clare. A rather large glacial terminal moraine rests outside the north country's gate. It had been worked at over the years by several road gangs, yet in 1917, it still defied the Good Roads boosters. The sand was soft and shifty and was most difficult, first for the teams and then later for the automobiles. A wagon only moderately loaded was so onerous to the horses that three stops were needed before the crest was reached. A few years later, it would be a testing laboratory for the purchasers of automobiles who wanted to try out the performance of the gasoline buggies.

C. H. Kleman said he'd give $50 toward putting an adequate covering of gravel on it. Considering that the state's generosity of $1,300 and Hatton's contribution of $1,000 would still not meet the expenses, we can see that it was truly a prodigious problem, at least under the township road system. A group of men went out to see Mr. Cornwell about some assistance toward the gravel, but he knew what they were after before they opened their mouths. He reached for his billfold and held it out to them. "How much do you need?" he asked by way of greeting.

THE COUNTY ROAD COMMISSIONS LEAD OUT

Michigan had 59 county road commissions in 1917. Forty-eight of them planned to take advantage of the Federal Road Act, as they let bids for 958 miles of Reward Roads. Township Commissions planned to add 442 more miles, and plans were on the Lansing desks for a grand total of 2,856 more miles of roads. As with most things in life, however, the days of cheap road construction were gone. More sophisticated specifications and higher wages had driven the cost of road construction to $3,500 per mile. The projected cost of the 1917 roads were thus $4,900,000, but only $3,666,419 would be available. If all roads projected were built in 1917, $14,896,000 would have been needed. Michigan was about $10,000,000 short of having sufficient funds to do everything the farmers were now anxious to have done.

THE AUTO'S INFLUENCE

What had caused the tremendous change in attitudes? In two words, the answer was HENRY FORD. Until the farmers began buying the automobiles, they never realized that roads were a paying proposition. In 1911, Ford began turning out his tin lizzies in large numbers. Clare farmers began buying them in 1915. From that point on, you couldn't hold them down. Also, the war was on, and the young men were having to think about broader horizons. Gone were the days when they were content to take their leisure at the neighborhood Pedro party. Speed was in the air! Speed was in their blood! Automobiles were on their mind, and those roads were the impediment to their goals, so better roads had to be acquired and rapidly, too.

Indeed, in 1917, the following projects took off:

WEST MICHIGAN PIKE — (Charlevoix, Cheboygan, Emmet, Grand Traverse and Manistee Counties)
MACKINAW TRAIL—(Emmet, Wex-

Henry Ford: The Man Who Put America on Wheels.
Photo courtesy Ford Motor Company

ford and Osceola Counties)
EAST MICHIGAN PIKE—(Cheboygan, Iosco, Alcona, Arenac and Presque Isle Counties)
MERIDIAN PIKE — (Roscommon, Crawford and Otsego Counties)

In 1918, roads were planned for the following:

1. Detroit via Saginaw to Mackinac
2. Gaylord to Mackinac
3. Little Traverse Bay to Charlevoix

ROADS AND ALCOHOL

During the summer of 1918, the Good Roads Campaign met in Detroit. By now, the state's hotelmen had taken over the association, and they wanted a wine and beer amendment. Since the Volstead Act, the hotelmen thought they were being unfairly burdened with problems not of their making, but their voices were drowned out by the patriotic citizens who wanted to "muzzle old 'Kaiser Bill' ".

The last year of the war saw another important proposal being made. Article X, Section 10 of the 1908 Constitution stipulated tht "the state may contract debts to meet deficits in revenue, but such debts shall not in the aggregate at any time exceed $250,000."

A proposed amendment would raise that limit to $50,000,000, which would in turn be used for highways in the poorer counties. When it passed, Sheridan Township let one of the earliest contracts under this provision for 5.6 miles. At last the townships in Clare were going to have their gravel roads.

The Automobile Intrudes

Transportation in northern Michigan was confined to trains, teams, bicycles or "shank's stage" prior to 1900. Longer trips by necessity had to be taken by trains, if time was a factor, and often it was. Citizens not having business near railroads could catch a stagecoach sometimes, but most preferred their own private means, with two-wheeled cart, buggy, wagon or sleigh in the winter time being the most common in use.

Keeping these moving and parked vehicles out of each other's way was normally left to the driver, but the towns tried, usually in vain to regulate them when they came through the business districts.

Village councils would spend many hours discussing where to put the horse watering troughs, hitching rails and the feed barns, but their advice was seldom heeded by the truculent teamster when he came to town. Likely as not, regulations concerning the horses and wagons would be ignored, and the village fathers didn't want to alienate the businessmen's customers.

Questions about street right-of-way, also thoroughly thrashed out in the town hall meetings, were ignored on the village streets. The farmer, being independent in nature, seldom stopped to consider his town neighbor's views. When time came for his Saturday shopping and drinking, he would act as though he were the only person in the world. If he was pushing his horses at a fast gallop coming near the town limits, he would keep the same pace as he crossed the pedestrian walks which the council had caused to be laid facing the business houses at the street intersections. On these, the town residents had

been given reason to expect a fair amount of consideration for their safety. The farmer, however, thought very little about all of these little courtesies.

His crude habits finally forced some action in towns like Farwell and Clare. Phillip A. Bennett, the editor of the CLARE SENTINEL attempted to straddle both positions when he wrote in 1894, "The streets belong to the teams and vehicles, and the pedestrian has no more right on them than teams have on the sidewalks."

Most adults in towns like Clare realized that the problems would basically have to be resolved by the townspeople, and hopefully the farm cousins would take the hint and conform to some sensible rules. Generally the women and children used the wooden cross-walks as the law stipulated, but men and rowdy boys made the streets their arena.

The educational processes were ones which continually had to be gone over and over by the council, the town marshal and responsible adults. Traffic safety wasn't something that came easily to the students of public affairs, but that wasn't the only troublesome spot as the northern communities began making room in their thinking for the coming revolution in personalized transportation. If the teamsters would only park their wagons far enough down the hitching rail so the rear of the box would clear the cross-walks, it would help. Also, if they would engage in their greeting of friends after the horses had been taken care of, instead of straddling the cross-walks with their rigs, the ladies and other law-abiding citizens wouldn't have to step off the wooden cross-overs into the often churned mud of the streets.

SUPPORTING THE MECHANICAL AGE

A complicated mechanical device such as the auto needed many supporting services before it could be successfully left on its own. Streets and roads would have to be in ample number and their physical condition would need certain minimum considerations, such as width and surface strength. Bridges would also need to be sufficiently strong, but a more critical area was in their repair and maintenance. The fledgling petroleum industry moved into Clare just ahead of the auto, but they were supplying fuels for lamps, stoves and stationary engines, not mobile monsters.

Standard Oil moved into Clare during the 1890's, and by 1896 they were ready to expand their permanent facilities if the city council would issue the permits. A request to the city council for permission to build tanks and a warehouse was made, and in due course was favorably acted upon by them. Kerosene and gasoline were the major source of revenues, but lubricating oils were used by all types of farm and industrial machinery, and they also contributed to the gross sales and profits of "John D". The company purchased a team of heavy draft horses to pull the tank wagon.

Not so directly related to the automobile's approaching entry into Clare, but still critical to its widespread acceptance, was a little-noticed meeting held in Port Huron during July of 1900. A short paragraph in the CLARE SENTINEL in June gave the details. It told how the "International Good Roads Congress" planned to organize itself on a permanent basis if enough delegates showed up. They did, and Andrew Patrula of St. Louis, Missouri was elected president, while the Honorable Martin Dodge became the Director of the "United States Good Roads" inquiry department. He was hoping for a brisk business in the immediate months and years, and Clare's residents, while not paying much particular attention to the group, should have been wishing him well.

THE ROADWAYS

Most municipalities in Michigan had someone who carried the title of "Street-Marshal". His primary job was to drag a split log over the main trail as conditions warranted. If a load of gravel was needed to fix a low spot, an appeal to the city council would be made, and sometimes the necessary authority was given for its purchase. In 1902, Clare gave its marshal authority to grade McEwan Street, with no limit on his expenses.

There wasn't much road work done during the wintertime, however, and teams entering town did so at their own risk. Occasionally, a large v-shaped wooden affair would be dragged down the streets and walks if enough snow warranted it. When ice prevailed, horses often would fall to the roadbed and be unable to get up. During February, 1904, a severe ice storm toppled horses like tenpins. "Several farmers had to brace their horses to keep them erect."

Sometimes a road bee would be called for a mid-summer Saturday in town, and all the farmers were invited to bring their teams and wagons to town where many shovelers were waiting to load or unload the dirt or gravel. Clare had one of these bees in June for the purpose of repairing and claying Goodman's Hill, north to the river. "Bring your eatables, and 'Jake' (Mason) will do the rest . . . Liquid refreshments will be on tap all day", was the come-on.

A DREAM

In the towns and cities of southern Michigan, the Interurbans were all the rage. Up north, however, they were not so attractive, financially, even though Col. Boynton periodically made his sales pitch to communities such as Clare, Gladwin and Mt. Pleasant, He envisioned a route connecting South Bend, Niles, Grand Rapids, Greenville, Winn, Mt. Pleasant, Clare, Gladwin, West Branch, Rose City and Alpena with fast, convenient electric cars, but it never was to be for patrons north of Winn.

A solution to the needs of the isolated citizen was chugging along on the city streets of Detroit in 1904. Enough automobiles were operating there between May and September to cause 33 accidents and one death. An automobile was speeding down a boulevard in that fair city when a pedestrian stepped in its path and became the first victim of a hit-and-run driver in the state.

Injury and death didn't slow down the love affair Detroiters and other Michigan residents had with the automobile. Indeed, it seemed that hundreds, if not thousands of men became captivated by its marvelous possibilities. Some, like Floyd E. Doherty, late of Clare, but employed at the state capital as an electrician, used their spare time and their mechanical skills to modify and perfect the machines. Doherty noticed that the electrical connection between the auto and the battery was a troublesome thing, especially since the battery had to be removed frequently for re-charging. He came up with a spring clamp connector that wouldn't loosen during operation, and was granted a patent on the idea. E. V. Chilson, the parts manufacturer, heard of it, looked at it and agreed to use it.

A BIG PROMOTION

Businesses changed hands often in the small towns, and concerns like the Clare Hardware and Implement Co. were often purchased. Lewis and Patrick proposed to unite their need for local acceptance and the automobile with a big drawing contest in 1906. Every purchase of one dollar or more entitled the customer to a ticket, good for a drawing six months later, supposedly in September.

A drawing of the prize, a 1906 Oldsmobile, was widely promoted. Customers flocked to the little store on McEwan and Fourth Street, each leaving their dollar bills behind and taking a raffle ticket with its visions of future happiness in exchange. The store sold good merchandise, and it's well they did, for it's not known if the prize was ever awarded to a hopeful motorist.

Someone was either lucky enough or wealthy enough to purchase a car in Clare by 1909, for we read of Belle Coulter and a companion being injured in Clare's first accident. The children had been up in Arthur visiting Belle's uncle. As the auto was travelling just south of Clare, it "slewed into a ditch" and upset. Miss Stockwell, the friend, received a broken arm and Belle was rudely thrown onto the ground, but otherwise not badly hurt. The driver wasn't injured, but the automobile was heavily damaged by the first accident in Clare's history.

How or where the automobile was fixed isn't known, but it must have been a rather formidable problem as there were no garages in town at the time, and wouldn't be until 1911 when David E. Ward established one on First Street at McEwan.

The lack of garages didn't deter the adventurer however, and the motorists continued to ply the sand and clay trails in the county. By mid-summer of 1909, one rather rugged vehicle chugged down Tough Street in western Freeman. That roadway wasn't locally known as a difficult stretch of highway without reason.

During the early years, the automobile was a blasted nuisance much of the time. Frequently the critter wouldn't even run at all. On the days it did condescend to sputter, it would have to be run over treacherous roads. After a rain, it was often impossible to go beyond the first mud hole. If, perchance, the excursionist was caught in a summer shower, a drenching for the passengers was a certainty. Few models sported any kind of a top, either permanent or temporary. Windshields were another luxury not often enjoyed.

It's no wonder the early automobilists were either wealthy or were sportsmen, preferably both, since the mechanical monsters were expensive to begin with and expensive to maintain. Additionally, they needed a strong arm on the crank to start the engine wheezing. Tires would frequently "blow" and they cost upwards from $40.00. Batteries would last one year and they carried premium prices also.

Around Clare, the only men who had the wealth and the need or desire for one of the early beasts were A. J. Doherty, Floyd, his son, C. W. Calkins and Dr. F. R. Gray. A year later, in 1910, L. E. Davy, Clark Sutherland, Tip Calkins and Dr. Clute joined the exclusive ranks.

This was the first prize in the Lewis & Patrick Hardware promotion during 1906.
Photo: Oldsmobile Division

Farwell's wealthy sportsmen included banker Floyd Oliver, Franklin Littlefield and William Armstrong. Harrison had only one auto, and that belonged to the Hughes family.

WHOA!

Men who grew up around horses and had driven them over a period of time found the transition to the auto particularly difficult. They had long been accustomed to the horse doing most of the driving, starting and stopping the buggy, and also doing most of the thinking. This perhaps accounts for the numerous accidents, both during the equestrian era and the time period which immediately followed it.

The young people had fewer bad habits to unlearn, and they rapidly adapted to the automobile and its demands for stern driver control over it. The Doherty boys were indulged by their famous father, as he was away from home on his many involvements in business, government and political affairs. Frank, Floyd and Fred would drive around town, and occasionally they shared the steering wheel with sister, Lydia.

One day early in the auto age, probably around 1912, Clark Sutherland's daughter, Avis, got an irresistable urge. She came home from school and saw that big, black car just sitting there, waiting for something to happen. She grabbed the keys, cranked it up and tore off down Fifth Street, heading west. Marshal Clark saw her cloud of dust and heard the engine backfire several times. He was nearly as frightened as the horses who were being nudged to the side of the road by their drivers to wait for the speeding car to pass on by in a haze of dust. Marshal Clark hot-footed it down to the Clare County

The revolution in personal transportation is presented here during 1918. Shown on North McEwan Street are sleighs drawn by horses and oxen. The automobile was about to replace them both. The Ideal Theater now stands on this spot.

Farwell in the pre-auto days, 1910.

Bank, leaned over the desk and shouted, "You tell her to keep her speed down, or someone's going to get arrested!" Well, banker Sutherland had been completely taken by this sudden turn of events, and he was at a loss for words. Shifting his big cud of tobacco to the other cheek, he stared at the marshal and then uttered, "Women drivers!"

Littlefield had an easier time of it in Farwell when his daughter, Hazel Grace, tore down the main part of town in 1914. There weren't so many formal rules governing traffic in this town, but her exploits behind the wheel soon made the rounds, and teamsters going to Farwell began keeping an eye out for her, just in case.

Franklin, the only son Josiah had, bought a 1912 Ford car which he drove back from Detroit. He became a common sight on the streets when his machine ran. There were no garages in Farwell for several years, and he became the town's first mechanic. The better he became, the more he drove. There were no Ford dealers in Clare County yet, so he had to make his selection of Fords from the black models Johnson had on hand in Mt. Pleasant.

Older drivers had more trouble with the horseless carriages. When they were finally able to coax some forward speed from the four-wheeled monsters, panic frequently set in as they began to consider means of slowing them down. Old fellows would be heard yelling at their machines as they roared down the street, "Whoa! Durn ya! Whoa!"

ORDINANCE NUMBER 65

There was beginning to be enough traffic on the streets of Clare in 1910 to warrant a few rules, so the city council passed an ordinance which limited automobile speeds to twelve miles per hour, but they didn't instruct either Street Marshal Clark or constable Mack Duryee how they were going to enforce it. All Mayor Will Adams said was, "Enforce the law!"

The first method Marshal Clark tried was to have a small boy standing on one of the street corners several times a day. When a car came along, he sent him racing along side, running as fast as his little legs would churn. Clark estimated that a ten-year-old boy should be able to keep up with an automobile going no faster than the speed limit for five rods. If the auto outpaced the lad, a summons was issued to the driver for an infraction of Ordinance No. 65.

This method didn't work out very well, as the drivers caught on very quickly to Marshal Clark's speed trap. His next attempt to control the drivers was more clever. He measured the distances along the major streets between the wooden crosswalks, and then prepared a reference table for optimum lapsed time between the sounds made by the vehicle hitting those wooden crosswalks, and from McEwan Street, he could look north and south and when an automobile approached, he would begin checking his pocket watch. At least twenty and seven-tenths seconds had better elapse before the second thump registered. If an automobile was going east and west, he expected thirty-six seconds to go by, as those blocks running in that direction were longer.

This system worked quite well, especially after a stop-watch was purchased. Anyone could be stationed on a street corner, and speeding motorists were without an excuse or an alibi.

GASOLINE FOR THE PUBLIC

Lewis and Patrick put a barrel up on a couple of saw-horses early in 1910 behind their store on McEwan. They began offering petrol to the public on a limited basis, but soon the demand increased to the point that they had to install a larger supply, and a better method of dispensing it. An underground tank hooked up to a hand pump served the purpose quite handily.

The next motoring season found a second source of public gasoline when John Gardner buried a tank south of the railroad tracks. "My gasoline is superior to that found in most small towns," he said. "My customers get clear quill."

Both gasoline purveyors were kept busy as more and more residents were making vehicular purchases, and there were more motorists taking in the town from neighboring districts. Dr. F. R. Gray purchased a Ford to help him in his rural calls.

One day he took John Grimason on his R.F.D. route in an experiment. Both wanted to know if the auto could reduce the time

Looking north on McEwan Street, Clare, 1920.

required for the twenty-seven mile course laid out by the postal authorities. Normally the distance would be traversed in about two hours and forty minutes. This time one hour and fifty-seven minutes had been required.

Dennis Cross, another carrier thought about this a bit and went right down and bought his own car. Cross ran his route in one hour and fifty-one minutes, and he made over one hundred starts and stops each day, yet "--from an economical point of view, it seems that part of the mail carrier equipment in the near future will either be a motorcycle or an auto, but for the worst roads---Dobbin will still haul the mail."

ANOTHER ACCIDENT

C. W. Calkins and James S. Bicknell were motoring down in Gratiot County one April day in 1910, when they "nicked" a horse as they attempted to ease by a three-horse team. Calkins had previously braked the vehicle behind the team, but as the car passed on the left, a horse jumped the traces and the car hit it and broke its leg. The farmer wanted $200, but Charley denied any responsibility. Later some lawyers came to Clare and tried to get him to pay $250, but he rejected this offer also. When the judge rapped his gavel down on $175 during the Fall term of Circuit Court, Calkins decided not to let this opportunity go by.

MICHIGAN'S FIRST AIRPLANE FACTORY

1910 was a noteworthy year for other reasons. The Brooks Boat Company of Saginaw looked at their boat-building prospects and decided to try their hand at building airplanes. Theirs became the first such factory in Michigan, as they negotiated with Mr. Armstrong of the partnership between Curtiss and the Wrights, to oversee the company. Parts were manufactured, but not assembled. They would sell the airplanes knocked down to a would-be-aviator. The pilot would also have to be a mechanic.

Out near the Clare Colony in California,

Mrs. Dan Jackson, late of Grant Township, wrote a letter to her cousin, Nora O'Neil, back home. She said that her husband worked on a large corporation farm which was near the big California air-ship race site in 1910. "Planes came from all over the world," she said. "One from France had a woman passenger, and it received $1,000 for a three round trip course...The parking lot covered three to four acres and it was filled with autos...There were at least 100,000 people at the races," she concluded.

Times were changing rapidly now! The citizens of Clare County were being amazed at the mechanical age whether they left the area or not. Cadillac, for its 1912 County Fair, contracted for a Flying Machine to perform acrobatic tricks in the sky and also to take passengers for a short ride, and they invited Clare's residents to come, see and ride.

Progress and change weren't always cheap, however, as officials at Cadillac had to pay as much for the airplane as they did for the balance of the entire fair. But when that "Baldwin Red Devil" took to the air, it was the "greatest event in the history of this section". Children from Clare County were admitted free of charge to the exhibition on Thursday, and they stood, awe-struck at the daring aviator. The motorcycle races were exciting also, but nothing stirred their imaginations like the soaring "Red Devil", flip-flapping through the air with such breathtaking stunts.

The automobile was such an insignificant factor that summer to the children, that they scarcely noticed its presence. The first county auto dealership was established by the Doherty Bros. in 1912. Those big Buick touring cars which gleamed alongside the sidewalks raced the boys' imaginations though, and James Bicknell, one of the young in heart, succumbed to the lure of the machine age. Mayor William Murphy was the next victim, and Farwell banker, Floyd Oliver, became the third proud owner of a Buick. Two more cars were sold before the driving season ended in October. Obviously, Buick was building a better automobile, and Clare's residents were buying them.

W. D. Ireland had been to the big auto

show in Detroit during 1911. He became excited as he examined the 150 different models on display there, and as he walked past the Overlands, Regals, Paige-Detroits, Carhartts, Whites, Oaklands, Cuttings, Imperials, Patterson 30's, Cole 30's, American Travelers, Black Crows and the Alpenas, he purposed in his mind that he would have one of these beauties, one way or another.

In 1912, he took on the franchises for the Reo and the Flanders 20, and imported display models to Clare. He thus became the second auto dealer in the county.

MORE ACCIDENTS

Northern people may have become familiar with the automobiles, but the horses were terrified of those machines which roared along, belching fire and smoke from their engines. Mrs. Fred Irwin knew her horses would be frightened by the monsters, but she couldn't keep them under control as they encountered a car in southwest Vernon, and her rig was upset after the horse bolted and became a runaway. Her baby was thrown out of the overturned rig, and mother and child were severely injured.

About the same time, a car owned by A. J. Doherty was cruising near Vance Warren's place in Vernon. Their family dog was standing in the road, disbelieving what it saw approaching. Too late it realized that the automobile was about to manufacture one dead dog.

THE HARD SELL

During April, the Doherty Bros. put together an ad which featured the 1912 Buicks. Model 28, a 35 H.P. roadster, sold for $1,175; the Touring Car Model 29 with the same horsepower retailed for $1,250; a light roadster, Model 36 powered by 25 horses, could be had for $950. The economy model sported a 16 H.P. engine and could be purchased for $550. The prestige car, Model 43, was a beautiful touring car and developed fifty surging horses beneath its bonnet. $1,800 would put this fabulous car on the roads of Clare County.

So well-written was this ad, that G. S. Garber, the manager of the Saginaw Division of the Buick Motor Company, wanted 35 copies of it for his sales department to examine.

David Ward, the city character, Jack-of-all-trades, mayor to be, future sheriff, bootlegger, auctioneer, blusterer, promoter and yet gifted citizen, decided that an automobile repairing facility would be a paying proposition, so he opened a garage on First Street at McEwan. He stocked an inventory of gasoline, oil, batteries, tires and the more common minor parts which failed so frequently. He had a small machine shop in back for the manufacturing of parts which couldn't be purchased, and he had a blacksmith forge available for more extensive metal fabrication.

From this beginning, he soon launched into his D. Ward Oil Company which in turn, evolved into the Oil and Drum Company. He sold gasoline and kerosene both wholesale and retail. "We meet all competition," he said, referring to Standard Oil.

DETROIT'S GROWTH

When you had this much activity in the hinterlands, you could pretty well assume that there were larger goings-on in Detroit, and indeed this was the case.

In 1902, there had been two small plants turning out automobiles. Production figures were never larger than a few score horseless carriages during the early period, and those cars only ran when they felt in the mood. Their individuality and contrariness caused more than one owner to roundly curse the day of purchase. Other times, spectators laughed and ran alongside the sometime moving vehicles, poking fun at the owners, causing in general, a bit of defensiveness on the part of the motorist.

By 1912, there were thirty factories in Detroit turning out 150,000 automobiles. 50,000 men were employed, and not a few were from Clare County. A person who had the foresight to invest a few thousand dollars in the right company would by now have a controlling interest in the corporation. Estimates of $35,000,000 were given out by the

Buick Model 16 Roadster, 1910.
Photo courtesy Buick Motors

promoters of the industry, who were waxing eloquently. Indeed, some of the early stock, worth a fortune in 1912, was peddled for over a year without a taker. Around 1912, the stocks frequently were paying 100% returns on an annual basis. Gross sales were $138,000,000.

Detroit, with its population now grown to 500,000, produced $276 worth of automobile for every person living within its environs. Truly it had almost overnight become the automobile capital of the world.

Such breathtaking statistics may completely overshadow such an insignificant news item coming out of Hatton on May 17th, but those four automobiles which came to that community were just as revolutionary to the future development of the automobile as were the impressive sales figures.

A STOLEN CAR

When young people are peppered with high-powered advertising, they sometimes lose their ability to be merely a disinterested spectator. Dennis Cross found this out when he parked his new automobile on the main street, near the post office. A few minutes later he was told by a youth that his beautiful machine was now being driven south out of town by a school boy. Dennis was panic stricken! There was that big new roadster of his going down the road to who knows where. "What if it's wrecked?" he thought. "There's no telling what these durn fool kids will do!" he said to a by-stander, but his fears were unfounded. Soon he heard the "chug-chug" of his prized machinery up on Vernon Hill. A few more seconds and it hoved into view! Cross didn't say much to the kid when he pulled it up to a halt in front of him, but he sure gave his big, black beauty a close going over.

USED CARS FOR SALE

The headlines of the CLARE SENTINEL didn't scream out this momentous news, but there it was on page four. "We have some nice second-hand cars for sale cheap," said the advertisement of Ireland and Higgins. In the same issue, they promoted the new Flanders 20.

Lewis Sunday from Arthur came down and looked over the offerings and decided that he needed a better one to take him on his official rounds as sheriff.

Business was booming in the auto trade.

The Doherty Bros., who had been servicing cars in the Dunwoodie Bldg. on the northwest corner of Fifth Street and McEwan, thought things were becoming too crowded. They had a machine shop in back with lathes, drill presses and the forge took a lot of space also. Then there were the big automobiles which were driven into the building for servicing. The only trouble was, the automobile season lasted for only part of the year.

A. J. Doherty, the father of the Doherty Brothers, was approached about this and he thought that a larger building, complete with machine shop, auto servicing and storage room for the autos during the off season could be a paying proposition, so he had a 28½' x 131' building erected on Fifth Street, facing north, but behind the Opera House. His boys moved their business into it when it was completed.

HARNESSMAKER TO AUTO HUCKSTER

One of the more important tradesmen to a community had been the harnessmaker, but now a new wind was prevailing. The big catalog companies were able to deliver harnesses to the farmer's door for less money than they could be hand-sewn, and many farmers had been taking advantage of the Sears and Roebuck offerings.

Grant Terwilliger, the skilled harnessmaker, saw the handwriting on the wall, so he took on the Overland franchise for 1913. He began by promoting the Model 69T for $985, hoping that the "T" designation would do half as much for him as it did for Henry. The car boasted a self-starter and 30 H.P. Five passengers could ride comfortably on Timken Roller Bearings, and for just $50 more, a Warner Speedometer would be supplied. If a person were interested in the interior decor, a $50 top and boot could be added. An additional $25 would cause a windshield to be installed.

It was a beautiful car, and it sold well in

Alice Doherty driving an early left-handed Buick.
Photo from the Margaret Wherly Collection

Clare. Perry D. Brown, the big farmer and land holder, bought the first one delivered in town. Mrs. A. E. Mussell purchased the next one.

Junius Roe, the Colonville merchant, was twenty-five years old when he took over the Dunwoodie Bldg. garage from the Doherty Brothers. In 1913 he was successful in securing the Buick franchise for the year, evidently negotiating more successfully than the Dohertys, but then perhaps his brother, Dr. J. B., who was a dentist, helped him during the negotiations. A younger brother, Alfred, soon joined the new garageman. A few weeks later, a gasoline tank was installed alongside the garage on Fifth Street, and the Roe garage began doing big business.

Clare was beginning to look like a motorists' town.

MORE ACCIDENTS

The automobile was now being taken for granted by everyone, including the horses, but mishaps still occurred. Dr. F. Gray upset his auto while attempting to cross over a narrow wooden bridge in the townships, and was pinned under the turned-over vehicle for about two hours.

Another incident involved an auto which

Dr. Clute poses with his new automobile in front of the Calkins House in 1914. On the cart is Glen Lloyd, and Frank Doherty is on the running board. On the steps are Rose Jerred, Jennie Pierson, Agnes Pierson, and Earl Dwyer, manager. By the utility pole is a Leffingwell boy. Phillips is on the water wagon.

frightened William Marlin's horse. He was taking the family for a ride one evening in May. A car coming up behind the buggy caused a run-away, but first the horse wheeled around and around in the street, throwing William Marlin out. His wife and daughter were still in the buggy as the horse began tearing through town. Acting coolly under pressure, Mrs. Marlin lowered the child over the rear of the buggy when they reached Anderson's Drug Store. She jumped when the runaway approached the Calkins House. The horse turned on East Sixth Street and was caught when it attempted to go toward Seventh Street.

Dr. A. Mussell, driving an Overland, attempted to pass between two rigs, one of which belonged to Mr. and Mrs. James Lower. He hit Lower's hub, throwing Arthur Lower out of the buggy. Mr. Lower was half in and half out of the buggy as his wife struggled, successfully as it turned out, to bring the team under control.

In late September, Clare was having a street fair. A rope was strung across the road to keep traffic and pedestrians out. Dr. William Clute, decided that he wasn't going to let a rope keep him from driving down the street. Aiming his auto at the center of the rope, he hit it a good lick, and damaged his auto at least $144 worth.

Since the fair had been a flop, some suggested that the city might pay the damages to re-inforce the lesson that the street carnival had not been a profitable venture, but it wasn't to be. "If Dr. Clute wants to take absence from good common sense," said one citizen, "then he'd better pay for his foolishness out of his own pocket."

A FORD FRANCHISE

Ford automobiles were sold in Rosebush and soon, in Clare. F. H. Broderick, a local garage man, in 1913 acquired the first franchise, but when he refused to hustle the cars, the company revoked his "agreement". They gave it to I. E. Hampton, formerly of Sheridan.

"Ike" didn't wait for some factory representative to come around urging him to sell cars. He knew that the Model T was a winner and he sold them in large quantities.

PROSPECTS LOOK GOOD

Business became so brisk for Alfred Roe that he bought the building north of the Dunwoodie location that William Haley had used for his office. He built a 33′ x 132′ garage and machine shop and moved in on May 8, 1914.

"The auto industry is in its infancy and no doubt the coming season will see another good increase in the number of cars owned in the territory. With two well-equipped garages, this city will be able to take care of the demand in first class shape," said Seymour Andrus in the CLARE SEN—TINEL.

Business was brisk, so "Ike" Hampton purchased the Doherty garage on Fifth Street. A more complete line of repairing was to be done, including tire vulcanizing. Most com-

monly used parts were kept in stock, and the machinery to make nuts and bolts was kept well oiled for use.

Everyone, it seemed, was driving cars in 1914. R. V. Rule, the Arthur school teacher purchased a new one, as did the L. M. Converse family, Frank Lamoreaux, W. E. Green, M. D. Clute, D. W. Rowe, John Quinn, F. C. Alley, B. S. Alley, Jim Duncan, William Armstrong and his sons George, James and Irwin. George Payne bought a Ford Truck so he could deliver groceries in Greenwood. Other autos were owned by Dr. Reeder, E. B. Brown, Charles Richardson, Dan M. Faye, A. R. Canfield, John Mahoney, Hamilton L. Leston, F. A. Ballard, Arthur D. Johnson, J. T. Brown (who was head of the first two-car family in Clare), J. A. Olson and Dr. A. E. Mulder, plus all the earlier purchasers. Soon J. F. Brand came rolling through town in his 1914 Oldsmobile Sedan. Herb Allen purchased an Oakland late in October, and Clark Sutherland bought its twin.

Legend has it that these "snowmobile kits" were invented here in Harrison and then marketed by the Ford Motor Company. Many RFD carriers owned them, but they weren't held in high favor by the owners, as they were expensive to maintain, and they wouldn't track well in a rutted road.
Photo: Mid-Michigan Bank Collection

A 1913 Model T Ford was converted to this utility pick-up.
Photo courtesy Ford Motor Company

GASOLINE VS. ZOLINE

Rumors were circulating in 1914 that sometime soon, automobiles would be able to run on water plus a couple of other substances commonly available in any drug store. The basis for this claim was a racing test made at the Indianapolis Speedway during the summertime.

John Andrus, a Portuguese inventor from McKeesport, Pennsylvania, discovered that napthalene and another substance could be combined and a combustible fuel would be produced. The AAA agreed to make the test, and so a Marmon 41 auto was modified to use the new fuel. It operated 1,030 miles in two days and averaged 59.95 miles per hour.

Russell Huff, test engineer for Packard Motors supervised. A professor from Michigan Agricultural College, Andrus and a man named Fisher completed the team.

The product from the still which was set up at the track was put into the car in five gallon quantities. The big Marmon 41 averaged better than 16 miles per gallon, which was about 400% better than the car normally got on gasoline.

C. J. Vincent, another engineer at Packard Motor Co. reviewed the tests and said, "It's better in every way than gasoline." Standard Oil was interested in this experiment, as were a lot of motorists.

THE 1915 SEASON

Alfred Roe leased his big new garage in January to J. T. Brown and Son, and he went to Detroit to learn electricity. Junius, his brother, had about four months to live at the time the garage was leased.

Brown had picked up the Oakland franchise for 1915, and as he planned to sell a lot of cars, he needed a good facility from which to work.

During the big auto show in Detroit, eight-cylinder cars were said to be the main feature of the popular national event, but the work horse in Clare continued to be the Ford.

WHERE ARE THE CHEVROLETS?

W. C. Durant organized the Chevrolet Motor Company in 1911. He sold the car with the familiar bow-tie rather successfully before 1914, when the car was designed as a light six-cylinder. Back in 1908, Durant had seen the basic Chevrolet emblem design on a hotel wall. His room had wall paper with this bow-tie motif repeated over and over on it. Tearing a piece of wall paper off, he put it in his luggage and brought it home for future glory.

J. T. Brown picked up the 1915 Chevrolet franchise and soon sold the first auto of that name in Clare. Brown also sold the Monroe, which was an economy car at $460.

During 1915, the farmers began buying the Fords in large numbers. Ike Hampton drove back caravans of six each week and he had six more coming in by freight. He complained that he was on the road too much of the time driving cars back to Clare.

In April the city council took up the matter of the hitching post. Opinion was divided, but many thought the wagons parked along the streets were a hazard to the increasing traffic and additionally, the tradition was most unsanitary, as the gutters were filled with horse droppings. When the council decided to leave them on McEwan, a critic said, "It seems that some in Clare are like the Chinese. They hate to give up any customs of their ancestors, but sooner or later, it will come to them and (we'll) give up the hitching rails."

A BOOM YEAR

Henry Ford offered to rebate fifty dollars to each Ford owner who purchased a vehicle between August 1, 1914 and April 1, 1915, if he sold 300,000 cars in a year's time. Ike offered each customer thirty dollars for his chance on a rebate, but everyone turned him down. Joshua Fuller, R. W. Fairbanks, F. P. Davis, Claud A. Reker, J. E. Doherty, John Garchow, Charles E. Davis, L. M. Converse, "Jess" Hampton and W. J. Maxwell began keeping track of the sales statistics around late March, 1915.

MODEL 49 T. C. (7 Passenger)

Oakland Model 49 Touring Car, 1915.
Photo Courtesy Pontiac Motor division

W. E. Noble loved to drive his 1912 Oakland touring car.
Photo courtesy Pontiac Motor Division

The famous Model T Ford, 1915.
Photo: Detroit Public Library of National Automotive History

The 1911 Chevrolet

Alfred Roe returned to Clare in May with a franchise for the "Wonder Car", the Maxwell. "Every road is a Maxwell Road" was the slogan used. One owner claimed he had put 38,000 miles on his car in only 18 months. Selling for $695 f.o.b. Detroit, it appeared to be a bargain. No less a bargain was the Monroe, which sold for the same price in Clare. This model also sold well!

The Clare Hardware and Implement Co. accepted the 1915 Overland franchise and pushed Model "83" for $750. "This is the largest four-cylinder car manufactured in 1915," Lewis said. A Roadster sold for $725, and Model "80", which was a big touring car, sold for $1,075. A floor model in Brewster green with fine hair line striping of clear ivory-white was a spectator's delight. It also had a five-bearing crankshaft, and developed 35 H.P.

A ROAD RALLYE

So numerous were the autos in August that fifty owners paraded them throughout the Coleman, Herrick, Clare, Dover, Brown, Cornwell and Harrison districts. This was a big social event, ostensibly booming the Chautauqua in Clare, but in reality, it was an ego trip.

J. M. Davis bought the building that Thomas C. Holbrook and Joseph Ladd from Franklin owned on Main Street. It was adjacent to the John O'Callaghan Feed Barn and the Bicknell Bldg. He built a 40′ x 100′ auto facility and put dark red paving brick on its front. This garage was soon being called the "big garage", and Ike Hampton would

eventually be selling and repairing Fords in it, but Roe leased it first.

F. H. Broderick, meantime, opened a garage in the Haley Building. He was an excellent mechanic and paint man, and would be hired by Hampton soon to fix the Fords he knew so well. His wide experience as the late manager of the Bell Telephone Company's office in Clare made him a valuable employee.

A CROSS-COUNTRY TRIP

John H. Wilson, Carlos Reading, Dr. A. E. Mulder and Perry Wilson motored east to New York City and Niagara Falls in what was probably the first locally organized tour. Next year Dr. Mulder would go on

When the fan belt slips off the pulley, the driver must replace it. This photo was taken in 1921.

another trip, but this one would take his son's and wife's lives.

Prior to this date, there wasn't much discussion about auto insurance, but perhaps the regular agencies were selling it with no questions asked. The Citizens Mutual Insurance Company in Howell began its corporate existence in September of 1915, and was the nation's first mutual auto insurance company. It sold yearly coverage for $6.50. Regular insurance had been costing as much as $42.50.

THE FIRST FATALITY

Noah Cousineau, Floyd Kirkpatrick, Alfred Hickey and Elton Allen left Clare in Allen's car for the annual Farwell Labor Day celebration in 1915. The car was traveling at a high rate of speed about three miles west of Clare when it approached the big curve. One of the passengers was heard by Fabian Hinkle to say, "Slow down!"

Allen, who was driving, and Hickey, in the front passenger seat, weren't injured, but Cousineau was thrown against a pole and fatally injured. Kirkpatrick hit the same pole, but fell on Noah. Cousineau was treated by a doctor, but he died three hours later.

A short funeral was held by the Free Methodists as Mrs. Carlos Reading sang a hymn, and lay preacher Rev. J. A. Allen preached a short sermon. Fellow workers from the Clare County Bank blinked back tears as his father and brother took the body back to Big Rapids for burial.

TIME FOR NEW RULES

Cars, trucks and horse-drawn vehicles were all over town during the fall of 1915. The city council looked at the chaos and decreed that, effective October 1, 1915, the following rules would be enforced:

1. The speed limit in the business district is 10 miles per hour. Elsewhere it is 15 miles per hour.
2. Keep to the right side of the street.
3. When passing another vehicle, pass on the left.
4. Stop as close to the curb as possible.

Members of the Schunk family pause for this 1919 photo.

Workmen are shown retrieving the Allen automobile which took the life of Noah Cousineau in 1915.

5. Park at a 45 degree angle to the curb.
6. Cross the street on the cross-walks.
7. Use hand signals before turning.
8. Turn front and rear lights on when running. Rear lights are permitted when standing.
9. Bicycles must have a bell or horn, and a light at night.

Even though the rules weren't designed to present a hardship, they caused many problems, so City Marshal Clark, with Earl Dwyer and Charley Johnson, stationed themselves on McEwan at the Fifth Street, Fourth Street and Third Street crossings and directed the drivers into the right hand lanes. The streets were filled with autos and teams were stacked every which-way, both before and after the men tried to sort out the vehicles.

This 20th Century was sure a bummer!

A BUS SERVICE

Enough traffic had been building toward Houghton Lake so that a regular bus line was the next logical step. A ten-passenger, low-geared car was especially built for this run, which made two round trips a week, beginning in May, 1915. The fare was five cents a mile. The published schedule called for the passengers to depart Mt. Pleasant at 7:00 a.m. and arrive in Houghton Lake twelve hours later.

DRIVERS LICENSED

A new state law took effect in October, which made it impossible to secure a license to drive if a person was under 18, and illegal to drive without the legal document. Of course that wouldn't stop the boys from jumping onto the running boards of cars and having their own taxi service, albeit a non-voluntary service in most cases, nor did it stop the occasional unlawful joy rides.

HARRISON'S FIRST AUTO AGENCY

Up until this time, auto sales in the county had been located in Clare. When Reo Motors came out with their "Reo The Fifth", Hughes Brothers in Harrison negotiated the right to sell it. Their seven-passenger touring car model exuded strength and power, and sold for a relatively modest price of $1,250.

1916 NOTES

William H. Caple went to Jackson to pick up a factory fresh "Jackson". On the way back, he collided with an interurban car of the Michigan United Traction Company near Mason, and completely demolished it. A brother, Walter, was in the car with him and received the most injuries, he being unconscious three hours.

DAVIS AND FEIGHNER AGENCY

J. M. Davis arranged to form a sales partnership with one of the Feighner boys. They sold the Oakland at the Big Garage that Davis erected the preceding season. Then "Ike" Hampton decided to vacate the Doherty facilities and purchased the Alfred Roe building next to the Dunwoodie Building. He bought a house from Holbrook and moved it to the rear of the 33' lot and put an addition onto the garage. Before he moved in, an offer came to trade the Roe building for the garage that Davis had just built next to the Feed Barn. The deal was completed and the Ford dealership was established on

The automobile liberated Michiganians. 1922.

McEwan Street between Bicknell's store and the Feed Barn.

When Hampton moved out of the Doherty facility, Valmour Armour opened a private auto repair service there which lasted until the draft beckoned him.

The Oakland Automobile changed its franchise again, this time with D. E. Mater becoming the agent. The big eight-cylinder monster sold for $1,585.

THE COUSINEAU ESTATE LAWSUIT

The big trial of 1916 was put on the June Circuit Court docket, and A. J. Lacy returned to Clare to handle half of the trial. It was a hotly contested case, but the jury came back with no verdict. Suspicions about Allen's drinking circulated, but were never proved, and the question of his responsibility for the death of Noah Cousineau on Labor Day, 1915, went unresolved.

It was tried again in December, but not much more success was coming Lacy's way. Carlos A. Reading, a friend of both J. A. Allen's family and the Cousineaus, fought the ploys and the jury came back with a verdict of ''no cause for action''.

ADDITIONAL CAR FRANCHISES

There were several other exotic cars sold in Clare before World War I. For example:

WILLYS-KNIGHT—sold by Clare
                    Hardware
                    Company—1916

METZ   —sold by L. H. Thompson—
         1917 ($600)

FORD   —sold by Fred Bingham
         (sub-agency in Farwell) 1917

ALLEN —sold by John Norton—1917

SAXON —sold by F. A. Ballard and
         Dr. L L. Kelley—1915 ($395)

DORT   —sold by J. E. Dohety—1918

DODGE —sold by Thompson and
         Williams—1919

ADDITIONAL GARAGES

Guy Georgia—Operated in the old Roe garage.   1916

J. T. Brown and Son Sales—''Fisk Tires'' 1916

H. C. Hall and Earl Anderson—on W. Fourth St. Catered to Fords 1916

Webb and Gallagher—(Now Clare Hardware) 1916

Guy Georgia and L. A. Wood—1916

Buick Model E-44 Roadster, 1918.
Photo courtesy Buick Motors

Farwell Garage—(McGinnis—proprietor) 1916

Will J. Stephenson—Tire vulcanizing 1917

Harrison Garage—1917

Fred Bingham Garage—Farwell 1917

John H. Rawson—Farwell 1917

H. D. Kratz—Auto livery in Clare 1917

Pete Bailey Garage—Harrison 1918

William Mott Service—Farwell 1918

A. Cuvrell—Auto painting in Farwell 1918

MORE ACCIDENTS

The rates of accidents had increased proportionately to the number of automobiles which took to the roads. Perhaps newer and thus inexperienced drivers flooded the poor roads beyond their capacities and caused some of the problem. Another explanation may have been the additional moving targets made it difficult for pedestrians to locate a safe median to stand on, and of course, more vehicles on the road meant a lineal increase in accidents, normally.

Clare's second traffic death involved Dr. Mulder's wife and son, Eugene. They were killed when the family car attempted to cross the Michigan Central Railroad tracks, locally known around Ypsilanti as the Geddes Crossing, an unmarked, partially hidden crossing. The Mulder family was motoring to the Michigan State Fair on September 6, 1916 when it was hit by a 70 mile per hour rain.

Mrs. Howard Raymor was hit by an auto on a snow-covered road. This accident was most unusual, as cars up to this time were only operated during the fair weather months.

Dr. Mussell had to check on a patient of his in a Bay City hospital one day in May of 1917, so he asked Archie Parks to be his traveling companion on the long drive. Three miles west of Bay City the car went into a ditch and both men were considerably injured. An ambulance carried both men to the hospital toward which they had been traveling.

Frank Pringle had his car upset in September 1917, and his collar bone was

The Ford Garage in Harrison.

Dr. Mulder

broken.

Tires which blew out were very dangerous to the early cars. In October, 1917, an Ohio car was ditched by a blow-out near the Bert Waite farm. Two families were riding in the car and several people were injured.

A THIRD FATALITY

Late in November of 1917, James McGoogan was injured in an accident in front of McIntosh's farm on Maple Road. John McAninch, a relative, came and took him home, but he had been injured more seriously than had been suspected. He died shortly after arriving home.

An accident near Temple upset a wagon driven by Mrs. Clarence Davison. William Mooney, an older man who was known locally for his recklessness, met Mrs. Davison's car in the center of the road and didn't give the right-of-way. When the horse finally lurched to one side, it threw a youth by the name of Barlow into a ditch, but he wasn't hurt. Mrs. Davison sued the car's owner, a Mr. Fuller, who was a passenger in Mooney's vehicle.

Young sports liked to drive their autos down the rural roads at night with no lights showing on the vehicle. A farmer from Arthur, who had been put into the ditch once too often, warned them, "I'm going to carry rocks in my wagon, and they're going through the next windshield of the car I meet with no lights showing."

Floyd Doherty was hurt when the tire he was fixing threw a heavy rim against his face, crushing his nose, eyes and forehead. The tire had a broken rim and he had started to dismantle it before all of the air was out of it. Even cars that weren't moving could cause accidents!

C. M. Jones lost control of his car while turning out to pass a buggy which had James Nevill and his daughter in it. He knocked both passengers out of the wagon and the auto turned turtle. No one was hurt in this accident.

During the Model T days, almost as many Fords "turned turtle" as stayed upright, yet they could easily be rolled back onto their wheels. Little damage was done because there were no windshields, and the passengers were almost always thrown clear of the rolling vehicle. A quick check of the oil and gasoline and the old Tin Lizzie was off in a cloud of dust, racing into the history books.

Farming

Addison P. Brewer was a lumberman who owned considerable property in Clare County back when the timber was still standing. He, along with Jesse Hoyt, was here early in the logging days, hav'ng "cruised" the virgin forests of Michigan extensively. Brewer was the timber cruiser, or land-looker, for the St. Mary's Canal Company, which had been given a grant of 750,000 acres of land by the Federal government, as a subsidy to build the locks at the Soo.

Jesse Hoyt was the financial wizard and baron who made his first fortune on the Great Lakes with his numerous ships plying the waters right after the Erie Canal was opened. His second fortune was gained in timber and a third fortune was sequestered in his financial dealings when Saginaw began to move ahead, having a dominant financial position in the banking business. He also had banking connections back in New York within the family's banks. Jesse was a major domo in the building of the Flint and Pere Marquette Railway company, one of the land grant railroads, and the only completely successful one at that.

Brewer and Hoyt saw the potential agricultural worth in certain soils around Dover even when the trees were standing, but Hoyt's death in the 1880's left only Brewer to develop the idea of farming the cut-over lands.

It was Addison P. Brewer, therefore, who pushed the settlements around Dover and Sheridan during the 1870's. Grant, as well as certain parts of Sheridan, were deep into agriculture well before 1900. Immigrants from Canada, New York, Ohio and Pennsyl-vania populated these early homesteads, but some also came from Europe, Germany and especially England. Brewer significantly assisted them with hard-to-come-by dollars by donating generously to churches, fairs and "bees" in the Dover, Clare and northern Isabella communities.

This early settlement and development of early Clare County has been covered extensively in the book MICHIGAN'S TIMBER BATTLEGROUND, published in 1976. The second phase of Clare County's agricultural development comes into focus around 1900, when the holdings of J. F. Brand were sold to immigrants who were moving in from Ohio and Indiana because state internal taxes there were considered excessive. Turnpikes and canals were placed upon the tax rolls, and the farmers in those states felt they were being asked to shoulder too much of their costs.

This tax-revolt syndrome pretty much characterized the attitudes of these early settlers in northern Sheridan and in practically all of Arthur. It was to have a retarding effect upon internal public improvements which were needed if growth was to continue, especially the roads and ditches which drained some of the low ground. Experts were being sent out by the State of Michigan, offering free advice about a variety of topics, including the following: farm animal husbandry; home-making; crops; home life; diseases and their control; roads; schools and also certain breeds of cattle, hogs and sheep. However these immigrants usually turned a deaf ear to them if taxes were involved.

59

THE FARMERS' INSTITUTES

Some concomitants of the state's interest in agriculture were the Farmers' Institutes, held in most counties in the north. Just when the first one occurred isn't known, but A. J. Doherty was its president during 1899 and 1900, and he probably helped initiate its activities to go along with his large Vernon farm.

They were organized on a county-wide basis, with the several townships having a contact person whose job it was to co-ordinate their activities, and to promote the common goals. Essentially the institutes were informational, but since they were held during the months of January and February, (periods when activities on a non-animal farm were limited) they became social events eagerly looked forward to by the ladies, especially. Residents in towns such as Farwell and Harrison often had some of their leading citizens in leadership positions. William Murphy, merchant and mayor of Harrison was one of those non-farm people who actively supported the Institute. Joseph E. Ladd, postmaster at Harrison, was another, although he did have a farm in Hamilton Township.

Wise, Vernon and Gilmore Townships in Isabella County normally participated in the Clare County Institutes, as their residents were an intrinsic component of the Clare community. Speakers from other districts were frequently brought in to speak on various topics. For example, L. W. Oviatt was the guest authority on sugar beets. He discussed the profitability of raising beets in the mid-Michigan regions. Since he knew the topic thoroughly, he discussed weeds, planting, harvesting and marketing with the men. The women folk were treated to home-making topics while the beets were analyzed.

Dr. Dunlop spoke on the topic, "Why many businessmen are farmers". Clark Sutherland, who had a large farm under a hired manager in Sheridan, talked about "Shorthorns and the bank-book". Since he was the cashier at the Clare County Savings Bank, as well as a farmer raising registered Short-horns, the topic was appropriate for him. Arthur J. Lacy, a recent immigrant to Clare, and an attorney, spoke about "Farmers and the public schools". His emphasis was upon a high school education and its value to the rural citizen.

The most pressing problem, roads, appeared on the 1900 agenda also. CLARE SENTINEL publisher A. E. Palmer talked about "Good roads and the county system". He was the first one to begin addressing the farmers about the problems connected with the old pathmaster system, but he wasn't the last. A County Road Commission wasn't adopted by Clare until 1930.

Dr. L. L. Kelley turned the office of President over to Josiah Littlefield in 1902, and he immediately set about bringing in more outside experts for the January 1903 meeting. Peter Voorhees, Oakland County's most successful stock breeder, and Professor Dean from Michigan Agricultural College were engaged to bring a new light on animal husbandry. F. F. Rogers of Port Huron, a strong advocate of good roads and a consulting engineer for the Michigan Good Roads Commission, attempted to nudge the farmers toward an acceptance of improving the country roads. His comments about their monetary worth generally fell on deaf ears. These men weren't psychologically ready for increasing their taxes, or for the adoption of a road system which nullified their local control over road-building and maintenance, even though it meant enduring inferior roads.

Clark Sutherland reported to the 1903 meeting that the aggregate value of farm products totaled $100,000. Some of this was from the sale of eggs, butter and poultry, but most came from beef. The concerted effort to turn Clare into the "Market City" was off to a good start.

F. A. Carncross was elected the new president for the 1903-1904 year, and his selection indicated the direction in which the organization was heading. In 1902 he had moved in from Ohio as part of a tax revolt among the farmers who objected to the taxes levied by the turnpike and canal authorities there. He was a truculent opponent of high taxes, which translated into opposition to the drainage ditches and roads.

By 1904 the farmers became sophisticated

enough to move beyond discussing crops and animals. The Wise Farmers' Club met at Alvah Servis' place and discussed the most important crop on the farm—their children. Mrs. Frank Lamoreaux spoke about the subject, "What constitutes a 'finishing-education' in the rural home?" and Clark Sutherland's topic covered co-operation between the home and the school. Having served as board member for over sixteen years, he indicated that "When complaints of children were looked into, nine times out of ten, the fault lies (sic) with the child"

The 1904 Farmers' Institute was attended by over 400 farmers. The walls of the Doherty Opera House were plastered with thorough airings about "Sheep" and "Good Roads"—topics which were just coming into their own. Professor Grawn from Central Normal College at Mt. Pleasant came up on the railroad to lead the discussion on school problems.

Alfalfa was the main discussion topic in 1909, and several farmers were induced to plant their fields to this new crop. As an experiment, D. E. Alward agreed to plant an acre, and so did Joseph Hudson. John Hudson planted two acres up the road a bit, north of Dover. "Court" Kleman planted three acres in 1908 and reported that he had cut three tons from it already.

Most of the farmers were limiting their forage crops to clover, and their hayfields were generally in the forty-acre category.

Dairying was being talked about by the Institutes around Isabella and Clare counties, replacing the high interest in sheep. Prices for wool fluctuated so dramatically from year to year, that farmers weren't able to plan on showing a profit very often. Also the early mutton breeds had been replaced by the fleece producers and this market was being closed off to the farmer as he attempted to salvage something from his large flocks.

Another trial balloon was going up in 1910, and that was the Pomological Societies' offerings. Professor H. J. Eustace from Michigan Agricultural College was imported for this discussion. He talked about spraying, San Jose scale, profits and of course, marketing.

By 1917, the Institutes had served their purpose and it became very difficult to draw crowds. An effort was made to focus attention on certain problems in agriculture by sending an Agricultural College Train among the counties. Wheat, dairy products, alfalfa and fruit were the major subjects featured.

When World War I rolled around, many of Clare County's big farms were owned by absentee landlords, who were called "gentlemen farmers". Wealthy businessmen in Illinois, Indiana, Ohio and even Kentucky purchased large blocks of land and farmed or ranched. They hired farm managers who pretty much ran things as they thought best, and they thought that beef and dairying were the best.

J. F. BRAND

Farming in Grant and Sheridan Townships, the Shea Settlement, the Doty Community and a few other districts was legitimate. Much of the other so-called farming could be better labeled "lumberjack

The J. F. Brand family, 1917.
Photo: Hoyt Public Library Collection

farming''. Several localities were dominated by occupants who eked out an existence on the land, but subsidized it by the stealing of timber from certain parcels of hardwood or cedar. More than one man who dealt in timber purchased back his own logs, as township farming was a cover for the primary occupation of many county residents.

Proper development of county farms had to replace these illegal activities, but some soils which were on the homesteads were not conducive to success. The loamy-clay soils in Arthur and northern Sheridan Townships were in the first rank, however, and these could support productive farming techniques.

The State of Michigan in 1892 and 1893 conducted experiments in Clare and Roscommon Counties, relative to the testing of certain crops grown on the so-called pine barrens. A two-year trial failed to give any hope for their eventual utilization by modern agriculture. The official report concerning the Roscommon sixty-acre plot said, ''All the ingenuity of the skilled agriculturists employed by the state, however, has a success only in illustrating the fact that barren pine lands are a poor investment if purchased for agricultural purposes.'' They concluded by suggesting that the state let the land lie fallow for a generation to see what nature would do.

Beginning in 1896, J. F. Brand of the Saginaw lumber firm of Brand and Hardin, began to put into operation a plan he formulated in 1889. After the timber was removed from a 4,000-acre tract, he dis-

covered that the soil was what he suspected from the start. He judged the soil to be of excellent agricultural potential. Following the example of Addison P. Brewer, he began to promote the sale of farm lands to immigrants from Ohio and Indiana.

He planned to retain a rather large farm with about a thousand acres for his own personal use. The surplus would then be available for modest or even non-existent down payments. Many of the settlers on his lands purchased farms for five dollars an acre, and even half of this was credited to the purchaser for stumping the land. Brand also hired several of the men to work on his farm, thus giving them hard cash to supplement their crops.

THE OHIO COLONY

George Cooper led a caravan of seven prairie schooners to the Brand area in 1902. These Ohio families lived in their wagons until negotiations could be completed with the Saginaw farmer-lumberman. Then log cabins were erected. The farming began in earnest as soon as the families had shelter.

Brand hired William Rhodes to be the foreman of his ranch, and by 1902 he had cleared one hundred sixty acres and planted fields of clover and timothy in forty-acre quadrants. Grains such as wheat, oats, rye or barley were grown in twenty-acre fields. Adjoining the main Brand farm was a large two hundred forty acre field which was used for the registered Herefords during the non-winter months. A herd of four hundred cattle was to be grazed here, but in the early years, about one-half that number were pastured.

Many of the Ohioans were hired to stump the main farm, as well as to help erect the barbed wire enclosure around a section of land.

C. W. PERRY FARM

South of the city of Clare was located a collection of successful farms. Wise, Vernon and Gilmore Townships in Isabella County had agricultural soils of unrivaled possibilities. Most of the homesteads were less than thirty years old, even though there were numerous blackened stumps standing as a mute witness to an era now in history. The main crops were hay, wheat, corn, sugar beets and clover. Good fences were restraining the cattle and hogs from irritating the neighbors, and school houses were numerous enough to keep the children busy and corralled as well.

The Perry farm extended right up to the city limits of Clare and contained two-hundred acres. Good buildings and a house for manager Andrew Mitchell made an elegant setting for the large flock of Shropshire sheep Perry delighted in raising. In 1902, Perry was the number one authority in the whole region.

THE DOVER FARMS

The Brewer farm, managed by brother-in-law Daniel McMaster, and the Joe Hudson farm were probably the best in the whole county. South a few miles was the big Doherty farm and it, too, compared favorably with the Dover entries. Other farms as small as eighty acres were earning a thousand dollars a year for the owner, if they

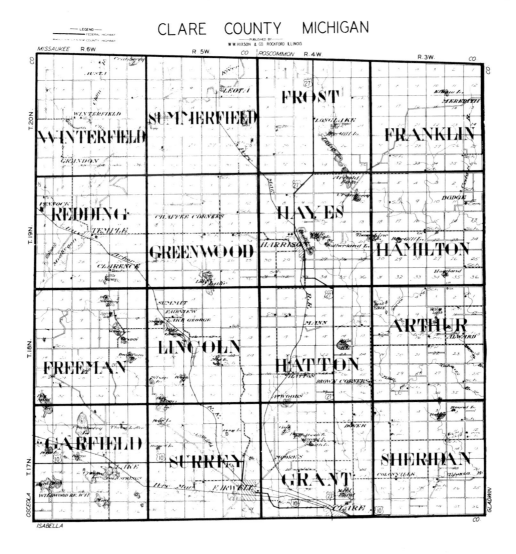

were managed properly.

Hudson's farm consisted of three hundred twenty acres, nearly all of which were clay loam with clay subsoil. He raised shorthorns, Shropshires and Percherons after the twentieth century dawned. Prior to this time, he worked winters in the woods and grew cash crops in the summer, which earned him his immense real estate holdings.

Many other pioneers were still living on their grubbed-out homesteads in the northeast corner of Grant Township, and they too were enjoying relative success in agriculture. The size of their holdings was smaller, being around eighty acres or so.

QUINCE BUSH FARM

Sheridan Township is located very close to the city of Clare, and its fertility of soil is excellent in many locations. One large farm, located only two miles east of Clare in 1903, was Clark H. Sutherland's four hundred-acre Quince Bush Farm. Substantial buildings, barns, sheds and other outbuildings on an improved road made this one of the show-places in the area. When Sutherland began to create a modern establishment in 1894, there were few buildings standing. Only fifteen acres were ploughed and the remaining acreage was unstumped.

Stump removal was more costly than buying raw land outright, and this farm was no exception. Later, farmers would try burning, then finally in frustration, dynamite was used in great quantities. Most men learned how to safely use the volatile compound, but not a few were injured, some even fatally, by it.

Most cattle barns were about 40' by 100'. Sheep barns generally were 20' by 200', and the hay barns would range 40' wide with lengths between 100' and 200'.

Perry's farm was basically a sheep establishment. and his buildings reflected it. Hudson, Brand, Myers, Brewer, Littlefield and Sutherland concentrated on cattle, although sheep were raised also.

Alvah Servis was an excellent shorthorn cattleman, and this became the main product on Quince Bush Farm. Beginning with a nucleus of sixteen superior shorthorns, he

A Stilyard stump puller.

rapidly built a herd of outstanding stature. This was the seminal beginning of the later herds in northern Isabella and Clare Counties. Sutherland's was, in fact, one of the first thoroughbred cattle farms in this district.

THE SHEEP RANCHES

Most of the big farms were in reality an extension of a businessman or an otherwise independently wealthy entrepreneur. Big money could not be earned on the farm by erecting large buildings and parading two-score registered cattle and a few heifers on a few thousand acres. The wealth behind these establishments came first.

Perry D. Brown came to Clare County from Durand in 1899. He had a vision of putting together a vast fortune from the land itself, and he knew it couldn't be from the show-place type farm. Learning about the stretches of wild, cut-over land in Hatton

Ralph Stephens' threshing machine on the C. W. Perry farm in Vernon Township, October, 1917. (L-R) Frank Battle (water boy), Robert Archamboult (engineer), John Phinesy (fireman), George Seil, Ford Barber, Bill Wilson, Earl Phinesy, Vern Renner.

Photo from Jim Grove Collection

An experiment in barn shapes resulted in this unusual circular barn, which is located on M-66 in Osceola County.

The normal dairy-hay storage barn with a stone foundation.

Barn raising bees used the talents of nearly every member in a community. The rounded rafters were the specialty of local carpenters.

The Hudson barn in Dover.
Photo from the Leah Garchow Collection

The rounded roof on this barn is a unique Clare trademark.

The Wilson house in Harrison, circa 1895.

Homesteads were functional during the early years. A windmill, a team of horses, a barn and a house were nearly all the farm family needed to survive.

Township, he purchased well over a thousand acres of it for one dollar an acre. He organized a company, Brown, Cole and Calkins, and fenced the land in. The summer of 1900 found several carloads of Montana lambs being unloaded in Hatton, and placed on the summer range. They gained about 40% in weight and then were sent to Shiawassee for the mutton market, since they were a mixture of Rambouillet and Delaine Merino.

The following year, Riverdale Stock Farm, one mile west of Clare, was purchased and mammoth sheep barns were erected. Twelve hundred sheep were wintered with a loss of only nine. Six had died during the preceding summer, and so the mortality rate was excellent. Inasmuch as the farm hadn't been developed at the beginning to supply all the feed needed, Brown fed each sheep $.90 worth, and this carried them through the winter months.

Wool was selling for a premium in 1902, and Brown sold all he had for well over $1 a sheep, thus recouping his expenses for feed.

The next year he imported more spring lambs for the 1,300 acres in Hatton to go with his Riverdale's 800 acres. Sheep raising in Clare County had been proven to be a financial venture of merit.

Imitation is the tangible evidence of success, however, and when the others began establishing ranches of two, three or even four sections of land, then one could be sure that his methods were acceptable. Hammond and Dodge purchased 1,800 acres, G. K. Brooks purchased 1,240 acres, H. Hawley bought a section of land, John Robertson negotiated 920 acres, Philip Geeck bought 160 acres and P. D. Brown added another 930 acres to go with his already considerable holdings, and this was only the Hatton story.

Lincoln Township, lying west of Hatton, also had wild land which up to now was of dubious value. N. P. Leland purchased 920 acres to supplement Ammi Wright's three sections of land and the woolies were established in rather quick fashion. Nathan Church still owned two sections of land in Redding, and H. S. Cruikshank of Mt. Gilead, Ohio, owned a section of land in Garfield and Gilmore. Powell and Co. moved into Franklin and ran 200 cattle and

1,200 sheep. The Page Wire Fence Company purchased the D. A. Blodgett farm in Frost Township and put its 1,100 acres, along with another 1,500 near Long Lake into cattle and sheep. Long and Eldridge purchased two sections at Dodge, and Surrey tracts were held by Littlefield and also by Dr. L. L. Kelley. Russell and VanWormer of Toledo owned one section north of Farwell.

In June of 1903, there were 7,000 sheep on these big ranches alone, and carloads were being added almost daily. 14,000 were grazing in short order.

The Montana imports were of the wool-producing breeds, and the Canadian stock was essentially for mutton. If the sheep were to be winterized, as was contemplated by many, the wool producers would have to be accented.

Western lands were experiencing drought conditions about this time and the numerous streams in Clare's wild-land townships were widely promoted. The rolling hills and the relative cheapness of land seemed to presage a glowing future for wool and mutton.

The old mill pond site in Clare had a small electrical generating plant located over the dam, but it had become idle through obsolescence. Callam and Cornwell, (no relation to William Cornwell) owners of the riparian rights, attempted to promote a woolen mill here to go along with the sheep industry now emerging, and to supply the raw material for the Wolsey Knitting Mills located near downtown Clare.

Callam replaced the flume pit with an overshot water-wheel capable of producing 285 horsepower of electricity in anticipation of an impending woolen mill, but no capitalist stepped forward to move the project along in 1903.

WOOL BUYERS

Over-wintered sheep were being sheared in 1903 for 100,000 pounds of wool, an increase of one-third. Many eastern buyers came to Clare to purchase the long wool varieties, but some ranchers had only the short fleece breeds. Competition for the eight-inch fleeces was keen and the price was excellent.

The amount of money earned in the sheep markets is determined by a variety of conditions, most of which the rancher had no control over. For instance, the land in Clare generally didn't suffer from drought, but when other areas did, the price of wool went up handsomely. During wet years, wool prices plunged to break-even levels. Other factors included the market demands based upon the season, availability of shipping cars, and having sheep to sell when a buyer was around.

Recognized sheep experts, such as C. A. Kleman, who later moved his own sheep operations to Hatton Township, were able to become financially well off by waiting for a price rise of ¼¢ a pound. Sheep ranchers, however, didn't deal in the hundreds of thousands of sheep annually like Kleman, and they needed more stable markets to succeed.

As more and more ranchers began wearing smiles, other farmers operating on a smaller scale changed over to sheep. Littlefield bought three hundred from Brown, and George Robinson took two hundred for his Gilmore-Garfield farm.

In 1906 sheep ranching was near its apex. Wool was selling for 25¢-30¢ a pound, and there were thousands of animals bleating in the outlying townships. Almost overnight the weather in the western states became wetter and Clare County's sheep market collapsed. By 1911, nearly all of the ranches had been converted to cattle, beginning the modern era of stock farming which continues even now.

Before the collapse, there were several wool buyers in Clare and Harrison. Farmers would load their wagons with the fleeces and head for the Burch and Wyman Grain Company, Wolsey and High, W. Lee or George Schunk, all in Clare. Later, after 1911, there was steady but less frenzied sheep ranching in Hatton and Hamilton.

Monroe Holderman, Chris Iutzi, Homer Keupfer, Leon Keupfer and Cyrus Buerge of the Mennonite settlement consistently produced wool from their flocks. The Collins Ranch in Arthur was that township's major producer.

George Brooks, Ed and Lem Johnson of Durand, followed Perry Brown into Hatton and established what was known as the Johnson Ranch in 1906. They bought in just ahead of some local speculators who believed that all land along the Harrison Branch would soon appreciate in value and make them richer.

Speculators from Clare included George Benner, George Easler, Dr. Reeder, James S. Bicknell, T. S. Dorsey, L. Burch, J. R. Goodman, James Duncan, Joe Hudson and D. E. Alward.

Some Hatton farmers, such as the Krells and Nasses, continued their steady, conservative old European ways and eventually diverted attention away from Dover, westward one mile and toward the town of Hatton.

Court A. Kleman formed a partnership with the Johnson Ranch in 1906, and over 2,000 sheep were imported the first year. Later, when Kleman ran the ranch alone, he would pasture five to seven thousand sheep and winter fifteen hundred or more.

NOXIOUS WEEDS

Canadian sheep brought with them the thistles which were native there. The thumb area soon became over-run with this pest driving the farmers to distraction. Western sheep brought sand burrs primarily, but these woolies were responsible for milkweeds, wild carrot, ox-eye daisies, Russian thistles and quack grass. The last one quickly

Josiah Littlefield and his flock of woolies.

The Kleman Ranch house.

A load of wool from the Powell ranch. John Woods is shown by this wagon parked in front of the Hughes Brothers' Store in Harrison, 1909.

Photo from the Budd-Hosler Collection

became the worst pest in the state, according to Dr. Beal from Michigan Agricultural College.

There were laws enacted on a state level which attempted to deal with these noxious weeds, but the township highway commissioners and overseers weren't especially diligent in enforcing them. Periodically a notice would be placed in a newspaper that, as of a certain date, all noxious weeds were to be cut.

The trouble was that one farmer who was negligent could reinfect neighboring fields by not complying with the laws on time. Many a quarrel broke out over this noxious weed problem. One farmer said, "If the laws are right, let them be enforced. If they're not right, let them be repealed."

GOPHERS

Soon after the weed embroilment came another western pest, the gopher. They spread from Lincoln into Freeman and became a major hazard in Garfield by 1915. There were so many of the little critters that an epidemic was said to be raging.

FERAL DOGS

Another more serious problem to the ranchers was that of the dogs which ran loose. They frequently penetrated a sheep range and raised serious havoc by wanton killings. Killing for survival food is one thing, but senseless slaughter of thirty to fifty sheep in one night was inexcusable and absolutely intolerable. Dog taxes were established to provide a fund for re-imbursements to farmers who suffered these infringements upon their ranges and pastures but they were never able to control the problem. W. L. Kinney of Winterfield tried in 1909, however, by killing eleven dogs in one flock in June.

Resolutions passed by the state Grange meeting at Saginaw in 1909 reflected the concerns of Michigan's heartland, but the dogs continued to plague the ranges. B. S. Alley, the Garfield Township farmer and ex-Indiana attorney spoke eloquently to the Grangers, state officials and local law enforcement officers, but the plundering dogs continued to put a serious strain upon the ranchers. Even bringing the sheep in each night didn't solve the problem of marauding dogs.

CASH CROPPING VS. STOCK FARMS

A young couple starting out in life could begin farming by renting a "forty" or an "eighty" and planting grain crops which would come to the market quite rapidly. Grandiose plans for a beef-raising operation would necessitate a rather large-size farm, fields for pastures, substantial buildings, tools, equipment, a house and livestock, certainly not a small undertaking.

By 1900, there were several families which

Every farm family tried to be as self-sufficient as possible. Here, a Woznack hog contributes to a full larder.

Photo from the Woznack Family Collection

The last load of sugar beets from 1916.

The Cornwell Ranch cut its own lumber for building this barn, 1905.
Photo from the John Hartman Collection

were established long enough so that the boys would have grown up in Clare, but they were often not among the monied citizens, especially if they were farmers. Nevertheless, these farm boys would have an edge if they chose to make agriculture their life's work. Some boys desired to leave the farm and they either went west to Oregon, Washington, California or sometimes into western Canada. A few married and migrated toward Detroit or Flint and the automobile factories.

Just as often as not, some young marrieds would head north into the rural districts where they could cash-crop farm. Their trail could be documented by their announcement into the rural communities, and then around the next February or March, realities hit them hard, and a notice of an auction sale of their personaal property would be made public. Perhaps a chattel mortgage at the bank would become due in about a year from the onset of their "farming", and the auction sale would announce the anniversary of their agricultural career.

Contracts for peas, cucumbers, clover, potatoes and later, beets would help stabilize many through the lean years, but weather often worked against the marginal capitalists. Gophers, army worms, weeds and other nuisances collectively added their negative qualities to the balance scales, and the young farm families often were found wanting.

Stock farms which were built upon a reasonable combination of acreage, buildings, livestock and weather had a better time

of it. Diseases and weather conditions didn't inundate these farmers so universally.

Hogs, poultry, sheep, horses, beef and dairy animals were the basis for success in Clare County agriculture.

A good infrastructure was in place in Farwell and Clare by 1910. Harrison was greatly stabilized when the Harrison Elevator Company was organized in 1912 by ten stockholders. They acted as brokers between the farmers and consumers for the amount of $23,801 the first year, chiefly for wool, potatoes, chickens, hogs, peaches, berries, cream and eggs. Ortho Boulton, Arthur Long, Charles S. Page, Maron F. Caner, Joseph Ladd, F. W. Town, J. R. Brown and John Quinn were the Harrisonites. A year later, the stockholders were increased to 91 and the farmers were marketing large amounts of their products.

Grist and flouring mills were operating in Farwell and Clare early in the century. The Callam and Cornwell Electric Rolling Mill had the flour milling capacity of eighty barrels per day. They processed flours to several qualities and marketed each under a separate brand name.

HORSE BREEDING

Horse breeding was another major enterprise locally. The Clare Percheron Horse Breeders Association was organized in 1903 to purchase "French George", a stud promoted by John Crawford. When the stallion was purchased in 1903, he was four years old, weighed 1,625 pounds and cost $2,000. Coming directly from the Michigan State Fair, where he took first place, he was housed in Thayer's Feed Barn.

Daniel Crouse, Carl Belling, S. A. Leitner, William Morrison, John H. Smith, Nelson Carrow, W. J. Maxwell, Duncan Roe, William Wirth, William Duncan, John Kurz, Herman Ross, D. W. Denno, J. H. Shroeder, Allen Gerow, John Presley, Frank Gorr, Henry Wild and R. W. Fairbanks each bought a $100 share of French George.

In 1907, the Farwell Horse Breeders' Association imported a stallion, reported to have been registered in Paris. Rohrabacker and Hunt, bankers in Laingsburg, bought a note from the Association for $1,048. John Crawford again was the broker, but this time he swindled the locals, or attempted to. When Crawford took the note to the Laingsburg bank, he had to sign as an individual for the face amount. In his fancy dealings, he wound up having to pay the note himself, and then tried to collect from the Farwell stockholders. It turned out all right in spite of Crawford's tricky efforts to swindle the bank and the local farmers. The stud stayed and produced a tidy profit over the next few years.

Levi Willey purchased "Frederick" in 1915 and boarded him at the feed barns around the county. Good sires quickly upgraded the quality of the draft horses around here, and many were soon sold to the Army which then transported them to Europe and the Great War.

MICHIGAN STATE FAIR EXHIBITS

Citizens of Clare County in the 1890's generally spoke in negative terms about its future as an agricultural district, and many put legs to their opinions and moved on. They had come with the lumber industry and generally saw things from that perspective. As the trees were depleted, the men and women began to focus their attention upon the stumps, not infrequently blackened by the forest fires which periodically swept through, burning up the garbage from the lumbermen.

A new era was on the horizon, but the spectators could only see the disarray of the dying scene. In 1901, A. J. Doherty became a senator from this district, and his elevation to that office boded well for Clare. His many talents were used in several positions during this time, but a key one for the farmers was his position as Executive Secretary to the Michigan State Fair Board.

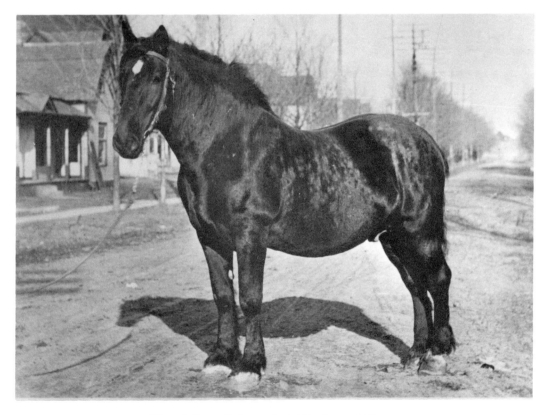

"French George", the syndicated Percheron stallion.

Clare County presented this excellent exhibit at the 1906 Michigan State Fair. (L-R) Dr. L. L. Kelley, Maron Caner, _____ and John Jackson.
Photo courtesy of George MacQueen

Doherty was chided frequently for having a farm up in the pine barrens, and his fellow legislators poked much fun at him. The Senator knew what the soil was like up here in the heartland, but not many others did. So he asked the Clare County Board of Supervisors to send an exhibit to the State Fair in Pontiac.

Dr. L. L. Kelley from Farwell was put in charge of the exhibit, after E. R. Chapin of Winterfield introduced the resolution in 1902. In September of 1903, Dr. Kelley took two satchels of county agricultural products to Pontiac. Small as it was, it won third prize and $20.00.

The CLARE SENTINEL, under the direction of Edgar G. Welch, began to collect pictures and a written story about the Brand, Perry, Sutherland, Hudson and Brewer farms. These were run as feature articles in the subsequent weeks. By 1904, a large "puff-job" was ready to be done on Clare County farms. Beautiful photographs of these farms were printed for distribution at the State Fair.

John A. Jackson and A. M. Howard joined Dr. Kelley in Pontiac and did an excellent job of putting the "pine barrens" myth to rest.

In 1905, the county took second place in several categories and by 1906 broke into first place. Fruits and dent corn were judged to be the best in Michigan, and grains and vegetables were in second place. The following year, and 9,000 pamphlets later, Clare took four first places, including: a) the entire exhibit b) grains and vegetables c) fruits d) corn.

The old "pine barrens" were doing pretty well!

Senator Doherty was doing quite well also, and those friends who, a few years ago, were chiding him for living in such a benighted country, now wanted to be invited up to the new Garden of Eden. The Senator was receiving so much attention these days that he began to think in terms of the Governor's office.

To accommodate the traffic to Clare, he had a beautiful English Tudor style manor built which was befitting a governor's prestige.

Prices of farm land began to soar, and several of the originals sold their farms for handsome profits around 1909-1912.

Many ex-Clarites said, "What a fool I was to leave that land for some stranger to show its value," and lots of strangers were anxious to show the short-visioned just how foolish they were.

As the price of land went up, generally the better type of farmer came in. Gone were the days of the lumberjack farmer. Ahead were the days of the stock farms and the stable farm communities.

W. C. CORNWELL

The Saginaw Beef Company, owned by W. C. Cornwell and Harris, began operating in Arthur Township around 1903. A year later, substantial buildings had been erected and beef cattle had been imported in rather large numbers. Brand was selling wild land in the same district for $5-$8 an acre. Cleared land, however, was selling for $75-$100 an acre. The Cornwell Ranch had a spread of at least 1,280 acres, most of it not cleared in the early days.

By 1913, a model dairy operation was operating with built-in feed carriers, gutters which were cleaned by power twice a day, individual cow watering basins, calf pens, bull pen, water tank and a King-Ventilator system. Thirty cows were milked on a regular basis, most of them registered Holsteins, with the milk being used for cream. Later a dairy was added, which distributed milk door to door.

MYERS BROTHERS RANCH

A significant part of the Ohio Colony was the Myers Ranch, operated by Frank, Jacob and W. E. Myers. They came with their Prairie Schooners, and soon hacked a thriving farm operation from their 840 acre tract. The common trait the brothers had was a willingness to work hard. By 1905 they had 80 acres cleared, three houses and three substantial barns built, plus a large herd of beef cattle.

The main house on the Brand farm.

William Haley—cattle buyer.
Photo from the Albert Haley Collection

POWELL CATTLE COMPANY

North of Arthur Township was land which had an uneven quality. Regardless, a group of men from Bowling Green, Ohio purchased 6,353 acres in Franklin, Frost and Hayes Townships and established a $40,000 ranching operation. Some sheep were run by these men, but primarily cattle browsed over a large range of scrub land.

THE CATTLE BUYERS

The large meat-packing companies in Detroit and Chicago had employees, or agents, who covered the rural districts frequently, looking for saleable livestock. The small packing-houses used the services of commission men who bought animals for several interests. One such agent was William Haley.

Haley had an interest in the Haley and McMullen Company on Dix Avenue in Detroit. Working from an office in a building across the street from the Calkins Hotel, general attitude was "The more that come, the better it is for both them and the county," as was expressed by Perry Brown.

More than half of Greenwood Township was first-class farmland. Six school districts and four good schoolhouses were organized. Many houses were well-painted, with barns and fifteen-year-old orchards bearing good harvests of fruit. One of the best farmers was William Smith, the township supervisor. Maron Caner was improving his farm at this

John B. Phinisey
Photo from the Allen Family Collection

he forwarded out of the Clare rail yards thousands of carloads of beef animals.

Upon the occasion of his severe goring by a bull in a Detroit stockyard, the DETROIT JOURNAL said, "... Haley is one of the best known cattlemen in Michigan." (February 1912) and indeed he was. His practiced eye could tell what the beef would grade, and he could estimate weight to within ten pounds.

In the years just prior to World War I, John Jackson (Jr.) was also in the cattle buying business, and shipped frequently out of the Clare stockyards.

1904 AGRICULTURE

The new type farmer had been coming into the county for about two years, and the county was being developed rapidly. The

Mrs. William Hosler of Greenwood Township. Mrs. Hosler was an early pioneer.
Photo from the Budd-Hosler Collection

time as well. A. E. Doty had been farming in the new style for several years by this date.

Hamilton was mostly undeveloped, except for the Irish community centered around Sections 25 and 26. Four school districts were organized and two buildings were functioning. The Pennsylvania settlement up in Section 8 wasn't established yet, but some stock farms had begun. John Shea, William Sullivan and Andy Hagen were the main farmers.

Winterfield farms were likewise in a boom phase of their cycles. J. B. Hamer grew excellent "dent" corn and took high honors at the State Fair. The Grandon Cheese Factory had begun in 1903 and was thriving.

On the state level, San Jose Scale was wreaking havoc on the apples, and field mice had damaged the fruit trees quite severely in February and March. Creameries were in full stride across the state, as were the numerous local cheese factories.

A well drilling rig, 1900.

The John Phinisey family of Vernon Township
Photo from the Allen Family Collection

In Vernon, Senator Doherty had volunteered his farm for an experimental station to study the Hessian Fly in the wheat fields. It wasn't much of a pest yet, but the U.S. Department of Agriculture wanted to devise a method of control before it was needed. Doherty reported some rust on local wheat, but the total amount of attention paid to this small U. S. Experimental Station was out of proportion to its contribution to state agriculture.

As the county developed its stockfarms, the Harrison site for the county fair was down-played by the southern townships, and a new fair was being promoted. It was projected for Clare by the Northern Isabella and Clare County Committee. Two hundred farmers gathered in Clare in February of 1905 to plan for the summer fair.

During 1904, a "ridiculous" street fair had been held, and the only ones happy with

Springtime was a busy season on the Schunk farm. John Hartman is shown driving the white team as Stan Schunk drives the black.

Photo from the Hartman Family Collection

it were the "shysters" who promoted it. The Board discussed the merits of a thirty acre site west of the Union Depot, but the $2,500 needed to fence it was a barrier to its development. In the end, they purchased a site at the foot of Vernon Hill, but east of McEwan Street. It was known later as the David Ward racetrack after this "fair board" had run its course.

GARFIELD FARMING

The soil lying north of an imaginary line in the township was generally inferior. South of this line, Bert Scott had purchased two hundred acres in 1901 and was raising twenty cattle. J. T. Owen ran the same number of cattle, but he also planted fields to clover, corn, potatoes and an orchard. William Smith had migrated in from Oakland County and was farming about a hundred acres in Section 25. Another Oakland County farmer in Garfield was L. Knowles. He had eighty acres. Walter Nauxwell had two eighty-acre parcels. He too hailed from Oakland. Thomas Maltby

farmed three hundred acres in Section 26. Al Tryon ran cattle and farmed a portion of Section 26.

Robert Carson, a land speculator, bought large tracts and sold them on land contracts with modest payments in a manner similar to Brand, but actually, he was in real estate. Carson had some fields fenced with wire, but his main crops came from the orchard, which supplemented the income from his land contracts.

The oldest farmer in Garfield was Cornelius Powlison, who had one hundred twenty acres on Section 14. He, along with Dresdan Bryan, were good farmers, and they ran cattle to stabilize their operation.

Alfred and Henry Tryon were active farmers in the township also at this time. Henry was a Spanish-American War veteran. They were cattlemen primarily, expanding to an upper-peninsula operation, but not as successfully as in Garfield.

Wise Township had the most wire fencing up, around crops as much as around the pastures. These farmers were sturdy tillers of the soil, but some raised stock on the side. James and George Hersey, E. W. and C. A.

Allen, Charles Armentrout, W. R., J. H. and W. J. Jennings, Milo Lamphere, Peter Murphy, E. L. Potter, P. M. Loomis, William Maxwell, James Phillips, Charles Church, James Irvin, I. G. Woten, John Roe and E. Carpenter were the main consumers of barbed wire products.

BURCH AND WYMAN COMPANY

John T. Horning built an elevator in Clare and operated it for many years. When he died, it was sold to Burch and Wyman Company in 1905. They immediately modified its facilities to handle field beans and to retail coal. Half of its $10,000 capital stock was owned by the Saginaw Milling Company and the other half had been retained by Burch and Wyman. H. H. Carr of Saginaw was the president and Jay Wyman served as vice president. M. Burch was the general manager and held the office of secretary-treasurer.

They bought F. B. Doherty's lime, cement and coal business and moved toward supplying the rapidly developing farm community around the "Market City".

The interdependence of the county farmers and the regional markets was evidenced many times by happenings outside the immediate districts. For instance, when two eastern brokerage houses went broke in June of 1903, they caused Barnaby Produce, dealers in Midland, Clare and other heartland communities to fail the succeeding month. Inasmuch as they were large purchasers of eggs, dairy products, potatoes and other similar type agricultural products, this loss of an outlet hurt the farmer who depended upon these cash sales.

Generally though, others would step in and attempt to take advantage of the situation. Winans and Anderson of Rosebush, operators of the elevator there, leased Doherty's warehouse about a month after the Barnaby failure and did a large wholesale business with the farmers in the "Market City".

This style of threshing machine was the backbone of the crop farmer. Contractors would take their machines and a crew from farm to farm. Most were steam powered.

Nathan Bicknell's old warehouse is on the left in this 1910 photo.

Potatoes were a big cash crop, but the amount of cash they brought the farmer was dependent upon the weather in Michigan, as well as in the other potato states. If the weather was favorable here and unfavorable elsewhere, Michigan farmers were able to pay off the farm mortgage, and quite possibly purchase some livestock for a more dependable future farm income. 1903 was just such a banner year locally. 1905, however, was just the reverse, and many auction sales took place in the spring of 1906.

Little by little, the resources of the county were being discovered and developed. Those townships that were able to sustain clover, wheat, potato, rye and corn production were cultivated and contract threshers were in full competition for the business. Early machines required many men to handle all of the facets of the operation. Manufacturers, however, brought out new models early in the twentieth century, which reduced the number of assistants needed to operate them.

The popularity of steam tractors and other mechanical equipment was immense, and several contractors operated in stiff competition with each other, often to the point of threshing grain for less than their expenses.

Stump pullers were in this category also, and a farmer could hire his stumps removed for less than he could extract them himself, unless of course, a "bee" came over and stumped for him. D. C. Evans of Sheridan had a puller in 1905, and he bragged about the forty-seven stumps he pulled in one day, using three men and a team. Some of the stumps were so huge that it required two teams to haul them away. He extracted five hundred forty from a Sheridan farm in 1905.

Accidents of the most unexpected variety often accompanied work in these fields. William Davy, helping his father pull stumps southwest of Farwell during May of 1905, was standing between his father and an uncle. A bolt of lightning came right down to him and killed him. The other men were unhurt.

Other times, a chain which had been wrapped around the stump would come loose. or the cable hooked onto the evener would break, and men standing in the path of the vengeful cable would be cut in two, or at the least, sustain broken bones. The "stilyard" type puller was the worst machine in this regard.

John List, a Hatton and Clare citizen, invented one which "screwed" the stumps right out of the ground. Even though it was safer to use, it was expensive and slow, and the machine shop on Vernon Hill in Clare soon folded. An attempt to manufacture other mechanical marvels was only marginally successful, and World War I put List out of business.

CREAMERIES

In April 1887, there were one hundred milk cows in the Clare market area. An agent from the Fairchild Creamery in Port Austin came to town looking to establish a creamery, or at least a station here to collect the farmers' surplus cream. Conditions hadn't progressed to the point that farmers were able to take advantage of this opportunity, even though there were several dairies in town. At least 2,500 cows were needed by a creamery.

Davis and Rankin next proposed a creamery in Clare and sent Mr. Fairbanks by railroad in April of 1893 to check it out. Eventually a collecting station was established near the railroad depot and some

Steam engines of this type were used by threshing crews all over northern Michigan in the pre-World War I era.

cream was sent out on the Ann Arbor Railroad to a creamery near Owosso. Vernon farmers sent their surplus cream to the Herrick Cheese Company operating in Wise Township. In 1902, this factory was making cheese every day, as R. Johnson had been engaged to be the new cheesemaker. A year later, a cheese factory began operating in Winterfield's Grandon Cheese Company plant.

Senator Doherty offered $5,000 to a cheese factory if it were built in Vernon Township and ready to operate by the spring of 1904. He wanted it put on his Kilarney Farm, so as to avoid Clare taxes. He incidently had fifty cows in a milking condition, and the surplus milk was a considerable problem to him.

The Switzer Creamery opened a butter factory in Clare during 1904 to go along with their other ones at Hersey and Evart. E. Switzer proposed to expand even more during the 1905 season, if there were enough farmers willing to increase their dairy herds, but sheep continued to be the Cinderella story until 1911.

R. D. Johnson of Clare started his Spring Brook Dairy in Clare in June of 1906. He delivered milk by tickets, selling twelve quart tickets for fifty cents, while a dollar entitled a patron to twenty-five quarts of fresh milk. Cream sold for twenty cents a quart.

Aden S. Retan had been operating the Lakeside Dairy near Crooked Lake during the same year as Johnson, but he sold at auction his eight milk cows and equipment. There weren't enough customers in the area to take advantage of his services.

CLARE, THE "MARKET CITY"

Clare, being the nexus of two railroads and a central collecting point, soon became a major cream depot for the Owosso Creamery as previous shipments of cream from here proved successful. E. F. Dudley was sent to manage their station, and offered to pay the same price for the cream here as the competitor had offered for cream delivered to the Owosso plant. This savings on the freight

Paul Nass is shown here with his steam engine.

Elzey and Fred Smalley (right) in front of the Smalley Wagon Shop in Clare, 1910.

The round roof style barns were popular because they were stronger and could hold more hay than the usual gable.

meant dollars to the local farmers. Butter made from this cream was sent to the New York market.

Merchants in the county began selling cream separators to the farmers so they could take advantage of the rapidly expanding markets. The F. B. Doherty Hardware Company sold the "U.S. Cream Separator", while the "Iowa" was sold by J. R. Dunwoodie. The "Dairy Queen Separator" was promoted by Dan Mater.

Mt. Pleasant acquired a milk condensary in July of 1908. The building was 70' by 276' by 24', and handled 50,000 pounds of milk daily. They produced 13,000 pounds of evaporated milk and 11,000 pounds of condensed milk. Thirty-eight employees worked in the plant, and fourteen men drove the collecting wagons farm to farm. The SENTINEL said, "Mt. Pleasant is lucky to secure this plant," and indeed they were. Farmers were soon able to clear $83.89 per cow per year.

The Michigan Creamery Company estab-

lished four cream collecting routes for their butter factory in Clare. They shipped the butter and other dairy products to Owosso, Alma and Saginaw. Within a few weeks they were buying live or dressed hogs, veals, eggs, and poultry in rather significant quantities. Their warehouse north of the tracks on McEwan Street put muscle to the slogan (The Market City) that Clare was now using in its boosting propaganda. Their operation began in mid-February, 1909. Cream delivered to the station brought 30¢, while hauled cream netted the farmer 28¢.

J. M. Davis of Clare purchased the Marion Creamery and scouted the idea of establishing another in Clare so that a condensary could be operated. Unfortunately for Clare, the condensary never materialized, although a creamery was finally put into operation here by him, with the title of the Clare Creamery Company.

During 1911, the Bi-County Agricultural Creamery was located at the entrance to the fairgrounds on 1st Street in Clare with Mr.

The barn on Albert Haley's farm in Arthur Township. The degree of semi-ellipticity depended upon the carpenter. Angus MacLeod built his in a half-circle.

Barberee as the buttermaker. A year later, Towar's Wayne County Creamery Company was operating in Clare, as was Swift and Company. Farmers had no trouble finding buyers for their cream.

1912 was a banner year for the "Market City" in other market lines as well. J. M. Davis quickly increased his purchasing of farm products and most of the former sheep ranchers were now banking solid, hard cash. Several of the other collecting stations cheated farmers by devious methods such as short-weighting or not even giving the farmer payment for cream for a month at a time.

Davis always paid the farmers in cash, and he paid a fair price. His twenty employees were kept busy preparing his carload shipments on a regular basis. He had forty agents in the districts surrounding Clare, and the poultry, beef, butter, eggs and allied products gave a solid cash base to the dairy farmers in the north.

Frank Lamoreaux and Fred Hubel promoted a condensary in Clare during 1914. Lamoreaux knew the vice-president of a corporation which operated several condensaries. Bert Parsons, the vice-president, came to Clare and attempted to line up 5,000 cows within an eight-mile radius of Clare, but they couldn't be found.

The reason a condensary was so attractive is simple. Cream enabled a farmer to earn approximately $50 per cow a year. A man who shipped whole milk with a 3.0% butterfat content netted at least an additional $30 a cow. With the price of milk being determined by hundredweight instead of butterfat, it's no wonder the Isabella farmers soon

went to the Friesian-Holsteins.

When the first condensary fell along the wayside, the Towar Creamery Company said it would build in Clare if 2,500 cows could be brought under contract. William H. Caple, who had by now purchased the Doherty farm, and C. C. Harris were the ones attempting to bring the loose ends together for a Clare factory. The Towar Company had come to Clare in 1912 and used the bicycle shop of Aaron O. Fish for a collecting station, but it never grew beyond the bicycle shop.

The farmers were deprived of their condensary income when negotiations failed, but by 1915, W. E. Vance, now managing the Farmers' Independent Produce Company located on West 4th Street, was paying out $300 in cash for cream on Saturdays. This company built the cement block building later used by Thayer Dairy, Inc. for storage.

The Farmers' Independent Produce Company contrived to expand its product line and shipped chickens by the railroad car lot. An enclosure was attached to the rear of the building and held the incoming crates of chickens until a car was available for shipment. There was a great variety of breeds and many mongrel chickens, but the Barred Rock breed predominated.

A carload of chickens would weigh approximately 16,000 pounds and brought prices ranging around 10¢ a pound. A few years later, poultry was dressed here and shipped, packed in ice, in the refrigerator cars.

Robert Archamboult became Vance's replacement for manager in 1919.

Home delivery of milk during the war was

A load of Manton potatoes being hauled to the potato buyer in 1924.
Photo by Bayes Photography

handled in Clare by the Fair Grove Dairy and the Schaeffer Dairy. Both used Holsteins in 1918, and in their own sphere, circumvented the misfortune of the condensary balloon.

THE BIG DITCHES

The big farms in the Saginaw Valley didn't develop until the big drainage ditches were dug in the earliest years of the twentieth century. Large floating dredges were used to chew canals into the swampy lowlands south of Saginaw and near St. Charles. Once drained, this land became very prolific for many types of crops, especially sugar beets.

Sheridan Township in Clare County and Wise Township in Isabella County had similar swampy locations, and some farmers around 1904 began to wonder if the time wasn't ripe for a local drainage system to lower the water table in their fields. Residents around Loomis were the first to consider such a move, but the tax-paying farmers were considering a project that they could work on during the off-season, so as to hold down their taxes.

As the proposed Loomis drain progressed on paper, a $20,000 price tag began to dampen some of the earlier enthusiasm. Nevertheless, discussions during the summer seemed to indicate that the drain ought to be dug, and that the starting point should be in Section 5 of Wise Township on John Marlin's farm. In August, Link Bergey was given a contract to start, with the ditch's depth to be determined in October when the water level was stabilized.

In February of 1905, massive timbers were hauled in to build the ditching machine on the job site. It was to be 14' by 56' and could float on the water it uncovered. Somehow the contractor built a big hole and started to assemble the dredge, which was able to carve a channel nearly twenty feet wide and eight miles long.

"Some people rejoice at the prospects of swamps disappearing. Others make wry faces at the prospects of high taxes, but at the very least, the $17,000 ditch is a go," reported the CLARE SENTINEL on February 3,

Ditching in Vernon Township

1905.

Speculators who had picked up the cut-over lands began to unload their holdings before the big taxes took effect.

J. W. Maples and Jasper Snider of Loomis were employed on the dredge, along with seven other men. Each "tender" was a blacksmith and a skilled mechanic, and worked under the daily direction of W. Horning from Saginaw.

The big drag-line scoop bit into the swampy debris and chewed cedar trees, stumps and everything else with each bite. Each day the machine progressed toward its goal by twenty rods.

By May, the machine was near Loomis and had to be moved south of the Pere Marquette tracks, but there was a problem. The railroad didn't want to build a bridge. One suggestion was to dig out the embankment, float the dredge through and let the railroad worry about what it could do to rectify the track problem, but this idea didn't satisfy the contractor either.

In the end, they dammed up the ditch and floated the dredge over the tracks. The railroad wasn't happy with this, but it was the best offer they had. So W. T. Weir was given $200 and he arranged to put the ditcher on the south side.

The ditch was so impressive that others wanted to drain their own lowlands. Vernon Township especially was anxious to get started on its own dredge.

SHERIDAN'S DITCHES

Isabella County's ditches were a breeze to plan, organize and build compared to Clare's. Drain Commissioner Schunk was approached by a few farmers, notably from Sections 14 and 24, about a ditch to drain their farms. A previously proposed ditch which would feed into Stoney Creek was abandoned in December of 1904 after the farmers began to estimate their next year's taxes, but not without severe bickering in the neighborhood.

That project included Hatton, Grant and Sheridan Townships, and would have straightened the McEwan (now called McCuron) and Stoney Creeks, but some pretty plain talk at a meeting in Dover between forty-five men convinced officials that this was an extremely unpopular issue.

About a month later, in January of 1905, a hundred men met at Dover and discussed the "Big Ditch" which was to take the place of the Stoney Creek project. John W. Hampton said, "The moment these projects are turned into a county drain, expenses will increase and those taxes will stay on the books for years." Some forty others agreed with his view of things and elected him president and business agent of an ad hoc group which was going to fight the ditch.

Dr. L. L. Kelley from Farwell was serving in the Michigan legislature, and A. J. Doherty was holding a senate seat during this squabble. Hampton asked Kelley to spon-

The sixteen room house of Joseph Hudson in Dover. It was torched by an arsonist.
Photo from the Leah Garchow Collection

Most of the ditching machines were made on the job site. This one was used in Wise Township.
Photo from the John Stough Collection

sor a bill which would decrease the power of county drain commissioners. A. R. Canfield immediately suspected the real intent was to remove Commissioner Schunk because he was a Democrat.

Canfield's paper, the COURIER, ignored the next two meetings held in Dover, but the SENTINEL was ready for the fight, and it was a heated one.

Governor Warner signed the bill which Kelley and Doherty had herded through the legislative chambers in March of 1905. There were similar drains being contemplated at the time in Isabella, Gratiot, Saginaw, Cass, Shiawassee, Ottawa, Barry, Montcalm, Van Buren, Alpena, Berrien and Cheboygan Counties, and this bill killed them all.

Judge Stone of Gratiot County ruled in July of 1905 that this law was misleading, dishonest and stealthy legislation in that it attempted to take authority away from Drain Commissioners and give it to the Boards of Supervisors. He ruled P. A. 21, 1905 void.

Schunk then hired W. W. Harper to survey Stoney and McEwan Creeks. His estimate was in the $20,000 range, but opponents placed their own price on the ditch and said $40,000 was closer to the real costs.

Fred Hudson, who had a farm on Section 24, dug eighty-seven rods of ditch, but he couldn't connect to a water course. About the same time, W. H. Virtue was quarantined to his farm because of some epidemic his children had come in contact with, so he dug sixty rods of creek drain on his property during his hiatus from the outside world, but he, too, was short of an outlet.

These two acts, coupled with a few other farmers' problems caused the bellicose turmoil, in that ten men could effect a valid petition, but a hundred or more would be forced to pay.

The County Board of Supervisors entered the picture before the courts ruled the law invalid, and stopped the drain proceedings in a special meeting held May 13, 1905. All of

Ditching in Vernon Township.
Photo from the Stough Collection

Schunk's expenses were allowed by the Board, but his future actions were limited to filling out paper forms for the Board's consideration. As the meeting broke up, everyone was satisfied, but the Democrats less so than the Republicans. Many farmers attended the hearing, but not one good word was said in public in support of the drain. Someone explained later, "It was hard rap at Schunk, but as his bill was allowed in full, he kept his silence."

Thomas McGivern began work on an approved drain in Sheridan, but as the drain fund had been drained, he was forced to wait until January, 1906 for his money. $400 was the first installment. By August of 1906, the McGivern drain was completed before the construction of the German Lutheran Church over near the Gladwin County line, and farmers there were encouraged to continue expanding their farms.

During the summer of 1906, an Ohio man came up to the area and decided that he could succeed here with the drain now making the farm land tillable. Little by little, the men reduced their hostility to the ditches. In the beginning, however, the early Ohioians were practically without money, and as they watched their expenses with an eagle eye, they turned many public meetings into chaotic affairs.

Sheridan had recovered sufficiently in 1909 to consider building a drain in conjunction with Wise Township. This one was to be four and one-half miles long and was to start north of Loomis and angle east, south-east toward the Gladwin-Midland county line for an outlet. It essentially aided northeastern Wise Township, but "the coloured settlement in the vicinity of Midland County pushed the project."

Another drain was dug in 1914, commencing on James Phillips' farm in Wise. It was known as the Lamphere Drain. The ditch was nine feet wide and six feet deep, and the big dredge scooped out half a wagon load each cycle. It moved about twelve rods a day and excavated five feet of muck for about $5.00 a rod.

Vernon also had its own ditch, as did many of the other townships at about this same time. Nowhere else did the farmers raise the strident objections that the Sheridan farmers did in 1904 and 1905. Results from the ditches soon proved their worth, and even the Ohio colony lowered its vocal objections to the drains.

Scion of the Loomis family

THE QUALITY OF RURAL LIFE

The quality of living in the rural districts was given a bad reputation by the early lumbermen who farmed as a diversion from their other activities. They viewed the under-developed governments, roads, lands and the thin soils with undisguised disdain. Public opinion makers, basing their views upon thin foundations and the testimonies of the many recently disillusioned hard-scrabble farmers who were forced off the farms by the economic facts of life, added to the soiled reputation of the north as a place to live. Not all of those who lived on those farms agreed with this assessment, however.

Mrs. Carrie Brewer, living in Wise Township, loved the healthy air and the purity of life which could be enjoyed on these farms. She gave a speech to the Wise Farmers Club in November of 1904, mentioning the healthy foods available in pristine freshness to the farmers, but not to the city dwellers. She also alluded to the temperature differentials between rural districts and even cities the size of Clare, remarking how much more difficult it was to breathe air which wasn't as pure nor as cool as country air.

Large cities had problems more serious than the quality of air, which would make them undesirable for the farm youths. The easy wealth of the city was viewed as a vice, and reports reaching the rural resident of extravagance, corruption, luxuries, art and beauty which came, either with the wealth or because of it, was discouraging to mothers and fathers who contemplated their sons and daughters being attracted to it.

Wealth was the problem! Because wealth was such a powerful magnet, attracting even more wealth, it was capable of establishing its own morality or code of ethics. The Thaw trial in 1906-7 revealed to the farmer a dark shadow which was settling in on the nation and would infect the patriotic citizens with an unhealthy virus.

"Shall we forever be compelled to be carried forward in the mad rush to build up the big cities where land prices have soared so high? . . . What causes land prices in Chicago and Detroit to (rise) even to hundreds of dollars for a square foot, while in this vicinity, we can buy a big farm for the same amount? Who makes possible the wealth of the big metropolis? Who pays tribute to it? The rural community, the farms, the mines, the forests, they all pay tribute to the big city. Thither go our boys as new offices and new departments are created, and thither in some form or other goes our tribute to the a part of the hard-earned dollars of all our rural communities.

"Sooner or later, the best thought of the nation must face the question: Is it not the part of wisdom to face them now, ere centralization has gone beyond all limits?"

The June issue of McCLURE Magazine in 1909 addressed itself to the problem of the cities draining the best blood from the country. ". . . while with our vast domains, there is no immediate danger, the problem of elevation of rural life does loom up on the horizon. An emphasis on the means of transit is indeed needed. Automobiles, trolleys, wireless telegraphy, aerial navigation (all may assist) the hastening of an anti-toxin to check the poison of the big city in the body politic."

Within the district, there were those who weren't as philosophically introspective, but they began to put tangible supports to the enhancement of rural life. The Farwell Woman's Club, which was organized in 1903, always was interested in promoting civic and school enterprises, if they bettered the community. Youngsters in the high school looked forward to the annual Spring Music and Art Night, which Mrs. G. E. Lamb spearheaded, thus continuing the goals Dr. and Mrs. Grillet had infused into the original committee.

Wise Township farmers organized a social club which met in various homes and served the needs of the community before the Grange replaced it with a more structured organization soon after the turn of the century. But the club which created the most community spirit and promoted a whole town was the Hatton Farmer's Club.

Its conception was in the person of Austin Trumble, the merchant of the Brown's Corners Store. He had been a newspaper writer in Evart before he came to the county in 1893, but preferred life in the rural areas.

His country stores were the literary centers as well as being the post offices, gossip centers and business exchanges. Upon selling the Brown's Corners store, he went to the Tonkin settlement of Section 32 in Arthur and again provided the stimulation for a lively community.

As R. F. D. came along, these little country stores lost their central role in the community, and Tonkin was a casualty when the post office was removed.

Moving over on the railroad where the Harrison Branch passed near the town hall, Trumble opened his third general store, and achieved a success in the community far beyond anyone else in the country's experience. Quietly at first, he and a few neighbors would gather for an evening social, and then rather suddenly, the whole neighborhood joined in. The Hamlins, Durfees, Hilemans, Marlins, Hains, Smiths, Hebers and Pervorses formed the central core, but Trumble remained the stem-winder.

His trusty pen was soon jotting down grandiose bits of propaganda about Hatton that attracted settlers into the area to farm the sandy soils. Through his Herculean efforts, Hatton became famous for something besides the dangerous hill on the railroad coming south out of Harrison. Hatton became the most exciting little community in Clare County between 1910-13.

Just before Trumble's health failed and he moved to Danbury, Texas for a few days, some reader of the CLARE SENTINEL in July of 1912 wrote about this remarkable man and his Hatton Farmer's Club.

HATTON

About 12 miles northeast of Clare
Upon the P. M. track
There is a little junction
The first of it is Hat.

Some of the settlers are batty
About the little place.
Poor folks! They do not realize
The place has run its race.

A certain man moved to that spot,
Tried to revive the land;

But when you get there, you will find
A great big pile of sand.

The town has a brand new scribe
He's full of wind galore,
But he's a fine and dandy fellow
There's always "Welcome" on his door.

They are worrying now about the crops,
Afraid they won't get cars this fall
Enough to carry them all away,
You'll need them — Keep them all.

They have a brand new Sunday School
And have had a social, too.
Every time the train pulls in,
They begin — "Why, how-de-doo!"

Sometimes it's a pack peddler,
Sometimes it's creamery cans,
But they're just as tickled as they can be
To live there in the sand.

So never mind, it's lots of fun
To read the Hatton news.
We fight to get the Sentinel first,
It drives away the blues.

Trumble came back from Texas within two weeks of his arrival there, because he couldn't take the humidity, snakes and heat. A grand-daughter he had raised since her mother died, provided him the nursing that he required in his Harrison home. Friends from Hatton traveled to Harrison, where the Hatton Farmer's Club reconvened, but the magic was fading from Hatton. Successive Reward Road turn-downs by the farmers brought low the mighty town of Hatton.

An effort to rejuvenate the town in 1913, when the Pittsburg Oil Company leased drilling rights on 3,000 acres, failed as the test holes were dry. The Hatton Improvement Company didn't improve it much, and soon the farmers moved on to more fertile lands.

In the early pioneer days, men sought to get ahead by depending upon their own efforts, and many thought the way to do it was to push the other fellow down. The second generation, which became the farm communities, saw that the way to get ahead

The barn on Charles Scott's farm in Coldwater Township.

The older wooden bridges collapsed nearly every time a steam tractor attempted to use them.
Photo from the Dover Historical Society

was by putting the welfare of the community ahead of the individual. This new order of affairs was known as "the get-together call".

This building-up effort by the Grangers emphasized the home, school and church, but with the home forming the anchor. All of these efforts at informal and formal community development were excellent as far as they went, but the main problem the farmers faced was the dire shortage of money.

Crops such as potatoes were unreliable as an income source, because weather and supply determined the value of the crop. When weather was bad and the crop was light, prices would be very high, but let a good crop year like 1914 come along, and the price dropped below the cost of production.

"The cheapness of land in the north was off-set by the dearness of capital. This discouraged cattle-buying and hiring help to clear and drain property, build barns and silos. The farmers were so financially burdened that the schools were forced to receive much of their support from the Primary Fund." It also handicapped the Pere Marquette Railroad in its financial distress so severely that the tracks and maintenance deteriorated to sub-standard levels. The impoverished farmer had no opportunity to ride out bad seasons or farm losses, and the auction sales gave hard evidence to the severity of the problem.

STATE HELP FOR THE COMMUNITY

A proposed bonding district to drain wetlands similar to the Federal Irrigation Districts in the West was defeated in the Michigan Legislature in 1916. This so-called Croll Amendment was to provide authority to borrow capital. Already on the books was the Federal Land Bank Authority, but it would require a favorable county vote before it could be utilized to fund a local drainage district.

The Smith-Lever Bill began to supply

some money ($1,200 a year to Clare County in 1916) to advise farmers about drainage districts, and also about other problems concerning the land. For instance, real estate promoters who were "sharks", selling land to immigrants in a most unconscionable manner, pushing grazing lands to families who needed tillable land, were sharply restricted.

The Public Domain Commission, chaired by A. C. Carton in 1916, suggested that a public starch factory ought to be built, so that surplus potatoes wouldn't drive the prices down on the farmers. They suggested that perhaps potato flour or alcohol might also help ease the pressure on prices.

William H. Wallace of the Michigan Sugar Company offered to do for the potato what his company had been able to do for the sugar beet, but nothing came from this.

Many concerned leaders meeting in Cadillac in May of 1916 pulled together many experts to tackle the problems of northern Michigan agriculture. The Grand Rapids and Indiana Railroad sent Mr. Hartman, its soil expert, to go along with delegates from Grand Rapids Chamber of Commerce, Gleaners, Granges and Michigan Agricultural College. Most of the larger counties such as Alpena, Saginaw, Wexford, Newaygo and Isabella sent their own county agents to begin the state's task of finding a solution to the chronic problems of northern Michigan.

Dean Shaw, from M. A. C., said to the convention, "When a farmer fails here in the north, he spreads the word that it's not a good place to farm. That isn't true! What is needed is to farm the crops that can be grown in the north on northern soils."

The meeting generally agreed that one of the best ways to farm in the north was with cattle. "The northern farms can raise all the cattle Michigan needs and more. No farm should be less than 160 acres, and the wild land should never be cultivated, since it is suitable only for grazing," was their report.

Meanwhile, the struggles went on. New farm buildings were erected when farmers could scrape enough dollars together, hiring Milo Lamphere, Walt Pettit or Angus McLeod to build the characteristic round-roofed structures.

Accidents happened from time to time, which created more grief for the hard-pressed tillers of the soil, such as when Eugene Schutt's tractor blew up while threshing Charles Hoover's crop, buring down a barn full of hay and grain — already stored for winter.

GASOLINE TRACTORS

Gasoline tractors came into the area during 1914, and one was used by George Turbush on his Vernon farm. His 15 horsepower Bates engine pulled a two-bottom plow in the springtime and provided power to operate a hay baler, haul a manure spreader and run a buzz saw, among other things. The Brand and Page farms purchased tractors in 1915 which could pull even more plows, and the revolution rolled on.

Farms began gaining modern conveniences such as acetylene lights from a home-made generator built from a kit in 1914 also. The generator was filled with a gas producing stone sold by Union Carbide, and water was added once a month. This produced a stable, safe lighting system for nearly a quarter million homes at the outbreak of World War I.

Outbreaks of Hog Cholera, Hoof and Mouth disease, coupled with potato blight, San Jose Scale, army worms, fungus, flies and various other problems kept the farmer busy coping with life. Soon other problems related to the introduction of the automobile in large numbers on the rural roads were swamping him from other quarters.

An early Fordson tractor.

A 1918 Ford one ton truck. This was the first production chassis of the Ford Motor Company truck line.
Photo courtesy Ford Motor Company

The farmers were strongly encouraged to purchase tractors by the State of Michigan. One thousand were bought by Governor Sleeper for re-sale in 1918. Their value soon became apparent to tillers of the soil.
Photo: National Achives GSA 165-WW-173-9

Through it all, many farmers were living well enough so that they could retire when the time came, and most moved into Clare. By 1915, a colony of approximately twenty had survived to their golden years and were enjoying the fruits of their labors.

WORLD WAR I AND CLARE FARMS

Beginning soon after the war broke out in Europe, prices for agricultural products began to rise spectacularly. Men who barely had enough to pay the taxes now were thinking in terms of an automobile, roads, tractors, silos and other out-buildings.

Beef raising soon took on major importance in the western townships as Thomas Sotham, late of Lake George, had become Secretary of the Hereford Breeders Association in Lansing. He promoted the region assiduously and many out-of-state monied men bought large tracts for beef herds. When critics would mention the West, he could list the advantages of Lincoln, Freeman and Garfield Townships. "Did you ever hear of cattle dying in Michigan for lack of water?" he would ask. "In the West, coyotes, wolves and mountain lions are a constant menace, even though dogs are kept, and losses there are never less than 10%. You never have those losses in northern Michigan," he expounded again and again. "Michigan lands up to a section in size are waiting. Her cities are full of millionaires. All that is needed is a vision of the potential wealth in the northern counties," he concluded.

THE MILLIONAIRES'S COUNTY

It didn't take long for the word to get around. Rich men began buying the sections of land. Men from Kentucky, Chicago, Detroit and Indiana soon were running large herds of cattle and immense flocks of sheep

Will Cleveland
Photo from the Cleveland Family Collection

A 1914 steam engine and thresher parade in Missaukee County.

as the war drew nearer to America's shores. Henry Ford purchased two sections of land in Greenwood and brought his tractors here for their shakedowns. He hired local men to manage his farms, but often came to look things over.

Thomas Sotham sold his 2,000 acres in Lincoln Township to Warren T. McCray of Kentland, Indiana. McCray owned one of the finest herds of Herefords in the nation, and he put some of his better animals on the ranch near Lake George in 1917. Annually he sold $95,000-$125,000 worth of premier blooded stock. One animal sold for $20,000.

D. C. Stevenson, an attorney from Chicago, picked up 1,200 acres in Hamilton and ran cattle and sheep during the war. Dell Baldwin, Hill and Cameron along with the Stehle ranch all ran big operations.

The war put a pressure on the farmer that only millions of starving people can exert. Propaganda coming from Washington led him to believe that only his efforts applied to the maximum could save the hungry and starving masses in northern Europe, Poland, Belgium, Russia and the Middle East.

When the weather remained cold and wet during 1917 and 1918, the farmers who attempted to raise field corn for shipment abroad were keenly disappointed. They however produced much beef and many dairy products for the masses of dislocated refugees from a world gone amok.

This big push finally resulted in a condensary for Clare, as The Borden Company completed its plant in November of 1917, and the small dairy farmers began to reap the benefits which Isabella County farmers had been enjoying several years earlier.

Through it all, the farmer thought he had it tougher than others who lived and reveled in the city. An unknown author penned a poem which gave vent to his lament. Its title tells the story:

THE SAD CASE OF THE FARMER

Oh, the horney-handed farmer, what a
hapless lot is his,
As he toils from the city where he
thinks all glory is;
There is dirt upon his trousers as he
plows the stubborn soil,
And he doubtless oft is weary of the
never ending toil.
But he may as well remember as he
sadly works away,
That few people in the city merely
loaf day after day.

Oh, the horney-handed farmer with his
old brown jumper on,
He must work away till sunset and get
busy at the dawn;
He must toil for little profit while the
years drag slowly past,
And be right back where he started
when he's through — Poor soul! — at last,
But he may as well remember that
the cities are full of slaves
Who are working, not for glory, but
just onward to their graves.

The Great Experiment

Idealists often see great complex issues in utterly simplistic terms. Profound questions are easily reduced to an oversimplified quality. If it is positive, it becomes good! If the quality is negative, it is bad! The number of idealists in an era seems to vary much as the pulse of an active animal, and their enthusiasms wax and wane as the society evolves or matures.

Michigan certainly has had its days of idealism. When the lumbermen came through the heartland of the state in the Nineteenth Century, the cause of law and order suffered, and this became an evil in the eyes of some observers, as they sought to counteract it with the Red Ribbon Societies. Reformed drunks, businessmen, churchmen and mothers of growing children would often lay aside other concerns, gather their forces, march and "Dare To Do Right."

When the Twentieth Century dawned upon northern Michigan, a great expectancy was in the air. The immediate years which preceded saw the acceptance of mechanical devices such as the adding machine, typewriter and telephone by a willing public. The automobile had finally been put on the roads of America, and the airplane was soon to be airborne. Indeed, marvelous things were bursting from the creativeness of man.

But there was a "spot" that bothered the maturing communities. It seemed to linger on from the boistrous era when the Canucks stomped the wooden sidewalks with their river-driving boots, leaving large gouges where their caulks bit into the wooden planks. That spot — that canker — was the saloon!

Saloons were of a different world, and they generally had been placed in a location not frequented by children and the genteel ladies. It was an unwritten understanding that lewd women and brawling men made the saloon their bailiwick, and the more sophisticated folk weren't wanted nor welcomed in them. Noises from them would often flood the night air, however, and their influence and environment affronted many people. A town with a developing concept of its future looked upon the saloon with disdain and not a little scorn.

As A. J. Lacy, mayor of Clare during these changing years expressed it, "there are times of awakening and regeneration of the conscience within the communities... when the moral sense of a people (has been) offended and public sentiment is aroused." In times like these, public sentiment is aroused, and strong action usually follows in quick succession.

"It is in this spirit we approach the coming election whereat we are to cast our votes upon the question: 'Shall the manufacture of liquor and the liquor traffic be prohibited in Clare County?'" he said.

That was precisely the big question before the voters in the spring election of 1909, but that wasn't the only question of the day. Inherent in this problem were minorities rights in a pluralistic society and also the enforcement of laws by the state.

Lacy, speaking before the Methodist Episcopal Church in Clare, March 21, 1909, dissected the "Local Control" question into the moral aspects. "In the decision to be made, the moral responsibility upon every elector is as great as rests upon the whole of the electorate, because this is a moral ques-

Oliver Beemer's Saloon, which was located next to the barber shop in Clare. (L-R): Jim Hickey, unknown, George R. Brown, George Gailey, Wes Ort, Hugh McGuire, Tug Wilson, Jim Graves, William Dwyer, Jim Alger, Mike McGuire, William Parrish, and Howard (Chick) Brown, age 12. This photo was taken in 1898.

Photo from the Jim Grove Collection

tion," he said.

In other words, every person in Clare County who was registered to vote in 1909 had the responsibility to weigh the problem of prohibition and its impact upon the public. If the communities would be better served by the absence of the saloons and their by-products, a vote for local option was necessary. If, on the other hand, the liquor traffic and the saloons presented no untoward influence upon the county, then "Local Option" ought not to be supported.

Michigan "drys" had two courses of action open to them at this time. One was a statewide repeal of its "High License," and the other was the enactment of liquor controls on a county by county basis. Eleven counties had elected to go the dry route prior to 1909, and these included Barry, Clinton, Gratiot, Midland, Missaukee, Oceana, Osceola, Oakland, St. Joseph, Van Buren and Wexford.

They opposed being in a partnership with the liquor industry, which is essentially what a state license of saloons and liquor implied. Lacy made this clear to a Baptist audience one Sunday evening as he said,

"I have no word of abuse for those who are engaged in the liquor traffic, because the business is legalized and I do not wish to heap abuse on all of your heads . . . for we, the people are all in the business. Listen to the contract of (that) partnership:

"We, the people, parties of the first part, for and in consideration of the sum of five hundred dollars per year to be paid to us in advance, agree to and with those who desire to engage in the liquor traffic, parties of the second part, that there may be conducted in your name (we being the silent partners therein) a business which the United States Supreme Court holds is a 'nuisance' and which 'is prejudicial to the public health, welfare and safety,' for the sale of an article which our Michigan Supreme Court holds is 'a dangerous commodity,' and we, the first parties, will without further charge to the second parties, agree to support the paupers the business makes, even if it bankrupts the county, as it has in Clare County; and we will prosecute, incarcerate and support all of the criminals the business produces; and we

will make divorce laws granting decrees to women who deserve them because of the habitual drunkenness, extreme cruelty and non-support of their husbands, who chance to be among our best patrons; and we will found charitable and industrial institutions and children's homes for the care of children from broken homes which our high license system helps to make; and we will hire sheriffs, deputies, marshals and police officers to try to enforce the law, and watch the towns by day and night, to keep the drunks out of sight so as not to offend public decency or attract general attention; we will dedicate our State Constitution to Almighty God, so that we will be on speaking terms with the Deity, and pray to Him to 'give us this day our daily bread,' for there will be some who will be unable to buy it; we will hope for a ready answer to our supplication 'forgive us our trespasses,' for this unholy contract is one of them; we will hold one hand aloft towards Divinity, humbly praying 'lead us not into temptation,' while we make a grab for this five hundred dollars with the other, evidently not letting 'our right hand know what the left one is doing;' we will first get our public clutches on the cash, and pray most earnestly to 'deliver us from evil;' we also agree that the second parties may organize a 'Keep Your Mouth Shut' association, for the purpose of dictating nominations, receiving pledges, electing offices, proposing legislation and lobbying it through . . . in fact to run the government if this association is sharp enough to fool the people sufficiently to enable it to do so . . . but there is one thing the first parties reserve . . . the right to terminate this agreement of co-partnership at the spring election of each year."

And that was what the spring election of 1909 was essentially about.

SECURING A POSITION ON THE BALLOT

During the fall of 1906, a petition asking for a county wide vote on local option was submitted to the Board of Supervisors in Harrison, but they rejected it on a techni-

The Women's Christian Temperance Union are shown marching in Ann Arbor in 1909.
Photo: Michigan Department of State Archives

cality. Their stated objection was that it didn't have the ten day notice given before it was filed with the Supervisors. The actual problem was that it severely shook the Board up, as they didn't know the pulse of the county and they wanted to go back to the townships and count noses.

In January the Local Optionists were back, this time with a petition to Judge Dodds for a Mandamus, seeking the legality of the petition which had been circulated in the fall of '06. Prosecuting Attorney John Quinn said towns having saloons would be liable for damages in case the local option vote carried when liquor licenses were normally to be renewed.

Lewis Sunday, Supervisor from Arthur Township, said Quinn's ploy was just an attempt to keep the vote away from the people.

Some "wets" placed an ad in the SENTINEL under the pseudonym of Michigan Publicity Company and took liberties with eight Cadillac businessmen, quoting them, saying that "Local Option" wasn't

working in Wexford. Rev. Quinton Walker, a dynamic opponent of the saloons went to Cadillac and interviewed those who had been quoted. W. L. Sanders, Henry Ballou and W. H. Yearned denied having made the alleged statements, and had in fact supported the "drys."

There was a rapid escalation of the public debate now, and men from Osceola and Gratiot Counties took an active part in Clare's campaign to force the saloons to close. They wrote letters to the editors and made speeches at every opportunity.

The CLARE SENTINEL took a position of not accepting any ads which were either for or against the "wets." Letters, announcements and so on were accepted by the editors, but Edgar G. Welch only seemed to be receiving propaganda from the "drys."

"TEMPLE, THE NUISANCE"

Missaukee and Osceola Counties were "dry" along with Wexford in 1908, but they were nibbled to the point of desperation by the saloons of Temple. The Ann Arbor Railroad Co. was making frequent passenger runs between the counties of Missaukee and Wexford, and sober men could travel south in the early evening and return with a snoot-full along about 11:00 p.m. Indeed, many people voiced the opinion that the only profit shown by the Ann Arbor road was earned by hauling drunks.

Marion and Cadillac merchants and churchmen were anxious to staunch this hemorrhage in their communities, and on March 19, 1909, a delegation met with the natives of Temple. The Temple Band led the cortege through the burg to the Township Hall, where the meeting soon took on the atmosphere of a Methodist prayer meeting.

Elder Brown spoke first and gave the moral background. J. F. Piper, the town of Marion's leading business representative declared that " 'Local Option' is a winner! We are now having to extend less credit and old accounts are now nearly all paid up,'' he intoned.

An observer from a big city newspaper said this is "a novel way to convince Temple, which has been a pest in the past, that 'Local Option' has real merit."

C. W. Perry took this opportune time to join the bandwagon, and declared to a Clare audience that he supported the move to close down the saloons. Carlos A. Reading, another attorney from Clare had joined Perry on the speaker's platform, and he had glowing words for the "drys." "A 'Local Option' is a part of a great national movement for National honesty and personal responsibility,'' he said to an applauding audience.

Perry said, "Enough money has been paid out in ten years to build a brick building all the way from the Pere Marquette crossing to the Calkins Hotel,'' and the audience just loved it. Up until this time, he had kept his own counsel, but many had suspected that he supported a clean-up of the town. Now he had stood up in public, and declared in a strong statement, his sentiments.

Others in the county must have been encouraged because the vote went favorably toward the "drys" with a 63% margin.

Isabella County, voting during the same April election, gave the "drys" 93% of their votes, as they swamped the saloons.

A TIME TO CELEBRATE

As soon as it appeared that the "drys" would win, the Farwell Band boarded the 8:20 p.m. train and headed for Clare. There, the streets were filled with the winners, and men temporarily ecstatic beyond control grasped each other's hands in happiness.

W. C. Fuller, C. W. Perry and A. J. Lacy finally made their way to the balcony of the Calkins and spoke to the assemblage. A review of the long campaign and how the "wets" had shamefully attacked Rev. Quinton Walker was made. They graciously gave credit to their Catholic and Lutheran neighbors who also voted dry in spite of what some people thought they might do.

When word came that the Clare Saloons would quit cleanly, not attempting to hang around with blind-pigs, the noise became deafening and the speakers could no longer be heard.

Unfortunately, no such commitment was made by the other nine saloons in the county, and their illegal actions would keep the marshals, sheriffs and prosecuting attorneys busy for a long time to come.

Now that victory had been gained, the other part of A. J. Lacy's speech took on more meaning. Referring back to a speech made before the Baptists, also that March, let's examine in more detail what else he had to say.

"Under the Local Option Law as under the high license law, a man has a legal right to get so full of the 'elixir of life' that he can't see through a ladder, but he is not permitted to sell, furnish or give 'Old Kentucky Embalming Fluid' to others.''

This was one of the problems law enforcement officials would soon face. If a man (or woman) was able to secure, legally or illegally, enough whiskey to stew him to the gills, the law couldn't touch the customer. Many businesses catered to the practice of sending beer, whiskey and other intoxicants to a mail-order clientele. Purchasers would buy in case lots or in gallon amounts, and the railroads would express it right to their homes.

Druggists were also permitted to sell intoxicants to those who had a medical requirement for the drink. Doctors of course would have to provide prescriptions, but physicians such as Drs. Clute, Mussell and Sanford were very accommodating and not many who had a taste for liquor suffered for long. Things were so loose that drug stores after a while didn't even bother with the slip of paper from a physician, a practice that Lacy foresaw when he said the problem of getting someone to make a complaint will be the first step in the law's enforcement. "The proper course is complaint, warrant, arrest, bail, trial, conviction and punishment. The remedy offered by law is adequate, if every citizen will do his duty," he said.

During the boistrous lumbering days in northern Michigan, finding complaintants was rather difficult. Law officers would make arrests, but legally speaking, according to Lacy, at that time they had no more obligation to initiate the arrest than did any other citizen. Their official responsibility was to act upon a citizen's complaint, after the prosecuting attorney had been notified.

If a citizen failed to make a complaint against a person breaking the law, he was himself part of that lawless community.

Lacy went on to explain why the problem would be difficult to handle.

"The disposition of the average citizen to believe that when he has cast his vote that all his duties in this regard are shifted from his shoulders to the shoulder of some officer upon whose head he heaps abuse for the failure to do that which he should have done, results in widespread lack of law enforcement. We emerge from the booth, absolved from all the duties of citizenship, receiving only to ourselves that great inalienable right of every American citizen to kick . . . a right, the enforcement of which requires but little knowledge, no brains and less than moral courage."

There was no toleration in Lacy's philosophy for the law officer who failed to do his entire duty, but the brunt of law enforcement depended entirely upon public opinion, and a public opinion which, according to the speaker, had been traditionally fickle.

With a prescience of great importance, Lacy concluded his remarks to the Baptists with this statement:

"The fickleness of public opinion is historical and proverbial and not the least among the martyrs are those who as officials have sought to enforce the law above the standards of the time."

When these chickens would come home to roost would be another day, but during the springtime of 1909, it was a season to rejoice over the defeat of the evil saloon.

THE SLOT MACHINES

Isabella County had fewer saloons initially than Clare County, and the issue of "Local Option" was not as keenly contested by either side. A light voter turnout nevertheless gave strong support for the "drys." The county also moved at the same time against Dan Larkin and his slot machines. They outlawed them with law #5923 of 1899.

Clare County had no experience with these devices until Larkin moved his inventory into Crooked Lake, Farwell, Temple, Harrison and Clare. Overnight, the county was flooded with the little one-armed bandits and they became immediately popular with the now fast drying-out ex-saloon patrons.

Sheriff Sunday let it be known that he was declaring war on the "slots" and that he meant business. It had been a long time since any sheriff in Clare really meant to clean up the county. Old timers had to think back to Sheriff George Graham and his crusade against Jim Carr in the 1880's to find a similar example.

THE SALOONS CLOSE-UP

As the clock ticked its way towards 11:00 p.m. on April 30, 1909, the saloons celebrated their last hurrah! Men drank with both hands as they sought to drown their sorrows about the dry tomorrows in their future. Less than a week later, Albert Whitlock became the first drunk arrested after the law padlocked the saloons down. He had come to town to buy some fishing tackle, but took several nips from a bottle he had on his person. Marshal Dwyer arrested him a few hours later for being "drunk and disorderly." Justice A. E. Maynard fined him $7.50.

STATE WIDE PRESSURES

Eighteen wet counties voted dry in April, 1909, bringing the total of local option counties to twenty-nine. Wayne, Washtenaw and Macomb Counties countinued wet, but Oakland had previously gone dry.

In Lansing a bill was introduced to supress the liquor lobbyists and another was introduced to restrict liquor traffic via the mails and railroad express. Senator Wetmore, Republican Caucus Chairman and leader of the administrative forces, threw down the gauntlet. Senator Ming from Alpena, the President Pro-tem accepted the challenge and named a Committee of three to arrange patronage and the Senator was given a cuff on the wrist. The Senator wasn't ready to lead a crusade for prohibition in 1909.

THE LAW AND ORDER LEAGUES

Farwell had established a very vigorous Anti-Saloon League in 1908 under the direction of retired Methodist minister, the Rev. D. C. Jones, late of Leota. When the saloons closed, he helped found a Law and Order League under the direction of W. C. Fuller. E. W. Brown, Charles Stinchcombe and Josiah L. Littlefield were the officers. An Executive Committee consisting of Watson Honeywell, Sam McGoogan, C. E. Bingham, William Mott and Henry Winters was also organized. They, along with thirty other residents, agreed to establish a fund of $750.00 to police the liquor problem.

Clare organized a similar Law and Order League. Rev. Quinton Walker became its active and ever vigilant president, and the former members of the Anti-Saloon League transferred their members to the new committee. These men were: Frank Ballinger,

L. E. Davy, A. S. Rhoades, James F. Tatman, Levi Shafer, Edgar G. Welch, J.H. Wilson, William H. Bicknell, A. J. Lacy, C. A. Reading and S. Bogardus. A thousand dollar fund was planned for, of which $750.00 was raised in cash. More than thirty others joined this watchdog group, including Clark Sutherland and A. W. Tibbits.

Rev. Quinton Walker was a very highly educated man, having gone to college eight years. He had been in business down in Jackson before he turned his talents toward the church and its responsibilities to the community at large. He was a strong speaker and spoke boldly against sin, liquor and crime. Few residents of the county and surrounding territory escaped his ubiquity during the anti-saloon campaign as he went everywhere and anywhere there was an audience; large or small, old or young, male or female, friend or foe, official or citizen, it mattered not to him.

Walker had organized the VanBuren County "dry-option" campaign four years prior to his Clare assignment by the Methodist Church, so he knew from these campaigns that there would be a need for vigilance in this county, especially when the Board of Supervisors gave him a 22-0 vote. But some voices were so faint, it was hard to hear their assenting remarks to place the liquor problem on the spring ballot in the first place.

FIRST STEPS

Clare city began organizing itself for "dry" law enforcement in May. At the regular meeting, a spirited contest was on by some council members to keep Carlos A. Reading from being named to the city attorney's position. Reading was "dry" and perhaps too zealous for some of the "wet" ones left over on the governing body, such as Mason, Dwyer, Mater and Smalley. "Anyone but Reading" was their slogan! They considered A. J. Lacy much more desirable than Carl, so his name was put on the table. Only Axford and Lange favored Reading, and they had just been elected by the new wave of public opinion, but Lacy was to leave Clare, within the next sixty days or so, for Detroit and much fame. His sudden departure was rumored to have been encouraged by an irate husband whose wife was dallying with some of the townsmen too much.

A MAJOR LAWSUIT

William Miller, a twenty-year-old son of Mary Miller from Grant Township died in December of 1908 from injuries he received jumping from a train while under the influence of drink. Both of his legs were cut off and a five thousand dollar lawsuit was commenced against Pat "Paddy" Coyne and Oliver LaFave, the ex-Cadillac saloon keepers who had moved over to Temple when Wexford went dry. Coyne's attorney suggested that Mrs. Miller take a cash settlement of two hundred dollars, but she wouldn't agree to that offer. What she finally settled for was never made public, but Coyne had long been the "King Bee" of Temple and he was still a very cocky man even after the spring election which legally closed his saloon. He probably got off quite cheap!

Several petit court cases were routinely handled as Marshal Dwyer acted on the complaints of the citizens. Not many overt cases were noted in the early weeks because so many of the alcoholics and bums had stocked up before April 30.

CARRIE A. NATION

Mount Pleasant normally imported famous speakers for its Chautauqua programs, but the more illustrious for name recognition would have to be Carrie Nation. On a July Sunday in 1909 she had some time free, so the Clare people enjoined her to speak at the Doherty Opera House.

A full house greeted her that afternoon, and responded affably to her jabs at President Taft, the Masonic Lodge, the Republicans and of course the saloons. She kept the audience laughing most of the time, but her language was coarse and her humor was in the same mould.

"The common language of the saloon is damn, and it's a damned business from beginning to end. It damns everything connected with it and it's a damn shame that we have put up with it so long," she said, as the audience roared louder with each succeeding phrase she expostulated.

"Why, I've been in jail thirty-three times for fighting in a saloon!" Then turning to one side she stared at a man and said "Why do you laugh — because I got out thirty-three times?"

She warmed up to politics after a spell and noted "There is no stronger party in Hell than the Republican Party." Then, appearing to become solemn, she said, "Once in a jail I was placed between a lunatic and a cigarette fiend. I naturally preferred the lunatic."

Carrie Nation was espousing a variety of causes in 1909, and woman suffrage was one of them. " 'Tis not good for man to be alone', " she said in her officious manner, then changed her inflection and concluded mischievously, "not even at the ballot box."

Before she left she praised landlord Calkins for keeping a fine hotel, but she scolded him real good for having a Schlitz beer advertisement in the dining room. Amid a rollicking and happy audience she began her trek to the depot where she would make connections back to Mount Pleasant and her evening lecture.

Passing S. C. Kirkbride, who was sitting in front of the post office, she railed at him for having a cigar, but he took it in good spirits and smiled at the long-skirted firebrand. Kirkbride had long been involved in politics also, but his style was one of conciliation, not confrontation. He watched her clamber into the bus which took her to the train. "So long, Carrie! Watch what you drink!" he said.

COYNE IN COURT AGAIN

A son of Alason S. Holbrook jumped from a train near Pennock and was mangled by the wheels of the cars. His father sued Coyne and La Fave for ten thousand dollars and in so doing, "stirred the cesspool too much for some people.''

Attorney Gaffney from Reed City and John Quinn, the elected prosecuting attorney from Harrison, defended Coyne and La Fave. Quinn claimed to be quite embarrassed by his compromised role. ''It's an embarrassing position for me to be in, holding the official position I do in this county and defending those saloon keepers,'' he said in court.

Attorney Savage, acting in the role of plaintiff's attorney, bowed to Quinn and said, ''We accept your apology for being connected with the defense of this case. Let us cast the mantle of charity over Mr. Quinn for his shortcomings.''

On the stand, La Fave testified to three violations, and he modified his testimony again and again. So rank did it become that Judge Dodds asked Attorney Lacy, ''Do you mean, Mr. Lacy, that this man doesn't know whether he is guilty or not guilty until the jury tells him?''

If those were the ground rules, then all of his admissions of law infractions didn't make him guilty, because the next door neighbor of Coyne's was on the jury and he admitted later that he would never vote to convict his friend.

The jury deliberated for several hours, but the vote was always eleven to one. Coyne and La Fave had done nothing for which they were legally guilty. The Holbrook boy, though a minor, had died and no one was guilty.

Many people in Harrison asked, ''How could such a man get on the jury?'' and no one could give an answer!

Coyne was tried a third time during 1909. This infraction was for transferring his liquor business to his farm just outside of town. Mrs. Coyne was alarmed at this turn of events and called Sheriff Sunday. Bill Artcliff was ''visiting'' with Paddy when the official call was made.

Coyne told Artcliff to turn the tub over and place it on top of the liquor and then sit on it. This he did just before Sheriff Sunday knocked on the door.

''I hear you have some liquor around here,'' said the sheriff.

''Is that so? Well take a look around and see if you can find it. Let me know. I'm getting a taste for it about now,'' replied Coyne.

So the sheriff and a deputy made a search in the basement and outside in the sheds, but didn't find any. ''Guess I was told a story by someone,'' he said and turned to go.

Mrs. Coyne was in the background all of this time and was dismayed that the law officers didn't find the barrels of whiskey out in the barn under some hay. When they were uncovered, Sunday pulled the plugs and the sequestered stock all drained into the ground.

''I'm glad it's gone, Sheriff. I just can't keep away from the stuff,'' Coyne said. But he did, for at least ten days, as that's the sentence Judge Dodds handed out to him.

The last big lawsuit Coyne had was commenced by A. S. Brooks. Ten thousand dollars was the amount of this suit, and it was tried in September of 1909. A jury of twelve men listened to the case and then brought in a ''not guilty'' decision.

Three deaths directly traced to his saloon and one blind pig on his farm brought the weight of the law down on his head to the extent of ten days in jail. If his wife hadn't uncovered the evidence, he would have escaped even that punishment.

THE BLIND PIGS

At least four blind pigs were active from the very beginning of ''Local Option.'' Willis C. Dunlap of Farwell ran one in conjunction with L. D. Sillaway, the ex-saloonist, and Arnold Lett, a local liveryman who hauled it in his wagons. Dunlap stored it at his place. Mrs. Dunlap was greatly disturbed over her husband's chronic alcoholism and had joined the Farwell Women's Christian Temperance Union (W.C.T.U.). She became its very able president and caused a lot of heat to be brought upon the Farwell Bootleggers, chief of whom was her drunken husband.

John Rodabaugh was another heavy violator of the liquor laws. He was arrested so many times that he and the judge were on a very familiar basis. He knew which jail cell was his and he knew all the protocol of the courts. He wouldn't even show emotion when the judge passed sentences, barely standing in front of the bench long enough to have the gavel to pound out his term in prison or jail.

A third blind pig operated out of Garfield, but it managed to escape since so many of the township's citizens did what A. J. Lacy suggested would happen. Observed liquor violations caused no official complaints and the law officials were only able to successfully apprehend one violator, Dresdan Bryan.

Lewis Johnson was arrested and brought to trial in 1909, but his peers were not in the convicting mood. Likewise Henry Look, the Hersey turn-key who went to Temple in 1910 for a snoot-full, and fell into the Muskegon River, otherwise he wouldn't have been noticed. Other than the wet clothes he didn't suffer any loss.

James Wilton was one of the few who were found guilty. He had a fine of eighty dollars and twenty days hammered down on him. Henry Vining, another non-Clare County resident was tried in 1909 and relieved of fifty dollars. He was given free room and board for twenty days also.

Other than these cases, very few arrests were made in the townships, and far fewer convictions were handed down. The Law and Order League had a few cases pending, the largest of which concerned Anna Mussell.

THE DRUG STORES

Osceola County went dry before Clare County and of a consequence had more practical experience in handling the ingenious ways enterprising people had in both selling and consuming wet goods. Under the local option law, the town marshals were to make weekly checks with the drug stores, checking their records for infractions of the law.

Wine could be sold by the druggists for sacramental purposes, and alcohol could be retailed for medicinal, scientific and mechanical purposes, but all of these had certain restrictions. When the sales of alcoholic beverages began to increase in volume beyond what could reasonably be accepted, Dan Young, prosecuting attorney in Evart became outright belligerent towards the enforcement practices in Clare. "That you have men who openly violate their oaths is a stench upon the name of Clare. Are there no honest, law abiding citizens with enough courage to make a complaint?" he railed at the readers of the CLARE SENTINEL.

SECURING THE EVIDENCE

The suspicion in town pointed rather heavily toward Mrs. A. E. Mussell and her drug store, as she had a very large number of seedy customers coming and going from her business on McEwan Street. Some members of the Law and Order League began to pay her more than normal attention.

She received by express eight barrels of alcohol for every one that E. A. Anderson signed the bill of lading for, indicating that it had been received. The town marshal, checking the store records of Mrs. Mussell didn't indicate that she was dealing with that large a volume of business.

Lucius Converse "happened" to near the trains as they came to town and overheard two men. One said, "Let's go to Mussells and get some booze." Converse followed the men, but believed they couldn't get it without a prescription.

The new arrival in town went up to Mrs. Mussell, said a few words to her and waited while she took a bottle from the shelf, went to the prescription room for a moment and then returned. She handed the bottle to the customer, which was quickly placed in his back pocket.

Converse followed the man as he left the store, encountering E. G. Welch nearby. Assigning the surveillance job to Welch, Converse made a phone call to Rev. Walker, the president of the Law and Order League.

Meantime the man who was later identified as Koeppe from Toledo, settled down in the alley between the former saloon of McDonald's and Lackie's Hotel. Welch then joined Converse and Walker as they entered the drug store to learn more of the details.

Mrs. Mussell denied selling the liquor to any such man that Converse described. She said she sold some medicine to someone who may have fitted the general appearance of the fellow, however. "He had heart trouble," she explained.

Converse led the league's members back to the alley where Koeppe now was with two other companions. They had been passing the bottle around and not much was left, but Converse wondered if he could have a "sip."

No questions were asked, and the bottle was handed to him, now holding only about two teaspoons of the liquid. Converse took a mouthful and determined that it was whiskey.

He took the bottle back to the store and said, "Mrs. Mussell, I've got the bottle!"

Mrs. Mussell then admitted that she did wrong. "I don't know why I did it," she explained. Then she tried to settle the matter out of court, but the Law and Order League wasn't in a compromising mood.

A formal complaint was lodged, and she appeared before Justice Maynard. John Quinn handled the prosecution and C. W. Perry was defending Mrs. Mussell. The trial was quite well attended as the community respected this woman who so faithfully ran her drug store that it ranked among the elite of the state. Her numerous friends refused to believe her guilty until it was proven in court. On that account, they should have had very few qualms.

Prosecuting Attorney Quinn quickly went over the salient points in the case, and turned the problem over to lawyer Perry. Perry, who was a softspoken person and highly esteemed by everyone, called his first witness.

Mrs. Hemstreet of Grant Township took the stand. She produced a bottle similar to the one in question and testified that her son-in-law Koeppe had left it at her home. She further testified that he was "troubled with a weak heart."

That was all Justice Maynard needed to hear, and he dismissed the case. "There is insufficient tangible proof for a conviction," he said.

John Quinn, the man charged by the courts to defend the law, said, "This is the weakest case yet."

The courtroom emptied, and many of Mrs. Mussell's friends walked her back to her place of business, where they celebrated her victory.

A. J. Lacy's words of warning were coming back to remind many that an attempt to "enforce the laws above the standards of the times would make martyrs" of many.

THE STRUGGLE GOES ON

Regardless of the problems encountered in Clare with the local option law's enforcement, other communities pushed on. Nineteen more counties voted to go dry in 1910 and a large movement in the non-big city districts was under way. Counties such as Muskegon, Crawford, Montcalm, Huron, Montmorency, Grand Traverse, Cheboygan, Manistee and Isoco were the major targets of the State Anti-Saloon League.

Other little problems kept poking their heads up across the state, one of them during July of 1910. Rumor had it that beer could be served legally at all barn raisings, and many farmers jumped at the chance to build barns that summer, but also, the Attorney General of Michigan said that he knew of no such support for such a statement. Of course that didn't stop the barn buildings nor the parties that accompanied them.

ANOTHER VOTE ON LOCAL OPTION

A petition was circulated by the "wets" in January of 1911, asking that the question of local option again be put to the voters in April. Naturally enough the "drys" weren't very anxious to conduct another campaign as they were very exhausting to the principals involved. "Considering the effect the election of two years ago had upon the community, it was hoped that we wouldn't have to go through that ordeal again this spring. Our businessmen are working together for a common good and it would be regretted if anything disturbed this harmony," said Rev. Quinton Walker.

The Eli Ramey Card and Lunch Room in 1924. Eli is on the left. Ben Hickey is on the right. This was the David McPhall Saloon before local option.

Those members of the Community who preferred things a bit "wetter" didn't think that a vote favorable to their side should be regretted at all!

However, Walker was magnanimous enough to say, "There are those who may feel just as strongly that the saloons should again be allowed to operate. They are entitled to their opinion." He didn't intend that they could be successful in their campaign to undo everything that his Anti-Saloon League of Clare and the Law and Order League had put together, nevertheless.

The problem in Isabella wasn't as pressing because every elected official except the county Surveyor supported the dry side. Clare had many officials who openly worked against the law they were sworn to uphold and so local option had many problems connected with it.

The vote in April, however, was favorable to the anti-saloon forces and Clare remained, on paper at least, a dry county. The liquor still flowed in the outlying districts and someone complained to Prosecutor Quinn that Dresdan Bryan of Garfield was running a blind-pig in Lake. He quickly confessed and was given a token fine by the magistrate.

Weidman, a community south of Lake, cracked down severely and successfully it seems. "No teams are hitched at Jockey Row any more," was the report from that community. "Nor are children crying for their fathers in the evening as they formerly were," it continued.

By 1912, the routine of things had pretty well settled into a pattern. "We handle a case of beer or a package of whiskey the same way we handle a hat or a suit of clothes shipped through us," reported a local express agent in Clare. Sometimes an alcoholic wouldn't be able to slip into town for his medicine often enough or his shipment hadn't come through, and he would be reduced to drinking horse liniment.

The dried out addicts wouldn't be able to differentiate many times which was the liniment and which was the whiskey, so varied was the purity of the express shipments. A Congressional investigation of the tricks and secrets of the compounders disclosed the fact that many of the best known and high priced brands of whiskey and brandy contained but a small percentage of the genuine stuff. Had the consumer known that he was drinking acetate of potassium, sulphuric acid, blue vitriol, ammonia or other similar compounds, he might have paused to consider his course of action, but most reveled in blissful ignorance.

Bourbon whiskey was sometimes made by adding an oil which consisted largely of fusel oil which had been treated with acetate of potassium, sulphuric acid, ammonium oxalate and black oxide of manganese. Scotch whiskeys which were expressed in, often were made by adding a small quantity of real Scotch whiskey to a mixture of oil of birch and spirits. Cognac was compounded from spirits flavored with cocoanut oil and colored with burnt sugar. In addition, there were other tricks only known to the practitioners. These weren't revealed to the Congressional investigating team.

So lethal did the mixtures become that tolerant Americans became alarmed, and not a few joined the "drys" in an effort to stamp out the adulterators. Archbishop Ireland had no earthly use for the saloons and compounders, so he began speaking very heatedly in 1912. Appearing before the National Convention for a Total Abstinence Union of America he said, "The saloon is our greatest enemy. It blights our national growth." Others began to think the same way also.

TOO MANY PRESCRIPTIONS WRITTEN

Dr. Clute was the type of a person who acted pretty much as he saw fit. If a ruling by the town was unreasonable in his estimation, it was ignored. The whole question of "drys" versus "wets" was to him a silly exercise in stupidity, and he had no reservations about bending the law or even the intent of the law if a man needed some medicine to get him through the night.

Pearl Calkins from Farwell was twenty-four years old in 1912, and suffered from an excessive fondness for alcohol. He often asked Dr. Clute for a prescription and just as often was given a piece of paper which entitled him to some relief.

Pearl's mother had requested Dr. Clute to not give her adult son any more prescriptions. Dr. Clute told her that her son had a weak "palpitating heart" and needed a drink now and then to strengthen it, so he ignored her request.

Then on December 20, 1912, Pearl came to Clare on the passenger train. About noon he clambered onto the ladder of a freight train heading towards Farwell. Calkins, being in a condition to not feel much pain, but evidently with a stronger palpitating heart, fell under the wheels of the freight car. His body was dragged a distance even after his legs had been cut off.

An inquest was held and his death was ruled accidental, but Enoch Andrus, the new editor of the CLARE SENTINEL, and the replacement for Rev. Quinton Walker in the Law and Order League, challenged the finding. He went after the jury and Dr. Clute for giving prescriptions to known drunks. Drug stores which sold prescription alcohol to addicts weren't let off any easier.

"They (the jury) could have learned that he was a man in the habit of becoming frequently drunk," he charged.

"There is not a shadow of an excuse for a physician to give a prescription to an alcoholic. It was an utter and gross perversion of the law, and yet this kind of business had been going on here week after week, month after month, and the people of Clare have sat supinely for it," charged Andrus.

A few days later Dr. Clute was arrested for giving the son a presciption, but he denied having been instructed by Mrs. Calkins to desist writing prescriptions. He further went on to explain about the weak heart business and concluded by saying that he didn't think any one in the community would criticise him for helping to make a weakly palpitating heart beat more strongly.

Andrus said in return, "A community can accept a stronger palpitating heart now and then, and a prescription for this can be tolerated, but we don't want an epidemic of stronger palpitating hearts in Clare."

There was insufficient evidence against the doctor, and so on the third of January he was released. The Pearl Calkins case was closed along with his.

THE COUNTY TREASURY IS EMPTY

Since 1909 the high license fees of five hundred dollars for each of fourteen saloons stopped coming in to the county treasurer's office, and by 1913 the coffers went dry. Prospects for 1914 were the same, and the Board of Supervisors didn't desire to increase the tax load on property, so Clare was in a genuine dilemma. What could they do? Someone suggested opening the saloons back up and taxing them at one thousand dollars apiece. Everyone laughed at first, but then they thought about it some more.

Nearly everyone in Clare County that wanted to drink was being supplied by the express company or the drug stores anyway. Besides, there weren't very many fines coming in from the courts even though Sheriffs Sunday and Brown had tried to make the system work. So "Why not? What can we lose?" they thought.

In April of 1914 the voters in the county went to the polls, again to decide between the "drys" and the "wets."

Just before the election, a delegation of "drys" went to Governor Ferris and complained about the current prosecuting attorney, Joe Bowler. They told the governor that Bowler wasn't very agressive about prosecuting the violators who were practically operating in the open. They strongly objected to his presenting the cases in such a manner that he seldom produced any convictions even after he was prodded by the Clare County Law and Order League.

Earlier, during the first half of 1911, when Bowler had taken office, he produced twenty-three convictions from twenty-three arrests, but then he was aided by Will Adams, the new mayor of Clare.

Bowler and Adams had first hounded the druggists with their wrath. "This promiscuous dispensing must and will stop," they said. They meant it too, at first.

Now, three years later, they had become weary of chasing the same people week after week, month after month. Lacy's warning about the over zealous law officers was coming true.

Joe Bowler had lost heart since he felt that he was all alone fighting the crusade for the masses, but all he ever heard from the "good people" were their kicks about his not doing more against the violators.

A DETROIT FREE PRESS reporter was in Lansing and he picked up the charges made by the Clare people to the Governor. One reporter came to Clare, and Bowler told him, "There has not been one intoxicated person arrested in Clare in more than two months, and there hasn't been a drunk on the street for a period longer than that."

Mrs. Mussell was still importing her eight barrels of alcohol regularly, while Anderson was receiving his customary order of one. Dunlop normally receipted delivery for one barrel and a box of whiskey. Dr. Clute would write seven hundred and forty-four prescriptions during a two month interval about the time Bowler was speaking. Mussell and Dunlop individually wrote half the number Clute churned out.

A member of the Law and Order League filled the reporter in on some other statistics. "There are thirty known alcoholics who are habitually sold alcohol and whiskey in illegal quantities. One man received thirty-three and a half pints, another thirty-five, and a third bought twenty-nine."

This wasn't exactly the story Bowler told the reporter, but the League spokesman said, "Go look at the records. They'll tell you that the drug stores have been furnishing liquor to Indians and also to minors."

A trip back to Bowler's office brought the response that he had taken the records to his farm because they were so bulky. He also admitted that he didn't know the local option law as well as some members of the Law and Order League, nor did he search as diligently for violators.

The reporter asked to see the records, so Joe said that if he wanted to come back in a week, he'd make them available.

A week later he told the reporter that all of the records were destroyed! That took care of that!

The League, however, wasn't going to accept this effrontery to the law and they began making so much noise that the druggists and physicians got together and called for a truce. Finally a statement was hammered out which read:

"This agreement, reached not at the behest of any faction, provides for the following:

a) Physicians will not issue any more prescriptions, except at the bedside of a sick person, or due to some equally extreme case of necessity;

b) Druggists will not furnish any liquor to persons except those have a valid prescription as stated above.'

As a condition to this agreement all litigation which was then pending was dropped, if it pertained to the liquor laws. They also agreed not to prosecute on any other charges except violations of the next agreement.

Together they pledged the following: "We desire that all local personalities and ill will be discontinued and a spirit of good fellowship and friendliness will hereafter prevail." A further mention of the good offices of Mayor Cole in bringing together the warring parties, then came the signatures of Drs. Mussell, Sanford, Clute, Dunlop and druggists Anna Mussell and E. A. Anderson for the business and professional side. Rev. W. H. Irvin, Rev. I. W. Knight, M. W. Cartwright, J. F. Tatman, A. S. Rhoades and J. A. Allen signed for the League.

The spring election was held soon after, and its results superceded all of the good intentions. The saloons were going to open up again!

WHY DID THE SALOONS COME BACK?

Many people in the county were utterly dismayed. Where did the lofty purposes of the anti-saloonists go wrong? In seeking to find an answer, one citizen said:

"We don't want saloons, but if matters continue to go on as they have, we might as well have them."

Another expressed his concern over high taxes and the problem the county had in paying for its obligations.

Said one sage, "The majority of the voters said they wanted it wet, so it will be wet."

Wet it was going to be for two years, as it turned out, then everyone began to re-examine their course of action, and decided

to get in step with the state, as the majority of the counties now had gone dry.

Enoch Andrus had these words of comfort to the optionists, on the eve of their defeat. He said, "Now let everyone keep perfectly cool and sweet. Take your regular ration and don't lose any sleep. God is ruling the universe just the same as He was last week, and right will ultimately triumph."

A DEATH IN TEMPLE

A mile north and west of Temple a shack had been built alongside the Ann Arbor tracks. A man by the name of Harry Crill had been living with an Indian girl by the nickname of Big Mary in the shack.

Late on Sunday afternoon in April of 1913, James Howard went to Crill's shack and found Big Mary drunk and the man unconscious with a head wound.

Justice Davis was called, then Sheriff Brown, Undersheriff Mason, Prosecutor Bowler and Supervisor Cross. Dr. Carrow had been called in Marion and he arrived

Enoch Andrus

just about the time a post mortem was required.

His verdict was, "Death came by two blows on the head and acute alcoholism."

Coroner Lamb impaneled an inquest jury and its verdict was the same as the doctor's.

Big Mary was the most likely assailant, so she was arrested and taken to jail in Harrison.

Sheriff Brown began asking questions of the neighbors and he discovered that Crill had been in Temple several years. Before that he had been a school director and had come to the area looking for huckleberries. He married Big Mary sometime in 1911.

The hut was small, but filthy in the extreme. He had whiskey shipped regularly to him from Port Huron in six quart lots.

Big Mary went peaceably to jail, and it's a good thing too, for she was an amazon of strength.

A trial was held a month later with Judge Withey from Reed City on the bench. A jury found her not guilty, and she returned to her shack in the woods.

Several of the witnesses testified that it was the poor whiskey rather than Big Mary that caused his death, but others thought that fear of the anarchists in Clare County at the time intimidated the jury into an aquittal.

THE NEW SALOONS

Many men applied for the 1914 saloon licenses in Clare, including J. W. Calkins,

The Temple City Band, circa 1915.

The Dewey Shingle and Stave Mill in Temple.
Photo from the Anna Crawford Collection

J. M. Davis, George W. Easler, David McPhall, William Haley, Alexander Lackie, James Duncan and Arthur Thorpe. They vied with each other to pay five hundred dollars to the county and an additional three hundred dollars to the city of Clare.

Farwell voted to keep all saloons out of town, but Temple issued a permit to Daniel Carey of Mount Pleasant. Napoleon Barricombe of Cadillac had wanted to start a saloon in Farwell, and Barney Kerry of Cadillac requested permission to open a saloon in Temple, but both were turned down. Four saloons were licensed to operate in the county during the two years they were allowed.

THE EBB TIDE REVERSES

Clare voted to go back to the dry side in April 1916. In this regard, they were now in harmony with the flood of new counties and states which were being swept along in a mood of glorious euphoria. Seven states voted to go dry in 1915, thus "8,253,993 more people are freed from the saloon," chortled the anti-saloonists. They joined the other eleven states in abstaining from hard drink. Immediately the consumption of alcoholic beverages fell. Manufacturers produced 14,263,089 fewer gallons in 1915 than the year before, and drinkers cut their consumption by 41,771,427 gallons. Beer production dropped by 6,381,256 barrels and one hundred breweries went out of business.

Seattle was the largest city to go dry in 1916, and it was in the center of the lumber district. "If the lumbering regions can go dry, so can the rest of us," reasoned the remaining states and soon it was to be.

Chicago closed its saloons on a Sunday in October of 1915 and noted that there hadn't been a dry day in the windy city for over forty-three years. Judge Matchett, when he was asked about the law, said, "I didn't enact the law. I just interpret it."

Some of the Chicago residents rather liked the idea of having a dry day. Perhaps an extended period of time would be better, at least that's what Clareites thought.

Citizens who hadn't lived in a wet county had never seen drunks on the streets before, but in 1914 and 1915, two or three could always be seen hanging around the depot. Even some young boys were being drawn into the habit.

A newspaper offered its spaces free to any advocate of the saloon who could name one benefit which came from the "wet" option. None came forward to claim the offer.

MICHIGAN TREADS THE LEGAL ROAD TO PROHIBITION

In March of 1915 Senator Straight introduced a bill to put the sale of liquor on a statewide referendum. Seventeen other senators joined him as co-sponsors of the bill and others were expected to vote favorably.

Enoch Andrus, the Clare publisher, had lost a boy on July 4, 1913, when lightning struck the judge's stand at Dave Ward's race track. Another young man, the son of Henry Hanes, was also struck dead. In an article widely copied in other papers, Andrus compared death by lightning, which is instantaneous, to death from liquor, which is slow.

"God alone can control the forces that took our two boys, but every citizen can exercise a control which will take the lives of several boys," he wrote.

"If you are able to vote 'no' on the question of local control, you will be able to do what Mr. Hanes and myself weren't permitted to do. You are permitted to save the lives of your boys. Who would not prevent

the death of his son if he could?" was the question asked.

Who, indeed?

The answer began to come quickly! Governor Ferris had led the fight in Mecosta County and was now leading the fight in Lansing. Father Murphy of the Catholic Church spoke before the National Convention of the Anti-Saloon League in scathing terms as he burned the hides of the saloonists.

An assassin had attempted to kill Father Murphy in front of a Texas saloon in 1910 because he dared to be both a priest and a sworn enemy of the liquor traffic. "That would be assassin is my punctuation mark," he would assert.

"I want to make one quote that will be quoted across this county for years to come. I want to help place the Catholic Church in her true light before the minds of those who have wasted many a hard effort against an imaginary menace. I want to help re-unite the Christian forces in one great sweeping and victorious struggle with the age-long enemy of the cause of Jesus Christ.

"In the campaign about to be launched against all the saloons in this county, I want every Catholic in the United States, whether priest or layman, to be absolutely free to work for and to vote for National Prohibition." And they did, in large numbers across the length and breadth of the land.

THE MICHIGAN CAMPAIGN

Walter J. Hoshal, the ex-mayor of Burr Oak was selected to organize Michigan's campaign for prohibition. Beginning in Detroit, he opened with a hard hitting campaign.

"This organization isn't going to be run by long haired men, short-haired women or bald-headed deacons. The average person's concept of a prohibitionist is a long-haired, frock-coated individual. My idea is to get big men — strong businessmen — in back of this dry movement. Then the people will know it's not being run by cranks . . .

"Some people like to get up in church with four bald-headed deacons sitting on the

The so-called David Ward Racetrack. It was built to host a regional annual fair, but the one at Harrison put it out of business. Horse racing enthusiasts kept it busy, however.
Photo from the Foss Family Collection

front pew and talk about the evils of the liquor traffic and how it is raising hell with our young people. Well, that isn't my style! I don't dote on sob-stuff, about father going home drunk and kicking little Nellie in the head,'' he explained.

What he did dote on was the plain truth and he made people like it. He frankly admitted that he had never read the Bible and that he didn't even know the creed of the Methodist Church.

''I have my own creed and it has just four points,'' he said. The first point is my son! The second point is my daughter. The third point is, I want them to grow up in a community where there is no saloon. The fourth point is that I want my wife to live in a state where there are no saloons.''

By October of 1916, the ''wets'' organized their Home Rule League, and sought to soften the absolute prohibition against all liquor sales which appeared to be all but a certainty.

The ''drys'' didn't let up though. ''Through struggle and painful effort during the past quarter century the people have driven this infamous traffic from more than half of Michigan, and now it appears that one little step will undo all this work. Will it succeed? Not if we can defeat this Home Ruin League, it won't,'' shouted the ''drys.''

The anti-liquor movement began in Michigan eighty-four years before the 1916 date. Then, Secretary of War Lewis Cass abolished the liquor ration in the U. S. Army. ''Seventy-six years ago the state was overrun by a disorganized revival of all sorts of temperance societies whose object was to reclaim the drunkard. A movement had been ever since operated on the theory that they would never be able to save the drunkards as long as the grog shops stayed in business.

''But the counter-movement in Michigan has always characterized the kind of a fight the liquor defenders have made. They have always professed to be satisfied with the last step the prohibition people took, if they didn't take another.

"When the people wanted a tax on the business, they fought it without stint. When the excise tax was increased to weed out the swarming hosts of grogeries, the liquor interests fought hard for the old system.

"When it was proposed to give counties the option to limit alcoholic sales, again they shrieked that liberty was in danger of being slain. Then when the movement enlarged to the state level, they proclaimed that there was no finer method than the local home rule.

"Ten years ago, the liquor business in Michigan was warned that something was going to happen if it didn't take hold of the reins and drive straight. But at that time, the business was deluded that the "bar" decided to vote. That delusion is being dispelled. Now they are crying for home rule. It must be made known now that this is the cry of the (wounded) saloons," said the CLARE SENTINEL, on October 12, 1916.

THE MICHIGAN VOTE

Michigan voted in November 1917, and decided that it could do without John Barleycorn. An expected margin of fifty thousand soon mushroomed to a plurality of seventy thousand.

THE NATIONAL MOOD

The Great War had a major influence upon the national prohibition movement. The nations in Europe were so severely short of food that the millions of bushels of grain consumed in the production of alcoholic drinks seemed down right unpatriotic. There was a great fear that millions of our allies would starve to death in the winter months of 1917-1918 unless we shipped every spare quart of wheat, corn, barley and rye.

In September of 1917, all distilleries in the U.S. were ordered closed, and the crusade moved ahead one giant step.

The United States Senate passed a prohibition bill which made national prohibition effective as of June 30, 1919. The "drys" in Michigan were happy.

Some of the more skeptical citizens could have learned a few things from the experiences of Clare, had they taken the time to closely examine the checkered record of locally controlled liquor sales.

The warnings A. J. Lacy gave the Clare Baptists in 1909 should have been ample, but his words were ignored in the euphoric celebration all across the country.

"The fickleness of public opinion is historical and proverbial, and not the least among the martyrs are those who as officials have sought to enforce the law above the standards of his time," echoed Lacy.

Local Politics

A nation's personality is different from the individual personalities of the several states, yet there is in a macrocosm, a blending of all the nuances which characterize the separate states and their main issues. So it is within a state! The individual, local personality is generally different from the larger, but the relationship is discernible to a disinterested observer. Over the years, political causes and fortunes have been spawned from the backwaters of government in vast profusion, and just as with the prolificness of a spawning fish, few eggs are fertilized, and fewer still are matured into an adult. Political ideas, concepts and causes are as numerous and just as will-o'-the-wisp.

At one time in Clare County's history, (during the 1900-1912 era) politics bred locally were a microcosm of state and national politics, and the actors from the city of Clare so dominated Michigan's Republican and Democratic parties, that all state-wide campaigns were master-minded and executed by Clare's brilliant, if partisan, leaders. In 1910, the apex of Republicanism, the national campaign was master-minded by a local man, Dennis E. Alward, who had his National Campaign Headquarters in New York. He had cut his teeth on the political campaigns of Clare County and the State of Michigan. In no other community or state could the Pre-World War I national fortunes of the two political parties be better analyzed than in Clare County, Michigan. Truly, during these twelve years between 1900 and 1912, the heart of America was in perfect synchronization with Michigan's heartland.

Alward came to Clare in 1881 as a young man. He purchased the CLARE COUNTY PRESS during the Jim Carr days and helped bring him to the bench of justice. Joining George J. Cummins and A. J. Doherty, he was elected to the Clare County School Commissioners and between them, they guided an excellent educational system into maturity. Growing professionally as well, his horizons extended to Lansing, where he became clerk of the State Railroad Commission. Lew Miller, Secretary of the Senate, quickly discovered Dennis Alward's genius for systemizing complex issues and made him his assistant. A year later, Alward replaced his boss and was given the opportunity to re-organize the clerk's job. The proto-type he installed in the Michigan Senate at that time still is used by the legislators today.

The Republican party drafted him to be its top officer in 1894, and he guided it through the Cleveland and Bryan years so skillfully that in 1904, there wasn't one Democrat in the Legislature. During the 1910 national elections, Alward was given the job of organizing the national election from a New York office, but he was not so successful that year. Everyone agreed, however, that Alward was a political genius! Clare, of course, knew this much earlier. He was no vote-getter, personally, but he could tell within 1% where every vote in any precinct or district was coming from. His estimations were accurate to such an amazing degree that not a few wondered if he was a "psyche", or just out buying votes. He was neither. He did his homework!

A partner in this scenario was A. J.

125

Doherty, a vote-getter and a political leader from the elected ranks. Coming from New York State to Clare in 1876, Doherty was something of a black sheep in his family, marrying outside his faith. A few years later, some of his brothers, in-laws and other relatives joined him in Clare and took him back into their good graces. It was a wise move on their part.

Doherty's abilities centered around men. He was able to gather coalitions together for the resolving of very difficult problems. Complex issues which had a multiplicity of of vested interests were his specialty. Again and again, the state recognized his unusual genius and tapped him for service in the sticky Public Domain Commission, State Agricultural Fair Board, State War Preparedness Committee and finally on the sensitive War Appeals Board. In each of these assignments after his Senate days in Lansing, he had the top responsibility to perform superhuman tasks, and they were done skillfully!

A third Republican was S. C. Kirkbride, Clare County's party chairman. During the sixteen years that he led the party, his efforts were not rewarded with total county victories, just the successful harmonizing of men and ideas on a political battlefield as lethal as a military minefield. "Kirk" was unperturbed by victory or defeat, and he never smiled nor frowned. His nickname was "The mumified Peachereno". He was considered to be the shrewdest politician in Michigan, and a genuine old-time boss. He never denied the legend!

So the Republicans had three geniuses. An organizer, a leader and a brilliant strategist, all of the set pieces for a political chess game.

The Democrats were equally favored. Taking over a newspaper in Harrison during Jim Carr's lewd days, Alfred R. Canfield was but a youth of 16. Carr's bullies threatened and intimidated Canfield severely, and the lessons marked him for life. His brilliance with ideas was blended with a pragmatic philosophy, but stained with a bludgeoning habit. He seldom used the velvet glove when a sledge-hammer was available. Unpopular issues which ran counter to the community's standards became his own cause, and he

rushed into the battle with nostrils flared. Respectable citizens tolerated him usually, but moral crusades, such as Local Option, found him and his family feeling the heat of vengeful neighbors. Canfield was no quitter, and he was certainly a brilliant politician.

Coming to Clare in 1899 was the most intellectually gifted man the county had known. His father had a mill and store in Nirvanna, Lake County. A. J. Lacy was always precocious and mature for his age. Taking the lad to New York City when he was eight, the father left him in his room and went about important business. Arthur dressed, went downstairs, began talking with an older man, had breakfast with him and later was rejoined by the father. He did everything his father expected of him.

Lacy was a talented artist and could have succeeded in this direction had he so chosen. In addition, he was organized! In a collection, now housed in the Bentley Historical Library at Ann Arbor, are the little personal notebooks he carried everywhere he went while still a young teen-ager. The thoughts he so recorded are not the babblings of a child. He was a mature soul, even in his youth. Language, to him, was a tool, and his control of it was extraordinary.

Borrowing money from his father's uncle, he went to Valpariaso University and later to the University of Michigan Law School.

Perry J. Davis of Arthur Township, 1910.

Carlos A. Reading

Dr. L. L. Kelley

A. J. Lacy
Photo: Bentley Library, Ann Arbor

Senator A. J. Doherty, 1901.
Photo: Michigan Department of State Archives

Never was money for an education better spent, and he came immediately to Clare to prove it.

The third member of the Democratic team was C. W. Perry, another attorney, who came to Clare also, upon graduation from the University of Michigan Law School in 1877. A dignified man, he always dressed for the courtroom. C. W. Perry was a standout and would have been in any era. He led the county Democratic party for years in his black, swallow-cut coat.

Joining this brilliant, select group of men were the soldiers of the two parties, the ones who ran for political offices and suffered the casualties. They were the ones who sprinted through the minefields. Included in this group, the dominant Republicans were Carlos A. Reading, Dr. L. L. Kelley, George J. Cummins, Josiah L. Littlefield, A. E. Doty, William H. Browne, Francis J. Morrissey, John Quinn, Louis Sunday; Richard Emerson, Francis McKenna, Lewis D. Wright, William Temple, John Fleming, Jesse Updegraff and Thomas Maltby.

William H. Browne

The Democratic shock troops included John A. Jackson, Jacob Mason, William H. Caple, J. R. Brown, Arthur D. Long, David Ward, L. H. Thompson, David Jennings, John Gordon, Will Adams and George Benner.

These are the men who lived an epic life in the political microcosms of national politics. Their pettiness and their brilliance remain for us, even today, as a remarkable story and a significant part of our heritage.

THE SILVER ISSUE

The Panic of 1893 was a major turning point for American politics. Cleveland had just been returned to the White House amid Democratic charges that businesses and farms were saddled with the heavy hand of corporations and greedy capitalists. They demanded a return to the people of a government which would make available an adequate flow of currency so as to constrict the propagation of both tramps and millionaires. They advocated free and unlimited coinage of silver at the ratio of 16 to 1, with gold being the basic unit.

C. W. Perry

Thomas Maltby

The Panic was thought by some to have been engineered by the capitalists to make Cleveland look bad. Reserves of gold were reduced dramatically as foreigners cashed in their securities. Congress debated whether to repeal the Silver Purchase Act, with or without substituting free coinage. The platform calling for tariff reform was hollow with industry shutting down their mills and men out of work. Eventually the repeal was passed without free coinage, but by then, the treasury was bare, and gold was used for house-keeping expenses.

William Jennings Bryan strode to the front and began his national campaign for free and unlimited coinage of both silver and gold at the ratio of 16 to 1. His brilliant speech about being crucified upon a cross of gold gave vent to the passion and frustration felt by many. The Democrats were split between the gold-backers of the Cleveland hue and the radical silver advocates of Bryan.

Locally, in 1900, this translated into a Union Silver Caucus, which nominated and won nearly every political seat in the county. Only George McKeever and John A. Jack-son lost their bid for political office, those being Ward Supervisors from Clare. Robert Mussell was elected mayor of Clare and John R. Brown was the sheriff. Thomas C. Holbrook, John W. Dunlop, James Louch, Frank Mooney, Orlando Thayer, Elias Hubel, William Parrish and William Loundra took over the city of Clare. The only city Republican winner besides Supervisors T. S. Dorsey and J. R. Goodman was Albert Thurston, city treasurer. J. W. Calkins, the most popular hotelman in the north was defeated for mayor.

THE BOY MAYOR

Elected mayor in 1902, he was at 21, the' youngest mayor of any Michigan city. Taking over Clare's political fortunes as the Union Silver Caucus faded, was the mature intellectual, Arthur J. Lacy. He began his tenure by apprising the city council of both the immediate concerns and a long-range growth program which would enable the city to remain economically healthy while at the same time, enhancing its charms as a place to raise families.

At his prompting, the Business Men's Improvement Association was formed and began to "boom for new businesses. Streets

George J. Cummins

David Ward

were mentioned as a vital problem, especially if the rural patrons were to be enticed into the business district. He wanted a survey made of McEwan Street by a civil engineer who understood drainage problems. Surplus water on the streets was a blight upon the city's character, he thought, so he wanted cobblestone gutters and clay streets to resolve the problem.

Sidewalks, poplar trees and bicycle ordinances were all scrutinized and found wanting. Cement sidewalks were the only legiti-

mate construction, and no future plans ought to be made for wooden paths, he claimed.

Calling for a campaign to eliminate the burning of garbage on the streets and the planting of maple trees, he gave the council enough to do for the immediate future.

Looking at the schools, he said they were "the object of our pride and the worthy testimonial of the educational spirit of our citizens."

Concluding his inaugural speech, he said, "Local pride can only be cultivated by a policy of administration that brings the benefits of good government to the people at minimum cost and makes them feel its beneficient touch. Let us remember that we are the servants of the people, not their masters . . .''

It was a worthy program of enlightened leadership.

CANFIELD'S HEAVY TOUCH

Harrison had stultified Canfield's ambitions, and its role as the county seat was not dominant in political affairs, so he moved to the center of power and established the CLARE COURIER, a rabid Democratic newspaper in 1895.

The staid, comfortable Republican town was soon convulsed by the staccato hammer blows of a partisan pen, and his comments upon personalities caused many to take exception to his style. With the Democrats taking over governmental control under Lacy's leadership and John A. Jackson daily seeking out Republican causes and issues to confront, things became hot for the fair weather citizen. Lines were drawn, and glowing platitudes for public servants from pious statesmen were trammeled by the muddy, heavy boots of the crude wielders of ward politics.

"Probably no city in Michigan, similar in size, injects the strenuousness into local campaigns than does Clare. Just why the condition exists in this city may not be clear to the average citizen, but that it does exist, no one doubts,'' said Canfield in 1903. He didn't recognize his own influence in promoting the discord, according to this statement.

The town was not yet old enough to withstand this duelling which began with Canfield's arrival, and caused even the COURIER to be concerned over the bitterness which remained after the elections.

When Lacy ran for re-election, the Senator's son, F. B. Doherty, opposed him in a bitter contest. National issues were brought up, and the candidates were held to the national platforms endorsed by their party. One prominent Republican went to Canfield

and told him to play down the personal attacks on Doherty, or a serious loss of business would be suffered.

Canfield replied, "Whatever criticisms that may have been made were inspired by an honest sense of duty to the residents and tax-payers of this city. They are made without malice toward any individual who advocated the policy.''

CLARE SENTINEL Editor Welch, speaking for the Republicans, wrote that township supervisors need not run on their own views of tariffs, nor should city candidates, but their opposition disagreed, and the invectives continued.

Doherty lost the election, and Canfield lost much of his advertising revenue. It was a costly election.

Standing above it all was Mayor Lacy, who was taking the high road. Jackson and Canfield were the shock troops. In his second inaugural address, Lacy mentioned the great progress made toward improving living conditions within the city and the movement toward road improvements. An engineering study had been made by John White, which was noted by the state government in Lansing as an example of how a city ought to engineer its subterranean

Mr. and Mrs. Edgar G. Welch in 1908. He was a human dynamo in Clare and Los Angeles. Much of California's liberal educational philosophy can be traced directly to his efforts during the 1910-1920 era.
Photo from the Cleveland Family Collection

Civil Engineer John White lived in Clare with his family, but his job took him all over the nation. Here he is supervising a street project in Romeo, Michigan in 1920.
Photo from the White Family Collection

network. He extolled loftily the thought that "all proper favors, courtesies and privileges should be dispersed freely and impartially with equal justice to all, guarding and retaining, however, such natural privileges which rightfully should remain with the people." It was a speech fit for Edmund Burke.

He praised the street marshal, local bands and the citizens who watered their lawns. Mentioned also were the cemetery, school and taxpayers who excelled in their contributions to Clare.

One hard fact was mentioned that soon would ensnarl him and his party in a fight that would bring about defeat, and even a mortal blow to Canfield's Democratic organ. It was the inadequacy of the water department to keep sufficient pressures in the mains to handle routine consumptions. The relatively shallow six-inch wells were mineraled-up, and the railroad was talking of cancelling its $750 contribution to the Water Department. A "...new water system was immediately needed" by the city.

The spring election of 1905 saw the water proposal on the ballot. Four new wells and new trunk sewer lines with two gasoline engines to power the wells were included, as was an eight-inch water main extending the entire length of McEwan, connected to a new 75,000 gallon stand tank across from city hall. $18,000 was the amount asked for on the ballot.

Many prominent citizens spoke against it. A few wanted to wait until the school's $3,500 bonded indebtedness was repaid before any new commitments were made. Others thought they should put clay on McEwan Street first.

One of the major arguments which carried the most impact was that of the twenty toilets which emptied into the river within eighty rods of the major water inlet.

"Our water is putrid...few in Clare know how bad the water is. It has so much material in it that our fire hoses wear out more rapidly than expected...The valves are clogged and public health is endangered,'' said Alderman John High.

In addition to Mayor Lacy, the others who also supported the proposed new system were J. S. Bicknell, J. Mason, A. J. McKinnon, Perry D. Brown, T. B. Hirt, L. E. Davy, Dan Crouse, Dr. Reeder and John High. The voters also supported it 211-62.

John Muveen and Company of Chicago agreed to install the complete system for $16,750, and the bonds were sold to F. W. Noble and Company in Detroit for $17,300. It appeared that all was going according to plan.

Then city treasurer John Kirkpatrick reported in late April, after the election, that the city council had out-spent the tax revenues for 1904 by $1,500. He projected to the city council that the $9,000 in revenues for 1905 would probably be $4,200 short and that 1906 would see another shortfall of the same magnitude, plus $3,450 in the water bond repayment.

Roads, engineering, sidewalks, fire department and law enforcement all had to be supported from the treasury, but there wasn't going to be enough money to cover the expenditures. Spending was 40% in excess of revenues.

Collapsing wooden bridges cost $700 in 1905, and a stretch of road in front of St. Cecilia's Church required an immediate $150. Two more bridges were in imminent danger of falling in, just as was the financial structure of Clare.

Mayor Lacy advised the council, ''I suggest with much assurance that all expenditures be reduced to the minimum.''

Can you imagine the glee those Republicans had with the boy wonder? Kirkpatrick's books were loosely organized, and the revenues were only approximately known by those whose responsibility it was to know. ''The horse is gone. Quick, lock the barn door!'' wrote Edgar Welch.

When the water project was finished in the fall of 1905, the total cost had jumped to $22,000, and that wasn't the final figure. An extra well had to be sunk and two new triplex pumps purchased to go along with some of the hitherto acceptable trunkline. Some of the 10,300 feet of wooden water

mains were still holding firm, but sections nearer the standpipe couldn't take the newly increased pressures.

Lacy said in defense that ''. . . the water supply is ahead of whatever Clare has had before,'' which was true, of course. But the 1884 project had been installed for a total cost of $14,000, and the 1905 changes were using about 14,000 feet of iron pipe in addition to 10,300 feet of wooden water mains which were installed years earlier.

Lacy decided not to seek re-election in 1906.

An accounting showed that the water fund in 1905 was deficient by $4,232.72 and that $3,450 was due in payments on February 1st and August 1st of 1906. The council was in a very embarrassing position. They had campaigned vigorously against the free spending and wasteful Republicans, and in just three years, with little help from Republican council members, thanks to their vicious campaigning, they had made a shambles of the treasury.

George Benner, cashier at the local bank, agreed to run as a candidate for mayor, even though he hadn't previously been associated with the Lacy-Jackson-Canfield group. When he was elected, his surprise was as genuine as everyone else's. Yet, his ''. . . council (was) embarrassed by the debts of their predecessor.''

The campaign of 1906 was hard fought, as all had been since 1896. The SENTINEL fought the secret, hushed-up council meetings called at unpredictable times and never with a warning to any except the members by a special messenger about fifteen minutes before the appointed hour. In his paper, Canfield attacked the individual Republican candidates through innuendo and devious generalized ridicule. He made light of these secret meetings, saying that the Republicans' only concern was that they weren't in power and able to do the same kind of thing.

Welch said in his SENTINEL, ''The people are not deceived by the time worn method of your substituting personal abuse for facts and arguments.''

One citizen said of Canfield, ''His is a big bag of wind . . . just as he always resorts to when hard pressed for facts and hasn't a leg to stand on.'' Another said, ''He can deal out more personal abuse than all the other editors of the county combined.'' A third said, ''D--- his dirt! If I were you fellows, I'd go after his dirty record and show it from beginning to end. He is simply relying on your refusing to fight him with his own low dirty methods.''

THE SENTINEL TAKES
THE HIGH ROAD

Welch said, ''The COURIER sets up a wail that the SENTINEL is coming very close to libeling them. Bosh, Mr Courier! They know you too well to take any notice of such nonsense. You dare not make one specific charge, nor can you substantiate one paragraph of any issue that has libeled you.''

The Lewis Cass Club, set up by Mayor Lacy to promote national Democratic issues, met and voted to exclude reporters from the SENTINEL at their public meetings. Reports coming from the Democratic organization said that the SENTINEL was going to expose the graft in the city hall, and that was why they were excluded.

Welch retorted, ''We don't know of what graft you are talking about. If there is any, the people have a right to know before the election.'' He went on to cite the spending habits of the council controlled by the Democrats. He then continued, ''The SENTINEL has only one contention, and that is the council ought to follow the charter and make the legally required reports to the people according to the various sections.'' He concluded by saying that all city business ought to be done within the limits of the law and that appropriations should be done according to Section 14, Chapter 30.

The canvass of the election may have shown that the people were willing to be hoodwinked again, but the fact of the matter was, Clare County had the best Democratic party organization in Michigan during 1906.

The 1906 council went to the bank and borrowed money on a series of $2,000 notes, due on a six month rotated schedule. ''This was done in accordance with a policy to maintain the city's credit by assuming the debts contracted by the council (of) last year, even though such debts may have exceeded charter limitations,'' said the SENTINEL on August 17th.

Welch kept digging into the council's methods of operation and periodically wrote about a wrong doing or what he construed as an improper act. He became a real thorn in the Democratic side.

At the annual banquet of the Lewis Cass Club, Welch showed up, having been given a ticket by C. W. Perry. John Jackson met him at the door and wouldn't let him in. He said, ''Welch, you've got your gall!'' He attempted to force him to go away, but the commotion became so odious that others noticed what was going on in the hallway leading to the banquet room. Perry and Lacy both came over and assured the Republican editor that he was welcome. Perry later attempted to soothe things more by telling Welch that he deplored such narrowness.

A day later, a Republican came to Welch and attempted to divert him from the inquisition he was putting the Democrats through. Welch said in his paper that he would continue to expose the errors of the council because it was the public's right to know what the council was doing. At this time, the council was 40% over its spending limits which the charter prescribed.

MORE EXPENDITURES

By 1907 there were 120 water customers drawing water from the city mains, and the price of gasoline was very high. Fred Manseau of Traverse City was given a contract for $1,015 to install a coal gas producer. This new method was satisfactory to engineer W. J. Holmes, who had recently replaced A. W. DeBois as water engineer.

In 1908, the city, with its 1,500 population, had $40,000 invested in its utilities, not including the electrical generating plant and distribution lines. There were two miles of graded streets and four miles of cement sidewalks installed, and a bonded indebtedness of $17,000. Bills payable included: a fire alarm system, $719.34; balance on the sewer, $906.78; balance on the water tower, $1,350; the gas producer, $104.47 and the balance for the water mains, $600.

For this $3,680.59, the council sat transfixed with the enormity of it all for two years. More dollars than these were spent on printer's ink campaigning against waste in government and railing against one another. George Benner, the cashier at the Clare County Savings Bank, was the mayor during these years, and he couldn't bring the men together intellectually long enough to borrow $3,500 and then spread the cost over a three year period. Instead, the city was caught between the warring Canfield-Jackson clique and the J. R. Goodman-Welch antagonists and was being torn apart each council meeting, and nearly shredded at spring election time each year.

These same years coincided with the Local Option issue, and forces tended to polarize around the positive or negative merits of prohibition, only to be transferred to the political parties. To be a "Wet" meant that you had to be a Democrat. Not too much later, all Democrats were "Wets", and the good people in town were becoming very "Dry". Republicans became good — Democrats were bad.

Dr. Mulder was a "good" man, ergo, he was a Republican. Mayor Benner was a Democrat, though he tried to be an honest broker among some dishonest charlatans, but his task was too great. When the 1909 election came around, the good people won and the bad people were defeated. In short order, Mayor Mulder and the council agreed to borrow the $3,500 for two years, thus removing the thorny problem.

Former Mayor A. J. Lacy's Business Men's Improvement Association had been successful in wooing new businesses into town, and Clare had become a mecca for the exporting of agricultural products. The "Market City" warehouses were sending to eastern markets enormous quantities of poultry, dairy and grain-type merchandise. Twelve businesses in the railroad district were employing 147 people, churning $87,950 a month in wages and cash paid to the farmer. A million dollar market was centered in Clare. Cream, butter, hides, beef, pork, chickens and similar items were daily loaded only the cars and shipped out.

Near the Union Depot, the Clare Stockyards were shipping many hundreds of cattle and thousands of sheep to market regularly. Business was very brisk, and people's interests weren't limited to petty partisan politics any more. Even Canfield sensed it in his bones, but felt it more in his bank account. His paper was losing money in hemorrhagic amounts by attempting to promote the Democrat-Wet cause when it was such a defensive position to be in. In the end, a decision was made to take the COURIER out of the Democratic Caucus and to become an independent promoter of issues. It was the only choice he could make and still survive.

THE STATE CAMPAIGN OF 1906

A most unique situation prevailed in Clare during 1906. Dennis E. Alward was the state Republican Party Secretary, with an office in the Tatman Building, on the east side of McEwan. A. R. Canfield was the state Democrat Party Secretary, with his office over the Mussell' Drug Store, directly across the street. Both offices looked out onto the town's main street and at each other. From these two second story offices, the entire State of Michigan's elections were master-minded and executed in a classic campaign, which eventually went to the Republicans.

Clare County had the best Democratic organization in Michigan, and they were riding high in local politics, but outside, the party was getting killed at the polls. The Republicans had been manhandled locally, but Denny Alward had the state absolutely going in the Republican's direction. In September, both men moved their campaign headquarters to Detroit for the final showdown in November, which continued to be bad news for Canfield.

The 1906 election campaign followed what had been a clean sweep for the Republicans in 1904. Not one Democrat was holding a seat in the House or Senate. This pervasive influence by the majority party has never

Dennis E. Alward in 1913.
Photo: Michigan Department of State Archives

been duplicated in state affairs before or afterwards, but it nearly was again at this time. The Republicans swept the state, and also won most of the seats at the county level. They so completely dominated state affairs that their opponents wondered if they would ever again be sitting in the legislative chambers in any significant numbers. But in American politics, things have a way of balancing out.

When Alward was tapped by the national party to direct a successful campaign out of New York City in 1910, he was not riding a Republican trend, and his genius wasn't enough to overcome the Taft-Roosevelt split. Two years later, Governor Wilson became president on a campaign of isolationism and pacificism. It was hard to convince a smug, self-righteous and confident America that Europe's problems were staring them in the face. Their success at Panama blinded them,

and Taft failed to guide their political destinies properly. Alward couldn't save him or the country from the Democrats forever.

Alward had served in Washington D. C. in 1896 as the Superintendent of the House Document Room and later as a reading clerk. His first task was to read President McKinley's message to a special Congress on Tariff. He had a voice which was clear and booming. He was an impeccable interpreter of sounds and concepts. The reputation he had was that of one who never missed a word, comma or phrase. Once he was challenged by a New York congressman for the word "and", which he claimed Alward had inserted in the read text. While Alward was double-checking, a congressional colleague read from the Congressional Record itself, which quoted the critic as the one who had inserted it originally. The New Yorker was thoroughly squelched.

As 1911 came along, A. R. Canfield could see a Democratic trend developing, and he caused to be formed a "Boom Wilson Club" in Clare County. His eye was on the position that Alward had in the nation's capital. If Alward could handle it, so could he. Their careers paralleled so closely, one wonders about a destiny both were following. Precocious northern Michigan newspaper editors in the 1880's, political party leaders in Clare County during the 1890's, state party powers in 1900, state-wide campaign chairmen in 1904, alternating Secretaries of the Senate, Reading Clerk in Washington D. C. for Alward in 1896 — and for Canfield in 1912. It was a remarkable coincidence!

Alward sought the congressional seat of retiring S. B. Darragh in 1908, but his efforts to secure it were handicapped by his duties in Washington. He ran again for the 63rd Congress, but Francis O. Lindquist from Belding, running on a platform of opposition to artificial leather, beat him. Alward was defeated by this one-issue candidate, who retired from Washington after one term, after introducing one bill — an anti-leather law. He was a puny politician, but he beat the master organizer.

Alward returned to Clare, re-opened his law office, sold insurance locally, and then in 1915 moved to Lansing where he remained. His close ties to Clare seem out of place when his talents and record of astounding political legerdemain are considered. He was a gifted orator and was much in demand for state and national Memorial Day speeches, Fourth of July celebrations and political conventions. An outstanding man in his family ties and moral leadership within the city he was a worthy contemporary for A. J. Lacy, A. J. Doherty, A. R. Canfield, C. W. Perry and S. C. Kirkbride.

Arthur Lacy left Clare for a Detroit law practice during the summer of 1909, shortly after he had been appointed city attorney. His departure was abrupt and gives some credibility to the rumor that he was forced to leave town by a husband who didn't look kindly upon his dalliance with a married woman. There never was any public scandal involved with this, and it was only a rumor. Lacy joined the law firm of Maybury, Lucking and Emmons and then in 1913 was appointed by his friend, now Governor Ferris, to the Court of Domestic Relations with a salary of $6,000. Lacy also became the editor of the NORTHWESTERN REVIEW, a bi-weekly pamphlet booster sheet which promoted northwestern Wayne County. Lacy was on his way to bigger things!

An observer in Detroit said of Lacy, "He is using the same kind of ginger that made him mayor for four terms before coming to Detroit."

When Lacy left Clare, he formed a partnership with Joseph Bowler so that his pending law cases could be successfully concluded. Lacy came back several times and loaned his forensic skills to the courts and to civic affairs, but by 1910, he had outgrown the small city of Clare. Detroit and Michigan were his new horizons, and he mastered them both.

Becoming a friend of James Cousens, he moved into Detroit City Hall with him when Cousens was mayor. Cousens had purchased some auto factory stock from Henry Ford in the early days and soon amassed a large fortune. Lacy was the executor of this estate, as well as for that of Dodge, Mary Rackham and several others.

His skills in the courtroom won important precedent-setting cases, both in the lumbering industry and with the Internal Revenue Service Appeals before the State Supreme Court set several important landmark decisions for all of Michigan.

He was a giant of a man who lived until 1975. Clare was favored when he chose to begin his law career here in 1899. We had him for ten years while his brilliant skills were being honed to a razor's edge sharpness. He took a few lickings in politics here, as he did also when he ran for Governor in the 1930's, but he contributed much to our state.

THE POOR FARM

Soon after the county organized itself in 1871, a Poor Farm was established in Section 35 of Grant Township. Eighty acres were set aside and a "keeper" hired to oversee the

Postmaster S. C. Kirkbride and his clerk. The post office was on North McEwan Street on the east side between Fourth and Fifth Streets. 1915.

buildings, crops and harvest. A lady, usually the keeper's wife, would care for housing the indigent and preparing the meals. The Board of Supervisors were always approached for a cash subsidy, because the farm was never able to meet the needs of all those county residents who had welfare needs. George Whiteside and J. C. Arnold were the keepers during the Grant Township days.

When the county seat was moved to Harrison in 1879, a desire on the part of the Board of Supervisors to place the Poor Farm nearer to the county's capital city caused a new farm to be developed for the needy citizens. 160 acres in the Southeast Corner of Section 20, Hayes Township, were purchased and appropriate buildings were erected. The total number of permanent residents varied between six and fifteen, and a subsidy was requested in the amount of $2,000 to $3,000 annually. Normally a three-man sub-committee was appointed to oversee the farm and its account books. Things were run quite loosely, and a calendar with check-marks on the individual dates told how many meals were served on any given day.

The Poor Farm Committee would per-manentize the tally with their annual report to the Board of Supervisors. It wasn't a good system of keeping the books, but no one complained. "Keeper" Coit, however, wasn't happy with the farm nor with his duties on the farm. He had been a teamster during the lumber days and had a few dollars saved up, so he proposed buying the farm from the county.

For some reason or other, the farm was sold almost immediately to Thomas Coit for $1,400. Without any plans for the twenty residents, the county found itself with no place to house the indigents. Some were too ill to be taken care of in their homes, and a few were orphans. The county couldn't abandon them to the streets, although a few of the lesser enlightened supervisors suggested doing just that.

A debate grew up over the years which concerned the philosophy that governed the Poor Farm. One side argued that the county ought to make the property into a true model farm, with good breeding animals that county farmers could use to upgrade their own animals. The opposite group indicated that the proper role of the Poor Farm was little more than a boarding-house which should use every device possible to keep expenditures down until the poor souls could be removed to the paupers' field. This alternative seemed to be the dominant one.

Some Harrisonites thought that the people in Clare wanted to remove the Poor Farm from Hayes Township and place it once again in Grant. Asa Aldrich used his CLEAVER's editorial page to encourage this pseudo idea, and he caused it to fester beyond decent limits.

Aldrich had been the County School Commissioner but he lost out to Edgar Welch of Clare soon after 1900. Vexed by this loss, he used every opportunity to divide Clare County into northern vs. southern camps. In this campaign he was aided by L. L. Kelley's hatred of Clare. Factions that shouldn't have existed were promoted, nurtured and rewarded by Republicans vs. Democrats, North vs. South, Farwell vs. Clare, Wets vs. Drys, and the normal rivalry between the townships for roads and other legitimate expenses.

To the credit of W. M. Cross, Morris Brown, Mayor William Murphy, William H. Browne and L. D. Wright, they never gave aid and comfort to the Philistines. C. W. Perry, county Democratic Party Chairman, used his position to keep an even hand on the Supervisors, but those kibitzers seeking their own self-aggrandizements kept the kettle boiling for years. In this mess, fortunately, Canfield didn't join the agitators, or else the problem might have been irreconcilable. Aldrich never had the deft touch of Canfield.

Aldrich was appealed to by Welch to retreat from his trouble-making. He said, "It is important to the future unity of this county that this concocted issue of yours be promptly laid to rest." But the idea of fairness appeared to go right over Aldrich's head.

BOARDING THE INDIGENTS

Coit took private possession of the Poor

The Clare County Poor Farm Infirmary, 1911.
Photo from the Fanning Collection

Farm in the fall of 1907. He began imme-diately to improve the soil, buildings and animals, and within a year had the farm pro-ducing a profit, something never done while it was owned and supervised by a three-member committee.

The Board began the first of dozens of meetings called in subsequent years to plan strategies on how to resolve this Poor Farm question. Basic to their difficulty was the absence of anyone on the 1908 Board who could dissect the problem so it could be resolved, first, on the basis of philosophy, and second, on the pragmatic resolution of its physical plant. Instead, they grappled with how to accumulate $10,000 when only $11,000 was annually available for their total budget. The Constitution of 1850 limited the Board from spending more than $1,000 a year upon the townships without a popular vote. In April of 1908, a new Constitution was being voted upon as well as a $6,000 bonding proposal.

Clare County and the State accepted the 1908 Constitution, which essentially per-mitted the State to grow with the automobile age, but it also appeared to offer an escape for Boards of Supervisors which faced tru-culent property owners. The bonding propo-sal went down 1,140-439, so the Board turned to the new document and read in Article 8, Section 10 that one-tenth of a mill could be spread by them, or at least that's the way they interpreted it.

A. J. Lacy said that the new statute didn't mean that at all. Permission was given to the Board to transfer funds from their general fund equal to one-tenth of a mill for the construction of buildings, but they couldn't borrow money, nor could the Poor Farm Committee spread the $6,000 over on the townships.

With this turn of events, the Board looked again at its plan to transfer $5,000 from the General Fund into the Poor Farm Sinking Fund. They decided to submit a $3,800 bonding issue in September, and if that passed, to transfer the funds and build a brick infirmary. A fine plan, but the voters didn't want to spend the money on that barren pine land, which had stumps all over and not a building on it.

Robert Carson of Garfield was not in favor of the bonding proposal because "The final bill for a finished Poor Farm would total $20,000," he claimed.

Dr. Kelley wasn't in favor of the new site because he was trying to unload his Garfield stock farm onto the county for the nifty price of $7,500. "There's a thousand dollars worth of timber on that land," he said, seeking to justify his outrageous price on some real pine-barrens.

Joe Hudson favored letting the inmates have an acre of ground to putter around on, and then buying at wholesale, the difference in food still needed.

D. W. Rowe of Farwell just flat out opposed the whole Poor Farm idea. "The $11,000 projection is a fraud on the county!" he stormed.

Arthur E. Doty, John A. Jackson and William W. Harper, the Poor Farm Commissioners, wrote an open letter to all of the county newspapers in March 1908, trying to explain in simple terms what they were attempting to do, but it didn't change many minds.

J. C. Arnold of Clare, the former overseer of the Poor Farm when it was in Grant, said that he fed inmates for 4½¢ a meal for three years and that he received $25 a month to operate the farm. "The county made a mistake when it took the Farm out of Grant. They made another when they sold that farm and they're going to make another, if they don't vote 'No'," he said.

Well, how could anyone vote for making a third mistake? That's why the first $6,000 bonding issue went down.

THE SECOND PROPOSAL

Morris Brown of Greenwood Township summed up the county's attitude when he said, "It looks to me as though the deal was made so that it would be necessary to buy a new farm at once." Clare voters weren't having any part of any deal. No, sir! And that took care of the second bonding proposal.

Josiah Littlefield suggested that the county rent a boarding home to house the inmates until the whole affair could be resolved. The best way, he thought, would be to . . . "Sell the new farm — buy a developed farm and let the valuation go up while a good manager made it produce a profit."

No one really understood what the rationale was for all of this, and so they forgot it.

Denny Alward was in Lansing right after the second vote went down. Its rejection was carried in all the state's newspapers, because Clare was the only county without a Poor Farm. He was being kidded about it by some political friends when he retorted, "Clare is so prosperous that it enjoys the distinction of being the only county in the state that doesn't need a Poorhouse."

Dr. Kelley was also in Lansing, and he was asked to comment on Alward's statement. He said, "Clare doesn't need help in caring for its poor. We can take care of our own." From these two statements, a Detroit reported concocted a story about the lack of poverty in Clare County, saying that they closed down the Poor Farm for lack of inmates. It made all the papers during April, 1908. If only the truth were known, probably the other counties would have sent relief packages to the Board of Supervisors.

B. S. Alley, Garfield's supervisor, was upset over the proposed setting over of $5,000 from the General Fund, now that the people had voted down the two bonding issues. He also wondered how long Coit was going to continue boarding the county's inmates. Speaking to the Board, he said, "We've asked for bonding authority from the people, but the Board has never had the real facts needed to justify those requests, and we haven't had facts from the Poor Farm Committee for years." All of which was true, of course, but Alley had been on the Board in 1907 and part of 1908, and he let the slip-shod reports be accepted without dissent. His old Indiana days were coming back to him. Back there he had been a fire-eating attorney, but when his wife lost her health, he gave up his practice and became a quiet rancher in Garfield. Now he was becoming a fighter again, only at this point, two bonding issues had been turned down.

Elmer Clute
Photo from the Clute Family Collection

LET'S BUILD ANYWAY!

David Ward's view of "sell this farm and get another," wasn't the majority opinion, so the Board took the $1,000 available to them by law, plus $1,400 and began to put the buildings up. Architect Gorr prepared plans for a full basement, two-story brick structure, and the foundation was put in before snow fell in December.

Meeting at their next regular interval, this time during December of 1908, the Supervisors were still hoping to raise $12,000 for the infirmary and a barn. The county's lawyers were still divided over how much authority the new Constitution gave them for spreading more taxes. In the end, Lacy's opinion, that the Board didn't have the authority to use the funds if they were borrowed, prevailed. The Board didn't think for an instant that tax-payers would have permitted a one-year assessment, which would have doubled everyone's taxes, to take place—especially not for the Poor Farm.

In January, a motion was made to transfer $2,400 to the Poor Farm fund. The Board chewed this around for awhile, and split 11-11. The sum asked for was only 50% of the 1909 projected expenditures for the new infirmary, and for this reason it was rejected, but there was no more available.

Meanwhile, the county budget had begun to grow. In 1900, only $8,000 was spent. During 1908, $15,000 was eventually appropriated and 1909 was being projected for $23,500 plus the infirmary, or $30,000. The moss-backs on the Board were having night-mares.

Disgusted with the actions of the other members, Doty and Jackson resigned from the Poor Farm Committee. The new trio whose job it was to resolve the endless confusion were W. W. Harper, J. D. Dunwoodie and George W. Graham. None of these officials were Supervisors.

These men were up against it! They had a $10,000 building going up with prospects of only $2,400 being accessible to them.

Rented quarters were used for the inmates. This facility was designated as the Poor Farm in May. A special report made to the Board of Supervisors on May 7, 1909 said, "This farm is not fit to care for the paupers as it stands today. In some cases, the dead had to be taken out through a window . . .If a state inspector were to come along, there would be some doings right-off." Something would have to be done on this matter.

The Supervisors were becoming very short-tempered about the imbroglio they had made for themselves. For years they fought

Arthur D. Johnson

each other for control of the Board, and they charged each other with cooking up deals. The basic problem was that no one in either party was willing to let the other side organize the committees. It was feared, and properly so, that one party would penalize the other townships with higher-than-justifiable tax rates. Another factor was the county printing contract. Even though the Republicans had more Board members, Canfield or Aldrich always got the $600-$700 printing deal.

Every other consideration in the county was handicapped by the cliques and their fears. Kirkbride and Quinn normally traded their power for other favors and in eight out of nine years, the Democratic papers benefited by the county contract. When Local Option tore apart the normal party alignments, the 1909 Board had to write some new ground rules.

When it appeared that Dr. Mulder and Local Option were going to win, "Supervisor L. H. Thompson of Sheridan was given some soft soap about controlling the Board to get his valuation down for the township, and then innocently, 'Hank' started driving all over the county to line up support for Republican Doty as chairman. Grant Howard of Winterfield was similarly dealt with and Supervisor Gleason of Clare was easily handled by a place on the Equalization Committee," explained Welch, as he saw his chances for the county contract failing again. He continued his report about the Board's action: "Gleason and Doty call themselves Republicans, but voted for Canfield and against economy in the most notorious action of the whole session, but they were game, and never winced to the end."

Commissioner Kelley was picked by Doty to head the Equalization Committee, as it was believed that his prejudices against Clare would easily drive him into the hands of the "push", that is, in Doty's hands, by soaking Clare on the equalization.

The strategy worked well for the April 1909 session, but during the fall session, everything came unglued. Thompson was the floor leader and pushed through a plan to increase the State Fair Commission. When he laid the county printing contract on the table for Canfield, one of the Supervisors said, "Let's put it up for bids."

Another one, surprised, said, "What the h--l do you want to take it away from Canfield for?" And on it went until David Ward broke away, and the jig was up. The bids came back. 9¢ for the SENTINEL, 29¢ for the CLEAVER and 21¢ a folio for the COURIER.

Quinn rushed in with his observation that the partnership of Welch and Bennett prevented the SENTINEL from having the contract, because Welch was the County School Commissioner. Ward asked him if the law prevented the SENTINEL from having the contract, and the answer was a whisper, "No."

Dr. Kelley ignored Quinn at that point and moved the question with the understanding that the School Commissioner's printing should not go to Bennett and the SENTINEL. It carried! For the first time in nine years, the SENTINEL got a contract from a Republican Board.

The most amazing fact came after this meeting. Dr. Kelley's committee presented the fairest equalization the county ever had. Doty wondered what went wrong with Kelly.

A THIRD VOTE

The Board put approximately $4,400 into the Poor Farm between 1907 and 1910, simply by adding a few hundred here and a thousand there. If the infirmary was to be completed before 1912, it seemed prudent to ask the voters for their support. A barn was needed and some fences to keep some stock in and to keep other stock out, so a $5,000 figure was deemed reasonable.

The meetings were eating up a lot of tax dollars, and by October 1909, at least $1,400 had been paid out to the Supervisors for per diem allowances, meals and travel. The continued mistreatment of the indigents in the rented quarters threatened to bring the state down on their heads at any time, and the men who had played politics with county affairs were even becoming alarmed over the chaos. Doty tried to cover himself by working a deal for a projected Highway Com-

mission job, so he resigned from the Board. To his chagrin, the new job didn't come through, and J. E. Bruce had his Supervisor's seat.

With Doty off the Board, things began to work more smoothly. William H. Browne assumed the chair and began bringing order out of the nightmare. He wasn't able to ensure a favorable bond vote, however, so economies were made all up and down the line. Monies saved were plunked into the infirmary. A year later, the plumbers moved in and completed the interior.

Inmates were admitted in May of 1912. Two years later, a $1,400 barn was built, and everything looked brighter. Yet even in 1915, no one had resolved the debate. Was the Poor Farm to be a model county farm to help farmers improve their own stock, or was the infirmary simply a place to warehouse old, used-up humans? Was the Poor Farm just a place to keep them off the streets and out of sight until their carcasses were removed to the potter's field, which was on the corner of the new farm?

Much concern for the indigents began coming from the county. The indigents should be treated not as unavoidable nuisances, but as deserving unfortunates, who were temporarily down on their luck. A sensitive community was no longer going to tolerate the incredible political infighting which was so evident during the J. R. Brown, A. E. Doty and William Frye reign. With men of compassion and good will coupled with a more fundamental understanding of the role a Board of Supervisors should play, coming onto the courthouse scene, prospects for Clare were looking the brightest they had ever been. Even the war in Europe couldn't dampen the progressive spirits of the men now vying for the Supervisor jobs.

Social Life

Pawnee Bill sent his railroad advertising car into the northern areas ahead of his "Wild West Shows". July of 1900 found both the advance car and the Show in the heartland area. Big, colorful pictures painted on the freight car were designed to entice every young lad to begin saving his nickels and dimes for a big show, "Coming soon in your area." But Pawnee Bill and his kindred brothers had been in Clare and Farwell before with their shows, and at least one person remembered from past experiences, that a person's own greed and willingness to take the other fellow's money played right into the showmen's hands. He said, "The person who will take $10 or $15 from a showman on one of their fake games is just as much of a rascal as he thinks the faker is . . . You can't beat a man at his own game."

Evidently there were enough people out there willing to give it a try, because the railroad shows came through every summer and made their stops close by, permitting those shysters living in the rural districts to try besting the fakers. The Wallace Shows unloaded in Clare during July of 1904, and Sun Bros. pulled their Progressive Railroad Show into town during August of 1905. These two groups made an annual tour of the isolated towns and brought excitement and mystery into the lives of the citizens who, perhaps, understood all too well the sense of boredom which settled over the north prior to World War I.

It wasn't the fact that people didn't have things to do! On a farm, or in a home, there were gardens to grow, animals to care for, weeds to pull, beans and cucumbers to pick,

younger brothers and sisters to watch, and not a few youths were employed on jobs outside the home, perhaps in a shingle or lath mill.

Machinery was quite common now, but the design of the machine was slanted toward production, not safety, and many a lad lost fingers in a shingle-making machine. Youths ten, twelve or fourteen were employed on these vicious finger and hand eaters, but they were still dulled by the monotony of things.

Even a railroad show was a dangerous place to work, perhaps because of the long hours and the continual setting up of the tents and cages and their removal to another town, only to be hurriedly erected again and again. Most of the circus or wild west show employees were overworked, as the forty-hour week never was applied to their craft.

When the Wallace Show came to Clare in 1904, they unloaded their fourteen railroad cars from a siding. One of the men, thought since to have been exhausted from lack of sleep, was run over by a car while the Ann Arbor engine was switching the cars around. The man's arm and head were severed from his body as the wheels passed over the prostrate figure. The railroad people weren't even aware of the accident until some time after it happened, which indicates the way things were done by these types of shows.

After a morning of frenzied setting-up of the tents, and the placement of the animals in their temporary shelters, it soon became time for the customary parade. All of the stops were pulled on this one, and music enticed young and old to come and see the mysteries of a menagerie or the spectacular collections in the museum. Ten cents could seem awfully small to a youth with a vivid imagination, and it seems that the imagination needed to be stimulated about once a year. Truly, the railroad shows brought a dimension to the hinterland that wasn't possible to duplicate in any other way. The animals on parade, accompanied by the exotically costumed actors and hucksters seemed to make these annual affairs worth waiting for.

A year was fifty-two weeks, and no matter how great or how exciting an event may be, the human mind usually needs more frequent stimulation than once annually. Parties, games, picnics, excursions, trips to neighboring towns to root for the home team—all are needed, and more, too! Consider the impact of the motion picture machine upon a rural community. The mysteries of far-off places could now be brought to a room where scores of eager little faces stared transfixed by the thrills of the unexplored.

EARLY MOVIES

The Doherty Opera House scheduled the Colonial Motion Picture Company for a performance to be held in November of 1903. Big "flyers" went out about the new machine which would bring to Clare spectacular scenes of "The Great Train Robbery". How disappointed everyone was when news came of a fire in Alma during its showing there, and that everything was in ruins; the machine, the films and the dreams. The excitement and the expectations of seeing the famous movie on the walls of the opera house vaporized into nothing. Yet fires often accompanied these early arc-lighted machines, which produced high temperatures close to the celluloid films. Some of the drama associated with these early showings personally involved the patrons as they sought safety from the flames.

By 1905, Gramophones were available in the local hardware stores, which enabled listeners to hear band and other instrumental music, as well as stories told by some of the professional story-tellers from the era which

produced excellent acting on the thousands of opera house stages all over the country. Entertainment for the masses had taken another giant step.

THE FIRST MOVIE THEATRE IN CLARE

Whitney and Sutton of Mt. Pleasant established a regular showing of one and two reel movies on 4th Street in a room equipped with a large white sheet on one end and wooden benches scattered in a somewhat regular manner for the patrons to sit on. They called it the STAR THEATRE in 1906. A year later they sold it to George W. Lee, who continued to run it for a while.

Dr. Dunlop had a second-story room over his Medical Hall vacant in 1907, so he decided to open the ORIENTAL THEATRE. This was patronized quite heavily by the Clare public.

The name was changed to "Vaudette", a play on the word Vaudeville, and used by many. It continued to do well, so well that it took too much time away from the drug store. Dr. Dunlop leased the show business part of Medical Hall to E. N. Whitney in 1910, and sold it to him a year later.

Whitney envisioned a nickel theatre where a person could come in and see a one-reel movie for five cents. However, he first needed a projector which could be used over and over, and which was operated by electricity. Clare was approaching a more regular type of entertainment which hitherto hadn't been available so frequently.

THE TEMPLE THEATRE

Lee O. Garrison from Indianapolis was hired by Mr. Hamilton to paint scenes on the walls of a building to be known as the TEMPLE THEATRE. It was the former STAR THEATRE, and had been purchased by the present owner from George W. Lee in 1908. "When he gets the TEMPLE completed, it will be the neatest vaudeville theatre in Michigan," was the puff-job handed out by the SENTINEL just before the building was sold to Fred H. Northquist of Cadillac.

Northquist changed the name to the PALACE THEATRE after a fire in the spring of 1911 nearly destroyed it. W. T. Wier was hired to come in and refurbish the interior and to put fire-proofing on all the walls and the ceiling. Its grand opening was to feature the Cadillac wrestler, Al Wolgast, as he mixed it up with a young man named Moran. Wolgast was trained by Clare's champion wrestler, Edward C. Pettit.

PRINCESS THEATRE

The first real, full-time movie house in Clare was the PRINCESS THEATRE, owned by the Princess Photo Company, and managed by Hackett and McKerring. Its grand opening in the Dunwoodie Block on the northwest corner of 5th Street and McEwan, was July 4, 1912.

All of the theatre's furnishings were purchased in Detroit and moved to Clare. The difference in this theatre was that it would show three-reel movies and illustrated songs daily for a ten-cent admission fee. "It's going to be managed under a different plan than the others," was the promise by McKerring, who had six years experience operating theatres in Michigan and Wisconsin.

MOVIE THEATRES REGULATED

In 1914, the State of Michigan enacted laws which prohibited indiscriminate showings of movies in buildings which were not safe for the public. Hazards created by the volatile films and the high temperature arc lights were more than a nuisance; they were a menace to life and limb of all who watched. Even legitimate educational films, such as those of Professor Taft from M.A.C., could not be shown unless certain safety standards were present. He planned to teach farmers during their Institute Conventions held around the state, with movies made especially for the occasion.

FREE MOVIES

Community-spirited groups looked at the movies and decided that the children should be exposed to some of the historical, educational and comical productions being offered by the film industry around 1914. Saginaw hired an auditorium and showed certain films to several groups of children for the first time in February. It was such a success that the practice was soon emulated by others. Farwell and Harrison, for example, began showing free movies on a regular basis, and other small towns followed the practice for years. Scores of thousands of youths in northern Michigan saw these highly informative movies during their hey-day.

Itinerent movie groups, which flourished during the pre-World War I era, were put under a lot of pressure, both by the free movie concept and the enforced safety laws. Not a few had to close up shop because the halls used formerly could not meet the new state licensure standards. There were good reasons why these laws were so strict. The villages of Walkerville and Dollarville were nearly wiped off the map by fires caused by these itinerants.

MOVIE STARS

Movies were developed from Thomas A. Edison's Kinetoscope, a coin-operated peep show of 1894. The first public showing of a moving, animated subject was held two years later in Koster and Bial's Music Hall in New York City. Eighty Vitascope machines were sold in 1896, and were the fore-runner of the basic motion picture projector. Vaudeville houses used these machines in cities and rural districts to fill in the time between their live acts, but they never saw the potential of a full-time movie house. That came from others.

Early movies used fifty feet of film as their standard length until machines of larger capacities were developed. Then reels of 1,000 feet, containing a hodge-podge of topics and subjects were spliced together. Quickly, events and film producers pressured further refinements, and the ten major producers banded together in what was called the Motion Picture Patents Company. They purchased a license from Edison and attempted to monopolize the industry.

Before their dominance, short films could be shown before audiences of 50-90 people with a piano player providing the background drama. These shows ran continuously and cost a nickel. Within four years of their development, 8,000 of these nickelodeons were scattered across the nation, including Dunlop's in Clare. Its great feature was "The Great Train Robbery", and the locals flocked to see it over and over again, many having missed it in 1903.

Edison patented his machine here, but in Europe, he forgot, or didn't want to pay $150 which would have protected his rights. As it was, many of his mechanical problems were solved by European mechanics, and the movie industry was propelled ahead rapidly by his omission.

French, German and Italian picture producers soon began turning out movies longer than the one or two reelers that was the American standard fare.

Longer movies required more thoughtful planning and acting. Soon movie stars began replacing "Pawnee Bill" and "Buffalo Bill" as the heroes for the young. Billie Burke, Pola Negri, Gloria Swanson and Clara Bow were early female leads and played opposite men such as Douglas Fairbanks, John Gilbert and later, Rudolph Valentino, the most famous of all the silent stars.

PIANO PLAYERS

During the "silent" era, local piano players were employed to accompany the flickering screen. Miss "Joe" Terry and Miss Flossie McKeever were two who worked for McKerring in his PRINCESS THEATRE, building the suspense in the impressionable audiences.

The "Battle of Gettysburg" was brought to Clare, and all the old Civil War veterans were invited for a free showing. They came from all over the county in 1914 and re-lived that fateful battle which sealed the doom of the Confederacy.

HARRISON'S FIRST THEATRE

Professor E. O. Chapman, a salesman of motion picture projectors and allied fixtures, sold to Mrs. O. Hallett all she needed to open Harrison's first regular movie house in May of 1914. She decided to show films on Wednesday and Saturday only. A year later, Mrs. Charles Roe opened the DREAMLAND THEATRE and began to show movies on a more regular basis. For some reason or other, the theatre was closed down during the winter months.

Farwell received its first movie house in 1916, when I. Naldrett converted an empty hall into a theatre. A year later, he purchased a new machine and put films on the screen regularly.

Towns such as Farwell, Temple and Harrison were treated to the medicine shows and the Stereopticons, prior to the theatre's introduction to their locale. When the movies began to be shown on a regular basis, these forms of public entertainment fell by the wayside. Many a delighted audience received their offerings with favorable applause over the years, and these early offerings were valued services to the towns.

OPERA HOUSES

The Doherty Opera House was erected in 1891 and furnished a reliable accommodation for the traveling vaudeville and stage shows which flooded the small towns with some good, and some terrible entertainment. A circuit was followed by most of these troupes, and the opera house was one of the main stopping points.

Farwell's opera house came in 1909, after Littlefield rebuilt part of the main business district. A fire in 1907 had destroyed several buildings and a few businesses. His new opera house came along about the time the movies were hitting the north woods, and many of them were shown in his establishment.

Harrison also had a large opera house, which served that community for years.

The George Dawson Pool Room and Cigar Factory in Clare, 1907.

Later, fire came along and destroyed this large wooden edifice, as also happened to the house in Farwell.

Over the years, productions of "Faust," "Peck's Bad Boy," "Merchant of Venice," "Uncle Tom's Cabin," "A Royal Slave" and "The Girl of Nevada" were all performed on stage, plus dozens of others. Each season, at least one minstrel show hit town, and generally two per season gathered large audiences.

These shows were quite well attended, but some which came to town without adequate advertising, lost money. Dancing, fights, bowling, roller-skating and similar activities were held in facilities other than the Opera houses. In Clare, Duncan's Hall, the building once used as Grant Township Hall and later by the G.A.R., and known up until 1930 as Haley's Hall, was the most commonly accepted site. Audiences could be large enough for an adequate "gate", and after all, that was the main reason the shows must go on.

Lecture courses were sold by season tickets, and four would be the minimum number of lectures or entertainments. A season's contract would run at least $275, with tickets selling for $1 and children gaining admittance for 50¢.

Duncan's Hall was used at other times for group dancing lessons, and teachers, such as Professor Fivenson, would travel by train to the various communities where he held pre-sold lessons for the season. Fivenson conducted classes in Farwell and Harrison during the late World War I era.

Locally produced dramas and comedies were interspersed in the various public buildings. Some of these were good-to-

excellent theatre, but most "could use more seasoning," as the local reviewers would say.

Audiences had a wide level of tolerance when it came to stage shows. Professionals were held to a more strict standard, while local amateurs were able to get by with inferior plays and performances. Professionals were also looked upon with more than a small amount of jaundice, as their reputations were often sullied by some members of the theatre who had ambivalent moral standards.

OPPOSITION TO THEATRES

Initially, the saloons opposed these burgeoning movie houses for the same reason the churches did; they took away their clientele in large numbers. As the novelty wore off, the saloons lessened their animosity a bit, but the churches began to increase their opposition as the star system developed. Many of the early actors and actresses retained the bad public reputation so often found with theatre groups. At one time, being a stage performer was synonymous with being loose with one's sexual habits, and to this, the churches stood in firm defiance.

THE LITERARY SCENE

Farwell, Harrison and Clare had public libraries which circulated some of the more common works. Adventure books for boys and romances for girls were stocked. Western-based stories and a bit later the Tom Swift series, delighted many. Will Carleton, the Hillsdale poet, was well respected throughout the state, and his works were widely read, even though he made periodic trips through the communities reciting his poems for a fee. When he came to Farwell in November of 1910, he read his "Darling Bess", "The Christmas Baby", "Uncle Nate's Funeral", "While the Drums March By" and several others. He surprised everyone by not reciting his most famous work, "Over the Hill to the Poorhouse". This one he read on his return trip in 1914.

Matie (Hinds) Hunter

Ladies of the Congregational Church in Clare sponsored his last pre-World War I visit to the county.

Edgar Guest, also a much-respected poet, came to Farwell during World War I and read several of his patriotic pennings. "America", "The Letter", "Boyhood Memory", "War's Homecoming", "The Things that Make a Soldier Great" and "The Soldier on Crutches" were the ones which had a war flavor to them, but he also recited "It Takes a Heap of Living to Make a House a Home".

The State of Michigan had a traveling library, and 300 titles were available for circulation. "David Harum", "Hugh Wynne" and "Richard Carvel" were well received.

By 1912, the TABARD INN LIBRARY was available for Clare citizens. A fifty-cent membership fee entitled a person to a book and a carrying case. When the book was returned, another could be taken out for a very nominal sum. E. A. Anderson had the service installed in his drug store, and most of the seventy-five books were checked out.

As soon as a hundred members joined, the book supply was doubled. This was a very popular service.

An author of note spent considerable time in Clare with his friend, James A. Tatman. James Oliver Curwood came up from Owosso for fishing and boating on the local waters. Their favorite fishing hole was on Shingle Lake in Lincoln Township. Once, on a trip to Cranberry Lake, the men came upon two fishermen whose canoe had capsized earlier while hunting ducks. There were so many weeds where they upset that swimming was out of the question. Without doubt, Mr. Chase and his companion had been snatched from an early death.

SWIMMING

Children of all ages love swimming. Youths in and around the Clare communities were no exception. Wildwood Beach at Eight Point Lake was popular with many Lansing people after roads made motoring a common experience. Budd Lake was the site for many out-of-state resorters who heard of Harrison's sublime climate and easy accessibility. A city park was established on the lake by Harrison in 1903, but it never received the care required for a family site until 1905.

Gasoline powered motor boats were introduced onto the lakes in 1910 or so. Sailboats were beginning to make an appearance on Lakes near the railroads at about the same time. Later, when autos were common (around 1915), tenting out was popular at Lake George, Temple, Freeman, Crooked Lake, Windemere, Budd and Cranberry Lakes, as well as along the rivers and streams.

W. B. Cook catered to resorters with boat rentals, groceries and cabins on Eight Point Lake around the time of World War I. Many cabins were being built on lake lots on most of the larger lakes during the same era, and the children would spend their leisure time sunning themselves or frolicking in the cool waters.

Boys often ganged up and made for the old swimming holes in rivers, streams and lakes. When the group consisted of all males,

The neighborhood baseball team, Clare, 1906.
Photo from the Thurston Family Collection

they frequently bathed in the nude. One popular swimming hole, just north of Clare in the Tobacco River, was made to order for the boys, as the water was deep enough, and a tree with a large limb from which a rope had been suspended for a "swing" out into the middle, made the perfect site. Unfortunately for the boys, or perhaps they secretly wanted to shock the town's adult population, their habit of skinny-dipping wasn't looked upon with much favor.

Boys in the early days of Clare were warned of a sound thrashing if they cavorted nude within forty rods of the bridge, but that didn't stop the practice completely. Annually, along about June or early July, the city fathers would implore, then adjure the boys, "Swim suits are cheap, boys. It's a simple matter to comply with the law and decency. Avoid trouble and cover up."

Most of the "thrashing" came in the form of periodic verbal whippings the boys received in the newspapers.

WINTER SPORTS

When the cold weather set in, swimming lost its appeal. Roller skating, wrestling, sledding parties, Flinch, Keno and eating then took over. Some of the avid fishermen had shanties on the larger lakes, but many fished out in the open on the ice. Basketball and polo were played overhead of the Clare Hardware store in town. Exhibition wrestling, featuring out-of-town and state wrestlers, made tours regularly. Duncan's Hall was the local site for this public display of strength and agility. Quite a bit of betting took place at these matches.

For the daring souls, parachuting became a sport accepted by the community, but not many local boys took up this pastime. Exhibitions of the sport were featured at the county and regional fairs and became almost as common as the airplane, which is to say, it wasn't all that universal. Farwell had the first airplane flight ever in Clare County, that being during the Labor Day celebration of 1915. The County Fair in Harrison featured an airplane in 1916.

Auto racing cost Floyd Doherty a leg in 1911, when he went to Omaha for competition, but that never dampened his or other boys' dare-devil stunts. The main detractor from auto racing was not having a vehicle

The latest beachwear of 1915.

to race. For those whose pocketbook couldn't take the heavy expenses, motorcycles were a good substitute. There were many of these all over the county during the 1911-1918 years, several of which were involved in accidents of one type or another, but a broken rib, leg or arm was considered a reasonable price to pay for the thrills.

The first annual state convention of motorcycle enthusiasts met in Bay City, June 18, 1914, for a four-day competitive meet. Several fellows went from Clare, but none raced.

DOG BREEDING

Several men took to Field Competition locally, and bred dogs to enhance their skills. The Saginaw, Midland and Clare area sportsmen in 1902 organized the "Sportsmen's Field and Trials Club". Their first field day was held in Clare during October of 1903, and 112 members showed up. E. H. Waller of Clare, owner and trainer of the dog, Claravoint, took a first prize and also won the all-age stake over a number of veteran dogs. He was out-classed only by

Lou Rodfield, owned by M. W. Tanner of Saginaw. Mr. Tanner was president of the club, which fielded two hundred dogs.

This group of sportsmen was responsible for the introduction of several species of game birds into the area, including the Chinese pheasants, grouse, partridge and quail.

Other types of small game hunting were common, and one day's trek often resulted in fifty to a hundred rabbits per hunter. Larger game, such as deer, were heavily hunted by the "meat harvesters". To conserve this source of food, the county was closed to deer hunters for several seasons during the period of World War I.

THE TOPPERWEIN'S SHOOT

The Remington Arms Company sponsored a Mexican husband and wife shooting team which toured the nation giving exhibitions of remarkable shooting skills. In September of 1909, the Topperweins came to the Clare Gun Club's field near the Tobacco River and showed the local residents how rifles could be used. To start with, the man held a hand extended to one side, holding on to a clay pigeon. His wife drilled .22 bullets into five pigeons thus held. Next he threw four clay pigeons into the air at one time. She drilled holes in each of them. Then he threw the same holey pigeons into the air again, and this time she put the projectile through each of the holes.

The Fourth of July Picnic at Lake George. Most of these people were relatives of Clark Sutherland.
Photo from the Homer Douglas Collection

William F. Hunter—a man who lived up to his name. This was taken in 1910.
Photo from the Jim Grove Collection

She threw a small-sized marble into the air, and he picked it off. He could hit anything he wanted, or for that matter, what anyone in the audience wanted. He shot an outline of an Indian's head against a tinplate background with remarkable artistry and resemblance to reality. Laying the gun down, he threw four eggs into the air, then ran twenty feet, picked up the gun and broke all four before they hit the ground. Next, using a mirror, he shot a potato out of his wife's hand.

Climaxing with a target shoot, Mrs. Topperwein joined both local teams, and collectively they hit 92 bullseyes out of 100. The shooting Topperweins never missed a shot. Fred Cimmerer, a young lad at the time, witnessed the half-hour demonstration and later declared, "They could shoot any gun with absolute accuracy. There has never been anyone like them in Clare, and probably not in Michigan."

The Remington Arms Company said they were the best shooters in the world, and for once at least, the press's snow job was probably an understatement.

THE BANDS

Each town had its own band, and sometimes local neighbors, such as the Brand district, had their own. Dover, Temple, Harrison, Farwell and Clare all had musical groups. Henry Heisman, the Harrison dry goods merchant, organized one of the better ones, and he continued to direct it until he sold the store and moved to Midland. Before he was in Harrison, he had organized a Clare group.

Dutch Eager faithfully led the Farwell band for over thirty-eight years. Under his baton, sweet music effused for Labor Day parades, special holiday concerts, summer evening musicals and, of course, the inevitable band competition days. His bands were very good.

Dr. Mulder, S. C. Kirkbride and Professor Northey all led bands in Clare, although Kirkbride's was considered an orchestra and Northey's was a military band. Music was available for every occasion. Dr.

Mulder loaned his talents to the M. E. quartet, Dover band, Clare band and other groups. He often entertained the musicians at his home, and he purchased several instruments himself, so the bands would have a wider range of sounds.

Adolph Krell of Dover was a very well-trained musician. He played the violin and cornet well enough to become a member of the Minneapolis Symphony.

Chamber music accompanied dinners, graduation, smokers and other similar meetings. The opera houses used the Charley Butts orchestra of Harrison. They also played for various social clubs which met around the county. As the draft began taking the men regularly, a band of some type would play before the train pulled out for Camp Custer. If a dinner was served to the men, chamber music was featured before the group marched to its departure point.

Music was everywhere! Vocal groups and soloists were much in demand. Edgar Welch, Mrs. George E. Lamb and L. M. Converse were the most active soloists. Churches used many musicians in their services, including the faithful organists. Some of the most notable of these were Mrs. John Galliver, Elsie Collicut, Grace Giberson, Elvia Baker, Maud Rhoades and Miss Louie Louch.

THE CLUBS

The most apparent aspects of social life in this era were the ad hoc clubs, which formed overnight and lasted a year or less, only to be replaced by other similar clubs. Flinch clubs, Block, Select, KayKaKee, Pioneers, Thimble, Pleasure, Tango and Keno are some examples of their common denominators. More permanent clubs, such as the Aid Societies in towns, and also organized by the rural churches, were very common. Women's clubs of all sorts, as well as the gourmet club, The Alfabata Society of Harrison, flourished.

Convivial get-togethers over ice cream, sledding, harvest or any other excuse was a good enough reason for a sociable evening. Picnics for immigrants, such as the Hoosier-Buckeyes or the Ohio Colony, were also

Clare County fashions, circa 1910.
Photo from the Schunk Family Collection

baseball. If a young fellow enjoyed the sport to the exclusion of all else, a religious conversion experience might change his priorities all around. For example, the Rev. L. D. Bodine was, in his youth, a superior baseball player, good enough to play with Rex DeVogt on the Boston Red Sox team, had he pursued the game, but he never went big-league. Every day of the week and especially Sundays, L. D. played baseball, he thought baseball and he dreamed of baseball at night.

During a conversation experience at a Free Methodist camp meeting, he was convinced that his time could be better spent than living a life of baseball. He took his former enthusiasm for the game and put it into his ministry — that of pastoring churches all over northern Michigan. He was good at this vocation also, going full-tilt for his church.

L. D. never played ball again, but he often umpired games. To him, his former passion for the game almost became a sin to his life, and he avoided sin. The only negative comment he had for others on the

quite common. Church groups, however, had the most organized gatherings, and they collected lots of people for their festivities on a regular schedule.

There were the more formal groups as well, including the G.A.R. and the Women's Relief Corps, Knights of Pythias, the Masonic Lodges with the Eastern Stars. These were very active, as were the farm groups such as the Grangers and the annual Institutes, which filled the empty time slots, if there were any. The list could go on and on, but the activities of other clubs were similar to the ones listed.

A FORBIDDEN DANCE

Over the years, it is amazing to see the focal points of a community's approbation shift to the opposite ends of the spectrum, and things once approved becoming off-limits. Sometimes the problem would be

Jenny (Bingham) Littlefield

baseball subject was, "Don't play on Sunday."

In 1914, Rev. Clarence F. Seastrum, a converted dance instructor, held a revival in Luther. The tango was making the circuit during this time, and it became the focal point of his attention. It seemed that the popularity of the dance competed directly for his audience and prevented their conversion. He likened the dance halls to recruiting centers for the brothels of the larger cities and cited a Detroit raid by the vice squad as his evidence. "A large percent of those women were there because the dance influenced them," he said in February, 1914, according to the SENTINEL.

Rev. Seastrum wasn't the only one breathing fire down on the tango. Rev. Fr. O'Conner of Mt. Pleasant also declared war on it and told his parishioners that ". . . it will not be tolerated in any of you." President Grawn of the Normal College didn't

encourage students to indulge in the tango either, as noted by the SENTINEL on January 23, 1914. Some were persuaded, but many young people who became less obvious participants, were active dancers, nonetheless.

HORSE RACING

Horse racing has always made blood run a little faster in the northland. Early fairgrounds legitimized the race tracks and they helped draw audiences. As the fair shifted to Harrison from Clare in 1882, racing was accelerated there also. Horse breeders, trainers and drivers didn't give up racing just because the track was in Harrison. McEwan Street frequently was cleared for a two-dollar bet which had begun as a friendly discussion.

In 1901, the Clare Firemen's Field Day

The members of the play, "Safety First". Back row, L-R: Maude Hayes, Claude Hayes, Beulah Conrad, Jack Harrington, Bertha Wellman, Bert Greer, Anna Greer, Al Wellman, Betty Gundler. Front row: Mrs. Huntington, Mary Green, Iola Matthews, Jessie Duncanson.
Photo from the Jay Green Collection

Every live-wire town in central Michigan had horse racing, even if there were only two or three commercial buildings in it. This is the Austin, Michigan raceway.

began, ostensibly to benefit the firemen and the department, but it took on all the trappings of a county fair, complete with racing, games, bowery and music.

Chan Lloyd, the McNeil Brothers, Dr. Stirling, William Van Vleet and Clair Coulter were the major owners of equestrian talent. "Blinkey Ben", "Ridpath", "Little Jew" and "Isabell" were the horses usually seen tearing down main street during the Fireman's Field Day. Once in a while, outside horses from Mt. Pleasant were imported to change the odds a bit. Ridpath, the chestnut stallion, was usually the winner, but Chan Lloyd's Little Jew, ran a good race for a gelding.

Most races were not held in Clare, and so the horses were taken to Mt. Pleasant, Midland or Saginaw for their real challenges. Seventy-five people from Clare usually showed up whenever local horseflesh ran, which gives some idea of the commitment people had for the sport.

In 1908, the Clare and North Isabella County Fair Board was organized to develop a race track on the south end of Clare. David Ward was president and Dr. Charles Stirling became the vice-president. A mass meeting was held on May 27th to sell shares to the public at a dollar each. Most of the horseflesh enthusiasts in town were on the Board of Directors and they included: J. R. Goodman; Phil Bennett; Thomas C. Holbrook; Jacob Mason; Dr. James Reeder; Chan Lloyd; F. E. Alderton; W. N. Cole; William Van Fleet; George Benner; Dr. A. R. Mussell and Dr. Sanford.

In July a year later, the track was receiving its finishing touches. President Ward said, "Racing will be fast in this burg soon and it won't be on main street either."

The opening matinee was held August 14, 1909 with "fleet footed steeds" entered from Clare, Coleman, Evart, Northville and Gladwin. Trotters and pacers were allowed. Ward also scheduled a five minute automobile free for all race to follow the three minute horse races. This was the first auto racing held in the country.

William Van Fleet drove "Donal Wood", a three year old horse from Northville, into the winner's circle on opening day. Men paid twenty-five cents to watch the spectacle and the ladies were admitted free.

The race track was scheduled full clear up until fall and each week saw familiar horses being challenged by out of town entries. The original concept of a county fair type grounds in Clare gradually went by the boards as baseball, horse racing and practice runs by the horse trainers more and more monopolized the facilities. Over the years the races held their key role right up to the first frost, when the audience began to seek other diversions and to take care of projects which had been delayed too long already. The ponies had to wait for the next spring before the town would become transfixed by their photo finishes.

The best fair was held in 1910. There was still enough enthusiam around for the assorted exhibits to be brought together and the farmers had more in common with the northern townships in Isabella than they did with the pine barrens of the northern tier in Clare county. The weather was excellent for crops that year and the townspeople were enjoying the out of doors to its maximum extent. Baby shows, exhibits of all types, baseball, musical ensembles of all types and the fast horses all added up to a spectacular success.

During 1912 the heavy spring rain collected on the low lying ground and flooded the track itself for an extraordinarily long time and even covered the floor of the exhibition hall. There was a scarcity of livestock for the fair and the net result was a very discouraging scene for the few fair goers who bothered to show up. It was the beginning of the end for the fruit and vegetable exhibits which the youths had regularly brought in for display. Dr. Charles Stirling perhaps anticipating this down trend sold his prize race horse "Dan T" to a party in the Soo during February.

The better horses were going to the other tracks around the surrounding counties which hosted the Central Michigan Circuit and Ward finally signed on in an attempt to revitalize the racing card in Clare, but the peak had been passed.

Regular county fairs in Harrison and Mt. Pleasant were too much competition and horse racing wasn't enough to keep the local business men contributing a subsidy. The automobile was now in rather substantial numbers in town and it gave freedom to the well to do class and they would rather go out of town to do it.

BASEBALL

Competition between the towns of Farwell and Clare wasn't very sportsmanlike during the first two decades of this century. There was a certain amount of envy, jealousy, hatred and fierce community loyalty involved every time these two teams met. Hired players would be brought in just for the games and they weren't necessarily hired for their ability to play baseball.

A large following escorted the teams to the playing fields and often times they protected their own players from a severe mauling when things got out of hand out on the playing field. Other times the grandstands would empty and join in the fun. Blood was shed most of the times these teams met and broken bones were expected about once a season because this was a very vigorous rivalry.

There were good ball players on all of the northern teams and the quality of play was keen. The best ball player developed locally was Rex DeVogt. He was a catcher who went from this area to a semi-pro team in Detroit, then to a minor league team in the New England League, then out to the Pacific northwest for two years of seasoning. He was brought back by the parent Boston Red Sox in time to be the battery mate of George Herman Ruth, who at the moment was baseball's premier pitcher. Rex was an excellent catcher and stayed in the big leagues for several years.

There were other players who could have played in the big leagues if that had been their goal. Just before the turn of the centurey, A. R. Mussell had a phenomenal arm, but the life of a major leaguer in those days was somewhat different than it is now.

Traveling teams of semi-professionals would barn storm through the north woods from time to time and challenge the local hot-shots. Often as not they whomped it to the amateurs. In 1913 the Boston Bloomers came to Clare and played the best athletes which the town could muster. The final score was 2-1 in favor of the Boston team, but some observers thought the pitcher, catcher and short stop were men. That didn't change the final score, but it did help to ease the

The 1911 Farwell Baseball Team: Mgr. Rowe; Cline, Pitcher; Updegraff, first base; Gardiner, second base; Richmond, center field; B. Cline, right field; N. D. Watkins, booster; McGinnis, shortstop; Lou Gee, center field; Saxton, catcher; Oliver. third base.

The Sheridan Township Baseball Team of 1910. A. T. Carrow is fourth from the left, and Stanley Schunk is sixth.
Photo from the Schunk Family Collection

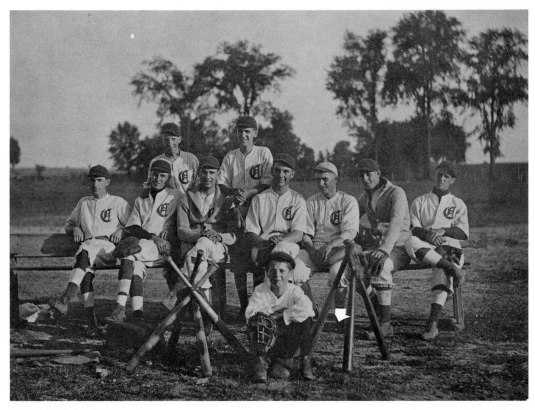

The Clare High School baseball team, 1912-13. (L-R rear): Earl Foss and Percy Wilson. (front) Harry McKerring, Kyle McKinnon, Raymond Potter, "Babe" Stone, Joe Paige, George White, and John Forbes. The batboy is Emerson Hickey.

humiliation of losing to a girls team.

1914 found Clare playing in the Hub Circuit along with Coleman, Alma, Ithaca, Shepherd and Mt. Pleasant. Osborn and Morrissey were the team's pitchers and Clark their battery mate. Will Adams was the president of the club which had the following shareholders: James S. Bicknell; C. C. Harris, George Benner; David Ward and J. M. Davis. H. P. Hubel was their manager.

Lake George had a team which played in a league with Wexford and Missaukee teams. Harrison and Crooked Lake played local teams usually.

FARWELL'S LABOR DAY CELEBRATIONS

Balloons were imported for Farwell's first Labor Day program in 1910. There were horse races to go along with several ascensions and a large crowd attended the festivities. A baseball game was scheduled between teams from Lake, Gilmore, Farwell and Lake George. It isn't known which event brought the most people to town, but everyone agreed, the first Labor Day Celebration was a tremendous success. A year later ox teams were put on the racing card along with several vaudeville acts, water fights, a big tug of war between Gilmore and Surrey farmers and of course the inevitable horse races.

F. E. Oliver was the stem winder, assisted by Marshal Almond Powell, Secretary Sam B. Pizer and William Burston, treasurer. The second year's program took off from where the first one stopped and again, it was well supported by the surrounding community.

During W.W.1., ex-Governor Fred M. Warner was the key note speaker. Patriotism

Main Street in Farwell on a Labor Day. Ice cream could be purchased in the restaurant-bakery at the left. Earl Updegraff's grocery was next to the Michigan Creamery Company's station, followed by Henry's Meat Market. Another grocery store was on the street corner at the far right. The Roys Drugstore was across the intersection.

oozed from the entire program as it did from every thing done in the county that summer. The nation had a big job to do in Europe, but first the country had to get its citizens behind the program and the men who were now going into the cantonments via the draft. Civilians were plumped up by the elected officials as they were exhorted to sacrifice for victory.

THE COUNTY FAIR SCENE

C. W. Perry and John A. Jackson went to the World's Fair in Paris during 1900 and returned extolling the wonders of the twentieth Century. Indeed, if the fairs held in all of the communities, cities and states had anything in common, it was the advancement of new ideas. Machines and technology through the fabulous exhibits held promises of a glowing future.

Clare county used the State Fair held in Pontiac to promote its agricultural assets beginning in 1902, but it was in 1905 that it was done with a professional touch. Three

thousand pamphlets were distributed which bragged up the county in a most flattering way. This promotional gimicry was a success both for the exhibits and also for the infusion of new money into the so called pine barrens. Sheep ranching, orchards, cattle and grains all were successfully boomed by L. L. Kelley, Robert Carson and John A. Jackson. Maron Caner was a promoter from a year earlier who helped the men get their materials together. A. J. Doherty was the current Secretary of the Fair Board and he was pleased with the success of the local effort to put Clare on the map. A. E. Doty and James Hamer continued to exhibit Clare products even after the Fair was moved to Detroit.

The regular county fair held at Harrison moved along regularly. There were balloon ascensions, horse racing, baseball and the popular vaudeville shows every summer and the popularity was sustained at a high level even when David Ward and his race track idea cut into the exhibits from Clare.

J. B. Haskins of the Howard City Fair Board summed up these annual events about as well as anyone. He said, "There is no

The 1906 Farwell Concert Band. Front Row, L-R: Tom Hilson, Ron Barton, Charlie Belding, John Armstrong, Dan Rowe, William Burston, Carl Updegraff, Nate Trumble. Middle row: Bernie Weisman. Albert Weisman, George Heyward. Back row: Linus Gardner, Wilmot Carpenter, Fred McGuire, Oass Row, Percy Saxton.

The village of Farwell during the World War I era.
Photo from the Littlefield Collection

single element in American Life today that develops a greater degree of neighborliness and friendships than those that result from the population of the whole community working shoulder to shoulder boosting for a common purpose.''

A. M. Fleischauer, Secretary of the Tri-County Fair Board at Reed City said, ''Too much value cannot be placed on the county fairs. Here the farmer can exhibit his very best and others can judge for themselves what is suited for the district he lives in.''

In a nut shell, fairs promoted change and they also gave the citizens a standard by which they judge their own efforts. No other community endeavor could fill the role so well.

Law and the Citizen

Essentially, there are two types of crimes which the law recognizes, civil and criminal. Civil cases are the most common in society, and these range from simple ordinance violations to the more serious fraudulent schemes of shysters and professionals. Most of the local problems before the automobile came along were caused by personal wrong doings between citizens, and generally were not felonious. For example, Clare had a bicycle ordinance which prohibited riding on the board and concrete walks, yet riders invariably chose to ride on them anyway.

City officials didn't know what to do in 1900, as there were so many violations of this ordinance that it was impossible to enforce things even-handedly. One of the main causes were the poor streets. A recently accosted bicycle rider said to the Justice of the Peace who was about to rap a five dollar fine on him, "There is not a city in the commonwealth with streets so poor as those in Clare . . . the problem isn't with us riders, it's with the city. Fix the streets and we'll ride on them."

"That's a mighty fine point you are making, young man," said Justice Carpenter, "Pay the clerk five dollars."

Three years later, Mayor Arthur J. Lacy asked the city council to repeal the onerous ordinance. He agreed with the harrassed bicyclists, saying, "Let's fix the streets instead of issuing tickets," but a lot of tickets had been issued in the past.

PROFANITY IS FINED

Some friction points could be wiped out by a decree from the council, and others were more difficult to handle. Laws and ordinances were on the books which protected society and members of a society from those crude types who choose to consider everyone as oafish as they are. It was illegal to use foul and profane language in front of a lady or gentleman as David Hoffman found out. He had gone to many homes in the communtiy and then used indecent langauge upon the housewives. Several ladies complained to Under-Sheriff Welch about this, so he took James S. Bicknell with him to assist in locating the culprit. Hoffman was found and quickly fined fifteen dollars, with a strong admonishment to leave town rapidly. He believed in strong admonitions earnestly!

Another type of annoyance to town folk was the "flasher." Farwell was treated to the nude body of R. I. Lloyd for a whole week as he kept one step ahead of the village marshal in 1912. Lloyd hailed from Indiana and carried everything except an outer coat in a sack. Justice Mauer took his money, and Lloyd took his advice. The women and children in town were delighted with this give and take arrangement.

Sometimes the problem between citizens was not illegal, just an irritant to one party or the other. A lady in Temple had just about all that she could take, but there was nowhere that she could go for relief except the newspapers. She wrote an open letter in September of 1913 to "the party who stuck his nose in another party's affairs." She wrote, "If that party would kindly go about his own business, perhaps he'll have all he can do." Whether this bit of advice was accepted isn't known, but it's hoped that it was.

A STOLEN GOOSE

Just before Christmas, 1917, a Sheridan man was observed carrying a goose in a gunny sack over his shoulder. When asked where he got it he answered, "Halstead and Feighner" (local merchants in Clare).

"Since this man is a well to do farmer and respected citizen in Sheridan, his name won't be mentioned, but most people steal geese at night," was the not so friendly chiding.

A RACKET

Some men continually traveled between towns, looking for ever new pastures, to try their swindling schemes upon unsuspecting businessmen and women. A telegraph alert to Under-Sheriff Welch told about two men who worked over Lake county pretty well, and now were heading east, probably to Clare.

Welch got on the trail and located the pair as they jumped off the train just as it was leaving town. The crooks never suspected that Welch and Loundra were at least as smart as they were, but they were given the opportunity to make their acquaintance while being escorted back to Baldwin.

F. Molar and W. Minis would present a twenty dollar bill for small articles and then slip another paper bill in its place before actually handing it over to the merchant.

A FAMOUS MURDER CASE

George Paradie, his wife and thirteen month old baby boarded with the W. B. Curtis family on West Seventh Street during June of 1902. During the afternoon of June 19, the ladies were in the kitchen hulling strawberries. Suddenly, the baby, Fennel Paradie, screamed and both women rushed to the crib where they found the baby horribly burned about its mouth. The mother picked up the child and ran to the Lewis home across the street.

Verne Martin was selling vegetables door to door in the neighborhood when the commotion was going on. He was asked to get a doctor, and Dr. F. C. Sanford was summoned to the Lewis house, where the child was screaming in extreme pain and agony. Two hours later the child died from carbolic acid inhalation.

Mrs. Paradie asked Anna Curtis, the thirteen year old daughter of Mr. and Mrs. W. B. Curtis, what she had done to her child. Anna said nothing. From the burns on the mouth, face and neck, it appeared that the carbolic acid was poured from a bottle commonly sold in a drug store. An autopsy performed on the child in Manistee by Dr. L. L. Kelley, with Dr. Langin assisting, showed no carbolic acid in the stomach. It was pointed out that embalming fluid would not have neutralized it.

Anna was arrested on a murder charge and taken to the county jail. John Quinn, the Harrison attorney, was asked to defend her. His first action was to secure her release with the posting of a three thousand dollar bond put up by Nathan Bicknell, J. Dunlop and J. W. Calkins.

Prosecuting attorney George J. Cummins asked A. J. Lacy to assist him with the case, and he began by locating the evidence. A bottle of carbolic acid, with about half a tablespoon of its contents removed, was found in the Curtis woodshed by Bessie Travis the next day. Bessie worked in the Curtis' boarding house regularly, and her cleaning chores led her to the bottle's discovery, hidden away.

Clyde Horning, clerk at Dunlop's Drug Store identified the bottle as one he had sold to Mr. Curtis the Saturday evening preceding the poisoning. He recognized it by the label.

Anna Curtis was brought to trial during September of 1902. Judge Peter Dodds presided. Her attornies were John Quinn, H. A. Sanford of Mount Pleasant and W. P. Corbett of Detroit. George Cummins and Arthur J. Lacy handled the state's case in the trial held in Harrison. Forty-five prospective jurors were questioned before Ole Amble, Charles Keehan, Albert Gleason, Fred Cosgrove, D. Bryan, John Pfannis, Elmer Havens, Charles Cahoon, B. C. Spohn, Louis Brazett, E. Hutchins and L. Williams were accepted. There were none from the Clare or Grant Township areas.

This trial was a landmark case because in only two other instances in the entire nation was a child so young charged with murder.

The trial started slowly with Thomas Despers of Manistee testifying about the identity of the body. Clyde Horning next testified about the bottle, and Verne Martin, a twelve year old vegetable peddler gave his version of the case. James F. Tatman testified for the Coroner's Jury, which he chaired.

Mrs. James Duncan, who had been at the Lewis home, testified that she found traces of acid on the child's crib clothing in the boarding house.

George Paradie next took the stand and testified that Anna Curtis didn't like children. His opinion was supported by Annie Goodknecht who said she saw Anna giving the baby a ride in her wagon the Sunday before its death.

"I remarked to Anna how nice the baby was, but Anna replied, 'I hate the little brat. I'm going to kill it,' " she testified.

Nora Houck testified that she took a bottle of carbolic acid from Anna during a Sunday school class, but that she had demolished it after confiscation.

While in jail waiting trial, Anna acquired a mouth and tongue burn somehow. Sheriff J. W. Updegraff said that the burn came from hot tea, or at least that's what she told him.

Dr. Langin testified that the burn couldn't have come just from a hot liquid. It had to have been much more dangerous. He suggested that it could have been caused by carbolic acid.

During the lengthy trial, Anna was kept overnight in the county jail, since she couldn't be released at this point on bail.

Assistant Prosecuting Attorney Lacy dissected the evidence in a very methodical manner, giving both sides to the evidence

submitted to the court, but all the while making a strong case for the prosecution.

George Cummins "undoubtedly made the plea of his life in his final presentation of the case to the jury," but the case was circumstantial at best.

William P. Corbett, the Detroit attorney, pointed out to the jury that the prosecution had to prove "deliberate intent" on the part of the girl; that she had the "capability of forming the intent" and lastly, that she "committed the crime." He made it hard for the prosecution.

The trial ended late Saturday afternoon during the week of September 15, 1902. Defense attorney Sanford stressed in his concluding remarks that Anna Curtis was only thirteen years old. "She is only a little girl, not yet fourteen and in the eyes of the law, she is innocent," he pleaded. "A child who is so young is not capable of forming an intent to commit a crime of this magnitude," he said.

Thus in the eyes of the jury, "They succeeded skillfully in making the prosecution prove not only the crime, but also the intent." This Cummins and Lacy did not do, and the jury found the young child "Not Guilty!"

After the trial was over not everyone was happy with the verdict, but everyone thought that the officers of the court had done their duty well, and "The people are rejoiced to see that so far as possible, their selected servants do discharge the duties of their offices," reported the CLARE SENTINEL, September 18, 1902.

ANOTHER MURDER

On the afternoon of March 31, 1903, Silas Burr, one of the merchants of Crooked Lake, came to his death. He was in the process of selling his grocery and patent medicine store to Dr. Verum H. Worden, and was in the company of Dr. Worden at the time of his death. Both men were riding in a horse drawn buggy on their way to the county courthouse in Harrison, when Burr was taken violently ill, dying soon afterwards.

During the morning of the 31st, the papers

transferring the property were made out in the store. After dinner, both men started for the county seat, to verify the title's lack of incumberances.

Dr. Worden returned home with the dead man's body across his knees and reported that death had overtaken his companion when they were near Lake George. Mrs. Burr speculated that perhaps the tumble her husband had recently taken was more serious than suspected and had weakened his heart fatally.

Silas Burr was taken to Vassar for burial. Meanwhile, Mrs. Worden claimed that she had paid Mr. Burr nine hundred dollars as part payment for the business just before he left for Harrison.

She had taken no receipt for the money, and at Mr. Burr's alledged request, no mention of it was made to the widow. Suspicion was aroused, and the body was taken out of its grave and an autopsy was performed by Dr. H. Morris.

He found no surface markings which indicated violence, and the heart was perfectly normal. The lungs showed normal hypostatic congestion, certainly nothing that would lead to an inference that they caused death. The liver, bladder, kidney, brain and spinal column were all examined and nothing was discovered of a fatal nature. These organs were all placed in glass jars and turned over to Sheriff Updegraff.

Dr. E. D. Reed, chemist at the Michigan Homeopathic Hospital in Ann Arbor, examined these organs on April 10, 1903. They were all normal except for an area which was free from fungus about three inches in diameter on the stomach. He tested the area and found it was alkaline with potassium cyanide. The poison was also found in other parts of the stomach. Dr. Reed determined that there was enough poison in the stomach to cause death. Silas Burr had been murdered!

Now the question, "Who killed Dr. Burr?" had to be answered back in Crooked Lake.

Dr. and Mrs. Worden had agreed to remain in custody at the county jail until results of the autopsy were known, seemingly very confident of the outcome. As soon as

Reed's verdict reached Harrison, a warrant was placed in Sheriff Updegraff's hands, and he served it on the Wordens in jail.

DR. WORDEN'S CHECKERED PAST

Verum H. Worden had been married at least five times in his sixty years. He drew twelve dollars a month pension, and this was said to be part of his charm in the eyes of women. He first got into trouble by marrying a woman without getting a divorce from his first wife. He had claimed that his attorney indicated to him that the divorce was final, but it wasn't. Worden spent five years in Jackson for this one, and gained the reputation as being a good prisoner.

He was sentenced from Sanilac county for bigamy and he married Ada J. Teller, a young girl in Huron County. It seems that Worden planned to marry again, this time to Mrs. Pritchard, but she fell ill, mortally ill it was feared, so she asked him to marry her daughter, Phoebe. A doctor was called and

Dr. V. H. Worden

The Clare County Courthouse and Jail, 1890.
Photo from the Fanning Collection

through his concoctions, the mother recovered, only to discover that her sixteen year old daughter was just fifteen. A family council was convened and concluded this marriage to the youngster null and void, so he married the buxom widow, his mother-in-law. At his trial in Mount Pleasant three of his wives were present in the court room but not one of them would testify against him, while the adolescent, Phoebe May Pritchard, was in the county jail for immorality.

Judge Dodds gave him ten years in Ionia, but Governor Pingree pardoned him after three. He next went to Indiana and West Virginia where again he married, this time to Etta May Brammer, his present wife. Etta abandoned seven children in Indiana ranging in age from seventeen to seven years of age, evidently disbelieving the stories of Dr. Worden's past.

"'Tis said that Dr. Worden has had eight wives and that more than once he has been married to both mother and daughter, but the truth of this is buried in the remote past. But to have had five wives, to have been in prison twice for matrimonial experience, to have been pardoned by two governors, and now to be confronted with the charge of murder, is a record not supposed to be the acquisition of an ordinary man, said the CLARE SENTINEL on June 11, 1903.

At the trial held during the first week of October, the jury found Dr. Worden "Guilty" and his present wife "Not Guilty." He was sentenced to life imprisonment and taken to Marquette. His wife went back to Indiana and her seven children.

ANOTHER MURDER

In April of 1916, a body was fished out of the Tobacco River, just below Hubel's Bridge on Grant Avenue, a half mile west of Clare. He was dead before his body was placed in the river. There was no identification on the fifty year old male, although there were three letters tatooed on his right forearm. He was never identified.

DR. CARPENTER ASSAULTED

At the turn of the century, Dr. Carpenter was a local druggist in Clare. Just after closing time one evening in August, the merchant was locking up the rear door when two young men approached him. They asked for some cigars, so he unlocked the door as the men told him to put up his hands. Turning, he saw two guns pointed at him. The doctor, a very muscular man, knocked the gun out of the hand of one man and made for him. His physical aggressiveness frightened the two so much they ran away. He started for home again when these two came up to him and threatened to shoot him if he didn't stop. He didn't stop! They didn't shoot. When he reached home, one of them stepped into his pathway and offered to shake hands as "It had all been in fun," said the gunman.

The doctor knocked the fun loving gunman to the ground and called for help. The other assailant ran away from the doctor who had no sense of humor.

AN ASSAULT IN GARFIELD

Millard F. Robinson owned a sawmill west of Crooked Lake and operated it several years, hiring many of the local residents at various times. As he prospered, he took to wintering in a home in Farwell, going to the mill from time to time in a supervisory capacity. He always made it a practice to pay his help on Saturdays in cash.

A local farmer, O. H. Keyes, had engaged the Benn brothers to work for him, cutting down trees for the Robinson mill. Robinson had previously told the boys that he would pay for the logs delivered to the mill, and by the end of the week about half of the logs had been brought in by sleighs.

Robinson came out to pay his mill hands when he was accosted by John and Noah Benn who were in the company of O. H. Keyes. They demanded fifty-four dollars,

which was the price for all the timber, half of which wasn't delivered yet. The mill man demurred, but the ruffians persisted, even knocking Robinson to the ground. One of the boys kicked him about the head and face. To save his life, he agreed to give them the money.

While the boys made their escape, the older man, O. H. Keyes, held a gun on Robinson. Later he claimed that he had no part in the attack, but Sheriff Updegraff didn't believe his story, and had him arrested and placed in jail.

Robinson had never hired the men, as they worked for Keyes, yet he was forced to pay more than Keyes had coming. During the struggle, Robinson heard Keyes tell the Benn brothers to "Give it to him!" and he thought that the three were in cahoots to rob him.

It turned out that others had heard of a plan to rob Robinson, and a man had come to Farwell to warn him, but missed connections somehow. Another man in Garfield attempted to head off the mill owner as he too had heard a rumor about a planned robbery.

The Benn brothers were located across the state line, south of St. Joseph County, working in a mill. Updegraff asked an Indiana officer to arrest the boys and bring them to the state line, thereby saving Clare County about one hundred dollars in legal requisition papers. The boys were lodged in jail on five hundred dollars bond, while Keyes was held on a bond of four hundred dollars.

A trial was held in June of 1903 at Harrison. John was found guilty and sentenced to eighty-seven days in the Detroit House of Correction. The others were found "Not Guilty."

A SHOOTING AFFAIR

John Herring was a Vernon farmer who had cattle usually on his farm, but once in a while, they escaped his inadequate fences and ate whatever was available, which meant his neighbors' crops and gardens.

A. C. Geer found that he was feeding

more cattle than he owned, so he went to Herring and asked him to keep his cattle home. Again the bovines broke through the fences and dined on a newly planted field of clover which Geer had plans for.

A second time Geer went to the Herring farm. This trip he was in a nasty mood and told the offending farmer that some cows were going to be shot if they got onto his property again.

They did!

Geer went and got his gun, returning about the time Herring appeared on the scene. Not even bothering to talk, he lowered the gun and shot in the direction of Herring.

Rumors began to circulate like wildfire, some blaming Geer and others blaming Herring. One rumor had it that Geer was only in Vernon a year when he decided that his neighbor was such a bad man that he deserved to be shot. Another rumor had it that Herring sat in his buggy, taking the bullet into his body without moving so as to protect his little girl who was with him.

Justice Gray in Rosebush held Geer over for trial in circuit court with bail fixed at two thousand dollars. What the courts determined in this case isn't known, but Geer moved from Vernon in 1912.

FARWELL POST OFFICE

John Saxton was the postmaster in town for many years, but during 1903-1904, the problems which caused him the most difficulty, were all of the burglaries. Every few weeks, they broke out a window and burgled the safe. Normally only fifty dollars or so was taken in cash, and about the same amount in stamps. It was getting to be a down right nuisance, this call from the village marshal about 2:00 a.m., informing him that the office had been broken into again.

During July the mail depot was broken into for the third time in 1904, and this was beginning to get under Saxton's skin. "Why don't they blow up the safe and clean the place out?" he said in exasperation. So three weeks later, several sticks of dynamite were used on the Detroit Safe Company's masterpiece, and the door was warped so much that it was ruined.

Less than a hundred dollars worth of currency and stamps were taken, but several hundreds of dollars worth of damage was caused by the explosion. Since a heavy thunderstorm raged at the time, the exploding dynamite never caused a second notice.

Circuit court dockets in Clare County for the next several sessions only contained the usual rapes, adultery, timber stealing and chancery cases, but the hanger-ons and sensation seekers never found out who the Farwell burglar was.

JOHN C. ROCKAFELLOW ESTATE

During December of 1908, the court regulars were treated to a spectacular case, when the estate of the late John C. Rockafellow was contested in Harrison. Rockafellow was a very successful businessman in Clare and served in a variety of city and township elected offices. John was a talented man!

Upon his death in 1900, George Benner, cashier of the Clare County Savings Bank, was appointed the executor of the healthy estate. Two children, Arthur and Carrie, were to receive the assets. Arthur lived in Evart and Carrie had married Henry A. Stroupe, a Pere Marquette mail clerk living in Manistee.

There in Manistee, the Stroupes became acquainted with the "Flying Rollers", a sect from the Benton Harbor Benjamin and Mary Colony. In 1906, the Stroupes moved back to Clare and held meetings in the local Baptist Church for a week, then they were found out and asked to terminate their special meetings.

In 1907, the Stroupes moved to Benton Harbor and subsequently Carrie assigned her share of the estate to the Benjamin and Mary Colony as she became a member of the group, dependent upon it for her support.

Arthur, her brother, wasn't very happy over this turn of events, so he brought suit to prevent George Benner from giving the assets of her estate to the Colony. A brilliant array of legal talent was brought in and many of Harrison's and Clare's prominent citizens testified about every detail of the Rockafellow's and Stroupe's personal life imaginable. Even the Stroupe's five children were brought into the case presided over by Judge Miner of Owosso.

Mr. Rowe, secretary for the sect, took the witness stand and presented a most unique personality to the court. His long beard and whiskers were a sensation to say the least, and probably had much to do with the jury's finding Carrie Rockafellow Stroupe incompetent and therefore incapable of properly handling her portion of the estate.

There may have been other factors which influenced the jury such as: the sect believed that sex could be practiced only after a state of perfection was reached here on earth; Mrs. Rachel Goodman testified that insanity was present in Carrie's side of the family; Mrs. Robert Friedeborn testified about her religious background; and finally Mrs. Minnie Marr testified about the notions Carrie had concerning food she permitted her children to eat. All of these together seemed to indicate an imbalance in the court's eyes, but the Benjamin and Mary Colony appealed the case. The money in the estate was worth going after.

A PETTY LARCENY

Mrs. Frank Parrish worked for the Calkins hotel over a period of several months as a domestic servant. The family wasn't financially well set and J. W. Calkins advanced her several hundred dollars so she could buy a home in Clare. Mrs. Parrish then repaid "Tip" Calkins out of her weekly pay, a few dollars at a time.

She had refunded the advanced money almost in its entirety when the family sold the house and moved. They paid the balance still owing to her former employer and parted company.

One day "Tip" was browsing in the Holtry Shop down on 3rd Street when he was amazed to see most of his missing chinaware on sale. He inquired as to the origin of the china and was told that Mrs. Parrish had sold it to him just before she and her husband moved to Petoskey.

Well, now, "Tip" was a nice fellow and all of that, but this was a bit too much! He had a warrant issued for her arrest and it was served in Petoskey by a local law official. A Clare law officer went to the northern city and escorted her back for her day in court.

"I forgot to return the dishes," she told the judge. "Mrs. Calkins often gave me food to take home to the family and I forgot to return the dishes," she added.

"Fifty dollars and ten days to help you remember the next time," snapped Judge Elden.

A GREENWOOD CHARACTER

George Payne was a country storekeeper in Greenwood township during the first decade of this century. He was known for strange behavior and most considered him a weird character, but nonetheless, a normally agreeable man. He had a streak of accommodation in him and would help everyone that asked. A neighbor of his had need of a co-signer down at the Harrison Bank, so Payne put his signature to the note and forgot about it. Six months later, the bank came to him and demanded that he pay the note which was due as the original maker seemed to have disappeared.

Payne decided that he wasn't going to pay the note and the bank had made up its mind that he was. Cashier Weatherhead filled out the necessary papers for Sheriff Louis Sunday and Lew decided to run out to Greenwood and deliver them. Payne had heard that the sheriff was coming and had declared to a customer that "No one was going to serve any papers on anyone in my store."

The customer waited for Sunday to arrive and informed him that the storekeeper had a revolver and was going to shoot him if he stepped through the door. Now Payne's reputation with firearms was well known and many a person had been run off the property with Payne right behind him brandishing a gun.

Sheriff Sunday thought about it, and took the advice of Payne's friend that he wait a while so he could cool down. Before he left, he shouted into the store, "Mr. Payne, I'm going to come back some day and I'm going to serve these papers on you whether you are dead or alive." With that he took off for Harrison.

Returning to the bank he told Weatherhead that it "Tisn't worthwhile, shooting a man who is a little off."

A week later he sent word to Payne that he was coming out with the papers and that he was going to deliver them. "Either you accept the papers or I'm bringing your body back to the undertaker."

Pulling up in the vicinity of the store, Sheriff Sunday called out, "Mr. Payne, are you going to be good or am I going to have to kill you?"

Payne returning the call, shouted, "I'll be good Sheriff, come on in and get my guns."

So Sheriff Sunday walked in and the guns were handed over. Papers were served on the grocer without a murmur and the man was taken to Harrison where he posted a $600 bond. Later he was arraigned before Justice Young who told him, "You be good, or I'll put a heavier bond on you."

"I'll be good, Judge! The sheriff can come out and get all of my guns any time he wants. I'll be good!"

And he was. Sheriff Sunday collected the guns and the bank collected its note.

A BULLY

John Empey was an overgrown bully, the type that pushed people around when he was young and never got out of the habit. He physically beat up people from time to time and law officers would arrest him. Just as often the fellow would beat the case as he was a "charmer." Then in 1912 he was arrested for assaulting a man by the name of Waller. Judge Maynard heard the case, but a jury of twelve women turned him loose. Joe Bowler the prosecutor didn't have a good day in court, but Empey and C. W. Perry, the defendant's attorney did.

HORSE THIEVES

Each town had at least one livery barn where a person could walk in and rent a buggy and a horse or two. Drummers, or traveling salesmen, used the railroads to move between towns, and then working out of a central location, they would rent a rig and cover the rural districts. Generally the hotels had their own livery service close by for the convenience of their guests. The Calkins, the Lackie House, the Parkview or the Commercial House would have their own.

During October of 1903, William and Ross Toland came to Clare and checked into the Lackie House on West 4th Street. The next day they rented a team and wagon, saying they intended to drive east of town about seven miles or so. In the evening they still hadn't returned, but word was that they went through Mt. Pleasant, heading south. Another report came in, indicating that they were in Marion and that the team was pursued out of Weidman by the Isabella county sheriff who was chasing them so closely that they abandoned the team in Marion. The two had stolen some blankets in Weidman on their way through.

Under-sheriff Welch took a train for Marion, but saw the men walking along the railroad tracks near Lake George. Leaving the train at Clarence, he commandeered a possee and a section hand-car and gave chase. The two were just outside of Lake when they were caught. Welch handcuffed them and they were marched ten miles on foot to Clare unassisted. The possee took the handcar back to Clarence.

The two brothers were arraigned for stealing horses and placed under a $500 bond. Landlord Lackie later discovered that his team had been driven over one hundred miles in just under thirty-six hours. He was very angry with the pair of thieves.

A COMMERCIAL BURGLAR

George Church was arrested in September of 1903 a week after Roxbury's home was broken into. Davy and Company was entered and systematically looted over a period of time, but no evidence was available which indicated how the burglar got into the store. One afternoon, Mr. Davy was walking past the Church's apartment in a downtown location when he noticed a pair of lace curtains, similar to a pattern which was unaccounted for in the store. Davy asked his chief clerk, Jennie Sexsmith, to slip over to the Guild which was meeting in the Congregational church and look around. She did and found a variety of things which were missing from the store.

On the following Friday, Mrs. Church was observed carrying a bundle which contained a shirt which also had come up missing. This was too much of a co-incidence for L. E. Davy and he asked for a search warrant for the married couple's apartment. Mrs. Church was indignant when the officer came to serve it. insisting that there was a mistake being made by someone.

A large amount of dry goods identical to the local supply stocked at the Davy & Company store was found. George Church insisted that he had purchased them in Grand Rapids. Later he signed a statement that he had entered the store after the lights were out by prying out the coal scuttle and letting himself down by a plank. He attached the garments to a rope and hauled them up.

W. E. Elden, armed with a search warrant, found two lamps and some other goods taken from a barrel in a shed which had a mysterious fire a few days earlier.

Church worked for the Ann Arbor railroad as a foreman and had moved to Clare in April from Canada.

On Monday following his arrest, Rudolph Schaeffer observed Mrs. Church burying a package out near the bridge north of town. He waited a day and then after thinking about it some, his curiosity got the better of him and he dug the package up. There was an electric dark lantern without its dry cell. Such a lamp had been used in the robbery by the Roxbury's night time visitor. Mrs. Roxbury had been awakened by the burglar downstairs and had alerted her husband. As they lay in bed wondering what to do, footsteps came up the hallway indicating that he was now upstairs. The bed-room door was opened carefully and a light shone upon the bed, but both of them pretended they were asleep. The man went to the dresser and took things from the top and also some jewelry from a drawer. The man was a cool professional burglar.

George Church was sentenced October 3rd to Ionia for a term of 1-15 years. Deputy Sheriff Green escorted Church to jail and then the next Monday he was taken to Ionia. Mrs. Church returned to Canada the same day.

THE PROFESSIONALS

Beginning in 1907, a trio of professional crooks began making life miserable for local merchants and law officers. Marcell Cour, Roy Jackson and Ward Louch started their careers with stealing a revolver from W. T. Weir's store. The cartridges were pilfered from Lewis and Patrick's hardware store and O'Connor's grocery contributed $11 from the change drawer.

Since the lads were local students and this was the first time they were in trouble, no one wanted to give them a police record. Justice W. H. Elden said, "At heart, these boys are not bad, but they are out late at night, drifting." He could have added that they were also seen standing around on the corners, smoking cigarettes, but that might be giving them too much of a black mark on their record, although they had been using the weed for years.

The boys were put on probation and a suspended sentence. "No liquor! No tobacco! And you be home by nine every night," he told them. "A violation of this parole and you could receive fifteen years." was his final warning.

In December, Marcell Cour violated his parole and was sentenced to a term of six months to fifteen years. He and George Baldwin had broken into a house in Midland where they were caught.

Cour came from a good family in Clare, but "He is a truculent youth" said a local law officer. Some one else indicated that the town had winked at some of his earlier problems. "If only some one had taken the time to deal with him earlier he wouldn't be in trouble now" was the comment made by Edgar Welch, the editor of the CLARE SENTINEL.

While Cour was in Ionia, Louch began using tools belonging to the Clare Furnace Company. He had removed them from the company's foundry a few weeks earlier. Banks in Midland, Mt. Pleasant and Farwell were broken into and the tools were suspected of being used in those bank jobs.

Since Marcell was a first time offender in the eyes of the law, his stay in Ionia was short. Upon his release, he teamed up again with Louch and they began a full time career in petty and not so petty thievery. Five dollars taken from the James O'Connor store, then small change came up missing in Anderson's Rexall Drug Store. Tatman and McKeever's store was next and they missed some petty cash. All of these little incidents were too small to make much of a fuss over.

In 1910, Clare was known all over as the "Market City" as they had boomed the slogan hard. The warehouses down by the railroad tracks had their walls pressed out most of the time with produce and farm goods. One morning the manager of the Michigan Produce Company noticed that some furs were missing from the back room. A few nights later more furs seemed to be pilfered. A little later a side of beef was taken and the problem was taking a very serious turn for the worse.

Joe Davis, Clare's law officer began to surmise a few things and he started to press down on Cour and Louch. They felt the heat from the law and tried to get away in an automobile they hired, but Joe took off after them and pursued them toward Midland. Sheriff Sunday telegraphed ahead to Midland, Saginaw and Bay City, asking for some help in bringing these fellows in.

A police spotter saw them drive into Bay City and soon the pair were resting under the shelter of the law. They claimed they were two brothers by the name of Brown and lived in Cadillac. They were on their way to Toledo.

Sheriff Sunday didn't let their tall story detain him and he went to Bay City and brought them back as guests of the county.

"They were checked into the county guesthouse" was the comment of the Clare COURIER. Within ten days they escaped on foot heading for Clare. Under-sheriff Jake Mason waited for them at the north end of town where he gathered them in and gave the "brothers" a free ride back to Harrison This time they stayed put.

In October of 1915 they escaped from the Harrison jail again only to be re-captured in Bay City the following April. Blood hounds were used to track them down as they were after the Kandy Kitchen was burglarized in Clare, but both times the pair eluded their pursuers. By now Judge Dodds began to become weary of this pair. The next time

George and Edward White in 1909.
Photo from the Edward White Collection

The second Ann Arbor Railroad depot at Lake George. The first one was a box car. A later one, the third, was much nicer, but was razed in 1955.

Photo from the Jim Grove Collection

they were brought before him he gave them more than the three years he had meted out in 1912.

While the two were on the loose after the county jail break in October, they went to Detroit and tried to pawn some stolen property. The Detroit police eventually caught up with them and extracted a laundry list of jobs they had pulled in the central Michigan area. Those city police were impressed that ones so young and had been given so many chances to go straight had muffed their opportunity.

Returning to civilian life after their last prison trip, it is assumed that a major change took place in their lives because Cour did come back to Clare and took a job as an auto mechanic.

OUT OF TOWN SPORTS

Gene Pettit, Clare's deputy Game War-

den, was a very aggressive enforcer of the state's conservation laws. Stories of his apprehensions are legion and his reputation traveled far beyond the county line. Out of towners who came to the lakes and streams of our fair county expecting to break a catch limit law soon came to respect his ability to anticipate their wrong doing. Lake George was a favorite area for patrol, but he was well known in Crooked Lake, Harrison and on the reaches of the Doc & Tom stream as well as all up and down the Muskegon River.

He was a fearless enforcement officer and would often tackle a whole covey of men who had stretched things too far. One group of Mt. Pleasant sports were heard muttering to themselves, "That damned game warden!" Edgar Welch said, "May his memory long remain in the minds of the Mt. Pleasantites." No doubt that's just what happened.

ARSON

This crime was suspected by many to be the most common in the county during the early years and even on into the twentieth century, but it was a crime very hard to prove. Lumberjacks often torched property of a former employer if they felt they had been wronged in some way, and many of those men had a very touchy ego. A blacksmith in Sheridan was feared by many and he carried the reputation of an arsonist to his grave. Many local residents found their barns going up in smoke after an encounter with him.

Feuds in Garfield resulted in at least two arson jobs and a suspected dynamiting of another, but then it was hard to prove any of these. Law enforcement officers received very few written complaints against those who people feared, and so arrests were rare.

Gottlieb Hoefle lived in a house on 1st Street in south Clare. A bulky figure of a man was observed under Hoefle's window during the night, but not much attention was paid to him at the time. A little bit later, about two o'clock in the morning, smoke was detected and the mother escaped with a daughter from the burning house. Mr. Hoefle wasn't home at the time and so he wasn't injured by the flames.

John J. Oliver owned the house and was selling it to Hoefle, but the sale hadn't been completed yet. Some insurance covered the house and contents. No further information ever came out on this fire which nearly took the lives of two female residents of Clare, but then arson fires hardly ever had arrests associated with them.

A BOARDING HOUSE THIEF

Mrs. Archie Norman kept a boarding house at her Long Lake residence, feeding and housing about a dozen men or so at a time. She kept chickens and a garden on her Frost Township property during the second decade of this century.

Every morning the men would come down to a breakfast of eggs, potatoes, coffee and bread. Her board was well respected and men waited to fill any openings that would come along.

One morning, in the spring, a new mill hand moved into her house placing his belongings in with another room partner. He went to work and returned home after a long day wrestling with the logs. Early next morning Mrs. Norman was busy in the kitchen when the men trooped in and sat down waiting for the food to arrive. Presently Mrs. Norman brought in a platter with about two dozen eggs on it. She handed it to the newcomer and he, without hesitation dumped the whole platter of eggs on his plate, and handed the empty dish back to the cook.

The other boarders just sat there. They were stunned! Not knowing what to say, they said nothing. Mrs. Norman went back to the kitchen and cracked two dozen more eggs and fried them. Returning to the dining room she handed the platter to the same fellow and he looked at them, thinking, but then he passed them to Peter Oman, the one room school teacher in Long Lake. Peter took his two eggs and passed them on.

Not a word was said in the dining room about the incident, but at the mill the men felt more in their element and they began to ride the green horn so hard about his faux pas that he quit his job, went to the boarding house and packed his turkey.

A man who would take all of the food at a common dining hall table wasn't made to feel very welcome. If he had been a wife beater, a drunkard or a common chicken thief he would have been more easily tolerated.

Problems in Conservation

A little pond east of Clare in the northeast corner of Section 35 was called Mud Lake by the locals. It was about five feet deep during normal times, and weeds grew in it, along with the rushes. Edgerton Switzer, the local creamery operator, wanted to plant an orchard on the site, so he put in a tile connecting the trapped water to the Tobacco River. Some thought it was an improvement, because the pond was an unsightly view. Others expressed an opposition to its demise, as it lowered the water table four feet in the immediate area.

Some farmers had lands which were water-logged during the spring and early summer months. This exposed water table prevented the raising of potatoes and other crops which couldn't stand having wet feet, but alternate crops could have been tried had there been an inclination in that direction. Unfortunately, drains were put in and the environment changed—without a second thought or regard for the dependent wildlife which used the moist areas for their homes.

Switzer was really a creamery owner and butter-maker, rather than a conservationist or orchardist. Soon after the trees were bearing fruit, he leased the farm to R. E. Hood of Cadillac and moved his family to Muskegon in 1910. He also ran the butter factory at Hersey and owned a partial interest in the Marion Creamery.

A POLLUTED RIVER

Midland County officials looked at the Tittabawassee River flowing through its townships and noticed that the quality of water was being lowered. Tracing the contamination in the summer of 1908, they discovered the St. Louis Sugar Company dumping its tailings into the river, resulting in a large fish kill. The county sued the sugar company for the pollution and asked for an injunction to halt the dumpings.

In Clare, a sewer which emptied into the Little Tobacco River in the downtown district polluted the water which passed in front of the Geeck property. His cow drank the polluted water, and although everyone knew it could cause diseases such as typhoid or dysentery, there was no money in the city's budget to correct the problem. The sewer opened into the rear of Mrs. Clute's property, and required an extension of several hundred feet to the river. "Everyone admits the sewer ought to be extended to the river, but there is no money to pay for it," said Mayor Adams.

FISH PLANTINGS

The water quality in the streams and rivers in the county was excellent before the lumber was cut off, but it suffered from surface run-off pollution after the ground cover was partially removed. Periodically, violators would take too many fish out of the streams, using nets, spears, dynamite or whatever. Often a fisherman would return with two tubs of trout taken in a day's fishing from a hole on a small stream. A few of these heavy expeditions, and the breeding stock of a species would be severely curtailed. To re-

179

place these losses and also to introduce new species into an area, fish plantings were carried out by the state fish hatcheries. The railroads would transport the milk cans of fish, and locals would take them to various spots in a stream or lake and deposit the contents into the fresh water.

Ed Whitney planted trout in the Tobacco River in 1878, and W. W. Green planted carp in Budd Lake during the late 1880's. A large shipment of 50,000 trout was distributed to the streams of the county out of Harrison, and also in Five Lakes, Chard, Halstead and Mud Lakes.

Shingle Lake received three cans of trout in 1904, as the train stopped on the tracks for the plantings from the state's hatcheries. (The Ann Arbor's baggage master emptied the cans.) Fuller's and Harris' mill pond were replenished in 1912, as the re-stocking took place every few years in the various counties.

DUAL UTILIZATION OF RESOURCES

Public enroachment on private water impoundments was not serious in the early years, but with the building of dams to supply electrical power, as well as for other purposes, fishermen would often be careless with their debris, angering the owners. They were even known to break a fence or two. This dual utilization of a public resource would long be a problem to officials and taxpayers, and many a vexious argument ensued between sportsmen and property owners.

In town, the Clare mill pond was used by many boys for swimming without the supervision of adults. B. F. Cornwell, co-proprietor of the mill warned that the waters around the intake were dangerous, and that several boys had been rescued by older companions recently. Children as young as five years old were swimming in the deep water near the intake line. "If the practice continues, it's only a matter of time before one of them will find a watery grave," he warned.

DEER

Game laws were enacted before the turn of the century which regulated when game birds, turkey, deer, squirrels and birds of prey could be harvested. Bears, squirrels and certain birds such as hawks, owls and crows were considered undesirable, and there was no closed season on them. Deer could be hunted between November 5th and the 25th. No dogs could be used, but there was no limit on the number that could be killed.

Parties of men would come into an area and shoot everything that moved. An example of this occurred in 1910 when a Shepherd party killed a truckload of deer off the Harrison Branch north of Meredith in one day. They loaded them into the baggage car and took them home for their wives to preserve by canning.

ICE HARVESTING

Before refrigeration became mechanized, ice was the only source of the cold available to preserve food during warm months. A law was passed by the Legislature in 1899 which provided that all harvesting of ice on ponds, lakes or streams had to be accompanied by a sign or barricades of rope, chains or poles positioned three feet high and a sign which warned of thin ice. Failure to post the danger warnings was worth ninety days in the county cooler and/or $100 in fines.

Sometimes a woman or a child would walk across Dewey Lake, heading for school or church, after the ice had been recently harvested, only to fall into its frigid waters. Most had a difficult time extricating themselves from the trap, as the ice forming on the cut-over waters couldn't sustain their escape efforts. A few, but not many, perished in county lakes, due to the ignoring of the law by the ice harvesters.

ARBOR DAY

Arbor Day was a time for the planting of trees in Michigan to replace those that were removed by the lumberman and the fires. In

1904, Clare began pushing the custom, because men who had travelled in the southern counties noticed how much more pleasant those communities were, when they had groves and shade trees dotting the landscape. In northern Michigan during the early years, relatively few trees were allowed to grow. The roadways had a few species which escaped, and a woodlot here and there interrupted the bleak horizon with elm or maple saplings. About 1900, a complete reversal in the attitude of the northerners took place. Poplars were replaced with desirable shade trees in town, and lawns were encouraged to grow. A few lawn mowers were sold, giving a chamber of commerce type promoter the opportunity to say, "The work has already begun again this spring. Let the work go on beautifying the town." So on Arbor Day, 1904, the town turned out and planted scores of maple trees along the streets of Clare.

A BAD SLUR ON CLARE SOILS

Professor Roth, University of Michigan's forestry expert, became involved with Clare County in 1906 when the DETROIT FREE PRESS quoted him in a November article. He said that most of the northern lands weren't fit for the plow.

D. E. Alward said, "His description may fit some localities, but it doesn't fit Clare County." Alward claimed one of the reasons for the late development of Clare farms was that rich men held the land off the markets for years.

So Prof. Filbert Roth came to the county at the request of Alward and looked around. His trip naturally included Farwell where Littlefield had his affairs centered, and the two began discussing reforestation. The Public Domain Commission was also bringing the public's attention to the task of re-covering the denuded landscape. Roth suggested that Littlefield consider Blue Spruce, White Pine, Norway Pine and Catalpa seedlings for the barrens around Farwell. By 1909 Littlefield had reforested a tract of land with one of these suggested species.

The Public Domain Commission began furnishing trees one year later to any resident who would plant the seedlings which were being grown at the Roscommon nursery. Yellow Pine, Red Pine, Scotch Pine, Red and Norway Spruce were available. Prices ranged between $2 and $15 a thousand for the two to six year old seedlings. Most of the offerings were about eight inches tall, but the height varied considerably, some being two feet.

Professor Roth came back to Farwell in 1912 and spoke at the Congregational church. His main purpose was to look over the county, checking on the progress of the reforestation projects. After viewing the local efforts of conservationists he said, "Things are vastly improved."

There were others who had an interest in the pine barrens. For example, State Immigration Commissoiner Augustus Carton had the responsibility to encourage settlement by new immigrants. He concentrated on foreigners who were now coming to the country in large numbers. They were seeking land which could support their agrarian styles of living, but these people wanted something besides a field of stumps. As new growths of deciduous trees came on, he thought that game birds could be introduced and that perhaps large swampy tracts could be set aside so the real estate sharks couldn't sell them to the unsuspecting foreigner. Since Carton had been a member of the Public Domain Commission at the time, he was quite familiar with the problems the northern communities had with the cut over land, and he knew that the only way to effect change was to work with the policy making bodies officially charged with that responsibility. These suggestions, plus others, he laid before the Public Domain Commission in 1912.

The legislature at his suggestion set aside land for the Michigan National Guard encampment at Grayling as one more use for the sandy soils of the north. Previously, the Guard held its annual maneuvers'near Ludington on leased property.

In 1917 Prof. Cobb of Mt. Pleasant Normal College showed some lantern slides in a Farwell church depicting several reforestation projects around the north. Many of the audience took the hint and ordered hundreds of seedlings for spring planting. It was at this time that many black walnut trees were set out as they could be purchased from a state source for about two cents a-piece.

SONG BIRDS

What few birds were able to exist in the pine woods were driven out of the north when the land cover was removed. As the second growth took over, the bird population increased and the varieties included more open field types as well as the light woodland species. Governor Ferris had helped them in their comeback by declaring an open season on the marauding cats in 1913. Not all of the citizens agreed with this law, but there were so many prowling felines running loose that it became an accepted fact of life. The one bird which seemed to thrive on the new environment was the robin. It was the only song bird holding its own.

A meeting held in Clare during 1904 by Prof. Hedrick of the Michigan Horticultural Society disclosed that most people favored killing all of the robins off. "The bird is a pest," one person is reported to have said. Finally a member of the audience spoke up and said, "The robin isn't a good for nothing bird. He is a good worm destroyer."

European partridge were imported in large numbers by sporting clubs and individuals. W. C. Cornwell and William B. Mershon purchased this particular species and turned them loose, but illegal hunters shot them out of the sky about as fast as they could be brought in. When a few seasons had gone by and there were no appreciable numbers in the woods, Cornwell asked the sheriff and the deputy game wardens to enforce P.A. 311 of 1907. This law stipulated that the partridge was a protected bird and that violators could be fined and jailed. Cornwell said, "Give the bird a chance to adjust to the country and soon it will be able to withstand moderate harvesting."

Governor Ferris was on a crusade during his years in Lansing. He wanted to make the entire state a better place for people to live life to its fullest. This meant that all citizens must be allowed to more fully utilize their own potential. Education was a high priority, but so was the environment. He would tell audiences about his own boyhood experiences when he and his father would sit in the shade of some trees which they had planted earlier. There were birds now nesting in the grove and the cacophony of their songs were etched in his memory, providing him some choice points of references for his stories. As he regaled his audiences he would invariably say, "Let us take heart and plant more trees. They will become the homes for birds which will make our towns better places to raise our families."

Arbor day was more than a day for planting trees in the spring time. To him it was a focal point for his conservation efforts and he used his high state office to its fullest extent. Ferris may have been a maverick at times for the orthodox politicians, but his feet were firmly planted on sound conservation practices. Many of the beauties we now take for granted are the legacy of this gifted man.

Of course Ferris wasn't the only one who spoke out on the topic of conservation. Forest fires were long a bane upon the northlands and Deputy State Forestry Warden J. H. McGillivrary related to members of Clare High School in 1914 that fires damaged bird populations as well as emaciating the trees and wild animals. He cited the 1911 forest fire which cost the state four million dollars. Not even computed, he said, were the losses in bird and wildfire categories. Preventive methods and an increased vigilence reduced the fires and losses to $23,000 in 1913. "All boys and girls have an important job in this conservation," he said.

During 1914 there was a little ditty making the rounds which eloquently tells the status of things better than statistics. It went like this:

"We wish again
    to fish in Michigan."

Slowly but surely the lessons of wanton waste were being learned, even though in most instances they were absorbed the hard way.

REFORESTING MICHIGAN

Lumbermen in 1906 began to see the problem of exhausted forests as a great financial loss to themselves. The end of lumbering in Michigan was plainly visible to more than a few. Ten years previously these capitalists had been busy converting the trees into money, but now that they were nearly all gone, they wanted the government to assist them in staying in business. The barons computed the supply of lumber to be 1,475,-000,000,000 feet and since a season's cut was forty five billion feet, they reasoned that in only thirty three years all of the lumber would be gone.

They asked Congress to place an embargo upon the exportation of logs. They also requested that all company owned tree plantations be exempt from taxation. The CLEVELAND LEADER thought that the two suggestions from the lumberman's associations weren't likely to pass, yet it concluded, "It is clear that some such measure must be taken soon."

In Michigan during 1906, the state had a property tax levied against every parcel of land privately owned, or not exempt by some legislature or governmental authority. The rate wasn't high and the valuation placed upon the parcel was something a township supervisor would normally compute. Locally owned property often was treated more leniently than absentee owned land. In the past, during the lumbering era, the court dockets were filled with litigation related to this disequal treatment.

With the timber down, the sandy hills had lost much of their commercial value and many tracts weren't worth the taxes assessed against them. The state would then become the new owner under a reversion procedure. Following this, a tax sale would be held and the land either auctioned off or placed into the Public Domain Commission's custody. A period of dormancy usually followed.

Garfield township had a lot of land which went back for taxes, but in reality much of it was fertile enough for grazing or cultivation. Robert Carson, W. H. Wilson and John Brown were the three most likely new owners of these reverted tracts as they bought heavi-ly, usually paying less than the amount of taxes owed to the state. Fifty thousand acres of Clare county land reverted to the state in 1906-07, but these speculators were able to put forty seven thousand acres back onto the tax rolls.

Robert Carson said, "Yes, I bought considerable land last year, but I've sold practically all of it already on a contract with very little actual money from the purchasers." He went on to explain, "People with money don't want to go onto a place and do all of the slaving necessary to make it a farm. Many of those who buy from me go onto the land with practically no money, yet many of them in a few years will come through with good farms."

W. H. Wilson and ex-sheriff John R. Brown sold most of their purchases to the sheep ranchers who were bitten by the woolly bug around 1904. The state collected twenty thousand dollars for the fifty thousand acres and new money was annually being paid into the state treasury in large amounts. In short, these speculators were in reality performing a substantial service to the county and state.

The Public Domain Commission decided that the raw land ought to be planted to something which could produce a harvest quickly while at the same time filling a real need. Some argued for planting trees which could be used by the paper industry as a crop of poplars matured every fifteen years. Others thought a more substantial tree was in the best interest of the state. Michigan railroads consumed a large number of road bed ties each year as the early installations used untreated ties. Black locust wood was dense and strong enough to be a preferred replacement. The fact that they resisted rotting when placed on the ground made their cultivation a good choice. A grove was discivered growing near Traverse City and thousands of seedlings were soon growing in the Roscommon nursery. Later they were transplanted all over the northern sand hills. E. L. Sprague of Greenwood was one of the first to suggest this tree and A. J. Doherty handled the Lansing connections making it possible for this common sense suggestion to take root.

In 1909, the Legislature had a heavy discussion about taking northern pine barrens out of private hands for a generation to see what nature would do about restoring their productivity. Senator Foster from Gladwin and George Cummins were one hundred per cent opposed to this line of reasoning. They wanted the land put back into private hands because of the tax revenues. Schools received much of their support from the Primary Fund and this was fed by these state tax collections. It was later that the state contributed to each county an amount related to the total acreage in escrow.

The Clare County Board of Supervisors gave a flat footed endorsement to the concept of placing these lands back on the tax rolls. During a session in 1909 they passed a resolution which was sent to Lansing stating very clearly their opposition to the state set aside concept. The problem probably went deeper than just wanting to tax the land. Many men were convinced that the pine producing soils were actually slandered by the down staters when they said the soil was worthless. Some of it was, of course, but they didn't want to mis-label the entire county because of a few swamps. In addition, many still felt that outsiders and especially those who lived in the state's cities benefited more from the timber than did the county residents. As they saw it, northern Michigan's resources were expended as a sort of tribute to the southern counties. When roads, colleges, railroads or other improvements were needed by the southerners, the practice had been to use the timber lands. So large was the need by the other counties that few sections of land were available for the homesteader under the Homestead Act of 1862, and the farmers had to make do with stump lands. City men became millionaires off the resources of Clare county and the local resident barely was able to pay for a minimum standard of living.

When the city legislators wanted to tell the north how to use their lands in 1909, it was more than they would accept. They were not about to sacrifice the north's resources again.

Sam Bruce, Greenwood Township Highway Commissioner, stated it quite well when he told the Board of Supervisors in April, "The real issue is not to fight forestry, but to fight a movement to condemn the northern half of the state to benefit the southern half."

In May, the Flower's Forestry Bill was advanced to the House where it was killed on the floor. Detroit wanted to tell the rest of the state what to do, but this was in the time when the quantity of square miles determined the number of representatives more than population. There were several extreme things contained in the bill which pushed city priorities ahead of the rural interests. Representative George Cummins said, "There must be a recognition of proceeding from what is sanely to better conditions (sic) not just a million acres made into a state forest with one stroke."

By now it was clear that it would not be a simple thing for the Legislature to create a state forest. Land which had been reverted to the state around Roscommon had been under the custody of the Public Domain Commission for about a decade when this whole problem surfaced in the form of the Flower's Bill. Senator Foster went to Roscommon and looked around the public land already set aside. He was not impressed. His report showed that a total of $56,000 had been spent on the reserve up to 1909, yet there was less actual timber standing a decade later than was originally placed under the custody of the Public Domain Commission.

This fact alone wasn't the real reason a state forest was facing heavy sledding, but it gave the northern communities something to use in the floor debate going on in the Legislature. "There is a need for practical forestry," said Foster, "but the utter failure of the cities to treat the subject from the standpoint of the northern communities is the principal reason for the failure of the bill."

FOREST FIRES

Michigan's Forest Warden, Pierce, denied that the three great forest fires of 1871, 1881 and 1908 plus the smaller one in 1894 caused direct losses of forty-four million dollars in timber. He said the figure was closer to $2,500,000. This is very difficult to accept. There were 949 townships in thirty-six counties which were in the fire district, but eighty two townships failed to even report their fire losses, so the state didn't know which of the two conflicting amounts was the correct one. It was this lack of precision which presented the legislators with an indefinite problem and of an undefined magnitude.

The best way to resolve those issues in 1909 was to give them to the state's number one trouble shooter, A. J. Doherty, the ex-Senator. He was appointed the new Public Domain Commission Chairman in June. Explaining the problem to some friends in Clare, Doherty said that the problems facing the state were large, but "The Commission has just been organized. We'll feel our way very carefully to avoid mistakes . . . We are inventorying state lands to find the present status of reforestation in the reserve.

"We are also going to do all in our power to prevent forest fires this season. We have a fund of $10,000 for this purpose. Already there have been a number of fires in the Metz region, where so many lives were lost last year (1908). We are going to compel the railroads to equip their locomotives with serviceable spark arrestors. Without doubt, several of these fires were caused by locomotives not properly equipped."

True to his word, the legislature passed all of his suggestions into law. Within a very short period of time he brought the forestry problem closer to its solution.

In November of 1909, the federal government appointed Higgins to the position of state forester. His philosophy called for an emphasis on second growth, rather than seedlings in the national forest. His headquarters at Traverse City oversaw four rangers who assisted him. They were situated in Alcona, Iosco, Oscoda and Ogemaw counties.

Not everyone agreed with Higgins. Many thought that an active program of re-forestation from seedlings was a more direct approach and therefore a better policy. W. A. Rose, the ex-land Commissioner, ex-Civil War soldier and ex-state official believed in taking direct action if that was what the

situation called for. He planted thirteen thousand yellow and white pine seedlings saying, "It'll take fifty years for these trees to reach maturity, but let's begin now."

F. C. Martindale, a member of the Public Domain Commission agreed with Higgins, but he sought their common goal a bit more indirectly. His suggested course of action was to take all lands not fit for agriculture to be withdrawn from sale and to appraise such lands for their forestry use, with the state paying a local tax on all such land held in reserve. He reasoned that if the unproductive land was bringing in some tax to the local governmental units, they would be more amenable to the second growth concept. In this he probably was correct.

Another problem which confronted the Commission was the irregular shaped tracts and their scattered locations in the northern countries. W. B. Green, a district forest ranger, thought that the two holders of these parcels ought to exchange certain of their holdings so each would have contiguous forests. Doherty agreed that there was no merit in each forestry unit being responsible for the scattered forty acre parcels so they traded and evened up their preserves as best they could.

The reforestation plan for 1909 called for two large reserves, one being six by twelve

W. N. Ferris

miles and the other extending six by six miles. Doherty wanted a large planting so the young trees could serve as an object lesson to the residents. Enough seedlings were available so that individuals who already had seen the light could begin on their own reforestation project. Several residents of Clare county were in step with the Public Domain Commissioner including Will Adams, Charles Rockwell, and Josiah Littlefield.

W. C. Cornwell took the Commissioner at his word and planted a large number of seedlings on his Arthur township ranch. He reported a year later that they were all growing vigorously. Some more of the non-lumberjack farmers were added each year, but still the northern hills looked desolate compared to the lush greenery in Indiana and southern Michigan. Too few people were paying enough attention to the reforestation project.

Commissioner Doherty was a well traveled man and he knew that the initial efforts were pitifully small compared to the need. Using the Public Domain Commission as his platform, he began to urge all farmers to cultivate a woodlot on their farms. "There ought to be scores of woodlots in every township," he declared. "The need for a timber crop is every bit as vital as the supply of firewood. An apiary is an excellent addition to the permanent farm as is a sugar bush. A stand of trees will soon make the difference in the farmer's outlook if he will but make the effort," he concluded.

Acting upon Martindale's suggestion, the state in late 1909 withdrew 112,000 acres from the resale schedule and planted three million pine seedlings in the Reserve. Secretary Carton thought it was a mistake since pine trees grow so slowly. He suggested the pulp tree would be a better investment as they mature in fifteen years.

Another person who had an opinion on this subject was Robert J. Rayburn. He thought that farmers who owned land adjacent to the state lands ought to be supplied with seedlings with the state picking up the taxes assessed for the period of time required to grow a crop. When the timber was harvested, then the state would be re-imbursed

for its trees and taxes. Looked at from the pine lands around Alpena which was his home, this suggestion makes some sense. The individual would still be able to retain his land and the state would accomplish its goals as well. His plan could have been a benefit to everyone, but it was not to be.

The main problem with using the Houghton Lake-Roscommon Preserve as the only test site was the spectre of fire. It didn't require some old person to recall the past when it came time to consider this subject. Nearly every person in the north had personally lived through conflagrations which blackened the sky for days at a time. The terror which emanated from these fires was vividly etched in the forefront of their minds. In 1910 regular patrols were instituted by the Commission. Twenty five mounted police regularly rode the fire trails of the 275,000 acre preserve. The areas which had recently been harvested were more closely watched than the newly seeded tracts. Their success in controlling small fires enabled them to become the prototype of the later instituted fire warden system.

REAL ESTATE FRAUDS

While the trees were slowly re-growing, land still owned by private parties was used as a come-on for real estate promoters especially in Chicago. Considerable amounts of land was secured by graft through the machinations of second echelon officials in Lansing who turned titles to thousands of lots over to these bunco artists. In turn these lots were sold to individuals for higher than reasonable prices as they were touted to be resort property. Unfortunately for the new owners, most of these lots were nowhere near the water and were in effect useless to the purchaser. There were no provisions for individuals to gain access to the beautiful lakes in Roscommon and soon the majority of these lots once again became the property of the state when the $3 or $5 tax assessments failed to come in. The Public Domain Commission moved into this fraudulent scheme and clamped down on the Chicago operators. Since there were others in the real estate game also selling similar lots, the practice didn't stop completely, but the number of bilked buyers decreased significantly.

Soon traffic into the area was increasing to the point that the railroad couldn't accommodate them all. Public roads were being boomed by the Hotel and Resort Owners Association in these years and the road bees which improved the connection between Harrison and Houghton Lake made a real contribution to resorters going and coming in the northland.

A TURPENTINE FACTORY PROMOTION

While the state was wrestling with the esoteric problems of re-forestation, thousands of private tracts were cluttered with the ubiquitous stumps. To the private land owner they were a nettlesome problem because of the expense involved in their removal. Unless they were used for fences, these cumbersome remains of the lumbering era represented an investment of about $75 an acre to remove. Normally this was a direct cost because there was no economic gain to be derived from the sale of the stump.

Into this dilemma strode the Wolverine Turpentine Company, which appeared to offer an opportunity for the farmers to salvage most of his expenses. They further promised to remove from Clare county and its environs the unsightly stumps. B. F. Getchel of Evart was the local representative and he came to Clare in September of 1911 looking for a site which was near the railroad over which most of these stumps would have to travel. Two sites were selected. One was the now moribund Horning property just west of the Union Depot and the other was the Riverdale Stockfarm of Perry D. Brown's, lying one mile west of town.

The plant itself needed to be quite large and a large storage site would also be required. A Reduction Building 86' x 194' was planned to be adjacent to the Distillery which was to be 50' x 125'. Their operating schedule called for a start up in February of 1912.

An office was established temporarily in the Jackson Block and the construction phase began. Foundations were put in on the Horning site and then a decision was made to use cement block construction instead of wood. This necessitated newer and heavier concrete footings. When the workmen went about rectifying this mistake, some of the locals were given some reason to suspect the wisdom of the promoters. One brave soul even predicted that the whole affair would be a flop. Those were brave words in the Market City of Clare.

Joseph Yost of Lansing joined Getchel in Clare and sought out C. W. Perry, Clark Sutherland, J. M. Davis and a few others. They explained that the factory would be greatly strengthened if some local funds could be raised to help defray the heavy expenses of building the plant. One hundred thousand dollars was suggested to the local men as a desired amount of capital to be used in this wonderful addition to Clare's business community.

Meanwhile, G. A. Livermore was given a contract to make ten thousand cement blocks in his Evart factory. He was capable of making nearly four hundred a day and so by November 17th, he had seven thousand on hand. J. H. McDonald of Evart was hired to put the block walls up. During December a high wind came along and blew the entire south wall down. Since this was the main wall, this was a severe loss.

Clare's support would be forthcoming after the building was up, but now the company had a difficult task of even doing that much. They had expended their paid in capital on options of large tracts of stump land and so they had not enough to finish the buildings. No new money came in to continue the project and all of those visions the Clare people had of stumps being turned into money, just disappeared.

Lawrence Jackson sued the company for the back rent on the office space he furnished and this caused the company to fold up. Upon being told that the company was now gone, he said, "Our visions of transforming stumps into products ready for shipment to Pittsburg have been dispelled. All we have left is the spitoon and a small bottle of turpentine.''

Clare's big chance to become an industrial center was lying in the heap of broken and disheveled concrete blocks. The loss to the community and the stockholders was 100%. The farmers who thought the factory was too good to be true were correct, but they didn't gloat over the fact that they had been right all along.

GOVERNOR FERRIS AND REFORESTATION

Governor Ferris took office in January of 1913 and he immediately was faced with several problems, not the least of which were the forests of Michigan. The Michigan Forestry Association meeting in Saginaw on December 12, 1912, came up with a list of suggestions. They wanted the state to stop selling land fit for timber growing if that tract was larger than one hundred sixty acres. Their plan was to reserve this property for the seedlings which were now coming out of the nursery in Roscommon. They also suggested that the Governor appoint a competent state forester, whose office would be in Lansing. One of the roles they suggested for this new administrator was assistance to land owners who desired to plant trees.

The real kicker in their laundry list of recommendations was a proposal to exempt all timber land from taxes. Even though Ferris was a conservation minded man, he was unable to consider this scheme. One thing he could do however, was to re-appoint A. J. Doherty to a six year term as chairman of the Public Domain Commission. Every one understood that when dealing with public policy and private interests only a skilled politician and administrator could handle the task. Doherty at one time wanted to be the Governor of Michigan and he probably still had his eye on Lansing, but he could not serve his state more than by guiding us through this troublesome problem of our forests. Fortunately for us he accepted the appointment. The beautiful woods and forests we now enjoy are his legacy to us.

The Doctors

HEALTH SERVICES

Clare County had a very favorable ratio of doctors to citizens during the lumber era. Practically anyone who had the urge to be a doctor or owned a drug store could be one. Most were only superficially trained and the quality wasn't especially gilt-edged overall, but there were good physicians taking care of the needy. One such doctor was an ex-Dutch army physician who had served in the Boer Wars according to local lore, but he was loath to discuss those days. Dr. Donders practiced in the western townships, especially Garfield, as he lived in Sherman City of Isabella County. During Social Security days he was unable to qualify as his early years were a hidden past with no documentation available. His shadowy beginning didn't interfere with his qualifications, and he practiced until he was nearly one hundred years old.

Before the advent of hospitals in the county, hotels would often have a room or two which could be set aside for extended treatment, especially of the itinerants or those wounded by accidents. The Central Hotel served that role in Clare, Farwell had its Rust House and Harrison was serviced by the Northern or Commercial Hotel. Doctors would look in on the patients and a nurse was normally close by.

NURSING HOME

Most communities had their own little semi-hospitals where skilled nursing was available. Indigents were normally cared for at the County Poor Farm where an infirmary of sorts tended their needs, but not adequately. Clare and Mrs. Joseph Presley boarded up to six recouperating patients at a time. Her place was the best in the county between 1900 and 1912, the year she died. Joseph tried to continue on his own, but he had not the skill of his second wife. She was a jewel!

EPIDEMICS

Essentially there were two types of epidemics, one which afflicted the young and the other didn't discriminate by age. Scarlet fever periodically swept through an area, and the best remedy would be isolation or a quarantine of the victim. If the plague was widespread, schools would be shut down also. Clare County had a mild outbreak of 'La Grippe' during February and March to go along with its Scarlet Fever in 1900.

Cities such as Saginaw would be harder hit by the epidemics which hit in cycles. The flu, or La Grippe as it was called, struck in 1901 and caused considerable misery, but few fatalities.

PNEUMONIA

Health officers began treating this new health menace as an infectious disease in 1909. Instructions from the State Board of Health went out to county health officers who in turn took appropriate measures to inform the physicians currently treating patients in the county. Dr. James Reeder

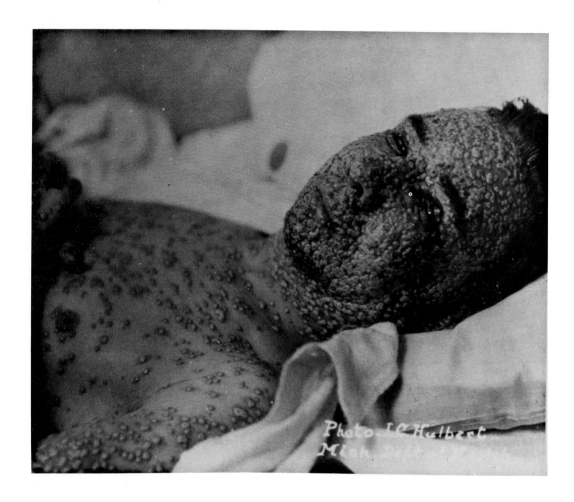

An extra severe case of small pox.
Photo: Michigan Department of State Archives

would frequently travel by train to the towns and check on things. Records began to show pneumonia replacing consumption as the number one killer in Michigan during the early decade of the new century.

Clare County had a lot of diseases extant during April of 1904. The records showed ninety-seven cases of small pox, eighty-eight measles, sixty-one pneumonia, fourty-four typhoid and twenty-eight diptheria cases during this month alone, with typhoid taking the most lives. It was virulent in other parts of Michigan also, including a major epidemic in Escanaba.

SMALL POX

Small Pox was feared by nearly everyone, as it could be passed on so easily from one person to another. Saginaw's barbers reported a very heavy rate of infection. In Clare, not a few deaths resulted, but its greatest impact was in the fear which accompanied its prevalence. Notwithstanding the fear, its lethalness was genuine. Authorities ordered deceased victims of small pox to be buried without public ceremonies, thus the danger could be limited to a few. One not able to avoid exposure was the undertaker.

Charles Thurston, an undertaker in Clare during this epidemic contracted the disease from a dead victim. He isolated himself in a room and remained completely alone for nearly two weeks, nursing himself and taking food which was set inside the door of his room by the family. Killer diseases were not something to take lightly!

The whole region along the Pere Marquette railroad from Kalkaska to Stratford was quarantined in March, and ticket agents weren't allowed to sell tickets to Sharon, Moorestown or Spencer. Michigan was experiencing a high death rate due to the outbreak which claimed 13.9 victims for each one thousand population. Pneumonia only took a total of two hundred seventy-one, while T-B claimed two hundred eight during the same time period. There were two thousand, nine hundred thirty-seven deaths in March of 1904 in Michigan. By May, the epidemic had run its course with only three people succumbing to its evil.

Animal disease could sometimes be passed along to humans, but generally, the distemper which ravaged the horse population wasn't such a threat. A farmer might lose most of his animals and suffer financial ruin, a calamity almost as lethal as other diseases. In 1904, horses were dying all over the county, and the veterinarians were kept busy disinfecting the contaminated areas.

T-B was a continuing problem in Michigan and deadly all during the pre-World War I era. To meet some of the needs of the victims, Governor Warner proposed in 1910, a T-B Hospital for the state, and appointed Dr. Frank R. Gray of Clare to serve on the new hospital's Board of Control. A delegation of Harrisonites came to lobby Dr. Gray about locating the facility in Hayes Township. They said the altitude and lakes, along with the central location in Michigan favored the site. People from Grayling didn't agree with this assessment however, and successfully lobbied its construction there.

The nation had a high death rate due to T-B, but Michigan was lower. Isabella normally lost twenty of its citizens each year and Clare mourned nine, both well below Michigan's rate.

DIPTHERIA

The catastrophic diptheria epidemics hit the heartland of Michigan during the 1880's. Then, the children were taken from their families in groups of two or three at a time, but four children in the same family has been noted in MICHIGAN'S TIMBER BATTLEGROUND. Still the disease came back again and again to buffet the children. One such child, Martha Conrad had her breathing completely blocked by the thick membrane which formed in her throat. Dr. Reeder was treating her when her breathing stopped. Reacting quickly, he, along with Dr. Thomas Maynard who had been summoned to assist, performed a tracheotomy which restored her breathing. Recovering consciousness she said, "Its nice to be alive again," a quote, along with her picture, which appeared all over Michigan in December 7, 1906. She was a frail child and didn't survive more than three or four years, its sad to say.

In 1911, the John W. Horan family in Arthur took sick and contacted Dr. Clute who diagnosed the problems as quinsy and follicular tonsilitis, and treated them accordingly. When the family didn't recover as rapidly as expected, a call went to Dr. Reeder who diagnosed the problem as diptheria, and quarantined the whole area.

Dr. Clute didn't take this affront to his medical skills lightly. He went back, took throat samples and sent them to the State Health Department in Lansing. Their report

Thurston Brothers hand-built this hearse on an Oldsmobile chassis. It was the first motorized hearse-ambulance in the county.

Photo from the Al Thurston Collection

said approximately, ''There is no diptheria culture present.'' So Clute went to the newspaper columns February 24, 1911, and gave Dr. Reeder a verbose boxing lesson about medicine. He impugned the good doctor's medical skills in diagnosis, since according to Clute, nearly every case that came to his attention resulted in a diagnosis of appendicitis and a subsequent removal of that organ. Clute said many things that he probably wished he hadn't, but when his wrath was hot, he made the reading of the local newspapers a very interesting occasion.

Dr. Reeder in rebuttal, contacted the State Board of Health and they told him that while they didn't find diptheria germs present in the culture, they couldn't rule it out either. He took to the newspaper also, and in a very rational letter attempted to explain what he did and why. When the affair was over, Horan's family recovered, but the doctors weren't speaking to each other for a very long time. No one else contracted diptheria, so probably both men could claim victory. Clute, because he felt the diagnosis was wrong, and Reeder, because he felt that

Dr. and Mrs. F. R. Gray

his quarantine stemmed the epidemic before it got started.

Diptheria continued in the district until the 1920's when a vaccine was developed to prevent its slaughter. Modern medicine scored a major victory with the wiping out of this scourge.

TYPHOID

Health officials long suspected that contaminated water was the cause of this deadly disease which is taken into the body via the mouth. Treatment of the disease was minimal until the advent of sulfur drugs, but prevention was possible during the early decades of this century. Of course that doesn't mean that it was prevented, because in many isolated instances it went through families like a land roller, leveling them all.

Most of Clare County's problem with this killer surfaced in the period between 1908-11. Farm families became the victims primarily. For instance the Burt Turner's children were left orphans when he and his wife, Altha, died in the fall of 1908. An uncle from Ohio came up and took the four boys back from whence they came five years earlier.

Hatton Township was hit quite hard in 1910, but then so was the rest of Clare County. Typhoid was widespread in the nation in 1909, with more people affected than there were cases of cholera in India. Five hundred thousand cases were reported resulting in a ten percent mortality rate. ''The prevalence of typhoid fever in the United States is a national disgrace,'' re-

Dr. William Clute

ported the CLARE SENTINEL on July 19, 1912, but it wouldn't be for long. Authorities went after the problem and scrubbed it out of the mortuary books.

SCARLET FEVER

Two small epidemics hit the region in 1912 and 1917. Officials acted promptly in both instances and the disease was contained before it emaciated the children.

INFANTILE PARALYSIS

This disease's first appearance in Clare County was in August of 1911. Its reputation preceded its entry into the northland, and adolescents and younger children began their summer vacations with a certain dread, knowing that August and September were becoming very dangerous periods that they had to face.

Dr. Reeder's transportation

SMALL POX AGAIN

Two rather formidable small pox outbreaks took place in the area. During the spring of 1910, Harrison had forty cases which the authorities knew about. Mannsiding School was hit hard and forced to close. By May 20th, the epidemic was over and public get-togethers commenced again. Coleman had two cases, and Clare schools closed two rooms which had been in contact

with the disease. The cases were all mild, and the infection from a Flint family was quickly put behind the inhabitants of Clare, although at times, victims appeared on the streets during the later phase of the disease and alarmed not a few.

Saginaw, however, was subjected to a terrorizing epidemic that fall. Every citizen in town had to be either vaccinated or quarantined for twenty-one days. Hundreds came out of the ordeal with pock-marked faces as forty-four died.

During the height of the danger, no one could leave Saginaw without fumigation, at least not legally. One drummer who rode the train into Clare was not allowed off because he bragged about his outwitting the authorities. November 13, and Monday the 14th were set aside in Saginaw and every person was implored to become vaccinated.

The Clare City Council unanimously quarantined all clothing which had come from the Saginaw steam laundries as part of the routine services offered here. Until the siege was over, no laundry could be sent to or received from Saginaw. Health officials met all passengers at the trains and demanded to see their certificates of vaccination. If they had a valid one, they were allowed to detrain for fumigation. Those who objected found themselves back on the trains.

Marshals Orrie Smith and Thomas Dwyer rigidly enforced Dr. Maynard's orders, especially with anyone coming from Saginaw's direction.

The Saginaw outbreak spread to Charlotte, Petoskey, Evart, Lapeer and environs. Dr. C. S. Knusman went to Lansing and explained to the State Health Board the situation as it appeared to him, the County Health officer of Saginaw. He quarantined every person not vaccinated, but he wasn't sure that he had the authority to be that inclusive. The governor thought the problem was serious enough and concurred with the edict. The governor then sent troops to seal off the State Home in Lapeer when a severe outbreak infected the inmates in November.

Terror and alarm spread throughout Saginaw and the citizens didn't need much prodding from city health officer Dr. C. L. Grube. All public assemblies were cancelled.

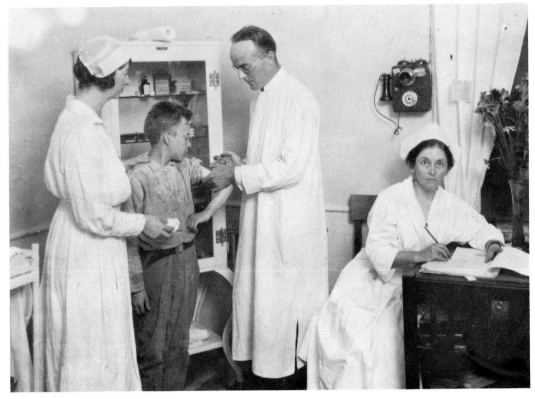

A young lad being given toxin-anti toxin as a preventative for diptheria, the child killer.
Photo: Michigan Department of State Archives

Family Thanksgiving get-togethers were banned as formaldehyde candles burned nightly in all public buildings.

Vassar, Midland, Mayville, Brown City, Reese and finally Clare barred all Saginaw passengers from alighting, according to the SAGINAW NEWS in November. Within a month of the quarantine, the epidemic peaked out, and gradually the worst was over.

A milder epidemic hit all of northern Michigan in the fall of 1917. A state health officer dispatched into the region upon the first case coming to the attention of a doctor, ordered all school children vaccinated. Some parents objected to their children having to be vaccinated and refused to comply. A meeting in the public restrooms in the Calkins basement, indicated that parents didn't want their children exposed to the disease if it could be contained. The school officials then and there decreed that no child could be admitted to school unless they had a success-ful vaccination and a good scar to prove it.

With this, the problem was contained locally, although a case was reported in the Hyslop School of Gilmore Township March of 1918, and another in Greenwood Township.

THE SPANISH FLU

La Grippe made its annual foray into the northern communities usually in the springtime or late winter. A mild outbreak in March of 1915 wasn't unusual, and it soon passed. In Europe, soldiers on the eastern front came into contact with a strain associated with China's borders, and a wave of sickness hit Russian and German troops in 1916.

The virus mutated and migrated into France and Spain where it changed again, this time into a more virile form. Soldiers were hit with this quite hard in 1917, but most recovered. American troops coming into Europe in larger numbers in late 1917 and early 1918 were met with this deadly "Spanish Lady", as it was being called over there. Nearly everyone was affected by it, but not all suffered the ravages that were to be so widespread in the United States during the fall and winter of 1918.

The pandemic was sweeping around the world in a vicious fashion as the war caused great problems to many. Poor diets, rest and sanitation added their bit to the plague. When it hit concentrations of adults in camps and cities, the deadly virus knocked them off like flies.

Between October 4, 1918 and April 21, 1919, Saginaw had 3,914 cases of influenza resulting in the deaths of 170 people. Camps like Custer, Great Lakes, Fort Sam Houston, Camp Travis or Fort Wayne had nearly that many deaths every week. The flu was overwhelming the army and navy.

One particularly sad coincidence surrounded James Garrity, a sailor stationed at Great Lakes. He died in January of 1918. A cousin, Albert Looker died a week later, and an additional cousin, John Ansil died within a month. Hamilton Township suffered three casualties in the war very quickly. In total, twenty-two men out of Clare's four hundred and fifty soldiers and sailors, died from the flu. A rate of nearly 5%.

While the flu hit hard in the district, the population of the heartland communities wasn't as concentrated as military camps and cities. Schools, church meetings, all public gatherings and casual visiting were on the list of discouraged activities, with most schools all over northern Michigan being closed from October until January 1, 1919.

The flu while debilitating in and of itself, nevertheless wasn't the direct cause of most deaths. The body was so ravaged by a three day bout with the virus, that pneumonia swept in and finished off the weakened victim. Survivors often had enduring complications such as meningitis, mastoids, or damaged hearts from secondary reactions. Dr. Kuno Hammerberg, then a young lad of nine, was walloped by the flu, a respiratory affliction and rheumatic fever. He survived the punishment, but his body needed about two years to fight off the Spanish Lady's

heavy hand:

Fifty-nine county deaths were directly related to the flu*, twenty-two of them being in the prime of life and serving their country. The county, however, never reached the epidemic proportions cities attained, and even reported the crest having passed through when Michigan was just approaching the maximum infections.

When the epidemic began, officials at Camp Custer volunteered to set up mobile medical units to assist communities which were overwhelmed. Within two weeks, Custer itself was under siege with the Medical Corps reporting 6,888 cases or 17% of the Army sick at a time. The hospitals were so full that men were released to "A" companies in all of the battalions to recover. Every regiment had a barracks reserved for men who showed any indication of coming down with the disease, and nearly everyone in this quarantined area contracted a virile case.

Doctors worked day and night in the military hospitals as well as in the cities and rural areas. General Laubach, commander of the 14th Division, requested fifty doctors for immediate detachment to Washington Hospitals, but his request was turned down. There weren't fifty doctors which were in surplus anywhere in the country. Doing the next best thing—selecting three hundred men who had some knowledge of medicine, he created his own corps of medical personnel.

Some towns offered to send nurses to camps, but the military didn't want to infect others, so they refused the offers. Trained nurses went anyway in large numbers and relieved the bone wearied staffs in camps and city hospitals all over. Mrs. Floyd Doherty for example went to a camp in Iowa, and a Farwell nurse went to Ford Hospital.

As the epidemic gathered its forces, the state and nation went on a campaign to disperse the people so the space between bodies would make it more difficult for the germs to spread. All institutions were ordered closed in New York, Philadelphia, Washington, Detroit, Cleveland, Chicago and elsewhere. Troops about to be assembled for shipment overseas had their orders cancelled, and the staging areas on the east coast were

*See Appendix for those who died.

nearly deserted.

The concentration of the population downstate alerted officials to the problems and Clare County isolated its citizens before the disease barely got off the ground here, but it was still deadly enough.

The CLARE SENTINEL said, ''The epidemic which is raging in various sections of the country seems to be about stationary here in town. New cases seem to arise about as fast as old ones recover. No deaths have occurred on account of it recently and all recover quickly when they are properly cared for. This week will probably see a marked improvement in this matter.'' This October report was premature, however.

Winterfield schools opened up in the first half of November, and Freeman Township missed the entire October bout, which was the most devastating epidemic ever sustained in Clare County. Greenwood on the other hand, had a 100% contraction of the disease.

During November of 1918, flu deaths accounted for more deaths than the war up until Armistice Day, and after that, of course, combat fatalities dropped way off. Seventy eight thousand were reported dead in forty-six cities in the first half of November—all across the nation.

When 'Peace Sunday' was proclaimed for November 17th, people gathered in churches and gave thanks for victory; but the flu flared up again and went rampaging in the communities that celebrated. 'Peace Sunday' was celebrated nearly everywhere, and the flu epidemic was rejuvenated.

A few weeks or months after the flu had run its course, T-B began taking over. This was a delayed repercussion, and it was feared nearly as much as the flu.

The doctors of the community worked overtime during the outbreak and rumor had it that some took drugs to keep going. Dr. Clute went without sleep so much that he hardly left his auto. He had a chauffeur who took him on his calls and those few moments constituted his night's quota of slumber. His relatively abbreviated life span was said to have been caused by this flu epidemic.

Fear induced a lot of wierd reactions in the way people attempted to deal with the virus. ''Some people wore a cotton ball soaked in a concoction of carbolic acid around their neck, probably hoping the germs couldn't stand the odor and would go away. Other equally intelligent people would wear asafoetidas of camphor, onions and other inhuman odoriferous charms about the neck, perhaps on the homeopathic theory that 'likes cures like'. Some people drank a pint of whiskey each day while others put sulfur in each shoe on a daily schedule,'' according to Dr. Clute.

The CHRISTIAN SCIENCE MONITOR said that fear was the cause of the Spanish Flu epidemic. ''Indeed, fear is the provoking cause of all evil of every sort,'' it claimed in January of 1919.

Dr. Reeder took issue with their logic and said in the SENTINEL, ''a bullet may kill a soldier whether he fears or not. Likewise a microbe attacks humans whether they fear or not. If the Christian Scientists would come out and say that bullets didn't kill soldiers, fear does, people would be better able to evaluate their reasonings.''

It may really have been fear that provoked the Spanish Flu epidemic. It it was, America was in a terribly fearful state right on the eve of victory.

DEATH RECORDS

A new law went into effect for Michigan which required a more accurate and timely registration of deaths in September of 1903. Licensed embalmers were eligible for appointment to become sub-registers of death. Previously, township clerks kept those records, but they weren't accurate at all. A relative of the deceased might show up a year later and register the death if it was done at all, and officials would be greatly limited in their ability to keep reliable control over their mortality figures.

CHILDHOOD DISEASES

Some diseases were always present, but in a dormant stage during these years. Measles, chicken-pox, whooping cough, and ague, the catch-all name for any illness which resulted

Harold and Edna Potter

in the 'shakes', were the major ones, although diptheria still raged off and on until the end of the war. Smallpox vaccinations were available around 1912 but many didn't avail their children to its protection.

Lock-jaw cases were numerous immediately after the July celebrations each year, as firecrackers, toy pistols, and gunshot wounds caused most of these. Rabies was another threat, generally to children through dogs who had contacted the disease. Simon Utley had a dog which was bitten by a rabid feral animal. Next, the stray got into the hog pen and bit a hog. Utley shot the stray dog, the hog and quarantined the others in an attempt to control it. The Utley dog worked his way loose and ran towards Farwell. Someone shot it and gave it back to the owner, who then sent its head to Ann Arbor for a diagnosis.

RABIES

Cattle weren't immune to wild dogs which had rabies either. Lewis Rawson lost two young heifers in Gilmore Township to a wild dog in 1907. He and some neighbors went out and began killing the ferals, bringing down about fifty free roaming canines.

H. H. Hinds, president of the Michigan Livestock Sanitary Commission came to Garfield and Gilmore and then ordered men to shoot every dog running at large. Hundreds of dogs were put out of circulation, and the incipient epidemic was brought under control.

STATE CONTROLS OVER HEALTH INCREASES

Health problems in the state were at best, under weak controls by the authorities, mostly because the state of the art hadn't progressed significantly for several years. Antibiotics were still in the future, but sulfur was available for all that it was worth. Michigan was inundated by men who had varying degrees of medical training and skills, and scores traveled a circuit, promising grandiose cures for every conceivable problem.

Dr. A. B. Spinney for example, set up an office each month in the Calkins for the afflicted to come in for either a treatment or a fleecing. He promised cures for epilepsy, paralysis, blood poisoning, eye and ear diseases as well as piles.

Dr. W. R. Soper, working out of Evart, limited his traveling road show to curing cancer. "If I fail to remove the cancer there is no charge," he said. And then there were the drugless healers who practiced; some of whom were the hypnotists, chiropractors, and Christian Science practitioners.

Governor Ferris wanted to bring these medical people under state control so he promoted a bill which went into effect in 1913 and 1915 to limit the services and advertising doctors could promote. "Michigan is at present a camping ground for all kinds of medical fakirs," he said in his State of State Address, January 3, 1913.

An example he used was a famous catarrh remedy, which was vaseline with a wintergreen smell. It sold for a 3,000% mark up on it. The United Doctors Specialists who claimed to cure chronic diseases in one day only, was also pointed out. Both of these examples were pertinent to the Clare area.

When the law took effect, the Dr. A. B. Spinney Maternity Hospital in Ionia was the first such facility to be closed. It also incorporated the registration of births, and the treatment of the newly born infant with a prophylaxis to be applied to the eyes as a precaution against veneral disease's effects.

Once the state began becoming more aggressive in these affairs, other rules and regulations followed. Drinking cups had to be removed from all public places, such as trains, boats, depots and so on. Travelers began carrying their own collapsible metal cups which were commonly used. This was the goal of legislators for years, but vested interests somehow or other prevented its passage.

Cigarettes were another problem, and in 1915, the Morford Anti-Cigarette Bill was passed 85-0. This law was enacted because some high school boys went to Lansing and pleaded with the legislators to pass a law which would protect them and their fellow students. From March 1915 on, it was unlawful for a minor to smoke or receive cigarettes. After the bill went to the gover-

nor's desk, there were many legislators who began feeling uneasy about its enforcement, but it went on the books anyway.

Green oranges were the target of health officials during 1911 as many were coming into Michigan. Some were poisonous, and the Florida Citrus Exchange offered one hundred dollars for the first railroad car confiscated by officials.

Meat products were loosely regulated and there were many humorous jokes poked at some of the current practices. In 1912, when the cream buyers were scouring the rural districts, one correspondent to the CLARE SENTINEL said, "With cream selling at thirty cents/c.w.t. (sic) cows are too valuable to turn into bologna when dogs will do just as well." One hopes that this was all in jest, but current practices don't support such assumptions. A lady reported a few months earlier of finding dog toenails in a ring of bologna.

Farm patrons who came to town on Saturday were hard put to find bathroom facilities. Men could patronize the saloons and they always had toilets available. Women and men who didn't frequent the drinking establishments had a difficult time of it, even after the 1915 law was passed which mandated towns to provide public bathrooms.

Manager Brown of the Central Gas Co. in Clare, upon hearing of a petition the rural ladies had presented to the city of Clare for compliance with the two-year-old law, suggested using the Calkins basement. This was looked into, and a large room fronting on the south and west corner was made available for the public. Chairs were provided and it made for a very comfortable gathering spot for rural and town folk. This facility stayed in use until May 15, 1918 when a new proprietor took over the hotel. Henry Rohr wanted to turn the meeting room into a sandwich shop with soft drinks available, and he did in June. The ladies were pushed aside again.

A WAR ON CATS

Governor Ferris was a very blunt man. He had a streak of independence which

199

comes easily from a man who is convinced that he is on the right track. His interest in conservation was widely known, and he caused a law to go on the books which made it open season on maurading cats. When the trees were cut down, birds had a hard time surviving, especially when cats were allowed to run loose. "We need more birds, not more cats," was his favorite line, when asked about his views.

He also had some other pretty sound views concerning marriage laws. It was not uncommon for close relatives to marry or for mentally deficient to produce twice as many children as normal families, so he proposed legislation which regulated the marriage laws of these groups. To highlight the problem, he proclaimed February 9, 1913, as "Eugenics Day" in Michigan. His rationale was that "degenerates and disease victims are multiplying twice as fast as the normal population in Michigan . . . our prisons are getting more crowded . . . saloons are out of control and the bawdy houses are wide open."

The bill he proposed was similar to one submitted in 1911. This time it succeeded in passing the legislative hurdles, but its ninety day waiting period and a six week application for marriage licenses were substantially modified.

The federal government was moving in a similar direction at this time also. The 'Mann Law' which prohibited certain aspects of white slavery was being tested in the famous Wilson case in Chicago. In March of 1913, a year before the case was decided, D. C. Murdock came to Clare, gathering primary information on local prostitution. The results were to be published by Clifford G. Roe, who was the Assistant District Attorney in Chicago. "It should make for interesting reading, if they got their facts," said a local observer of the Clare scene.

TELEPHONES

The new century found the northern communities still nearly isolated from the outside world except for magazines, newspapers and mail itself. Quick communication was available if the telegraph was sufficient for the needs of the citizen, or sometimes contact with Rosebush could be made over the line strung by A. J. Doherty in the later part of the 1880's. In the southern part of Michigan, many independent phone companies were in the process of being absorbed by the aggressive Michigan Telephone Company, based in Marshall, Michigan.

The Bell Company bought exchanges in Detroit, Ann Arbor and Jackson early in 1900 plus about twenty-five percent of their state trunklines. Competition by the Erie Telephone Company was strong about this time, as the Central Michigan Telephone Company was absorbed in February of 1900; but independent phone companies in Gratiot and Isabella retained ninety percent of their stock, thus preventing their being taken over. When the new State Telephone Company was consolidated with the Michigan Telephone Company, rates were jumped from twelve dollars per year to eighteen dollars. Business phones increased to twenty-four dollars.

Clare had a Citizens Telephone Company operating its "Central" out of the Central Drug Store in March of 1900. Service by the new company was said to be "excellent". The big phone company in town as the century dawned, though, was the Union Telephone Company. Sixty subscribers were 'on the line' and connections to one hundred forty-eight towns were worth bragging about. Harrison was serviced by the Citizens Telephone Company.

The Michigan State Telephone Company purchased the Citizens and by May of 1900 had pushed ahead aggressively and commandeered sixty-three phones in Clare, many of which were also subscirbing to the Union Network. Their efforts to become the major telephone company in Mt. Pleasant moved along and they began improving their equipment, replacing the old magneto system with a battery. The operators appreciated this, as about two thousand five hundred calls a day had to be "ground" out by the hand generator. To pay for this expansion, the Michigan Telephone Company borrowed five million dollars from the Old Colony Trust Company of Boston.

One hundred customers were now on the system in 1902, so Union moved its "Central" to the bank and F. B. Doherty went out into the hustings seeking to begin the organization of the district independent phone companies. The only trouble with his plans was in the person of Charlie Calkins. Calkins was now managing the Michigan Company which took over Citizens. He moved his "central" out of the drugstore, and located it in the more spacious quarters of the Clare Hardware Company's office on the second floor.

Doherty, promoting his company, said that he'd provide "all-night" service as soon as a hundred subscribers were enrolled, a number nearly on the books in 1902. The Michigan phone put that many on in a month's time as the North Arthur Telephone Company was organized by L. W. Sunday in cooperation with Calkins.

Connections were being made nearly every day as the construction crews were working Grant, Sheridan, Colonville, Dover and Arthur. Winterfield was connected to Marion when the Grandon Independent Telephone Company was installed in 1903. Farwell organized an independent company with a Union line to Clare.

When all of the phones were connected, Charlie made a trip to Farwell and bought the whole network, thus depriving Union of Clare of that district. Calkins didn't slow down now as this was the key year in determining who was going to be dominant in Clare, Union or Michigan. Lines were extended to the Herrick Roadway Company in Sheridan, Stevenson Lake, and another to Arthur Township. An extension through Arthur connected Harrison.

Union put a line to Sheridan and another to Dover as thirty more customers were enrolled.

Over in the Saginaw and Flint area, the Valley Telephone Company began swallowing up the independents, trying to stay ahead of the monopolistic Bell Company. In Clare, Calkins was doing his best to avoid a later take-over as he aggressively entered into contracts with the following independents: Wise Telephone Company; Sheridan Roadway Company; Gilmore Union Telephone Co.; Mannsiding Telephone Co.; McDonald Independent Telephone Co.; Lake Telephone Co.; Pleasant Valley Telephone Co. (eastern Grant Twp.); Greenville-Clare Independent Telephone Co. (W. Grant); and Maple Grove Telephone Company.

Frank Bowers replaced Calkins in 1905 as the Michigan manager, only later to be replaced by C. F. Broderick. Union appointed George Wall to take Frank Doherty's position, as A. J. was pushing his electrical generators for more capacity, and it was too much to run both utilities, especially with the competition the Bell Company was exerting.

By 1918 the competitors were reaching for a dominant position in Mt. Pleasant. Recent rulings by the State Railroad Commission allowed one company to become a monopoly if there were two competitors. In the settlement, Union took Mt. Pleasant and about

half of Isabella, Mecosta, Clinton, Midland, Shiawassee and Saginaw counties and a monopoly in Gratiot and Montcalm. Bell was permitted Rosebush and the townships north to go with Clare and the Harrison independents which had come along in 1914. These were the Maple Grove Telephone Co., 1st Ward Telephone Co., Swedish Telephone Co., Union and Bell.

The last independent company organized during this era was the Mud Lake Telephone Company in Lincoln Township, organized in February of 1919.

Michigan Bell bought out the Union Company operations in Clare on July 1, 1919.

ELECTRICITY

Clare and Harrison began the new century with a modicum of electrical power, nearly all of it being dedicated to lighting the streets until midnight, unless the moon was full, in which case no lights were turned on. The first generators which turned out Clare's electricity were steam powered. A proposal by the Tobacco River Milling Company, which owned the dam site on the mill pond in Clare, was turned down in favor of the local townsman.

In May of 1900, the original contract with the Doherty Light and Power Company was expiring. The city wanted more lights, especially near the depot, and extensions on both ends of McEwan Street. There was some agitation for the city's purchasing its own equipment but a council member said, "Mr Doherty is in a position to light the city and run the water works for less money than the city can possibly do it."

By June, and agreement had been reached which called for A. J. to build a three hundred dollar building to house the steam generators and to furnish water for a sprinkler on main street, plus lights in the hose house and city hall. Four additional arc lights were to be installed and all candle power to be increased to twenty thousand. The street lights were to be operated from dusk to twelve each night. All of this cost the city only $188.48 each month.

A. J. had leased the Milling Light and Power Company's generator down on the dam, and incorporated its output to supplement his steam generators. He constructed a 64' x 64' building and transfered the sixty horsepower boiler there and added a new heavy duty two hundred horsepower boiler to be the main power source.

Harrison's lights were furnished from the Pittsburg Steel Company's generators, which supplied their stave mill with electricity, but since the voltage varied so much, the lights weren't as satisfactory as the gasoline lamps.

A. J. Doherty had first proposed to the city in 1895, ten arc lamps for the main street and immediate area adjacent to it, plus supplying the water pumps with steam for one hundred twenty five dollars a month. The city rejected this by saying, "We need better terms than your first offer." They suggested one thousand two hundred fifty dollars a year and the counter-offer of one thousand three hundred dollars was accepted.

The lights, mounted forty feet above ground were turned on April 25, 1895, as a new superintendent came into town during March to make the final arrangements. C. H. Clark became a partner to Doherty and supervised most of the operation.

Farwell didn't have electric lights until a special bond issue passed in November of 1915, although the Case House in 1905 installed its own lights, becoming "The best lit building in Farwell."

LIGHTING ACCIDENTS

The new facilities helped relieve some of the night's darkness, but in November of 1903, Tom Holbrook, who went across the street, returned to his store and ran into a wagon which had parked in front with a long piece of well pipe protruding beyond the body of the wagon. As he was trotting at the time, the impact with the pipe knocked out five teeth, plus himself.

Another mishap took place in the Lewis and Patrick's hardware store about a month later. A gasoline lamp began to leak, and soon flames engulfed the lantern and the surrounding fixtures. The firm's tinsmith saw the flames, grabbed one of the Ajax fire extinguishers the town had placed all around town, and threw the dry charge on top of the fire. The flames were snuffed and a major fire had veen averted. A. R. Canfield was impressed! He said, "For incipient fires, the Ajax is certainly a deceivable extinguisher."

The winter of 1904 was cold, and a lot of ice formed on the mill pond in Clare. Along about the last of February, some ice dislodged one corner of the Callam and Cornwell's electric powerhouse and fifty feet of the dam was torn out on the north end. Since the spiles were undamaged, a new clay bank was all that was required to put things back in operation again. Some problems, though, were more serious, and required a large outlay of money.

The new dynamo Doherty had hooked onto his two hundred horsepower boiler in 1901 burned out and it took three thousand dollars to replace the 2,300 volt generator. A poor transformer was the culprit this time.

A NEW ERA DAWNS

A. J. negotiated a third five year contract with the city of Clare which extended his responsibilities to the town until 1911. Before this termination date, a new power company from Mt. Pleasant, the Chippewa River Power Co. proposed to build five dams between there and Midland. They began a bidding campaign with the city of Mt. Pleasant in May of 1909. The total head on the river, they computed to be one hundred twenty-three feet.

Another company was also planning and building dams in Michigan, namely, the construction and holding company of Consumers Power Company. They were going to build a series of dams on the AuSable River, beginning with the "Cooke" which was completed in 1911. Its completion opened up a great demand for electricity which was more than the company expected at first. Soon fourteen other dams were on the way, finalized by the Foote Dam with its ninety foot head.

Immense power was now being generated

This utility pole was located in Clare at the corner of Pine and Fifth Street.

by the ten thousand horsepower turbines and water was backed up eight miles by each one. One hundred forty thousand volts of surging energy zinged down the wires to the Zilwaukee transmission point, thus proving the potential E. A. Cooley and J. C. Hewitt had suspected. (see: *Future Builders*, McGraw-Hill 1973, pp. 151.)

The Chippewa River Power Company never completed its dams before the Consolidated Light and Power Company came along and purchased its assets. Consolidated took over the Doherty Light and Power Company, but not the dam, because the estate of William Callam, the builder of the electrical facility, negotiated its return from A. J. before Consolidated's deal was completed. Henry B. Tingley was appointed manager of the dam site and also was the head miller for the Callam Milling Company.

Consolidated, meanwhile, took over the contract for supplying the electricity to Clare, and Frank B. Doherty stayed on as the local manager. His new office in the Dunwoodie Building, 5th Street at McEwan, contained a supply of electrical accouterments, and the homes and businesses of Clare were now in a position to be serviced more adequately than before.

This period of time between 1909-1914 was one of great expectancy and actual expansion in this region. Farwell even began thinking about a municipal electrical plant, but it wasn't finalized until a bond issue was approved in 1915. The Clare franchises suffered from the voltage variances caused by the Callam generator, so Doherty was glad to see that contract expire back in 1911. It gave the steam generators a commanding lead in Clare, and wasn't again headed until the dams on the Chippewa began to come on the line.

Consolidated Light and Power Company hustled its five dams to completion so it could take on the task of supplying the electrical needs of several small towns in the Isabella area. With the purchase of the Schultz-Prindle interests for $18,000, J. L. Hudson, president of Consolidated began looking for the fifty towns he needed. To start with, they ran a power line from Beaverton to Clare, thus giving service twenty-four hours a day to four mills, two elevators and one printing office.

THE GRANGE OBJECTS

Consumers was negotiating heavily with bankers from New York, and the Consolidated Company was being strained by its underfinanced expansion. In 1914, the Grange adopted the following resolution at its state meeting: "We view with apprehension the growing tendency toward monopolizing the water power of the country, and we urge congress and the several state legislatures to enact early legislation to prevent a water monopoly and to preserve as far as possible, that most inexhaustible source of power for the welfare of all the people."

Where the money should come from, if not the financiers and monopolists, wasn't stated. The gargantuan problems weren't addressed either, and they probably didn't understand the technical problems which small water-powered electrical procedures scattered along the streams and rivers would entail.

THE 1915 SQUABBLE

The Consolidated Light and Power Company had gone into receivership about the time consideration for a new electrical contract between it and the city of Clare was to be negotiated. Some men in town thought that the concept of a municipal power plant had merit, especially when Consolidated's future was so clouded with financial burdehs.

Mayor Will Adams didn't want to consider a proposal by David Ward that the city buy the mill site which the Callam Estate still owned. They had sold the mill to Jones, but the generators were retained by them. Jones had a clause in the agreement which said that he could purchase electricity from the Estate for ten years at two cents per k.w.h., with no limits on how much he could use. A few thought that Jones could expand his Clare Roller Mills and the city would have to furnish all the electricity he wanted for two cents.

F. E. Doherty, now manager for Consolidated's interests, wrote a letter indicating that municipal ownership wasn't all that wonderful. He made three major points: first, most such plants are mortgaged for all they are worth; second, the interest paid by the city is equivalent to the profits a share-

holder would receive; and third, most municipal ownership is really private ownership under municipal control.

A petition, which had been circulated earlier and was signed by over two hundred citizens, called for a termination of the contract with Consolidated when it was due for renewal. Mayor W. L. Adams himself had signed it before the embranglement centered upon purchasing the Callam dam site. Two hundred signatures in a small town the size of Clare were hard to ignore.

An ad hoc citizen's committee did some rapid calculations and estimated that the gross revenue from the sale of electricity would be $500 each month times ninety-six months, or a total of $48,000. Expenses calculated at $1,200 a year for interest and $1,500 for labor would at the maximum, cost $22,080. Since the total price of the facility was only $18,000, a tidy profit ought to be earned, they reasoned.

The committee began roasting the council members during the regular meetings. "When has there been any figuring done to save the taxpayer in the way of lights?" asked E. C. Aukcompaugh. "Why did the council spend so much time in looking up high rates in parts of Michigan when you should have been looking for better rates and services for Clare?" asked George Easler. Finally, Charlie Grill asked the council, "Why are we being billed at ten cents k.w.h. rather than four cents?" To these questions the council had few satisfactory answers.

The city requested a report on the condition of the Callam dam and started by asking engineer S. B. Wiggins, the man who had installed the dam in 1892 for Alden Varney of Detroit. A representative came in his place to the Clare City Council and made a report that a replacement for the dam would cost $66,000, including eighty acres of land at twenty-five dollars an acre. A new dam site was projected at $52,400, and he said that a salvage price for the pond and facilities would exceed the Callam price of eighteen thousand dollars.

However, William Ryan, a mill man with thirty years' experience, said the mill ought to have a concrete foundation and structure, but barring any abnormal conditions, the dam ought to be good for a few more years.

With this, A. R. Canfield stood up and said, "In the event of an accident, necessary repairs either to the dam or wheel pit, it would be necessary to close down the plant, thus throwing the city and its private consumers into darkness as well as to materially handicap every institution that was using the current for power."

Dr. Dunlop then asked that a referendum be placed on the spring ballot for $25,000 The next meeting was a special one, and Tom Holbrook asked for the same referendum. The council moved to adopt it for placement on the April 5, 1915 election.

Paul Leake wrote an article in the MICHIGAN TRADESMAN and quoted in the CLARE SENTINEL April 2, 1915, hit very hard against public ownership of utilities. He claimed that most municipal light plants were failures.

Editor Andrus of the SENTINEL said the key question was, "Can a municipally owned generating plant be made to succeed under any circumstances, or is it the nature of the case doomed to failure? No man should favorably vote for the dam lighting project unless he feels reasonably sure of its ultimate success."

When the vote was cast, the dam went out the window. Within a week, the city council met secretly and signed a five year contract with Consolidated Light and Power Company. City clerk Seymour Andrus wasn't notified about the meeting or the vote, but approximately thirty-five citizens heard about it and were present for the contract signing.

"We think this is the rottenest deal ever in Clare," one of the witnesses said later. Others were trying to negotiate for some replacements to the council, although the new term of office was just one week old.

There was a lot of talk about a recall vote, but when everything settled down, Consolidated was still generating electricity. The sparks came from the disgruntled die-hards who felt betrayed, not the burned out transformers.

Within a year, the Detroit Trust Company, acting as Receiver for the bankrupt Consolidated Light and Power Co. sold the assets to J. L. Hudson, its former president, through W. A. Pelzold, treasurer of the J. L. Hudson Company in Detroit.

Farwell voted in November of 1915 to put in a municipal power plant identical to the one Roscommon had installed. Both were successfully operated.

Harrison, however, had a different problem. When the Pittsburg Steel Company went out of the stave business in 1909, the O.D. Cleveland Company took it over. All new equipment was installed in 1911, but the whole system went dead in December of 1915. Everyone had to go back to gas and kerosene lanterns. "The city had to resort to the Standard Oil System," observed a wag.

The Clare facility was allowed to run down by the Detroit group and when the problems of war and the acute shortage of coal hit in 1917, the city adopted an ordinance (#95) which permitted the purchase of electricity from the O'Keefe's plant, after a favorable vote was held in the spring of 1918.

CITY GAS LINES

N. J. Brown, manager of the Mt. Pleasant Light and Fuel Co., came to Clare February, 1916, and presented Clare with a proposition to furnish them cooking and lighting gas. The company needed access to street right-of-ways for the gas lines, and attempted to entice them with the statement, "As wood becomes increasingly scarce, it might be used as a replacement for that in heating the homes."

Donald M. Canfield was in Washington, D.C. at the time the gas franchise came up for the public airing in Clare, and he wasn't aware of it, nor was he consulted in any manner about it. The proposition had gone to the City Council for a vote when he pulled into town in March.

Incensed because he had been left out of the discussion, Canfield attempted to scuttle the franchise. In an open letter appearing in the CLARE SENTINEL, March 23, 1916, N. J. Brown said:

"Every town has its wise dictators and unless their O.K. is obtained, they balk, kick over the traces and try to break the bulwarks of prosperity and property.

"You underestimate the wisdom of your people! You are not their boss, Bossism is dead! You are not their dictator. They will not follow your lead . . . You would have the gas franchise defeated so other interests would be benefited . . .

"You are the 'lone-star' whose luster is tarnished by self-interest. The grumbler is always willing to find excuses for exercising his specialty."

Mayor David Ward called a meeting open to the public in Davis' garage March 28, 1916, and one hundred fifty men showed up. C. W. Perry spoke after Brown had concluded his remarks. A straw vote showed about eighty percent affirmative.

A letter from the Consolidated Light and Power Co. stated that they had no interest in the gas franchise and had no desire for it to be defeated at the polls.

With that the town went to the polls and voted "yes" for a thirty year franchise. The gas lamp posts were to be kept painted and meters furnished to the customers without charge, and the gas could not be sold for a rate higher than $1.40.

Clare's project was completed by January 1, 1918, right at the height of the severe coal shortage. The gas service had been installed in Mt. Pleasant, 1906, while Midland gained its benefits in 1916.

The pipe line from Mt. Pleasant was laid in a trench one foot wide and two and a half feet deep. Five carloads of pipe were used, and it had cost the company ten thousand dollars just for the material.

Three large compression tanks were ordered, two for Clare and one for Mt. Pleasant, to keep an even pressure on the lines. The big steel chambers were 36' x 8'.

As the ditches went through Vernon, old logs which had been thrown in the soft spots were snagged, but the machine kept on moving ever northward.

An open house held in Clare in August, 1916, featured a gas hot water heater which kept the temperature an even one hundred forty degrees Fahrenheit. It was the hit of the whole show! W. H. Elden won a gas range, which was the door prize. Clare was on the front burner at last!

Schools

The county of Clare encompasses nearly 570 square miles of swamps, lakes, rivers, hills, plains and forests of varying densities. Scattered over these 364,000 acres were the homes, farms and businesses of approximately 8,000 citizens, 2,000 of which were of school age, as determined by the school attendance law enacted in 1870. Communication and transportation within the county, with its sixty-plus school districts, normally was by horse-drawn carriages, trains or "shank's stage".

Had all of the school children been evenly distributed, each square mile within the county would have contained 3.5 students. Of course, this density was never reality, because people lived in towns, rural communities centered around churches or country stores, and on fertile farm land which could support a family. In practical terms, this meant that 42% of the county's population was concentrated in Arthur, Grant and Sheridan Townships, including the city of Clare.

A pattern for rural, one-room school distribution usually had children living within 1½ miles of their instructional centers. A township would have between three and eight school districts, each governed by a three-person board. A director, moderator and inspector were the positions usually held by men, but women sometimes filled the roles. Funds for hiring the teacher, paying for the heating wood supply, plus one coat of paint each year, were supplied from the State's Primary Fund. Two to seven dollars were available each year, depending upon payments from the railroads and other cor-porations. Most districts had to supplement the state's contribution with monies raised locally.

When the Panic of 1893 (which many people attributed to the Republican capitalists reacting to the Democratic victory in 1892) hit the northland, most school boards sought to reduce expenses to approximate the lower amount of Primary monies. Since a teacher's wage constituted 75% or more of the budget, most savings were sought in this direction. Women worked for less money than men, so men's contracts were usually terminated. Women became dominant in the rural one-room schools just before the new century arrived, and were receiving about $25 each month.

Town schools, such as Farwell, Clare and Harrison kept a man on to be the Superintendent, but all of the others were hired on the basis of cheap wages.

THE EIGHTH GRADE GRADUATE

A high school diploma wasn't a common document in the early years for many reasons. Often a student would be orphaned or the father would die, leaving the family in dire economic straits. If a lad was twelve or older, he was expected to take on his share of financing the family. Before 1905, this meant that the County School Commissioner had to approve a request made through the local school administration before the youngster under fourteen could drop out of school. Permission was granted quite freely prior to 1905 in Clare County, especially while Asa Aldrich was Commissioner.

If a lad or lassie was fortunate, they would eventually become candidates for graduation from the eighth grade. This was considered to be a red letter day for the student and family. Teacher-administered tests were given to the students, and generally, with some help from a friendly tutor during the examination, most qualified for the diploma. However, beginning in 1904, all candidates had to assemble in a central location for the County School Commissioner to monitor their examinations. Twenty-two applicants took the test during that May, and not one eighth-grader passed.

The teachers were all summoned to Harrison in June of 1904, and the "riot-act" was read to them by Commissioner Edgar G. Welch. Most of those who intended to remain in the teaching ranks hustled off to Mt. Pleasant, where they began to learn a few things about standardized tests.

Since graduates of the eighth grade were eligible for admission to the normal colleges, many had by-passed the high schools, opting for a two-year program which certified them as teachers by age sixteen. Now, with more formal class work, these young teachers went back to their one-room schools and tried again. In 1905, of the forty-eight who attempted the examination, thirteen passed. A year later, thirty out of sixty-seven were successful. Some eighth graders were having to spend three or four years in order to graduate.

Gradually the tests became common knowledge, and the teachers began teaching toward those questions which would be asked. The percentage of successful candidates began increasing impressively, and everyone was happy. It is questionable, however, whether the students learned what was necessary.

CONSOLIDATION EFFORTS

Garfield, Winterfield, Harrison, Farwell and Clare had graded school systems in 1905. This meant that more than one teacher taught in a district at a time. It had other implications as well in accreditation of curriculum, in adminstration, as well as in financial support from the state. Some districts which had five or six students eligible for schooling found themselves operating a very expensive per pupil program, while other boards had their costs down to $2 per pupil per month. Sparsely populated districts, such as Frost's District in Section 13, found their costs to be $11 per student per month. Legislation in 1903 permitted rural school districts to pay for transporting students if they decided to consolidate, or to farm out tuition students, so residents of Section 13 sent their younsgers to the Long Lake District.

Prior to this time, in 1894, the districts two miles east of Clare unsuccessfully attempted to consolidate. Pratt, Brown, Bradley, Lansingville, Phinisey and a fractional part of Grant-Vernon Townships were involved. The respective school inspectors

A Sheridan Township School

met and attempted to iron out the problems, but to no avail. When education became more popular, schools consolidated frequently, but there were always mitigating circumstances which governed the moving of children too far from their local neighborhoods.

TEACHER ASSOCIATION MEETINGS

Teachers organized into local or county associations quite early. Usually the agenda for their meetings covered routine subjects, such as what to teach and how. One January, Superintendent Linaberry from Harrison and Superintendent Downs from Farwell bundled their teachers into sleighs and trekked to Clare. Superintendent Hutchison had his clutch of school "marms" waiting at the schoolhouse, and the meeting began when the frozen young ladies thawed out. The teachers were told, "Teach down to the third grade how to determine the location of a forty acre field before you teach them how to 'bound Patagonia'."

They also were told to have the playground leveled so the students were able to use the facilities. "Trees should be planted, coat hooks put up, keep the dipper off the floor, . . . don't let the little children spill water onto the wooden floors, . . . Keep things on the chalkboard for the little ones to do while (you are) drilling the older students, . . . Be sure the maps are hung straight and keep fresh decorations on the walls for the students to look at and appreciate," they were told. Finally they were admonished, "Praise the students frequently!"

THE 1891 SCHOOL HOUSE BURNS

During the night of September 26, 1900, a fire started in Clare's nine-year-old two-story, masonry building, damaging its interior extensively. Blame for the fire was placed on kindling, stored near the coal bin. How the flames began, no one ever knew. All that was known at the time was replacement cost, which totaled $20,000. A month earlier, insurance coverage had been increased 50% from $10,000.

Classes were held the next Monday in the various churches and halls, of which there were several available. Meanwhile workmen began to gut the interior, replacing all of the floors, fixtures and plumbing. The old 1892 coal furnace was dusted off and a small gasoline driven fan was attached to circulate the heated air. Both were inadequate. Plans in 1908 called for a new steam plant, large enough to heat the second floor in place of the old small, coal-fired, hot air system, but a $10,000 price tag came along with the new boiler.

Some wanted to get by with a $3,000 system, although it probably wasn't adequate now that all four rooms on the top level were being used. Bennett, the former local Superintendent said, "Confessedly, many of our young boys have been going to the devil lately, . . . All that many of us can do for our children is to give them an adequate education." From appearances, there must have been a lot of boys on their way to Hell, because the Board at the next meeting agreed to the more expensive system. All opposition had quieted down.

The reconstructed school retained all of the exterior walls. From an outside glance in 1902, the school hadn't changed at all, but a new floor and interior walls replaced all of the original construction. A superintendent's room, recitation room, science laboratory, oak woodwork, green walls, cream ceilings and pink halls greeted the visiting taxpayers. In addition, each room now had a blackboard, electric lights and bell, chipped glass interior doors, individual seats for each student and an elegant teacher's desk. $25,000 had been expended on the school after the fire, and the district was left with a $10,000 debt, but it was manageable.

The high school was projected to take care of one hundred scholars. As a comparison, the Kindergarten class enrolled twenty-five, while the first grade checked off eighty-eight eager boys and girls thirsting for knowledge. Forty students was the normal number enrolled in each class, however. When graduation time came in June, those students who were successful with their eighth-grade examinations usually vamoosed!

In 1903, high school students were in extremely short supply. Superintendent W. D. Riggs was the last of the "economy" administrators, as finally the policy of 1895 to reduce all school teacher salaries below even that of a farm hired hand had taken a heavy toll on an adequate, minimum faculty. Forget what Mayor Lacy said about the local schools in his first inaugural address. The truth of the matter was very simple: the Clare school was in a deplorable condition. In addition to the poverty wages paid to teachers, the fact that graduates of the eighth grade could enroll in Mt. Pleasant Normal College was the most insidious reason of all. Most young people were considered by themselves and by their parents to be educated by the time they reached the eighth grade.

The Board of Education began looking at this problem head-on, but when President C. W. Perry suggested paying the teachers more money, he was challenged by a moss-back board member, "Why should we pay good money for poor teachers?" He had the same philosophy as the old woodsman who

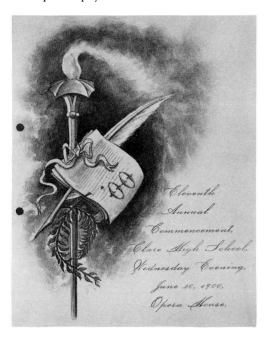

Graduation time in June has traditionally been an important part of a student's life. Helon B. Allen was the class orator, while Belle Ironmonger presented her essay.

entered a cold room in wintertime, kicked the cold stove and shouted, "Warm me up and then I'll throw some wood in ya!" Several in the community would have been satisfied if the school house had been closed down.

It took many years for the patrons to realize that the low wages paid to teachers had driven out the qualified educators, and that in their places were men and women who were incapable of producing an acceptable product. Sheridan District Number Two was one of the first to see the connection between good wages and good teaching. They hired Emery McLaughlin in 1905 for $50 a month, twice what the rural school had been paying. Other districts began offering $30, $35 and $40 to men, but two women were hired at $40. A salary that high created quite a stir in the county, but Commissioner Welch's philosophy of paying a decent wage began taking hold. He said, "It is far better for districts to offer a fair price to a teacher, and demand a good one, thus keeping the ranks filled, than to reduce wages so low the best seek other occupations . . . Get a good teacher, pay him what he earns, and hold him up to his best efforts."

SCHOOL HOUSE CONSTRUCTION

Log school houses were not unheard of in Clare County, even back in the 1870's, but most were of "frame-construction". Sheridan had one log school on Section 35, and Grant had one on Section 21, but beyond this, they were scarce. The reason is that the county had lots of sawmills in the early days, and it was easier to build with lumber.

After Meredith was dissolved as an incorporated town in 1899, the permanent population had re-located itself onto what fertile farmland there was in the township. A few families began farming in Section 31, so a schoolhouse was required. Lyman Sears, the Harrison jeweler, and Charlie Butts headed up a "bee" which built a log school house in 1900. The cracks between the logs were chinked with chips, then plastered and whitewashed. Two windows were on the north and south sides. Inside, the floors had wide,

The Hardwood School in 1916.
Photo from the Virgil Newman Collection

rough planking, and a teacher's desk which had been nailed together from wide boards. Students' desks were commercially manufactured, but the ones purchased were all for older children. The wee ones had trouble climbing up onto their seats.

The school itself was scheduled to be established in Section 32, but the old railroad grade cut west of there in Section 31, so one acre of land on a small knoll just over the line was selected as the site, in order to make use of the Meredith railroad grade. The children climbed wooden steps to get to the boarded-in school yard. A plank was fastened onto the top of the fence, and in nice weather, the children clambered up on it to eat their lunches.

On the school property was an abandoned cook stove, left there by the lumbermen. The boys rigged it for operation, then covered it with boughs of sumac for a clubhouse effect. A neighbor boy who didn't attend school came over before recess and started a fire so that the children could cook food brought from home. Eggs and potatoes baked in ashes were the normal fare. Memories of those burned potatoes were selective, and the

pupils of the log schoolhouse remembered the delicious times they had in their "wigwam", as they called it.

Of the county's sixty school buildings, ten were of brick, thirty-eight were frame, six were stone and six were of other types. Eleven schools had full basements. Thirty-three buildings were situated on stone foundations and eleven were supported by cedar posts dug into the ground. Heavy timbers were used for plates and then normal balloon type frame construction followed. An average one-room school was 23 feet by 28 feet by 12 feet. In the rear, normally, a woodburning stove with a long-run of smoke pipe heated the room, theoretically.

Those buildings had such poor insulation qualities that students roasted on one side and received chill-blains on the other. Ventilation was poor, which tended to make them unhealthy places for children. Pneumonia, flu, colds, T.B. and all the childhood diseases were nurtured by the one-room school. It takes no Sherlock Holmes to discover why so many youngsters didn't survive childhood. Sitting in refrigerated classrooms during wintertime with wet feet, and drinking water from a common dipper immersed in a pail of water added extra perils to their survival struggle.

Eventually, Indiana began to promote major changes in its educational system, and Michigan was dragged along with their tested improvements. In 1901, a bill was passed in Lansing which permitted townships to establish their own rural high schools. Winterfield and Grandon took advantage of the new law, and the Grandon-Winterfield High School graduated its first seniors in 1903. The Honorable D. E. McLure of Lansing gave the address, and Reverend A. L. Woodcock preached the baccalaureate sermon on June 14th.

Towns such as Temple, Leota and Clarence either terminated their financial responsibility to the graduates, or if the board so desired, they helped subsidize the tuition costs and sent eager scholars to a high school district. In 1909, the Legislature passed P. A. 65, which revolutionized Michigan education. From this point on, a student that wanted a high school education could receive it free. The local school district was responsible for providing either a high school or the tuition, up to $20 each year

for their young citizens. A student could elect which school system to attend as long as it was one of the three closest.

TRANSPORTING STUDENTS

A law passed in 1903 permitted rural districts to transport students. Just how they were moved from one district to another isn't known, but probably the school provided a horse-drawn buggy to convey the pupils. Greenwood students who were sent to Harrison boarded with local townspeople, as did most of the other older students from Hayes and Hamilton. Sheridan, Arthur, Hatton, Grant, Wise and Vernon sent boarding students to Clare. Farwell collected its scholars from Gilmore, Surrey, Lincoln and Freeman. Redding students went to either Grandon or Marion.

THE SUMMERFIELD FIRE

District Number 5 in Section 26 was the only school operating in the township, other than the Leota school. In 1903, an unhappy

The new Farwell School in 1908.

Mrs. Vick, on her third attempt, finally burned down the school house. Sheriff Updegraff gave her free room and board in Harrison. The pupils had to walk or ride to the Town Hall over in Section 22, about three miles away until a new building replaced the torched structure.

Other fires also took their toll. One cold February 12th morning, three school houses burned, including the Redner, a Sheridan structure and Gilmore's Glass District. Each teacher was responsible for checking on the stove's condition regularly, then reporting to the Director any repairs or changes required. Leah Hudson, teaching in the Redner when it caught on fire, had reported to her Director that the smoke pipe was becoming filled with soot. Two weeks later the fire took care of the problem.

About 10:00 a.m., Miss Hudson (later married to William Garchow) thought she heard funny noises in the attic, but her attention was on the recitation exercise, and she didn't pay much attention to it. Suddenly a McNeil boy shouted, "The school's on fire!" Keeping control of the students, Leah calmly told them to gather all their books and take them home. Then they marched over to the coat rack, put on their cold weather garments and went home, all but one older boy. Miss Hudson sent him for help. Snow was falling, and a strong wind hindered the young man, but he persisted in locating Mr. Magnus, the closest school official. By the time men began arriving, the floor was burning from the collapsed roof. The loss was total.

Because enough time was already in to meet minimum state requirements, no school was held until good weather arrived.

Even though school fires were too frequent, not one student was ever killed, or even injured by any of these conflagrations. It's a testimonial to the teachers and pupils that this record was created.

In December of 1913, Hamilton District Number 5 lost its school to arsonist Fred Speck. He had been a little unbalanced for some time prior to the fire, which he started late in the evening. Again, no one was injured. Sheriff John Brown boarded him in Harrison until the court decided what to do with him.

WHAT ARE SCHOOLS?

In 1904, the Clare School District was spending $26,000 a year and had a debt of $2,000. Less than 75% of the eighth graders completed their examinations successfully, and annually the high school only produced four or five graduates. "Does our school warrant this outlay of money?" asked Commissioner Welch. "The small number of graduates makes it doubtful that we are receiving our money's worth," he said. "If three-quarters of our eighth grade graduates would go on and finish their education, in a few years our community would see a general uplift."

This was the era when cigarettes were gripping hard on the boys, and ten of the high schoolers began hanging around the street corners during school hours. They represented 25% of the whole high school enrollment. The Board attempted to deal with the general malaise by hiring an extra teacher, but the problem was more deeply ingrained within the community.

Many drop-outs later took correspondence courses through the International Correspondence School for a charge of $10 to $120 each, plus postage. One drop-out later went back to a high school teacher who had strongly urged him to finish his education. He said, "Well, it's come true, just as you said. Now I wish I had stuck to that algebra ... I'm taking the next best route and learning it by correspondence, but it's harder and more expensive."

Welch thought the problem was even deeper than the drop-out level in the high schools. He said in 1904, "... Many in high school and clear down to the sixth grade think they have learned it all."

Some of the students who applied for I. C. S. programs were denied admission. The would-be correspondent was told, "your place is in the public school." But not many boys believed them. Only nine males graduated between 1898 and 1904 from Clare High School, and four of them were tuition students from the townships.

Clare High School Class of 1909 at a reunion in 1960. Back row (L-R): Florence (Smith) Towne, Gladys (Lackie) Gade, Flossie (McKeever) Kane, Christine (Tatman) McDonald. Front row: Kirk Sutherland, Richard Bogan, Arthur Gilmore, Thomas Holmes.
Photo from the Flossie Kane Collection

Even though schools were so characteristic of every frontier town in Michigan, their real value in elevating the individual beyond the simple reading, writing and arithmetic hadn't seeped through. Lofty ideas which the philosophers debated so vigorously over the centuries never left a mark on most of the crude residents of Clare County. A day to day struggle with life sapped most of the energies of boys, girls and adults to the point that they emerged here on earth in bodies condemned to limited maturation of their mental and social capabilities.

Habits of physical abuse reduced even those years to that of pain, frustration and a definite ceiling on their personal developments. Parents with limited insights tended to pass on to their offspring their own narrowness of purpose and aspiration in life. Teachers, and even Superintendent Roode, were said to have beaten children with canes, broom handles, measuring sticks or whatever

else was available. Schools were incapable of changing the young unless they had more time, as well as adequate insights, to stretch the minds of students toward the horizons. Fortunately, help would soon be on the way.

THE NEW TRUANCY LAW

What the local citizens didn't know intuitively, the State of Michigan understood, and so it passed a new, tough truancy law in 1905. Commissioner Welch began to bear down so hard on the teachers to enforce it that they reported every student who was absent on Monday mornings as truant. Soon C. J. Pease, county truant officer, was swamped with work. Because the law made him responsible to the sheriff, he only took complaints from the schools, but enforced the laws through the legal channels. Sheriffs Updegraff and Sunday put on extra manpower over the years, and collected $3.00 per truant child from hundreds of parents. Parents, kids and teachers were having a hard time adjusting, but Welch kept their feet to the fire. The custom of parents taking their children out of school to work at age 14 was a tough one to break around here, since the local Superintendent could request the County Commissioner to excuse children from school if they were needed to work at home.

In Michigan, there were over 5,000-fourteen-year-old children working ten or more hours a day under the old school attendance law. An amendment was made to the 1905 law two years later, making it illegal to be out of school if the youth was under sixteen. Then the local parents really began to scream! Welch was taken to task harshly, and people were rude to him for asking that

---

"NOT FAILURE, BUT LOW AIM IS CRIME"—LOWELL

HARRISON, MICH., *May 2* 1914

Florence Hilborn

Your standings made at the State Eighth Grade examination are given below.

Required standing is, minimum, 60; average, 75. Your standings follow:

Arithmetic	- -	*63*
Geography	- -	*76*
Grammar	- -	*68*
Civics	- -	*95*
U. S. History	- -	*82*
Spelling	- -	*78*
Orthography	- -	*73*
Reading	- -	*95*
Penmanship	- -	*98*
Physiology	- -	*86*
Agriculture	-	*94*
AVERAGE	- -	*83*
Passed	ASA H. ALDRICH,	
~~Failed~~		Commissioner

Florence Hilborn's eighth grade state test scores indicate the curriculum changes affected by Governor Ferris. Asa H. Aldrich once again was the elected county school commissioner.

---

the law be enforced. Of course, this was during the days when Local Option was on the books, but not closely enforced. Welch had the same dilemma about which Lacy warned the Baptists when they pushed for liquor controls. He said, ''The fickleness of public opinion is historical and proverbial, and not the least among the martyrs are those who, as officials, have sought to enforce the law above the standards of the time.'' Welch approached this point in 1908.

ACCREDITED SCHOOLS

Superintendent of Schools, Phillip A. Bennett, during 1900, began the necessary foundation work for the Clare schools to become accredited by the University of Michigan, then, as now, a sought-after endorsement. Finally, on February 20th, 1908, the goal was reached. Bennett and his successor, W. D. Riggs were gone, but J. Q. Roode completed the requirements at long last.

It isn't known whether the Grandon-Winterfield High School received this recognition for superior standards, but it continued to matriculate six or seven graduates every year up to World War I. No record exists of Farwell's having met the University's standards, but it is assumed that both Harrison and Farwell qualified prior to World War I.

SPORTS IN THE CURRICULUM

For seven years prior to 1903, not one city boy graduated from the Clare High School, but after football was introduced in 1901, four city boys were encouraged enough to grind out the four years. William Dwyer, Charles Jackson, Neil Bidwell and James Tatman broke the long hiatus. The ''Huskies'' played teams from Cadillac, Midland, Mt. Pleasant and Coleman, among others. Baseball had long been a favorite sport, but a boy didn't have to attend school for this activity.

Girls played basketball all over the county, and a school wasn't alive and functioning if

The Clare High School 1906 football team. The members include: (left to right) (L.E.) Fred Stone, (R.E.) Will Henderson, (R.T.) Max Pelton, (L.G.) Frank Ross, (R.G.) Michael Archamboult, (C.) Frank Jackson, (Q.) Leo DeVogt, (L.H.) Hagel, (F.B.) Carl Dorsey, (R.E.) Cunningham, (G.) Herbert Jennings, Coach Wells, and Superintendent J. Q. Roode.

a team didn't play the other communities. In 1913, Clare's basketball team was of championship caliber, and so was the following year's team.

Each year saw more and more boys and girls staying in school as the truancy law encouraged the parents to keep sending their children, and sports encouraged the child to want, to attend classes. Clare was able to graduate eighteen students in 1909, the greatest number up to this time.

Custom had it that the boys gave the graduation orations, while the girls read essays, played the piano or sang. The valedictorian was expected to give an address equal to the occasion. J. Q. Roode, Superintendent during 1905-1909, shepherded the 1909 class to its triumphant day. He coached Edward Shaw to project his voice off the wall facing him some fifty feet away in the Doherty Opera House, as he was the best scholar. Bernie Weisman, a tuition student from Farwell, was another good student, and so he orated also. Since so many boys were speaking, Roode said to Flossie McKeever, "Flossie, why don't you play the piano? Your voice is so soft they probably couldn't hear you anyway."

In that class of 1909 were orphans, night telephone operators store clerks and others who worked out their "town board" at the hotels and restaurants. This was not a pampered class! Rather, they represented a new type of student who recognized the value of an education. Kirk Sutherland, Thomas Holmes, Leo DeVogt, Art Gilmore, Richard Bogan and Edward Shaw all made glowing careers for themselves in business, photography, law and railroading. They were a credit to the county, and some of them achieved national fame for their skills.

The Clare High School football team of 1919-20. (L-R rear): Eddie Hubel, Roy Cimmerer, Ensley Hubel, Orlando Thayer. (front) John Groves, _____ Elliot, Royal Wilson, Don Waller, Clare Dyer, Percy Stough, Emerson Hickey. The school building shown here burned in January of 1920.

WOODBRIDGE N. FERRIS

W. N. Ferris, president of the Big Rapids institution named after him, came to Clare in September of 1909 to talk to the teachers. Without waiting for formalities, he waded right into his current crusade: fossilized teachers. Observing the lack of intellectual perception on the part of students, he correctly assumed that much of the blame was theirs.

There were ninety-two teachers present as he began warming up to his topic, "Building of a Man". "Stretch their minds with philosophy, and then let them follow your example," he said. Lowering his voice and slowing his rate of delivery, he began to speak about sexual indiscretions which were common in the era. "I hate with righteous indignation any of my ancestors whose sexual sins make it harder for me to be a man," he intoned.

Before he finished with them, any sexual deviant present must have wished for a trap door to open up and bring relief. Ferris stressed again and again that students could not grow beyond the examples those teachers lived. They were the patterns which young lives had to emulate if they were to be successful.

His missionary zeal was to become famous four years later as he took up the cause of a clean social environment when he became governor in 1913.

Ferris did more than chide teachers for their sins and cats for eating birds. He was a solid education man, and he worked effectively to consolidate the one-room school districts into sizeable geographical areas, so the so-called Township Unit School could flourish.

THE PUREST SOUL

Ferris might have had foreknowledge about the personal lives of some Clare County teachers, but there was one whose life was almost saintly. Coming to Greenwood Township in 1908, Estella Groves contracted T.B. and died April 22, 1910. Her body was buried in Greenwood Cemetery,

The Ferris Institute, circa 1918.

W. N. Ferris in Clare during his successful campaign for the governorship in 1912.

having endured for only 24 years.

As a teacher, she was superb! Her sweet, gentle manner endeared her to everyone in the district. When she became sick from the unhealthy school building, the community was shocked, for death always followed the onset of T.B. Why should this "innocent lamb" be subjected to this horrible disease?

Her death and funeral were much noted in Greenwood, and her casket was escorted to its final burial spot by a very large number of friends, students and companions. She was abundantly loved and greatly missed. "Her's was the purest soul." it was said.

SANITATION REFORM

Too late for Estella Groves, but not too late for those who came after her, were the new state laws which sought to take the danger of disability and death out of the schools. John D. Pierce, often called the "Father of Michigan Schools", began in 1911 to wage a heavy campaign against poor ventilation, inadequate lighting, uneven temperatures and unsuitable seats, which resulted in physical disabilities, general depression, lassitude, headache, dizziness, lowering of resistance to disease, the contraction of pneumonia, T.B., influenza, curvature of the spine, near-sightedness and so on.

Thirty percent of the students were said to be suffering from some disability or other. The main culprit was ventilation. A standard thirty cubic feet of air per occupant per minute was established, and light approaching from either side was a new minimum standard. In this crusade, Pierce was joined by Dr. Robert L. Dixon, Secretary of the State Board of Health.

MOVIES IN SCHOOLS

Thomas A. Edison, himself a victim of having left school too early, had invented the system for successfully showing moving pictures in the 1890's. In 1912, he began using his machine to show films 80 feet long, which could be mailed in pill boxes to the nation's schools. As he envisioned it, each school would purchase a machine, then regularly, he would send out from his laboratory, films on the mosquito, honey bee, Typhoid fly, air, sea, creatures and so on.

Anticipating a big demand, he sent his photographers to Africa, South America, Europe and Asia to build the library he needed.

WOMEN VOTERS

In 1912, all school elections were open to women if they were taxpayers and if they were a parent or a guardian. Paying a dog tax wasn't enough to qualify, it was decided, and so the eager female citizens had to hurdle another obstacle in their march to the ballot box.

REFORMING THE RURAL SCHOOL

State regulations were coming out of Lansing on a regular basis during the 1910-1918 era. Everything from attendance, teaching days, school plant, grounds, play-ground equipment, health, vocations, calendar and so on were decided by the state. In 1912, another regulation was pro-mulgated. The Legislature had given authority to the State Superintendent of Public Instruction to define required subjects. Luther L. Wright began the task. He decreed that 3rd graders should study nature and that 8th graders were to study agriculture for half of the year. His idea was to make the schools more related to the actual social life the students lived in.

His edict helped to quash the endless memory work which had forced the students to memorize the hundreds of bones in the body. Rather, the child was to be instructed in how to care for his teeth, skin, eyes and ears. Lessons in prevention of drowning were to be given, as well as first-aid, sanita-tion, fly and mosquito control and finally, public speaking. Reading was still the number one subject, even after the reform.

When W. N. Ferris became Governor, he went after all of the school buildings. "Most are unfit for livestock to occupy . . . They rarely furnish adequate light, never supply pure air and few are comfortably heated . . . On the whole, the schoolhouse is destructive to the health of children," he claimed. Another improvement prohibited school board members from running for partisan offices.

One suggestion he gave, that of uniform text books, met with fierce opposition from ex-State Superintendent Pattengill. "If there is one thing I hate, it's a uniformity of text books," he said.

Ferris's campaign to upgrade the school houses picked up steam in the fall of 1913. Of the 7,234 one-room school houses, there were only 2,075 with heating and ventilating systems, and only 499 of these were in the basements. 3,772 were overheated and stuffy, he claimed. 1,270 schools had a drinking fountain. Only 151 schools had paper towels. 4,463 schools had satisfactory water, but thousands of students sat in seats which were so high that their feet dangled.

"If this state has the power to compel parents to send their children to schools, it has the power to compel the districts to provide proper facilities to gain a proper education," he told the State Board of Education in 1913.

Gradually, things began to take shape, and more students were receiving an edu-cation adequate to their needs. Superinten-dent Fred L. Keeler of Mt. Pleasant was appointed by Governor Ferris to replace L. L. Wright. His job was to translate Ferris's pronouncements into action. His idea for keeping kids in school was what he called the "6 and 6 plan". All grades beyond the 6th grade were to be departmen-talized, and those lower stayed with one teacher all day. "Several cities in Michigan have tested this program and conditions in Michigan are ripe for adopting the plan," he said.

State law over-ruled local preference every time, but often the rural district officials didn't know the law. In 1915, when the Brown School burned, Director Alwood

The Farwell High School Orchestra of 1914. Back row (L-R): Jay Bellinger, A. J. Campbell (superintendent), Paul Goltree, Guy Perry. Middle row: Milward Rogers, Leone Rowe, Ruth Milliken, Lou Milliken, Lou Gee. Front row: Frank Graham and George Bailey.
Photo from the Littlefield Family Collection

called a meeting to discuss a replacement for the thirty year old building. Three separate bonding proposals had been defeated by the voters when J. F. Bowler came out to their board meeting in July. He told them that they didn't have to build a school building for their children if they didn't want to, but the law required them to furnish schooling to the children. If there was no building, the children would have to be transported out of the district. He assured them that they would have to pay transportation and tuition costs in addition to enduring all of the inconveniences.

The Board decided to vote one more time. A 20-3 decision permitted them to begin construction the next morning. The new school year was voted on, and an eight-month year was accepted. "The new school started off like a new 'Henry' (Ford car)," said Charles Garver, moderator for the burned out district.

SOCIAL CENTERS

With the passing of the husking bee and the spelling contests, the schools lost a community of spirit. In the cities, schools were being opened only a few hours a day for about three quarters of the year.

"In the northern communities, the school house is the center of community affairs and is a social center. The school house should be the meeting place for many social groups and organizations where topics of community interest may be discussed and our citizens trained in the democratic system," wrote Seymour Andrus in the CLARE SENTINEL in February, 1916. "Schools are not meeting this if they don't serve as a place for training our people how to live and work together."

The 1914 Farwell Girls' Basketball Team. Back (L-R): Inez Parker, Fleda Richmond, Ruth Hinds, Anna Sherman, Ruth Milliken, Bess Brown. Front: Referees Miss Cuvrell and Georgia Shumway.

The replacement school at Brown's Corners, Arthur Township.

The Russian School, Hamilton Township.

Hamilton Township School in District #3, 1912-13.
Photo from the Shea Family Collection

The Elm Grove School in 1915.

Sheridan Township School Number 3 in 1915.

THE STANDARD SCHOOLS

In 1916, the Department of Public Instruction set certain standards for heating, ventilation, lighting and sanitary conditions. If a school met the conditions, they were awarded a blue metal sign to attach to the front of the building. It was a badge of great prestige.

World War I broke out as Clare was gearing up to meet the Standard School criteria, but the noble idea was installed in several districts, including Franklin #3, Arthur, Leota, Redner, Sheridan, Lincoln #3 and #4, Elm Grove, Freeman and two districts in Redding before the war shut things down. When peacetime came, several years elapsed before the next Standard School was completed. This was the Reynolds School, built in Frost Township in 1924.

It's picture-taking day at the rural school.

WORLD WAR I AND THE SCHOOLS

President Wilson called up the Michigan National Guard to meet the Mexican Border problem prior to our entry into the European conflict. Many local high school boys had enlistments which had to be served, and a few went to Texas with the 32nd Regiment. Then returned individually after a year or so. These men had the experience needed by this country when the war broke out in April of 1917, and they were rushed back into camps and to overseas assignments. Their continued exposure to combat conditions on the fragile front lines caused many casualties.

High school graduates were premium men, and the army used them in responsible positions. Fred Stone, a graduate from Clare and Michigan Agricultural College, was an engineer, and his skills earned him a high rank. Several others were taken for medical doctors, nurses, truck transportation and so on. Skilled men were in heavy demand by the war effort.

The war came on suddenly, even though it had been brewing for years. President Wilson took this nation through those years with his anti-preparedness cliches and wasted an opportunity to build machine guns, artillery, planes, trucks and rifles. Due to his party's isolationist philosophy, the young men paid heavily with blood for this folly of gross underpreparation. Not a few of these lads were put on the front lines with inadequate familiarization with the basic tools of war.

The home front was even more disorganized and chaotic! Food was in short supply in Europe, and President Wilson's administration began propagandizing the farm districts to plant extraordinarily large crops to avoid starvation conditions in Europe during the fall and winter of 1917. As a result, many of the high schoolers either left the classrooms in April to enlist or to begin the great effort on the farmlands. So many left, including girls who went to the farms, that for all practical purposes, school was cancelled by April 20, 1917.

Graduation ceremonies were abbreviated, as most graduates weren't present. The military camps and farms had claimed many

Most of Clare County's rural teachers received their certification from this institution, Mt. Pleasant Normal.

of the educated youth before their schooling was complete.

Next to be hit were the teachers. Wages were still low, and the war offered higher wages to anyone who would go to the centers where skills were in desperate demand. Several of the male teachers left the teaching ranks, leaving the locals wondering if they weren't mortally wounding our educational system. The largest casualties were in the students' ranks. They quit school almost enmasse and went to join the "war effort".

Enrollment during World War I declined. Many families moved away, and those who remained were engaged on the farms. Clare's student body, which numbered 417 when the war started, dropped 36, or 9%. Considering the Primary money at $7.50 per student, $270 was involved, a sum of some importance to the treasurer, but not overwhelming.

School students worked hard during the warm weather of 1917. They stayed on the job, ensuring a large harvest, even though school had resumed with the fall term in September. So many of the older boys and girls stayed on jobs that school officials began a campaign to get the kids back in school. They took the government's propaganda too seriously.

A severe fuel shortage in the state caused discomfort to the pupils in the town schools, but the rural schools burned wood, and so they weren't so severely affected. Later, when the outbreak of diphtheria and flu, as well as a food shortage, hit locally, schools were closed from two weeks to thirty days in February, 1918.

The flu epidemic in October of 1918

closed every school, church and public meeting place for three months. By the time the war was over, a significant number of children had gotten out of the school habit, and a national campaign was carried on in January of 1919 to re-enroll those youngsters who had dropped their education prematurely.

Accidents and Disasters

Considering all of the potential lethal hazards there are in the average day, the miracle is that so few are injured fatally. Taken over a life time, it's amazing that more people do not meet a violent death. Pioneers of all types face the most serious challenges to an attainment of grandparent status. It was so in the pre-Revolutionary Colonial days, lumbering days and also in the gold-rush days. A second generation comes along and enjoys the fruits of their forefathers and escapes most of the hazards just a few short years removed. Most, but not all!

Frank Doherty was working in his store in late June of 1900, when the elevator's big wheel broke, letting the platform drop all the way to the basement. The shaft fell right after the carriage, hitting him a glacing blow on the arm. As it turned out, he received only a flesh wound to the right arm, but had he been standing three inches closer, there would have been another fatality added to record.

Lumbering had moved out of the lower peninsula, practically, by the turn of the century, although some hardwood was still to be cut. The upper peninsula was now the scene of hundreds of men working both above and below ground. In 1903, mine disasters in Iron, Marquette and Dickinson counties took ninety-one lives. This mortality rate was higher than that of the lumber woods.

The mid-state region in 1904 registered deaths on a much more limited scale, fortunately, but deaths of lads such as Ole Larson of Sheridan seemed equally brutal. He was fourteen years old and swimming near the old Herrick School when life ended.

A married man riding in a buggy with his wife Nancy seemed to have life's challenges pretty well in hand, when all of a sudden the horse bolted, breaking away from the buggy, dragging David McAninch to his death because the reins were twisted around his wrists. The horse turned and the husband hit a stump. Just that quick, pretty, young Nancy was a widow.

Many less traumatic accidents occurred nearly every day, it seemed. Young Charley Mitchel, living with his grandparents, the James Gerrens, for the summer was badly hooked by a cow. His left ear was torn off and nearly his left arm, but he did survive as Dr. Sanford gave him the best modern medicine had to offer.

Two young lads, Ben Welch and Ford Denzen, were playing around the Pere Marquette stockyards that Bill Haley used so frequently. Ben fell, breaking his arm in two places. Denzen jumped down to fetch Dr. Carpenter's skills, when a freight train rolled over his foot. When it passed, the lad jumped free. Dr. Reeder removed a section of Denzer's great toe.

Dr. Frank Gray attended an adult almost the same day out in Dover. Orville Saunders cut off two toes while chopping wood early September of 1903.

Temple didn't have a regular doctor in town, so when an accident occurred there, Dr. Carrow from Marion might be called, or the patient could be scooted down the railroad to Farwell or even Saginaw. Arthur Cole was hit by a flying knot in the Dolph stave mill. X-rays taken in St. Mary's Hos-

The Doherty Brothers hearse. This photo was taken in 1897.
Photo from the Coleman Centennial Collection

pital showed his eye to be ruptured, but not beyond recuperation.

DYNAMITE

Dynamite was a problem to the farmers, because they didn't use it properly, many times letting it freeze. The nitro-glycerine would then settle to the bottom, where it became very dangerous to handle, but not fit for use in blasting.

Clyde Sloanes was a farmer in Coldwater Township near Crooked Lake in 1908. He and a neighbor were feuding, it seemed, when one night in May, some dynamite blew his house to splinters. Not a door or window was left. Suspicion fell on the feuding neighbor, but it could have been unstable dynamite.

That same year, the Kanaar boys out in Arthur wanted to blow some stumps. Frost came early and the brothers, Harry and Lewis, took the frozen dynamite and put it in the kitchen stove's oven. One of the twenty sticks caught fire, and Harry grabbing it, began to rub it vigorously on the hot stove top to put the flames out. Instead, it exploded, followed by the balance of the blasting supply, killing the two boys instantly. The mother, Mrs. James Quick, was standing outside the kitchen door when the blast went off. She survived long enough to tell neighbors what happened, then she too expired. Harry was never found. His body was "blown to atoms" as the accident was reported. All three were buried in Cherry Grove Cemetery, with the funeral being held in the Balsley Schoolhouse.

D. M. Wood of Grant Township didn't learn from this explosion, or at least he didn't remember its lesson. Thawing some dynamite in his kitchen during the middle of April, 1910, he blew the house to bits—but no one was injured.

James Ferguson and his wife lived north of Farwell in 1916 and they weren't getting along with each other, yet they continued to share the same house so as to save the expenses of a divorce. Each used the kitchen to prepare their meals, but at different times. Late in October, the wife was getting ready to use the kitchen, it having been just vacated by her husband, when it blew up. Someone put a stick of dynamite in the firebox, and quite naturally, suspicion fell on Jim, since he was the only one who had been around.

The Farwell Post Office either had a lot of dynamite being shipped through its facilities, or else someone kept coming back and putting a few sticks under the safe. In May of 1908, the postmaster, Saxton, said, "for the 'x'teenth time, the safe has been dynamited. This time it's ruined." There had been many severe explosions that night, but a heavy electrical storm was raging at the time and no one paid any attention to the disturbance down at the post office.

Dynamite was used by Roy and Ed Coffell in 1910 when they found that dynamite could temporarily stun fish when thrown into a dammed-up pond. Newton's dam up in Hatton was blown out in July of that year by these two who presumably were fishing, but some farmers took to blowing dams if their streams were blocked by others. They were arrested by Officer Pettit!

Boys found dynamite a dangerous business also. Gerald Boulton and Ray Green were both severely hurt when they lit two dynamite caps with a match in September of 1915. They lived in Hatton. Boulton was the most severely injured as his arm was carried in a sling for a while, and his eye was feared for. Sometimes these accidents really were accidents, and other times, they were the result of foolishness, or maliciousness.

GUNSHOT WOUNDS

Rufus H. Gephart was out hunting on October 7, 1908 in Arthur Township with his son John. Standing on a stump to get a better view, he rested his left arm on the end of the barrels. Suddenly the rotten stump gave way, and both barrels discharged into his abdomen. He was buried in Montpelier, Ohio. John W. Richmond of Harrison was killed in 1905 by a head shot from an unknown gun.

Many accidents were caused by the guns or the person carrying them. Out in Garfield Township, it was said in 1908 that a citizen hunting in his own thicket would put his shoes on backwards so that if a stray bullet knocked down a man, he could get hid before being apprehended. This may have been said in jest, but the early settlers and Indians used to do the same trick in pioneer days.

The small sawmills were still taking their pound of flesh whenever something unusual happened. Warner Hess, working at Rilett's sawmill in Sheridan during 1908, was riding the carriage to change the log after each cut. On one trip, the sawyer reversed the direction unexpectedly and threw Hess onto the circular saw. His left hand was cut off. Dr.'s Gray and Clute attended him in town.

WEATHER CALAMATIES

Cyclones or tornados came through every so often, and scared the wits out of people. One baptized Farwell and Clare on July 13, 1900, but it stayed above the tree tops near towns. Several trees were uprooted by its raging winds.

Crooked Lake was visited by a black twister, touching down on M. F. Robinson's and Alfred Tryon's barns during May of 1909. A year later, a two mile path northward from the Pratt School in East Grant felt the sting of nature's wrath. Buildings on L. H. Thompson, Chan Lloyd, Fred Hudson, D. Mater and John Harpster farms were hit.

Five months later in November, the temperature dropped from 76° to 10°F in a few short hours as several vicious tornados roared through most of Central Michigan. Millions of dollars worth of damage was done by the widely endured storm, but Owosso was the worst hit. Locally, Vernon Township buildings took the brunt of it.

The next storm didn't hit until 1921. By then the COURIER thought these types of storms to be rare. The Bowler barn was flattened and then the tip of the whirling mass touched Charles Grove's new barn before it leveled Christian Heuschele's and

John Larman's. C. B. Lloyd had some buildings scattered along the countryside right after the storm passed over.

LIGHTNING STORMS

The denuded hills and plains of northern Michigan were ravaged again and again by the most violent electrical storms than can be imagined during the early years of this century. Some theorized that the trees provided some measure of neutralizing effect on the weather, and when they were gone, nature ran amok.

A spring storm hit Sheridan Township in 1903 especially hard, setting fires to many buildings and killing horses, cattle and hogs. Nelson Carrow reported three horses killed by one stroke of immense voltage. A year later Hamilton was hit by lightning, then hail. The farms of Wm. Nash, George Van Horn, George Stockton, John Myers, Orr Campbell, Charles Keanester and Sam Wilson were covered with ice and water six inches deep. The peas and potatoes were ruined.

The Latter Day Saints area was hit by lightning again in 1905. Some relatives from Hamilton were meeting in Elder Joseph Bitler's home when the bolt came down the chimney to his right side and hip and out his shoe, shredding it. It burned a hole in his foot. Charles Bitler had his arm and a path across the chest burned, as the flash came out of his left shoe, shattering that one also. William Bitler had two daughters in the same room, but neither of them were injured. The lightning continued across the floor to a hole where it went down and grounded out. It's a wonder no one was killed.

Three weeks later a million dollar storm ripped through Gratiot County and parts of Isabella. One hundred thousand dollars worth of buildings were destroyed in Gratiot alone. Alma, St. Louis, Kalamazoo, Detroit, Mt. Pleasant and Forest Hill were subjected to immense hail, and wheat crops were leveled. Rain poured out of the skies as masses of coal black clouds seethed overhead. Hurricane winds drove the fist sized hail

onto and through roofs and sidings. One report said hail thirteen inches in diameter smashed every window facing north in the whole town of Alma. An extraordinary amount of rain fell in Vernon, Wise and area, including eight inches in Clare. Hailstones in Vassar covered the ground to nearly a foot in depth. Sheridan Township said this was the most water on the ground at one time in over seventeen years.

Fourteen months later another electrical storm roared into Greenwood, Hayes, Frost and Franklin townships. Lightning strikes were continuous for one half-hour, and hail which accompanied it broke every window in the Clare County Courthouse exposed to the wind. Since most of the exposure was toward the north, the one hundred forty windows broken were nearly all that were in the building.

Charlie Pfetsch was hit on the head by several very large hail stones and was seriously hurt. The tall chimney on the Poor Farm was toppled at a loss of several hundreds of dollars. A path two miles wide marked the storm's path through central and northern Clare County, killing Clarence Robinett with a wayward bolt.

By now, salesmen cruising the country looking for customers, had no trouble disposing of their lightning rods. Nearly every farm building began looking like a porcupine, and some went out and planted a grove of trees around the homestead.

Lightning visited Clare on July 4, 1913, when a full day of activities was scheduled. A baseball game was interrupted abruptly when a dark cloud descended over the fair grounds on East 1st Street. A large crowd had gathered for the races Dave Ward was promoting, when a bolt struck the judges stand. Two young men fell about twenty feet to the ground, dead. Arthur Andrus and Ray Hanes of Sheridan were carried into the recently completed Women's Building to keep the stunned crowd from eyeballing the tragedy. Others, including Dr. Mussell, Thomas Dwyer, J. M. Davis and R. A. Leffingwell who were officials for the races, received severe shocks as well, but not in the fatal magnitude the boys' bodies accepted.

Ernest Beal, standing under the judge's

The dam goes out again on Dewey Lake in Clare.
Photo from the Al Thurston Collection

stand, was shocked severely. He was treated by Dr. Clute in his office downtown.

Speculation about the cause of the electrical strike centered around the number of autos that were lined up along the track. The first heat of the second race had just started when the bolt hit. Young Andrus had only a few days previously been graduated from law school. He was buried in Riverside Cemetery, Hastings. Hane's funeral was an immense one, and it had to be held in the front yard. He was buried in Cherry Grove.

A month later, another terrifying electrical storm hit in northern Michigan, and just as regularly, old timers would say, "This is the worst storm we'd seen in 'x' years," with the 'x' varying with the old timer's memory. It did seem, though, that the August 8, 1913 storm was in a class by itself. Thirty-seven barns were set on fire in Isabella County alone. Clare area barns hit were: Wm. Becker's in Grant; The Kleman Ranch barn with fifty tons of hay; W. R. Lansing, Wise;

J. M. Seeley in Vernon; Jesse Burgess of Gilmore and the Perry Brown sheep buildings on his Riverside Stock Farm.

Farwell had its own private storm in November of the same year. The Parkview Hotel was hit, and its roof burned. No one was injured in this minor league storm.

DAMS

The Callam and Cornwell dam washed out in February of 1904 when fifty feet of the north bank was taken out by an ice build-up. It went out again in June of 1912 when floods caused a large opening in the eastern embankments. Workmen hauled in more clay and plugged it up one more time.

Farwell's dam went out in 1909, and a law suit went through the courts to determine who should pay for the two bridges which were swept out. Dr. Kelly, speaking as Supervisor for Surrey, said Fuller ought to pay all replacement costs. A limited outbreak of typhoid fever occurred with this break, and was a greater threat than the loss of a roadway into town.

Saginaw experienced ten feet of water in May of 1912, and five hundred homes were completely cut off by the high water. Street car traffic was stopped all over town. A man riding a horse over a bridge was swept off the structure and drowned. The next spring, floods accompanied the gigantic spring storms and washed out a mile of Ann Arbor railroad track near Mesick. The Billings dam in Manton washed out, as did Reed City's.

"The worst storm in twenty-five years" took out the Harrietta fish hatchery, the Boardman River Dam and the Mayfield Dam, killing night watchman John Hawthorne. All train traffic on the Manistee and North-eastern railroad was cancelled as tracks were washed out in several locations.

Wind, rain and hail pounded the battered northern communities that memorable spring of 1913.

STEAM SCALDS

Children received most of the scalds as mothers left mop pails to tend a pressing chore, or a toddler tipped a pail of hot water. The child would teeter back and forth, grabbing the lid as it fell. Scaldings also happened to adults. Fabian Hinkle, working down at the local stave and shingle mill, carried his tea and soup in a syrup can. He hung the bale over the pressure relief switch holding it down. Normally this procedure didn't cause any problems, but one night the fire got very hot and the relief valve wasn't able to function.

When Hinkle took the pail from its resting place, the contents had been heated above two hundred twelve degrees Fahrenheit. Prying the lid off it immediately turned to steam and scalded his face horribly. Mrs. Hugh Henderson living in east Grant essentially did the same thing. She was a new bride, having been married a month and had a few things to learn, but the scalding she received took her young life. The husband sadly returned to Canada after he buried her in

Cherry Grove.

Three year old Beatrice Gerlitz of Hayes Township was scalded to death in February of 1917. Details of her death are not known, but her parents Paul and Etta were deeply saddened by her untimely accident.

Jacob Walters was a railroad fireman. His job was normally a difficult one without the fear of mortal burns, but an accident near Durand killed the fifty-nine year old man when the steam escaped back into the cab as the engine rolled off the tracks and onto its side. He was buried in Farwell in September of 1918.

Firemen on the steam locomotives often were scalded when the engines went off the tracks and upset. One fireman, working out of Saginaw, but living in Farwell, was in a wreck. His body was so badly scalded that it took nearly thirty operations to make him presentable to the public again. He was given a small life time pension by the company.

HOUSE FIRES

David Smalley's Sheridan home developed a roof fire during threshing time in 1910. The crew saw it, and took their water tank over to the flames and put it out. The engine probably started it. Another fire took place when David McPhall was at the John Cunningham auction sale. The home burned to the ground. He had partial insurance coverage.

A Hebrew peddler living south of Wm. Duncan's in Vernon had his house destroyed in January of 1902. U. Livingston was out on the road at the time and didn't learn until a week later that his thirteen children were homeless. He carried no insurance.

A man by the name of McIntyre moved into David Wood's house in the same month as Livingston's fire. He too was out of his household goods, and Wood was short one house.

A fire at Atwood Siding in Surrey Township took the home of an elderly couple during a cold January day in 1903. Wm. Mailson and his wife were away at the time and they lost everything. Merchants and

A wreck on the Pere Marquette Railroad, 1910.

neighbors pitched in and settled them in a new home, with clothes and a ten dollar bill. They moved temporarily into the R. D. Johnsons' home. No insurance covered this loss.

Barns burned from a variety of causes. Often a new crop of hay and the winter's supply of grain would be consumed along with the animals. John Neithercutt suffered such a loss in 1903. He had eight hundred dollars' insurance to cover a fifteen hundred dollar loss. Wm. Kube's barn, which was fifty feet by sixty feet, along with thirteen tons of hay and all his farm implements burned. The cattle were driven out by his wife. Kube had been attending a Republican political meeting when the flames hit. A clover huller belonging to "Arm" Allen was destroyed, and no insurance was available to replace the four hundred fifty dollar machine.

E. H. DeVogt, the local photographer lost his Clare Studio in 1903 and his Beaverton studio in 1909. His gallery, photos, negatives and cameras were destroyed. With these losses went a priceless treasure trove as he had camera crews covering the entire northern lumber regions during the 1880's— 1900, and he knew every camp. His ledger books which listed the pertinent details of the hundreds of camps and their foremen were destroyed. The glass plate negatives were the most serious loss, but his report of the fire mentioned the gallery as the greatest casualty.

During 1910, the L. Belcher home in Gilmore burned, and also the R. Martin home in Vernon. A storm which swept through one Sunday evening, whipped the flames causing total losses. March has always been a bad month in the central part of Michigan for fires.

BUSINESS DISTRICT'S FIRES

Fires were feared by everyone, but the town's business districts were the most vulnerable to wide spread conflagrations. Nearly every community of any size organized some type of a volunteer fire department to meet the forthcoming battles, for they were positively assured that they would come. Clare had a well organized fire fighting brigade in

Clare's first automotive fire truck.

Dr. Dunlop's Medical Hall. This drugstore was the town's first brick building. It was destroyed by fire.
Photo from the Jim Grove Collection

1900. A. R. Canfield was its captain and would remain at the top rung for many years. Albert Lasher served as Lieutenant and T. S. Dorsey was the secretary. Hose Company No. 1 was captained by James Louch, with Ed Hawkins serving as his Lieutenant. Pipemen were E. Goodman and James Daugherty. Hose Company No. 2 was headed by Captain M. N. Dehart, assisted by Lt. Fred Loomis. Pipemen were Sam Northy and C. H. Johnson.

In 1901, several small arson fires were set, one on the second floor of the bank building, in the closet which separated Dr. Lamb's office from Lawyer Perry. An hour after this was put out, the Doherty warehouse was set on fire. The arsonist used kerosene in both blazes. A month later, a locomotive pausing near Gorr's mill, sent sparks onto the lumber piles. While the firemen were fighting this problem, J. F. Tatman's store was set afire.

William Sines said he saw the arsonist fleeing from the rear of the store carrying a kerosene can. Within an hour Sines was dead, and foul play was strongly suspected. Since the alledged arsonist was identified as A. J. McKinnon, and his reputation was being rapidly downgraded, he wrote a letter to the COURIER, denying any part of a plot to collect insurance on his grocery store next door.

In 1903, J. E. Doherty took over the Hook and Ladder department, assisted by Lt. James S. Bicknell. Lt. C. S. Clark had joined Hose Company No. 1 replacing Ed Hawkins. Their big challenge came in August when five frame buildings on McEwan Street were observed on fire around 2:45 a.m. The businesses were between 4th and 3rd streets, and swept the business district south of 4th Street. Destroyed were: John Jackson's Meat Market, E. H. DeVogt's Studio, George McKerrachee's Harness Shop, Enoch Fish's bicycle shop, T. Smith's furniture and clothing shop, D. J. Fox jewelry building, J. S. Bicknell groceries, Ed Gilmore's restaurant, and the Friedr. Lange bakery building. These were old buildings, some of which were built after a devastating fire in the same block back in the 1870's.

Late February in 1904 the fire hydrants were all frozen and people were holding their breaths, hoping that spring would come before a major fire arrived, but the Exchange Hotel fire came first. A hose was strung from the Althouse factory, but it was too late. "Con" Mullen, the current proprietor had several heating stoves going during the cold night, and one overheated. Hotels in those days were heated by several space heaters. The Lackie House, later known as the Central Hotel had seven chimneys, with long runs of smoke stack pipe going through the various rooms. Its a wonder that this hotel didn't burn also.

Harrison experienced a fire in May when the O. D. Cleveland Heading mill burned. Kilns and lumber piles all went up in smoke. So important was this business to the town, that one thousand dollars was subscribed for its re-construction. This same month, fires were raging all across the upper peninsula as the dry spring made the whole region a tinder box. Homesteads were burned as well as lumber camps. Moorestown in Missaukee County also suffered a severe loss when the Buehler saw mill went up in a fifty thousand dollar fire.

THE JULY 1904 TORCH FIRE

Ora Dawson, son of George E. Dawson of Rosebush came to Clare for the extravaganza which would extend for five days, climaxing on the 2nd of July. Evidently the street fair and public entertainment wasn't enough for his liking, so he set fire to the O'Donald barn on 5th Street. The flames swept south to 4th Street where it set ablaze the Clare Hardware's warehouse and its stock of farm wagons. Flames now spread east and west engulfing the homes of Robert McCartney and Roy Bray, as well as the dress shops of Mrs. Sines and Mrs. Pete. It stopped before burning Sam Young's property.

The other part of the blaze moved into the rear of the businesses which fronted on McEwan and began just north of the Clare Hardware, which was on the corner of 4th and McEwan. Sweeping south with increas-

The fire during the street carnival in Clare, 1904.
Photo from the Jim Grove Collection

ing furor, it destroyed the following: The Tatman building, W. P. Lewis' Cigar factory, Marie Sexsmith Millinery Shop, A. J. McKinnon's store, Silas Creeper's shoe repairing service, the Doherty building, the Thomas Maynard building, Del Kump's barber shop, James Louch Shoes, George W. Easler furniture store, James Dunwoodie blacksmith shop, the McCormick Co., Enoch Fish's bicycle shop, the telephone office, Mrs. W. D. Mckenzie's millinery shop, the IOOF Lodge, and the D. J. Brewer camp meeting room. Davy and Co. suffered a scorched front.

Several businesses temporarily relocated, while some such as Mrs. McKenzie moved out of town. Owners of the business lots planned to rebuild with fire brick buildings, placing fire walls between each one. They saw how A. J. Doherty's fire wall on the opera house stopped the progress of the flames moving north, and the lesson would be remembered. An alley was placed behind the new stores for servicing, as well as safety.

A problem which the fire accented was the shortage of fire hose, so the council bought another five hundred feet. Another handicap was the substandard quality of the water system to fight major fires. Some thought the mains were large enough, but larger pumps were needed. Others thought a new supply north at the river would solve the bottlenecks, but all knew that something had to be done soon. Mayor Lacy considered this to be his number one problem and he began working on it.

The buildings destroyed were landmarks from the lumbering era, and one, the Lewis Cigar Factory, had served as the drugstore building for Henry Trevedick, Clare's first druggist.

James F. Tatman bought Maynard's building and prepared to erect a forty six foot by ninety foot building on the two lots. Overhead he planned to have office spaces, one of which would house the State Republican Central Committee and Dennis Alward. Tatman, sorting through his charred remains, found the safe and opened it. All the school records were there in excellent condition. He was serving as the school board's secretary at the time.

Dawson's part in the fire didn't come to light for two years, and then by a simple statement he made to a friend. He hadn't been in his right mind for years and was the slave of cigarettes. Since this was the beginning of Clare's big move toward temperance, you can imagine what kind of ammunition this gave the prime movers.

The CLARE SENTINEL was strongly anti-cigarettes and bore down on the half-dozen high school students who smoked on their way to school each morning. Welch promised to name them unless they put away the filthy habit.

In 1906, the dry spring caused another spate of forest fires in the upper peninsula. Dozens of lumber camps were burned out. Back in Clare, the Dunwoodie block burned, taking down a grocery store, the billiard hall, a tailor shop and the Riley Parrish residence. Clare's new fire alarm system was about two months late for this blaze. The city council arranged to distribute widely in town seven fire-alarm call boxes which a citizen could use to telegraph the news of a fire. They didn't work very well, but since the telephone central office closed down during the early morning hours, this was the only way to rapidly alert the town.

Lake George had a large fire for its size in June of 1906. A freight train was switching cars when sparks caused a lumber pile to ignite. Two thousand five hundred dollars worth of lumber and three railroad cars were burned. The ice house and F. A. Luce's store were threatened with the extreme heat, but men were able to control the fire with water.

A fire in the western half of the business block bounded by 4th Street, Beech Street and 5th Street wiped out a fire trap, but the losses were sorely felt nevertheless. Those establishments which burned out in March of 1907 include: M. E. Whitney's poolroom, W. H. Elden Implements, Mrs. Courtland's Millinery, J. E. Smith Bakery, James Campbell's building, C. W. Perry's barn, W. T. Weir's second hand store, the Michigan Telephone Co., the Clare Electric Light Co., A. E. Mussell and Son store, and the W. S. Cooley barn.

The new water system worked better this time and the Mt. Pleasant Fire Department equipment, which came up by train, helped

Nearly every business house on the east side of McEwan Street between 4th and 5th Streets was destroyed by this arsonized fire.
Photo from the Jim Grove Collection

contain the flames to the western half of the vulnerable block. Water department engineer, Wm. J. Holmes arose from a sick-bed and started the auxillary pump on the reserve six inch wells. He had to be helped back to his sick-bed, but his heroic efforts saved a greater loss of property.

Harry DeFoe climbed a light pole and cut a hot wire with his pliers. As they melted from the heat a fellow standing on the ground said, "I wouldn't have done that for all of Clare."

Three months later, Clare was hit again with an immense fire. Only ten firemen responded to the blaze as it was vacation time. Flames hit the Foss bakery, Dwyer building, Mrs. Parmeter's meat market, Dr. Mulder's building, Wm. Lange shoe shop and Silas Creeper's shoe repairing facility, in back. Some of these businesses were struck repeatedly by fires which were started in other buildings or by arsonists, but they were the ones who stood the losses.

Harrison's Pittsburgh Steel Company's stave mill was the next casualty. When this building went down, along went the town's electrical supply. The local fire department responded ably and salvaged as much as possible, but this fire about did in the weakening lumber business in town.

Farwell next felt the flames as May unfolded in 1909. Three store buildings were consumed and several businesses were wiped out including: J. F. "Asa" Leonard's grocery store; D. R. Wait Grocery; C. I. Mauer Grocery; Myrtle Sifton Millinery; Silloway and Boucher Billiard Hall; Weisman's store; the J. W. McMichael's store; Farwell Banking Company; K.O.T.M. Hall; D. I. Elder furniture store; and the Bell Telephone Office. Most of this loss, as was usually the case, had no insurance underwriting it.

Fred Wait lost a lot of timber when a forest fire went through Sections 6 and 7 of Freeman and over into 31 and 32 of Redding Township in the fall of 1908. He had to salvage the scorched logs before insects and rot destroyed them. His losses were high.

A small fire in the new Jackson Block damaged slightly the telephone office, the Nedry and Johnson Studio, Mrs. A. S. Krantz Millinery and the Jackson Meat

The "Calkins" after the January 20, 1920 fire.

Market. Most of these losses were covered by insurance in 1909.

Temple lost its Ann Arbor railroad depot in March of 1910 when a train threw sparks on its roof. A heavy wind fanned the flames and within an hour, ashes were all that remained.

Two of Clare's remaining four original buildings were destroyed in August of 1910. The Avery VanBrunt Grocery in the Bogardus Block and the George Brown barber shop were all that remained of the 1870's. The feed barn owned by John O'Callaghan and built by W. S. Cooley and Charles Whitney burned. George Hersey owned it at the time of the fire. O'Callaghan re-built a barn which still stands on McEwan street near the 3rd Street corner.

The store building next door was built in 1878 and was owned by J. E. Ladd of Hamilton, burned and was replaced by the Big Garage which eventually Hampton's turned into the Ford Garage.

A more surprising fire was the brick building conflagration of Dr. Dunlop's Medical Hall. It was Clare's first brick building and housed the Idle Hour Nickle Theatre upstairs. The A. S. Rhoades grocery store south of the brick structure wasn't burned, but Dunlop suffered a total loss of his drug store.

Rodabaugh's restaurant down on 4th Street, next door to the Central Hotel was burned when a worker spilled some gasoline while filling the stove storage tanks. Duff McKinnon was injured, but the flames were put out by the firemen.

1910 was to claim another business house. The 1890 structure which Wolsky (since changed to Wolsey) began burning about 2:00 a.m. Dr. Gray returning from a rural house call spotted it and sounded the alarm. Even though there was no wind, the intense neat laid to ashes the stores of L. E. Davy and J. H. Wilson, Thomas Holbrook, Featherby and Co. and the quarters of the Masonic Lodge. The Central Hotel was scorched a fourth time. Holbrook suffered the greatest loss as he had a large Christmas inventory destroyed. The block was not rebuilt for years afterwards.

Theatres were a dangerous place in the early years because of the intense heat given off by the arc lamps and also because most early buildings had no exits except in the front of the building, right where the flames would have ignited the film. State regulations would soon force all theatres to have exit doors at the rear, and this made the movies a safer place to attend. During August of 1911, however, the Temple Theatre had exits only in front. Twenty-four people were in the audience, and they escaped only with great difficulty. The firemen were having a general meeting at the time and all forty-one showed up. Otherwise a loss of life could have been expected.

Harrison's entire south side business district consisting of all original buildings burned in February of 1912. Structures which served the community well since 1882 were nothing but ashes.

John Mauer lost his clothing stock in 1912, when a fire swept through the James Duncan building. He lost $4,800 in stock, about half of which was covered by insurance.

St. Cecilia's was having services early one February morning in 1914, when an electrical short started a fire which damaged the alter, walls and roof. Firemen soon controlled the blaze.

Floyd Kirkpatrick had leased the Mussell Drug Store and he was the next victim of a fire which started in March of 1917. $5,000 worth of insurance covered most of the loss which started in the debris piled in back of the store. W. H. Elden suffered $2,500 losses and Thomas Holbrook again was victimized by a fire not of his own making. The Wilson-Davy Company next

door suffered smoke damage. Drs. F. C. and Burt Sanford lost their offices, as did Drs. Roe and Mussell. L. C. Hulbert lost his studio which was overhead.

The last fire in this period of time was set in the old creamery building used by Jay Wyman and Patrick O'Toole. One Hundred twenty tons of hay were burned and hundreds of dollars worth of eggs were destroyed. Plans were made to replace it with an elevator.

Many towns lost more property, and certainly more lives, than did Clare County's. Gladwin, for instance, in 1900 lost sixteen buildings worth $50,000. For a time it seemed the whole town was doomed as a high wind prevailed all during the battle. Albert Bergan burned to death in the disaster, as the fire started in the billiard hall where he resided. It was an immense disaster for the town.

Coleman lost most of its business district in just one hour during February of 1904. Everything from Washington to Railroad Street on the west side of 4th Street went except for a small shoe shop. Water pipes were frozen here too, and firemen were helpless to prevent the Post Office destruction along with the Bower's Saloon, Myer's Jewelry Store and Frank Small's saloon. Dr. McKay's office burned along with the Union Telephone Co. and the Allen General Store.

Marion's business district burned in November of 1904, when a $200,000 fire wiped out the town. Eight hundred residents in town suffered as every church and store was leveled by the flames which started in the Opera House block.

Two successive fires baptized Beaverton in 1909. Two-thirds of the town was desolated by the $50,000 fires. It was thought that a saloon was the point of origin for the first fire, but smoldering sparks ignited the second and more devastating flames. Firemen couldn't control the wind and there wasn't enough water in the hoses to bring the inferno to heel.

Midland lost $75,000 worth of business property in August of 1910 as it suffered its worst disaster. There had been a series of small fires, and finally the big one came in

August. Reardon Bros.' big store was the main loss, but offices for professional people, lodges and the Bell Telephone were not insignificant.

Residents in Michigan were glad they didn't live in Minnesota or Manitoba during October of 1910. Thirteen towns were on fire and residents were jumping into wells as the flames passed overhead. Eight hundred died and five thousand were homeless. Two thousand people were missing and the worst was expected as bodies were piled like baked loaves of bread. Fiend fire was visiting the lumber regions with the terror northern Michigan communities experienced too often in the 1890's.

Iosco County in Michigan suffered a catastrophe just as traumatic when $3,033,375 worth of property was incinerated in 1910. Oscoda forests were swept by a half million dollar disaster and towns all along the eastern shores of Michigan fought to preserve life. Alpena, Alger, Turner, Otsego, Cheboygan, Presque Isle, Antrim, Mackinac, Charlevoix, Posen and Roscommon were facing flames that turned their happy homesteads and communities into charred remains of black ashes and smoldering timbers. Villages on the Michigan Central R.R. were isolated as the railroad ties were burned up. Rails were warped by the heat and fleeing passenger trains were derailed into the hot flames. It was a terrible disaster for northern Michigan.

Heavy rains finally came along and put the fires out. Slowly, news came out that original losses were highly exaggerated as they normally are, but the total losses exceeded $3,988,928.

Prof. C. L. Hall of the University of Michigan's forestry department in 1912 said, "There is no excuse for having forest fires. Means to fight the fires is antiquated. The cost of protecting U.S. forest lands is three cents a square mile. Michigan loses hundreds of times this amount in timber to say nothing of lives and towns."

A fire went through Lake City again, this time in March of 1912. An entire block of businesses were wiped out, including eight stores. The fire hydrants were frozen in this town's hour of need, also.

Perry, Michigan was burned when sparks from a passing Grand Trunk Train dropped onto the elevator. Losses here amounted to $200,000. Men standing on the M-E church roof put out six fires before the battle was won.

Reports from Lansing said that one hundred house fires were caused by old fashioned candles burning and then falling onto something combustible. In 1914, over two million dollars worth of property was threatened in February alone.

Lake George felt the forest fires again in 1917 as the pasture around F. A. Luce's barns burned. He lost some sheep to the flames, as did Erastus Bigelow, who also lost his recently constructed house. The fire traveled as fast as a mare could run, and threatened to do even greater damage, but the wind shifted and caused the fire to turn on itself.

FIRE INSURANCE COMPANIES

Farmers sought to protect themselves by forming mutual fire insurance companies. One of the more successful ventures was the Clare, Lake, Osceola Counties Mutual Fire Insurance Co. They began in 1905 and gave modest protection during the early years. By 1910 the company had been renamed the Tri-County Mutual Insurance Co. of Reed City, and later it merged into the Hastings Mutual Insurance Co. which still operates today.

Churches

One characteristic of the viable communities in the northern counties during the developmental years was the pervasive influence of the churches upon them. By the time the new century dawned over the heartland of Michigan, churches from many denominations were in full stride, providing personal religious experiences and ameliorating services to a population buffeted by the crude lumbermen and some pioneers. They were well attended, but poorly endowed financially, as almost everyone was hard pressed for money.

Two of the oldest churches functioning in the county, the Methodist-Episcopal and the Congregational, were making plans to rebuild their edifices in the first decade of the twentieth century. The Congregationalists dedicated theirs in November of 1909 and the Methodists during the month of September, 1910. Other congregations such as the Catholics, Seventh Day Adventists, Baptists, Church of God and Free Methodists were building their first permanent structures around the turn of the century.

Societies of the Church of God were located in Elm Grove, Eagle, and Colonville. They used the local one-room school houses until at last the church families decided that it was time to build their own structures.

Father Malone of Midland was assigned to build the Catholic church on North McEwan Street during 1900. He assisted in laying the corner stone during August. The parish was small and the numbers were not wealthy; nevertheless, they had completely paid off all of the costs by 1905. William Haley and John Doherty paid the last $115 sometime during December of 1904. As the work grew locally, Father McAllister promoted internal organizations and caused a cemetery to be dedicated in 1910 by Bishop Richter. In Harrison, Father Miller from Gladwin held mass for the neophyte congregation as late as 1912.

The Baptists were established in Sheridan township by the Clutes, Langins and Herricks around 1888. A sister church was organized in Clare about the same time. They thrived quite admirably as group activities were part of their total worship program. For example, young people had their frequent socials, but the whole community was invited to share their Thanksgiving dinners every November. They probably came as close to emulating the Pilgrims' prototype of feasting as any group in the county.

The rural communities which grew up around a school house or a country store frequently held interdenominational or undenominational church services. Towns such as Clarence, Temple, Grandon, or Dodge hosted intermittent or irregular services, depending upon a circuit preacher or traveling evangelist to organize them. Other farming communities organized their own societies and then sought out a denomination to send a regular minister to their church. This is essentially the way the Colonville, Elm Grove and Eagle Church of God societies were started. They met in the local school house under the leadership of a lay preacher, but were energized from time to time by an outside evangelist who came in for a series of "revival meetings". The Eagle church felt the need to build when Elder Frank Bates was pastoring the charte. Elm Grove was established as a result of a great revival meeting the Rev. McNutt conducted during 1915, the year of the great world wide period of revival. Colonville had been organized by traveling ministers of the Free Methodists, but they joined the Church of God when Rev. M. D. Rogers came to the county in the 1890's.

The Latter Day Saints had moved into the county comparatively early and were strong in Hamilton, Garfield, Surrey and Silver Lake. They, too, used school houses, with the main ones being the Amble, Phelps and Bass Lake. A congregation in Farwell used the Knights of Pythias hall. It isn't known where the Greenwood, Loomis and Redding congregations met. Elder J. J. Cornish, H. DeGeer and George Bailey were the spiritual leaders and they were the ones who defended the faith from those outside the church. Rev. M. D. Rogers was one such minister who delighted in debating the alleged issues with these Mormons.

Seventh Day Adventists met in tents when they first moved into an area. In Clare, they held services on a lot at Sixth Street at Hemlock in 1912. Later they moved an old building in from Sheridan Township and turned it into a church building. The Episcopal church resumed its meetings after a short suspension about this same time.

One of the most significant community efforts the churches cooperated in was in conjunction with the Sunday School Association. Greenwood, Hayes, Frost and Summerfield, along with northern Hatton perfected an organization with F. Weatherhead as president. Mrs. Page, Mrs. Ritter and Arthur Sharland were the lay people in leadership roles. Rev. A. F. Light was the stem-winder and co-ordinator.

Methodist churches in Winterfield, Redding, Garfield, Gilmore and Leota were established in school houses and then later expanded with their own structures. All, that is except Leota, which built a church first and then held school in it until the district was operating. Winterfield bought a superannuated school in 1904 and moved it to the

James Hunt farm, a place just west of its original site in Section 16. Rev. James Caterall was its pastor during this transition. Gilmore's church building burned in 1904, but its sixty families decided to rebuild. It was a stable Methodist society, having been founded twenty-one years prior to the fire. A replacement church was dedicated in 1907. It was this same year the Rev. C. W. Jones, assisted by Missionary C. D. Petershans, built and dedicated the Leota church.

The German Lutheran congregation had fifty families when it began building in 1904. Rev. H. Grimm pastored the church during this construction and encouraged $2,000 to be subscribed. It was almost enough to pay for the entire building program. Herman Lange, John Kurz, Carl Belling, C. C. Stoll, Christian Krell, Fred and Joseph Bauer, John Schroeder and Julius Schaeffer were the senior members. Sheridan had a congregation in 1907 under Pastor H. J. Reithmeier, and circuit churches were filled by the regular pastors in the rural communities. Lake George, Hamilton, Hermansdale and others were temporarily on the circuit. Eventually the Hamilton one became a permanent

The Eagle Church of God, dedicated in 1916.
Photo from the Kleiner Family Collection

The Church of Christ purchased this church from the Clare Baptists.
Photo by Dexter Elden

247

This was the Methodist-Episcopal Church in Clare between 1910 and 1978. The windows were made by Tiffany's of New York.
Photo by Dexter Elden

Saint Cecilia's Church of Clare.
Photo by Dexter Elden

249

The Clare Baptists organized in 1882. This was their first permanent church building.
Photo by Dexter Elden

This is the second sanctuary used by the Clare Congregationalists.
Photo by Dexter Elden

251

The Clare Church of God.
Photo by Dexter Elden

A country church.
Photo by Dexter Elden

church society.

The new towns were fertile fields for the various churches to organize. Many of the incoming citizens were members of the orthodox Protestant denominations, but they found it easy to transfer their membership to the energetic preachers who fanned out into the thinly populated districts. The Free Methodists were the most successful of these aggressive evangelical ministers. They were the dominant Holiness church of the time period and held regular meetings at Temple, Gilmore, Mann Siding, Clarence and Clare. From these sites, the preachers would fan out in a circuit and the outlying areas were effectively reached with the gospel. They brought with their doctrine a degree of plainness which was in harmony with their life styles. They eschewed church organs, pianos, neck-ties, stained glass windows and ostentatious living. Their preachers breathed hell-fire and damnation, but the people loved it. There was a willingness to be subjected to this type of ministry because the frontier people were essentially a plain people and they did not go in for luxurious living, which they equated with sins of the flesh. In 1916, during the world wide revival, those living in Europe, under the guns, also approximated

Reverend and Mrs. James Gregory in 1900. He was the Free Methodist minister at Clarence.

this plain living. The less indulgent they were to their own creature comforts, the closer they felt themselves to be toward their God. The Free Methodists and other Holiness people had long held the same views. This denomination was a very strong influence for clean, plain living. They believed what they preached and acted accordingly.

The Clare Free Methodists included J. A. Allen the Clare merchant, Charles Arrand the planing mill owner, Ed Yoemans, Cora Cope, Frank Lamoreaux, who owned the gravel pit which supplied the covering for most of the local roads, Floyd and Henry Couch, George, William, Jeremiah and George Jr. Feighner, and Mrs. Del Kump. In Gilmore when their new church was dedicated in 1919, there were over three hundred people in the audience. This building was formerly in Weidman. It was moved out into the Gilmore community and placed upon a stone foundation.

Common to most of the Protestant churches were their regular "revivals." Inherent in this name is the assumption that there was something that required reviving since the former life had become moribund. Two or three of these churches would combine their efforts for a series of protracted meetings, traveling to the different locales for the preaching. Methodists, Congregationalists, Baptists and the Free Methodists were the major supporters of the revival technique.

A "revival" swept through the Brown Corners area when the Rev. R. A. Allen from the City Rescue Mission held interdenominational services in a local grove during 1913 near the Balsley school house. The effects of his efforts were continued over the next decades and helped make this a wholesome community to raise a family. The type of sordid living so often found in the frontier community was not a common trait of the Arthur township families. The revivals which periodically renewed the churches intensified the concern people had for the present and also for the future. It was enough in the way of internal discipline to foster a pious people. Colonville, Eagle, Lake, Cherry Hill, Elm Grove, Long Lake, Herrick, Lansingville, Gilmore, Clarence and Dover all experienced religious resur-

The Free Methodists held annual encampments in Cadillac prior to their permanent move to Manton. This photo was taken in 1902.

gences when their communities were hosts to the revivals.

So effective were their techniques in changing the individual that other churches modified their structure to include them. St. Cecilias, for example, invited Jesuit Missionary Rev. M. J. McNulty to Clare for a one-week mission in 1914. He gave lectures which answered the question "What must I do to possess eternal life?" Other evenings were devoted to church doctrine. The net effect was not dissimilar to the Bible thumpers.

CAMP MEETINGS

The summer extravaganzas were the camp meetings, up until the Chautauquas began arriving around the area in 1914. Union camp meetings for the various districts were hosted in Arthur, Harrison, Greenwood, Grant, Gilmore, Frost and Redding. Usually a tent was set up for a main meeting place, while small tents were clustered around it. Meetings went on as long as two weeks or so during the summer months and were

favorites for the kids.

The evangelical churches such as the Methodists and Free Methodists had conferences along with the camp meetings, and these lasted an additional week. The church fathers would meet and discuss the late year and plans for the coming campaigns against sin. Ministers would be re-assigned to different circuits at this time. Reed City, Cadillac and Manton were the most commonly used locations for these larger conference-size camp meetings. A modern business man would not find the conventions he goes to much different in purpose from these once a year pepper-uppers.

THE CHAUTAUQUAS

The orthodox Christian, Protestant and Catholic, responded to the message of Christ in a personal internalized mode, and normally that person who assimilated the ethic of Christ or a denomination was deeply influenced by it. As a by-product of the individual's new outlook on life, a pervasive climate was established in a community which was different from the individual's personal code and experience, yet very similar in important points. Honesty, fidelity, moral rectitude and dedication were basic to a healthy religious experience. Undue loyalty to one's church, circle of friends or denomination often led to intolerance and bigotry. There was a super-abundance of bigotry going around in the north as the minorities became more numerous. The old line Protestant churches felt threatened by the Mormons, Christian Scientists, Seventh Day Adventists and Catholics, and individuals said things which would have been better left unsaid.

An ameliorative force which moved into the northland during these days was the Chautuaqua. The first one held in Michigan was at Bay View in 1886 with a camp meeting atmosphere set by the Methodists. The Grand Rapids and Indiana Railroad offered special excursion rates to Petoskey, and its patronage was high from all over Michigan. After the Toledo and Ann Arbor Railroad came through to Cadillac in 1887, almost all of southern Michigan was close to a rail line which offered an economical ticket to Bay View.

Mt. Pleasant decided in 1910 that they ought to have their own Chautauqua, and so a week was set aside in July for its festivities. Ex-Governor Yates from Illinois was the featured speaker. Reports had it that a couple of musical groups were weak, but otherwise the series of meetings was commendably handled. Four years later Clare began hosting its own Chautauqua.

A big tent was unloaded in Clare during the week prior to July 14th by college boys who traveled full time with the popular entertainment. They, along with a local promotion committee, organized the big project which stayed in a town for four or five days. College girls would arrive in town the first day and care for the babies and young children, thus freeing up the mothers for the lectures and musical programs.

Professor Dr. George P. Bible, President of State Normal School in Pennsylvania, was the main speaker. Governor Robert S. Vassey of South Dakota, Professor Ganse, Superintendent of Schools in Panama and

Dr. Harry C. Hill of Peoples' Church of Indianapolis were the "names" who drew the crowds. Each was a superb crowd pleaser and they lectured in the main tent on their own special day. They traveled a circuit for several Chautauquas which operated simultaneously all over the heartland.

Superior talent was booked for these summer institutes and a wide variety of musical groups performed. The 1914 program listed an all girl orchestra, the Illinois Glee Club, a cartoonist, a baritone solist named Tom Morgan and a university orchestra from Wisconsin. On the last day, Judge Collins of City Court, Indianapolis gave an animal mimicry and bird song demonstration which was a superior entertainment.

All over the nation the Chautuaquas were well received. Former President Theodore Roosevelt called them "The most distinctive thing in the country." Judge Ben Lindsey called the Chautauqua the fourth institution in American life. The other three were the home, church and school.

While the Chautuaquas were originated by the Methodists at Lake Chautauqua, New York in 1874, they had been accepted by all citizens, and most everyone attended the programs. Railroad fares were the greatest handicap people faced when they wanted to take in one of the earlier productions, but by 1910, they were put on in localities all over the country. Clare sponsored these annual popular entertainments until the mid 1920's. Then things changed and their popularity waned.

The infinite amount of good done by these Chautauquas will never be known, but they produced a salve for communities, and helped heal the bitter strife which denominationalism promulgated. Church and secular leaders worked side by side over the years to sell the reasonably priced tickets to the rural and small town citizen. If there was one force which blended the foreign born and native sons together in the years prior to World War I, it probably was the Chautuaqua. It did for the nation what a religious experience did for the individual. The wholesomeness of American life during 1900-1940 probably was attributable to their annual presentations all across the country.

This healthy community spirit wasn't so powerful that all denominational bickering was stifled however, and there was considerable animosity exhibited between the Protestants and Catholics. During the war the YMCA became an important influence in the Army camps for the Protestants and the Knights of Columbus were recognized by the government as the Catholic counterpart. Canteens were hurriedly built by the YMCA organization in every camp and overseas installation which the military operated.

On the other hand, the Catholic organization wasn't as successful in its fund raising activities, and there were many camps without a building or chapel to hold services in. Because the YMCA, through Rev. Russell H. Bready, believed that every young man ought to maintain home patterns as much as possible, they made available the YMCA's for the Catholic services. A spokesman for the Protestant organization said, "I want every Protestant boy to feel that his church is keeping right up next to him in this hour of great struggle, and I speak to you as a Protestant minister from a Protestant pulpit when I say that I want every Catholic boy to feel that his church is keeping right close to him as the church of his Protestant chum.

"If Protestants and Catholics must antagonize each other, please let it wait until more peaceful times . . . In these times, let us pray together, let us work together until the stars and stripes are tacked to Kaiser Bill's flag staff in Berlin."

THE MISSIONARIES

India was a wide open mission field in 1900 and many Americans were drawn to its opportunities. Clare was developed enough to export its own missionaries, although there were home missionaries mining the smaller communities at the same time.

Mattie McKinley was in India and C. E. Parsons was serving in Shangai under the China Inland Missionary Board early in this century. Another Clare girl, Clara Bruske, had married missionary Rev. E. A. Rayner who was scheduled for the Phillippines in 1904. She joined him and their children were raised there. They returned to Clare in 1911. Edith Crane was a missionary to China in 1904, but it isn't known how long she served. She witnessed the Boxer Rebellion.

Farwell's contribution to the Chinese Mission field was filled most capably by Dr. and Mrs. Dennis Smith. They left San Francisco in 1914 and served as medical missionaries until 1928. Those were tumultous years for China and their first hand experiences with the Revolution were recorded in their letters home. These letters are a valuable primary source of imformation for historians who wish to understand the Chinese conundrum better.

SUFFRAGE

The church as an institution has always influenced the society in which it operated. Its influence on the Red Ribbon Societies, Temperance, Prohibition and Suffrage is widely acknowledged. It provided the troops for the crusade spearheaded by the Susan Anthonys, Jane Adams and Frances Willards. Local efforts to move the Suffrage Movement along were considerable, and many alliances were made. In March of 1919, Emiline Rhyder of Harrison, an eighty-three year old woman was able to go to the polls and vote on all of the current political questions. She had been permitted to vote five years earlier in the local school elections since she was a taxpayer, but in 1919 there were no restrictions of this nature. Participatory democracy had taken a giant step, mostly because of the women from the Christian churches.

City of Clare

Almost without exception, the early civil governments of Clare were in the custody of the Republican party and under the personal benign leadership of S. C. Kirkbride. Although he never had held an elective public office, Kirkbride dominated the entire county. His rule was to be challenged in 1895 when A. R. Canfield moved down to Clare from Harrison and began publishing his COURIER, a rabid Democratic newspaper. Four years later, Canfield was joined by A. J. Lacy directly from the University of Michigan's Law School. Between these two, the town was converted temporarily to the party of Cleveland. It was a major political re-alignment, perhaps facilitated by the major changes which overshadowed individuals during the onset of the new century.

By definition, the first generation of citizens in Clare were the pioneers. They were the lumbermen, railroad builders, homesteaders, fledgling entrepreneurs, farmers, roustabouts, law breakers and civilizers. They came into a frontier country and made it serve their own peculiar needs according to the best and worst goals they held collectively and individually. Clare County had some excellent frontiersmen. Clare County also had some of the worst frontiersmen ever noted in Michigan's history, but these two types co-existed in a stable accommodation of each other's vested interests. The church people avoided certain parts of town because they belonged to the saloon crowd. Likewise, the brawling men and bawdy women stayed out of the respectable residential districts. No one had to enforce this separation, it simply existed.

Commercial warehousing, stockyards, shingle mills, saloons and bagnios were near the railroad tracks. Hotels which were located in that area catered to the seedy element in society. Three blocks north of the railroad district was the elegant and highly respectable "Calkins" house, one of Clare's major claims to fame in 1900.

The pioneering generation had finished all that it was going to do to Clare by 1900, and many of the originals were being replaced. It was almost as if the individual knew that he had lived out his purpose, and that it was time to leave. Many of the off-spring of these restless pionieers also felt the climate changing and they began their exodus to Montana, Idaho, Oregon, Dakota, California, Washington and the Canadian provinces.

As lumbering faded from the northlands rather quietly, a large surplus population had been created by 1900. There was a very limited demand for woodsmen, river drivers, mill hands and railroaders, and had those workers continued to stay on, much economic distress would have been encountered. There wasn't much going on in the heartland of Michigan during this transition period to indicate that there would be a better tomorrow. All that was apparent was a dying industry dragging down an entire county to poverty levels. Most eyes were fastened on the death throes of the old, not on the birth pangs of a new society. Many of the older generation considered Clare's economic life-span to be approximately forty years, and death was just around the corner.

Human types who thrive under frontier

conditions are stifled when a robust, unstructured society no longer exists. As Clare was now structured, these pioneer types had to be free from the restraints being imposed on them. When the railroad "boomers" came through looking for settlers in the western states, these restless ones began moving on. The citizens who stayed watched sadly as their friends pulled up roots and departed. Buckets of tears were shed by both groups during this transition as thousands of residents migrated west.

Young boys who grew up during this era struggled with school discipline on one side and the lure of freedom on the other. Many lads were trapped by a beguiling idea that they could be happier out of school and out of Michigan. One such lad wrote his story fifty years later. Here is how he recalled his move west.

"Being one of ten children, and there not being much work for either my father or brothers to do, my parents made arrangements with an older brother to take charge of me if I was able to successfully make the journey to Cosmopolis, Washington. On the very last day of the special westward rates, I had my ticket in hand, ready to board the north bound noon train for the Pacific Northwest. My fare had only cost thirty dollars.

"Ma had packed my telescope valise with baked cookies, cakes and bread. She figured the sandwiches, jelly tarts, dill pickles, and preserves would see me through the week long train ride to the Pudget Sound district. I'll never forget that after the third day, the food was so dried out, my seat mate thought I was eating oatmeal.

"My older brother, Glenn, had sent forty-five dollars for my car fare and other expenses two weeks earlier. Since I had never been away from home, I never had any respectable clothing, so that became an important project before leaving. Pa was so laid up with rheumatism that he couldn't leave the house, and I was sent to town alone, the day before my departure west, to buy some kind of a suit.

"Not knowing what I was doing, I had bargained for an eight dollar suit which the shopkeeper layed away for me to pick up the

Thomas Holbrook

next day on my way to the depot. Of course I didn't do the right thing and when I told Pa what the suit cost, he said, 'I wish I had been there. I could have gotten a better bargain than that . . . Don't take it! Tomorrow get into town in plenty of time, go across the street to that cut-rate clothing store and jew them down.'

"The next morning, early, Pa went into much detail about the finer points of buying clothes and everything else that had a quick sales pitch. I was in trim shape to buy my traveling clothes.

"Ma packed my telescope with food and what clothing I owned. During the packaging of the sandwiches, she sniffled a lot and fought back tears just as she had for the others of her brood who had already broken away and were on their own. But at sixteen, I was the youngest to go so far from home.

"Pa was not able to go a piece of the way, but Ma walked with me across the pasture that was in the direction of town. At the fence, Ma stopped, and then kissing me, told me to be on my way. After a few minutes, I turned and looked back, and there she was, still standing as I had left her, with the apron up to her eyes, her shoulders shaking as she was grieving for a son who was now thrown into a world she knew only too well. She knew of the dangers in the lumbering districts and the tears she shed were tears of love for me. I never realized before this moment that Ma had loved me. She was always so busy with the younger kids, baking, dish washing and clothes mending and she always seemed to be scolding me or Frank. I wanted to run back and hug her and tell her how much I loved and cared for her, but I didn't. Quickly turning away I walked into town, anxious to get my new suit and to be on my way.

"Our farm was next to the railroad on the north side of town, and as the train neared the old homeplace, I lowered the window and waved good-bye to my childhood and the parents who loved me so much more than I ever knew.

"Pa wrote in a letter that he had seen my handkerchief waving as the train pulled by and out of sight. He was lying in bed and Ma had helped him to the window. They both cried for their son."

THE EMIGRANT TRAINS

A large scale movement of people was under way between 1900-10, and the railroad "boomers" were part of the reason. They would spread rumors and stories about the west, about how easy it was to become rich by jumping at the opportunities now opened to men and their families. Special trains would be made up, traversing a district and picking up whole families on their way west. Passenger fares were so low, that no one could say he couldn't afford to go.

The Clare Union Depot in 1913.
Photo from the Jim Grove Collection

Later, those who didn't find the western states a paradise and sought railroad transportation back to Michigan, found the rate had increased by three hundred or four hundred per cent.

Big changes in the communities of northern Michigan were taking place in the first decade of the new century. The old generation was having to make way for the new. The frontiersmen and women either died, moved or adjusted. They had to, as there was nothing else they could do. A revolution was sweeping out the old and bringing in the new agrarian society.

As if on cue, the log cabin of pioneer saw mill owner, George Boorn, burned in the spring of 1900. This was probably the first actual residence in the geographical area that became Clare. There had been lumber camps within the village, built by the McEwans in 1868, but the single family cabins came later. Peter Callam had thrown his canvas tenting over a large tree limb in the summer of 1870 down on First Street, but again, that was a commercial enterprise, Clare's first general store. The original home in Clare was gone as the century began to unfold. It was as though the old slate was being wiped clean.

On March 27, 1900, an Ann Arbor train, specially designated for a migration to North Dakota, pulled into Clare and fifteen families loaded their possessions onto it. The fare was fourteen dollars and twenty-five cents for each passenger, and baggage rates were correspondingly priced. The big attraction in the Dakotas at this time was the placement on the market of government land, as reasonably transferred to the modern homesteaders as to those who qualified under the Homestead Act of 1862.

Oregon had been the popular destination for other Michiganians two years earlier, but by February of 1900, Oregon was sending out warnings through the Central Labor Council, to avoid making the trip. "Sharks" had oversold the availability of land and jobs. The city of Portland was overwhelmed with immigrants, and some were near starvation. The prime movers in these mass exoduses were the railroads. They had been given tremendous grants of prime timber land, but they needed people to buy the cut over lands, as well as customers for goods shipped from eastern markets. If enough settlers would come in, immediate and future business would make the railroads very solvent financially.

California had also been boomed as a land flowing with milk and honey, except there, orange groves were touted. Tens of thousands of acres were sold for these future orange groves at prices starting around one thousand dollars an acre. That promotion was so bald that even the unwise began to catch on. Oregon never had those high prices for farm land, but more acres of prime agricultural soils were being sold than existed, by about two hundred percent.

Nevertheless, the footloose and restless generation went west anyway. Saskatchewan absorbed a large number of Clareites with the lure of its vast, fertile wheat plains available under acceptable prices and conditions.

WHY DID THEY LEAVE?

Demographers have been able to construct a theoretical population mobility model for some types of economies. For instance, in agrarian lands, if a population increases for three decades, a maximum sustainable level is reached. Next, the population begins to export its surplus population. In Clare's case, it exported the lumbering population, not the agrarian, because one hadn't developed in the county at this point.

Out they went! Sixty Isabella and Clare families boarded a train for Idaho in April of 1903, crossing Lake Michigan on the car-ferries, through Wisconsin, Minnesota and the Dakotas. The promised land was further west. The West! What a powerful magnet that slogan produced. People were hypnotized by the lure of the Pacific regions.

When the townships emptied out, land prices dropped, enticing farmers from Ohio and Indiana to come in. Generally, those farmers who came into the county during the 1900-10 decade were far better suited to build farms, pull stumps, drain swamps and to till the soil than the frontiersmen, but

they were the malcontents from a highly taxed state, and low taxes were enticements strong enough to draw them here in their schooner wagons.

Even though the local assessors placed high valuations on property owned by absentee citizens, property taxes assessed were not heavy burdens for the wealthy barons to bear. Ammi W. Wright, A. P. Brewer, J. F. Brand, Wellington Burt, Edmund Hall, M. H. Church and others were the largest holders of vast tracts of stump land. What they planned to do with them isn't clear, but probably they were speculating, hoping that something would cause the price of the pines barrens to go up. If this is so, they were in luck.

Discussed in the agricultural chapter is the development of these large blocks of land, first by the sheepmen, followed later by the stockmen and dairying interests. Clare's place in all of this was to be the supplier of capital, goods and a shipping point for agricultural products. The new immigrants coming into Clare, replacing the departed lumber era frontiersmen, were the storekeepers, bankers, insurance agents, professions and others of the service related castes.

1903

If there was ever a pivotal year for the city of Clare, it had to be 1903. Death claimed Christopher Clute, Edmund Hall, James Louch, Isabell Alger and Captain Gardner. Each of these represented an important type of role in a frontier society. Farmers, lumbermen, tradesmen, hotel keepers and the Civil War Veterans were dealt a major blow by these deaths. Nathan Bicknell, one of the dominent retail merchants on Main Street, retired, even though he was only fifty-six. His health was failing, but sons Wm. H. and James S. were well integrated into the business community. They would ably carry on, using the same work ethic which had guided the patriarch.

Fred Lister and Charles O'Donald were two local men who had gathered a sizeable amount of cash by operating their lumber, shingle and stave mills effectively. By August

The main building on "Wall Street" in Clare (West Fourth Street) was this Central Hotel. It was also known as the Lackie House for years. Homer Douglas is standing on the left end. Landlord Lackie is on his left. 1914.

1903, these two had perfected their Citizens Bank plans, and so they opened their doors for business. O'Donald, however, was not destined to enjoy the fruit of their wealth, as he died within a month. Lister continued on with the help of George Benner and J. R. Goodman, their cashier and teller respectively.

The Clare Rolling Mill was erected during 1903 on N. McEwan Street, in the railroad district, by William Callam. Callam was related to Clare's first businessmen and postmaster, Peter Callam, and he always had strong ties here. Taking personal and business risks rather freely during his younger days, William was a wealthy man by 1900. He was willing to put some of that money to work in the town he loved. A new turbine water wheel and generator was put in the mill down on Dewey Lake, and electricity was generated. Copper wires were strung around Cherry Grove Cemetery on their way to the new flouring mill, where electrical motors turned the heavy machinery.

The Calkins brothers owned the Clare Hardware in 1902 when they built a modern brick building. A year later, Lewis and Patrick from Ovid, bought the business, with Lewis becoming the tinsmith. Both men knew how to run a competitive store.

Mayor Lacy's Business Men's Improvement Association was able to agree upon some type of food processing plant being built here, suggesting a canning factory like the one at Fremont. Clark Sutherland and John A. Jackson thought that one was too large as it employed one thousand two hundred workers and cost fifty-two thousand dollars. However it did one hundred thousand dollars worth of business in 1902, an amount equal to the total beef market in Clare. The temptation to begin a corporation was strong, but it was resisted. Instead, they opted for a pickling station installed by the E. G. Dailey Company of Detroit. Seventeen large brine tanks were installed on the west end of Seventh Street at the railroad tracks, as well as a fifty-six foot by sixty foot building. Each vat was ten and one-half feet in diameter and eight feet deep. Two hundred acres' growth of cucumbers were dumped into each vat.

William Callam

John O'Callaghan owned a livery stable in Clare, where a few horses were sheltered while their owners took care of their business. In 1903, he built a large sixty foot by one hundred fifteen foot feed barn, housing eventually up to one hundred horses at a time. It faced Fourth Street and was behind the Flouring Mill.

A fire in August of 1903 forced several large construction projects in the same block. Friedr. Lange's old bakery was finally burned down, as were the Bicknell stores. Late in August, four car loads of bricks were brought onto the building site and a new thirty-three foot by one hundred foot dry goods store was constructed. It has withstood the elements for over seventy-five years.

Wholesale businesses came to town when Wyman and Danley arrived in 1903. They took over the Doherty warehouse along side the Pere Marquette railroad, connecting it to a poultry processing plant. Twenty-five men dressed chickens and forwarded them to the eastern markets from this location.

Wyman and Cruickshank, wholesalers also, bought warehouses alongside the Ann Arbor railroad for their hay purchasing and forwarding business. A year later, Burch and Wyman took over the Bicknell warehouse, and began buying grains, later processing beans and providing elevator services.

The last major change effected by Mayor Lacy was the Clare Furnace Company. It was capitalized for ten thousand dollars and began building brick foundry buildings for casting the internal heat radiators. This brick building has been used over the years as part of a large lumber yard. It too stands, even after seventy-five years of service.

Not everything projected for 1903 came to fruition. Dr. Dunlop said he and John Northon would open a third bank in Clare. It was scheduled to open by August, but it never came off.

Fred Stanley's potash factory was put back into operation during November, having suffered from a fire earlier during the soft-soap production year. This was more successful than the concrete brick factory C. W. Calkins wanted to build. Calkins estimated that twenty thousand could be manufactured a day, but the ten thousand dollars needed for capital even made Fred Lister and C. W. Perry go slow. They were the town's bankers, but in 1903, too many projects were eating into their reserves.

Finally, the Davy and Company made plans to brick up their old wooden store on the northwest corner of McEwan and Fourth Street. Construction was to be commenced during the spring of 1904. The dying town of Clare wasn't dying anymore. It had come alive with vigor in 1903, and soon eighty percent of the county's business would be centered within its corporation limits. The corner had been turned under the direction of Mayor Lacy, but he was helped by Fred Lister, C. W. Perry, Clark Sutherland,

The O'Callaghan Feed Barn, 1903
Drawing by Holly Maxwell

William and John Dunlop

E. A. Anderson

James S. Bicknell, Wm. H. Bicknell, L. E. Davy, George Benner and Edgar G. Welch.

Dr. Reeder, taking over the task of beautifying the town, enlisted Will Adams, and between the two of them lawns, maple trees, flowers, a park and terraces were heavily promoted. On Arbor Day, 1904, a work bee uprooted scores of poplar trees, and replaced them with Norway and Sugar maples. As Dr. Reeder said, "Let's look ahead a few years. We'll see the results of our efforts and Clare will have beauty galore."

Reeder had divided the city into twelve districts and a leader was assigned the task of rooting out the burdocks, and removing the unsightly debris from the town. Dr. Reeder's "bacillus aestheticus" spread rapidly throughout the town.

THE GROWLER

Cheerful people began asserting themselves in town, and the rapidly developed sheep lands west and north of town encouraged them to continue. Efforts by the city's promoters, however, ran into the soured old men who thought all of the changes in town were foolishness. Here is how one Clare businessman described an encounter he had with a "growler".

"The corner grocer and delivery boy were busy sorting out the apples from a barrel for a fruit display, when the growler stopped by. They didn't notice his entry and were startled to hear him speak.

"'Things are coming to a pretty pass in this town when them goslins what call themselves businessmen are talking about giving a bonus for 'nother railroad. They seem to think that every new moon the people are s'posed to shell out about half of

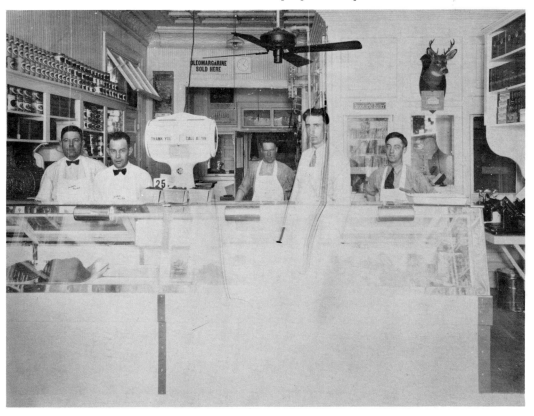

Jackson's Meat Market at the corner of Fourth and McEwan Streets. (L-R) Lawrence Jackson, Frank Jackson, George Wilkie, Elmer Osborn, and Emerson Hickey.
Photo from the Jackson Family Collection

their earning's for some 'paper-collared' chap that blows in here with a hatful of schemes for boomin the town.'

"The grocer regained his perpendicular posture after being doubled up in the apple barrel for several minutes, and as soon as he regained his breath regularly, he ventured the suggestion that a few months ago, if memory served him correctly, the visitor was strongly opposing the establishment of a wagon factory in the city, because the promoter asked for fire protection for his plant and the privilege of blowing a whistle three times a day.

"'Yes, I was agin' that buggy factory idea because they don't amount to nothin'! Down where I come from the town gave three hundred dollars for a buggy factory and after running it two years, it burned up. The feller said he'd double the size if the town would give him another three hundred dollars. We didn't do no sich thing, and he left. Guess he thought we were easy marks.'

"Some people think a canning factory in Clare would be a good thing. It would furnish a market for a lot of truck that don't now meet with a ready sale.

"'Hah! Durn nice institution for a town, that is. Run about three months in the year and the balance of the time a roost for chimney swallows and cobwebs. When they do run, they hire kids and old women for fifty cents a day and make about thirty-seven percent for the owners. The farmers have enough to do now and don't want to raise no truck garden. Such establishments are a damage to a town.'

"The grocer was becoming unhappy with the visitor. 'What sort of industry do you think would add prosperity to Clare?' he asked.

"'I can tell you in a minute. We want a steel mill like they're got down in Pittsburg. Something that amounts to somethin! A sugar factory, a cement plant, a 'biler factory, a ship yard or a cotton mill. Them's the kind of things that does a town some good. When you fellers get any of them to locate here and get started so I can see they are stayers, I'll give just as much as any other man of my means to encourage them. These little one-horse concerns are a nui-

sance to Clare.' "

Grumpy old men who down-played the efforts of others who were attempting to improve the town weren't limited to the pool-room gang. Dr. A. E. Mulder, the town's dentist, was directing two bands in 1904. One was in Clare and the other at Dover. Each one needed a place to meet for practice. The Clare site was the upstairs of City Hall. As part of the 1903 efforts, the rooms had all received a coat of fresh paint.

The council members instructed the mayor to tell Dr. Mulder about the habit some of his musicians had of spitting tobacco juice on the floor, ignoring the spitoons. Mulder countered by saying his bandsmen didn't chew when they were practicing and so the tobacco juice found on the floor probably was left over from the late election.

The next meeting the council voted four to one to oust the band. Councilman James Bicknell thought the band ought to be accommodated somehow, but he wasn't present when the vote was taken. A month later, the council, under Bicknell's urging, rescinded their vote and offered the upstairs room to the band.

By this time the musicians and Dr. Mulder were a little sore at the council and found a practice room over in Haley's Hall. The bandsmen passed the word that, "Come next Memorial Day, don't you be expecting free music."

THE HOUSING BOOM!

A robust business expansion in 1903 led to the 1904 housing boom. Dr. Maynard built a new house on 6th Street and Fred Lister spent ten thousand dollars for a new home on N. McEwan Street. James Alger, W. P. Lewis, Rev. J. H. Lowe, Mrs. Fall, Phillip Ripenberg, A. C. Gordanier, Joe Hudson, Mrs. A. E. Mussell, George Easler, Ruben Immick, James F. Tatman and Frank Doherty all either built new homes or substatantially improved their old ones. Over one hundred thousand dollars had been invested in new housing during 1904. It was a banner building year.

mercial sector continued throughout 1904 and 1905, as the ''torch-job'' on the business district in July had wiped out many important retailers. Replacement buildings were fire proofed as brick was used in the several business blocks.

Businessman, actor, father, and civic leader George B. Wells.

Photo from the Wells-Carlson Collection

Davy and Company had completed the re-organization of their seventy-five thousand dollar business which operated in Clare and Evart by moving along with their new store building in early 1904. The company had started in Evart during 1882, utilizing an eight foot by ten foot room. Now there were forty employees and they were the leading businessmen on the Pere Marquette railroad. The Clare store opened in 1894, but had outgrown its quarters twice previously.

The Clare Furnace Company erected its two brick main buildings in 1904. W. H. Pierce and Herman Lange were the carpenter and brick mason foremen, as a large number of men composed the construction crew. An office for George Wells had been included in architect O. M. Sutherland's plans, and it was placed in a corner of the smaller building. The company next ordered enough iron and steel raw materials to carry the company during its first two years of operation.

Other construction projects in the com-

MATTIE McKINLEY

In 1905, Mattie McKinley returned home. She had been a public school teacher in Clare during the early 1890's, but sensing a ''call'' to become a missionary to India, she prepared herself for a mission station in Darjeeling. Traveling by way of England, she arrived on the mission field in 1899, under the auspices of the Methodist-Episcopal Church. There she labored among the children who came to her little mountain school for five years, teaching them about her Savior, Jesus Christ.

Her mother, living in Clare, had become an invalid in 1903, and now was dependent upon others for the most basic services. Upon hearing of her mother's condition, Mattie realized that her return to Michigan was not in the too distant future. Taking the only means of transportation available, she arrived back home in June.

The Epworth League of the local M-E Church prepared a banquet in her honor for June 23rd. She arrived a week prior to this homecoming dinner. Rabbi Louis Wolsey, a Jewish leader laboring in Little Rock, Arkansas, came back to honor his childhood friend. Three hundred others also attended the lovefeast held in Duncan's Hall. The room and table's decorations had been purchased in Saginaw and were elegant. Clare wasn't stingy in its efforts to honor the young woman everyone admired so much. The Kirkbride Orchestra played during the meal and Frank Brownson's ten waiters catered the huge repast.

The Reverend Joseph Dutton of Mount Pleasant acted as the toastmaster so skillfully that an observer noted, '' . . . so well did he perform that even those who knew him were surprised.''

Prof. Loomis of Central Normal gave a toast to ''The American Girl.'' He compared the low standards of the American man and how girls had to move outside the normal marriage channels to meet their own superior standards.

Rabbi Wolsey, without expressing belief or disbelief in Jesus Christ, used the teachings of Christ as a comparison to what Mattie McKinley believed and did with her life. He eloquently told of her sacrifice and that of Christ's, showing that both lives had been dedicated to others. So eloquently did he present the lives of Christ and Mattie's that a minister remarked afterwards that his fondest wish was to be skillful enough to present the message of Christ as effectively as Rabbi Wolsey. At another time, during a service held in the Congregational Church, Rabbi Wolsey preached the most effective Christian sermon heard in years and many were converted to Christ under his preaching. He was a great Jewish Rabbi, but in Clare, the town he grew up in, he had learned about the Savior in the Methodist Church, and it didn't take much to get him talking about the Christian way of life.

D. E. Alward, another who knew Mattie as a child, spoke next. His comments were directed toward her decision to leave Clare for the Mission Field and how hard it was for her numerous friends to accept her foreign service. " . . . She realized the pleadings of her friends were from the heart, not the mind. They weren't to dissuade her from her mission life overseas," Alward said.

After all of the speeches and warm words of praise and admiration had been showered upon her by the community, Mattie McKinley rose to respond. There wasn't a dry eye in the auditorium as she told in her humble way of her love for Christ, for the hungry little boys and girls in far off India, and for those she left behind on the mission field. Emotions were high all during her response, but she heightened them more by saying, "I am not a martyr! I have been privileged to carry out the Great Commission of our Lord. If there is one who is deserving of your kindness it is my sister, Mrs. George Dawson, for it was she who enabled me to leave Clare in the first place."

Turning slightly to her left, she raised her arm and pointed in the direction of a little log cabin lying on the eastern edge of Clare. Inside was her mother, a bed-ridden invalid. Mattie had left a world where she was highly honored for her skills, compassion and love and had come home to be a dutiful servant for her mother.

Concluding now, the emotional tension was so high that every person was dabbing at their eyes. Each one understood that this brilliant woman had given up everything life was offering her because of love. Her love for a helpless mother.

Mattie McKinley was Clare's favorite young woman! She later became the favorite of a local preacher in the M-E Church in Wise Township, the Rev. Wm. W. Younglove, and they married. Together they served churches in California and again back in Clare.

Rev. Younglove was a remarkable man in his own right. During the Civil War he was but a teenager as were so many of the Union soldiers. His commanding officer entrusted an important message from the front to him, and it had to be delivered to the White House and President Lincoln. Quickly, amid the confusion of battle, Pvt. Younglove made his way to the nation's capitol.

Approaching the White House, he saw a door which was open. He went inside and nearly bumped into the President himself. Lincoln took the message, read and signed a receipt for its safe delivery. Then the President inquired of the messenger boy, "Did you come directly from the battle?"

"Yes Mr. President," was the reply.

"Would you join Mrs. Lincoln and myself for supper? You must be hungry!" offered the President.

And so Pvt. Wm. Younglove joined the war leader and his family for the evening meal. The President himself asked the Lord's blessing before the dining began. One thing led to another, and Mrs. Lincoln suggested that a good night's rest would be in order before the long journey back to camp. The President agreed, and so Pvt. Younglove was taken to a bedroom in the White House, where the exhausted youth of sixteen years, fell into a deep sleep.

The marriage between Mattie McKinley

Looking north on McEwan Street in 1905. On the left is Brown's Barber Shop, next to Oliver Beemer's saloon and Eli Ramey's sandwich shop.

and Wm. Younglove was a natural. Both were outstanding Christians and served the Methodist Church faithfully. Mattie died first and was buried in Cherry Grove. Rev. Younglove died in 1938 at the age of ninety-two. Their grave stones lie adjacent to each other in Cherry Grove while their souls await Resurrection Morning.

MORE THAN COMMERCE

A city is more than a business district, more than houses and streets. A city is a complex organic living and thriving community with a multiplicity of inter-related interests, joined for the purpose of helping each other survive if not to thrive. Consider then the impact of the mail order catalogs upon the local merchants and the community. In 1906, these catalogs were a serious problem to the merchants. The CLARE SENTINEL on December 7, 1906 wrote the following article. It was entitled, "Mail Catalogs."

"In business relations, a man has the right to trade wherever he pleases. But it is to be presumed we all trade where in the long run we, as we suppose, best get our money's worth. There has been much said pro and con on the question of patronizing mail order houses, especially raking farmers over the coals. Investigation reveals however, that farmers are not alone in this. Not a few of Clare's families, including merchants, are known to take a chance every now and then to trade in some distant city, going in person, or sending by mail. But of course, their own particular business should be an exception to their own rule when it comes to home patronage . . .

"Statistics show that the average farmer pays out for the things he uses and does not produce, a little over six hundred dollars each year. If he spends this with a mail order house, he will have a net savings of about ten percent per year. This, for a period of ten years would amount to six hundred dollars. The value of this man's farm, if of average fertility, depends upon the surrounding markets, schools, churches, roads and etc. Suppose he is one of five hundred farmers owning an average of one hundred sixty acres each and whose farms lie contiguous to a small town of one thousand inhabitants, with the usual number of stores, markets, schools and so on. Farms in the area would usually be worth thirty dollars an acre. Now suppose these five hundred farmers spend their six hundred dollars with the merchants in this town. Give them the sixty dollars a year they might try to save. This would amount to thirty thousand dollars a year and three hundred thousand dollars in ten years. The money would stay in town and would be invested in other enterprises and at the end of ten years, the town of one thousand inhabitants would be a lively town of two thousand or three thousand citizens, and with more and better stores, schools, churches, and roads with factories and mills employing hundreds of laboring people and an ever increasing market for farm goods. Now his farm is worth forty dollars an acre instead of thirty dollars. For the six hundred dollars squandered in his home town, he would have received one thousand six hundred dollars in value for his farm, to say nothing of the increased values of the community.

"Let us contrast this with a community giving their trade to the mail order houses.

"The money that would be deposited in local accounts is sent by mail order to distant cities. The bank getting few deposits and more and more calls for loans to meet maturing obligations of merchants whose business is gone and whose stock of goods are unsaleable because there is none to buy them, closes its doors and leaves town. The smaller businesses and less prosperous dealers soon follow, and half the business rooms and many residences are empty. The remaining business . . . discharge their help, who then leave town. Property in town depreciates in value, everybody wants to sell out and no one wants to buy. As values decrease, the relative tax rate increases and there are not adequate funds to pay for public utilities, a paid fire department can't be maintained. The water works closes, insurance rates go up, manufactures close down, employees are discharged and there is an exodus. The minister leaves, the high school closes down and grass grows in the streets.

"Realizing at last the havoc he has wrought, he thinks to escape the consequences by selling his farm, he finds alas,

The Del Kump Barber Shop on West Fourth Street. Del "Komp" had the reputation for giving the quickest shaves in northern Michigan. Travelers would stay overnight at the Calkins to try out his skills, often with side-bets of $5 on his time. Homer Douglas stands by the number one chair in the foreground. Jackie Mason is the third barber at the rear.

The family of Senator Doherty

273

Alvey Powers with his children, Clifford and Josephine. Their dog was named Jack. This photo was taken north of First Street on McEwan in 1910.

there is no buyer. His farm like the property in town is undesirable, becomes unprofitable. In attempting to live for himself alone, he has engulfed himself in the common ruin induced by his own thoughtless folly. He has paid the price that all must pay who attempt to live narrow, selfish uncharitable lives. In his greedy impatience to seize the utmost dollar, he kills the goose that might have indefinitely continued to lay an ever increasing supply of golden eggs."

The blame could be placed on the farmer's shoulders for the demise of towns such as Grandon which had a high school, churches and a small business district, but the continuance of a community is everyone's concern and responsibility. Clare for example left the problem of increasing employment for workers to the mayor and city council. They talked up the strong sales points of

Clare to everyone who would listen, and some businesses were brought into the city by these political leaders. The "kickers" often sat around and blamed someone else for not improving things.

In 1907, the Clare Knitting Mills needed to expand. William Wolsey, the owner had helped establish the Clare County Savings Bank in 1885 and he continued over the years to build Clare. In 1905 there were twenty-two employees working full time in the old gospel hall which had served many others over the years. There were approximately two hundred women who knitted mittens and wool socks at home. Two years later, thirty-five employees were working full time and their business was growing.

Mayor Lacy said, "Let those who glibly talk of what ought to be done, get together and put in some capital for the development of industries already on Clare soil." It appears that a successful group was put together, for the knitting mill continued several more years.

THE BANKERS

William Wolsky, Clark Sutherland, C. W. Perry and Louis Weisman started the Clare County Savings Bank in 1885. They were the only bank in Clare or Farwell, although Col. L. Saviers of Ithaca had opened his bank in Harrison two years earlier. Little Jake had a modified bank in Farwell when

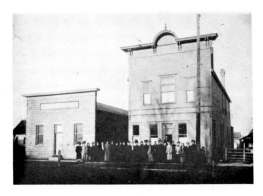

The Wolsey Knitting Mills on North McEwan Street in Clare. The two-story building may have been the original Grant Township Hall built in 1872.
Photo from the Brooks Family Collection

The Wolsey Mill girls in 1905.
Photo from the Brooks Family Collection

he was a partner to George Emrick during 1879, but he only exchanged currency and sold money orders. This is not the normally accepted definition of a bank.

R. H. Jenny, a local mill man, sold his interest in the Savings Bank around 1905 when his Upper Peninsula mill took up much of his time. In Marquette he put together a vast fortune and became one of the state's more wealthy men. A son, E. Burt Jenny, started a National Bank in Dowagiac and then projected one for Clare in 1911, but a bookkeeper's mistake kept him busy just trying to save his Dowagiac institution. His sister, Gladys Jenny, who had grown up in Clare went on in 1911 to become the first female deep sea diver. She utilized the cold waters of Lake Superior for her diving. All of the glowing plans for a third bank in Clare were fruitless.

Fred Lister and Charles H. O'Donald started the Citizens Bank in 1903 with ten thousand dollars. In 1908, the bank received a state charter and its capital had been doubled about the time President Lister died. He suffered from cancer.

Wm. Haley became the new Citizens Bank President and Dr. Mulder joined J. W. Calkins, James Duncan, Mrs. A. E. Mussell, W. H. Virtue, and N. A. Bloom on the

William Wolsky (Wolsey)

This building still stands on the southwest corner of Fourth and McEwan Streets in Clare. The site was formerly used by William Wolsky in the 1880's and the Wilson-Sutherland Dry Goods Store, 1905.

Fred Lister

Louis Weisman

Clark Sutherland

J. Stuart Bicknell

The James S. Bicknell family. In back, left to right, are Donald, Nathan, and Josephine. Stuart is in the center. In front are Alberta (Long), James S., and Mark. Circa 1918.
Photo from the Bicknell Family Collection

Board of Directors. He guided the bank through a healthy growing period and then sold his interest to State Treasurer A. E. Sleeper. J. W. Calkins and James Duncan also sold their stock to outsiders, James McCall of Yale, Michigan becoming a lead- ing Director. That same year, Wm. H. Bicknell purchased bank stock and became a Director. Donald McNair of Crosswell ran the day to day operations until May, 1911, when James S. Bicknell replaced him as cashier. At that time Jim was already well respected. The SENTINEL said of Bicknell, ". . . no one doubts that he will make good in his new field."

By 1913, James S. Bicknell had become president of the bank, and many of the outsiders had withdrawn, although A. E. Sleeper was still a Director.

The Clare County Savings Bank was prospering also, becoming a repository for state funds. This was somewhat unusual for a small bank, but it had been well managed in 1893 during the panic, and it was still ably managed as Sutherland served as cashier.

Finally in 1914, Wm. Wolsey (Wolsky) sold his stock to James McKay and his nephey Louis Weisman sold to George V. Collins. Joseph Hudson was elected the new President. James McKay became the bank's 2nd Vice President.

During late 1914, the Federal Reserve System was introduced in Clare, and soon began giving leadership as well as controls to county banking practices. Clark Sutherland was a member of "Group Five" of the Michigan Banker's Association which was established to implement the Federal Reserve System.

As conditions changed among the owners over the years, plans were finally completed for building a modern bank building on the southwest corner of 4th Street and N. McEwan. This was the site of William Wolsky's (Wolsey) dry goods and clothing store during the 1870's. Offices were projected for the second floor and all banking rooms were to be on the street level.

Practically speaking, not too much else was added in the way of large business changes prior to the end of the Great War. Social events were scheduled by the various fraternal lodges, fair boards, race track promoters and the Civil War veterans who began facing the "low couches" in Cherry Grove with a heightened realization that it wouldn't be long before the last roll call would be made, and the "Boys in Blue" would answer reveille "Across the River".

Appearing in the SENTINEL during June of 1911, a poem entitled "The Passing of the Boys in Blue" appeared. Here is how it read:

THE PASSING OF THE BOYS IN BLUE

There is coming a time
When the funeral chime
of the bells will be ringing at dawn,
and the coffin and pall
will be saying to all
that you, my dear comrades, have gone.

There is coming a year
When the few who meet here
will speak of their comrades, the dead.
and they'll tell what you've done
and the glory you've won,
but you will not hear what is said.

There is coming a day
In the sweet month of may
when your memory shall fill all the hours
and blossoms and bloom
will engarland your tomb
but you will not see the sweet flowers.

There is coming a night
In whose dim feeble light
I see visioned the passing of all
and not one of your hand
is there left in the land
you have answered your final roll call.

There is coming a morn
When this land that was born
as a home for those freedom has blessed
will herald your fame
and hallow your name
and hold sacred the place where you rest.

Then let us who may
Rejoice in our day
that we hold each as guest and as friend,
and let us not shirk,
but continue the work
they leave to us, on to the end.

Those were noble thoughts penned by an unknown author in 1911, but the old boys weren't to be put away so soon. As the 50th Anniversary of the Gettysburg Battle approached, plans were made by several of the Clare veterans to trek once again to Seminary Ridge. A special train was being made up in Detroit to transport the returning army.

A Civil War field gun.

George MacLane, one of the few Confederate veterans living in the county, joined H. Hughes, S. P. Dowd, Philo Smith, J. W. Reed and George M. Clark on that special train. The state of Pennsylvania agreed to feed both Union and Confederate veterans and the U.S. Army brought in tents and bunks, setting up a bivouac between Cemetery and Seminary Ridges.

The "Greys" and the "Blues" visited the battleground together in an amiable comradeship above and beyond what either side had expected. The fierceness of the battle had long since been forgotton. Now most Confederates realized what an awful curse slavery had been. During those July 1913 days, many commented on their defeat as being in the best interest of the nation. There developed a strong bond of friendship between these former enemies as they talked of battles and leaders. Their generals were analyzed from strictly a military view point, as if their own lives hadn't depended upon the decisions, or lack of decisions, those leaders had made.

It was a momentous moment for the vet-

erans of Clare and also for the entire nation.

The years passed by, and the old veterans were now becoming too feeble to march the long distance to their G.A.R. monument in Cherry Grove. Automobiles were provided in 1916 and the thirteen survivors rode in the Memorial Day parade. Never again would their feet march in tune to the old war drum. Its staccato beats were just a memory now,—or were they?

THE OLD WAR DRUM AWAKES

It is standing in the corner of the littered
lumber room
and the dust upon its rawhide head is pleading
for a broom.
But the old war drum is silent now, it has no
voice to call,
Like a dry, decrepit veteran, it leans against
the wall.
But hush, hush, hush!
Don't you hear the war drum beat?
Don't you hear its rumble, rumble, rumble, rum?
Lean and listen! To your ear
put your hand and you may hear

Faint and far, the rumble, rumble, rumble of
the drum!

But a ghost of ancient echo is the war drum's
warning low
from the far off fields of carnage, from the
battle long ago.
From the gory Shiloh maelstrom, from the
Chickamauga hell,
From the first Antietam caldron where the flower
of manhood fell.
Ah, hear, hear, hear!
Can't you feel the war drum throb?
Can't you sense its rumble, rumble rum?
For the moment close your eyes.
It is not a mere surmise
'Tis the real rumble, rumble, rumble of the drum!

They have borne it in the morning when the
bugler blew the notes.
Rousing regiments to marshall and assault the
cannon throats,
and the drum has mixed its rumblings with
the bugle and the fife
Calling men to make for fatherland the sacrifice
of life.
Oh list, list, list!
Don't you know the war drum's voice?
Can't you catch its rumble, rumble, rum?
Stand a little space aside
Let the drummer beat with pride
Louder now the rumble, rumble of the drum!

Yes, we hear its solemn rumblings as it leads
the charging lines
In the wilderness, at Resaca, at Fair Oakes,
Seven Pines:
Hear its deep basso profundo as it halts upon
the heights—
Peerless Pickett's launching legions in the fury
of the fight.
Yes, hark, hark, hark!
'Tis the war drum's tongue awake!
Hear its voice the rumble, rumble, rumble rum!
Doff your hat and heave a cheer!
Why, the drummer's here—he's here!
Beating out the rumble, rumble of the drum.

Thus I saw the ghostly drummer on a morn
in latter May
When beyond the littered lumber room a band
began to play
And I turned for a moment for a glance along
the street
Where a thin blue line of veterans went by on
weary feet.
"Ah, hush, hush, hush!"
Called the monster within.
"Hush and hear the rumble, rumble, rumble,
rum!"
Was the war drum come awake
Or my heartbeats did they make
All the mighty rumble, rumble, rumble of the drum?

The final resting place for those who defended our country faithfully to the end.

Clare county had two cities in 1900. Clare was chartered as a fourth class city in 1891 so it could sell its revenue bonds on more favorable terms. There was probably a bit of competitive spirit in the decision to seek a city charter and the origin of it probably was in the Board of Supervisor's meetings. Under the county system of government each township was entitled to one supervisor on the Board while each city was entitled to a supervisor from each ward. Clare and Harrison established three wards after the chartering and so each had more representation than did Farwell which was represented by the supervisor from Surrey. Clare was situated in Grant township and so that supervisor might be persuaded to vote favorably to the city's interests. Harrison relied upon Hayes' township supervisor in a similar manner.

When Clare secured the city designation it jumped ahead of Harrison, which was only a village. The competition between these two towns during this heavy politicing is covered in MICHIGAN'S TIMBER BATTLEGROUND, published in 1976. To summarize briefly, both towns became fourth class cities in 1891. Since Clare was the smallest city in population upon its chartering the granting of a city status to Harrison, with less than half of Clare's numbers, makes the whole affair almost absurd. For many years Harrison was the least populated city in Michigan. It may still be even in our time, but that didn't matter then when those extra ward supervisors meant political power in the county.

As the lumbering era closed down about 1900, Harrison almost ceased to function.

Indeed if the county seat had been located elsewhere, in all probability, Harrison would have been another ghost town. It almost was as it turned out anyway. There were a couple of heading and stave mills operating on the bolts of logs which the fires missed, but until the resorters began coming in during the 1920's, things were pretty quiet.

A canning factory was boomed for the town in 1903, but there weren't enough truck farms around to make it pay. The boom let out a slight sigh and went away.

Sometime during 1909 fires got into the roundhouse and destroyed it. A stave mill owned by Cleveland also was destroyed. Since the city's electrical power was produced by the mill's steam generator, the town was back to supporting "John D." The mill machinery was dug out of the rubble and shipped to Leota, a town that was still going strong.

In 1905, Harrison Postmaster Dudley was discovered by Postal authorities to be $500 short in his funds. His alibi was failing eyesight. "My eyes have been giving me trouble and I must have burned the receipts by mistake," he told the Federal Judge who heard his case in Saginaw. The story wasn't believed and he was found guilty of embezzling federal monies. President Roosevelt appointed A. S. Young to replace Dudley.

During the transition, robbers broke into the Post Office and took about $300. The question every asked was, "who's going to stand the loss?"

The banking laws of Michigan enabled the bank in Harrison to become a State Chartered Bank, so in 1907 Col. Lemuel Saviers was directed by the newly enlarged and more

Harrison in 1910.
Photo from the Fanning Collection

Harrison's big supply house in the 1890's. William H. and Farwell A. Wilson are standing on the left.
Photo from the Floyd Wilson Collection

adequately capitalized Board of Directors to change the name to the State Savings Bank of Harrison. Saviers was retained as President and Fred Weatherhead was made an officer along with C. R. Giddings who was the Cashier. C. S. Harrington, N. White, A. S. McIntyre, O. H. King, C. H. Page, Fred Weatherhead, E. J. Hughes, E. G. Hughes, W. H . Wilson, J. B. Joos and L. Saviers owned the $20,000 paid in capital stock.

Soon after the first of the year in 1908, some burglars blew the Post Office safe and took off with $10. Postmaster Young raised a fuss over the fellows who destroyed his safe and then escaped on a velocipede which had been borrowed from the Ann Arbor railroad in Clare. It developed that the crooks stole the vehicle in Clare, rode it to Harrison on the Branch, broke into the Post Office and then escaped all the way back to the Ann Arbor Freight house where they replaced the machine on the platform. "The hoo-doo that has followed the burglary scarcely yet seems lifted," reported the CLARE SENTINEL

on January 17, 1908.

Life went on, however, and the townspeople continued their own interests. The bands, orchestras and parties kept most of the local residents busy. On Memorial Day, the City Band directed by Henry Heisman led the parade to the cemetery where the boys in blue saluted their fallen comrades. Summer time found the county gathering for the county fair in late August. Then a bit later the school children heaved a sigh and trudged back to the one-room schools or the graded systems in the towns.

Jesse Allen, in an attempt to juice up his newspaper, the CLEAVER, took in a partner from Greenwood by the name of Charles H. Roe. "We're going to put Harrison on the map," said Roe in 1912.

During May of the same year, Clinton Bower went swimming in Budd Lake. Something happened and he went under the water. A. R. D. Calkins noticed his frenetic thrashing as he came up the second time. As he rushed out to him, Bower had just gone under the third time. Calkins dove again and again. Finally, after five minutes he found him in about fifteen feet of water. The water was cold and its numbing effects had something to do with a successful resuscitation. Calkins was only nineteen years old at the time, but he exhibited a maturity not possessed by men twice his age. Others swimming in the lake were not so fortunate and it claimed not a few, including some who fell through the ice. Fishermen spudded holes all over the surface, but the real danger was in the areas recently harvested by the ice men. Either they didn't put up the required signs or the youths were negligent. Regardless of whose fault it was, far too many perished in the middle of winter.

East of Harrison, in Hamilton Township, the Mennonites began moving in during 1915. Some came from Kansas, but most were easterners seeking out fertile soils for their agrarian style of life. A stable community developed in the Amble school area and their thrifty habits enabled Harrison to increase its commercial interests. Another religious group in Hamilton was the Latter Day Saints. A cluster around Silver Lake in Lincoln township and the Bailey group in the general area of Hamilton's Section 15 added more conservatism to the old lumber camp sites.

During the war years, the area suffered from the flu just as everyone else, plus the normal attrition due to the draft and the lure of the munition factories of Detroit, Flint and Saginaw. The sale of Ford trucks to the Greenwood and Hamilton farmers sparked an interest in roads. As the roads developed, resorters began using them and soon the whole area started to blossom like flowers in a warm May. Hotels were built and others were improved as the patronage was increasing quite regularly. Fred Double built a small hotel in Section 27 of Frost Township in 1917. Its location favored resorters on Blue Gill Lake, but Long Lake might have had more growth potential.

As towns went, Leota and Harrison hadn't yet reached their social maturities as late as

The Harrison Savings Bank.

Harrison, Michigan, circa 1920.
Photo from the Woznack Family Collection

Some of the Budd family's relatives drove up to Greenwood Township from Ohio in this automobile during 1918.

William Henry Wilson
Photo from the Floyd Wilson Collection

1917. Mrs. Loecy was a Harrison resident who took in washings to support her family. She raised vegetables in each summer in the garden located to the rear of her house. Adjacent was a small barn where a cow was kept for milk. If there was a family that had to scratch to make ends meet, this was it. Her industry, however, wasn't appreciated by someone in the neighborhood, for one evening in August of 1904, someone removed the bell from the cow and turned her loose in the garden. As you can imagine, in one night's foraging, that cow ruined her garden and with it all of the vegetables that she was planning to can for the family's coming winter requirements. This dastardly deed was almost a death warrant to the family, but "Such was the low miserable act of some scoundrel Monday night," reported the CLARE SENTINEL.

LEOTA

When Meredith died, the railroad was taken up and laid in the direction of the Muskegon River, terminating in a town later called Leota. The lumbermen had stripped all of the cork pine long before this date, but there were ample bull pines and hard-woods in the surrounding townships. In addition there were numerous logging railroads still intact. In 1896, Leota was about to become a lively little river town.

It's true, of course, that Leota was a wild little town, but it never could equal the lawlessness of Meredith and probably didn't even want to. The log drives from the Roscommon direction were petering out and in 1907 they ended. It was in this year that the Rev. C. W. Jones came to town. He was a retired Methodist minister who assummed the role of a home missionary. The fact that Leota didn't have a church or a school house seemed to weigh heavy on Rev. Jones, so he enlisted the aid of a young man, the Rev. Petershans to help him convert the town to Methodism.

The rowdy element didn't relish the idea of Leota having a church, and of course, this meant practically the whole town. Undeterred, Jones purchased a lot and ordered some building materials. Working alone, he singlehandedly cut the timbers which served as a foundation, and then nailed the structure together. The first outside assistance he received from the local townsmen was when he put the rafters up. One middle aged man began to feel sheepish about the reception he was given by the hard drinking crowd of mill and river workers. While he was pounding away on the roof the rowdies stopped to jeer at him, "Come on down old man, you don't have much longer to live. You'd better join us for a drink before it's too late." But the old retired minister just kept on pounding the nails into the shingles.

Log houses and cabins were common in early days, but the rural districts had more than the towns. This one stands in western Freeman Township.

A picnic for Sheridan and Wise Township residents, 1910.
Photo from the Schunk Family Collection

Lake George's Post Office, circa 1900. Harry Moyer is on the left.
Photo from the Jim Grove Collection

An interior photo of Mike Fanning's Harrison store.
Photo from the Fanning Collection

Later that day, when the resolute old gentleman's wife was standing on the ground passing materials up to him, a group of men came back and gave him a hand with the high work. A few more came around and helped set the windows and trim work. Before long the church was finished on the outside with the exception of a paint job. By November of 1907, the church was completed and most of the $600 was raised locally. Mill owner Rhoades put in nearly half of the required amount. There were still the hecklers around when the photographer arrived to take a picture of the new church and they thought it would be funny if they stood in the background behind Rev. Jones holding up their cups of beer. Acting as if the men weren't there, the photographer began snapping pictures, catching the sots in their glorious buffoonishness.

The pictures having been taken and the camera disassembled, the men suddenly realized what complete idiots they had made of themselves. Rev. Jones and his dignified wife never once said a cross word of reproach to these men and that seemed to have made it worse. They slinked off and that was the end of the boorishness in Leota.

A week later thirty children came to the church building and school was in session.

Rev. and Mrs. Jones conducted the first weeks of classes without incident. The town, meanwhile, had formally organized a school district and arranged for the hiring of a teacher who would take over the instruction for the remainder of first term of school. Some of the youngsters had attended schools outside of the district, but many had their first encounter with the three ''R's'' at this time.

Now that the town had a church, a school and some respectability, it rapidly became a better place to raise a family. Soon more and more men brought their wives and children to town, placing a heavy burden upon the supply of housing. The mills, kilns and related employers were able to secure a more stable type of worker and they continued to live in Leota for some time. A community spirit next infused the river hamlet with a more mature outlook on life. The hard-drinking river hogs of yesteryear were being replaced by the family men and their dollars were now being spent on furniture, clothing and taxes instead of booze. Since the soils around Leota were deficient in humus, they were highly vulnerable to drought conditions. Any family which intended to succeed in Summerfield township therefore was required to find sustenance in a non-agricultural role.

Raw materials for the local mills were limited to coarser pines and abundant elms, oaks and maples.

During the last stages of World War I the town began to lose much of its steam and the railroad began thinking about pulling up its tracks. The state supervisory agency gave permission in April of 1922 and the first rail was taken up. Leota was to be greatly reduced in stature until the automobile age once again put it on the map.

Peter Oman's General Store at Crooked Lake.

This ruling by the State Public Utility Commission was the first one since a United States Supreme Court decision authorized the P.U.C. to abandon railroads which were no longer profitable to operate. Those who lived on the river were not very happy with this distinction, but they were not about to let their town die. The resort set found their way over the sand hills to the Muskegon River in sufficient numbers to keep a minimum town going, but the growth of the new Leota was slow.

FARWELL

Portland cement became the rage in northern Michigan in 1900. The towns which had been hewn out of the woods by the lumbering crowd had been burned over once or twice and some were burned completely to the ground. Summit, for example, was a Surrey township burg which was completely destroyed right down to the foundation piers. Those villages which had some compelling reason for existance had a decision to make.

Frank Burns in later life. He was a river driver in Temple.

The village of Farwell

This is the building Josiah Littlefield owned in Farwell. It was set on fire by an arsonist several times.

George and Alie Palmer
Photo from the Palmer Family Collection

"If the fires cannot be stopped, how best can a town insulate itself from the devastating effects of the flames?" Two courses of action were available. First, the town's fathers could clear cut the immediate area and remove the potential combustible materials; and secondly they could build stores and commercial buildings out of masonry products. Those towns which survived began using bricks and concrete in large quantities, replacing even the existing structures. The new wave of town building or re-building required mortar and bricks.

Michigan had several cement plants, but more were on the drawing board. One was scheduled for Petobago Lake near Elk Rapids during March of 1900, probably utilizing the marl which was indigenous to the lake. Others were boomed for plants near Brighton, Linden, Cass City, Kalamazoo and elsewhere. It appeared to be a hot item and a town with its eyes on the future perhaps ought to look into the possibility

of securing its own. Clare did, and the Clare Portland Cement Company was organized in May of 1901 to use the marl at Five Lakes in Grant township. It planned to produce one thousand barrels of Portland Cement a day. Estimates of the potential reserves were in the range of over a hundred fifty years. The stockholders were expecting to generate profits of at least fifty cents a barrel and so they had visions of banking at least $150,000 each year.

Another company was established to dig

Lou and Monce Gee

The Sam Henry Brick and Tile Company of Farwell.
Photo from the Cecil Davison Collection

the marl out of Coldwater Lake and transport it to Mt. Pleasant where it could be turned into the profitable cement. A two million dollar paper corporation was set up and a plant designed by engineers to produce at least 540,000 barrels of mortar a year. An option on two hundred forty acres was made around Coldwater Lake, and a railroad grade was planned with terminals in Mt. Pleasant and Coldwater. Exactly what happened to this speculative company isn't known, but no doubt its fate could be quite easily traced.

In 1902 there were eleven cement factories in Michigan producing 1,665,999 barrels each year. By 1903, production had doubled. Sixteen factories were operating in 1904 and it seemed the boom would go on for ever. Nearly a thousand employees were working in the factories which had a capitalized cost of $7,840,000. Fourteen of the factories used lake-marl for their basic raw material. In 1904 the largest plants were in Union City, Coldwater and Quincy.

It was in June of 1903 that Josiah Littlefield decided to build a Portland Cement factory in Farwell. Two months later the Alpena Cement Company had him in a Clare County Court, charged with a processing enfringement. The courts gave Littlefield enough encouragement so that he was able to continue the company, so he hired Robert Wentz of Nazareth, Pennsylvania to be his process engineer. Two years later the kiln hadn't yet been installed, but the thinking now was to haul limestone from Petoskey rather than to use lake marl. More capital was needed to build a railroad spur and Littlefield went out to raise $50,000.

In September of 1907, the Farwell company was sued by the Hill Clutch Company. Evidently there was not enough paid in capital to keep the construction costs current and the judgement handed down by the Clare County Circuit Court case was the largest granted up to the point. It is questionable whether there was a larger judgement when the Lake George and Muskegon River Railroad was sold for back taxes by the State in the mid 1880's, but those records aren't readily available.

With the judgement in favor of the Hill Clutch Company against it, the company fell back and attempted to re-group. A new effort was made to raise $100,000 via five per cent bonds due in ten years, but even expected dividends of twenty per cent weren't enough to bring it in. The prospectus of the Farwell Portland Cement Company said:

"We are trying to establish this great and growing industry right here in your midst. If it can be carried to completion, every resident of Clare and Isabella counties will be benefited thereby."

A year later, Circuit Court Commissioner William H. Browne accepted a bid from the Joliet Iron Works in the amount of $11,000 for salvage rights to the bankrupt company. In addition, the now defunct company owed three thousand dollars for taxes, and the winning bidder had to pay this sum before the plant could be dismantled.

It is said that the introduction of rock limestone in Alpena and the process which was used to turn it into cement made the Farwell enterprise obsolete before it was even begun. Technology probably had been more the cause of Littlefield's failure than anything else. It is probably, too, that the hauling distance between Petoskey and Farwell was equally the problem.

Each town of substantial size had its brick factory, and Farwell was of the required size in 1910. In addition there was a cement tile factory using the Burnham patented machines. There are many buildings in town even today, which were built entirely of Farwell-produced bricks. Farm fields in Surrey and Gilmore are drained by the cement tiles produced by the Henry Brick and Tile Company.

Banking in town had long been a problem to the merchants, because the closest bank was in Clare. Louis Weisman, a local dry goods merchant, was one of the original stockholders in the Clare County Savings Bank of Clare. He and his brother in law, William Wolsky (later Wolsey), were joined by C. W. Perry, Clark Sutherland and others to charter the bank in 1885. Because it is so difficult to carry on a business without the facilities of a bank, Weisman asked his partners to create one for Farwell. They did, and $10,000 was subscribed. E. H. Smith, the local Pere Marquette station agent, was made the first cashier. The Far-

John Henry in his Farwell Meat Market, January 10, 1913.
Photo from the Gee Family Collection

well Savings Bank opened its doors in October of 1903.

Before a year had gone by, R. H. Jenny, O. S. Derby and Carrie Stroupe bought stock and were added to the Board of Directors. They now collectively owned a 20' x 50' building which had cost $2,500. A modern heavy duty safe with a locking arm which had to be unscrewed each morning, was located behind the "L" shaped counter which Thurston & Son of Clare had custom built for the new facility.

By 1918, the bank had $500,000 in capital stock, loans and surplus. President John S. Weldman had been chosen to replace Clark Sutherland as President, and Floyd E. Oliver had replaced Smith.

Most of the local retail stores changed hands frequently, but some stayed in business for two or three years. Leonard, Ritchie and Stinchcombe were early 1900 grocers while Palmer, Henry and Brown were three of the many butcher shop owners. There were legitimate reasons for a change in ownership, such as a fire which wiped out the independent merchant, but usually it was economics. Farwell just didn't have enough business to keep every one going. The business district was swept by fire every so often, but the block owned by Littlefield was more prone to the flames than any other. More than a few figured that some one was out to get the town's leading business man, and if that meant a fire, then so be it.

What passed for the local Chamber of Commerce attempted to induce new businesses to locate in Farwell from time to time. Cheese factories were promoted, and one was successfully launched soon after 1905. There was a cucumber-collecting station with brine tanks in town, and it operated successfully between 1900-1918. The cheese factory was locally owned, being a co-op. Thirty-five men put up the money to get it started. Twenty four of them were local farmers and the other eleven were merchants. It had cost $2,750.

In 1886 Farwell had built its water supply system, but by 1900 it had been stretching its capacity to service the village. A fire came along in 1903 and burned the installation down, including eighty cords of fire

wood, which was its source of power. The town carried no insurance on the five thousand dollar facility, so it had to issue a series of bonds in order to rebuild.

The mill pond was built early in Farwell's commercial lifetime, and it served as a reserve of hydro power to grind the grain and as a source of fishing. It had gone out prior to 1900, leaving a wave of typhoid fever in its wake. A heavy spring rain in 1909 threatened and then took out a section of the earthen embankment south of the mill. A wave of water cluttered with debri rushed downstream and took out a smaller dam one mile east of town. A bridge was ripped from its foundation, and the Hinkleville dam was damaged so that it, too, was destroyed. Someone telegraphed ahead to Clare warning them of the impending wave of water. Hurriedly the gates at Dewey Dam were lowered and seven inches of water escaped. The new water just about equalled the amount released and so a state of equilibrium was once again maintained.

A law suit was commenced by the township road overseer against Fuller and Harris, owners of the mill and dam. The document charged the mill owners with maintaining a water level too high for the spring time, thereby causing the minor disaster. A forty-foot section of the road way was carried away and the source of Farwell's water supply was now without fire protection, as its pumps could not operate. Someone suggested that a temporary earthen dam be built, impounding some water around the intake. Eventually enough water was trapped and the tank filled. A roadway was rebuilt, this time using more clay in its foundation. The courts later decided that the milling company was indeed at fault, at least partially, and they had to pay for the new roadway.

The water system was a hit-and-miss affair, and it was often inadequate to its responsibilities, especially if a larger than usual fire happened along. The big fire of 1916 was compounded by the water department's inability to provide water in a timely manner. The engines just couldn't pump water fast enough to maintain hose pressure. The recently built brick structure which housed the Calkins and Schlegel store and the Littlefield Opera House was the main casualty of the defective water system.

On the eastern end of Farwell was the Park View Hotel. It had been named the Rust House when it was built in 1872, but then it had three stories. As the lumbering era phased out, the hotel continued, but business was not what it was. A fire came along in the 1890's and the floor on top was ruined. A decision was made to remove the entire roof and top story, and so the hotel was now about the size which the diminished town needed. Its ownership was in various hands over the years and finally its name was changed too. At one time it was called the Farwell Hotel, but that didn't last long. When the park was dedicated across the street the name was changed to Park View Hotel and then finally to Parkview Hotel.

A competitor to the Parkview was the McGinnis Hotel and was located on Main Street also. It was torn down in 1914 so that a residence could be built for John Warner. From this date on, only one hotel functioned in town.

During July of 1918, the log house George Hitchcock built in 1870 was dismantled and moved to Crooked Lake for a summer cottage. It appeared to the town's residents that this was necessary, and they resented the loss of their original building. Another loss of importance took place in 1918 also. During the war there was a need for scrap iron, and so Littlefield junked the mill machinery that had been lying dormant in the planing mill. An era which began in 1881 had come to an end.

Below are listed the names of communities or districts within Clare county or its immediate environs. They were named for a school district, country store, church, farm family, a cross roads nick-name or even a telephone co-operative commonly called something or other Roadway Co. At times the names were used in fun but someone took it serious enough to begin referring to the area by it. Such is the origin of North Chicago for Hatton. Clare then by inference became Little Chicago. Later people thought that the city was so tough that it resembled Chicago of the Dillinger era that it attained its pseudonym, but that explanation will not bear out if we examine history.

Allen	a school district in Hamilton township (No. 5)
Alward	a post office in Section 14 of Arthur
Amble	a school district in Hamilton (No. 4)
Andersonville	in Sheridan township
Attwood Siding	north of Farwell on Ann Arbor Railroad
Austa	Post office in Winterfield township on Section 3
Austin	Brand Farm area, Arthur township
Balsley	A school district east of Cornwell Ranch
Berryville	near the Wildcat school in Sheridan
Bessie	School District No. 4, Arthur township
Big Mud Lake	Section 31 Freeman township
Brand	community around Section 33, Arthur
Brinton	Post office, Coldwater township, Isabella
Brown Corners	Section 25, Hatton township, a church and school. Also a country store.
Brush College	A school near Alward, Arthur township
Caner	School No. 1, Greenwood township
Carrow	School district on Section 21, Sheridan township
Cherry Hill	Freeman township school district
Chaffee's Corners	North east Section 16, township
Chippewa Station	Post Office on Pere Marquette railroad
Clarence	Post Office Section 25, Redding township
Colonville	Section 20 Sheridan township, school, store
Crooked Lake	Post Office, Garfield township
Dago City	community east of Crooked Lake with 130 population
Delaney Corners	Gilmore township
Doc and Tom	School District on Sect. 2, Freeman township
Dodge	Post office on Section 12, Hamilton township
Dover	Post office, store, school, Grant township
Eagle	School, church on Section 5, Sheridan township
Ehle	School No. 2, Hamilton township
Elm Grove	School, store, Section 11, Sheridan township
Five Lakes	Section 9, Grant township
Fairview	settlement on Ann Arbor railroad, Section 8, Lincoln
Farwell	Post office, 1915 population: 522

Floodwood	School east of Muskegon River, Winterfield township
Fordsville	West of Clare one mile
Grandon	Post office, school, Winterfield township
Gut Lake	School No. 7, Grant township
Hardwood	School near Brush College, Arthur township
Harrison	Post office, 1915 population: 543
Hatton	Post office, 1915 population: 55
Headquarters	School No. 1, Frost township
Hermansdale	School, church, N. E. Arthur township
Herrick	School No. 4, Section 27, Sheridan township
Herrick	the new name for Lansingville, Wise township
Hoodoo Valley	near the Russell school, Vernon township
Kidd	School No. 3, Franklin township
Kirby	School No. 4, Winterfield township
Lake George	Post office, 1915 population: 61
Lamont's Hill	southwest part of Clare city
Leota	Post office, 1915 population: 57
Little Chicago	nick name for Clare in 1914
Lochabar	School, Section No. 8, Surrey township
Lonesome Avenue	Eagle area, 1910
Long Lake	Post office, population 1915: 34
Mann Siding	Section 16, Hatton township
Maple Grove	School, Section 28, Surrey township
Meredith	community, Section 13, Franklin township
Moore's Crossing	Section 19, Grant township
Myers	School No. 7, Arthur township
Nester Dam	Section 14-15, Arthur township
North Chicago	nick name for Hatton. A pun by Austin Trumble
Norway	School No. 3, Redding township
Pennock	Post office Section 7, Redding
Phelps	near Silver Lake, Lincoln township
Pig Toe Alley	Eagle area, 1910
Pleasant Valley	a telephone district, E. Grant and west Sheridan
Podunk	Hamilton township
Randall	School Section 14, Grant township
Redner	School, Section 27, Hatton township
Rinckney	Temple area
Riverside	Arthur township
Robbins	School No. 4, Greenwood township
Sharp	School No. 1, Franklin township
Silver Lake	Lincoln township
Slab Town	School No. 3, Sheridan
Smith's Cross Roads	???
Summit	railroad town on Ann Arbor, north of Farwell
Temple	Post office
Three Lakes	Section 11, Garfield township
Tonkin	Section 32, Arthur township
Valley Center	
Vernon City	community of Clare in Vernon township
Wall Street	West Fourth Street in Clare, 1908-12 era
Wallace	School, Section 6, Arthur township
Windover	School, Section 14, Freeman township
Winterfield	School, post office, Section 16, Winterfield
Wychoff	School No. 2, Franklin township

War of Woes

On January 17, 1913, the CLARE SENTINEL carried a short news item to the effect that an imbroglio between Roumania and Bulgaria threatened to precipitate a war between the European nations. There were twenty-five thousand Albanians killed by the Serbs at Kossovo, Turkey during January and the Emperor of Austria-Hungary was calling up the army reserves. News dispatches from Vienna, Sofia and Bucharest all carried somber messages: War was on the immediate horizon for much of Europe.

The United States and Michigan were more interested in the Panama Canal, a new president and woman suffrage, and the dark shadows in Europe seemed so far away. Governer Ferris had given his State of the State address and his emphasis on eugenics appeared to be far more important to the heartland resident. Conservation was having a favorable press as it was being promoted by the Public Domain Commission, and the gravel roads commanded more attention from the farmer than the Bulgarian affair. In some localities, recent immigrants from eastern Europe took sides, but there were very few southern or eastern European immigrants in northern Michigan at the time.

Memorial Day still meant the Civil War veterans would march from the center of town to the cemeteries in most northern Michigan communities, although there were a few veterans of the Spanish-American War who took part in the "homage" to the Boys in Blue. Aaron Austin, Henry Tryon and Francis Whitacker, 1898 veterans from Garfield township joined the Surrey, Gilmore and Lincoln ceremonies in Farwell each year, as did many of the local citizens. Edgar G. Welch, past editor of the CLARE SENTINEL, Oscar Ethridge, Donald McKinley, Albert Wilson, Harry Webber, Zepher Yoder and George A. Bowen were the other recent veterans living in Clare county.

Summers were enjoyed by the youngsters because the Fourth of July promised them much more fun and merriment than the other seasons. The sacrifices made by the Revolutionary War soldiers, sailors and civilians had long been forgotten, leaving only a celebration of the nation's birth. Some young men had joined the Michigan National Guard and went to summer camp near Ludington, but their least imagined prospect was a war either in Mexico or Europe. The new Democratic Chief of State, President Wilson was a non-interventionist of the first order and he even went so far as to reduce the number of battleships and cruisers coming down the ways. Peace to him was a full time job and he worked diligently at the avoidance of conflicts. His style was diametrically opposed by Theodore Roosevelt who often clashed with other nations as he showed the American Flag in Panama and the Pacific.

A year later, in February of 1914, Lt. H. B. Post was killed when the engine of his hydro-aeroplane exploded five hundred feet over a lake. Lt. Post was the best aviator the Aero Corps had at the time. His death during an attempt for an altitude record was widely reported because of the novelty of the aeroplane and the rarity of deaths caused by it.

THE WAR BEGINS

Tucked away on page eleven of the July 31, 1914 CLARE SENTINEL was a paragraph long news item which explained that the Austro-Hungarian government had declared war on Serbia. Germany had paved the way by announcing a rejection of the English proposal to bring the four powers together. President Wilson announced that all Americans would be brought home. Locally that meant Rudy Schaeffer and his brother Julius would be returning soon. Rudy had gone to Germany to study the Munich trade and vocational schools as a representative of California and the United States. His brother had joined him in Germany after the study was completed. They visited the paternal homeland, staying with relatives.

President Wilson asked Congress for $2,500,000 to expedite the return of the 100,000 Americans in the war zone. The armored cruiser "Tennessee" carried eight

Henry Hinkle, U.S. Army, 1899.

million dollars in gold to cash checks the returnees weren't able to convert locally. Most ships which plied the commercial lanes were foreign owned and ocean traffic came to an immediate standstill. All, that is, except the American vessels.

In Michigan the National Guard held its first encampment at their new Grayling facilities, having moved from the leased campsite at Ludington. Members of the 2nd Infantry fired their guns for the first time in Crawford county. Their field problem in 1914 reflected the nation's dilemma as it sought the proper strategic direction to take. The Engineers, Signal Corps and Infantry used a full complement of horses and wagons to "attack and defend a wagon train." Governor Ferris went out to the camp to observe the maneuvers in mid-August. He pronounced the Guard ready for any attack the Indians could muster. He wasn't so confident about the type of war unfolding in Europe, but then he didn't need to worry about that. President Wilson was determined to have peace and that ought to suffice.

THE WHIRLPOOL DEEPENS

In Europe the interlocking alliances began

Jim Clute, Michigan National Guard, 1915.
Photo from the Clute Family Collection

to suck the nations into two large armed camps as five great nations of the world squared off to begin killing each other. The British navy was put to sea with orders to "Capture or destroy the enemy." Germany on the other hand sent her armies marching through Belgium and into France in a war of annihilation. Eighteen million men were in uniform by mid-August, warring upon each other like an angry host of praying mantises. The momentous decision for which the world had been waiting was finally handed down. Patriots on both sides cheered the coming of the holocaust and numerous parades were held by the opponents in their cities, eager to be on with the extermination of their enemies.

Many recent immigrants from Europe to this country were summoned back to their homeland for induction into the military forces. The nation's largest cities were especially hard hit as these were the repositories of the newly arrived. Many had filed their first papers of citizenship and had married in this country expecting to escape the European carnage, but it was not to be for some. As early as September 1914,

Detroit had to place hundreds of young families on its welfare rolls as the bread winners had been recalled to the war. New York, the coal regions of Pennsylvania and Chicago were the hardest hit by the edicts coming out of the east. Relief agencies set up to care for the displaced families in Europe had first to care for the American families torn by war.

The war moved into the braggadocio phase early when Count Zeppelin promised to lead an invasion force of airships over England, "I shall teach France's great ally a lesson even if I have to hang for it later," boasted the addlebrained inventor. But he was only saying what the other Germans believed. He and his fellow countrymen had a deep hatred for everything British. Americans returning home told of the fearful pressures being mounted against England. Most of the witnesses were sure that the Kaiser would snuff out the country in short order.

England, reacting to a mortal threat to her survival began intercepting American ships on the high seas and removing the European reservists returning home for a military life. Some Americans objected to these seizures, but it was perfectly legal if not acceptable to the American public. Thousands of Germans were captured and placed in prison camps by the Royal Navy.

Relief agencies in the United States recruited hundreds of nurses and scores of doctors for European service. Later ambulance drivers, medical technicians and other non-combat personnel began arriving in Europe on ships flying American flags. On board also were the first shipments of

The German Cavalry pause for this historical photograph prior to their riding off to war in 1914.
Photo: National Archives GSA 111-SC-95844

German Chancellor von Hollweg
Photo: National Archives GSA 111-SC-95775

food supplies for England, France and Belgium. The broad scope of the war soon became apparent to the Americans and it caused a great division among them, as so many recent immigrants had not yet been emotionally assimilated in their new homeland. President Wilson, sensing this, asked the nation to remain neutral in thoughts as well as in deeds. The United States stood ready to sell food, machinery, clothing and weapons of war to any nation that had gold enough to pay for them.

The practical effect of this even-handed policy was limited because the British navy had practically forced the German merchant fleet into ports for the duration. American beef which reached Europe jumped five cents a pound. Hats which were produced in Austria and Germany increased fifteen per cent. Tea and coffee were in extremely short supply and soared in price. Liquors of all types and wines carried prices nearly twice as high as pre-war supplies. Leather for European shoes came from Russia. When the war erupted those supplies were cut off and American leather and shoes were in heavy demand. One casualty of the war was the Christmas toy. Germany made over ninety per cent of the world's supply and overnight this production stopped. The "War of Woes" as it was called back in 1914 had no time for children or children's games. For the next four years men would be playing with the tools of death and destruction.

In August, Germany threatened Paris itself, and was repulsed when armies were only twenty-five miles from the capitol city. British and French forces fought along a front hinged at Precy. Fighting vigorously, they pushed the Germans back away from Verdun and gained their first victory over the Alliance armies. The massive assault masterminded by German strategist Von Schlieffen had failed because Moltke shifted his ersatz troops to the left wing at the crucial moment when he should have retained them. The quick victory Germany saw in the west was gone, even though eventually they must win because of their superior might.

THE GERMAN-AMERICAN DILEMMA

The mid-western states were populated by millions of citizens who had much German blood in them. Even before 1776 the persecuted Germans fled Europe in large numbers. After 1848 even more Germans migrated, settling in the Ohio Valley, Michigan, Wisconsin, Illinois and Iowa. If those Americans with German blood should favor the Kaiser, President Wilson's "neutrality in thoughts and in deeds" would really take on a more serious tone. Many people attempted to rationalize the problem so that France and England would gain their moral support. As some saw it, Germany had two types of citizens, one favored the militarists, thinking that they had a divine right to rule. They were the caste which produced the duelers, militarists and an aristocracy. It was this group that gave so much offense to the world. They so dominated world opinion that the word "German" meant arrogance. Forgotten were the poets, musicians, artists, industrious workers and dedicated family men.

The other Germany was totally different. From this larger portion of the population came the great souls who made Germany the great nation that it was. Its teachers, scientists, civic administrators, poets, musicians, idealists and patriots came from this autocracy. To this Germany America's Germans traced their heritage. From its hosts came our teachers, our professional men without number and others who wielded their craftsmanship for the benefit of all America. "If a German-American sought a connection with the country which gave him birth, he should look in the direction of the nobler autocracy. If he be truly an American citizen, if he places reason over emotion, he must withold support from the Kaiser," said George R. Catton, the late president of the Benzonia Academy in a speech at the Clare Congregational Church September 1914.

As the war unfolded its grand design, local people started to feel its impact. Stewart Mayhew, a regular army enlisted man from Hamilton Township returned home in October and related how unprepared this

Baron von Richthoven and his squadron await another military award in 1917.
Photo: National Archives GSA 111-SC-95773

305

nation was for a war such as was being waged in Europe. The same month Julius and Rudy Schaeffer returned to Clare from the war zone. About that time the Clare Knitting Mills received a huge order for woolen socks from the English and French armies. They signed a contract to deliver 90,000 dozen pairs of blue or black military quality socks prior to December 15th. The $175,000 order had been computed with each pair of socks costing seventeen cents. It was the largest single order of the entire war for the county and it had come in the first year of the carnage.

The war had not gone especially well for the English and French allies, called in those days the Triple Entente. France suffered casualties totaling 590,000 up to December 1st, of which 100,000 were killed in combat. The English were buying prodiguous quantities of food from us as they sought to break the rapidly developed submarine blockade on the homeland. At the same time we sold war goods and food to the Germans, angering the English who began harassing our neutral ships on the high seas. So serious did this become that all natural good will felt toward the English was in serious jeopardy. A serious note was sent to the Court of St. James, warning them of consequences which would follow if they continued their tactics.

The war reached this continent via Canada. Its close political and economic ties with England brought them into the war in its first phase. Many of Clare County's families were of Canadian descent and they returned home for future military service. In February of 1915 a major war scare erupted when three unidentified planes were sighted over Brockway, just sixty miles from Ottawa. All of the capitol's lights were turned off and the mint was completely darkened as all of the Dominion's gold was stored there. This was the first time the mint was completely darkened and showed to America the type of hysteria the western allies were

The Kaiser distributing the "Iron Crosses".

A fifteen inch siege gun used by the Germans against Verdun. The Americans captured it when the enemy was driven back toward their homeland.

developing.

During March, a former German merchant ship was outfitted by an American flag and crew and set sail for Europe. Captain Edward Breitung who lived in the Upper Peninsula had radioed the French that he was sailing with 11,000 bales of cotton. They took the hint and captured the ship on the high seas, towing it to a port in England. A major question of maritime law was involved in this brazen act, but its resolution wasn't reported to the public.

Another major international crisis hit in May when the "Lusitania" was torpedoed resulting in 1,149 deaths. No warning was given to the ship as one hundred-plus Americans were killed. Multi-millionaire Alfred G. Vanderbilt and other first class passengers continued their dining, thinking that the ship couldn't sink. All of them died for their fallacious reasoning. From this point on, it was difficult to be neutral in their thoughts.

The war was being graphically brought home to the county in May 1915 when the Princess Theatre showed its first war newsreel. The carnage was vividly seen by many of the local residents and it, too, had its impact upon their thinking.

AGRICULTURE DURING THE EARLY PHASES

Beef, pork, wheat, rye, cheese and other similar farm products began to increase in value as soon as the war broke out in July of 1914. Large shipments left Clare regularly for shipping ports on the east coast and also via Canada. The farmer who didn't have the capital for animal and dairy production relied on shipments of grains and potatoes. The men who cast their lots solely with the potato didn't prosper because the crop didn't ship or store well. As a consequence its price stayed low. Later when the public was asked to eat potatoes so the grains could be exported to Europe, the price improved some, but never to the levels the marginal farmers desired.

The Michigan Company operating out of a Clare warehouse near the Pere Marquette freight house, began buying eggs in large quantities. They were forwarded to Canada for quick transportation to England. One worker put a note in a crate of eggs asking for a reply. It came several months later stating that the eggs arrived in good condition and that some Kent residents had them for breakfast. The note also related things about the war not normally found in print. Because of the submarines, many eggs found their way to Davy Jones' locker.

Commercial ties to England such as the shipping of eggs and other farm produce helped forge strong bonds of friendship in spite of Wilson's admonition to the contrary. Theodore Roosevelt was another who attempted to destroy the neutrality scheme of Wilson's. He traveled all over the nation ·· 1915 speaking forcibly about "Preparedness for War or Preparedness for Peace if that is the way you see it." His views were widely accepted, especially when he spoke about the navy. The Republicans for years had commissioned two new battleships each fiscal year since 1900, but Wilson and the Democrats, immediately upon assuming office in 1913, reduced capital ship construction to practically nothing. This was the time when men were out of work and factories closed down in droves. He compounded the problem further by failing to develop airplanes, machine guns, military transport, artillery or even rifles. His biggest blunder was in artillery and the development of the manufacture of artillery shells. The 1915 Chautauqua speakers criss-crossing the country agreed with Roosevelt and they spread the lack of preparedness philosophy where ever they went.

Bethlehem Steel on its own had gone ahead with the development of armored steels which could be used by the navy and later, it turned out, by the army for its tanks. The company further offered to sell plate steel at cost plus overhead expenses, as determined by the Federal Trade Commis-

sion, but Wilson and the House of Representatives rejected the offer.

Dow Chemical Company prospered during 1915 as they produced huge quantities of chloroform for dyes and the war. In addition, the British blockade had effectively removed much foreign competition from the German dyes and these were superior to the American product. Dow continued to turn out the indigo dyes and they made rather substantial profits on the inferior product.

In October Congressman Loud began pushing for a larger navy. William Jennings Bryan, the old enemy of a strong military posture was gone and the spectre of Germany's forty battleships cast a shadow over America's thirty-four. England of course had seventy-six, but America was definitely in third place and holding.

During the fall of 1915 General Swayne attempted to increase the British army by three million men. He stressed that the nine to ten million men under arms in Germany were a formidable foe. A strategy of wearing the enemy down was not capable of bringing victory. He showed by projection that Germany's winter casualties would be greater than the allies, and if England could only begin the spring campaigns with an additional three million men, Germany would see that she couldn't win and would stop the war. Alas, it was not to be!

As 1915 drew to a close, the Democrats clearly realized that a weak army and navy was the prescription for national suicide and they began to heed the American people who had moved strongly toward England and France in spirit and in deeds. The Canadian press was having fun with Wilson's attempt to remain neutral. The MONTREAL STAR on November 26th said "Why doesn't the U.S. arrange to fight the Germans on Monday, Wednesday and Fridays and the English on Tuesday, Thursday and Saturdays. For variety they could fight the Mexicans on Sunday, unless the churches would consider this blasphemous."

Fortunately America didn't have to fight the Germans or the English in 1916. The joust with Mexico was enough to indicate the army's lack of preparation.

ISOLATIONISM AND PACIFICISM

The "War of Woes" broke upon England not unexpected, but totally unprepared for. Lord Roberts had traveled the island nation for years preaching preparedness, but there were few who listened. As the German armies swept toward Paris in August of 1914, the British Expeditionary Force was landed on the continent with the minimum of credibility. General Moltke was unaware of the army's presence for nearly two weeks, so impotent was its effect. The regiments sent over were without proper weapons, uniforms, shoes, transportation and other fundamental tools of warfare. In England there was an embarrasment in their amateurism. Yet even that nearly disastrous experience was lost upon the Americans and its leaders. Lord Northcliff who now was bemoaning his own lack of foresight said, "I doubt that America will really prepare for any war." He had gone through England's sleepy period when Lord Roberts alone tried to arouse a nation to the coming danger. Everywhere Roberts went, he met the stock reply, "I didn't raise my boy--- etc., etc."

In England, the average citizen had laughed at the men who carried the warning. In America, if anyone except General Wood and Theodore Roosevelt had cried out, they would have been laughed at also, but as it was, many Americans were alarmed by the nation's lack of preparation. Wilson and the Democrats, however, were victims of their own demogoguery, and it was hard to change their tune. When war came the dreamers quickly folded their tents and slithered away. "England today would give all that a century of preparedness would cost if she could only turn back the hands of the clock" said Lord Northcliff as reported by the CLARE SENTINEL January 16, 1916. The casualty lists of the belligerents released that same month indicated that he was probably correct. 14,960,000 casualties had been suffered up to the end of December 1915 and twenty per cent of these were deaths. 21,000,000 men were now under arms in Europe, yet America slumbered on.

Judd Lewis the patriot wasn't asleep though. His concern for preparedness was so strong that he wrote a poem entitled "THE PACIFIST" and was widely distributed.

I want the world to know that I'm
  an active pacifist.
I would not rudely slap a fellow man
  upon the wrist.
I never hide my money, I never
  lock my door.
I think its wrong to bar and bolt
  our mints and banks and store.
For a burglar would not burgle if we'd
  fling the portals wide
And show there was no protection for the
  heaps of wealth inside.

They'd say, "That is a trusting gink,
  see how he trust us.
'Bo, we will not rob him of his
  skad."
No, let him keep his dough, we'll
  go around the corner
Where the man has got a gun
  a dog and bolts his doors
And windows every one.
He thinks preparedness is the thing
  and he's prepared to shoot
And so we'll risk our lives and rob
  that old galoot.
And so the man who's not prepared
  he does not lose a yen
And the man who totes not a gun
  he meets no hold-up man.

Oh, when will men see this great truth
  and wipe out robbers by leaving
Access to their vaults
  and to their treasures free.
And then will all nations sink their ships
  make crochet hooks of guns
And holler loud to all the world,
  "We're the unprotected ones."
When nations do that sort of thing
  that I am longing for
Strong nations won't oppress the weak
  and there will be no war.

CHRISTIANITY AND THE WAR

The years just prior to the war saw a strong world-wide resurgence of religious piety and revival in the Christian churches and many denominations were greatly strengthened. Europe was especially swept by this phenomenon. England, Germany and the Netherlands felt the pervasive spirit of rebirth. When the war broke out, each nation besought the same God to favor its cause. The dilemma facing the Creator was similar to the American Civil War experience as noted by Lincoln in his Second Inaugural Address. Both sides invoked God on their side and troops engaged in fervent prayer on the eve of battle. In the trenches hundreds of thousands of men read and studied their Testaments. Belgium and France experienced a great revival in 1915-16. Liquor and luxurious living were considered taboo as the simple life became equated to religious piety.

Willard Price, writing in the June AMERICAN REVIEW OF REVIEWS for 1916 thought that the subtle renaissance of the world wide spiritual revival was more than coincidence. He thought that horrors and devastation from the war were responsible for solemnizing the world, and that they had the effect of driving people back upon divine security. "At any rate," Price said, "Christendom is faced with the greatest opportunity in its history."

Despite the heavy thundering of guns in Europe, Wilson hadn't understood their warning signals and he led our nation into its problems with Mexico almost totally unprepared. The army and navy had fewer men than their peacetime limitations and these days were anything but peaceable. When Poncho Villa gestured towards our southwestern border all Wilson could do was to summon the emergency reserves. He called out the National Guard and hustled them to protect the Texas border. Machine guns were purchased from England, and artillery wasn't even considered for deployment. The Guard units were issued civilian trucks to supplement their horse-drawn wagons, but they were not engineered for the requirements of modern war. So poorly were the Guard units equipped, that they couldn't even perform the task assigned them. Later some trucks were rounded up and placed at their disposal, but now the critical shortage was in drivers. A major recruiting drive was begun to locate automobile drivers from all over the nation.

In Flint Jim Clute had been test driving every other Buick which was coming off the assembly line in 1916. His job called for him to take every car, clock-wise around the track, one complete turn. This routine became rather tiresome, so the other test driver and Jim decided that they would

Every able-bodied man who could drive was encouraged to join the Army. Most of those recruited were sent to France with the A.E.F. in 1918.
Photo: National Archives GSA 4-P-23

reverse the direction of travel. Wouldn't you know it, before long one was going clock wise around the mile long track and they collided head-on. As expected, Buick foremen and supervisors poured onto the track, and one raised his voice to him and said "You're fired!" Out of a job, he joined the 31st Regiment in Texas and became an army truck driver. He was one of the few soldiers who crossed the Mexican border on wheels.

By now, President Wilson was trying to catch up with the country's mood, especially after New York's Mayor Mitchell called a public meeting to discuss the hap-hazard military call-up for the Mexican problem. Mayor Mitchell said, "I don't think anything demonstrates more clearly the prostrate condition of this country than what is going on in this city and in this state and in the other states today, when we see men called from the National Guard into the concentration camps, these fellows, the finest in the country, are responding only to find that when they get there, that there is no equipment, they are without horses, without the facilities for a successful campaign.'' He further compared the situation to the British when their first troops were sent to France without training or equipment. ''We need a policy which will put this nation on a war footing,'' he declared.

President Wilson responded to similar speeches in the past by calling the critics ''nervous and excited people.'' The president's actions gave them good reason to be nervous and millions of others had good reason to become excitable. Men were going to pay with their lives for this dalliance with the hyperbole. In the immediate situation facing the nation, the Guardsmen were sent to face a second rate quarry, but they were equipped as third rate soldiers.

UNIVERSAL MILITARY TRAINING

Professor Monroe Smith of Columbia University called for Universal Military Training. He claimed that a professional hired army was a thing of the past, while a volunteer army maimed the vigorous and spared the inert, the timid and the selfish men who sought escape from their responsibilities. He believed that if modern war makes it possible for the physically unfit to survive, modern war waged by a volunteer army makes for the survival of the socially unfit. To him there was no choice and no alternative to U.M.T. as it would balance the pluses and minuses of democracy.

During September of 1916, Germany was losing men faster than they could be replaced and so were France and Austria. Most analysts figured that Russia was the only belligerent who could fight on indefinitely, as she had an inexhaustible supply of cannon fodder. Some Americans compared Germany to the American south when General Grant bled it to death at Cold Harbor and the Wilderness. ''Germany must shorten her lines or face disaster,'' was the often repeated observation.

THEODORE ROOSEVELT IN BATTLE CREEK

The most outspoken critic of unpreparedness was criss-crossing the nation in 1916. None in the nation was more aggressive than the former president. At a meeting in Battle Creek Roosevelt said that Wilson's slogan ''He kept us out of War'' was something that Washington and Lincoln couldn't make. ''They chose war because it was for righteousness rather than perfidy,'' he said. ''The men who chose peace at any price are the heirs of the tories and the copperheads,'' he concluded.

Wilson was returned to the White House by a nation which wanted to believe in him, but they should have thought back to 1912-14 when the railroad sidings were filled with empty boxcars, idled because he shut the factories down and closed the ship yards. Poverty and unemployment were partners in the industrial heartland of the nation. City dwellers were given permission to slaughter the municipal horses for food. When war came to Europe munition orders poured in and the country ended Fiscal Year 1914-15 with a $200,000,000 surplus. This war had staved off an industrial crisis among the unemployed, it was widely believed.

During December of 1916, Wilson was begged by many important people to develop an army, but he wouldn't listen. His reliance upon the National Guard was incomprehensible to General Wood who publically chided him for his stubborn blindness. While the Guard was in Texas and Mexico, he made no effort to even bring the army up to its authorized levels. In October of 1916 it was 14,307 below its peacetime authorization and 34,307 below the new law's limits. When the new capital ship ''Arizona'' was launched in November, crews from three other ships were stripped and those ships immobilized, so short was the navy for manpower. The country in December began having more serious reservations about the man they had just re-elected and who was to lead them for four more years.

As the fateful year of 1917 broke over the horizon, Wilson said in a speech that America will have the greatest navy in the

An American ship passing through the Panama Canal during World War I.

This was the major catalyst for rupturing the peace between Germany and America.

At this turn of events everyone was up in arms, acting "nervous and excitable" as Wilson formerly had described it. Michigan Agricultural College offered its campus to the federal government for military training if and when needed. Central Normal College followed the lead and offered its facilities also.

With war only weeks away, Bethlehem Steel's offer to build ships at cost was finally accepted by the dilettante government. On its own in 1914, the steel company had begun modifications in its plants so it could turn out sixteen inch naval shells. A year later they signed a contract for 2,400 projectiles and they were delivered, but the government wouldn't take possession. In late 1916 they attempted to levy a fine of $495,744 for non-delivery. This was only a foretaste of the government's handling of the preparations for war and it didn't look good for the allies.

WE ENTER THE WAR

An extra session of Congress gave President Wilson authority to arm our merchant ships in mid-March 1917. With this action it became obvious to all of the world that war was imminent between America and Germany. The threat to our ships, however would come from the submarines. COLLIERS magazine in its March issue carried an indepth story of this underwater danger and depicted problems this country was to face in the immediate future. The seriousness of the problem was no longer the province of Wilson's nervous and excitable people as evidenced by the sinking of the American ships "Vigilancia", "Memphis", and "Illinois" around the third week of March. Fourteen lives were lost and Congress hurried through a defense appropriation bill for $115,000,000. A state of war existed during this week which was a full two weeks before the actual Declaration of War.

On April 5, 1917, Wilson went before the Congress and asked that a Declaration of

world, but he never mentioned it again in public. Volunteers sensing the ineptness at the helm stayed away from the army recruiters as the number of men hovered about the 100,000 figure. The navy by now was feeling the U-Boat pressure and warned that a break between Germany and America was not far in the future. Alarmed by an intensified German navy, Wilson called for the arming of our merchant ships, but until the Zimmerman note came to light in March no one seemed to care what Wilson thought.

THE ZIMMERMAN NOTE

The turning point in our destiny hinged upon a German plot to embroil Mexico in a war with America in exchange for the states of New Mexico, Texas and Arizona. When this message was sent through diplomatic channels to Von Eckhardt, it was intercepted and President Wilson published it in March.

War be passed and that an army of 1,200,000 men and 500,000 for the navy be approved. It was a popular request. Michigan's Governor Sleeper sent a telegram pledging $5,000,000 for troop support. Other states pledged similar amounts. A call went to all of the county residents to display the American flag. "If you don't have one, get one!" was the admonition. Within a day flags began flying from long poles, short poles and even from trees. Everyone had responded it seemed, but not quite. Out in Arthur township one German family didn't have the colors hoisted on a flag staff and some neighbors suspected their loyalty. About a week went by and then a delegation of neighbors visited George Pfetch and inquired about his lack of loyalty to his country. They found out that he didn't lack patriotic fervor, just American dollars. Someone donated a red, white and blue emblem and the Pfetches were now one hundred per cent red blooded Americans.

RAISE MORE FOOD

The Germans earned the public approbation of the "Hun" when they joined other European nations in a war against the Chinese during the Opium War. "Treat the Chinese like Attila the Hun" was the official policy of Germany, and her army did just that. Their abuse of the Chinese was absolutely barbarous and the title of disrespect became associated with the Imperial German Army. True to their Hun tradition, they brutalized the civilians of Poland and Belgium in a most dispiteous manner. Adults who were able to work were removed to Germany and placed in war production. Infirmed adults and children were deprived of food and shelter and starvation was every where.

One of the first official acts of the American government was to address ourselves to the problem of feeding the children who were still systematically being destroyed through starvation. The war had disrupted European agriculture and social life to such an extent that without great quantities of American food, colossal disaster awaited friend and foe

during the coming winter. It became the official policy of this country to raise all of the normal crops and in addition, every extra square foot of soil was to be planted to wheat, oats, rye and corn. Meat animals were to be produced at the maximum rate. Urban residents were strongly encouraged to plant large gardens. Soon Farwell, Harrison, Lake, Temple and Clare were plowed up and huge Victory Gardens were everywhere. These would be called Liberty Gardens a bit later and they raised Victory Cabbage, Victory Beans and Victory every thing else. Hardly a spare foot of ground could be found in the country.

County extension agents worked overtime looking for enough seeds to supply the zealous gardeners. Corn, oats, rye and other grain seeds were in especially short supply. W. Holmes Kennedy, Clare County Extension Agent hurdled over obstacles to locate seed beans, but when he did their price was so high that many farmers couldn't afford to purchase them. They were further reluctant to plant when there was no guarantee that the government wouldn't set a price which would be so low they couldn't recoup their investment. Acting quickly on this problem, the government gave the seeds to the farmers and set a policy of guaranteed prices which were high enough for a modest profit. Soon all of the beans were in the ground along with all of the seed potatoes which were lying around.

Business as usual in the county went by the boards as local Red Cross Chapters were being organized in every county and township in Michigan. Schools relaxed their attendance policies as high school age students flocked to the farms for the immense job of significantly increasing the food supply began. By May 1, most high schools were in such shambles that classes were cancelled until graduation time and even these were conducted on an abbreviated scale.

An all out effort to save the Belgium children was launched in Clare during May as money, clothing and food was collected. Herbert Hoover was appointed by Wilson to this humanitarian post and he went to Europe to survey the situation. It was worse than any one in this country understood.

The home front was the battlefield for food.
Photo: National Archives GSA 4-P-59

This is a World War I farm scene of a Chippewa farm. Every effort was made to harvest each bushel of wheat in 1917.
Photo: National Archives GSA 165-WW-172-3

Muskegon contributed its fair share for victory. The home front contributed funds for the YMCA, Red Cross and the Knights of Columbus. They also conserved food for the Allies.
Photo: National Archives GSA 4-G-25-9

The nation, states and communities were gearing up for an all out effort to avert a world famine, but the weather was one condition for which there was no control. Nevertheless, by the first of June, every acre of ground in Clare county which could possibly grow food was planted. Hundreds of Liberty Gardens as they were now called were tended by the town residents as well as the rural families. Potatoes was planted by everyone in the north and fortunately so for the government was planning to ship millions of bushels of wheat and other grains to Europe. Potatoes would be the one main stay of the American diet during the 1917-18 winter.

The city, village and county governments organized for war also. A war Relief Committee was established with Mayor Andrus assuming control in Clare. All charities were to be funneled through it and each church, fraternal and civic clubs and other interested parties were asked to send a delegate to it. This group took over the Belgian Relief Fund and the Red Cross chapter.

Men were needed for all types of war related work. The Bay City ship yards began recruiting workers as soon as the merchant ships were armed. They needed skilled millwrights and common laborers. The auto plants continued their civilian assembly lines but they added military trucks to the schedule. Packard Motors converted to military trucks and supplied a large volume of vehicles. The White Motor Company also churned trucks out in large numbers. Dow Chemical Company advertised for skilled and unskilled help offering three dollars a day for the latter employee. Concurrent with this siphoning off of men was the recruitment by the National Guard. Most of the local men had returned from Mexico and reverted to a stand-by status. On April 26th, eight of these men, members of the Guard, assembled in Clare for a trip to Army Drill Camp. Civic leaders took them to the Calkins for a farewell dinner. Then escorted by the Boys in Blue, they were taken to the depot. A band played several patriotic numbers and soon it was time for Walter Larman, Russell Alexander, Courtney Milam, Stuart Hay, Archie Parks, Fred Adams, Warren Hale

and Charles Jackson to go. Three hundred citizens including Boy Scouts, class mates and friends watched the train pull out of town. It was an ominous departure and everyone knew it. Only sixteen days earlier Percy Kissick, a former Sheridan township boy, was killed in France while serving with the Canadian Army. His family had moved to Ohio and then later to Saskatchewan. From there he enlisted in the infantry. Kissick was a nephew of Val Empey and a friend of scores in the county.

Two weeks later George Sheffield, Arthur Sheffield, Harold Wyman, Hal C. Bush and George McKeever were sent to Fort Sheridan. Bush was a teacher from the Bay City schools and McKeever was a local mill man's son. Together they began Officer Candidates School.

These bean sorters worked for five cents an hour during World War I.

THE DRAFT

America's responsibilities in Europe now demanded that a large number of troops be sent into the war zone as rapidly as possible, but the army was still extremely weak in numbers and equipment. Congress passed a conscription law in May and a general enrollment of the nation's young men was scheduled for early June. The navy had a modest number of men and a number of first rate ships, but they needed more men quickly. Secretary of the Navy Daniels put into operation a vast recruiting drive and started to bring in a half million men. Industry was gearing up its facilities as rapidly as possible and certain types of war munitions had already been put on stream from the purchases the French and English had made, but not in the type and quantity required by the army envisioned by the War Department. Secretary of War, Newton Baker from Ohio, sought an immediate

solution to the army's problem. Thirty two training camps were planned, half of them in the south and the other half in the north. Southern camps would use tents while the northern cantonments would require weather proof construction.

June 5, 1917 was the day announced for the men to register for the draft. Registrars oversaw the enrollment in town halls, school houses, township offices and even in barns as was the case in Freeman township. Socialists tried to persuade the potential draftees to boycott the enrollment procedure, but authorities in Chicago and New York struck them hard and quick and they did not have the opportunity to generate much public support. Clare County's Socialists were frustrated Democrats in Hatton. They weren't the wild-eye anarchists of the big city variety and so the local enrollments proceeded without incident. President Wilson had warned all who might escape the registration would face certain military service

New draftees arrived at Camp Custer, oftentimes bewildered, but usually patriotic.
Photo: Michigan Department of State Archives

This group of Clare County draftees had dinner at the Calkins House prior to their train ride to Camp Custer, November 21, 1917. Front row (L-R): Dr. Langin, member of the Exemption Board; George J. Cummins; unknown; Al Graham; unknown; Thurman Robinette; unknown; unknown; unknown; Al Perry; unknown; unknown; William Hawkins; unknown; unknown; Don Canfield; unknown; Henry Mooney; Sheriff Hutchinson. The man on the porch is unknown.
Photo courtesy Harold Fleming

eventually, so they should not attempt to avoid their duty.

Volunteers did not flock to the recruiting stations as many had predicted. Either the country's reluctance to become embroiled in Europe's affairs or a desire on the part of the men to avoid paying for Wilson's mistakes predominated. Some men such as Carl Holbrook enlisted in the medical branch and was assigned to a hospital which was then preparing to leave for Europe. It was predicted that he was to be Clare county's first American army representative in France. Albert Wilson a former artillery man re-enlisted, leaving his family in Harrison. Jim Clute, only recently discharged from the Guard, signed on again. In August these men were joined by the first draftees and all members of the National Guard as these units had been federalized.

At the time of the draft registrations, men could claim exemptions if they were clergy, government officials and or a few other high priority civilians. Some consideration was given to the family responsibilities a man had in this classification also. Whether they were classified exempt was dependent upon the county draft board and the county draft committee. Some favoritism was suspected as a few married men with children were taken

in some counties, but deferred in others. One farmer in Isabella county lived in Vernon. He was married and had six children, yet he was taken to Custer. Some thought that he didn't carry enough social prestige. To compound the tragedy further, he was later killed in France.

Clare county had a three member board also. They were accused of playing favorites by a few, but most thought Francis M. Morrissey, Robert Hutchinson and A. J. Doherty played it straight. One Clare resident was visited by a representative of the draft board in a semi social call. He suggested that Don Canfield wouldn't have to go as he could arrange things. At this overture, A. R. Canfield bristled! "Senator, if Frank Jackson and Fred Cimmerer can go, Don Canfield can go too!" And all three did!

Almost as soon as the registration was finished on June 5th, the draft machinery was put in motion by Washington. Provision was allowed for a large portion of the man power pool to be deferred but Indiana's acceptance rate was ninety per cent. This was much higher than Michigan's. Clare county registered 661 men. Gladwin signed in over seven hundred and Isabella had 1,753 show up. At Windover Lake in Freeman township, C. A. Gilmore organized a big patriotic affair complete with orations, glee clubs, bands and a picnic for the families while the young men signed in. Activities of this nature lent strong support for the draft. The actual enrollment was held in C. O. Gillman's barn.

THE SHERIFF'S PROCLAMATION

A large German population resided in Clare county and many still held citizenship in the old country, although their young families were all native born Americans. During the massive effort to unite the nation into a strong posture of support for Wilson and the country, several adults who could trace their roots back to American ancestors looked at these Germans and wondered if they represented a threat to this country. The Germans looked back and wondered how much they should fear their neighbor. Sheriff Robert Hutchinson decided that he ought to clear up the problems before they developed into something serious. He himself lived in the Eagle community where several German families resided. He knew them to have impeccable credentials and were the type which built America.

Sheriff Robert Hutchinson
Photo from the Hutchinson Family Collection

The letter was addressed to all citizens of Clare county, but he spoke especially to the foreign born. ''... No resident in Clare county need fear for his property and personal rights as long as he doesn't become lawless ... The United States has never confiscated property of foreign born and it has no intention of doing so now ... I declare that all residents will be protected in the ownership of property as long as they obey the law of the state and nation. I urge every citizen to not discuss the situation in a manner as to disparage a person's nationality.''

With the exception of a missing flag or two in the front yard or the heavy pressure upon the Germans to buy Liberty Bonds, little friction developed at this phase of the situation. Some neighbors talked, of course, and Fred Krell wrote a letter about a year later about some scurrilous comments which were circulated by a busy body. He said that he was as patriotic as the next person and Uncle Sam thought so too as he was a substitute mail carrier. This open letter put to shame the ones who were the gossips and they stopped their talking.

Packard Motor Car Company in Detroit announced a policy change in their handling of promotions. They said . . . ''In the future all native born or naturalized citizens would have first chance at all promotions.'' Foreigners would not be advanced for the duration of the war. There was a large nucleus of foreign born in Detroit at the time.

A GERMAN PROGRAM

By the end of the second week in June, things were quite well organized. The large scale food program was well under way and the high school students had regathered long enough to hold the abbreviated graduation ceremonies, although most of the young men didn't show up, and the program to relieve the Belgian children was in full swing. Now came some news from Germany which sickened even the most crass American.

England had effectively blockaded Germany early in the war. In turn, the Germans began to exploit their civilians, especially those in the captured territories, by denying food to certain classes which in the government's opinion couldn't help them carry on the war. As these neglected people died off in the controlled territory, corpses were collected and utilized in their Kadaverweriungeanstall facility at Evergnicourt. There the bodies were boiled to remove the fat so it could be used for lubricating oil. The remains were ground into a powder in a bone mill to mixed with pig's food or used as a manure for the fields. "Nothing can be permitted to go to waste," was the official explanation. In America this bit of news upset most everyone. "We no longer wonder at the outrages in Belgium. Now we understand how the Prussians can condone their submarine warfare," was the general view expressed in Clare.

Stories like this one put a spur to the efforts now going on in the county to collect money for the Red Cross, scrap iron for the factories and food for the allies. A patriotic pole was erected at the residence of D. McCrimmon in Vernon which C. W. Perry and other city big-wigs attended. Even when food prices jumped nine per cent in May and June it didn't cause much grumbling. Clare citizens now began to understand the full job to be done.

When the Red Cross funds were slow in coming in, the Clare chapter was given a new leader. Farwell organized a very active chapter under the direction of Mrs. E. R. Brown, Mrs. T. U. Fuller and Mrs. A. J. Chappell. They took matters in hand and secured regular pledge cards and scheduled knitting groups. Other townships also organized their chapters and knitting groups. Mrs. Carl Reading traveled all over the county helping each sub-chapter to have a successful beginning. Michigan became the first state to have all of its counties organized and Clare county was the first to have all of its townships functioning. Now money began coming in on a regular basis and the commitments which the county owed were met on schedule although most of the pledges were around a dollar a month.

THE NAMES ARE DRAWN

In Washington, a public drawing of the drafting sequence was held. All names in a county were placed on a card and then given a number. Only one number could be used until the next sequence was permitted. The numbering was done in ink before the lottery system was put into operation in the nation's capitol. Across the country there were about 4,400 districts. This meant that each number drawn represented at least that many potential draftees. Clare's first draftee was Walter H. Matthews of Hamilton township. He was followed by Cloyce H. Detwiler, Eber R. Johnson, John Reed, Bruce E. Pelch, Valmous Armour, Harold V. Lassen, Lee E. Ervin, Orin A. Mason and Bernard F. Park. The remaining 505 men were given a priority sequence so they knew where they were on the waiting list. The men drawn were sent from Clare to Custer in late July and then forwarded on to the new divisions being made up in the south.

Roy Tatman was one of the first to volunteer and now in August he wrote a letter home. "They gave me six shots, one in the left arm and five in the right. We eat baked beans, bread, potatoes, macroni, pudding and cold tea. Believe me it is good . . . We arise at six every morning for the day's activities . . . The rumor is that the 28th Regiment will be assigned to Georgia for further training. I will write you from there," he promised the readers of the CLARE SENTINEL.

CAMP CUSTER

A crash program of camp construction went on all over the country. Sixteen weather proof camps had to be completed before the draftees could begin their training. Men from all over Michigan were drawn to Battle Creek to begin the massive but hurried construction project. The government had purchased 6,000 acres of land west of the city and the farm families were removed almost overnight. They hated to give up their farms, but there was no choice in the matter.

Then came the two thousand construction workers. School teachers, principals and superintendents were prime candidates for this job as they normally were looking for summer employment. Joining them were the heavy construction mechanics, brick masons, plumbers, electricians, carpenters and unskilled workers. The task was to build 156 barracks 117' x 40' by two stories high. In addition there were to be an additional fifty buildings housing the hospital, fire department, power plant, water works, headquarters, YMCA and other assorted types of military structures. The sub-surface construction went on at the same time the barracks were going up. Otto J. Heber, a Hatton township resident and school superintendent and county school commissioner for Osceola was one of the local crew members employed at Custer.

Soon the draftees would come pouring into camp. The mess halls and other auxiliary buildings were pushed hard but they weren't ready when the first draftees were scheduled to arrive. Cooks, bakers, medical personnel, water works engineers, teamsters, telegraph operators and a whole complement of supporting workers were recruited. The Michigan Hotel Association was asked to train 960 cooks before the bulk of the men arrived. They immediately set about the task. All across the state they took trainees and had them trained in their hotel member's kitchen. When they went to camp, each of the new cooks was assigned three men for him to train. In this way there were sufficient food personnel on hand when the 85th Divison began showing up in late August.

All summer long the building activity went on at a frenzied pace. When September arrived most of the buildings were ready. but a few had to live in tents temporarily. In the south some of the draftees didn't want to report to camp when they were ready and thirty-five men retreated to a hide-out ready to fight it out. These men were part of the Mother Jones family, a splinter group of the I.W.W. or the Industrial Workers of the World, a socialist activitist group. Soon after they holed up, a deputy sheriff was shot. It wasn't much later that the whole gang was arrested. A few widely publicated fracases like this and the men were glad to get into a camp finished or not.

Camp Custer's Knights of Columbus Hall, 1917.
Photo: Michigan Department of State Archives

During 1917, massive and hurried construction efforts were made toward the completion of Camp Custer.
Photo: Michigan Department of State Archives

One of Camp Custer's fire stations.
Photo: Michigan Department of State Archives

THE CONSCIENTIOUS OBJECTOR

In a religious country such as America most every one believes in peace and in the sacredness of life as given by the Creator. Now that a war was being waged by the nation against fellow humans it was easy for some to question the efficiaciousness of service in the military. Bishop Henderson of the Methodist Episcopal Church had some views on this conundrum. His analysis of the problem was carried in the CLARE SENTINEL August 23rd, 1917.

"It is not ungenerous nor without historical ground to say that rights of conscience are too easily manufactured by sophisticated minds who are always conscientious enough to let the others bear the burdens, the hardships and the sufferings of life while they enjoy its benefits.

"The problem of serving the nation doesn't have as a premise, its roots in the theological at all. It is a state question and belongs in the domain of the state.

"The conscientious objector is opposed to war — to any war — even though in defense of all that God in the development of humanity has slowly evolved and made the heirlooms of the nations. But he is willing to enjoy all the benefits, social, political, cultural, commercial or others that these men have won or preserved for him at the cost of their own blood and suffering and death. For if all war is wrong, how does he wipe the bloody spot of guilt from his own hands by simply objecting to war, while he enjoys the benefits of wars? Is the receiver of stolen goods less criminal than the thief? Is the

Carl Spicer

The rifle range at Camp Custer.

beneficiary of a crime a partner in crime? Is such a man a conscientious objector at all?

"Should such a person be punished or interned for his opinion? No, a government doesn't have the right to punish a person for his opinion. The solution is, let the man have his opinion, but let him forever be deprived of the benefits of war, of all political, social and civil rights which have been wrested by war.''

From this rationale and others similar in tone, most citizens strongly supported the nation's present and future courses of actions. Men now began to enlist ahead of the draft and were taken into branches of service which could best utilize their skills. Fred Stone, the famous Clare resident and former football captain of the powerful Aggies while at Michigan Agricultural College had been graduated as a civil engineer. Going to Chicago he became a very skilled engineer for an Illinois railroad. Marrying a United States Senator's daughter he was in the higher echelon of society. His parents lived in Clare and he returned home after enlistment and just before he joined General Pershing in France. He was in charge of tearing up 1,000 miles of railroad track in this country and putting them down in France. This was the first major task this country faced as it began the massive build up in the European war. George F. Sanderson of Farwell enlisted and was sent to France in the early phases. He too was a railroad man. Unfortunately Sanderson was killed soon after his arrival over there. Stuart Hay joined Russell Alexander and Walter Larman in North Carolina where the 4th Division was in advanced training. Roy C. Larkin, a regular army man from Grant township returned home prior to his 10th Division's departure for France. Other enlistees caught up with their divisions as hurried preparations for open field warfare were carried out.

In late August, just before the Russians collapsed, scores of Isabella, Osceola, Clare, Gladwin and other area men were enlisting. The draftees were just beginning to leave for the hurriedly constructed camps all across the nation. Government officials speaking for Wilson denied that Russia would leave the war early. In support of this position they announced an additional loan of $100,000,000 bringing the total to $275,000,000.

Field kitchens at Camp Custer
Photo: Michigan Department of State Archives

An outdoor barber shop at Camp Custer.
Photo: Michigan Department of State Archives

GENERAL WOOD

In the second half of 1917, the national government had caught up with the warnings of Theodore Roosevelt and General Wood. The lack of preparation for war by most officials caused many to question their ability to lead the men and divisions in France. Many influential people pressured President Wilson to give General Wood an important assignment, preferably with the American Expeditionary Forces. The general's problem was that he dared to be right ahead of his time and his vocal warnings about the coming war had put Wilson on the defensive. It would have taken a pretty big man to admit the colossal mistakes and put in charge the one who had been attempting to point them out over the years, so General Wood was assigned to a minor post in Platts-

burg. A large public concern developed over this and a press release said that a more important assignment was being considered for later. In July of 1918 it was still raging and the President finally called him to the White House for a conference, but his services were never used in the war in any significant manner. If the general was disappointed at this cuff on the cheek, he never mentioned it. Many, many citizens thought that this little act of pique was measuring the man who was the president. General Wood was a war casualty.

SOME DISLOCATIONS

The summer was going rapidly now and a few problems began surfacing. Home canning demonstrations had been widely held in late June and July, but they weren't thorough enough and a few cases of ptomaine poisoning and botulism began showing up. On the draft matter, some thought they were being imposed upon by insensitive officials so the federal government established an Appeals Board. One was assigned for Arenac, Alcona, Alpena, Bay, Crawford, Clare, Cheboygan, Gladwin, Huron, Isabella, Iosco, Midland, Montmorency, Ogemaw, Oscoda, Otsego, Presque Isle, Roscommon, Sanilac and Tuscola counties with A. J. Doherty as its chairman. It heard appeals for all drafting problems initially, but then its scope was widened to hear all disputes related to the federal war regulations and programs. It was a busy board and normally held its meetings in Bay City, but A. J. had the authority as its chairman to hear individual appeals alone and to dispose of the problem as he saw fit. This was a very powerful position and generally speaking, he did not take much criticism for his handling of it.

On the home front the fellows who weren't able to pass their physicals or who had deferments felt left out of the glory which the military was now basking in. Someone came up with the idea of establishing a local unit of the Home Guards, complete with uniform, rifles and a band. W. E. Currie donated a large sum of money and others pitched in a few dollars and their uniforms were ordered. In December, the 80th Company of the Michigan State Troops were dressed in their new threads. They had been mustered in previously when Captain H. G. McKerring had assembled his troops on the Clare Race Track in September. There Major Phillips swore the unit into active service. Their service was essentially ornamental.

In Europe, the Russian troops began deserting the trenches and the war in the east was deteriorating rapidly. Lead elements of the AEF were now showing up in France as the 1st Division was scheduled to disembark momentarily. Engineers had previously gone to Chaumont in preparation of turning the area into a $100,000,000 base of operations. The French were anxious to get the Americans onto their soil as they planned to put the Amis into their trenches to make up

for their huge casualties. France had begun the war with one strategy and that was "Attack, Attack, Attack!" As their men were killed in astronomical numbers they eventually began to question its wisdom. Digging into the ground to avoid the machine guns and artillery they became paralyzed with indecision. The British had begun the war woefully unprepared. Soon, however, they began to send men over to France, and they took over the French strategy as their ally dug in. British homes were now taking the immense casualties and they too wanted the Americans to replace their vacancies in the ranks. Confident of their strategy they marched a whole generation into the machine guns of Flanders, Ypres, the Somme and Marne. It was a horrible strategy. Its execution first by the French and then by the British cost them a generation of its young men and in France's case, its national vitality. Even today, France still suffers from this immense blood-letting.

General Pershing had been tapped by President Wilson to lead the Americans in Europe. This man, who had suffered his own personal tragedy when his family was killed in a California fire, was a good choice. He protected his soldiers from the stupidities of the French and British generals who kept insisting during most of the early build up that he piece-meal feed his regiments into their divisions. Except for the momentous crisis of the last great German offensive in 1918, he kept the men out of their trenches. Pershing arrived in France in June of 1917. Two weeks later the first convoy of American engineers docked with their railroad. Somewhat later the 1st Division disembarked at St. Nazaire and on July 4, 1917 they marched through the streets of Paris and on to Lafayette's tomb. There Col. Charles E. Stanton uttered the famous remark which thrilled the world, "Lafayette, we are here!" The news media ascribed it to Pershing although he denied it repeatedly.

The 20th Engineering Battalion was recruited to manufacture lumber and timbers for the Americans to use in their Chaumont cantonment and later for their combat needs. Recruiters went all through the lumber regions of northern Michigan, Wisconsin,

The 20th Engineers were lumbermen recruited especially for A.E.F. They went to France in the early months and cut the timber for the trenches, barracks, hospitals and railroad ties. Without their skills, the war effort would have been seriously handicapped.

Photo: Natioinal Archives GSA 111-SC-24466

Minnesota and the Pacific northwest for lumberjacks, sawyers and other skilled lumbermen. They were members of the pioneer engineering units at Chaumont.

By late summer several Clare men had been shipped to France either as members of the Canadian Army or as the lead elements of the AEF. Courtney Milam was a member of the 16th Infantry Regiment of the 1st Division. He arrived in France about the time Capt. William C. "Chester" Halstead of the Canadian Army was made famous for his heroic capture of two machine guns and other acts of heroism. Chester came from Garfield township and had been home in Lake just before he went to France in 1916. He was a larger than life hero all over France and in England. The Canadian Army, needing heroes perhaps, chanced onto his exploits and gave him a big build up for propaganda purposes, but the men respected anyone who could take on the machine guns. Chester was destined to die in August 1918. William J. Wilson was fighting in a Canadian uniform and had been in the trenches since 1916. Victor Cooper from Hamilton and George Duncan were others who carried the Canadian flag into battle. James Flannigan was now in France although he was in an American uniform. In general, however, there weren't many Americans "Over There." The big build up of American forces was scheduled between March and June of 1918.

The first troops at Chaumont had to live in tents. This American camp site was selected because of its relative isolation from other French villages. Bakers, cooks, a hospital unit, well drillers, electricians, plumbers and other similar skilled craftsmen went to work immediately. Bakers and cooks began honing their skills by preparing large quantities of food and bread for the allies. The short rationed troops loved every bit of the experimental foods.

The $100,000,000 base was to have rails leading to it from Brest, St. Nazaire and LeHavre. One thousand miles of rails and standard sized locomotives, box cars and related equipment was taken up from the Pennsylvania Railroad company along with many of its personnel and set down in France. Section crews began the immense task of laying the rails right up to the expected battle areas. It was a bold conception and showed that not everyone in charge of things was asleep during our pre-war years.

As the "Sammies" began to emerge from the ships in larger numbers near the end of 1917, some friction developed between them and the allies over money. European Lieutenants earned between $366 and $466 a year. From this sum they paid for their clothing, food and personal requirements. An American private received $475 and he had to pay for nothing except his laundry. Members of the AEF were given an additional 20% making them comparatively rich by European standards. French privates were paid $2 a month and English Tommies were issued $7.50. It was no wonder the trouble developed. The Americans had food, money, soap and tobacco. It soon developed that they had their pick of the women and this was the problem.

The Red Cross now asked all chapters to forward all of their knitted goods to the camps where the state's draftees were concentrated. An attempt was made to send the knitted sweaters, wristlets and socks to the state's soldiers. Clare's quota was one hundred each of sweaters, mufflers, socks and wristlets.

AIRPLANES

A thorn of contention was the airplane. This country had invented the contraption and then developed it to a relatively sophisticated level, but during the 1914-16 years little happened. Europe on the other hand began using the machine in the war and they took over the development of engines and airframes. Admiral Perry in June of 1917 said that this country ought to send one thousand planes to Europe as soon as possible. By September a new liberty aircraft engine was developed far enough so it was expected to take over the propulsion of the American aircraft. It was capable of propelling a machine 140 miles per hour. This was the equal to any foreign engine. Plans were hurried and a goal of 22,000 planes was

American war planes used engines such as this Hispano-Suiza model.
Photo: National Archives GSA 111-SC-14019

set for the spring of 1918 using this new eight cylinder engine. It had a ratio of 1.75 pounds of weight for each horsepower developed. One engine we had was capable of producing 250 horsepower and could propel the plane 214 miles per hour. There was some talk of placing two or three engines on a single airframe and sending it into battle. It was clear that the American engineers had scored a major triumph, seemingly overnight, but it had been wrought by American industry, not the government. This late accomplishment was almost too late for this war, but it at least showed some of the potential of the post-war period.

THE 32nd DIVISION

The federal government nationalized all Guard units in August of 1917. Michigan had three regiments of troops, but they were not at full strength at the time of their federalization. The cantonment at Camp Custer wasn't completed on schedule so three thousand of the first draftees were assigned to the 32nd Division, the new designation for the Wisconsin and Michigan National Guards. They were sent to Waco, Texas where the division was being prepared for open field warfare that Pershing insisted upon. An additional three thousand troops were sent to Little Rock, Arkansas where the 42nd Division was being prepared. This was the famous Rainbow Division, consisting of Guard units from all over the country. The old Michigan National Guard regiments, the 31st, 32nd and 33rd Regiments were combined into two new regiments, the 126th Infantry of the 63rd Brigade and the 125th Infantry. Plans were drawn by the War Department and they indicated that this combat division was to be in France soon after the first of the year. Earlier plans to use the Michigan Guardsmen as a reserve for the Wisconsin Division were aborted because history books wouldn't give much ink to a series of reserve regiments scattered around the army. Michigan wanted and received a fighting unit which was capable of earning glory for itself. Most of the Clare men served in the 126th Regiment, and we

had scores serving with it when it was the sixth division to become a part of the AEF. Its early shipment to France enabled it to be involved in much of the heavy fighting during 1918.

LIBERTY BONDS

The government set a goal of two billion dollars for its first Liberty Loan drive held in June of 1917, and it was oversubscribed by fifty one percent. A second loan drive was set for October and a goal of three billion dollars. Its slogan was "Liberty Lights." Clare county had a quota of $80,000 in June and $172,000 for October. This quota was based upon bank deposits and while the county had four banks, two of which were

Buying Liberty Bonds was the patriotic duty of every able American. They were sold agressively by the government. Civic leaders, such as A. J. Lacy, were strong participants in the fund raising.
Photo: Archives GSA 4-P-233

in Clare, three actually drew heavily upon Isabella farmers for their business. It appeared to all that a very heavy sum was assigned to Clare. Nevertheless, the county went about raising the amount assigned. E. P. Darling, the old Civil War veteran from Farwell, bought the first Liberty Bond sold in the county. Joseph Reed, General Custer's personal buglar during the Civil War, bought the second bond. Reed left Custer just before he went west to his destiny at Little Big Horn. Reed came to Farwell.

Many of the county residents didn't have enough cash to buy a bond, so the banks used the document as collatoral and loaned eighty per cent of its value. A purchaser paid twenty per cent down and an equal amount each month. Even so the large quota caused a great burden to fall upon the county. Farmers were not in a position to purchase the bonds at the time of their offering and they didn't buy their share. It was said that the better off segment of the county's population didn't support this second drive either. On October 15, all school house lights were to be left on until 10:00 p.m. as a reminder for the citizen to support his government in this hour of great need. By appealing to the patriotism in each citizen the quota was finally reached on the last day of the drive. It pulled hard on the county.

In Detroit, Clare's former mayor, A. J. Lacy was traveling extensively speaking in favor of the Liberty Loans. During the second drive he went to factories, churches and theatres giving a speech similar to the one he gave to the men in a Detroit factory. Here is what he had to say:

"We are engaged in the most terrible war of all history. By spring there will undoubtably be over two million odd red-blooded American boys on the battlefields of France to fight for our beloved country and for Democracy and Humanity. These boys come from your homes and from the shops, the desks and fields of America. They are your brothers, your fellow-workmen, your fellow-citizens. You love them.

"Our army and navy must be munitioned, fed, clothed and all necessaries supplied to comfort our soldiers and sailors at the front and to render it possible for them to do their best, to win this war, to end it speedily, and to return home safe to us again.

"There are but two ways to pay the expense of a great war. One is by direct taxation, which would be confiscatory, and unbearable to the people. The other is for the people to loan their money from their earnings and savings to the government, the government paying interest for the use of the money, evidencing the obligation to pay the principal and interest by a government bond. I now show you a government bond. It is an obligation of the United States of America to pay the sum of $100 with interest at four per cent. Attached to this bond are interest coupons, and the total of the interest which this bond will draw will exceed the amount of the principal. In other words, the government pays you two for one for what you loan our nation at this time.

"This bond is the finest security in the world. It is secured by all of the property which is now or may hereafter be in the United States of America. It is the promissory note of 110,000,000 of the finest people that ever trod God's footstool, people who pay their debts at maturity. There never has been a time since George Washington took his oath as the first president of our nation, that our government has ever been one day behind in the payment of the principal or interest on its bonds.

"I would not insult your intelligence or patriotism by suggesting that you buy Liberty Bonds for the mere purpose of getting four per cent interest, although that rate of interest is attractive. Men! You are not the percentage patriots! The real interest you want on your investment is the interest of victory for our armies in the field.

"We are facing and fighting the most highly organized and stupendous military machine with which civilization has ever had to cope. It has no morals. It has no respect for anything that is sweet and decent in the world. There are no depths of infamy to which it has not stooped to strengthen itself. Men! You have read of the women of Belgium in the devastated districts who have had their breasts cut off. Do you know why their breasts were cut off? I will tell you.

Back of the German lines are maintained great camps of women, both married and single, who are brought there for breeding purposes, and German soldiers in the front lines go back to serve them as stock would be served. The wife of a friend of mine recently received a letter from an unmarried woman in Germany, in which she said she loved her 'glorious contry', for she had just given birth to 'her second official child.' Her 'second, official child!' My God, Men! How can a sane people get themselves in a state of mind where they can believe for an instant that a military aristocracy, a government can legitimately and officially father a child, to deliberately and methodically plan for its conception by a mother by a nameless soldier commissioned to be the father, and thereafter to be unknown to either the mother or that child! Official breeding for military purposes, the deliberate procreation of a race of bastards by German military efficiency. It is an offense punishable by death for any German soldier who is afflicted with syphillis to have any relations with one of these German breeders back of the lines, because if he did, he would contaminate her, and she in turn would contaminate other German soldiers, thereby breaking down the physical and military efficiency of the German army. But the military authorities, to preserve the morale of the German army permit those German soldiers so afflicted to treat Belgian and French girls and women in devastated territory as common prey, and they ravish and rape them and contaminate them. But, men, do you not see that when these girls and women are once contaminated, they in turn would contaminate other German soldiers who might later rape and ravish them; therefore, as a matter of military efficiency, these Belgian and French girls and women must be marked, and they must be marked by the cutting off of their breasts! The mutilated breast is an official danger signal to safeguard these hellish Huns in their campaign of rape and ravishment. Can a more hideous method of modern military efficiency be conceived in the mind of mortal man!

"Every German soldier is ordered to carry in his vest pocket an aluminum medallion upon which is written 'Strike him dead. The Judgement Day will ask no questions.' What does this mean? It means that German soldiers are taught to steel their souls and consciences against all things which might otherwise appear wrong and to do anything and everything without any moral limitations which will tend to terrorize the enemy, break down their spirit, and increase the military efficiency of the German Army. Horrible as has been the ravishment of Belgium, of Servia, of Poland, of France, of Armenia; terrible as have been all the crimes in this category, I sometimes think that the most diabolical and terrible crime of all the history of the world has been the crime committed by the military aristocracy against the people of Germany by the systematic teaching of the German people, generation in and generation out, that it is right to do wrong, and that any means are justifiable to attain the end desired, that only the strong should survive, that the weak and blotched should perish, — the crime of deliberate soul prostitution of one's own.

"Men! The United States of America has ever stood as the friend of the poor, the distressed, the weak. We do not stand for the outrageous practices and policies the military government of Germany has sponsored, and encouraged. It is reported on authority that there are now over half a million children under the ages of two in the devastated territory of France and Belgium, born of French and Belgium mothers who have been raped and ravished by the German soldiers. Red-blooded American patriots propose to assist in ending that sort of a program. This war has been denominated a war for the safe-guarding and preserving of Democracy. It is all of that and more. It is a war for Humanity. It is a war to protect womanhood from organized and systematized rape and slaughter, it is a war to save civilization. It is a war to preserve the right of unborn children to come into the world as the priceless fruitage of love, and to save for them the natural right to know their fathers and to be brought up in a home where the father and mother live together as husband and wife under the holy bonds of matrimony, instead of being launched adrift into this heart-breaking world as illegitimate waifs.

"If there are any here who are traitors or seditionists who love or sympathize with the kaiser and his red-handed retainers who are drenching this world with blood and submerging it in woe and distress; if there are here any alien brutes whose sense of common decency is so low as to cause them to approve of the diabolical practices of this hoard of Huns, we say to them: 'Let them go back. There is no room in America for them. Let them take their proper place in the front ranks of kaiser's heathen hordes.' We wish for them nothing better; we believe there is nothing worse. The kaiser and his armies are due for a first-class, fine and artistic trimming, and the United States proposes to assist in administering it. It will require of America millions of men, billions of dollars, untold sacrifice, and perhaps years of time; but I am sure I voice the American spirit when I say to you that we are in this war to stay and the war will end when the German military autocracy is crushed. And the way to crush it, is to crush German

sympathizers in America, first, and to do it now.

"But if a man of German or Austrian extraction and loves America, if he eliminates the hyphen from his name, and proves by his acts of loyalty and service that he is an American through and through, body and soul, first, last and all the time, then, God bless him, we love him, for he is as much an American as any native born who cannot trace his ancestry off American soil. But lip-service is not the test; his actions must speak louder than his words; let him act according to American standards of patriotism; let him show by voluntary service that his labor is a labor of love.

"When I look over this audience and see the glint of patriotism in your eyes, I know these things touch your hearts; that you love America as you love your lives, and that you would willingly offer your lives for your country, if need be. Men! It is not the lot of all to serve at the front. There is work to be done here. Two things must win this war: Men and Money. Those who remain here in confortable homes who sleep in warm beds, who are amply fed of food prepared by loving hands, who daily see the smiles of their children and wives each passing day, have their part to perform just as certainly as those who leave their homes, separate themselves from near and dear ones, and assume the more dangerous and hazardous service of the battle front and bare their breasts to the awful storm of everything that kills, that this monster that is clutching at the throat of civilization may be destroyed.

"Millions of clear-eyed, fine American men are going to the front, out of the trenches and over the top, wishing each other the best of luck, offering their bodies as a living sacrifice to the country they love and the world they cherish, and for your cause and mine. They have left jobs that paid them as much as your job pays you; they have left behind wives and babies as dear to them as your wives and babies are to you. They offer to make the supreme sacrifice. It is now for us to show them that we with joy and good-will fulfill the obligations of patriotism which equally devolve upon us. Without money, they go without food, without clothing, without munitions, without reserves —without you they perish.

A Russian general has recently been convicted of treason and shot because he sent poor Russian soldiers to the front armed with wooden guns, representing to them that they were merely to engage in military training. They met the German Army, an army equipped with the most modern military supplies the world has ever known and these poor misguided Russians were mowed down by tens of thousands; their blood was on the hands of that hideous monster of a traitor who sent them unprotected and unarmed into battle.

"But, men! If we conscripted an army, as we are now doing, and sent them forth to fight the battles of America, and failed to provide them with the munitions of war with which to defend themselves, with food to satiate their hunger, with clothes to protect against the inclemency of the weather! If we with our eyes wide open, did that, and they, too, were mowed down by tens of thousands as they inevitably would be, we too would be guilty of an act of traitorism similar to the atrocity committed by that demon of traitorsim, that Russian general. The only difference would be that his was an act of commission; ours would be an act of omission; the effect would be exactly the same.

"You have read of consolidating a position. When men go over the top out of the trenches, one half of them are armed with guns, grenades and bombs, and other equipment for fighting, while the other half are armed with picks and shovels. When the lines have advanced as far as they can, those with the picks and shovels work under a murderous shell fire from the enemy, to dig the others in and build new trenches. In the first year of the war, England, being unprepared, was at times so destitute of ammunition, that men were forced to stand in No-Man's land, and while their comrades were trying to dig them in, unable to amply protect themselves by the use of ammunition. I have been informed by a returned sergeant that at times they were limited to thirty rounds of ammunition for every forty-eight hours. Think of it, men; think of it! We do not want that sort of a thing to happen to American soldiers who are going abroad. They are entitled to the best and most there is in the world, and the American people propose to see that they get it. We are going to accept it as a glorious privilege to assist in furnishing our government with the money wherewith to purchase and supply all of their needs.

"How much should I subscribe? That is the question you are asking yourselves. I have but one answer. Let us measure our sacrifice by the sacrifice our boys are making when they offer themselves. Let us loan our money to the government to such an extent that we feel it; let us subscribe till it hurts, and then subscribe some more; let us buy Liberty Bonds till it distresses us, and then for some more. That is the test of real service and real patriotism. Men! You are not slackers; you are not mere talking patriots; you are not just verbal heroes! Remember, the man who merely talks is a hollow sham; he is no good! There is but one language that the brained stormed German nation can understand, and that is the eloquent language from the fiery mouthed guns in the hands of men at the front, and your money loaned to the government will enable our heroes to send those unmistakeable messages over the top. The supreme eloquence of today is in action rather than words.

"Remember you are giving nothing. You are merely loaning your money to the government. It is a kinder suggestion to you that it would be for me to say to you: 'Put your money in a savings bank,' because a bank pays but three per cent, and the bank may fail, and if we lose this war, the bank probably would fail! The Liberty loan is based on the finest security in the world, backed by the richest nation in the world, and pays a larger rate of interest than savings banks, and in addition, it performs the function of providing food, munitions, clothing, supplies, reserves, ships, and all other needs of our glorious army. Now, men, go to this with a will! A Liberty Bond will always be a source of pride and comfort to you in the days to come. When the boys come back again they will look you in the eye and ask you the question: 'What did you do?' Put yourself in a position to say to them: 'You went into the trenches; you offered your life; you took the hazards of the fight. I remained at home, but I worked, I saved, I loaned my money to the nation to enable it to buy you food when you were hungry, clothes to keep you warm, munitions to protect yourself and carry on this warfare; I did all it was in my power to do to supply you and safeguard you and aid you.' And he will grasp your hand, look at you straight in the eye and with pride say to you, 'You were a patriot as well as I; I could have done nothing without you; you could have done nothing without me; we saved the world from the enemy which was grasping at the throat of civilization and trying to destroy her and everything that is sweet and holy in the world.' And all he says to you will be true.

"I beg of you to make a record for yourselves in this great industry where you are employed. Make it a unanimous proposition. Do not let any man decline to render this service to the government; let it be a test of your patriotism today; let it be considered as a profound, yes, sacred duty; it is a duty beyond the power of language to describe or overestimate. Let a Liberty Bond be a diploma of your patriotism. The satisfaction of having done your duty will be a comfort to you as long as you live. Make it unanimous, Men, and do not fail."

THE FUEL CRISIS

During the summer of 1917, the government hinted that they possibly would roll back the retail price of coal before winter, and that's all it took for one of the worst foul-ups to develop. Wholesale coal dealers didn't want to be caught with a winter's supply of coal on hand, only to have the government roll back the price beyond its profit mark up, so they didn't order any coal during the summer months, and none was delivered on consignment by the mines. At the time, coal was wholesaling at the mines in Virginia for $2.85 a ton. Michigan coal sold at the mine for $4.40. Freight and

the retailer's profit were added and it retailed for approximately $10 a ton. The government's rumored roll-back of a dollar or a dollar-fifty was greater than the total profit margin. It was a probable money loser for everyone concerned. Nevertheless, the mines continued their production, storing it at the production site.

The way things developed, no roll back was ordered, but then there was no coal delivered in the hundreds of major cities of the nation east of the Mississippi. Along about late September some official caught on to the problem developing and alerted the public to the crisis just around the corner. The government for its part denied any intention to roll back the prices. Next the wholesalers sought coal cars and transportation from the southern pits to the cities, but there was such a congestion at the eastern ports of the nation that the railroad engines couldn't be freed up so the gondolas of coal could be delivered. In October the newspapers of Michigan began to delineate the problem, but not its solution. At last in January after the situation failed to rectify itself, President Wilson appointed his son-in-law, Treasury Secretary McAdoo, a federal czar of all railroads. The tie-ups around Boston, New York, Philadelphia and Baltimore were skirted and new shipments to France were routed to the southern ports. With a strong dictatorial hand at the helm, the railroads began freeing themselves from the confusion. In mid-January coal cars began appearing in the northern cities and towns. Farwell received a load of coal just as the last sackful had been given out. A car was sidetracked in Clare at about the same time.

East of the Mississippi, war production was seriously threatened that entire winter. The crisis became so acute that Federal Fuel Administrator Harry A. Garfield, the ex-president's son, issued an order closing all manufacturing plants for five days. The uproar in Congress was so strong that the edict was cancelled, but the factories had to close anyway, because there wasn't coal available. In Michigan, Administrator Prudden passed out a code of restrictions which hit every business in the state.

An incredible fuel shortage developed during the fall of 1917 because of bureaucratic bungling. Civilian efforts to conserve coal were essential, but proved not enough. The war effort suffered dramatically during the winter's coldest months.
Photo: National Archives GSA 165-WW-174-12

Eventually the towns and businesses began receiving more than one car load of coal at a time and the colossal mistake was slowly overcome. President Wilson sent out a memorandum which in effect told the regulating agencies to keep their ideas of what they might do in the future to themselves.

GERMAN SABOTAGE

Throughout this period of time there was a low-grade uneasiness in the country concerning the Germans and possible sabotage. Prior to the outbreak of hostilities between Germany and America, a huge explosion on Black Tom Island, New Jersey on July 30, 1916 rocked the countryside. One hundred railroad cars filled with ammunition exploded. Buildings were vaporized and others were knocked flat. Windows scores of miles away were shaken as $100,000,000 worth of munitions went up as the greatest example of sabotage on the American continent took place.

Early in 1917 Albert Kaltschmidt along with Maria Schmidt blew up the Detroit Screw Works and the Grand Trunk railroad tunnel at Port Huron. Albert was given the maximum sentence of four years at Fort Leavenworth and a $20,000 fine. Ida Kaltschmidt and Maria Schmidt were fined $15,000 each and sent to the Detroit House of Corrections for three years. Fritz A. Neef was convicted for his part in the tunnel explosion, fined $10,000 and placed in jail for two years. Carl Schmidt was convicted in a Canadian court for his part in the railroad tunnel sabotage.

During January of 1918, some Red Cross ladies rolling bandages in Midland discovered ground up glass deeply enbedded in the gauze. A rumor had been going around that this type of treachery was not uncommon. The MIDLAND REPUBLICAN said, "The poisoning of bandages used to bind the wounds of American and Allied soldiers is about on a par with the slaughter of innocent non-combatants."

It was no wonder then that the Germans were suspect in the larger communities.

However in Clare, the Germans owned farms and many had been here for quite some time. Neighbors knew them to be hard working industrious people and good friends to have in the community. Very few instances of overt hostility took place between the natives and the foreigners. However, the teaching of German in the local high school was dropped from the curriculum and French was added.

The city of Clare put a night watchman on the streets and especially near the warehouse district. Immense quantities of farm produce were coming into the "Market City" for forwarding to the east coast. "The menace of enemy plotters and their following traitorous ingrates is too acute to warrant any carelessness in matters of this sort," said Mayor Andrus in November of 1917. There were no incidents ever reported of any local treachery, however. This precaution, if it was taken for the German saboteurs, was not needed.

GERMAN TERRORISM ANALYZED

George R. Catton came back to Clare in 1917 and attempted to explain the intense hostility between Germany, France and the others. He claimed it was a matter of blood and environment. "The Highlands develop one type of citizen and the bogs another, he explained. Two thousand years ago when the race came out of the east only the hardy specimens survived, and certain traits became common to their leaders. "Now it is just simply a battle of monarchies," he claimed.

Catton admitted that German acts of treachery and beastly treatment of civilians was indefensible, but he added, "It should be the determination of the allies to smite German military power while abstaining insomuch as possible from resort to any of those methods of cruelty and terrorism that have so deeply disgraced the German name. Since the German government is so identified with those bad methods, let them remain a German monopoly. To retaliate would make matters worse, even at present," he said.

In preparation for the eventual show down with the world, Germany had built a vast industrial complex in Europe. In addition she sent spies into all the major countries of the world well in advance of 1914. A large scale peace offensive was designed to keep the future enemy weak and dis-jointed. To ensure that her own people would support the aristocracy, enlightened social welfare programs, pensions, health care, employment agencies and similar sweetners were instituted. Then the citizens were told that other nations were jealous of Germany and that the country needed to be armed heavily for possible attacks. The government controlled press then fed a diet of propaganda to the public over the years. The government also paid the teachers and told them what they could teach in the classrooms, thereby conditioning even the youth in the German way.

If there was a major mistake in the Kaiser's plans it was in the calculated brutal ruthlessness he showed the civilians. He thought that they would be neutralized if the German troops would act brutally. Instead, his deliberate starving of the Polish and Belgian children caused the largest array of nations to be gathered against one country since the dark ages.

"America," said Catton, "has always been for the oppressed of the world and in fact it became the asylum for the oppressed of all countries. Many of the Germans now in America were oppressed in Germany and so they understand the plight of all Europeans better than the other American citizen."

THE WORLD SOCIALISTS

Large numbers of malcontents were roaming Europe in the 1870-1910 era with a few emigrating to the United States. Most of them were poor, but some were the intellectual dissidents who were more theoretical than practical. Some of the more wealthy or dedicated socialists became the backbone supporters of the I.W.W. and other fledgling labor unions of the time. Sabotage and industrial strife was their lever to force changes as they reviled the capitalistic systems of the west.

Draft dodgers were encouraged and led

by these utopian seekers as the war came along. In Europe they crossed international borders with impunity and were instrumental in disrupting the internal affairs of Italy, France and England. Some Austrian Socialists went to Italy in November of 1917 and attempted to persuade the Italian soldiers to desert the war zone even as their political cousins had wreaked havoc and disruption behind the Russian lines and in their trenches. In northern Michigan this treachery of extra-nationalism was roundly condemned.

THE A.E.F. LEAVES FOR EUROPE

The draft caused 321 Clare county men to be inducted into the army, navy, aerocorps, marines, engineers, or artillery. Camp Custer was completed by the end of September although men had been coming in earlier than this, and the 85th Infantry Division was fleshed out with its full complement of men. Clare county men were serving in force with

Sergeant Homer Douglas in 1918.

the 32nd Division, the 42nd Division, 23rd Engineers, 26th Engineers, 4th Division, Aerocorps, Base Hospitals, Truck battalions as well as in many other infantry regiments. Some men were in England, France, Texas, North Carolina, Georgia, New York and Alabama. By the first of October the representatives of the county were well scattered.

Recruits who had been in camp for a few weeks came home for Christmas, some for their delay enroute furlough and others for the holidays. Many of those who paid visits to neighbors or had family get togethers never had another opportunity as death was ambushing a large number. The flu was to claim the larger portion both here and abroad. A last walk down a familiar path with friends, an evening with the old gang, a convivial meal and then it was time to go.

Sgt. Bernice E. Wright, a member of the 23rd Engineers wrote to his family just before he was shipped out. "Whatever comes 'Over There', we'll have to tough it out, for I believe it is everyman's duty to stand up for the Stars and Stripes."

Cpl. Walter Larman, home for the holidays spoke at several meetings. Speaking before a small gathering in the Grant township hall he encouraged the civilians to continue supporting the Y.M.C.A. and the Red Cross. "They are the best reminders of home," he said.

Lt. Clarence McDonald wrote home and said, "Now that some Americans are losing their lives, the soldiers here (at Custer) want to get in their lick. Many boys had been hoping to be left here are now anxious to sail. When some great principle is at stake and men feel that they are doing something for humanity, they accept the terrible hardships they know awaits them."

David Miller of the 126th Infantry Regiment said, "Don't pray that we be spared suffering. Pray that I may be given the courage and strength to stand it . . . If it should be that my life goes with my effort, why, what does it matter? It's a pretty good thing to lose one's life for and I am perfectly willing and glad to offer it. Compared to the issue at stake, one life is small."

And so the men went to the ports of embarkation, resigned to their fates, not knowing what the future held. Theirs was a confident belief in the correctness of their service and a willingness to serve that many civilians did not understand. These men were on a crusade, a crusade to make the world safe for Democracy.

THE SPANISH FLU

German troops fighting on the eastern front in 1915 came into contact with a new strain of the flu which had originated in the Far East. It was a mild epidemic and didn't cause too much discomfort. In the subsequent flu season it was exported to Spain where a mutation was believed to have taken place. This virus swept through the German and Allied armies, but even at this point it didn't reach its full lethal strength. The

Harriet Allen
Photo from the Allen Family Collection

end of the 1917 season saw a new and stronger mutation hitting the military camps causing many deaths including James Garrity and Arthur Looker, cousins from Hamilton. A month later, in late January Privates Vane Mickle and Odell Stratton died from the flu. In February, John Ansil died in an Arkansas hospital. If we include Pvt. Irving Reed who died of antiseptic pneumonia in September, there were already six county men dead from the flu and it hadn't reached the epidemic stages yet.

THE HOME FRONT

Changes were coming fast in the fall of 1917. Congress had just passed a federal income tax designed to raise fiscal support for the expanding war effort. Through some machinations the members of Congress exempted themselves from the tax which would have extracted $225 from their $7,500 salaries. It was a cheap thing to do and caused much negative comment. Some Congressmen said afterwards, "We didn't know that provision was in there." Its probable they didn't, but then they didn't take corrective action when then discovered it either.

Over at Mt. Clemens John Cross was arrested when he was selling bootleg whiskey to soldiers. He wasn't seen on the streets of Clare for a year. Two of his partners, Archie Boyer and Chris Reger were held for trial, but were let out on a $1,000 bail.

Food was being shipped to Europe and the middle eastern nations in large quantities as cold weather set in. Herbert Hoover, the food administrator for the country, asked

The flu epidemic was so severe in military camps, such as Camp Custer, that the personal linens and bedding were placed in the sun as much as possible.
Photo: Michigan Department of State Archives

The surgical ward of the base hospital at Camp Custer in 1918.
Photo: Michigan Department of State Archives

that Keno games not raffle off turkeys this fall. "With the shortage of food world-wide this year, its an unseemly thing to be doing," was his explanation. No where was the shortage of food more acute than in Poland where infants and small children were systematically deprived of food. The United States sent food packages through the Red Cross with the understanding that it would be given to the children and the German army was not to divert them for their own consumption. Most of the food went to the victims as intended.

In late December a trainload of eight hundred Belgian children arrived through the war zone. Mothers weeped as they had placed their tots on the train, choosing separation rather than the child's starving. The Red Cross shepherded the four to twelve year olds with the older girls holding onto the younger ones as they marched to the waiting cars. Tears streamed down the faces of the mothers and children as they parted. The Red Cross workers were touched as well and they too had stained faces. It was such a moving experience that even the German guards had tears. Little boys told the smaller ones to cheer up for they would soon have food.

When the train reached the Front, all of the German guards detrained, leaving a few Red Cross workers and the older children in charge. Slowly the train penetrated No-Man's Land and all of the fighting ceased while the precious cargo passed through. English soldiers assumed guard duties and escorted the train to Evian. On a platform waiting to receive the youngsters were American doctors, nurses and attendants with wheel chairs, ambulances and chaperones. Those able to walk were led down a street towards the orphanage. They shouted "Meat! Meat! We're going to have meat!"

The children were given a full meal and then tucked into bed with a full tummy for the first time in months. Many of the children hadn't been in a bed with sheets since before they could remember. Every day this scene was repeated and some days a thousand children were brought through the lines. Some trains carried adults and children, but the older people had a very high mortality rate, dying within a month. Yet the doctors said, "We can and we must save the children." Many people in this country agreed and they contributed money in generous amounts.

Regular pledges for the Red Cross were collected by the county and township chapters. Clare's quota was in excess of $1,200. The poorer people in the county were the biggest pledgers.

A third Liberty Loan drive was scheduled for the beginning of 1918. It was hoped that it would be better supported than the first two as many officials thought that the class of people with above average wealth failed to do their share. There was some criticism also focused on the farmers. On the very first day of the drive, the farmers in the Beal City area, mostly Germans, went to the banks and bought Liberty Bonds in large numbers. Isabella county met its quota the first day. Clare county had a tougher time meeting this quota also, but it had been reduced to $105,000. Farmers in Clare were in a better position this time and they were anxious to show their patriotism so they bought bonds here too. Men of wealth still held back from their fair share was the general consensus, however.

Before the war there were many men on the move all across northern Michigan. They were out of work and most wanted jobs, but there were some who were professional bums. They were called hoboes, a term which was too charitable. These men were ingenious for their methods of securing food and avoiding work. During peacetime, where the survival of a nation is not at stake or the lives of young men weren't jeopardized, this class of people was tolerable. Now, however, the slacker as he was being called, was unpopular. New Jersey, Maryland, and West Virginia passed laws which made it illegal for males ages 18-50 to be unemployed for the war's duration. The labor unions in a similar move agreed to a ban on strikes for the same period. For its share, the government said that all women who worked at jobs normally performed by men would receive the same pay.

Food had been essentially a problem in the

save

1- wheat
use more corn

2- meat
use more fish & beans

3- fats
use just enough

4- sugar
use syrups

**and serve
the cause of freedom**

U.S. FOOD ADMINISTRATION

With starvation stalking the Allies during 1917, every effort was made to squeeze sugar, fats, meat and wheat from the civilian bill of fare.
Photo: National Archives GSA 4-P-122

war zones, but now it was becoming difficult for America to take care of its own eating habits. Millions of extra tons of wheat, rye, oats and corn was shipped to Europe, stripping our reserves to the bottom line. We were feeding or supplementing the diets of 200,000 Finns, an additional 100,000 Poles, 50,000 orphaned children in Belgium plus a similar number in France, 2,000,000 soldiers in the American Expeditionary Forces and civilian employees in the British Expeditionary Forces. There was a generous amount of grain and meat sent to feed the civilians in France, Belgium, England and the other allies. It was obvious to the cursory observer that there wasn't enough for the normal consumption patterns to be continued. One plan called for the quality of flour to be lowered, using more of the rough parts of the grain.

The grinding capacity of the United States was 2,275,000 bushels of wheat a day and this provided 500,000 barrels of flour. The new lower quality would increase the daily production of flour by 17,000 barrels or enough to make 6,154,000 loaves of bread. Herbert Hoover said, "Any American customer who does not cheerfully accept the lower quality is neither loyal to the best interests of this country or to the boys in kaiki."

Mills in the country didn't change the name brands of their flours because it was assumed that everyone understood that all flours would be of lower quality. The mills, however, did put the wheat through an extra cleaning step before they made the first break. New silk screens from Switzerland were used for maximum extraction of flour as the food supply was stretched out.

The United States Food Administrator said in January, "These seventeen thousand additional barrels of flour will feed an army of six million for one day or an army of one million for a week." Newspapers had little slogans on their interior pages which read, "Help the Sammies over there."

In December of 1917, there were several ship losses. In addition crop failures abroad made it clear that the food supply produced abroad was even lower than expected. An additional 90,000,000 bushels of wheat and grains were taken out of our depleted reserves and shipped with no questions asked. The government later said, "Food was now the critical element in the war." Italy, France and England had only a three month supply of food in storage or on the way. When the American supplies stop, they begin eating into this reserve and begin their march to starvation. It was a gloomy winter for all of Europe.

WHAT IS A PATRIOT?

Americans were being asked to do a lot of things in the name of patriotism in 1917, but how could the average citizen measure his own degree of sacrifice and contribution? At what point could a person reasonably

The American woman marched with the Suffragettes and the armed forces in 1917. This USDA poster indicated her key role in the war effort.

Photo courtesy National Archives 165-WW-174-10

Posters were used for uniting the civilian population. This one emphasized the importance of food.

assure himself that he or she wasn't a slacker? Was there a check list which could be quickly looked over, which would automatically indicate the point when one turned into a patriot? Would planting a liberty garden, purchasing Liberty Bonds, rolling Red Cross bandages, working longer hours on the job or writing letters to the soldiers be the criteria one should use? Mrs. Charles Stinchcombe of Farwell thought this problem over and wrote a speech which she gave several times around the county. Here is the substance of what she thought a patriot was in January of 1918.

"As a mother and homemaker much responsibility rests upon us if it be true that the home is the foundation upon which the nation rests. Then if I am to serve my country, I must come close to God in prayer and there receive grace and patience to teach my children truth, honesty and justice; for unless these be persistently taught in the home and in school, we cannot hope to send out men and women who will be an honor to our nation.

"In spite of things which money can buy, are not the best things in life of the spirit? Who can set a value upon courage, honesty, high endeavor or noble thinking? Emerson declares that the soul of God is poured into the world through the thoughts of man. Pure, loving, helpful thinking! Who can measure its value or its power? Let us count time spent in prayer, in teaching our children to look up at the stars, in pointing out the beauties of sunsets and sunrise and in tracing the hand of God in the wonderful world of nature around us as time well spent, and talk of things which will encourage high thinking for 'as a man thinketh, so is he.'

"Then in order to best serve my country, I must not only do my work well at home, but I must concern myself with all conditions in the community that effect the home.

"Are we asking ourselves everyday, 'Lord what can I do to be useful in this dark hour of our nation's life?' Oh my sisters, let us not hurrah for the flag thoughtlessly, but remember that God gave America a great opportunity and we have only been partly true. With other nations of the earth, great blots of horrible sin, moral cowardice, selfishness and greed mar our pages of history. We ought to bow our heads in shame that this is true and promise God that as for us, we will take a bolder stand than ever for right and truth and justice.

"Let us observe meatless and wheatless days. Let us produce food of some kind if we can. Let us live on the plainest fare, not allowing one morsel of food to be wasted for "A country worth fighting for is a country worth saving for.'

"Let us darn and mend as never before and give and give where so much is needed. Buy thrift stamps, savings certificates and Liberty Bonds if we can, and be brave even as our boys 'Somewhere in France', 'somewhere in cantonment camp', and 'somewhere on our ships' of the oceans are brave. What great comfort and riches in the last words of the Great Teacher:
'Peace I leave with you.
My peace give I unto you,
Not as the world giveth,
Give I unto you.
Let not your heart be troubled,
Neither let it be afraid.' "

1918

At last the cumulative effects of naval blockades, submarine warfare, wholesale casualties on both sides, continual clashes of vast armies, collapse of Russia and poor weather had all negatively affected the world's food supply. 1918 was without question the year of food. Herbert Hoover, the United States Food Administrator gave part of the story in his report to the President in 1918.

"It is now possible to summarize the shipments of foodstuffs from the United States to the allied countries during the fiscal year (FY) just ended, practically the last harvest year. These amounts include shipments to the allied countries for their and our armies, the civilian population, the Belgian Relief and the Red Cross.

"The total value of these food shipments which were in the main purchased through or in collaboration of the Food Administration, amount to roundly $1,400,000,000 during 1917-18 FY. The shipment of meats and fats to allied destinations are as follows:

FY 1916-17   2,166,500,000 lbs
FY 1917-18   3,011,100,000 lbs
   an increase of   344,600,000 lbs

"Our slaughtered animals at the beginning of the last fiscal year were not appreciably larger than the year before and particularly in hogs, they were probably less. The increase in shipments is due to conservation. The extra weight of animals added by our farmers is also a factor. The full effect of these efforts began to bear their best results in the last half of the FY when the exports to the allies were 2,133,100,000 as against 1,266,500,000 lbs. in the same period in 1915-16.

"In cereal and cereal products reduced to terms of cereal bushels, our shipments to allied destinations have been:

1916-17 FY   259,900,000 bushels
1917-18 FY   340,800,000 bushels
                 80,900,000 bushels

1917-18 FY
Wheat   131,000,000 bushels
Rye   13,900,000 bushels
                144,900,000 bushels

1916-17 FY
Wheat   135,100,000 bushels
Rye   2,300,000 bushels
                137,400,000 bushels

"The total shipment from our last harvest including food in transit is 154,900,000 bushels of prime breadstuffs. In addition to this we have shipped or have enroute an additional 85,000,000 bushels of wheat which we did not plan for. At the time of this request, our reserves were more than exhausted. This accomplishment by our people in this matter stands clearly if we bear in mind that we had in FY 1916-17 from a net carry over as a surplus over normal consumption 200,000,000 bushels of wheat which we were able to export that year without trenching on the 'home-front' loaf. Therefore our shipments represent approximately our savings from our own wheat bread.

"This does not convey the whole measure of sacrifice on the part of our people. There corn which failed to mature properly and corn is our dominant crop. It was nine per cent below in total (of) the nutritional

349

The barrens of Michigan's Upper Peninsula were pressed into service during World War I. This is a stock Farm near the Soo.
Photo: National Archives GSA 165-WW-172-21

The harvesting of deer in 1918 supplemented the civilians' diets. This camp was in northern Michigan. *Photo: National Archives GSA 165-WW-170-C-1*

quantities of the previous year.''

While this report tells much of the difficulty we had in growing and accumulating the prodigious quantities, it doesn't tell the complete story. Americans normally consumed seventy-five pounds of sugar a year. French civilians used twenty-four. Even at that low consumption rate, there wasn't enough sugar to meet their needs, so we shipped them 85,426 tons by the end of December 1917 and promised to send an additional 100,000 tons in 1918. The federal government asked all Americans to reduce their consumption of sugar by fifty per cent. This came through a drastic reduction in candy manufacturing and a twenty per cent daily intake reduction in our diets. In Java there were 250,000 tons of sugar awaiting shipment, but that amount would have required the use of eleven ships for one year and the ships could not be spared. Pre-war Germany, the West Indies and the East Indies were the chief sugar producers, but now in war time, much of Europe looked to the United States to make up the shortfall.

During the first two Liberty Loan drives it was said that the farmers didn't do their share. Some talk was even mentioning the farmer as not doing his share in supporting the total war effort. It is probably true that they didn't buy the bonds in the quantities and dollar amounts as their urban cousins, but the average farmer was so poor when the war broke out that he found it difficult to purchase the seeds the government wanted him to plant in the spring. In addition, the nation was hit with the coldest weather and the wettest fall in nineteen years. This handicap alone made it difficult for the farmer to make favorable production records, and it dug into his pocketbook as well.

President Wilson asked all Americans in January of 1918 to make an extra effort to observe two wheatless days a week and one wheatless meal each day. He asked for one meal a day to be void of meat and that pork be eliminated from the Saturday meals. Restaurants were restricted to a nine hour business day on Monday when all of the other businesses were closed. Meat markets were open half a day.

Housewives began baking Victory Bread, which was any type of bread which used twenty per cent less wheat than normal. Corn meal, rice, rice flour, and potato flour was substituted. Citizens purchasing wheat flour at a grocery store had to purchase one third of their requirements in a non-wheat flour. Lots of them complained about this rule, but it was enforced nevertheless. The government was attempting to set a food policy which would enable it to engage in the war until 1921 which was the year they said it would finally be concluded.

During March each farmer was asked to plant five acres of spring wheat in hopes that the weather might improve enough for a harvest. Wheat was in extremely short supply when the additional 85,000,000 bushels were sent out of our reserves.

Michigan residents were encouraged to eat potatoes by state Food Administrator Prescott. ''Make sure they're Michigan potatoes,'' he said. ''Support your neighbor!'' In this regard the country was fortunate as 1917 had been a banner potato year. The tuber is bulky and contains a lot of water and as a consequence, they don't ship too well. ''Help eat our bumper crop and save wheat!'' was a slogan often repeated by the nation's newspapers and magazines. This bumper crop came about because the farmers took the government's advice and planted every acre and square foot of ground that was available. The weather co-operated favorably and a huge crop was the result. No one thought to allocate certain quantities because the war came on too sudden for the central regulators. Those Europeans would have loved to feast on potatoes, but shipping was at a premium and the northern Michigan product was left behind in huge piles.

Governor Sleeper, Michigan's wartime chief executive, made his State of the State address early in 1918. He indicated that we were producing army trucks by the thousands and U-Boat chasers in large numbers. Five million dollars had been given to the national government and another five million was used to purchase one thousand farm tractors. These would be sold to farmers, but the Governor felt that more machinery was needed on the farm if they were to produce the food being asked for by Herbert Hoover. The state took the lead in searching out and buying adequate seed corn for the spring season. Michigan's corn didn't mature and most of the crop went into cattle feed. A medical program was begun which identified carriers of V.D. and then its treatment. Law officers were called upon to nip the I.W.W. sedition in the copper country and a constabulary was organized to keep the peace and guard the locks, munition plants and warehouses. Soldier's families in financial straits were able to receive $10-50 a month from the state, if they were qualified. Certain highways were critical to the war effort and they were put on a construction schedule for the year. In addition, every county had by now been organized with a War Board, and they were charged with all of the official programs and bond drives.

In short, the state and federal government and the farmers were aware of the key role agriculture was playing in the war. Every effort was exerted to maximize food production and distribution. In the northern counties, other than the shipping off to camp of its men, food production was the major contribution to the war which was or could be made.

ANTI-WAR ACTIVITIES

Considering the diversity of America's population and its history during the Civil War when Lincoln faced such formidible dissonance from the Copperheads and their newspapers such as THE DETROIT FREE PRESS, there wasn't much disharmony in 1917-18. The major problem this country had in effectively concluding the war was promulgated by the Democrats themselves, and the reluctance of Wilson during the pre-war period to adequately lead the nation defensively. A continued litany during those pre-war years convinced, or at least encouraged a substantial body of Socialists, anarchists and pacifists that any form of war was immoral and that no war ought to be supported.

Once Wilson was persuaded by events to lead the nation toward a successful culmina-tion of the belligerency, he found that some had believed his rhetoric which not too much previously he had espoused. Potential enlistees in the army and navy stayed away in large numbers and the nation had no recourse but a large draft to swell the ranks of the skeleton army. Wilson at the onset asked for an army to number 1,300,000 men, but he soon had to up that figure after Pershing had gone to Europe for a survey of the problems. The draft which began in July was able to bring in large numbers of men, reluctantly at first, but soon willingly.

There was only the pre-war sabotage in the east coast and some other scattered incidents, but for the most part it was minimal. A German spy ring operated out of Washington D.C. and rather openly at that. It was only when the president was convinced that their overt activities were detrimental to this country's security that he closed it down. Before that he had given its network a tacit approval. In 1916 the Count Von Bernstorff spy ring increased its activity in the mid-west, probably in preparation for the coming rupture between the two nations, so Wilson moved to close down the $40,000,000 spy ring. Later a small group of eight spies was arrested when it was attempting to light a fuse in a navy arsenal at Norfolk, Virginia.

A scandal erupted in February of 1918 when it was discovered that eight clothing manufacturers had foisted off some shoddy goods on the army. Five million dollars worth of uniforms were involved, but this was nothing like the wholesale scandal in the Civil War. Again, there was a car full of beef which arrived at an army cantonment which was in a spoiled condition, but during the Spanish-American war, several of the beef packers connived to sell the army embalmed beef.

The most serious opponents the nation had were the Wobblies or members of the I.W.W. (Industrial Workers of the World). This organization appeared to have anarchistic designs for this country even as their philosophical cousins had sought to disrupt the internal affairs of Russia, Italy and England. They wore red arm bands and traveled in large groups, fomenting riots and civil disorders where ever they happened to be. Big Bill Hayward, George Andreytchine and Manuel Rey were the main ring leaders who attempted to disrupt the draft, copper mining and war related activities in the Pacific Northwest. Not much actual sabotage was laid to their account, but if the radicals had wanted to take this route, there was ample opportunity for them.

Eugene Debs was arrested in Canton, Ohio during June for his comments on the war. He had been a candidate for the United State Presidency four times and now, here he was charged with ten violations of the Espionage Act.

In September of 1917 there were over a hundred and sixty I.W.W. members arrested in Chicago and in the northwestern states. Trials were held all across the nation including Chicago and Grand Rapids. Seventy nine were sent to prisons for long terms and the remainder were given two year jail terms.

Senator LaFollette of Wisconsin made a speech in the fall of 1917 which many said was seditious and a minor fracas ensued when some members of the Congress wanted to impeach him and have him expelled, but this effort died rather quietly.

In central Michigan there were not many overt acts of violence between the German-born residents and the citizens. In Clare county, there was one night in late 1917 when two barns burned and that appeared to be more than mere coincidence, but it wasn't proved to be arson. S. C. Badgley and John Loar both lost their new hay, which had been stored for the winter, the same evening. Arson of one's neighbor had become rather uncommon by this date, but their German citizenship could have been the cause. These men had been residents of Arthur township for years and were known to be good substantial people, an integral part of the community. Neighbors came to their assistance and helped them through the winter. Actions such as these friendly overtures helped defuse a potential problem.

Under close scrutiny then, it appears that there was a minimum of anti-war or anti-German activity carried out, if we consider the possibilities which existed at the time.

SOME SHORTAGES APPEAR

Gasoline now had become scarce in the middle of Michigan and many owners had to put old "Lizzie" away for a while. Down in Mount Pleasant the Central Gas Company was having trouble making enough gas at the current prices. They were one of the few customers who had enough coal shipped in the previous summer, but their expenses kept climbing due to the war pressures. A letter was sent out to their customers asking for a voluntary increase of thirty cents a thousand cubic feet to make up for the doubled price of coal. Clare agreed to it, but when the Cadillac customers were asked the same thing, they said "No!" The local gas company there told them they had better locate a substitute soon, because they were going to close down their gas producers at the end of January.

Electricity was becoming scarce during the winter of 1917-18 as the producers had problems with their coal supply also. In Clare, the city was nearing the end of their options when the Callam estate, owners of the local hydro-electrical plant on Dewey Lake, offered to generate enough electricity to keep the city in essential services. To the city fathers this opportunity seemed to be a miracle.

On the war production front, the Ordnance Department had fumbled around for a year and still hadn't learned how to manufacture artillery shells in volume, nor did they have enough barrels. The A.E.F. was forced to rely upon the French and their 75's. Fortunately they had a proven system. The comments here were not very charitable to those involved. "Gold braid and years of service should not count for anything in the face of inefficiency. There are men in the United States right now who could in thirty-days time re-organize the munitions department and begin turning out adequate quantities," said the editor of the CLARE SENTINEL January 10, 1918.

England had similar problems over the years with moss-covered men who had outlived their thinking. The nation still respected these men who had given good and faithful service in former years, and it was barbaric to throw them out to a life of reduced honor now that they were too old. To remove their deadwood from responsible positions the English had created a House of Lords. There they could serve without hindering the vital interests of the nation. With the foul-ups in the American war effort coming with intolerable regularity, some thought this country should create its facsimile of a House of Lords and fill it with the "Old Boys"!

As the fuel crisis deepened, Michigan decreed that all businesses except the most essential classifications close for five days in January and then again every Monday until the situation improved and the coal supplies were nearly normal. In Farwell this meant that no water was pumped for five days except to fill the tank three times in case of fire. People went visiting their neighbors and the ones heating with wood never knew they had so many friends. Many residents who worked in the factories of Lansing, Flint or Saginaw returned home for the week as those cities and all others had closed down in conformance with the edict.

In the midst of all of these public dislocations, the federal government asked for a house by house survey of all food supplies available. Not a few were alarmed over this request and suspected the government was preparing to confiscate food which had been squirreled away by the prudent home maker; but over and over, the government stressed that it was not planning to confiscate excess quantities. They needed to know how much food was available to their citizens so they could send the excess to the allies, many of whom were near the starvation level.

Clare county Food Administrator William Caple directed the local inventory tabulation. He said, "Europe still calls for food and we must send it if the war is to go on efficiently." His re-assurance seemed to allay the local concerns and the inventorying went along smoothly after this.

Governor Sleeper appointed a county War Preparedness Board in each of the eighty-three governmental units. Locally he appointed John Jackson, postmaster of Clare; W. Holmes Kennedy, county Extension Agent and A. J. Doherty. Their task was to oversee all phases of the war effort including the bond drives, Red Cross chapters and agriculture. The state and federal government were planning for more strict measures in the future and this was their channel for local implementation.

The harvest of 1917 provided an ample supply of corn after the three billion bushel crop was put in storage. At the government's urging, an extra five hundred million bushels were raised. Because wheat was being shipped abroad in large amounts, the supply remaining for domestic flour was definitely limited. A suggestion from Washington pointed toward corn as a flour substitute. Corn bread, corn puddings, corn meal and corn cereals were all mentioned. "Corn flour mixed with wheat flour is a satisfying combination," assured the government.

It was re-iterated that on Monday and Wednesday one meal should be wheatless. On Tuesday one meal should lack meat of any type and pork should be eschewed on Saturday. All meals throughout the week should use fewer fats and less sugar.

The problem of finding and distributing adequate supplies of seed corn was tackled by the state War Preparedness Board. Estimates of 378,000 bushels of seeds were needed, and only Lenawee county had enough on its own. The thumb counties had about one per cent of their requirements. The desperate search led the Board to New Jersey and purchases soon followed. At harvest time it was obvious that the corn which was adapted to the eastern state's climate was not well suited for Michigan's. It was not a good harvest.

No one knew at this time how long the war was going to last, but it was very obvious to government officials that the United States had to play the key role in war production. They sent out memos in January that they expected the allied armies to be in confrontation with the Germans at least until 1921. All of their official planning was based on this projection. One of the major factors was the withdrawal of the Russians. This freed up a large number of divisions and also gave the Germans the breadbasket of Europe. What they didn't know of course was how complete the disruption of services and agriculture was in these districts.

Not everyone was this pessimistic of course. Some thought Germany had enough strength for one more major offensive thrust, and if it could be launched before the Americans entered the continent in force, the allies could still be defeated. With this in mind, several predicted a major German offensive early in the spring, probably in May. Frank Simonds, writing in the AMERICAN REVIEW OF REVIEWS, predicted the coming offensive, but he said it would probably come in Belgium. "1918 is the last year of the war for Germany," he said in January.

THE YANKS ARRIVE IN FORCE

When America entered the war in April of 1917 there were about 135,000 soldiers in uniform. The navy had another 75,000. German submarines had been sinking English ships at a fearful rate, far more in fact, than they had been telling their public. A three week supply of food remained in England when Admiral Sims conferred with First Sea Lord Jellicoe. It was a desperate nation! As Jellicoe outlined the war's progress and especially the difficulty with the submarines, Sims became convinced that he had to do something different from the dispatching of ships in isolation from each other. The British thought that bunching up the ships was too dangerous, but so few were arriving safely in ports, it appeared to Sims there was no alternative. He suggested to Jellicoe that from this point on, all allied merchant ships would sail in convoys of eight or more and be protected by fast military escorts who would ferret out and destroy the submarines which would try to sink the cargo carriers. Jellicoe frosted up at the impertinence of the American admiral and looked Sims in the eye. Sims didn't blink. Realizing that the English would soon be out of the war without the Americans, he relented and said, "Perhaps we should give it a try."

A month later, many American destroyers arrived in England after a hurried crossing of the Atlantic. Pausing only long enough to refuel they escorted the first convoy from Gibraltar to London, arriving May 20, 1917.

World War I aviators rammed their machines into the German observation balloons. This plane still hosts a destroyed airship.

In mid-June the American 1st Division sailed from New York under the watchful eyes of the navy. One hundred miles from the French coast, additional British warships joined them and shepherded them safely through several submarine attacks. Not one man was lost, thus proving that the A.E.F. really could be brought to France.

In spite of the government's foot dragging, army and navy officials had done their homework in a most thorough manner. Secretary of Navy Daniels rapidly put into execution plans for expanding the navy into a 500,000 man force. By the end of 1917 a "bridge of ships" was built across the north Atlantic and a flood of new type mines were dumped into the ocean between Norway and the Orkney Islands, blocking the German U-Boats from departing the North Sea. Now the men could be transported in safety and in large numbers. By March 1918, when the 32nd Division arrived in France, there were 100,000 men a month being shipped across. Most of them were carried in English passenger liners, but some German ships had been impounded at the onset of the war and they were pressed into service for the American troops. One such ship was the "Leviathan" and it carried 12,000 A.E.F. members a month.

Five divisions had preceeded the 32nd including the 1st, 26th, 2nd which was made up of army and marine regiments, the 42nd, which was the Rainbow Division and included units from all of the National Guards

Company A, 125th Infantry of the American 32nd Division marches through an Alsace town.
Photo: National Archives GSA 111-SC-14070

357

A platoon of the American 1st Division crossing the Mosel River in France, 1917.
Photo: National Archives GSA 111-SC-95743

and the 41st Division, also made up of Guardsmen. The 1st Division sent its men into the trenches on October 20th, 1917 at "Looneyville," the American corruption for the French town Luneville. It was there that America took its first casualties. The divisions which followed were put into trenches which were in the quiet sectors, giving them time to adjust to the pressures of combat conditions.

The war on the western front had stagnated to a fearful extent and the men had burrowed deep into the ground so as to avoid artillery and machine gun fire. Lice, standing water, mildew and rats became the enemy. It rained nearly every day at the front, or at least it seemed that way to the men who had to fend off the rats, grown big on the bodies of men killed in "No-Man's Land."

The 32nd Division was debarked from their transports at St. Nazaire and put into an area where they learned advanced combat techniques. General Pershing had insisted all along that they be trained in open warfare and that is the type of combat they would eventually be engaged in, but for the present they were to receive their baptism in the trenches. Food was in short supply in Europe and these men were introduced to the war first in the chow lines. W. K. Pommerening of Co. E 126th Infantry Regiment said, "Pershing had better send some food up here or he'll see us in our graves within thirty days." Things weren't quite that desperate, but they were bad enough. Pershing didn't send food, he sent for them instead. They were loaded into French boxcars large enough

Members of the 59th Infantry, 4th Division are marching through Lorraine, headed for the Rhine River.

for 40 Hommes or 8 Chevaux and began the three day journey to Champlitte where they were billeted in peasant homes. The French supply of food was no better than the American's, but they shared what short rations they had with their guests, nevertheless.

The German offensive Frank Simonds predicted began in March. Marshal Foch wanted to plug the Americans into French units, but General Pershing held fast against the request. The ineptness of the French and English at conserving the lives of their soldiers horrified Pershing. In April a second drive was commenced by the Germans and this time it was the British who wanted help as they were under heavy attack in Flanders. Pershing still held his men out of the fight. Then when the turning point of the war came, he sent the 26th Division to Seicheprey. A third drive was focused at Soissons and the 32nd Division was committed to that sector. The Rainbow Division was dispatched to Chateau Thierry, and between these two divisions he put the 2nd Division in a geographical location called Belleau Wood.

Advancing to the front, the 2nd Division was confronted with civilians fleeing, and the roads were almost completely blocked by the peasants and their carts. "The war is lost!" they said to the Americans as they passed to the rear. Either the Marines and Doughboys didn't understand French or they didn't believe that the German Army was their equal, so they continued their forward movement, entering Belleau Wood. There the battle was joined and after fierce encounters with the German machine guns, the Marines resorted to Indian warfare. Soon gun after

French civilians liberated by members of the A.E.F., 1918.

French civilians flee ahead of the Germans during their great spring offensive.
Photo: National Archives GSA 111-SC-14088

gun was captured or wiped out. Yard by yard they advanced, then it was mile by mile as the Boche fell back, out of the woods and then across the Ourca River. The German offensive had run into a buzz saw and they came out the poorer.

On July 1, the 32nd Division was pulled out of the trenches and moved towards Angeot. Three weeks later they were joined by the 4th, 28th, 26th and the 42nd Divisions for the Aisne-Marne Offensive at Chateau-Thierry. The Americans were taking the initiative for the first time. On the soil of France were 1,300,000 members of the A.E.F. Some had been seasoned in the quiet trenches and others had survived the main German drives, but for the most part they were as green as grass. The recently arrived ones were re-adjusting their sea legs, others were down with the flu and still more were under quarantine for an epidemic of meningitis. By the time of the September offensive, there were forty divisions across the water. Thirty of these were destined to enter combat against the enemy.

With the sputtering out of the big German offensive, their first line troops were joined by many second-rate troops from the eastern countries who didn't have the heart to fight, but there were enough Prussians around to make sure they did.

General Pershing was convinced that the only way to break the stalemate was to carry on a vigorous encounter in the open. Keeping his plans secret from his men, he had Col. George C. Marshall prepare the necessary support for the green troops to fight around the Meuse-Argonne sector while he feinted with his seasoned troops a bit earlier near Chateau-Thierry. There the veterans pushed the salient back into line and prevented their attacking the inexperienced forces when they jumped off September 26th.

THE ARGONNE

General Pershing took control of the Argonne sector from the French on September 22. He retained the greater part of the French artillery and they also made available 189 tanks. There were 821 allied aircraft situated at St. Mihiel. Amidst all of this disarray were the huge amounts of ammunition about to be sent toward the enemy. Pershing had all of his movements carried on

Hundreds of thousands of men were brutalized by World War I. Here are some of the Germans who paid the "supreme price".

The German gas generators are producing a gas attack on the Americans. 1918.

at night so the Germans wouldn't become aware of the increased activity. Rain fell on the tin helmets compounding the problem of shifting a half million men up to the lines. On the night of September 25, French mortars were brought up along with the American troops. Many of these regiments had not seen each other since their arrival in Brest or the other ports. The difficulty of securing the supplies required for the barrage prevented a long softening up of the enemy, but at 3:30 a.m. twenty seven hundred guns began a three hour bombardment. Windows twenty-five miles behind the German lines were being shook by the intense shelling.

At exactly 5:30 a.m. the whistles blew and the men went "over the top." Since most of the divisions didn't have tanks to break through the barbed wire barricades, engineers went forward with their bangalore torpedoes and blew holes in them for the infantrymen. A fog had shrouded the battle-

field and men wearing their gas masks carrying rifles "at the ready" presented an eerie picture to the troops. Walking at a deliberate pre-set pace to keep just behind the rolling barrage which was designed to remove or to at least seriously lessen the amount of enemy fire, the Yanks entered "No-Man's Land." Stepping around the rims of the artillery impacts, the men moved in unison. Four hours later they had passed through the entire system of trenches which the Germans had so laboriously constructed. Still the troops marched on behind the artillery, but now there were pockets of enemy resistance and the men fell behind their cover fire. The real fighting now began.

The assault troops were completely inexperienced, except at the training tables where the officers were shown what the terrain looked like. Near the middle of the long line of American Divisions was the German Command Post, Montfaucon! Marshal Foch said it would take five months to capture it, but Pershing had given the 37th Ohio National Guard Division one day to get the job done. It was an impossible task, but nearly accomplished even at that.

Secretary of War Newton Baker came from Ohio, and as a favor to him, Pershing gave the most important military objective to his favorite division. "I want to inspect the battlefield from Montfaucon in twenty-four hours!" Pershing told General Farnsworth. He was only late one day. Montfaucon was a promontory eight hundred feet above the valley and from its heights the entire Argonne battleground could be viewed. Ensconced in its bowels was the Crown Prince himself. Artillery spotters were able to call down fire on the advancing Americans about 10:00 a.m. when the fog lifted, although there was a lot of gas and smoke from the deadly warfare going on down below. Without tanks, planes or adequate artillery, members of the "Buckeye" Division stormed the bastion from the

west, and the 79th Division came at the key position from the south and east.

Montfaucon was about four miles beyond the jumping-off line. Advancing troops had to run at times to keep the backs of their enemy in their gun sights. Advancing now in the open, artillery was coming down on the Yanks, and one whole company of Buckeyes was killed down to the last man. Yet the advance went on, and the support troops were unable to bring supplies and food forward. Twenty-four hours later than General Pershing had planned, the Americans forced all of the enemy from the commanding heights of Montfaucon, but their regiments were shattered. The green troops had given a good accounting of themselves, but they were exhausted from the continuous fighting.

The 32nd Division which had been engaged a few weeks earlier in Chateau-Thierry now were moved westward and brought in to relieve the exhausted Buckeyes. They

An aerial view after the pre-dawn bombardment of September 26, 1918. Twenty-five hundred heavy artillery guns fired hundreds of thousands of shells into the Argonne Forest just ahead of the advancing Yanks.

strengthened the middle of the American line and continued the advance on schedule.

The 37th Division was pulled back and sent to Belgium where they again were put into action with the British. The Rainbow Division and the 32nd were to stay in touch with the enemy until the Armistice was called for November 11th.

Over one million men were in the Argonne Offensive and most of these had no previous experience at the front. Many had only minimal infantry training, and more were short of the advanced combat methods the earlier troops had. Casualties were high on both sides, and men who so recently had been home were now dead or in hospitals with grievous wounds. Regardless of the surge of battle casualties, they were less than everyone expected as the Germans sued for peace at last. As early as October 3rd, Luedendorff had told the Kaiser that there was no other choice but to ask for peace.

Food conditions in Germany were even more desperate than in France and Belgium. The Kaiser said, "Germany wants peace, but it must be a peace with honor."

The 85th Division arrived in Europe just before the last offensive, but it was broken up into regiments. One, the 339th, was sent to Murmansk to protect the huge amount of allied war supplies left when Russia pulled out of the war. The 338th was sent to Italy in an attempt to bolster their morale. The other two regiments were landed in France. There they were used as reserves, entering the fight after the first day. George Runyan of Farwell was sent to Russia with the "Polar Bears" although most of them were from Detroit.

Prior to the division's departure for Europe, a Clare family went down to Camp Custer to see their son and brother. As was the custom, they were invited to share the evening meal with the soldiers in one of the 150 kitchens.

Elsie, a girl of seven, watched the men dig in and begin eating with gusto. If something was wanted they'd grunt out an oath or two and the dish would be passed without further comment. The eating would continue without a let-up. Elsie was seated next to a soldier and he wasn't relaying much food

A German casualty of the air war.

along, so she turned to her mother and said, "Mama, why can't I be a soldier?"

"You can be if you want to," said the unthinking mother.

"Can I really!" she replied.

"Yes, you can if you want to." came the answer.

Then turning to the soldier beside her she said, "Damn you, pass me them beans."

THE CASUALTIES

Doughboys and sailors had been dying regularly and long before the Argonne Offensive, yet with this big battle, the number surged to its highest point and then fell off rapidly. The earliest Clare battle deaths were the Canadian soldiers who entered the fight in 1916. Percy Kissick was the first county battlefield death. The second was Captain William "Chester" Halstead, who was killed August 14, 1918. Another Canadian, Leo J. Cavanaugh was killed August 30th, 1918. All of these men died in France.

Cavanaugh's death vividly illustrates the tragedies which were played out during this era. His father, James Cavanaugh, came to Grant township in 1894 and built a farm house out near Arnold Lake. There he worked hard and raised Joseph, John, Leo and Loretta. All of them attended the West Grant School. Disaster hit the family in 1911 when the father died. A year later the mother was thrown from a wagon and killed when the team ran away and upset the vehicle. During the spring of 1913 Joe Bowler held an auction and sold off the property. Relatives from Canada came here and took the

Walter Larman

children back with them. In 1917, Leo was old enough to leave home and he came to Mt. Pleasant, but he didn't stay long. Heeding his country's call, he joined the Canadian Army and was sent to France. Fighting to defend both of his countries, he paid the supreme sacrifice. With his life he helped buy Peace.

Notices next came to the families of Sgt. Rush C. Davis in Greenwood, James Frizzell, David A. Johnson, David Miller and William J. Wilson. Two weeks after the armistice, John Larman was notified that his son Walter was Missing in Action. Around Christmas time he was notified that Walter Larman died in a Prisoner of War camp November 15, 1918. Larman had been serving with the 4th Division and was in the heavy fighting of the Argonne Offensive. He was wounded and taken prisoner three days prior to the war's end. The Germans had little medical help available, and none was furnished to the American sergeant who

was a true, red-blooded American.

Other men who died in France include Floyd Fakes, Gilbert Howard, William Kube, Kenneth McIntyre, Herbert McNeil, Charles Makin, George F. Sanderson and Charles Shaw. Most of these men died from the flu, but Howard and Sanderson were killed in railroad accidents.

Telegrams were sent to families telling of their sons' wounding. These went to the parents of: Ernest Allen; Valmour Armour; Floyd Austin; Louis Baker; Godfrey Beck; Byron Black; Dan Courtney; Martin Courtney; Alford Crandall; Milton Davison; Stanley Graham; Everett Hickok; Merle C. Howe; George Larson; _____ Lockwood, a Canadian soldier; William McKenna; Leo Malcomson; Courtney Milam; Carl Monday; George Pearson; Al Perry; Guy Perry; Louis Rutter; Roy Tatman and Orlie Weible.

It was a bloody war! The English and French lost an immense number of men, while America was more fortunate in so many ways. The deadly submarine war was eliminated soon after our entry into hostilities, and we had avoided the prolonged trench warfare which sapped so much vitality out of the allies. In addition, we had avoided most of the chaos Socialism was bringing to the Europeans. The Socialists and anarchists churned Europe into a vast conglomeration of splintered forces, each weakening the social fabric of the nations. But in a more subtle way, America had suffered more than she knew at the time. Her innocence was one such casualty.

FRANK WALSH IN RUSSIA

The Bay City Steam Shovel Company had hired Frank Walsh for one of their jobs in Russia. He arrived over there just ahead of the October Revolution and was a witness to much of the turbulence which continues to rock the world. He was the son of James Walsh of Vernon township. Arriving in Petrograd in July, he was immediately confronted with street riots, run-away inflation and absolute anarchy. He was lucky to escape from the city alive. By mid-August he was in Murmansk where he was to operate a steam shovel for the railroad. Russian men and women, as well as German and Austrian Prisoners of War did the common labor. Meals consisted of of hash, black bread and coffee. Three months later he realized that conditions were deteriorating very rapidly now, so he sold his suits, shoes and coats and boarded a tramp steamer bound for Liverpool. There, aided by the American Consulate, he made his passage back to New York and finally to Clare. He was fortunate to have escaped.

THE FLU

An earlier wave of the Spanish Flu had gone through Europe in 1917, inflicting many disablements. American Expeditionary Forces in France came into contact with the virus, but it was a milder version than what was awaiting the military camps and civilians during the coming October. Nevertheless, the troops having endured an ocean crossing in very congested ships were in a weakened condition, and they were felled like flies. The disease was able to totally incapacitate the victim for about two days. Severe pain and agony wracked the bodies of the Americans as their systems fought to throw off the effects of the germs. The heart, lungs, kidneys, liver, stomach and muscles were severely damaged in many instances, and the high body temperatures damaged many of their brains. Pneumonia quickly followed the disease and began to further attack the weak bodies. Deaths were numerous, and the hospitals piled the bodies in rows behind the main buildings. Deaths were attributed to secondary causes in most cases, of which pneumonia was the most common. Members of the military who died from the flu stateside include: John Anger; John Ansil; Oscar Babcock; William Dingman; Robert Elliott; Arthur Fox; James Garrity; Thomas Harvey; Arthur Looker; James McCollum; Vane Mickle; Irving Reed, Arthur Stinchcombe; Odell Stanton; Vern Wixom and Roy Wright. Stinchcombe may have died from diptheria.

Nearly half of the draftees and workers in Camp Custer were hit by the flu. The hospitals were filled to over-flowing and a separate barracks in each company was set aside for the victims. The men were asked to air their bedding each day in an effort to control the spread of the serious outbreak.

Great Lakes and other naval bases were swept by the epidemic in October, reducing the bases to skeleton crews and bringing daily routines to a minimum. The camps were hit the hardest because there were so many people concentrated in a small area. Then it moved to the civilians.

Early in the fall of 1918 it was apparent to the authorities that a major flu epidemic was going to hit the United States. In October, all schools, churches, public buildings and non-essential public meetings were cancelled or closed. The gathering together of crowds was absolutely discouraged by the War Boards.

Almost every school in Michigan was closed between the first of October and January 1, 1919, as officials sought ways of controlling the disaster. Rural schools, isolated from the population concentrations did not appear to suffer as much as the city folks.

Hospitals in the larger cities soon had so many patients that they couldn't handle them. The Boat House of the Saginaw Yacht Club was pressed into service, and many recuperating patients were transfered there. Nurses and trained medical personnel from Clare county went to the city hospitals, such as Henry Ford in Dearborn and Saginaw General, and helped the beleaguered staffs. One nurse from the county was sent to Iowa where a major outbreak had occured.

In Europe an epidemic of meningitis hit the front line troops in October, and many men from the 32nd Division were stricken, but none from Clare were made public.

Attempts to understand the reason for the higher mortality rates in camps were, and are at best, speculative. The flu bug hit the healthy as well as the run-down. Most of the men in the military were in prime condition, but they had been given massive doses of shots and stringent exercises. Many were taxed beyond their bodies' ability to handle the added burden. Another major reason, perhaps, was the serious crowding of the men into small rooms and areas. If the flu hit, it was soon passed on. Sick victims were taken to hospitals where everyone else had some form of a disability and was in a weakened condition, and there were no miracle drugs to knock out the side-effects. Aspirin, rest, a placebo and some tender loving care was all that was available. Sometimes an alcohol bath was used to lower dangerously high body temperatures, but all of the treatment was secondary or tertiary.

Civilians who died from this outbreak are listed below.

Mrs. Fred Akey	Thelma Keyes
Elmer Badgley	Ernestine Kliewoneit
Floyd Badgley	Cecilia M. Larman
Ford Barber	Chester Listenfelt
Augusta Belling	Ray Locke
_____ Bingley	Joseph Lutke
Percy Bond	Ray McAllister
Eva Boner	William L. McCarey
Mabel Boner	William McKinley
Mrs. Albert Bouchey	Charles McKinnon
Clarence W. Brown	Clayton McPhall
Edward Calkins	Charles Mitchell
Henry Clausohm	Samuel Morton
Mildred Fair Cuvrell	Mrs. E. A. Overton
Busher B. Dunlop	Venus Pelch
Mrs. Lee Ervin	Raymond Potter
Samuel Faught	Earl O. Rodabaugh
William E. Fish	Warren Rodwell
Adelbert Forbes	Durwood Ross
Peter Freed	Ruth Russell
Isol Gable	Leone Seibert
Joseph Gay	Hugh Shaver
_____ Giebel	Luch Shaver
Florence Harrington	William Shaver
Ada Harvey	Mrs. Wm. Vandelinder
Thomas Harvey	Olin Walker
August Hildebrandt	Burt Williams
Enid Howe	Andrew G. Wood
Jay B. Husted	Anna E. Wood

Funeral cortege for Walter D. Larman, 1919.
Photo from the Jay Bellinger Collection

THE KAISER QUITS THE WAR

David Ward, Clare county sheriff-elect sent a telegram on November 8, 1918 to Prince Maxmillian and the Kaiser in Berlin. He said:

"Upon receipt of this wireless you will have until November 11th to sign the American peace plan for a complete unconditional surrender. If it is not signed by 5:30 p.m. I will arrive by airplane with a warrant which reads:

'Bring the whole Royal family, dead or alive, regardless of cost, and place them in the Clare county jail at Harrison, Michigan for life. Their bill of fare will be Mutt and Jeff soup eaten with a muzzle on. I am a man of few words and a small amount of money with which to buy the soup.'

Signed D. Ward Sheriff-elect."

For the first time it is now possible to tell the real story behind the Kaiser's quick suit for peace and why he fled to Holland. The country really has Dave Ward to thank for ending the world's most serious war. The question which arises now is "Why didn't Dave end the war sooner?"

PRESIDENT WILSON AND HIS PEACE PLAN

The Congress gave Wilson scattered support, and most of what he received came from Republicans all throughout the war. At its conclusions he asked Congress to support "my" program..."I ask"..."I need"..."I"..."I"..."I". Mentioning "Our country" just once in his plans for a post war world, it is no wonder that problems erupted. The price for his folly and the Congressional foot-dragging would be extracted from another generation, but for now everyone relaxed as the Yanks had made the world "safe for Democracy."

Victory Sunday was celebrated on November 17th in most churches throughout the land. Locally the Rev. L. J. Teed preached his maiden sermon at the Elm Grove Church of God on this day, and it was one that was not forgotten by those who heard it. The whole county was in a euphoric mood and

The problems of peace received the attention of the Allied leaders at the end of World War I. Their collective failure to deal equitably with Germany and her allies led directly to World War II. President Wilson is shown here riding with President Poincare of France in December of 1918.

Photo: Michigan Department of State Archives

had been since November 7th, when rumors of an armistice hit Clare. A big crowd assembled and a band joined for the frolicing. Mayor Caple, Sheriff-elect David Ward and Joe Bowler gave the public the benefit of their wisdom and it was probably early the next day when Dave found out that the Kaiser had tricked him, that he sent his famous telegram to Berlin and ended the war all by himself. Most people considered the joke on themselves and resolved not to be snookered in again by some rumor. Until the war was actually ended, everyone realized that the boys "Over There" were still in great danger of becoming a statistic.

The actual Armistice was celebrated on the eleventh of November, just as it was all across this nation. The Farwell Home Guards boarded the train and headed for Clare where a big Victory Celebration was in full swing in front of the Calkins. Farmers,

children and parents of the boys joined in a thankful rejoicing that at last it was all over. The crowd was kept down because the Flu Epidemic was raging at the time and large gatherings were frowned upon by the authorities. The ones who showed up made up for the absent ones with their cheers and cries of joy.

Plans for a post-war Europe had been developed by the General Staff. It included a ten division occupation army which would stay in Germany until the peace treaty was signed. With the cessation of hostilities came the voices of 140,000,000 more hungry mouths and they all looked to the United States for satiation. The major reason the Kaiser quit the war when he did was the acute shortage of food in Germany for the coming winter.

All of the fighting and producing for the war had so seriously reduced the food supply that the best estimates indicated a three month ration for Europe had been gathered into the storage facilities. A desperate winter was in store for the former enemies and their allies. The best that we could do was to feed our allies and then send an additional twenty million tons, cutting into our own reserves drastically.

The Red Cross stayed on in France and the other countries where our people were serving, helping to return the American soldiers. Many of the wounded were escorted back by these brave women who donned the nurse's uniform and worked right behind the front lines. Irene McDonald was one of those modern Florence Nightingales whose hands staunched the blood from fresh wounds. Later she was assigned to a big Base Hospital unit in Paris, but she had served her country faithfully during the heavy fighting. Elsie Slater was another nurse who served in the Red Cross units abroad. She arrived on the scene in August, just in time for the big drives and the numerous casualties. She stayed on, tending the sick and wounded, and came back with some of the last members of the fighting units.

Almost as soon as the warfare stopped, President Wilson boarded a ship and arrived in France with an escort of ten ships. Chairman Hurley of the United States Shipping

Armistice Day celebration in front of Clare's leading hotel, "The Calkins," November 11, 1918.
Photo courtesy of Robert Kleiner and Ruth Wade

Board accompanied him to Europe to expedite the return of the soldiers. He planned to ship 300,000 men a month back to the states, using about thirty ships belonging to Australia and Germany. British and German liners were used originally to bring the men to France.

The ten dreadnaughts which carried Wilson to Europe, returned almost immediately with the largest shipment of American troops ever undertaken. Their return lessened the demands upon the available food supply and their departure was appreciated by the civilians as well as the Yanks themselves.

Germany was desperate for food and pleaded with the Allies to keep her citizens from starving. Some thought it was a ploy to secure better peace terms, but most remembered the treatment she had meted out to Bulgaria, Poland, Serbia, Belgium and Roumania when they stripped the countryside of food, leaving the civilians to starve. German women appealed to Mrs. Wilson and Jane Adams, asking in the name of humanity to help Germany. The question asked was "Did these women appeal on behalf of the women and children of Belgium and Poland?" There were stories told by the returning Prisoners of War that some had asked for water of the German women and they had spit on them. The CLARE SENTINEL in an editorial November 23rd, 1918, said, "We suspect a little genuine suffering is the only thing that will bring these people to their senses." And that is where most Clare people left the war.

A SOLDIER'S TRIBUTE

The war had uprooted hundreds of thousands of men from their families and their communities. These strangers were gathered together into the camps and there, amid a sea of faces, they began to look for a friend. There were many reasons they were drawn to each other; perhaps it was because they were lined up in a column of twos by their height. In other situations the men were assigned to a barracks or a company by the alphabet, and then again it might have been a work detail that brought them together for the first time. Regardless of the mechanism, the men sought and found a buddy to help them through the hard days of basic training. Since so many of the draftees were put into a division and kept there all through the war, it was easy to maintain contact with one's buddy.

A young man from northern Michigan enlisted in the Ohio National Guard in Cleveland because he was down visiting his brother in Lodi, Ohio, a town not too far from the big city. He was assigned to the 145th Infantry and shipped out along with the rest of the Division to Montgomery, Alabama for basic training. It was there that he met Frankie Elliott.

Frankie Elliott was now a young man of twenty one years, but he had been kidnapped from his parent's home when he was two. Taken to a foreign country by his abductors, he grew into adolescence among some people who treated him cruelly. From the age of twelve on, he was expected to work like a man. His was a very difficult life.

Finally when the war broke out and men

Robert B. Meek, 1917.

were being impressed into the service, Frankie determined to make his escape back to the United States. He had learned over the years a few details of his real parents by eavesdropping, and soon after his return to America he went to Pittsburg and found his mother. But he was a restless youth who had been on his own for too long, and the United States' entry into the war was all the excuse he needed to join up. He too had enlisted in Cleveland and went with the Division to Alabama. It was there the men joined each other in Co. K of the 145th Infantry Regiment.

Together the men found a comradeship neither had known before, and they both basked in each other's company. They both were happy and carefree for the first time in their lives and they loved every minute of each other's time and friendly banter. They went on week-end passes together and to the clubs and other forms of entertainment. Life had become meaningful to them both and they had reasons now to live.

Then the training period was over and the Division was packed up. The weapons and machinery of war were loaded on board merchant ships, and the men were sent home for a short delay enroute furlough. It was while home on this leave that the northern Michigan soldier buried his father in a Manton cemetery. A few more days and then it was time to return to the waiting ships in New York.

It was here that the two friends were parted. Though still on board the same ship, they were in different compartments and therefore they were let up on the deck at different times. After a rough crossing, the ship was placed in quarantine because several cases of meningitis broke out and the two lost track of each other for eleven weeks. The two met on a road in France, not far from the place Frankie had lived most of his youth.

Frankie was carrying a large combat pack nearly as large as he was. When the sergeant called a rest stop, Frankie threw off his pack and bounded over to his friend, Bob. Such a meeting! They talked of many things and then it was time to move out. The big push was on for the next day in the Argonne.

A week later the survivors of the Buckeye Division were in Belgium, getting ready to plug a hole in the British lines. "Hello, Burns," was the salutation heard above the roar and din of the confusion. At first Bob was all smiles at seeing his "Buddy" again, but it soon left his face. There was Frankie weighted down with his eighty-five pound combat pack and carrying a one-pounder. He was on the suicide squad. Bob was marching in the opposite direction and all he could say was "Take care of yourself, Frankie!"

A wave of the hand and then he was out of sight.

Company K marched along and Bob shuffled his feet in lethargic steps. He had a

Frank E. Elliott

feeling of guilt and it was not going to be removed.

Two days later the men were pulled out of the line for a rest, and Bob looked up his "Buddy". "Hadn't you heard," said the sergeant. From the look on Bob's face, it was obvious that he hadn't.

"A whiz-bang lit at his feet. If there wasn't another soldier close by to witness it, nobody would have ever known what happened. We couldn't even find his dog-tags."

Bob, staggered at the news and with head bowed low with grief, made his way back to his own company. He couldn't understand it at all. He was alive and soon to be on his way home. There was Frankie, a man who in the last year of his life had finally found a friend, then in the twinkling of an eye, it was all over.

Civilians may forget a war, but a comrade-in-arms doesn't forget the friendship forged in camp and on the battlefield. Robert Burns Meek never forgot his friend, Frankie Elliott.

Appendix

1918 FLU DEATHS

Akey, Mrs. Fred
Badgley, Elmer
Badgley, Floyd
Barber, Ford
Belling, Augusta
Bingley, _____
Bond, Percy
Boner, Eva
Boner, Mabel
Bouchey, Mrs. Albert
Brown, Clarence W.
Calkins, Edward
Claushom, Henry
Cuvrell, Mildred
Dunlop, Busher
Ervin, Mrs. Lee
Faught, Samuel
Fish, William E.
Forbes, Adlebert
Freed, Peter

Gable, Isol
Gay, Joseph
Giebel, _____
Harrington, Florence B.
Harvey, Ada
Harvey, Thomas
Hildebrandt, August
Howe, Enid
Justed, Jay
Keyes, Thelma
Kliewoneit, Ernestine
Larman, Cecilia
Listenfelt, Chester
Locke, Ray
Lutke, Joseph
McAllister, Ray
McCarey, William L.
McKinley, William
McKinnon, Charles
McPhall, Clayton

Mitchell, Charles
Morton, Samuel
Overton, Mrs. E. A.
Pelch, Venus
Potter, Raymond
Rodebaugh, Earl O.
Rodwell, Warren
Ross, Durwood
Russell, Ruth
Seibert, Leone
Shaver, Hugh
Shaver, Lucy
Shaver, William
Vandelinder, Mrs. William
Walker, Olin
Williams, Burt
Wilson, Wallace
Wood, Andrew C.
Wood, Anna E.

CLARE COUNTY
WORLD WAR I ROLL OF HONOR

Abbott, George A.
Acre, Vern A. AEF
Adams, Frank
Adams, Fred
Albertson, John C.
Alexander, Russell AEF
   30th Rgt. MNG 4th Division
Allby, L. Custer
Allen, Ernest AEF
   Wounded Feb. 1918
Allen, Floyd
Allen, John USN
Allen, Roy E.

Alwood, John L.
Amble, Elmer AEF
Ambrosier, Reynold
Amy, Glen Custer
Anger, John d. 1918
Archamboult, Robert
Armour, Valmour AEF
   Gassed October 1918
Armstrong, Edward—Custer
Armstrong, John
Austin, Arthur G.
Austin, Floyd AEF
   MIA (returned)

Babcock, Oscar d. 1918
Badger, Oliver
Badger, Walter
Bailey, Cassius
Bailey, George AEF
   Aero Corps
Bailey, Harvey S.
Baker, Charles W.
Baker, Godfrey AEF
   Wounded Co. E. 126th Inf.
Ballard, Freeman
Barber, Orla
Barlow, Percy—Camp McArthur

Barker, George
Barker, Louis R.
Barker, Orla AEF
Barrett, Clarence
Barris, Carl
Barry, Archie
Batch, James L. AEF
  Co. F 26th Engineers
Bauer, Carl
Bauer, Edward
Bauman, D. C.
Beard, Guy—Custer
Beard, Robert C.
Beck, Godfrey AEF
  Wounded Argonne
  337th Inf. 85th Div.
Bellinger, Jay
Bentley, Harley C.
Bergey, Leroy
Bergey, Ray AEF
  85th Division
Bergey, William H.
Bersette, George F.
Bersette, Irvin AEF
Bigley, Alexander
Bilgren, Anton (Major)
Bingham, Roy
Birdsall, Leo
Bitler, Joseph W. AEF
  302nd Stevedores
Black, Byron AEF
  St. Mihiel, Chateau-Thierry-
  Argonne
Bodkins, Charles W.
Bond, Percey E.
Bonham, Charles
Bouchey, Albert
Brackett, Walter T.
Brazee, Walter E.
Briggs, Ephrium USN
Bringold, Emil C.
Brown, Ralph
Brownell, Benjamin
Bruce, Thomas R.
Bruno, Charles
Bunto, Ralph OCS
Burch, Jesse
Burgee, William—Custer
Burns, Charles—Custer
Burton, Earl
Burton, Emerson
Bush, Harold
Bushong, William H.
Butters, Clyde
Butters, William
Calkins, Charles
Calkins, Edward
Campbell, Harry K.
Canfield, Donald AEF
  85th Division
Carey, Asa B.
  39th Machine Gun Co.
Carpenter, Edward C.
Carpenter, Wilmot J.
Carrier, Rex
Casterline, Orrin
Caughrove, Edward M.
Cavanaugh, Leo J. KIA
  Canadian Army
Cepela, Ladislaw
Chaffee, Emory AEF
  26th Engineers

Chapman, Floyd USN
Chapman, Lloyd
Charrette, Francis
Charrette, Wesley J.
Chester, Walter A.
Cimmerer, Fred AEF
  85th Division
Clark, Floyd—Custer
Clark, Ray AEF
Clark, Roy E.
Cline, Lenwell E.—Custer
Clute, James AEF
  Co B. 31st Rgt. MNG
  Motor Truck Bn.
Coates, Leo M.
Collins, George V.
Collins, Oard AEF
Colosky, Matthew AEF
Cook, Elsworth
Cook, Ralph
Cook, Roy
Cooper, Victor
  Canadian Army
Coors, Merrill F.
Cotton, Jesse
Cotton Lester
Coutler, C. Leroy
Courtney, Daniel J. AEF
  wounded
Courtney, Martin AEF
  gassed—Soissons 32nd Div.
Cowles, Jabez
Cowles, W. J. AEF
  28th Engineers
Cradit, Earl D.
Craine, Llewellyn
  a Bandsman
Crandall, Alford USN
  Torpedoed 1918
Davenport, Clifford G.
David, Charles R.
David, Sale
Davis, Joseph AEF
Davis, Lee M.
Davis, Rush C. AEF KIA
Davison, Milton AEF
  16th Co. M.M.S. 4th Rgt.
  Wounded
Denno, David R.
Detwiller, Cloyce H.
Devereaux, Henry
Dingman, William O.—Custer
  d. 1918
Dobson, Clifford
Doherty, Lear AEF
Doherty, Lawrence W.
Doherty, Wendell
Doornbas, Neal
Douglas, Homer
  85th Div. Aero Corps
Dowd, Rufus d. 1915
  Coast Artillery
Duncan, George
  Canadian Army
Durfee, Lewis A.
Durfee, Percival J.
Duttweiler, Clyde H.
DuVall, Earl
Dyer, Carter AEF
Dyer, Rolland B.
Dysinger, Clarence E.
Eberhart, Ralph

Elliott, Robert d. 1919
Elston, Harvey
Empey, John
Ervin, Lee Edd
Everest, Theo. A.
Fair, Floyd
Fakes, Floyd AEF
  d. 1919 Flu
Fanning, Bryan—Custer
Fanslaw, William H.
Farmer, Roy—Custer
Fear, Earl
Fisher, Eugene AEF
Fitzpatrick, Bernard
Flannigan, James AEF
Foell, Emil
Folkes, Floyd W.
Fookes, Lee
Fordyce, Egbert AEF
Foss, Earl AEF
  32nd Division
Foster, C. L.
Foster, Clinton H. AEF
Foster, Corliss AEF
  310 Ammo Train
Foster, George W.
Fox, Arthur d. 1918
Fox, Francis
Freeman, Martin
Freer, William J.
Frizzell, James AEF
  KIA October 1918
Gable, Clyde AEF
Gamble, C.
Garchow, Albert
Garchow, Carl F.
Gardner, Linas Lt.
Garrity, James USN
  d. 1918 flu
Garver, Forrest L.
Geeck, Edward D.
Giers, Emil F.
Gilbert, Del
Gilmore, Alwein
Goodrich, Carlos H.
Gorr, Arlie AEF
Gosine, Phillip AEF
Graham, Allen R. AEF
  Clerk on Gen Pershing's staff
Graham, Hugh
Graham, Jesse
Graham, John A.
Graham, Stanley AEF
  Co. E. 126th Inf. Wounded
Green, Charles
Green, F.D.
  Tank Corps
Griffin, Albert C.
Gruno, Herman
Gruno, William C.
Guest, Calvin J.
Guest, Forrest
Hagan, Andrew AEF
Hagan, Stanley
Hale, Warren
Hales, Ray H.
Hall, Perry C.
Halstead, Will C. Capt.
  KIA Canadian Army
Hamer, J. C.
Hammersley, Charles L.
Hamlin, St. Clair

Hammond, Archie
Hammond, Delos
Hammond, Lewis J.
Hampton, Frank A.
Hampton, Jesse
Hanley, Patrick
Harding, John C.
  85th Division
Harger, Riley I.
Harrold, Rollie
Harvey, Eslie
Harvey, Ralph
Harvey, Thomas D.
  d. 1919 Flu
Hatfield, John AEF
  Wounded
Hawkins, Bernard
Hawkins, Roy AEF
Hawkins, Will
Hay, Stuart
  30th Rgt. MNG
Hayward, Marion R.
Hayward, Martin Lt.
Hayward, Richard O.
Heintz, Henry A.
Heintz, Lee E.
Heiser, Ivan E.
Heiser, Martin F.
Hemstreet, Nathan S.
Herman, Edward F.
Heuschele, August C.
Hickey, Alfred AEF
Hickok, Everett AEF
  Seriously wounded
Hickok, Guy—Custer
Higgins, Charles H.
Hildebrandt, Albert
Hildebrandt, Fred
Hildebrandt, Robert AEF
Hileman, Will
Himes, Herbert AEF
Hintz, Henry E.
Holbrook, Carl AEF
  36th Base Hospital
Holcomb, Daniel
Holmes, Thomas
Hooker, Herbert F.
Hooker, Keith
Hornberger, Donald AEF
Hornberger, Harold AEF
  St. Mihiel, Chateau
  Theirry-Argonne
Horning, Floyd AEF
Howard, Gilbert AEF
  d. 1918
Howard, Roy
Howe, Merle C.
Howes, Alva P.
Howey, Bert F.
Hudson, Benjamin H.
Hulin, Earnest L.
Hursh, Starrie
Hutchins, Howard M.
Ickes, Charles R.
Irish, William AEF
  85th Division
Jackson, Charles
Jackson, Frank AEF
  Co I 7th Inf.
Jackson, Herbert
Jackson, Roy AEF
Jackson, William R.

Jarman, Glenn—Custer
Jennings, Herbert
Johnson, Bert
Johnson, Carl
Johnson, Charles AEF
  MNG Mexico 1916
Johnson, David A. AEF
  KIA 1918
Johnson, Eber R.
Johnson, George H.
Johnson, Harry
Johnson, John
Johnson, Seeley
Johnson, Verl
Jones, Howard W.
Jones, Kernie L.
Kapplinger, Charles—Custer
Keating, Jesse AEF
Keehn, Arthur
Keehn, Charles
Keehn, Ike
Keehn, Martin
Keller, Cornelius
Kennedy, Charles
Kennedy, W. Holmes
Keysor, Andrew
Keysor, Lloyd T.
Kipfer, William—Custer
Kirkpatrick, Floyd
Kissick, Percy KIA
  Canadian Army
Klann, John E.
Kleiner, Otto AEF
  Co E. M.T.C.R.V.
Kleinhardt, Charles E.
Knapp, Linton USN
Koch, Frank
Koepplinger, Frank
Koontz, R. B. AEF
Kotek, Harvey J.
Kretzer, Jno.
Kube, William W. AEF
  d. 1918
Ladd, Clarence O.
Lambertson, Abraham—Custer
Lamban, Howard
Lane, Spencer J.
Lange, Charles G.
Langworthy, Ralph
Larkin, Ray C.
  10th Rgt. Co. D
Larman, Walter D. AEF
  KIA 4th Division 1st/Sgt.
  P.O.W. Wounded 1918
Larson, George AEF
  1st Division Wounded
Larson, Joseph
Lassen, H. V. AEF
  Co. 12 1st Motor Truck Corps
LaVoy, Charles AEF
Laverty, John
Leitner, Lorin (Orin)
Leosh, Alvin
  A.W.O.L.
Levinson, Henry
Listenfeltz, Ralph AEF
Little, Andrew AEF
  107th Engineers
Little, Ernest
Lockwood, Johnson AEF
  85th Division
Lockwood, _____ Wounded
  Canadian Army

Lockwood, Wallace
Looker, Arthur USN
  d. 1918 flu
Loomis, Martin AEF
Lund, Ernfrid
Lynch, David Major
  DVM—Custer
Lynch, Frank J.
Lynch, Patrick
  Ambulance Corps
McClung, Harold AEF
McCollam, James d.—Custer
McCracken, Ward
McDonald, Clarence Lt. AEF
McDonald, Irene AEF
  Nurse
McFadden, Vincent
  A.W.O.L.
McGuire, Dennis J.
McGuire, Francis
McGuire, Fred O.
McGuire, Russell
McIntyre, John
  41st Co 11th Bn 160 Brigade
McIntyre, Kenneth AEF
  KIA 1918
McKeever, George Lt.
McKenna, William AEF
  Wounded in Marne—gassed
McKinley, Henry
McKinley, James
McKinley, John H.
McKinnon, Kyle AEF
  Co. L. 3rd Bn 340th Inf. 85th Div.
McNeill, Cecil
McNeil, Herbert Sgt.
  d. 1918 flu
McNeill, Andrew C.
McNeill, James
McNeill, Russell
MacLane, _____ Reg. Army
MacLane, Grant
Mahan Fred
Mahan, John F.
Makin, Charles W.
Malcomson, Leo AEF
  Wounded
Malosh, Clifford AEF
  7th Div. Army of Occupation
Maltby, Thomas
Manee, Paul AEF
Manwaring, Joseph
March, Stephen E.
Marlin, Blake AEF
  330 Machine Gun Bn
Marsh, John R.
Marshall, Leon
Martin, Stephen L.
Martindale, Earl C. Capt. DVM
Mason, Orin A.
Matthews, Fred AEF
Matthews, Walter—Custer
Mayhew, Arthur
Mayhew, Stuart
Maynard, Perry USN
Merrill, Carl E.
Mickle, Vane d. 1918 flu
Milam, Courtney AEF
  Co A 16th Inf 1st Division
  Wounded
Milkie, Enoch E.
Miller, Charles

Miller, David AEF
    KIA 1918
Miller, Frank Lt. AEF
    Quartermaster Corps
Miller, John AEF
Mills, George AEF
    32nd Division
Mitchell, Neal
Monday, Carl AEF
    Co I 126th Inf 32nd Division
    Wounded
Monday, William H.
Mooney, Henry
Moorse, Baldwin
Moore, John
Moore, Louis E.
Moore, Marvin AEF
Moore, Walter
    C Troop 6th Cav.
Moran, Walter H.
Morrissey, Burke C. USN
Morton, Earl H.
Muringer, Louis W.
Mussell, Dr. A. R. AEF Capt.
Naegle, Dewey
Neagle, George
Newman, Raleigh A.
Nicholls, Emmett
Nickerson, Bonnie
Northrup, Ruie
Nowlen, Wellington
Oberholtzer, Earl W.
Odell, Frank M.
Oden, L. E.
O'dette, Raymond B.
Oles, Harry B. MNG
    Co B 33rd Rgt.
Olson, John A.
Olson, Ove Lt. Alaska
Oman, Charles M.
Ott, Robert G.
Otto, Lewis E.
Page, _____ MNG
    Mexican Border 1916
Park, Bernard F.
Parks, Archie
Parks, John L.
Parrish, Ray
Pearson, Earnest
Pearson, George AEF
    Wounded
Pelch, Bruce E.
Pelcher, Thomas
Perry, Al AEF
    8th Inf. Teamster
    Wounded
Perry, Guy AEF
    128th Inf. POW
Peterson, Carl A.
Peterson Richard V.
Pettit, Edward Lt.
Phillips, Charles B.
Pike, Seer AEF
    Aero Corps
Pitts, James
Poe, _____
Potter, Raymond d. 1918
    Aero Corps
Poulson, Harold
Price, Clifford
Price, Earl F.
Price, Ferd H.

Ramsey, William H.
Randall, Clifford
Randall, John
Rawson, Ed
    Camp Lee, Virginia
Reed, Irving d. 1918
Reed, John
Reger, Adam
Rhoades, Walter
Rhodes, Reuben W.
Richmond, Arthur E.
Richmond, Cyrus
Ritter, Murl Lt. AEF
    51st Inf. 6th Div.
Robinette, Emmett B.
Robinette, Theron
Roe, Alfred
Roe, Charles Capt. AEF
Rogers, Dalton M.
    241 Aero Sqdn Kelley Field
Rogers, Milward AEF
Rose, William J.
Roth, Gleason AEF
    119th F.A. 32nd Division
Rulapaugh, Dale
Rulapaugh, Leon D.—Custer
Runyan, George A.—Russia
    339th Inf. "Polar Bears"
Russ, Elsie
    Red Cross Nurse
Russ, Fred
Rutter, Henry
Rutter, Henry
Rutter, Lewis
    shot one toe off
Sanders, Charles E.
Sanderson, George F. AEF
    killed r.r. accident
Sanderson, Otis AEF
Sanford, Burton Dr. Lt. AEF
Sanford, Charles
Saxton, Perry AEF
    Co. A 337th Inf. 85th Div.
Schaeffer, Peter AEF
Schaeffer, Rudolph
Schaeffer, Von Henry
Schilling, John
Scott, Myrl AEF
Schug, Fred
Schultz, Albert
Schultz, John
Schwanz, Fred E.
Seaman, Albert W.
Searsaw, George B.
Searsaw, William
Seaver, Berley
Sebert, Albert
Seferson, Arlington
Sersaw, Charles
Seymour, Elam
Seymour, William H.
Shaffer, Orlando L.
Sharp, Ralph AEF
    1st Division Army of
    Occupation Germany
Shaw, Clarence AEF
    d. 1918 flu
Sheffield, Arthur
Sheffield, George W.
Sheneman, George W.
Sherman, Earl C.
Sherman, James

Sherman, Milton
Sherman, Orville
Sherman, William
Shillinger, Gaius
Shimmons, Leonard
Shippey, Earl T.
Shorts, William H.
Shumway, Roy G.
Slater, Elsie AEF
    Red Cross Nurse
Slentz, Floyd Lt.
Sly, William
    Aero Corps
Smalley, Raymond
Smith, Arthur J.
Smith, John R.
Smith, Ralph E.
    301 Cav.
Snider, Henry
Solar, Lewis
Sowle, Harley
    Coast Artillery
Speer, Gordon
Spencer, Isaac
Spicer, Carl
Spicer, Ivan
Stanton, Leroy G.
Stevens, Ralph USN
Stillwell, Charles
Stinchcombe, Arthur USN
    d. Brooklyn Navy Yard
Stone, Fred Major
    Engineers AEF
Stratton, O'Dell
    d. 1918 flu
Strauch, Charles—Custer
Strauss, Louis
Strauss, Ralph
Strouse, Clair
Stuhle, Ralph
Sugar, Henry
Sutton, Jams O.
Schwartz, Herb—Custer
Swisher, Perry G.
Tatman, Roy A. AEF
    Sgt. 28th Regt Co E 51st Inf.
    Gassed
Teachout, Phillip
Tennant, Glen
Thayer, Earl C.
Tiedeman, Denzil M.
Treanor, Leo J.
    Aero Corps
Trowbridge, Ira
Tryon, Archie
    Camp Grant, Ill.
Tubbs, James
Updegraff, Carl T.
Utley, Ray
Van Valkenberg, David
Visnaw, Lloyd
Vosburgh, Louis S.
Vreeland, Bert M.
Vreeland, Bird M. AEF
    330th F.A. 85th Division
Wahl, William G.
    Co C 57th Ammo Train
Waite, Lyle E.
White, William D.
Waller, Ward
Ward, Delos AEF
Wardell, Will

Watt, Ray
Weaver, Fred A.
Weible, Otto AEF
  Wounded 23rd Engineers
Webster, Perry AEF
  85th Division
Welch, Leo B. USN
Wild, Harry
Willey, Andrew
Williams, Burt
Williams, Joy
  Coast Artillery

Wilson, Albert
Wilson, Allen
Wilson, Frank E.
Wilson, Joseph
Wilson, Norman
Wilson, Perry C. Lt.
Wilson, Robert H.
Wilson, William J. d. 1919
  Canadian Army flu
Wixom, Vern—Custer
  d. 1918 flu
Wood, Stanley B.

Wood, William
Woodin, Chancey—Custer
Woods, Edmond
Woods, John
Wright, Bernice E. AEF
  Co F. 23rd Engineers
Wright, Clark A.
Wright, Marion Charles
Wright, Nelson D.
Wright, Roy d. 1918
Wyman, Harold
Wyman, Walter E.

CLARE COUNTY TEACHERS
1900-1918

Adams, Hattie—Farwell 1912
Adgate,_____(Miss) Clare . . 1911
Aldrich, Asa H.—Harrison 1900
Alger, Edgar 1903
Allen, Irene—Brand. 1916
Allen, Bernice—Lyons. 1918
Alward, Gertude—Clare 1906
Amble, Charles—Hamilton. . . . 1916
Archamboult, Hazel—Leota . . . 1917
Armstrong, Josephine—Grant . 1906
Arnold, Adelaide—Clare 1906
Artibee, Alex—Harrison 1906
Artibee, Anna—Harrison 1904
Baatz, L. Ernestine—Clare, . . . 1912
Baatz, Susie—Clare 1912
Babcock, Flora—Harrison. 1904
Babcock, Thomas—Lake. 1914
Badger, Olive—Farwell. 1918
Bailey, Leora—Hamilton 1912
Bailey, Alva E.—Freeman. 1912
Barber, D. A.—Farwell. 1904
Barber, Fern—Arthur 1916
Barber, Maude—Arthur 1917
Barlow, Harriet—Lake 1914
Battle, Josephine—Owosso 1914
Bell, Alice—Sheridan. 1906
Bellinger, Alma—Mud Lake. . . 1918
Bellinger, Emma—Herrick 1918
Bellinger, Jay—Colonville. 1918
Bennett, Herman—Elm Grove . 1917
Bennett, Phillip A.—
  Clare. 1899-1906
Bersette, George—Harrison . . . 1919
Blackledge, Eleanor—Marion. . 1914
Blackledge, Frank—Farwell . . . 1917
Blevins, Gertude—Marion 1914
Bowler, Joseph—Grant 1905
Bowler, William—Clare 1905
Brown, John F.—Temple 1903
Brown, Laura—Clare 1901
Brown, Methvan—Harrison . . . 1904
Brown, Rose 1905
Bruce, Anna—Greenwood 1912

Bruce, Thomas—Greenwood . . 1917
Bryan, Nellie G.—Arthur 1912
Bunto, Elizabeth—Winterfield . 1914
Bush, Harold C.—Clare 1917
Cadwell, Coral—Temple. 1912
Cameron, Margaret—Clare . . . 1908
Campbell, Mellie—Harrison. . . 1904
Carpenter, Ella—Farwell. 1909
Carr, Anita—Clare 1914
Carter, Edith. 1905
Casey, Katie—Clare 1906
Casey, Frank—Harrison 1903
Casey, Mazie—Frost 1913
Casey, Joanna—Harrison 1907
Chapin, Edith—Winterfield . . . 1905
Chapman, Alice—Clare 1914
Chappell, A. J.—Farwell
  Superintendent
Clark, Edna—Clare 1906
Clegg, Anna—Clare. 1918
Cole, Laura B.—Clare. 1904
Conrad, Beulah—Clare. 1914
Converse, Zora—Shepherd. . . . 1914
Cook, Laura 1906
Cooper, Leitta—Leota. 1916
Cooper, Mary—Clare 1903
Cooper, Olin—Harrison 1914
Corey, Miss_____—Clare . . 1911
Coulter, Belle—Clare. 1909
Coulter, Lee—Clare. 1909
Cox, Frances—Temple 1912
Crane, Edna—Petoskey. 1914
Crane, Kathryn—Clare. 1908
Crane, Nellie L.—Boyne City . 1912
Crego, Gail—Clare 1906
Creol, Winnifred—Clare 1911
Crook, George—Sheridan 1908
Cudney, Ethel. 1917
Currier, Mabel—Clare 1901
Cuvrell, Juanita—Farwell 1914
Darling, Gladys—Harrison. . . . 1912
Davis, Vera. 1909
Davy, Florence—Clare 1912

DeBarr, Clara—Harrison 1906
Deits, Edith—Winterfield 1906
Dier, Miss_____—Clare . . . 1912
Dillingham, Laura—Harrison . 1904
Doty, Francis—Harrison. 1912
Dudley, Nellie C.—Harrison . . 1904
Duncanson, Jessie—Clare. 1915
Durfee, E. N.—Turner 1906
DuVall, Ethel—Clare 1909
Eberhart, Anna—Temple 1904
Eberhart, Eunice—Colonville . 1917
Eberhart, Nina—Winterfield . . 1906
Ehrhardt, Chris—Janitor 1909
Eisenhauer, Jessie. 1917
Eldt, Miss_____—Herrick . . . 1913
Empey, Anna—Grant 1906
Empey, John—Clare 1918
Empey, Mary—Sheridan 1912
Erhardt, Eunice—Colonville. . . 1916
Fair, Alvin. 1918
Ferrell, Irene. 1916
Finch, Inez—Lincoln. 1917
Fisher, Frank—Hardwood 1909
Fisher, Mabel 1909
Fisk, Lulu—Clare. 1911
Fordyce, Archie—Balsley 1918
Foster, Agnes—Grandon. 1909
Foster, Corliss—Greenwood . . . 1909
Foster, Olive—Frost. 1918
Frye, Helen M. 1909
Fuller, Myrtle 1906
Fulmer, Myrtle—Clare 1907
Gannon, Lillian—Winterfield. . 1909
Gardiner, Minerva—Farwell . . 1904
Gardner, Leota—Harrison 1918
Garland, Minnie—Greenwood. 1918
Garrity, Julia—Hamilton 1914
Garrity, Mattie—Hamilton. . . . 1912
Garrity, Maud—Hamilton 1909
Gaskill, Katie—Winterfield. . . . 1912
Gates, Hazel—Leota 1914
Gay, Kitty—Rosebush. 1918
Gee, Louis—Farwell 1914

Shull, Marguerite—Arthur 1916
Sifton, Emma—Rosebush 1912
Sifton, Mable—Clare 1912
Smith, Anna—Harrison 1904
Smith, Edna—Hamilton 1912
Smith, Emma 1909
Smith, Florence 1909
Smith, Gordon—Harrison. 1914
Smith, Mabell—Clare 1912
Smith, Maud H. Grandon Hi. . 1906
Snyder, Walter—Clare 1901
Sprague, Ila—Windemere. 1914
Stanley, Fern—Lochabar 1914
Stanton, Hazel—Clare. 1906
Stephenson, Faye—Sheridan . . 1916
Stinchcombe, Arthur—Farwell . 1915
Stinchcombe, Miss_____
   Lake, ... 1915
Stinchcombe, Frank—Farwell
Stinchcombe, Lester—Farwell . 1918
Stone, Lulu—Clare 1918
Stowe, Miss_____Harrison . 1911
Struble, Edna A. 1909
Sullivan, Agnes—Hamilton . . . 1914
Sullivan, Anna—Hamilton 1909

Sullivan, Frances—Hamilton . . 1914
Sutton, Belle—McKinley 1912
Sutton, James—Clare 1914
Swigart, R. G.—Clare. 1904
Swinehart, Mabel—Arthur 1917
Taggart, Mary—Eagle. 1909
Taggart, Marie—Clare 1912
Taggart, Sadie 1912
Tatman, Alina—Clare. 1904
Tatman, Christine—Clare 1909
Tatman, Marie—Frost 1904
Taylor, Cara W. 1909
Taylor, Edith—Harrison. 1914
Tenent, George A. Chippewa
   Station 1906
Terwilleger, Bernice—Clare . . . 1912
Terwilliger, Calvin. 1909
Thompson, George E. Clare. . . 1905
Thorburn, Myrtle—Clare 1908
Thorburn, Rose—Clare. 1909
Thurston, Carolyn 1909
Tibbits, A. W.—Harrison. 1904
Tolly, J. W.—Hamilton 1904
Towns, _____—Hatton 1914
Treanor, Leo J.—Clare 1906

Trofford, Emmogene—Farwell . 1904
Turner, Hazel—Bond 1912
Van Fleet, Lelah—Clare 1914
Van Valkenberg, Ina—
   Greenwood 1909
Von Leuven, Ruth—Clare 1915
Vreeland, Iva—Surrey. 1917
Walker, Quinton Jr.—Clare . . . 1912
Wall, Florence—Clare 1908
Ward, Winifred—Clare. 1906
Welch, Edgar G.—Clare Co.
   School Commissioner
Wells, Aletha—Harrison 1914
Westfall, Anna L.—Clare 1904
Williams, Bruce—Harrison. . . . 1906
Williams, Maud—Arthur 1904
Williams, Sprague—Harrison. . 1904
Wilson, Etta 1906
Witwer, Edith—Clare 1901
Wood, Miss_____—Herrick . . 1913
Woods, Laura—Franklin. 1918
Woods, Richard 1906
Worden, Hazel—Clare 1914
Wright, Bessie—Farwell 1914

Who's Who in 20th Century Clare County

Aaker, Mrs. _____—Temple, 1909
Abbott, Alfred—farmer, Sheridan
Abbott, _____—Hatton, 1914
Abbott, Clare—Dover, 1903
Abbott, David—Winterfield, 1909
Abbott, George—farmer, Hatton
Abbott, George—Dover, 1903
Abbott, Mary—Clare, 1900
Abbott, John—farmer, Sheridan
Abbott, John (Jr.)—farmer, Sheridan
Abbott, Silvers B.—Winterfield
Abbott, Thomas—Clare, 1911
Abbey, Neri—Freeman, 1917
Achard, Anton E.—Supervisor, Freeman, 1917
Acker, Carrie—teacher, Sheridan
Acker, Cecilia—Hatton, 1906
Acker, Grace—teacher, Harrison
Ackerman, Archie—Vernon Twp.
Ackerman, Charles—farmer, Vernon
Ackerman, David—Clare, 1920
Ackerman, Esther—Clare, 1929
Ackerman, Florence—Clare, 1929
Ackerman, Franklin—Vernon, 1917
Ackerman, Fred—Clare
Ackerman, George—farmer, Vernon
Ackerman, Hazel—Clare, 1932
Ackerman, Henry—Hayes
Ackerman, Henry—plumber
Ackerman, Jake—farmer, Clare
Ackerman, Jay—Clare
Ackerman, Thomas—Wise, 1917
Ackley, George—Sheridan, 1903
Acre, Delman—Grant, 1911
Acre, Ezra—farmer, Sheridan, 1917
Acre, Frank—farmer, Hatton, 1906
Acre, John—Arthur, 1918
Acre, Vern—A.E.F., Sheridan
Adam, Guss—livery, Clare, 1907
Adams, Ben—train conductor Clare, 1906
Adams, Charles—Gilmore, 1917
Adams, Chauncey—
Adams, Derrick—hotel manager, Reed City, Clare
Adams, Frank—WWI, Winterfield
Adams, Fred—WWI, Clare
Adams, Gideon—Grant, 1900
Adams, Gus—livery, Clare, 1907
Adams, Hattie—teacher, Farwell
Adams, Joseph—pioneer, Winterfield
Adams, Joseph—grocery, Clare
Adams, Leslie W.—WWI, Wise
Adams, R. J.—freight conductor, 1911

Adams, Roy—truck driver, Clare
Adams, Ruby—Farwell, 1914
Adams, Sarah—sold vegetables locally, Clare, 1914
Adams, Thomas—lumberman, Summerfield, 1906
Adams, Wm. L.—mayor, Clare
Adgate, Miss _____—teacher, Clare, 1911
Agle, Landy—farmer, Farwell
Agle, Wm.—1904
Akey, Ernest—Wise, 1918
Akey, Fred—Farwell, 1905
Akey, Peter—Clare, 1918
Albertson, Burleigh—1912
Albertson, J. C.—postmaster, Pennock, 1906
Albertson, John—WWI, Hamilton, 1918
Albertson, Louis—WWI, Harrison
Albright, Rudolph—farmer, Sheridan, 1903
Alderton, Salom—Clare, 1908
Alderton, G. A.—Surrey
Aldrich, Rev.—Harrison, 1915
Aldrich, Andrew—Harrison, 1903
Aldrich, Asa—publisher, Clare Co. School Commissioner, Harrison
Aldrich, C. N.—billiard hall, Clare
Aldrich, W. E.—insurance, Harrison
Alexander, Russell—WWI, Clare
Alger, Anna—Clare, 1915
Alger, Belle—Clare, 1908
Alger, Bessie—Clare, 1910
Alger, Byron—farmer, actor, Clare
Alger, Edgar—teacher, 1903
Alger, Ethel—Clare, 1900
Alger, Henry—lumberman, 1900
Alger, George—Clare, killed 1908
Alger, Isabella—hotel cook, Clare
Alger, H.—Clare, 1903
Alger, James—farmer, painter, Grant
Alger, Russell—Clare, 1900
Alkema, Hiram—pioneer, RFD carrier, Austa
Allard, James—Summerfield, 1917
Allbee, Arthur—mill hand, Leota
Allbee, Frank—Leota, 1909
Allbee, G. W.—Farwell
Allbe, Lloyd—laborer, Clare
Allby, L.—WWI, 1917
Alldread, Floyd—teacher, Clare
Allen, Aaron—Grant
Allen, Adron—Farwell, 1904

Allen, Albert—Civil War Vet, Vernon
Allen, Albert—farmer, Sheridan
Allen, Alice—Colonville, 1908
Allen, Armstrong—thresher, 1903
Allen, Bernice—teacher, 1918
Allen, Bert—W. Grant, 1906
Allen, Bessie—Eagle, 1905
Allen, Charles—Clare
Allen, Clayton—farmer, Arthur
Allen, Clyde—farmer, Wise, 1914
Allen, Dewey—farmer, Vernon
Allen, Donald—1921
Allen, Edgar—farmer, Isabella
Allen, Elmer—Grant, 1903
Allen, Elton—stockbuyer, Clare
Allen, Emma—Eagle, 1901
Allen, Ernest—WWI, wounded, A.E.F.
Allen, Eugene—farmer, WWI, Vernon, Sheridan
Allen, Everett—Sheriff, Grant
Allen, E. W.—farmer, Loomis, 1900
Allen, Florence—Colonville, 1908
Allen, Floyd—WWI, Clare
Allen, "Fon"—grocer, Clare, 1912
Allen, Frank—Clare
Allen, Fred—Eagle Area, 1908
Allen, Fred, Jr.—Eagle
Allen, Glen—Vernon, 1900
Allen, Grace—Arthur, 1903
Allen, H. B.—real estate, Clare
Allen, Herbert—Clare
Allen, Hugh—livery, Clare, 1914
Allen, Ida—1914
Allen, Irene—teacher, Sheridan, 1914
Allen, J. A.—grocer, Clare
Allen, James—farmer, Sheridan
Allen, Jennie—Eagle, 1901
Allen, Jesse—publisher, Harrison
Allen, J. D.—Vernon, 1900
Allen, J. D.—Clare
Allen, John—farmer, Sheridan
Allen, John—WWI, 1918
Allen, John—Garfield, 1914
Allen, J. S.—ashery, Clare, 1910
Allen, Joseph—Hamilton, 1912
Allen, Josephine—Grant
Allen, Leander—pioneer, Farwell
Allen, Lydia—Vernon, 1903
Allen, May—Clare, 1910
Allen, Maida—Eagle, 1905
Allen, Mourice—Grant, 1917
Allen, Norma—Clare

Allen, Norman—Eagle, 1914
Allen, Rev. R. A.—Arthur, 1914
Allen, Ray—Clare, 1900
Allen, Rexford—Clare
Allen, Roy—WWI, Temple, 1909
Allen, Ruby—Clare, 1915
Allen, S.—Grant, 1906
Allen, Sam—Farwell, 1918
Allen, Sara—Garfield, 1911
Allen, Scott—Grant
Allen, Shirley—Clare
Allen, Squire—1917
Allen, T.—Hamilton, 1906
Allen, Wm.—farmer, Vernon, 1903
Allen, Wm.—WWI, Vernon
Allen, Wm.—Grant, 1881
Alley, Bert—attorney, Garfield, 1905
Alley, C. R.—farmer, Garfield
Alley, F. C.—Garfield, 1906
Alley, Walter—barber, Lake, 1907
Alley, W. J.—farmer, Garfield
Allman, George—Surrey, 1918
Allman, Goldie—secretary, Surrey
Allman, H. B.—farmer, Surrey
Allman, Roswell—Surrey, 1917
Altenberg, Henry—Redding, 1917
Altschwager, Robert—tailor, Clare
Alverson, S. D.—Winterfield, 1906
Alward, D. E.—reading clerk of U.S. House of Rep., Secretary Central Rep. Comm., attorney, Clare
Alward, George—Arthur
Alward, Gertude—teacher, Clare
Alward, Hazel—teacher, Clare
Alwood, Annias—Arthur, 1905
Alward, Dolph—Hatton, 1911
Alwood, Floy—Browns Corners
Alwood, John—WWI, Hatton
Alwood, Russell—railroad, Hatton
Alwood, Warren—Arthur, 1900
Alwood, Wayne—Arthur, 1917
Alwood, Wm.—farmer, Arthur
Alwood, Wm.—Hatton, 1910
Amble, Charles—teacher, Harrison
Amble, Elmer—AEF, Hamilton
Amble, Ole—Hamilton, 1905
Amble, Seaver—sheriff, Harrison
Amble, Trygue—farmer, Hamilton
Ambrosier, A. M.—farmer, Surrey
Ambrosier, Reynold—WWI, Surrey
Ammon, Wm.—Leota, 1912
Amsden, Mrs. _____—Harrison
Amy, Glen—WWI
Ancel, Wm.—Frost, 1917
Ancompaugh, James—Clare, 1912
Anderson, Earl—mechanic, Clare
Anderson, E. A.—druggist, Clare, 1906
Anderson, Ethel—Clare
Anderson, Frances—Clare
Anderson, J. A.—farmer, Arthur
Anderson, Jean—Clare
Anderson, John—farmer, Sheridan
Anderson, Lelia—1911
Anderson, Lynn—Brand
Anderson, N.—Clare, 1903
Anderson, Wm.—farmer
Anderson, Octavia—Clare
Anderson, Wm.—farmer, Civil War Dover, 1900

Andrews, A. T.—Surrey, 1906
Andrews, Dan—Garfield, 1913
Andrews, Don—Lake, 1915
Andrews, Erve—Crooked Lake
Andrews, Ethel, Farwell Milling Shop, 1912
Andrews, Gerald—farmer, Clare
Andrews, John—Garfield, 1916
Andrus, Arthur—killed by lightning 1913
Andrus, Enoch—publisher, Clare
Andrus, Seymour—WWI, mayor of Clare
Angel, Joseph—Hayes
Anger, Allen—Surrey, 1906
Anger, George—farmer, Clare
Anger, Herbert—WWI, Frost, 1917
Anger, John—WWI
Ankney, DuLuah—Arthur, 1915
Ankney, John—farmer, Civil War Vet, Clare
Ankney, John—Arthur, 1915
Ankney, Kenneth—Arthur, 1915
Ankney, Mary Ann—1912
Ankney, Noble—Arthur, 1915
Ankrum, Ivan—driller, Clare
Ansil, John—WWI, Harrison
Ansil, Will—Long Lake, 1918
Antcliff, Henry—Harrison, 1908
Apel, Chester—Greenwood, 1917
Applebee, Cyrus—farmer, Sheridan
Applebee, F. R.—Sheridan, 1986
Applegate, Rev. F. W.—M-E minister, Harrison
Arbuckle, W. J.—Meredith, 1903
Archambeault, Charles—Harrison
Archamboult, Clara—1908
Archambeault, Clarence—Greenwood
Archamboult, G. A.—grocer, Clare
Archambeault, Hazel—teacher, Harrison, 1907
Archambeault, Jennings—salesman
Archambeault, John—Harrison
Archambeault, Maggie—Harrison
Archambeault, Michael—Clare, 1907
Archambeault, Robert—farmer
Archambeault, Robert, Jr.—mechanic and car dealer, WWI
Archambeault, Wm., Jr.—Clare
Archambeault, Wm.—1900
Archbold, A. J.—Vernon, 1918
Archer, Robert—farmer, Vernon
Armentrout, _____—Eagle, 1914
Armour, Elva—Clare
Armour, Mary—Sheridan, 1910
Armour, John—farmer, Sheridan
Armour, Valmor—mechanic, AEF Clare
Armstrong, Anna—Farwell, 1905
Armstrong, Edward—teacher, WWI Farwell
Armstrong, James—Farwell 1907
Armstrong, John—Vernon, 1886
Armstrong, John—farmer, WWI Vernon
Armstrong, Josephine—teacher Farwell, 1900
Armstrong, Linda—Farwell, 1900
Armstrong, Wm.—Farwell, 1900
Arndt, George—farmer, Arthur
Arnell, Will—Commercial Hotel owner, Beaverton

Arnold, Adelaide—teacher, Clare
Arnold, Albert—Wise, 1907
Arnold, Charles—Farwell, 1903
Arnold, J. C.—Civil War Vet
Arnold, Wm.—farmer, Grant, 1900
Arrand, James—Vernon, 1912
Arrand, Charles—Clare, 1913
Arrand, Charles, Jr.—Clare, 1914
Arrand, Gladys—Clare, 1917
Arrand, Harry—Clare
Arrand, James—carpenter, Clare
Arrand, James, Jr.—carpenter
Arrand, Martha—Clare, 1913
Arrand, Oral—delivery man, Clare
Arrand, Samuel—1913
Arrand, Thomas—livery, 1915
Arthur, Robert—farmer, Gilmore
Artcliffe, Edward—Greenwood
Artcliff, Mabel—1900
Artcliff, Wm.—railroad, Clare
Artcliff, Wm. C.—1922
Arthur, Moses—Winterfield, 1916
Artibee, Alex—teacher, Winterfield, 1903
Artibee, Anna—teacher, Winterfield, 1904
Artibee, Donald—pumper, Clare
Artibee, Joseph—farmer, Winterfield
Artibee, Moses—farmer, Winterfield
Artibee, Ralph—accountant, Clare
Artley, Mattie—Clare, 1900
Ash, Dr. H. L.—physician, Clare
Ash, M. J.—Clare, 1887
Ash, W. L.—Clare
Aschard, Tony—Freeman Twp.
Ashley, Idella—Clare
Ashton, Osmer—Franklin, 1914
Asline, Andrew—Clare, 1918
Asline, John—Clare, 1900
Asline, Dr. Norris—physician, Clare
Assamann, Henry—insurance broker, Clare
Athey, Fred—Arthur, 1907
Athey, George—Arthur, 1916
Athey, James—farmer, Arthur, 1906
Athey, Jennie—1909
Athey, John—farmer, Arthur, 1906
Athey, Wm.—Arthur, 1906
Atkinson, George—1916
Attwood, Chas.—teacher, Clare
Attwood, Warren—polisher, Clare
Aucompaugh, Ernest—A.A.R.R., baggage clerk, Clare, 1909
Austin, Arthur—Temple, 1917
Austin, Arthur G.—Temple, 1917
Austin, Arthur Z.—Temple
Austin, Clara—Temple
Austin, Cora E.—Temple
Austin, Earl—Harrison
Austin, Floyd—WWI, Temple
Austin, Fred—millhand, Clare
Austin, Henry H.—Temple, 1917
Austin, Jesse—1915
Austin, Melvin—lumberman, deputy sheriff, Clare Co., Civil War Vet, Grant
Austin, O. L.—Pennook, 1909
Austin, Thomas—farmer, Temple
Austin, West—Lake, 1914
Axford, Bert—A.A.R.R., Clare
Axford, Edward—Grant, 1906
Axford, Frank—farmer, Grant, 1900

Bassett, Edward—U.S. Navy, Garfield, 1908
Bassett, Lizzie—Garfield, 1907
Bassett, Rosa—Crooked Lake, 1906
Batch, James L.—WWI
Batch, Joseph—farmer, Arthur
Bates, Charles—farmer, Hamilton
Bates, Chester—farmer, Sheridan
Bates, Rev. Frank—minister
Bates, George—farmer, Arthur
Bates, Iva—Eagle, 1901
Bates, Jennie—Eagle, 1901
Bates, Orville—Eagle, 1901
Bateson, C.—Grant, 1904
Battle, Frank—farmer
Battle, Josephine—teacher, Clare
Battles, Elnora—Clare
Battles, Josephine—Clare, 1911
Battles, Wm.—farmer, Vernon
Bauder, Agnes—Clare
Bauder, Allen—Clare
Bauder, David—farmer, 1885
Bauder, Garet—laundry business
Bauder, Howard—Clare, 1908
Bauder, James Howard—Gilmore
Bauder, John—Clare, 1908
Bauder, Nathan—painter, Clare
Bauder, Robert—Clare, 1915
Bauder, Wm. J.—livery, Grant
Bauer, Carl—WWI, Grant
Bauer, Edward—WWI
Bauer, Fred—farmer, Grant, 1904
Bauer, Fred, Jr.—Grant, 1917
Bauer, Henry—Grant, 1903
Bauer, Joachim—Vernon City
Bauer, John—farmer, Clare, 1905
Bauer, John, Jr.—Clare
Bauer, J.—farmer, Grant, 1906
Bauer, Joseph—Dover, 1904
Bauer, Peter—Randall, 1918
Bauer, Sarah Ann—Clare
Baughman, Jonas C.—Wise, 1917
Baughman, Viola—teacher, Loomis
Bauman, D. C.—WWI, Hayes, 1917
Bawkey, Albert—Gilmore, 1909
Bawkey, Clarence—Gilmore, 1917
Bawkey, James C.—Clare, 1906
Bawkey, James—farmer, Gilmore
Bawkey, Wm.—farmer, Leota, 1909
Baxler, Daniel—lineman, 1908
Baxter, E.—farmer, Grant, 1903
Baxter, Esther J.—Hayes
Bayes, Otho Dale—bakery, Clare
Bayliss, M. George—Winterfield
Beacham, _____—Temple, 1900
Beadie, Randall—Civil War Vet, Clare
Beadle, John—auctioneer, Clare
Beadle, Randall—stock yards, Clare
Beadle, S.—Clare, 1900
Beagle, George—Clare, 1912
Beagle, John—farmer, Farwell
Beagle, John—Clare, 1897
Beal, Earnest—farmer, Vernon
Beale, Cleo—Clare
Beale, Ernest—store
Beale, Gladys—Clare
Beale, Wm.—Clare, 1915
Beam, F. E.—farmer, Harrison
Beamish, Evelyn—Clare
Bearse, W. E.—Eight Point Lake

Landing, Garfield, 1905
Beard, Elmer G.—Freeman, 1910
Beard, George W.—Freeman, 1906
Beard, Guy—WWI, Temple
Beard, Robert—WWI, Freeman
Beatty, Earl—Farwell, 1915
Beatty, Guy—Farwell, 1915
Beatty, Robert—Vernon, 1879
Beatty, Samuel—construction, Vernon, killed 1915
Beatty, Stewart—Farwell, 1900
Beauchamp, Felix—hotel prop., Meredith
Beauchamp, Josie—Harrison, 1907
Beavers, Lester—farmer, Harrison
Beber, Lew—Temple, 1913
Beck, Godfrey—AEF, Garfield
Beck, Horace—Delaney Corners
Beck, John—farmer, Arthur, 1906
Beck, Sam—Ann Arbor R.R., Clare
Beck, Wm.—A & P store mgr., Clare
Becker, Arthur—carpenter, Clare
Becker, Edgar—Clare, 1909
Becker, Edward—Clare, 1903
Becker, John—Hamilton, 1915
Becker, Louis—Clare, 1907
Becker, Oliver—R.R. mgr., Clare
Becker, Wm. E.—farmer
Becker, Wm.—Clare, 1910
Beckman, Linas Andrew—1917
Beckwith, A.—Arthur, 1986
Beckwith, S.—farmer, Arthur, 1906
Beckwith, William—farmer, Arthur
Bedin, Charles—Farwell, 1909
Beebe, Abyron—Civil War Vet, Clare, 1910
Beebe, Guy—Grant, 1917
Beebe, Jennie—teacher, Harrison
Beech, Marie—Clare, 1918
Beecham, Rev. D. C.—Evangelical preacher, Clare, 1908
Beeman, E. M.—music professor, Evart, 1900
Beemer, Arthur—Sheridan, 1900
Beemer, Charles—laborer, Clare
Beemer, Oliver—Clare, 1900
Beemer, Robert—Clare
Beer, Alfred—Garfield, 1912
Beers, William—farmer, Sheridan
Beining, Jno—Grandon, 1903
Belcher, Charles—P.M.R.R.
Belcher, Edith—teacher, Farwell
Belcher, Herbert—Lake, 1897
Belcher, L.—farmer, Gilmore, 1910
Belcher, Stephen—Farwell, 1912
Beldin, Charles—minister, Farwell
Beldin, Rev. O. N.—Cong. minister
Belknap, Frank—laborer, Clare
Bell, Dr.—physician, druggist, Harrison, 1910
Bell, Alice—teacher, Sheridan
Bell, Cora—Clare, 1900
Bell, Ernest—driller, Clare
Bell, Rev. E. Frazer—minister
Bell, Florence—Clare, 1900
Bell, George—Wise, 1917
Bell, Ira—Surrey, 1912
Bell, James—hotel, livery, Temple
Bell, John—Sheridan, 1915
Bell, Kate—teacher, Sheridan
Bell, L. H.—Clare

Bell, Mae—Vernon, 1910
Bell, Minnie—Sheridan, 1900
Bell, Murney—farmer, Sheridan
Bell, Thomas—farmer, Sheridan
Belling, Carl—pioneer, farmer
Belling, Paul—Grant, 1906
Belling, Seymour—Grant, 1914
Bellinger, Alma—teacher, Farwell
Bellinger, Arthur—W Grant, 1917
Bellinger, Emma—teacher, Farwell
Bellinger, Ida—Vernon, 1914
Bellinger, Ira—R.R. mgr., Grant
Bellinger, Jay—mail carrier, WWI, Farwell
Bellinger, Rufus—W. Grant, 1900
Bellows, Ralph—lineman, Clare
Beltnick, Roy—store mgr., Clare
Bement, J. H.—Clare
Bender, Clyde—farmer, Arthur
Bender, C. F.—Sheridan, 1906
Bender, Daniel—Arthur, 1900
Bender, Frank—Arthur, 1918
Bender, Henry—Temple, 1906
Bender, Katie—Grandon, 1904
Bender, Orville—farmer, Arthur
Bender, Wm.—1915
Bendon, Wm.—Harrison, 1916
Benn, John—lumberman, Garfield
Benn, Noah—lumberman, Garfield
Benner, A.—farmer, Sheridan, 1906
Benner, G.—insurance, Clare, 1900
Bennet, Alonzo—truck driver
Bennett, Audrey—1910
Bennett, Charles—Clare, 1910
Bennett, Don—5 Lakes, 1905
Bennett, Herman—teacher, Sheridan, 1910
Bennett, Jeremiah—farmer
Bennett, Jerry, Jr.—Sheridan, 1918
Bennett, John—Sheridan, 1918
Bennett, Rev. Lyman—M.E. minister, Isabella, 1905
Bennett, Mary—Sheridan, 1908
Bennett, Philip—publisher, teacher, superintendent Clare Schools
Bennett, Robert—Sheridan, 1915
Bennett, Rev. Thomas—Cong. pastor, Clare, 1916
Bennett, Rev. T. Porter—minister
Benson, Dewey, Clare, 1910
Benson, W. H.—Harrison, 1916
Bentley, Claude—8 Point Lake
Bentley, Harley—WWI, Garfield
Bentley, Libbie—Garfield, 1905
Bentley, Lyman—Garfield, 1904
Benton, Wilbur—Temple, 1903
Berdan, Leslie—Greenwood, 1906
Bergey, Bert—Loomis, 1914
Bergey, Earl—Wise, 1917
Bergey, Floyd—creamery, produce dealer, Clare
Bergey, Henry—Leota, 1917
Bergey, John—businessman, Loomis
Bergey, LeRoy—WWI
Bergey, Lincoln—farmer, Wise
Bergey, Mash—Loomis, 1914
Bergey, Ray—WWI, Wise
Bergey, Theodore—baker, 1912
Bergey, Vernel—painter, Clare
Bergey, Warren—Loomis, 1917
Bergey, Wm. Henry—WWI, Leota
Berkompas, A.—Winterfield, 1903

Bernier, W. J.— Clare
Bernthall, Rev. Leonard—minister
Berry, A. E.—clerk, Clare, 1919
Berry, James—Clare, 1911
Berry, L. W.—Freeman, 1914
Bersette, Ernest—A.A.R.R.
Bersette, Ervin—AEF, Harrison
Bersette, George—teacher, WWI
    Harrison
Bersette, Loren—Hamilton, 1909
Bertrand, Philip—attorney, Clare
Besant, Roy—Clare
Bessie, Cyrus—farmer, Arthur, 1906
Bessie, Jess—farmer, Arthur, 1906
Beyargeon, _____—Vernon, 1913
Bezze, Walter—Leota, 1915
Bicknell, Alice—Clare
Bicknell, Don—Clare, 1917
Bicknell, Frank—physician, Clare
Bicknell, James—banker, Clare
Bicknell, J. Stuart—banker, Clare
Bicknell, Josephine—Clare
Bicknell, Mark—banker, Clare
Bicknell, Nathan—businessman,
    Clare, 1874
Bicknell, Willard—businessman
Bicknell, Wm. H.—merchant, Clare
Bidwell, Bernie—Clare, 1915
Bidwell, Eula—Clare, 1907
Bidwell, Neil—Clare, 1903
Bidwell, M. E.—Clare, 1903
Bidwell, Neil—Clare, 1903
Biebush, Dora—Vernon, 1915
Bier, Wm.—1911
Bierly, George—Lake George, 1915
Bierly, Laurence—Lincoln, 1918
Bigelow, Erastus—farmer
Bigford, Caroline—Farwell, 1907
Bigford, John—Summerfield
Bigford, Wm.—Surrey, 1906
Bigley, Alexander—WWI
Bigley, Catherine—1915
Bigley, Jesse—A.A.R.R., Clare
Bilgren, Anton—WWI
Bilgren, Lillian—Lake George, 1916
Bilgren, Nils—farmer, Lincoln, 1906
Billings, Bert—Summerfield, 1917
Billington, Martha—Wise, 1911
Bilsky, Orval—Summerfield, 1915
Bingham, C. E.—farmer, hardware,
    Farwell, 1906
Bingham, Charles—hotel, Harrison
Bingham, Clare—1915
Bingham, Edith—Farwell, 1904
Bingham, Edward—Harrison, 1900
Bingham, Fred—mechanic, Farwell
Bingham, Rachel—Harrison
Bingham, Roy—WWI
Bingham, Sylvia—Harrison, 1917
Bingham, T. F.—Farwell, 1903
Bingley, Alexander—Harrison, 1917
Bingston, Herbert—Clare, 1910
Bird, E.—Temple, 1904
Birdsall, Albert—Clare
Birdsall, Chester—Greenwood, 1906
Birdsall, Elmer—Garfield, 1912
Birdsall, Glenn—Grant, 1917
Birdsall, Leo—WWI
Birdsall, Loren—1918
Birdsall, O. A.—Harrison
Birdsall, Rev. S. W.—farmer,
    minister, Greenwood, 1906

Bishop, Arthur—Clare, 1906
Bishop, George—farmer, 1905
Bitler, Charles—farmer, Hamilton
Bitler, Fern—Hamilton, 1915
Bitler, Joseph—farmer, Hamilton
Bitler, Joseph—AEF
Bitler, Lee—Hamilton, 1917
Bitler, Mae—1914
Bitler, Tilman Lee—Hamilton, 1917
Bitler, Wm.—farmer, Hamilton
Bitzer, Ralph—Wise, 1917
Black, Byron—AEF
Black, Ella—Farwell, 1909
Black, Ellis—Sheridan, 1912
Black, Maurice—attorney, Harrison
Black, Myrtle—1913
Blackburn, A. Lindsey—jeweler
Blackledge, Arthur—Winterfield
Blackledge, Cliff—sheep farmer
Blackledge, Eleanor—teacher
Blackledge, Frank—principal of
    Farwell, Winterfield, 1909
Blackledge, K.—farmer, 1918
Blackledge, Robert—Grandon, 1903
Blackledge, Sherman—1907
Blain, Franklin—farmer, Sheridan
Blain, Franklin, Jr.—Clare, 1907
Blain, Jim—Freeman, 1913
Blain, Steve—Freeman, 1914
Blain, Wm.—Freeman, 1914
Blain, Wm.—Clare, 1908
Blaine, E. L.—Sheridan, 1906
Blaine, Levi—Sheridan, 1905
Blair, Wm.—R.R. brakeman, Clare
Blake, Wm.—Redding, 1904
Blakesley, Charles—blacksmith
Blanchard, Cecil—barber, Clare
Blanchard, George—Farwell, 1916
Blanken, Cornelius—Clare, 1914
Blanken, John—bakery, Clare, 1914
Blashfield, L. I.—millwright, Clare
Blegan, John—Winterfield, 1908
Blevins, Gertude—teacher, Marion
Bleiss, Charles—Grant
Blender, Barnett—optometrist
Blett, E. B.—publisher, Farwell
Blinco, Wm.—farmer, Arthur, 1906
Bliss, Aaron T.—Clare, 1908
Bliss, C. N.—Sheridan, 1906
Bloom, John—Garfield, 1918
Blue, Charles—Hamilton, 1914
Blue, Wm.—Temple, 1903
Blum, Ben—Arthur, 1915
Blystone, Aura—Arthur, 1903
Blystone, Glen—Sheridan, 1914
Blystone, Juddie—Arthur, 1909
Blystone, Orson—Sheridan, 1901
Bodine, Rev. W. H.—minister
Bodkins, Charles—farmer, WWI
Bodkins, Hazel E.—Clare, 1910
Bodkins, John—farmer, Clare
Bodkins, J. B.—Sheridan, 1906
Bodley, F. W.—Redding, 1906
Bogan, Alice—Vernon, 1915
Bogan, George—Vernon, 1909
Bogan, H. H.—farmer, Hayes, 1900
Bogan, Marie—Clare
Bogan, Richard—superintendent,
    Clare Schools, 1909
Bogan, Thomas—farmer, Gilmore
Bogardus, Cornelius—Clare, 1873
Bogardus, Hilda—Clare, 1913

Bogardus, Simon—merchant, Clare
Bogue, Charles—farmer, Vernon
Bogue, H. H.—merchant, Harrison
Bogue, H. N.—Hayes, 1906
Bolan, Jess Ray—Grand, 1917
Boland, J.—Sheridan, 1906
Bolen, David—Vernon, 1911
Bolen, Edward
Bolen, James—pioneer, Vernon
Bolen, Thomas
Bolin, George—Greenwood, 1906
Bolle, Charles
Bolle, Cyriel—Clare
Bolle, Rene—farmer, Wise
Bolle, Walter—Wise
Bolton, F.—Hatton, 1906
Bolton, Orton—Harrison
Bolton, Silas—Hatton, 1906
Bolton, Nesley—farmer, Hatton
Bond, Emma—Leota, 1918
Bond, Fred—farmer,,Leota, 1906
Bond, Percy—WWI, Summerfield
Bond, Wm.—Arthur, 1915
Bone, Francis—farmer
Boner, Edgar—farmer, Arthur, 1906
Bonham, Charles—WWI
Bonnell, Albert—baker
Bonsing, Jacob—Surrey, 1917
Boody, George—farmer, Gilmore
Booth, Gladys—Arthur, 1908
Boots, Delos—Harrison, 1914
Boots, Peter—farmer, Harrison
Borah, C. R.—Winterfield, 1918
Bordel, Charles—Temple, 1904
Border, Allen—Vernon, 1912
Border, David—Vernon, 1912
Border, Frankie—Rosebush, 1917
Border, John—Clare
Border, Robert—Clare, 1917
Border, Seymour—Vernon, 1917
Border, W. J.—Clare, 1917
Borken—farmer, Sheridan
Born, Glen—chiropractor, Clare
Borst, Emma—Lake George, 1916
Borst, J. R.—merchant, Lake
    George, 1900
Borst, Mary—Lincoln, 1915
Borst, Susan—Lake George, 1914
Bostain, D. W.—Greenwood, 1912
Bostain, Lillian—Greenwood, 1918
Bothwell, C. C.—rancher, Lincoln
Boucher, Arthur—farmer, livery
Boucher, Harry—Garfield, 1915
Bouchey, Albert—WWI
Bouchey, Alfred—Vernon, 1912
Bouchey, Claud—Vernon, 1917
Bouchey, Gilbert—Vernon, 1912
Bouchey, Henry—grocery clerk
Bouchey, John—laborer, 1914
Bouchey, Willie—Clare, 1907
Bouck, Ira—Clare, 1907
Bouck, Oscar—livery stable, Clare
Boughton, _____—Clare, 1918
Boughton, Sybil—teacher, E. Grant
Boulter, Ethel—Harrison, 1907
Boulter, Florence—Harrison, 1903
Boulter, Jennie—Harrison
Boulton, Benna—Hatton, 1910
Boulton, Earnest—Harrison, 1934
Boulton, Frank—farmer, Hatton
Boulton, Ortho—farmer, Harrison
Boulton, Wesley—farmer, Hatton

Bowen, _____—Temple, 1913
Bowen, Flora—Clare, 1900
Bowen, John R.—Wise, 1917
Bowen, Willard—sawmill, Wise
Bowen, Wm.—pioneer, sawmill, farmer, Wise
Bower, Wm., Jr.—Wise, 1900
Bowen, George—Clare, 1909
Bower, Clinton—cigar maker
Bower, Fred—Clare
Bower, Glen—1917
Bower, Oliver—farmer, Grant, 1914
Bowerman, J. A.—farmer, Sheridan
Bowers, Frank—telephone co. mgr.
Bowler, Ellis—attorney, Clare
Bowler, Joseph—lawyer, Grant
Bowler, Margaret—Clare
Bowler, Patrick—lumberman
Bowler, Theodore—mail clerk, Grant, 1906
Bowler, Theodore—attorney, Clare
Bowler, Wm.—teacher, Clare, 1903
Bowne, Kendall—Clare
Bowne, MacLyn—Clare
Boyd, Fred—Ann Arbor R.R.
Boyd, Byron—R.R. conductor
Boyd, George—teacher, Clare, 1929
Boyd, James—merchant, Clare
Boyer, Edwin—Greenwood, 1909
Boyl, Rev. Elliott—minister, Clare
Boyle, Firman—farmer, Wise, 1918
Boyle, James—Clare, 1901
Boynton, O. L.—Clare, 1900
Bracey, Alice—Farwell, 1904
Bracey, D.—Harrison, 1907
Bracey, Dr. E. E.—physician
Bracey, Wm.—Negro, 1908
Brackett, Walter—WWI
Bradford, livery barn, Farwell, 1910
Bradford, Robert—Clare, 1917
Bradley, Angus—farmer, Grant
Bradley, Arthur—farmer, Grant
Bradley, Charles—Temple, 1909
Bradley, Clarence—Temple, 1908
Bradley, David—Temple
Bradley, E.—Clare, 1915
Bradley, Frank—Temple, 1918
Bradley, Fremont—Clare, 1903
Bradley, Harry—farmer, Clare
Bradley, Harold—farmer, Clare
Bradley, James—Loomis, 1900
Bradley, Paul—ticket agent, Clare
Bradley, Wm.—farmer, Sheridan
Bradshaw, C. E.—P.M. ticket agent
Bradt, Angus—Crooked Lake, 1906
Bradt, Lillian—Winterfield, 1903
Brady, George—1914
Brady, J.—meat market, Farwell
Brand, John—lumberman, Arthur
Brandon, John—farmer, Hatton
Brangon, C. W.—Winterfield, 1906
Brant, Charles—Leota, 1907
Brasington, C. L.—Farwell
Brasington, Glen—Vernon, 1917
Braisington, Jesse—farmer, Farwell
Brasington, M.—farmer, Clare
Branstettler, Charles—sheep rancher
Brasington, S. G.—farmer, Gilmore
Brazee, Walter E.—WWI
Braun, Bruno—Arthur, 1917
Braunstein, Samuel A.—Clare
Brayman, Arthur—R.R. brakeman

Brazee, Lory—farmer, Greenwood
Brazee, Martha—Greenwood, 1906
Brazett, Louis—farmer, Hayes
Brazie, Alfred—musician, Clare
Breed, (Chan.)—Farwell, 1900
Breese, Verna—Clare, 1918
Brezee, Walter—AEF, Hayes
Breeze, Wilfred—Clare, 1905
Breningstall, Jess—Temple, 1903
Bremer, O.—Hayes, 1906
Breningstall, Jess—Temple, 1903
Bretz, Paul—bank clerk, Clare
Brewer, Addison—lumberman
Brewer, Edith—teacher, Clare, 1900
Brewer, Elias—pioneer, Grandon
Brewer, Japirus—Vernon, 1918
Brewer, Ernest—Herrick, 1900
Brewer, Fred—farmer, Grant, 1901
Brewer, Henry—Clare, 1935
Brewer, Lena—farm, Clare
Brewer, Morty—farmer, Herrick
Brief, Daniel—Clare
Brief, Ira—Clare, 1914
Brief, Irene—Clare, 1915
Briggs, Ephrium—WWI U.S. Navy
Briggs, H. E.—farmer, Arthur
Briminstool, Ed—Garfield, 1915
Bringham, Edward—engineer, 1918
Bringham, Milton—carpenter, Frost
Bringman, Vera—Long Lake, 1912
Bringold, Amiel—Greenwood, 1915
Bringold, Arnold—farmer
Bringold, Carl—Harrison, 1910
Bringold, Christ—Greenwood, 1913
Bringold, Emil—WWI
Bringman, Milton—farmer
Bristol, Hiram—Norway Lake, 1900
Bristol, Oscar—Hayes, 1916
Broadbeck, F.—1908
Brock, Walter—Summerfield, 1912
Brockway, Harry—1916
Brockway, R.—lumberman, Hatton
Broderick, C. F.—telephone co.
Broderick, Frank—bakery, Clare
Broderick, Lola—Clare, 1919
Broderick, W. F.—merchant, Clare
Brodie, Alex—Clare, 1909
Brodie, Warren—Farwell, 1916
Bromson, David—Clare, 1903
Bronson, Frank—Clare, 1912
Brooks, Mrs. B.—Grant, 1909
Brooks, Charles—clerk, Clare
Brooks, Elmer—1910
Brooks, Ephriam—farmer, 1903
Brooks, Frank—Harrison, 1916
Brooks, Isabelle—1903
Brooks, John W.—1903
Brooks, John—Hayes
Brooks, J. W.—Grant, 1906
Brooks, Lucille—Clare
Brooks, Richard—Vernon, 1911
Brooks, Rozel—1918
Brooks, Ruth—Grant, 1909
Brooks, S.—Sheridan, 1906
Brooks, Thomas—R.R., Garfield
Brooks, W. N.—Sheridan
Brow, Hiram—Temple, 1915
Brown, Bertha—teacher, Harrison
Brown, Bert—Temple, 1909
Brown, Bessie—Farwell, 1917
Brown, C. H.—real estate, Temple
Brown, Carl—Harrison, 1914

Brown, Chas.—Garfield, 1886
Brown, Charles—Temple, 1914
Brown—mail carrier, RFD, Clare
Brown, Clyde—school teacher
Brown, Dan—8 Point Lake, 1919
Brown, Donald—Garfield, 1917
Brown, Dorr—Redding, 1900
Brown, Dott—Leota, 1903
Brown, Elizabeth—Grant, 1909
Brown, Ernest—postmaster, Farwell
Brown, Forrest—Frost, 1917
Brown, Frank—drayman, Clare
Brown, Franklin—Clare, 1914
Brown, Dr. Freeman—druggist
Brown, George—barber, Clare
Brown, Hazel—Clare, 1918
Brown, Henri—Clare, 1919
Brown, Henry—carpenter, Civil War Vet, 1909
Brown, Henry—Hatton, 1914
Brown, H. R.—Clare
Brown, Hiram—farmer, Temple
Brown, Hiram—farmer, Freeman
Brown, Howard—AEF, Clare
Brown, Hugh—Gilmore, 1917
Brown, Irving—Clare
Brown, James—mail carrier, Clare
Brown, J. O.—Garfield, 1918
Brown, James—Farwell, 1909
Brown, John—farmer, Garfield
Brown, John—teacher, Temple
Brown, John—sheriff, Harrison
Brown, John—RFD carrier
Brown, John—gas station owner
Brown, Joseph—Winterfield, 1913
Brown, K. W.—Farwell, 1917
Brown, Laura—teacher, Clare
Brown, Leonard—Clare
Brown, L. S.—Farwell
Brown, Lester—Clare, 1903
Brown, Lewis—Mannsiding, 1909
Brown, Lloyd—Clare, 1909
Brown, Mathew—city mail carrier
Brown, M. Clyde—teacher, 1908
Brown, Methvan—teacher
Brown, Minnie—Garfield, 1911
Brown, Morris—Grant, 1902
Brown, Nathan—well driller
Brown, N. J.—president, Central Gas Co., Mt. Pleasant, 1917
Brown, Norman—Greenwood, 1917
Brown, Ozro—Harrison, 1907
Brown, Perry—farmer, Grant, 1901
Brown, Ralph—farmer, WWI, Vernon, 1914
Brown, Ray—Sheridan, 1903
Brown, Robert—Gilmore, 1917
Brown, Robert—Vernon, 1917
Brown, Rosa—teacher, Sheridan
Brown, Roy—Clare
Brown, Silas—farmer, Hatton, 1906
Brown, Susie—Farwell, 1909
Brown, Susan—Clare, 1918
Brown, Thomas—farmer, Vernon
Brown, Tom—gas station
Brown, Varnum—Civil War Vet, Sheridan, 1900
Brown, Verne—farmer, Sheridan
Brown, Wm.—farmer, 1905
Brown, W. W.—the locomotive engineer in the Civil War's great locomotive chase,

Farwell, 1907
Brown, Walter—auto mechanic
Brown, W. R.—Harrison, 1910
Brown, Wright—farmer, Sheridan
Brown, Wyatt—Vernon, 1908
Browne, McKinley—Harrison, 1900
Browne, Theodore—Tonkin, 1904
Browne, Garfield—teacher
Brown, Wm.—Circuit Court
Brownell, Adelphia—Hatton
Brownell, Benjamin—WWI, Clare
Brownell, Charles—Clare, 1904
Brownell, Robert—Grant, 1917
Brownsell, Fred—Summerfield
Brownson, Frank—Clare, 1903
Bruce, Albert—Greenwood, 1918
Bruce, B.—Temple, 1914
Bruce, E.—Greenwood, 1906
Bruce, Edward—city engineer
Bruce, Ernest—Greenwood, 1917
Bruce, Irene—Greenwood, 1903
Bruce, J. W.—Greenwood, 1918
Bruce, Leo—Greenwood, 1917
Bruce, Lila—Greenwood, 1916
Bruce, R. W.—hotel, Temple, 1906
Bruce, Samuel—foreman of the
    Ford Farm, Greenwood, 1906
Bruce, Stanley—Greenwood, 1917
Bruce, Thomas—gasoline agent,
    WWI, Harrison
Bruckart, Elmer—Vernon, 1917
Bruckart, George—1899
Bruckart, Martin—farmer, Sheridan
Bruckart, W. H.—1916
Bruckart, Marie—Clare
Bruckart, W. H.—Clare
Bruckner, E. E.—store, Farwell
Brunni, Samuel—farmer, Hamilton
Bruno, Braun—WWI
Bruno, Charles—WWI
Brush, Clarence—laborer, Clare
Bruske, Bertha—Grant, 1900
Bruske, Clara—teacher, Clare, 1900
Bruske, D.—Farwell, 1907
Bruske, Louise—music teacher
Bryan, Almon L.—farmer
Bryan, Charles—Arthur, 1908
Bryan, Dresdan—farmer, Garfield
Bryan, Nellie—teacher, Arthur
Bryant, Elsie—Dover, 1903
Bryan, George—farmer, Arthur
Bryan, Nellie—Arthur, 1911
Bryant, George—blacksmith, Dover
Bryant, George, Jr.—blacksmith
Bryant, Laura—Clare, 1915
Bryne, Edward—1901
Buch, Christina—Harrison
Buckhart, C.—Clare, 1906
Budd, C. F.—pioneer, Greenwood
Budd, Elvin—Greenwood, 1903
Budd, Frank—Greenwood, 1906
Budd, Fred—farmer, Greenwood
Budd, Hazel—Greenwood, 1915
Budd, Isaac—Hayes, 1912
Budd, Ivona—Greenwood, 1916
Budd, Richard—Greenwood
Budd, Thomas—wagon maker,
    Civil War Vet, Greenwood, 1900
Budd, Wm.—farmer, Greenwood
Buell, Chas.—farmer, Clare, 1903
Buell, Fred—Clare, 1900
Buell, Laura—Clare, 1900

Buell, Mel —Davy Clothing Dept.
Buell, Mildred—Clare, 1900
Buerge, Alvah—Franklin, 1915
Buerge, Arthur—Hamilton, 1915
Buerge, Chris—Hamilton, 1914
Buerge, Cyrus—farmer, Hamilton
Buerge, Ida—Hamilton, 1915
Buerge, Ira—Hamilton, 1914
Buerge, John—Hamilton, 1914
Buerge, Joseph—Hamilton, 1914
Buffham, Aram—Winterfield, 1908
Bufford, D. E.—store owner
Bufford, Dennis—A.A.R.R.
Bullard, Dee—Wise, 1917
Bussis, Wm.—Wise, 1912
Bullock, Rev.—minister, Gilmore
Bulman, Edward—Grandon, 1904
Bulman, F. E.—farmer, Grandon
Bulman, Mathias—Winterfield
Bulman, William—Winterfield
Bump, Ace—grocer, Clare, 1903
Bundy, W. O.—Farwell, 1910
Bunting, John—Hamilton, 1917
Bunto, Ralph—WWI
Bunto, Elizabeth—teacher, Marion
Burch, Mrs. C.—Clare, 1903
Burch, George—farmer, Loomis
Burch, Glen—Sheridan, 1904
Burch, Jesse—WWI
Burch, Lyman—grain produce
Burch, Mahlon—farmer, Sheridan
Burch, Minnie
Burch, Russell—Clare, 1915
Burch, Wm.—Surrey, 1900
Burck, Daniel—Farwell, 1900
Burd, Hiram—Clare, 1907
Burdick, Daniel—Clare, 1906
Burdick, E. F.—funeral director
Burger, Wm.—WWI
Burgess, Floyd—farmer, Gilmore
Burgess, Frank—Gilmore
Burgess, Marcena—Gilmore, 1918
Burgess, Mark—farmer, Gilmore
Burgess, Martin—Winterfield, 1912
Burk, E.—farmer, Sheridan, 1906
Burk, Fred—teacher, Freeman, 1918
Burke, Daniel—Farwell
Burke, Rev. Earnest—minister
Burke, Ed—Farwell, 1900
Burke, Fred—farmer, Garfield
Burke, Malcolm—Farwell, 1900
Burke, Riley—Sheridan, 1911
Burley, Wm.—Surrey, 1906
Barnaby, Homer—1906
Burnell, Vernon—telephone co.
Burnett, Chas—farmer, Greenwood
Burnett, John—Greenwood, 1913
Burnett, W. W.—farmer
Burnette, John—Greenwood, 1917
Burnham, Alton C.—Clare
Burnham, Clarence—Vernon, 1917
Burnham, Loren—Clare, 1908
Burns, Charles—WWI, Frost
Burns, Frank—Temple, 1917
Burns, George—Leota
Burns, Jeremiah—Temple, 1917
Burns, J. S.—Loomis, 1900
Burns, John—Loomis, 1909
Burns, John—Freeman, 1903
Burns, Merlin L.—Temple, 1912
Burns, Robert—merchant, Harrison
Burnside, A. E.—farmer, Hatton

Burr, _____—Hamilton, 1905
Burr, Silas—drug store, Crooked
    Lake
Burrill, Lawrence—Harrison, 1912
Burston, Wm.—drug store, Farwell
Burt, Claud
Burt, M. C.—Clare, 1906
Burton, Burt—Vernon, 1917
Burton, Daniel—farmer, Hatton
Burton, Dayton—Garfield, 1906
Burton, Earl—WWI, Hatton
Burton, Edward—farmer, Garfield
Burton, Emerson—farmer, WWI,
    Hatton
Burton, Frank—Grant, 1903
Burton, George—pioneer, Grant
Burton, R.—Hatton, 1916
Burston, Will—drug store, Farwell
Burton, John—Farwell, 1908
Burwash, Arthur—Loomis, 1904
Burwash, Beatrice—Loomis, 1900
Burwash, Catherine—Loomis
Burwash, Frank—attorney, Loomis
Burwash, Persus—teacher, Loomis
Burwash, Stephen—attorney
Buscard, George—Farwell, 1909
Busche, Fred—Clare
Busche, Wm.—farmer, Loomis
Bush, Cassius—farmer, Freeman
Bush, Harold—teacher, WWI
Bushey, Gilbert—Vernon, 1900
Bushey, J. Henry—clerk, Clare
Bushong, Wm. Henry—WWI
Butcher, George—truck driver
Butler, Jacob—Hamilton, 1911
Butterfield, Frank—shoe cobbler
Butterfield, Mart—timber buyer
Butterfield, Ray—Farwell, 1914
Butterfield, Sam—Farwell, 1908
Buttermore, Al—Summerfield, 1910
Butters, Charles—Grant, 1914
Butters, Clyde—Sheridan, 1917
Butters, Clyde—Sheridan, 1917
Butters, Clyde, Jr.—grocery store,
    WWI, Sheridan
Butters, Frank—Eagle, 1909
Butters, J. W.—farmer, Sheridan
Butters, William—WWI
Butts, Charles—farmer, Franklin
Byba, Albert—Clare, 1915
Byba, Ark—Grant, 1909
Byroads, _____—Gilmore, 1900
Cadwell, Carol—teacher, Temple
Cadwell, Frank—Temple, 1909
Cadwell, Gertie—Temple, 1909
Cadwell, Jason—Temple, 1909
Cadwell, Pearl—Temple, 1903
Cady, Ervin—Vernon, 1917
Cahoon, Arthur—Farwell, 1916
Cahoon, Charles—pioneer
Cahoon, H.—Frost, 1906
Cain, Bertrund—Harrison
Cain, Glen—Clare
Calden, T. A.—Freeman, 1910
Caldwell, Rev. L. N.—minister
Cahhoon, E.—Hamilton, 1906
Calhoun, Leslie—farmer, Beaverton
Calkins, Burton—Clare, 1907
Calkins, C. W.—businessman
Calkins, Charles—WWI, Lincoln
Calkins, Edward—WWI
Calkins, Ervin—Rosebush

Calkins, Florence—Clare
Calkins, Irvin—Grant, 1918
Calkins, James—Clare, 1912
Calkins, J. M.—Farwell, 1912
Calkins, J. W.—hotel, Clare, 1900
Calkins, Lester—Rosebush, 1916
Calkins, Pearl—Farwell, 1912
Calkins, Peter
Call, Wm.—Sheridan, 1903
Callahan, Harry—Lincoln, 1910
Callam, George—farmer, Vernon
Callam, Wm.—lumberman, 1907
Callihan, Gerald—timekeeper, Clare
Callihan, Jesse—1900
Callihan, Lucille—Clare
Callihan, Naomi—Clare
Callihan, Ruth—Clare
Callihan, S. M.—Clare
Cameron, Cain—Temple, 1908
Cameron, Ertha—Temple, 1903
Cameron, Margaret—principal,
    teacher, Clare, 1908
Cameron, Roy A.—Temple, 1918
Cameron, Wm.—Wise, 1905
Camp, W.—farmer, Arthur, 1906
Campbell, Addie—Winterfield, 1903
Campbell, Arba—Mayor, Harrison
Campbell, Archie—Grant, 1904
Campbell, Benjamin—Surrey, 1900
Campbell, D. J.—barber, Harrison
Campbell, David—Harrison, 1908
Campbell, Charles—Harrison, 1917
Campbell, Eva—Harrison, 1903
Campbell, Edgar—Hamilton, 1906
Campbell, Frank—Hamilton, 1917
Campbell, George—Farwell, 1908
Campbell, George—Hamilton, 1917
Campbell, George, Jr.—P.M.R.R.
Campbell, Harry—clerk, WWI,
    Harrison, 1903
Campbell, Henry—mgr. opera
    house, Harrison, 1912
Campbell, Hugh—farmer
Campbell, James—Clare, Leota
Campbell, Jed—Clare
Campbell, John—Hamilton, 1917
Campbell, L. A.—Surrey, 1906
Campbell, Nellie—teacher, Grandon
Campbell, Ore—farmer, Hamilton
Campbell, R. B.—Surrey, 1906
Campbell, Roderick—Surrey, 1906
Campbell, Russell—Temple, 1903
Campbell, T. C.—superintendent
    Clare
Campbell, W. D.—Surrey, 1906
Campbeau, Archie—1910
Campeau, Arthur—Vernon, 1917
Campeau, Arthur—laborer, Clare
Campeau, Arthur, Jr.—farmer
Campeau, Leo—attorney, Clare
Caner, Jerome—Greenwood, 1909
Caner, M. E.—Greenwood, 1910
Caner, Marion—Harrison, 1910
Caner, Martin—farmer, Greenwood
Canfield, A. Ray—publisher, Clare
Canfield, Don—Clare Courier
    publisher, AEF, Clare
Canfield—Helen, Clare
Canfield, Henry—Clare
Canfield—probate judge, Harrison
Canfield, Pearl—Harrison, 1885
Canouts, Wm. S.—Clare, 1910

Capen, Albert—R.R., Clare
Capen, A. P.—Clare, 1915
Capen, Donald—Harrison, 1921
Caple, Reardon—Clare
Caple, Robert—Clare, 1911
Caple, Wm.—real estate, Clare
Capps, Elnora—Garfield, 1914
Carden, John—Lincoln, 1912
Carey, Asa B.—WWI, AEF
Carey, Carrie—farmer, Harrison
Carey, Jasper—farmer, Leota, 1906
Carey, John D.—Vernon, 1912
Carl, Roy—banker, Farwell, 1915
Carlson, Bernice—author, Clare
Carmen, M.—Greenwood, 1906
Carmen, Riley—pool hall, Leota
Carmichael, Angus—Clare, 1905
Carmichael, Duncan—pioneer
Carmichael, Edith—Clare, 1909
Carmon, R.—Greenwood, 1907
Carncross, Arthur—Arthur Twp.
Carncross, Eathl—Clare
Carncross, F. A.—farmer, Sheridan
Carncross, F. A., Jr.—farmer, Clare
Carncross, Frank—Vernon City
Carncross, Henry—1912
Carniff, Carrol—scout for oil co.
Carpenter, Art.—Freeman, 1906
Carpenter, Benjamin—Harrison
Carpenter, Benjamin—shoe repair
Carpenter, Bert—Clare, 1909
Carpenter, Charles—farmer
Carpenter, Charles—Wise, 1917
Carpenter, Edward—WWI
Carpenter, Edward—farmer, Clare
Carpenter, Edwin—Freeman, 1914
Carpenter, Ella—teacher, Farwell
Carpenter, Hope—farmer, Freeman
Carpenter, Joseph H.—physician,
    Civil War Vet, Clare, 1903
Carpenter, John—farmer, Surrey
Carpenter, Leander—Vernon, 1900
Carpenter, Minnie—Hayes
Carpenter, Orlo—Freeman, 1915
Carpenter, R. J.—Freeman, 1906
Carpenter, Stephen—Freeman, 1900
Carpenter, Wm.—Freeman, 1909
Carpenter, Wilmot—WWI, Surrey
Carr, Anita—teacher, Clare, 1914
Carr, Arthur—Sheridan, 1917
Carr, Christie—Arthur
Carr, Claude—laborer, Clare
Carr, David—farmer, 1914
Carr, Frank—1917
Carr, Herbert—farmer, 1888
Carr, Ira—Clare, 1914
Carr, Louise—1914
Carr, Nita—teacher, Clare, 1904
Carr, Richard—Arthur, 1906
Carr, Sarah—Arthur, 1880
Carr, Thomas—farmer, Eagle, 1917
Carr, Walter—farmer, Arthur, 1906
Carrick, Emmett—Wise, 1917
Carrick, Jacob—Wise, 1917
Carrick, Langton—Wise, 1917
Carrier, D. E.—laborer, Sheridan
Carrier, Dorothy—Sheridan, 1916
Carrier, Frank—Vernon, 1913
Carrier, George—Vernon, 1903
Carrier, _____—Clare, 1907
Carrier, Rex—WWI, Sheridan
Carrigan, Ford—Arthur, 1917

Carrow, Dr.—Sheridan, 1900
Carrow, Aaron—farmer, Sheridan
Carrow, Bessie—Sheridan, 1903
Carrow, Nelson—farmer, Sheridan
Carruthers, Faye—Crooked Lake
Carson, James—farmer, Redding
Carson, H. T.—1903
Carson, Robert—real estate,
    Garfield, 1900
Carson, Robert—Greenwood, 1917
Carson, Ross H.—Clare
Carson, William—1916
Carter, Bennett—farmer, Arthur
Carter, H.—Mannsiding, 1918
Carton, Ronald—Farwell, 1908
Cartwright, M. W.—photographer
Caruthers, J.—hotel man, Lake
Case, Edwin—hotel, Farwell, 1900
Case, Horton—Clare
Case, O. W.—Farwell, 1900
Casey, Francis—teacher, Harrison
Casey, Frank—teacher, Harrison
Casey, Jenna—Harrison, 1903
Casey, Joanna—teacher, Harrison
Casey, John—Hayes, 1906
Casey, Joseph—Hayes, 1906
Casey, Katie—teacher, Harrison
Casey, Mazie—teacher, Harrison
Casey, Michael—Hayes, 1906
Casey, Thomas—clerk, Harrison
Casey, Tony—mill hand
Cashin, A. F.—Mud Lake, 1916
Cashin, Lillian—Windermere, 1918
Casner, Leon—r.r. car inspector
Casner, Ione—Clare
Cassady, Claude—D.U.R., Vernon
Cassady, Floyd—farmer, Vernon
Cassady, John—Civil War Vet,
    Vernon
Cassidy, Floyd—Vernon, 1918
Casterline, Clifford—Winterfield
Casterline, Fred—Winterfield, 1919
Casterline, Orrin—WWI
Caswell, Miss G.—teacher, Clare
Caterall, Rev. James—M-E
Catterfield, Carl—lumberman, 1915
Catron, Paul—merchant, Frost
Catt, Wm.—Winterfield, 1906
Causgrove, Edward—mgr.
    telephone co., WWI, 1917
Cavanaugh, James—farmer, Grant
Cavanaugh, John—Grant
Cavanaugh, Leo—WWI, Grant
Cavanaugh, M.—Grant, 1908
Cavanaugh, Rupert—merchant
Cave, Charles—Harrison, 1914
Cea, Frank—Temple, 1903
Cepela, Jerry—Greenwood, 1918
Cepela, Ladislaw—WWI,
    Greenwood, 1917
Chaffee, Prof. C. B.—teacher
Chaffee, Chester—mail carrier, 1902
Chaffer, Clifford—1918
Chaffee, E. S.—merchant
Chaffee, Ellsworth—Clare
Chaffee, Emory—AEF
Chaffee, Floyd—Clare
Chaffee, P. P.—Greenwood, 1906
Chaffee, Russell—Clare
Chaffee, Sidney—Sheridan, 1904
Champman, Bert—farmer, 1916
Chapin, Anna—Winterfield, 1906

Chapin, Edith—teacher, Grandon
Chapin, Ethel—Temple, 1903
Chapin, E. R.—farmer, Grandon
Chapin, Laura—Temple, 1903
Chapin, Marshall—Clare, 1900
Chapin, R. S.—Winterfield
Chapman, Alice—teacher, Clare
Chapman, Edna—1916
Chapman, Eugene—Sheridan, 1904
Chapman, E. O.—superintendent
   of schools, Harrison, 1913
Chapman, Floyd—WWI, U.S. Navy
Chapman, Lloyd—WWI, Farwell
Chapman, Richard—blacksmith,
   lumberman, Sheridan, 1870
Chapman, Wm.—Lake George
Chapple, Alford—superintendent
   of schools, Farwell, 1913
Chapple, Elmer—cobbler, Clare
Chapple, Wm.—Vernon, 1917
Chard, E.—Winterfield, 1900
Charles, Alfred—Loomis, 1899
Charrette, Francis—WWI, Franklin
Charrette, Wesley—WWI, Franklin
Chase, _____—janitor, Harrison
Chase, Forrest—The Oil King, 1912
Chase, Kattie—teacher, 1900
Chatterton, A.—farmer, Arthur
Chester, George—Herrick, 1913
Chester, Walter—farmer, WWI
Childs, C.—Lincoln, 1906
Chisholm, Adam—farmer, Grant
Christian, Wesley—farmer, Lincoln
Christian, Clyde—Redding, 1908
Christian, Wesley—Redding, 1914
Christenson, David—Franklin, 1915
Christenson, Hans—farmer
Christie, Hans—Freeman, 1911
Church, Albert—farmer, Wise, 1913
Church, Charles—farmer, Clare
Church, Charles—laundry, Clare
Church, Dewitt—pioneer, Grandon
Church, George—1903
Church, Leroy—Cloverleaf Farm
Church, M. H.—Cloverleaf Farm
Church, N.—lumberman, Clarence
Church, T. N.—Redding, 1906
Churchill, A.—Hamilton, 1906
Churchill, Lewis—Hamilton, 1909
Churchill, Nelson—farmer
Churchill, Theresa—Hamilton, 1909
Cileax, Charles—Browns Corners
Cimmerer, Fred—AEF, Clare
Cimmerer, Henry—Vernon, 1900
Cimmerer, J. A.—Vernon
Cimmerer, Jessie—Clare, 1905
Cimmerer, Levi—Clare, 1915
Cimmerer, Roy—druggist, Clare
Clapp, E. C.—Harrison, 1910
Clapp, Floyd—Hayes, 1917
Clark, A. S.—Garfield, 1911
Clark, Alfred—farmer, Arthur
Clark, Ava—Clare, 1908
Clark, Benjamin—Clare, 1906
Clark, Bernie—Greenwood, 1916
Clark, C. H.—Temple, 1901
Clark, Chas—Civil War Vet, Maple
   Grove
Clark, Charles—Clare, 1907
Clark, Clifford—A.A.R.R., Clare
Clark, David—ice dealer, Clare
Clark, E.—Grant, 1906

Clark, Edna—teacher, Clare, 1903
Clark, Edward—farmer, Freeman
Clark, Ernest—Summerfield, 1914
Clark, F.—Hatton, 1906
Clark, Flossie—Farwell, 1904
Clark, Floyd—WWI, Garfield
Clark, Fred—farmer, Harrison
Clark, George—farmer, Arthur
Clark, Harold—Clare, 1904
Clark, Helen—Greenwood, 1916
Clark, Hugh—Clare, 1913
Clark, J.—Temple, 1913
Clark, Joseph—Garfield, 1912
Clark, L. D.—Clare, 1907
Clark, Linda—Farwell, 1903
Clark, Lucy—Clare, 1911
Clark, Percy—Clare, 1903
Clark, Percy—farmer, Arthur, 1894
Clark, Ray—AEF, Garfield
Clark, Roy—WWI
Clark, S. M.—Leota, 1906
Clark, Theodore—Clare, 1908
Clark, Thomas—ex-steamboater
Clark, Vera—Garfield, 1910
Clark, Vern—Clare, 1900
Clark, Victor—P.M.R.R., Clare
Clark, Wm.—Greenwood, 1916
Clark, Wm.—farmer, Garfield, 1905
Clarke, Thelma—Greenwood, 1916
Clausohm, H. F.—Elm Grove Store
Clayton, Doris—Vernon, 1913
Clayton, Mabel—Farwell, 1905
Clayton, Wm.—Farwell, 1903
Clegg, Anna—teacher, Clare, 1918
Clements, George—Sheridan, 1903
Clements, Wm.—farmer, Frost
Clete, Chas—Sheridan, 1906
Cleudenen, Andrew—Temple, 1911
Cleveland, Archie—Clare
Cleveland, Bert—mail clerk, Clare
Cleveland, Emily—Harrison, 1914
Cleveland, Harry—farmer, Clare
Cleveland, Ila—Harrison, 1908
Cleveland, Margout—Harrison
Cleveland, N. H.—farmer, Arthur
Cleveland, O. D.—merchant
Cleveland, Wm.—Clare, 1917
Clevenger, J. H.—Redding, 1906
Cline, A. J.—farmer, Farwell
Cline, Bruce—Farwell, 1917
Cline, Close—WWI, Lake
Cline, Dolph—Temple, 1912
Cline, Erma—Surrey, 1907
Cline, Lenwell—WWI, Surrey
Cline, Thomas—1911
Clink, Ernest—Grant, 1900
Clink, Frank—Grant, 1917
Clink, Fred—lumberman, Grant
Clink, Wm.—lumberman, 1903
Clock, Burt—Freeman, 1907
Clore, Mrs. Orpha—Harrison, 1900
Close, Levi—Lake, 1917
Clousolm, _____—Elm Grove store
Cluly, Elwyn—Clare
Clute, Andrew—farmer, 1905
Clute, Arthur—Sheridan, 1913
Clute, Christopher—Civil War Vet,
   Sheridan, 1903
Clute, Elmer—lumberman
Clute, Harold—truck driver
Clute, Irene—Clare, 1915
Clute, James—Clare, 1903

Clute, James—garage, AEF, Clare
Clute, Jay—Colonville, 1900
Clute, Jay—Vernon, 1900
Clute, Morrel—farmer, Sheridan
Clute, Rex—salesman, Harrison
Clute, Dr. Wm.—physician, Clare
Clutter, David—Surrey, 1906
Coats, Gertude—Clare
Coates, Joseph—Arthur, 1915
Coates, Leo—farmer, WWI, Arthur
Coates, Leo—Sheridan, 1909
Coates, Rev. W. J.—M-E minister
Cobleigh, Agnes—1909
Cobleigh, Bernice—Clare
Cobleigh, Donald—laborer, Clare
Cobleigh, Ezra—Vernon, 1917
Cobleigh, Ray—Clare, 1915
Cochrane, Clinton—Sheridan, 1914
Cochran, Clinton—Sheridan, 1918
Cochran, J.—Sheridan, 1906
Cochran, Robert—farmer, Sheridan
Coddington, Robert—Farwell, 1916
Codling, George—farmer, Arthur
Coe, Fred—farmer, Sheridan, 1906
Coe, Sylvia—Clare, 1911
Coffel, Arthur—Farwell, 1918
Coffel, Ed—Hatton, 1910
Coffell, Roy—Hatton, 1910
Coffman, H.—farmer, Arthur, 1913
Coffman, Orville, W.—1899
Cogan, Clarence—farmer, Clare
Cogswell, Eugene—Clare, 1903
Cohee, Alice—Temple, 1890
Cohee, Harry—Greenwood, 1917
Cohen, J.—Surrey, 1914
Coit, Thomas—teamster, Harrison
Colasky, Matthew—Gilmore, 1917
Colasky, Sidney—Lake, 1917
Colburn, F.—farmer, Sheridan
Colburn, Mary—Clare
Colburn, Maude—Clare, 1909
Colby, John—Vernon, 1910
Cole, A. B.—farmer, Sheridan
Cole, Miss _____—teacher, Clare
Cole, Addie—Surrey, 1906
Cole, A. B.—Elm Grove, 1917
Cole, Arthur—knot sawyer, Temple
Cole, Arthur—Summerfield, 1917
Cole, Charles—sawyer, Temple
Cole, Clifford—Elm Grove, 1918
Cole, Collins—Sheridan, 1915
Cole, Frederick—Sheridan, 1917
Cole, George—Clare, 1900
Cole, Laura—teacher, Clare, 1905
Cole, Len—pioneer, Grandon
Cole, Wm.—farmer, Clare, 1912
Cole, W. N.—livery, butcher, Clare
Colgrove, Rev. Will—minister M-E
Collard, James—farmer, 1910
Collard, Lana—Temple
Collard, Myron
Collard, Myron—WWI, Temple
Colley, Frank—Winterfield, 1909
Colley, S. C.—farmer, Surrey, 1906
Collicut, Elsie—organist, Farwell
Collins, Rev. _____—pastor
Collins, A.—Harrison
Collins, Burke—Clare
Collins, George—banker, WWI,
   Clare
Collins, L. H.—farmer, Grandon
Collins, Jason—Wise, 1917

Collins, Oard—AEF, Harrison
Collins, Ullman—oil pumper
Collison, Albert—Wise, 1917
Colman, Amos—1911
Colmus, Genevieve—Clare
Colmus, Jacob—farmer, Grant
Colmus, John—farmer, Grant
Colmus, John
Colmus, Peter—Grant, 1900
Colosky, Earl—farmer, Clare, 1900
Colosky, Matthew—Garfield, AEF
Colosky, Wm.—farmer, Gilmore
Colson, Sarah—Clare, 1900
Colvin, Mary—Civil War Widow
Colwell, L.—Harrison, 1909
Colwell, L. W.—farmer, 8 Point Lk.
Combs, Leslie—Clare, 1894
Comer, David—farmer, Dover
Comer, D. W.—farmer, Hatton
Comer, Herschell—clerk, Eagle
Comer, Kenneth—Clare
Comer, Klebra—farmer, Grant
Comer, Lloyd—Clare, 1909
Comer, Roland—Clare, 1913
Comer, Roy—Clare, 1905
Comer, Roy—oil producer, 1934
Comins, A. L.—P.M.R.R. agent
Comins, Clinton—businessman
Compeau, Archie—Clare
Compeau, Leo—Harrison
Compton, Wallace—Frost, 1918
Compton, Floyd—WWI, Clare
Compton, Wallace—farmer
Comstock, Burt—Sheridan, 1912
Comstock, Frank—farmer, Dover
Comstock, John—farmer, Clare
Conger, Nathan—Lake, 1916
Conklin, Andrew—pioneer
Conklin, Arthur—mgr. Union
    Telephone Co., Clare, 1916
Conn, Clara—1939
Conn, H. Ray—Harrison
Conn, Wm.—Harrison
Conner, Clarence—W. Grant, 1900
Conner, Wm.—Arthur, 1917
Conner, Isaac—pioneer, Arthur
Connor, Robert—Clare, 1900
Connor, Wm.—farmer, Arthur
Conrad, Beulah—teacher, Clare
    High principal, Clare
Conrad, Clara—Clare, 1907
Conrad, Freda—Clare
Conrad, Joseph—Clare, 1910
Conroy, L.—Dodge, 1909
Conrad, Martha—Clare, 1906
Conrad, Nathan—Civil War Vet,
    Vernon
Converse, Florence—Clare
Converse, Ethel
Converse, G. T.—A.A.R.R., Clare
Converse, John—farmer, Vernon
Converse, Lewis—Clare, 1912
Converse, Lillian—teacher, Vernon
Converse, Lucius—Vernon, 1900
Converse, Zora—teacher, Clare
Conway, Clara—Vernon, 1910
Conway, Leonard—1914
Conway, Michael—Franklin, 1913
Cook, A. L.—Garfield, 1916
Cook, Al—Garfield, 1918
Cook, Aaron—Civil War Vet,
    Garfield

Cook, Bertha—Freeman, 1909
Cook, Charles—teacher, Garfield
Cook Dick—pioneer, Winterfield
Cook, Ellsworth—WWI, 1918
Cook, F. W.—Freeman, 1918
Cook, J. L.—sawmill, Lincoln, 1906
Cook, Jennie—Garfield, 1911
Cook, John—Winterfield, 1906
Cook, Laura—teacher, Clare, 1907
Cook, Miss Lea—Garfield, 1909
Cook, Neal—Winterfield, 1906
Cook, Peter—farmer, Winterfield
Cook, Peter, Jr.—Winterfield, 1917
Cook, Ralph—WWI, 1918
Cook, Roy—WWI
Cook, Ruth—Freeman, 1915
Cook, Thomas, Jr.—Clare, 1913
Cook, Thomas—Gilmore, 1917
Cook, Virgil—Garfield, 1912
Cook, W. B.—planing mill, 8 Point
    Lake, 1906
Cook, Wm.—foreman, Clam River
    Drive, Freeman, 1900
Cook, Wm.—Freeman, 1914
Cookson, Alfred—Arthur, 1893
Cookson, Arthur—Arthur, 1900
Cookson, Edward—trucker, Clare
Cookson, Jacob—farmer, Arthur
Cookson, Milo—Clare, 1882
Cooley, B. A.—pianos, Clare, 1904
Cooley, W. S.—marble and granite
    business, Clare, 1900
Coolidge, Victor—civil engineer
Coomer, W. A.—1903
Coon, Sylvester—Civil War Vet,
    Farwell, 1900
Cooper, Alta—Clare
Cooper, Benjamin—Harrison, 1917
Cooper, C. J.—Frost, 1916
Cooper, E. P.—Long Lake, 1919
Cooper, Elva—Arthur, 1915
Cooper, George—farmer, Arthur
Cooper, Miss Leitta—teacher
Cooper, Mary—teacher, Clare, 1903
Cooper, O. J.—Frost, 1913
Cooper, Olin—teacher, Harrison
Cooper, Thomas—farmer, Harrison
Cooper, Victor—WWI, Hamilton
Cooper, Wayne—farmer, Arthur
Coors, Merrill—WWI, Surrey
Coots, Agnes—telephone operator
Conrad, Martha—diptheria,
    brought back to life by
    tracheotomy, Clare, 1906
Cope, Cora—Clare, 1909
Cope, Claude—1914
Cope, Ella—1911
Cope, Rev. Jonas—pioneer, farmer,
    Free Methodist minister
Corbin, Fannie—Clare
Corbus, W. C.—Loomis, 1900
Corbus, W. L.—Loomis, 1900
Corey, Miss _____—teacher, Clare
Corey, F.—Harrison
Corey, G. P.—Hayes, 1900
Corliss, Lafayette—Vernon, 1917
Corman, Alfred—salesman, Clare
Corner, Thomas—Vernon, 1900
Cornish, J. J.—Garfield, 1906
Cornish, Will—Garfield, 1906
Cornwell, Albert—Clare, 1901
Cornwell, B. F.—Rolling Mills

Cornwell, Frank—Clare
Cornwell, Vern—Sheridan, 1919
Cornwell, Wm. C.—rancher
Cosgrove, Catherine—Long Lake
Cosgrove, E. M.—telephone co.
Cosgrove, Francis—hotel employee
Cosgrove, Frank—Clare
Cosgrove, Fred—Leota, 1917
Cosgrove, George—Clare
Cosgrove, Katherine—Harrison
Cosgrove, Kathryn—Clare
Cosler, Fred—Temple, 1903
Costello, H.—farmer, Grant, 1915
Costello, Lloyd—E. Grant, 1915
Cotton, Blanchard—farmer
Cotton, Blanche—Arthur, 1918
Cotton, Calvin—farmer, Clare
Cotton, Frank—farmer, Clare
Cotton, Howard—farmer, Clare
Cotton, Jesse—farmer, WWI
Cotton, Lester—WWI
Cotton, Scott—Sheridan, 1914
Couch, Floyd—Clare, 1908
Cot, Frank—Leota, 1918
Coach, Henry—Clare, 1903
Couch, Henry Jr.—Temple, 1903
Couch, Iva—Clare, 1893
Couch, K. C.—twp. official,
    Temple, 1900
Couch, Ray—Clare, 1908
Coulson, J. H.—Clare, 1900
Coulter, Belle—teacher, 1906
Coulter, Clair—Arthur, 1917
Coulter, James—farmer, preacher
Coulter, John—Arthur, 1912
Coulter, Lee—teacher, WWI, Clare
Cour, Bernice—Clare, 1917
Cour, Jessie—Clare, 1907
Cour, Joseph—stave cutter, Clare
Cour, Marcell—blacksmith,
    auto mechanic, Clare
Cour, Pearl—telephone operator
Cour, Ramey—Clare, 1900
Cours, Arthur—Farwell
Cours, Rev. C. C.—publisher,
    Farwell, 1909
Cours, Merrill—Farwell, 1914
Court, Benjamin—Sheridan, 1901
Court, Grace—Sheridan, 1903
Court, Rolland—Sheridan, 1901
Court, Sidney—Sheridan, 1915
Court, Sidney—Sheridan, 1903
Court, Sidney, Jr.—Sheridan, 1901
Courthouse, Ralph—Arthur, 1910
Courtland, Mrs. E. R.—millinery
Courtney, Daniel—WWI, AEF,
Courtney, Edward—Vernon, 1917
Courtney, Martin—WWI, AEF
Courts, Sidney—Clare, 1911
Cousineau, Joseph—Clare, 1914
Cousineau, Noah—bank bookkeeper
Covell, Roy—Farwell
Covert, George—Harrison
Coville, Everett—Summerfield, 1914
Cowden, Harry—Clare
Cowden, _____—Clare
Cowles, Dan—Lincoln, 1917
Cowles, Harold—Leota, 1917
Cowles, Jabez—WWI
Cowles, Ralph—Lake George, 1904
Cowles, Thomas—1918
Cowles, W. J.—AEF, Grant

Cowles, Winfield—logger
Cox, Bessie—Temple
Cox, Charles—Clare, 1911
Cox, Frances—teacher, Temple
Cox, Fred—Temple, 1909
Cox, George—Temple, 1914
Cox, Kenneth—baker, Clare, 1904
Coyle, Frank—saw filer, Temple
Coyne, Jenny—Temple, 1918
Coyne, Patrick—restaurant, saloon, Temple, 1903
Cradit, A. C.—Grant, 1906
Cradit, Earl—WWI, Arthur
Cradit, Harold—Clare
Cradit, Joseph—Clare, 1903
Cradit, Wade—Arthur, 1917
Cradit, Wm.—Sheridan, 1903
Craford, Hugh—gas line worker
Craford, Mary—Garfield, 1909
Cragier, W.—Arthur, 1906
Craine, Al—Harrison
Craine, C. H.—Harrison, 1913
Craine, Llewellyn—WWI
Cramer, Frank—Long Lake, 1917
Cramer, Oresta—1916
Crandall, Abrum—Civil War Vet, 1914
Crandall, Alford—WWI, U.S. Navy
Crandall, Wm.—Greenwood, 1906
Crane, Charles—farmer, Harrison
Crane, Edith—Clare
Crane, Edna—teacher, Clare, 1914
Crane, Floyd—Harrison
Crane, George—pioneer, farmer
Crane, Kathryn—teacher, Clare
Crane, Llewellyn—Franklin, 1917
Crane, Nellie—teacher, Clare, 1912
Crane, Talcott—farmer, Winterfield
Crane, W. R.—Franklin, 1906
Crane, Z.—Redding, 1917
Craner, Ira—A.A.R.R.
Crapsey, George—Summerfield
Crause, _____—carpenter, Lincoln
Crawford, A.—Loomis, 1910
Crawford, Bill—Sheridan, 1900
Crawford, Clinton—oil-pumper
Crawford, David—Vernon, 1903
Crawford, David—meat market
Crawford, Eliza—Temple, 1900
Crawford, Ethyl—Harrison, 1903
Crawford, Joseph—Lake, 1915
Crawford, May—Redding, 1908
Crawford, Myrtle—Temple
Crawford, Samuel—Temple, 1903
Crawford, Thomas—hotel, Temple
Crawford, Wm.—farmer, Grant
Creeper, Silas—Clare, 1905
Crego, Gayle—principal, Clare
Crete, Charles—farmer, Sheridan
Crider, LeRoy—Greenwood, 1915
Criegier, Al—Harrison, 1904
Criegier, Frank—harness maker
Crigier, Neenah—Clare
Crigier, S. Walter—Harrison
Crill, Harry—Temple, 1910
Crippen, Sarah—Farwell, 1904
Crippen, Grace—Clare, 1907
Crist, Floyd—Clare, 1900
Criswell, D. E.—Freeman, 1918
Croel, Winnifred—teacher, Clare
Croford, Sam—Grant, 1903
Crofs, Eli—Clare, 1901

Cronk, John—Farwell, 1904
Cronkhite, Rev. _____—Baptist minister, Clare
Crook, George—teacher, Sheridan
Cropper, Wm.—Hamilton, 1908
Croskery, R.—Hamilton, 1917
Cross, Andy—Freeman, 1906
Cross, Dennis—Dover, 1904
Cross, Eli—Clare, 1900
Cross, Sarah—1903
Cross, Wesley—postmaster, Redding
Crossen, Thomas—Farwell, 1890
Crosset, Thomas—Loomis, 1900
Croston, Charles—Windover Lake
Croton, Charles—farmer, Freeman
Crouse, Daniel—blacksmith, Clare
Crouse, Oscar—Lincoln, 1916
Crowley, David—Vernon, 1910
Crowley, Theodore—farmer
Crowley, Thomas—Vernon, 1917
Croy, George—lumber, Farwell
Croy, James—Surrey, 1906
Crum, Allen—gas station, Clare
Crumrine, Samuel—Sheridan, 1911
Crysler, Amy—Harrison
Cuba, Wm.—A.A.R.R.
Cudney, C.—Clare, 1908
Cudney, Ethel—teacher, Clare
Cudney, P.M.R.R. agent, Clare
Cudney, Noel—Clare, 1909
Culbert, Dr. C.M.—doctor, Clare
Cuffman, Henry—Arthur, 1915
Culver, Ephraim—Clare, 1906
Cummins, George—attorney, Harrison, 1900
Cummins, _____—R.R. agent
Cunningham, Andrew—Clare, 1870
Cunningham, John—farmer, Clare
Cunningham, Raymond—restaurant
Cunningham, Wm.—farmer
Cunningham, Wm., Jr.—Clare
Cunningham, Wm.—Harrison, 1917
Cupples, Norene—Clare, 1900
Cuppernull, Byron—farmer
Curran, Weller—Temple, 1909
Curren, Fred—Temple, 1909
Curren, Wm.—Temple, 1913
Currie, W. E.—real estate, Vernon
Currier, Mabel—Clare principal
Curtis, _____—Crooked Lake
Curtis, Albert—Harrison, 1907
Curtis, Anna—Clare
Curtis, Darf—Wise, 1917
Curtis, E. G.—Harrison, 1910
Curtis, H. M.—Grant, 1906
Curtis, Wm.—Clare, 1915
Cusick, Harry—ice house, Lake
Cuthbertson, R.—R.R. tower man
Cutler, Anna—Winterfield, 1907
Cutler, Bessie—Winterfield, 1907
Cutler, Ethel—Winterfield, 1912
Cutler, John—Winterfield, 1912
Cutter, Lloyd—Vernon, 1917
Cuvrell, Archie—band director, baker, Farwell, 1914
Cuvrell, David—bakery, Farwell
Cuvrell, Juanita—teacher, Farwell
Daggett, Sanuel—Dover, 1900
Dain, F. M.—farmer, Farwell
Dain, Marion—sheep farmer
Dain, Wm.—Vernon, 1917
Dalton, Frank—Vernon, 1912

Dalton, John—farmer, Vernon
Dalton, Michael—Vernon, 1907
Dalzell, Sloughton—civil engineer
Damoth, Art—real estate, WWI
Danker, Walter—laborer, Clare
Danley, A.—Hatton, 1906
Danley, Glenn—Hatton, 1910
Darling, Bertha—bookkeeper
Darling, Carrie—Harrison, 1912
Darling, E. P.—Civil War Vet, Lake, 1909
Darling, Gladys—teacher, Harrison
Darling, James—Lincoln, 1905
Darling, Miles—RFD carrier
Darling, Roy—Harrison, 1912
Darnell, Clifford, Jr.—Lake
Darnell, Clifford—Lake
Darragh, U.S. Congressman, 10th District, Clare, 1903
Daugherty, Benjamin—Civil War Vet, Clar, 1900
Daugherty, Edward—farmer
Daugherty, James—Clare, 1903
Daugherty, James, Jr.—
Daugherty, Maggie—dressmaker
Davenport, Clifford—WWI
Davenport, Fred—Redding, 1918
Davenport, John—Redding, 1917
David, Charles—WWI, Sheridan
David, Frank—Harrison, 1918
David, Frank, Jr.—Long Lake
David, Stephen—farmer, Grant
David, S. A.—Sheridan, 1900
David, Wm.—farmer, Summerfield
Davids, F.—farmer, Arthur, 1906
Davidson, Harry—1918
Davidson, R.—Lincoln, 1905
Davies, James—Harrison, 1911
Davies, W. C.—jeweler, Clare, 1900
Davis, Rev. _____—
Congregational minister, Harrison
Davis, Albert—farmer, Vernon
Davis, Ann—Clare, 1916
Davis, Arvilla—Clare
Davis, Charles—farmer, Sheridan
Davis, Charles—1918
Davis, Charles—Temple, 1918
Davis, Clarence—attorney, Farwell
Davis, Clarice—Arthur, 1912
Davis, Dale—WWI, Sheridan, 1914
Davis, David—Farwell, 1916
Davis, Donald—Clare
Davis, D. N.—farmer, Arthur, 1906
Davis, Rev. E. W.—M-E pastor
Davis, Earl—Harrison
Davis, Eli—farmer, Sheridan, 1909
Davis, Ellsworth—Farwell, 1916
Davis, Emma—Temple, 1922
Davis, E. J.—farmer, Winterfield
Davis, Ernest—farmer, Surrey, 1914
Davis, Ethel—Arthur, 1907
Davis, F. E.—farmer, Redding
Davis, Frank—Farwell, 1909
Davis, Frank—brickmason, Clare
Davis, Fred—Harrison, 1918
Davis, Fred—farmer, Arthur
Davis, Frederick—Arthur, 1908
Davis, Franklin—farmer, Sheridan
Davis, Floyd—farmer, Redding
Davis, Fred—Winterfield, 1909
Davis, George—Temple, 1912
Davis, H.—farmer, Arthur, 1906

Dillenbeck, Lester—farmer, pioneer
Dillenbeck, Ray—Greenwood, 1919
Dilling, John—Freeman, 1907
Dilling, Oscar—Windemere Lake
Dillingham, Laura—teacher
Dillingham, Lila—Farwell, 1903
Dillsworth, Rev. _____—minister
Dimeman, Chancey—Sheridan
Dineen, J.—Temple, 1907
Dines, Berwyn—1903
Dingman, Jay—Winterfield, 1914
Dingman, Marshall—1907
Dingman, Roy—Temple, 1909
Dingman, Wm.—Sheridan, 1918
Dingman, Wm. O.—WWI, Sheridan
Dingwell, Fred—Summerfield, 1912
Dionise, John—Green Grocer, Clare
Dionise, Virginia—Clare
Disbrow, Rev. Arthur—Free
    Methodist minister, Clare
Disbrow, Frank—Clare, 1907
Dixon, Joseph—farmer, Vernon
Dixon, Olga—Clare
Dixson, Mabel—Vernon, 1913
Dixson, Wm. J.—pioneer, Vernon
Dobson, Arthur—Clare
Dobson, Clifford—WWI, Harrison
Dobson, Patrick—Harrison, 1904
Doda, Mable—Browns, 1909
Dodds, Dora—Sheridan, 1911
Dodds, Peter—judge
Dodge, Ralph—Vernon, 1917
Dodge, Wm.—farmer, Vernon
Doherty, A. J.—farmer, legislator,
    businessman, Clare, 1900
Doherty, Alfred—Clare
Doherty, Ed—Grant, 1904
Doherty, Esther—Clare
Doherty, F. B.—hardware, Clare
Doherty, Floyd—Clare, 1900
Doherty, Fred—1903
Doherty, John—undertaker, Clare
Doherty, Lawrence—WWI
Doherty, Lear—AEF
Doherty, Loran—Surrey, 1917
Doherty, Margaret—Clare
Doherty, Mary—Clare
Doherty, Michael—undertaker
Doherty, Samantha—Clare, 1909
Doherty, Wendell—WWI, Clare
Doherty, Wm.—Hatton, 1905
Dohm, W. S.—Hayes, 1913
Dolloff, Rose—Hayes, 1986
Dolph, C. L.—mill owner, Temple
Dolph, Norman—Temple, 1903
Dolph, Palmer—Farwell, 1916
Dondres, Dr.—physician, Garfield
Donkel, Shelburn—Clare, 1907
Doornbos, Neal—WWI, Winterfield
Dora, Alexander—farmer, Sheridan
Dora, J. P.—Harrison
Doran, D. M.—farmer, Greenwood
Dorian, Wm.—Temple, 1903
Dorney, A. J.—farmer, Grant Twp.
Dorning, A. J.—Clare, 1918
Dorsey, Carl—Clare, 1903
Dorsey, J. S.—Co. Clerk, Harrison
Dorsey, Thomas—probate judge,
    Clare, 1900
Dorten, Wm.—Redding, 1906
Doty, A. E.—farmer, Greenwood
Doty, Dora—Arthur, 1918

Doty, Francis—teacher, Harrison
Doty, Fred—farmer, Sheridan, 1906
Doty, Nettie—Harrison, 1912
Doty, Wilbur—laborer, Greenwood
Double, Fred—hotelman
Doud, Peter—Clare, 1915
Douglas, _____—blacksmith, Temple
Douglas, Albert—lumberman
Douglas, Charles—Temple, 1909
Douglas, Homer—barber, WWI
Dove, Alfred—Crooked Lake, 1906
Dove, S. H.—farmer, Civil War
    Vet, Garfield, d. 1916
Dowd, Montie—Clare, 1910
Dowd, Peter—Clare, 1903
Dowd, Rufus—WWI, regular army
Dowd, Samuel—Sp.-Am. War Vet
Dowd, S. P.—Civil War Vet, Clare
Dowling, E. P.—Crooked Lake
Downer, Arthur—Summerfield
Downer, Steve—Loomis, 1914
Downing, L.—Farwell, 1900
Doyle, Camey—Temple, 1909
Doyle, Effie—Long Lake, 1908
Doyle, Michael—Harrison, 1908
Drachenberg, Ferdinand—Harrison
Drake, F. F.—Sheridan, 1906
Drake, G. G.—farmer, Sheridan
Drake, G. E.—water works supt.
Drake, Howard—Freeman, 1914
Drake, I. L.—real estate
Drake, John—farmer, Gilmore
Drake, J. L.—Lincoln, 1903
Drake, Perry—Lake George, 1903
Draper, Flossie—Temple, 1910
Draper, George—Temple, 1917
Draper, J. H.—Lake George, 1903
Draper, Jerry—section foreman
Drew, Robert—pharmacist, Clare
Dubey, Joseph—Harrison
Dubois, Andy—Engineer, Clare
Dubois, Jesse—1915
DuBois, Kenneth—lineman, Clare
Dubreville, F.—Clare, 1904
Dudley, Alfred—Harrison, 1904
Dudley, Andy—Farwell, 1903
Dudley, Edith—teacher, Harrison
Dudley, E. F.—cream-buyer, Clare
Dudley, James—editor, postmaster
    Harrison, 1906
Dudley, Nellie—teacher, Harrison
Dudley, Wm.—editor, "Cleaver"
Duell, V. R.—Dover, 1915
Dunbar, Rev. F. G.—M-E minister
Duncan, George—Canadian Army,
    WWI, Clare
Duncan, Hilda—Clare, 1913
Duncan, James—grocery store
Duncan, John—farmer, Vernon
Duncan, John—farmer, Vernon
Duncan, Lionel—farmer, Clare
Duncan, Ralph—Clare
Duncan, Wm.—farmer, Vernon
Duncanson, A. J.—Clare, 1916
Duncanson, Jessie—teacher, Clare
Dunham, Fred—Temple, 1909
Dunham, George—Frost, 1906
Dunham, Jesse—Harrison, 1916
Dunham, Rolley—Frost, 1917
Dunigan, Robert—farmer, Gilmore
Dunigan, Wm.—Clare, 1907
Dunkle, Delos—Lincoln, 1918

Dunlap, Willis—Farwell, 1911
Dunlay, Mattie—Farwell, 1908
Dunlay, Pean—store, 1916
Dunlop, Donald—physician, Clare
Dunlop, Hilda—Clare, 1903
Dunlop, Dr. J. W.—druggist, Clare
Dunlop, John—druggist,
    WWI, Clare
Dunlop, John—Clare
Dunlop, Wm.—police chief, Clare
Dunnigan, Wm.—Clare, 1905
Dunsmore, J. W.—Summerfield
Dunwoodie, Florence—1914
Dunwoodie, James—mgr. Union
    Telephone Co., Clare, 1903
Dunwoodie, Lee—mail clerk,
    R.R., Clare, 1908
Dunwoodie, Lena—Clare, 1902
Dunwoodie, Robert—Clare, 1917
Durfee, Arthur—Hatton, 1913
Durfee, Clarence—farmer, Hatton
Durfee, E. N.—teacher, Harrison
Durfee, Lewis—WWI, Hatton
Durfee, Percival—WWI, Hatton
Durham, Araham—Harrison, 1917
Durham, Abel—Hayes, 1986
Durham, Mell—Mannsiding, 1918
Durling, Henry—Civil War, Loomis
Durnin, Charles—Vernon, 1890
Durnin, James—farmer, pioneer,
    Vernon, 1900
Durnin, Kathleen—Clare
Durnin, Marion—Clare
Duryee, Anna—Clare, 1900
Duryee, Rev. B. H.—Free
    Methodist Pastor, Clare, 1912
Duryee, Carl—R.R., Clare, 1914
Duryee, Josephine—Clare, 1913
Dusten, Ethel—teacher, Clare, 1903
Dusten, Rev. John—minister, Clare
Dustin, John—Clare, 1907
Duttweiler, Clyde—WWI
DuVall, Clifford—WWI, Lincoln
DuVall, Ethel—teacher, 1909
Dwight, Wm.—Crooked Lake, 1908
Dwyer, Daniel—Clare, 1913
Dwyer, Earl—mail service, WWI
Dwyer, Frances—Clare, 1900
Dwyer, John—Hamilton, 1909
Dwyer, John—R.R. foreman, Clare
Dwyer, Myrtle—P.O. clerk, Clare
Dwyer, Pearl—Clare, 1900
Dwyer, Raymond—Clare, 1919
Dwyer, Thomas E.—P.O. clerk
Dwyer, Thomas J.—farmer, cook
Dwyer, Wm. A.—Clare, 1903
Dwyer, Winnie—1903
Dwyer, Wm. J.—night marshal
Dyarman, N. G.—Sheridan, 1911
Dyer, Carter—livery, AEF
Dyer, Clarence—butcher, 1901
Dyer, Hazel—Clare, 1916
Dyer, John—Grant, 1906
Dyer, O. E.—livery, Clare, 1918
Dyer, Rolland—WWI, Clare
Dyer, Rolla—WWI
Dyer, Zack—P.M.R.R. fireman
Duke, David—jeweler, Harrison
Dyke, Florence—Hayes, 1912
Dykstra, Abel—farmer, Winterfield
Dykstra, H.—Austa, 1906
Dykstra, John—Austa, 1906

Dykstra, Wm.—pioneer, postmaster, merchant, Austa
Dysinger, Clarence—Arthur, 1918
Dysinger, Dan—farmer, Hatton
Dysinger, Forrest—Arthur, 1917
Dysinger, Jessie—Clare
Dysinger, Wm.—farmer, Arthur
Eager, E. J.—band director, Farwell
Eakins, Rev. J. E.—minister, Eagle
Earl, "Doc"—hotel owner
Earl, George—Temple, 1918
Earley, Clarence—Clare
Earley, Melvin—Clare, 1906
Earns, Arthur—A.A.R.R., Lincoln
Eartman, Edward—Hamilton, 1918
Easler, G. W.—merchant, Clare
Easler, Winnie—Clare, 1903
Easlick, Billy—Farwell, 1914
Easlick, Wm.—Farwell, 1918
Eastmont, _____—gas and oil
Easton, James—Clare, 1900
Easton, Pearl—Clare, 1903
Eaton, Carrie—Clare, 1900
Eaton, Marvin—publisher, Clare, 1900
Eaton, LeRoy—Harrison, 1917
Eaton, Ralph—farmer, WWI
Eaton, Roy—Harrison
Eaton, Sherman—lawyer, Clare
Eberhardt, Christ—Clare, 1900
Eberhart, Anna—teacher, Clare
Eberhart, Bernice—Clare, 1915
Eberhart, Eunice—teacher, Clare
Eberhart, George—Clare, 1903
Eberhart, Kenneth—Clare
Eberhart, Louie—Clare, 1905
Eberhart, Martin—Wise, 1912
Eberhart, Nina—teacher, Clare
Eberhart, Paul—farmer, Clare, 1874
Eberhart, Ralph—Clare, 1918
Eddy, Harold—milk tester, Clare
Eddy, Theron—postmaster, merchant, Alward, 1903
Edgar, I—Loomis, 1900
Edgecomb, Herbert—1915
Edinger, Rev. E. C.—Free Methodist minister, Clare, 1910
Edman, Abram—farmer, Arthur
Edwards, John—Herrick, 1903
Egbert, _____—egg man, Farwell
Egbert, A. J.—Clare, 1893
Egbert, Alva—Clare, 1903
Egbert, John—Gilmore, 1908
Egbert, Nathan—miller, Clare, 1900
Eggert, Clarence—Gilmore, 1911
Eggliston, Archie—Wise, 1917
Elle, Alfred—farmer, Hamilton
Ehle, Walter—drain comm.
Ehrhardt, Calvin—Clare
Ehrhardt, Chris—janitor, Clare
Ehrhardt, Eunice—Clare, 1913
Ehrhardt, George—Clare, 1905
Ehrhardt, George E., Jr.—Clare
Ehrhardt, John—merchant, Clare
Ehrhardt, Marguerite—Clare, 1911
Ehrman, Reuben—1900
Eichorn, Lilliford—Farwell
Eidt, _____—Farwell, 1915
Eisenhauer, Earl
Eisenhauer, Jessie—teacher, 1918
Eisenhauer, Vincent—Farwell, 1915
Elden, Mary—Clare, 1915

Elden, Dexter—Clare, 1918
Elden, Norris—Clare, 1903
Elden, W. H.—farm implements
Elder, D. I.—furniture store
Elder, _____—chemist, Farwell
Eldredge, E.—Hamilton, 1903
Eldridge, Rev. _____—minister
Eldridge, Elsworth—wool farmer
Eldt, Miss _____—teacher, Herrick
Elk, Wm.—Wise, 1917
Elliott, Florence—Clare, 1900
Elliott, Rev. Foster—minister
Elliott, James—farmer, Dover
Elliott, Joseph, Jr.—farmer, Vernon
Elliott, Joseph—Clare, 1887
Elliott, Leah—Vernon, 1918
Elliott, Lorender—Clare, 1900
Elliott, Rev. Lyle—minister
Elliott, Maud—1915
Elliott, Norris—Clare
Elliott, Robert—carpenter, WWI, Sheridan, 1912
Elliott, Wm.—farmer, Farwell, 1916
Ellis, Cash—farm laborer—Sheridan
Ellis, M. D.—jeweler, Clare, 1906
Ellis, Willard—Grandon, 1880
Ellis, William—Grandon, 1900
Ellison, Truman—farmer, Loomis
Ellston, Addie—Clare, 1914
Ellsworth, Homer—1912
Elston, Harry—WWI, Vernon
Emerson, C. M.—butter maker
Emerson, Edith—1915
Emerson, Jack—farmer, Clare
Emerson, Richard—Supervisor, Grant, 1903
Emerson, Wm.—farmer, Dover
Emery, Dolphus—Grant, 1917
Emery, E.—Hatton, 1906
Emery, Frank—Dover, 1904
Emery, George—farmer, 1918
Emery, John—Clare, 1918
Emmons, Lincoln—Summerfield
Emos, Ira—Lincoln, 1909
Empey, Anna—teacher, Clare, 1903
Empey, John—Vernon City, 1915
Empey, John—teacher, WWI
Empey, John, Jr.—Clare
Empey, Val—farmer, Sheridan
Empey, Mary—teacher, Clare, 1908
Enders, M. P.—furniture store, 1903
English, Ralph—Frost, 1909
Erdman, Edward—bootlegger
Erdmon, Amelia—Hamilton, 1917
Erhardt, Eunice—teacher, Sheridan
Erhardt, Wm.—Arthur, 1906
Erter, Dale—Clare
Erter, Harvey—Clare
Erter, Matt—Hamilton, 1915
Erter, Wm.—city engineer, Clare
Ervin, Lee—WWI, Winterfield
Ervin, Mason—businessman, Clare
Ervin, Thomas—Clare, 1908
Erwin, Charles—farmer, Surrey
Erwin, James—Clare, 1906
Eschennck, Fred—farmer, Grant
Esterline, Merl—Gilmore, 1917
Etile, A.—farmer, Hamilton, 1906
Evans, Benjamin—Clare, 1917
Evans, B. P.—auctioneer, Clare
Evans, David—farmer, Sheridan
Evans, D. E.—farmer, Sheridan

Evans, E. B.—1903
Evans, H.—Garfield, 1906
Evans, James—Clare, 1905
Evans, John—Grant, 1905
Evans, John—Clare, 1914
Evans, J. S.—Grant, 1906
Evans, J. C.—Temple, 1903
Evans, Solon—Garfield, 1915
Everdeen, LeRoy—Clare, 1900
Everest, Theodore—WWI, Redding
Everette, John—machinist, 1915
Ewing, Mildred—Winterfield, 1919
Faber, Aline—Farwell, 1918
Faber, Gattlieb—Denver Twp.
Fahnestock, Archie—Garfield, 1904
Fahnestock, F.—Crooked Lake
Fahnestock, John—lumberman
Fahnestock, Sworro—pioneer
Failing, Dewey—farmer, Clare
Fair, Alvin—teacher, Farwell, 1918
Fair, Floyd—WWI, Farwell, 1917
Fair, Forrest—Farwell, 1917
Fair, Henry—Isabella
Fair, Thomas—real estate, Farwell
Fair, Wayne—1906
Fairbanks, B. H.—Ann Arbor R.R.
Fairbanks, F.—Grant
Fairbank, R. W.—W. Grant, 1907
Fairchilds, George—poolhall, Clare
Fairman, H. A.—Loomis, 1910
Fairman, L. S.—Wise, 1910
Fakes, Floyd—AEF, Leota, 1919
Falconer, Bert—Garfield, 1911
Fales, Albert—Harrison, 1900
Falk, A.—Clare, 1903
Falk, Clara—1901
Falk, Ed—Clare, 1900
Falk, Frank—barber, Clare, 1900
Falk, Mary Ann—1910
Falk, Obadiah—laborer, Clare
Falk, Ray—Clare, 1907
Fall, Adam—Clare, 1903
Fall, Beatrice—teacher, Clare, 1900
Fall, Charles—Farwell, 1900
Fall, Clarence—laborer, Clare, 1915
Fall, Ethel—teacher, Farwell, 1905
Fall, Fred—farmer, Clare, 1902
Fall, Janice—Clare, 1902
Falor, F—Temple, 1909
Fawcon, Erma—Clare
Fancon, Harland—Clare
Fancon, Henry—farmer, Sheridan
Fancon, Horace—farmer, Clare
Fanning, Bryan—funeral director, WWI, Harrison
Fanning, Catherine—Harrison
Fanning, Helen—Harrison, 1916
Fanning, Louise—Harrison, 1916
Fanning, Marie—musician
Fanning, Michael—merchant, undertaker, Harrison, 1900
Fanning, Norbut—Harrison, 1918
Fanning, Wm.—Harrison
Fanslau, Carl—Arthur, 1918
Fanslau, Henry—Hamilton, 1917
Fanslau, Jacob—Hamilton
Fanslau, John—Hamilton
Fanslau, Karl—Hamilton
Fanslau, Michael—Hamilton
Fanslau, Wm.—WWI, Hamilton
Fanslaw, Charles—1918
Fanslow, Charles—Hamilton, 1900

Fanslow, Wm.—Hamilton, 1917
Farchand, Joseph—car salesman
Farmer, A. J.—granite works, Clare
Farmer, John—Vernon, 1900
Farmer, Roy—WWI
Farmer, S. G.—farmer, Clare, 1903
Farmer, Will—Vernon, 1900
Farnum, F. E.—supervisor
Farr, Bethel—Clare, 1914
Farrington, Arthur—Clare, 1900
Farrington, James—Clare, 1917
Farrington, Robert—building mover
Fast, Delmar—Garfield, 1911
Faught, Sam—plumber, Clare, 1916
Fay, Dr.—druggist, physician
Faye, Dan—Harrison, 1913
Fear, Earl—WWI, Vernon
Fea, Felix—Arthur, 1912
Feighner, Anna—Clare, 1915
Feighner, Erma—Clare, 1903
Feighner, Frank—Clare, 1900
Feighner, Frank—Clare, 1907
Feighner, George—Clare, 1903
Feighner, George, Jr.—Pennock
Feighner, Geneva—Clare
Feighner, Ivan—Mich. Produce
  Co., Vernon, 1900
Feighner, Jerry—Clare, 1900
Feighner, J. V.—Clare, 1906
Feighner, Ivan—Clare, 1903
Feighner, Malcolm—Clare, 1904
Feighner, Roy—printer, Clare, 1905
Feighner, Rev. Wm.—minister
Feller, David—Wise, 1903
Fenner, N. T.—Farwell, 1909
Fenton, James—1917
Fenton, John—Dover, 1909
Fenton, Robert—Harrison, 1917
Ferenerda, John—farmer, Lincoln
Ferguson, E.—Hatton, 1906
Ferguson, Dr. E. L.—veterinarian
Ferguson, Eugene—farmer, Vernon
Ferguson, Floyd—Harrison, 1908
Ferguson, James—Lincoln, 1916
Ferguson, James—plumber, Clare
Ferguson, Lawrence—Clare, 1910
Ferguson, Ted—Mannsiding, 1918
Ferguson, Thomas—Loomis, 1909
Ferrel, "Den"—Sheridan, 1900
Ferrell, Irene—teacher, 1916
Ferrell, John—farmer, Arthur, 1906
Ferris, J.—farmer, Grant, 1903
Ferris, M. D.—P.M. agent, Farwell
Fetterhoff, Rev. _____—pastor
Fetters, Llewellyn—shoe repairman
Fick, Alexander—barber, Sheridan
Fick, Chauncey—farmer, Vernon
Fick, Christine—Clare, 1906
Fick, Donald—Clare, 1898
Fick, E. L.—Hatton, 1906
Fick, James—farmer, Clare, 1900
Fick, Leonard—Clare, 1906
Fick, M. J.—Grant
Fick, Walter—Clare, 1903
Fick, Wm.—Clare, 1903
Fielbing, J.—Garfield, 1915
Fifer, Clyde—farmer, Arthur, 1914
Fike, Wm.—Wise, 1917
Finch, Ed—farmer, Garfield, 1903
Finch. E. B.—real estate, Clare
Finch, Inez—teacher, Lincoln, 1917
Field, F.—Farwell, 1903

Finch, George—truck driver, Clare
Finch, Gladys—Freeman, 1910
Finch, Henry—Surrey, 1907
Finch, Inez—Farwell, 1918
Finch, John—Farwell, 1916
Finch, Lena—Surrey, 1910
Finch, Louis—farmer, Surrey, 1906
Finch, M. W.—Lincoln
Finch, Verne—Farwell Grocery
Finch, Victor—Freeman, 1915
Finch, Warren—Garfield, 1917
Finnerty, David—farmer, Grant
Finton, James—farmer, Grant, 1906
Fisch, Henry—Hamilton
Fisch, Hy—Hamilton, 1906
Fisch, Leonhard, Hamilton, 1900
Fisch, Robert—Hamilton
Fisch, Walter—Hamilton, 1917
Fischer, Wilhelmina—Arthur, 1909
Fischer, Wm.—Farwell, 1912
Fish, Aaron—cream buyer, Clare
Fish, David—1905
Fish, Enoch—bicycle shop, Clare
Fish, Henry—Wise, 1917
Fish, Osborn—Clare, 1904
Fish, Othe—Garfield, 1914
Fish, Robert—Hamilton, 1906
Fish, Wm.—Clare, 1904
Fish, Wm.—Wise, 1917
Fisher, Albert—laborer, Clare, 1899
Fisher, Andrew—brickmason, Clare
Fisher, Bernhard—farmer, Arthur
Fisher, Christopher—Clare, 1908
Fisher, Eli—1917
Fisher, Eugene—AEF, Farwell
Fisher, Frank—teacher, Farwell
Fisher, George—farmer, Lincoln
Fisher, "Ike"—Freeman, 1909
Fisher, Joseph—Wise, 1917
Fisher, Mabel—teacher, Hatton
Fisher, M.—Hatton, 1906
Fisher, Peter—mail carrier
Fisher, R. G.—steam laundry, Clare
Fisher, Wm.—Surrey, 1917
Fisler, Wm.—Farwell, 1911
Fishley, Charles—Clare, 1904
Fishley, Fred—Clare, 1903
Fisk, Lulu—principal, Clare, 1908
Fitch, Charles—Clare, 1903
Fitch, Grover—Wise, 1917
Fitch, John—sawmill, Hinkleville
Fitzharris, E. J.—Surrey, 1906
Fitzmore, Robert—Clare
Fitzpatrick, _____—Clare, 1915
Fitzpatrick, Alfred—Clare
Fitzpatrick, Bernard—farmer, WWI
Fitzpatrick, Charles—Arthur, 1917
Fitzpatrick, Dennis—Clare
Fitzpatrick, George—Clare
Fitzpatrick, James, Jr.—Rosebush
Fitzpatrick, John—farmer, Arthur
Fitzpatrick, T. N.—Lincoln, 1906
Fitzpatrick, William—Clare
Fivenson, _____—dance instructor
Flanagan, C. A.—Clare, 1903
Flannigan, James—AEF
Flegal, Blair—Arthur, 1914
Flegel, David—salesman, Clare
Flegel, William—farmer, Grant
Fleming, Harold—Clare
Fleming, Ruth—Temple, 1903
Fleming, John—Civil War Vet,

farmer, Winterfield, 1871
Fleming, Rev. _____—minister
Fleming, Samuel—Grandon, 1903
Fletcher, T. D.—partner with
  Bicknell & Fletcher Groceries,
  Clare, 1903
Flint, Donald—Farwell, 1917
Flood, Chris—pioneer, farmer
Flood, John—Vernon, 1917
Flood, Leo—Vernon, 1900
Flood, Peter—farmer, Vernon
Flood, Peter, Jr.—farmer, Vernon
Flora, Clarence—Dover, 1913
Flynn, Harry—Clare
Flynn, Harry—Vernon, 1917
Flynn, Margaret—Clare
Flynn, Rosella—Clare
Flynn, Wm.—Sheridan, 1912
Fockes, Will—Clare, 1909
Foell, Clarence—1918
Foell, Emil—WWI, Surrey
Foell, Walter—farmer, Clare, 1918
Foell, Wm.—farmer, Farwell, 1918
Foland, George—Gilmore, 1912
Foley, Daniel—Isabella—1900
Folkes, Floyd—WWI, Frost
Follett, Feu—Farwell, 1909
Follett, M. J.—Harrison, 1900
Foltz, A. H.—Grant, 1906
Foltz, Hazel—Clare, 1909
Foltz, Jesse—farmer, Grant
Foltz, Marie—Clare, 1911
Fonner, F. W.—Vernon, 1917
Fonner, J. W.—Clare, 1911
Fookes, Audrey—Greenwood, 1909
Fookes, James—Greenwood, 1909
Fookes, Lee—WWI
Forbes, Adelbert—Clare, 1913
Forbes, Archie—Clare, 1903
Forbes, Francis—wagon maker
Forbes, Frank—Clare, 1904
Forbes, Henry—Wise, 1903
Forbes, Herbert—lathe mill, Wise
Forbes, Lillian—Frost, 1908
Forbes, Louis—Pennock, 1911
Forbes, Martin—Pennock, 1913
Forbes, Wm.—Clare, 1924
Forcy, Earnest—Clare, 1913
Ford, D.—Farwell, 1908
Ford, Dryas—Summerfield, 1900
Ford, Elmer—Clare, 1915
Ford, Fred—Clare, 1917
Ford, George—farmer, Vernon
Ford, Hattie, Union Telephone
  operator, Farwell, 1910
Ford, Henry—land owner,
  Greenwood
Ford, I. J.—Summerfield, 1904
Ford, John—laborer, Clare, 1902
Ford, John M.—lumberman—Clare
Ford, Merton—Clare
Ford, Miss M. M.—teacher, 1900
Fordyce, Archie—teacher, Arthur
Fordyce, Egbert—AEF
Fordyce, Earl—Gilmore, 1917
Fordyce, James—Gilmore, 1917
Foreman, Harry—Sheridan, 1917
Forsberg, Harold—Coleman
Forsyth, Ernest—1910
Forsyth, Mark—farmer, 1904
Forward, Mrs. G. W.—millinery
Forward, Wm.—farmer,

businessman, 1900
Foss, Calvin—Clare
Foss, Earl—baker, AEF, Clare
Foss, Ernie—baker, Clare
Foss, John—bakery, Clare, 1915
Foss, Mamie—Clare
Foster, Agnes—teacher, Frost, 1909
Foster, Carlis—teacher, Greenwood
Foster, Clinton—AEF
Foster, Clinton—WWI, Winterfield
Foster, Corlis—AEF
Foster, Agnes—teacher, Marion
Foster, E. E.—1900
Foster, Elizabeth, 1901
Foster, Frank—Clare, 1909
Foster, George—WWI, Winterfield
Foster, Grace—Winterfield, 1909
Foster, Lewis—Temple, 1918
Foster, John—Winterfield, 1917
Foster, M. C.—farmer, pioneer
Foster, Olive—teacher, Frost, 1918
Foster, Wm.—light house keeper
Fowler, A. E.—Grant, 1906
Fowler, Charles—1916
Fowler, F. A.—orchard, Arthur
Fox, Alonzo—Clare, 1900
Fox, Anna—Franklin
Fox, Arthur—WWI
Fox, Beulah—Clare, 1917
Fox, David—contractor, Clare, 1900
Fox, Francis—Arthur, 1917
Fox, Ivah—Clare, 1917
Fox, John
Fox, Lester—jeweler,
   optometrist, Clare, 1910
Fox, Wm.—Franklin Twp.
Foy, Chelsea—banker, Garfield
Francisco, Mrs. M.—Clare, 1911
Francisco, Theodore—Hayes, 1919
Franks, Harry—Garfield, 1917
Frary, Albert—Vernon, 1909
Frary, Charles—Clare, 1884
Frary, Sidney—Summerfield, 1906
Frary, Wm.—Vernon, 1908
Fraser, Stella—Temple
Frasier, Samuel—Harrison
Frazell, John—bakery, Loomis
Frazer, James—Rosebush, 1915
Freed, Anthony—farmer, Hatton
Freed, Ethel—Brown Corner, 1914
Freed, Giles—Clare
Freed, John—farmer, Hatton, 1906
Freed, Peter—pioneer, Hatton, 1882
Freeman, A. E.—Farwell, 1917
Freeman, Carl—mechanic, 1903
Freeman, C. H.—farmer, Farwell
Freeman, Charles—mill hand, Wise
Freeman, Franklin—Gilmore, 1917
Freeman, Irwin—sheep farmer
Freeman, Jasper—1911
Freeman, Martin—WWI
Freeman, Wm.
Freer, Wm.—WWI
Frees, Jerome—Clare, 1917
French, A. H.—Grant, 1906
French, Ethel—Grant, 1909
French, Nina—Grant, 1908
Froutz, _____—E. Lincoln, 1918
Frye, Helen—teacher, 1909
Frye, John—Temple, 1915
Friedeborn, Mrs. V.—Clare, 1900
Friedeborn, Robert—Clare, 1900

Friedenburg, Louisa—Hayes, 1912
Frisbie, Lyman—farmer, Farwell
Frisbey, John—Lake
Friz, A. N.—undertaker, Clare
Frizzell, Fred—Farwell, 1919
Frizzel, James—WWI, AEF, Surrey
Frost, _____—Harrison, 1918
Frost, Clara—Sheridan, 1908
Frost, David—Civil War Vet, Clare
Frost, David, Jr.—1903
Frost, Helen—teacher, Clare, 1907
Frost, Rev. L. C.—Cong. minister
Frost, Malissa—Sheridan, 1908
Frost, Nellie—Farwell, 1908
Frost, Rev. W. J.—Cong. minister
Frost, Wm.—farmer, Sheridan
Fry, Wm.—farmer, Redding, 1906
Frye, W. H.—Clare, 1900
Frye, Helen—Farwell, 1909
Frye, Minnie—Farwell
Frye, Wm.—Redding, 1903
Fuller, Alice—Farwell, 1906
Fuller, Dan—pioneer, Grandon
Fuller, Edna—Farwell, 1918
Fuller, George—painter, Clare
Fuller, Josh—Clare, 1915
Fuller, Martha—Farwell, 1908
Fuller, Myrtle—teacher, 1906
Fuller, Sid—pioneer, Grandon, 1900
Fuller, Thomas—teacher, Farwell
Fuller, W. C.—elevator and mill
Fullmer, Myrtle—teacher, 1905
Fulweber, C.—Freeman, 1915
Funnell, David—farmer, Clare
Funnell, Vernon—farmer, Farwell
Furney, Charles—Vernon
Gable, Ira—farmer, Harrison
Gable, Harvey—Hamilton, 1913
Gable, John—Greenwood, 1918
Gable, Verne—Hamilton, 1915
Gaddy, Chas—farmer, Grant, 1917
Gaedke, Otto—Ann Arbor R.R.
   brakeman, Lake George, 1903
Gaffney, Frank—Freeman, 1909
Gaffney, George—farmer, Osceola
Gaffney, John—Freeman, 1909
Gaffney, Wm.—farmer, Freeman
Gage, Rev. _____—minister
Gage, H. C.—Harrison, 1903
Gagnon, Chester—Greenwood, 1902
Gailey, Charles—farmer, 1903
Gailey, Flossie—Clare, 1903
Gainsforth, Jessie—housewife
Gainsforth, Roy—Gilmore, 1917
Galdeen, A. C.—farmer, Garfield
Gallagher, M.—Clare
Gallery, Dr. Arthur—farmer
Gallery, Reuben—Redding, 1916
Galligher, Byron—Clare
Galliger, M. B.—Clare, 1915
Galliver, Bert—Clare, 1903
Galliver, Ella—Clare, 1908
Galliver, John—P.M.R.R. agent
Galliver, Joseph—Clare, 1900
Galloway, John—ranch foreman
Galloway, Thomas—Hatton, 1894
Gallup, Clyde—1909
Gallup, George—attorney, 1900
Gallup, Jonathan—Farwell, 1914
Galvin, Charles—Redding, 1895
Gamacke, Joseph—lumberjack
Gamble, Clyde—WWI

Gamble, Edward—farmer
Gamble, George—Garfield, 1912
Gamble, Leon—garage, Clare, 1899
Gamble, Nina—teacher, Farwell
Gamble, Roy—Gilmore, 1909
Gamble, Wm.—Gilmore, 1905
Gable, Clyde—AEF, Surrey
Gammel, Chas.—farmer, Farwell
Gannon, Lillian—teacher
Gantz, D.—Elm Grove, 1918
Ganzlie, Charles—Clare, 1905
Garber, John—chemical engineer
Garchow, Albert—WWI, Grant
Garchow, Carl—WWI
Garchow, Fred—Clare
Garchow, John—pathmaster, Grant
Garchow, John, Jr.—1909
Garchow, Julius—Dover, 1910
Garchow, Marie—Clare
Garchow, Minnie
Garchow, Otto—farmer, Grant
Garchow, Theobold—1909
Garchow, Wm.—farmer, Grant
Garchow, Wm.—post office, Clare
Gardiner, A. M.—Farwell, 1909
Gardiner, E. L.—grocery store
Gardiner, Linas—WWI, Grant
Gardner, A. E.—Clare, 1909
Gardner, Ben—1912
Gardner, H.—Harrison, 1934
Gardner, Henry—Farwell, 1903
Gardner, Joe—Surrey, 1906
Gardner, John—implement dealer
Gardner, Linas—Lt., WWI
Gardner, John—hardware,
   music dealer, Clare, 1907
Gardner, Capt. John H.—Union
   Army Vet, Clare, d. 1903
Gardner, John—farmer, Hatton
Gardner, Leota—teacher, Harrison
Gardner, Minerva—teacher, Farwell
Gardner, Ray—Vernon, 1913
Gardner, Robert—farmer, Clare
Gardner, Will—farmer, Vernon
Gardner, Wm.—Harrison, 1915
Garland, James—Summerfield
Garland, May—Greenwood, 1903
Garland, Minnie—teacher
Garlock, George—tinsmith, Clare
Garn, D. F.—Clare
Garrabrant, James—Grant, 1915
Garrison, Wm.—Farwell, 1902
Garrity, Hazel—Hamilton, 1906
Garrity, James—WWI, U.S. Navy
Garrity, Julia—teacher, Hamilton
Garrity, _____—teacher, Hamilton
Garrity, Maud—teacher, Hamilton
Garrity, Thomas—farmer,
   post master, Dodge, 1906
Garshaw, John—Grant, 1909
Garshaw, J. W.—1903
Garchow, William—Sheridan, 1903
Garthe, L.—teacher, Clare, 1908
Garver, Bessie—Clare, 1910
Garver, Charles—farmer, Arthur
Garver, Ellen—Arthur, 1906
Garver, Forrest—WWI, Arthur
Garver, Walter—Arthur, 1917
Garwick, Joseph—Clare, 1903
Gaskill, Katie—teacher, Winterfield
Gaskill, Sam—farmer, Winterfield
Gasser, Wilburt—banker

Gates, Frank—Temple, 1908
Gates, Hazel—teacher, Temple
Gay, Beulah—Winterfield, 1918
Gay, Joseph—Clare, 1918
Gay, Kittie—teacher, Mannsiding
Gay, Ransom—Harrison, 1918
Gay, Robert—Grandon, 1903
Gear, Arthur—farmer, Vernon
Gear, Walter—Arthur, 1904
Gears, Wm.—farmer, Harrison
Gee, Blanche—Farwell, 1917
Gee, Harry—Farwell, 1910
Gee, Louis—Farwell, 1900
Gee, Rena—Farwell, 1917
Geeck, Bertha—Clare
Geeck, Clarence—Clare Lumber
   Co. mgr., Clare, 1903
Geeck, Edward—U.S. Army
   Aero Sqdn., WWI, Clare, 1911
Geeck, Nicholas—lumber merchant
Geeck, Perry—Clare, 1910
Geeck, Phillip—farmer, Clare, 1911
Geeck, Philip—gas station attendent
Geer, A. C.—farmer, Vernon, 1912
Geer, Ira—Frost, 1912
Geller, Byron—attorney, Clare
Genung, Glen—telegraph operator
George, Wm.—farmer, 1931
Georgia, Guy—auto mechanic
Gephart, Albert—farmer, Dover
Gephart, A.—Greenwood, 1906
Gephart, John—farmer, Arthur
Gephart, Marion—Eagle, 1904
Gephart, N.—Greenwood, 1906
Gephart, Rufus—Arthur, 1908
Gerber, Chas—Arthur, 1917
Gerkhe, Charles—Grant, 1921
Gerlitz, Anna—Hatton, 1906
Gerlitz, Pauline—Hatton, 1909
Gerlitz, Paul—farmer, Hatton
Gernsey, Julia—1907
Geron, James—1917
Geroux, Anna—teacher, Clare, 1912
Geroux, Edward—clerk, Clare
Geroux, Eli—farmer, Grant, 1919
Geroux, Melvina—Clare, 1911
Geroux, L.—Grant, 1906
Gerow, Allen—farmer, pioneer
Gerow, Ethel—teacher, Clare, 1910
Gerow, Doris—Clare
Gerow, Ethel—Colonville, 1908
Gerow, Floy—teacher, Clare, 1908
Gerow, Henry—Clare, 1914
Gerow, James—Sheridan, 1904
Gerow, Mose—Sheridan, 1907
Gerow, S. W.—Sheridan, 1906
Gerow, Wesley—Sheridan, 1917
Gerow, Will—Sheridan, 1917
Gerow, Wm.—farmer, Clare
Gerrand, Nelson—Harrison, 1914
Gerren, Bert—Vernon, 1917
Gerren, Floyd—farmer, Vernon
Gerren, John—farmer, Vernon
Gerrin, Floyd—teacher, Vernon
Gerrin, James—farmer, Vernon
Getchell, Walter—restaurant, Lake
Gibbs, Albert, Clare, 1905
Gibbs, A.—bank clerk, Clare, 1914
Giberson, Grace—teacher, Clare
Giberson, W. C.—Clare, 1900
Gibis, Alois—farmer, Grant, 1900
Gibis, Anna—Grant, 1909

Gibis, George—farmer, Grant, 1912
Gibis, Lawrence—truck driver
Gibis, Marie—Grant, 1907
Gibson, Charles—Harrison Grocery
Gibson, Dalzell—teacher, Harrison
Gibson F. D.—Harrison
Gibson, Frances—teacher, Clare
Gibson, J. A.—Hayes, 1906
Gibson, J. V.—teacher, Harrison
Gibson, James—farmer, Clare, 1903
Gibson, John—Farwell, 1917
Gibson, Paul—Harrison
Gibson, V.—Farwell, 1907
Giddings, Charles—Harrison, 1903
Giddings, Chas.—bank cashier
Gieble, Fred—farmer, Grant, 1903
Gieble, Gottfried—farmer, 1903
Giers, Emil—WWI, Harrison, 1910
Giers, _____—Harrison, 1910
Gilbert, Del—WWI, 1918
Gilbert, James—Clare, 1905
Gilcher, George—farmer, Sheridan
Giles, Willis—Hatton, 1915
Giles, Willis, Jr.—Lilly Lake, 1915
Gill, Auda—teacher, Clare, 1917
Gill, Clarence—Dover, 1902
Gill, Clarence—Dover, 1903
Gill, H.—Pennock, 1906
Gilland, W.—Summerfield, 1906
Gillean, Delmer—creamery, Clare
Gillet, Marie—W. Grant, 1919
Gillette, Edna—teacher, Clare, 1918
Gillis, Ada—Clare
Gillis, Idah—Clare
Gillis, J. Dale—laborer, Clare
Gillis, J. E.—livery, Clare, 1915
Gillispie, James—mechanic, WWI
Gillman, C. O.—Freeman, 1917
Gilman, Daniel—Civil War Vet
Gillman, Frank—Lake, 1909
Gilman, D.—Grant, 1906
Gilman, Frank—Clare, 1907
Gilmore, Alwein—WWI, 1918
Gilmore, Anna—Clare, 1900
Gilmore, Arthur—Clare, 1909
Gilmore, C. A.—farmer, Freeman
Gilmore, Earl—Clare
Gilmore, Edward—farmer, Grant
Gilmore, Ernest—Clare, 1913
Gilmore, Freeman—Freeman, 1908
Gilmore, Freida—Clare
Gilmore, Hazel—teacher, Clare
Gilmore, Karen—Windover, 1918
Gilmore, Herbert—Clare, 1900
Gilmore, John—Clare, 1900
Gilmore, Mary—Grant, 1909
Gilmore, Meta—teacher, Clare
Gilmore, Maud—seamstress, Clare
Gilmore, Minnie—1909
Gilmore, Paul—Freeman, 1917
Gilmore, Sylvester—Clare, 1906
Gilmore, Velma—teacher, Clare
Gilson, D.—Crooked Lake, 1904
Gilsen, Edward—farmer, Clare
Gilson, Wm.—farmer, Clare
Ginn, Mary—Clare
Glass, Ed—farmer, Gilmore, 1917
Glass, Frederick—farmer, Gilmore
Glass, Herbert—farmer, Civil
   War Vet, Gilmore, 1900
Glass, Herbert, Jr.—Gilmore, 1917
Glass, James—merchant, Dover

Glass, Lucille—Clare
Glass, Mabel—teacher, Clare, 1908
Glass, Malvina—teacher, Farwell
Glass, Stanley—Gilmore, 1917
Glassley, Perry—Redding, 1904
Glazier, M.—Woolen Mills,
   head salesman, Clare, 1900
Gleason, A.—Clare, 1910
Gleason, Albert—Franklin, 1904
Gleason, Dean—Harrison, 1900
Gleason, E.—Harrison, 1903
Gleason, Ethel—Clare
Gleason, Fred—farmer, Franklin
Gleason, Jessie—Clare, 1917
Gleason, Leon—Clare, 1903
Gleason, S. A.—farmer, Clare, 1903
Glosch, Anna—teacher, Harrison
Glosch, Otto—Greenwood, 1906
Gobella, J.—Greenwood, 1906
Godfred, L.—Grant, 1906
Godfrey, Milo—Surrey, 1906
Godkin, John—farmer, Arthur
Godwin, E.—Winterfield
Godwin, W. A.—farmer
Goheen, Omer—Freeman, 1915
Goheen, Wm.—Lincoln, 1917
Goisine, Phil—Harrison, 1915
Gooden, I. N.—Grant, 1909
Goodenough, Frank—general store
Goodenough, George—merchant
Goodenow, Charles—Clare, 1903
Goodenow, Elmo—Temple, 1903
Goodenow, H. N.—Clare, 1900
Goodenow, Velma—Clare, 1907
Goodknecht, Anna—Hatton, 1906
Goodknecht, Ethel—Clare, 1910
Goodknecht—Hatton, 1900
Goodknecht, Frank, Jr.—Hatton
Goodknecht, Fred—Hatton, 1900
Goodknecht, Jennie—1911
Goodknecht, Wm.—P.M.R.R.
Goodman, J.A.—Clare, 1903
Goodman, John—bank cashier
Goodman, K. M.—millinery, Clare
Goodman, Wm.—merchant, Clare
Goodman, Wm.—merchant, Clare
Goodman, Carlos—WWI
Goodrich, Ralph—WWI, Temple
Goodwin, Ora—farmer, Surrey
Goodwin, W. A.—Grandon, 1903
Gordanier, Karl—Clare, 1918
Gordanier, Archie—undersheriff
Gordanier, Belle—Clare, 1903
Gordanier, Carl—commercial man
Gordanier, John—Clare
Gordon, Rev. Frank—minister
Gordon, Glenn—Arthur, 1917
Gordon, "Ike"—Farwell, 1915
Gordon, John—Hatton, 1904
Gordon, Lora—Hatton, 1903
Gordon, Ray—Arthur, 1917
Gordon, Roy—Clare, 1915
Gorr, A. E.—AEF, Clare
Gorr, Barnard—Clare
Gorr, Dorothy—Clare
Gorr, E. B.—Clare, 1903
Gorr, Frank—farmer, Clare, 1903
Gorr, Mary—Clare
Gorr, _____—Vernon, 1871
Gorr, Raymond—Clare, 1910
Gosden, Ralph—Clare, 1917
Gosine, Oliver—salesman, Harrison

Gosine, Phil—WWI, AEF, Hayes
Gottschall, Mrs. G.—dept. store
Goudie, Alexander—Arthur, 1915
Gould, A. W.—Arthur, 1903
Gould, C. H.—undertaker, Clare
Gould, Florie—Garfield, 1909
Gould, Frank—Garfield, 1905
Gould, Fred—8 Point Lake, 1904
Gould, Grace—Clare, 1900
Gould, H. C.—Clare, 1915
Gould, Rev. H. V.—Evangelist, Dover, 1900
Gould, Orson—Clare, 1900
Gould, Oscar—Clare, 1900
Gould, T. C.—Garfield, 1909
Gould, W. F.—Garfield, 1911
Goultry, W.—Farwell, 1914
Gover, George—pharmacist, Loomis
Gover, Harry—Loomis, 1915
Gover, N. D.—store, Loomis, 1912
Gow, James—1908
Grace, S. L.—Loomis Grocery
Grace, S. P.—Loomis, 1918
Graff, Rev. Benjamin—minister
Graham, Allen—WWI, Farwell
Graham, Arthur—Vernon, 1917
Graham, Bert—Farwell, 1914
Graham, Clyde—Clare
Graham, Edward—career soldier
Graham, E. R.—Farwell
Graham, Ethel—teacher, Farwell
Graham, F.W.—1918
Graham, Floyd—farmer, Redding
Graham, George, Jr.—Farwell
Graham, George W.—ex-sheriff
Graham, H. A.—ex- supt.
   of schools, Clare
Graham, Hugh—WWI, Gilmore
Graham, Jesse—WWI, 1918
Graham, John—WWI, 1918
Graham, Joseph—farmer, Isabella
Graham, Luther—Surrey, 1915
Graham, Manson—Farwell, 1906
Graham, Orpheus—1912
Graham, Rollo—Surrey, 1907
Graham, Stanley—AEF, Surrey
Graham, Vera—Temple, 1914
Graham, Wilmot—farmer, Gilmore
Grandell, C. B.—Garfield, 1906
Granger, Arthur—Farwell, 1904
Granger, G.—Frost, 1906
Grant, Frederick—Winterfield, 1907
Grathwohl, Lawrence—tailor, Clare
Graub, Fred—farmer, Harrison
Graub, Freda—Greenwood, 1911
Graves, Burrell—Clare, 1916
Graves, Charles—farmer, 1917
Graves, George—bank teller, Clare
Graves, James—lumberman
Graves, James—saw mill, Sheridan
Graves, M.—Redding, 1906
Graves, Tessie—Greenwood, 1916
Graves, Thomas—Clare, 1915
Graves, Ward—Sheridan, 1908
Gray, Asa—farmer, Summerfield
Gray, Bessie—Clare, 1905
Gray, Rev. E. F.—M-E, Clare
Gray, Frank—Clare, 1913
Gray, Dr. Frank—physician, 1904
Gray, Dr. Harry—physician, Clare
Gray, Jessie—Harrison, 1909
Gray, M.—Meredith, 1917

Gray, N.—Meredith, 1911
Gray, Perry—Meredith, 1917
Gray, Dr. Robert—physician, Clare
Gray, Samuel—carpenter, Vernon
Gray, Thomas—Rosebush
Grear, M.—Hamilton, 1906
Grear, Wm.—Dover, 1908
Green, A. C.—farmer, 1911
Green, Albert—finisher, Clare, 1915
Green, Bertha—Harrison, 1912
Green, B. A.—Harrison, 1913
Green, Charles—WWI, Lake, 1917
Green, Christopher—farmer, Grant
Green, Dell—Mannsiding, 1918
Green, Dorothy—Clare
Green, D. S.—farmer, Hatton, 1906
Green, Earl—teacher, Harrison
Green, F. D.—WWI, tank corps.
Green, Florence—Clare
Green, Floyd—salesman, Clare
Green, Fred—Harrison, 1912
Green, George—Summerfield, 1906
Green, Gerald—Clare
Green, H. L.—Garfield, 1916
Green, Harry—Garfield, 1917
Green, Henry—Winterfield, 1912
Green, Henry—Garfield, 1918
Green, James—Harrison, 1964
Green, Jay—Clare
Green, Jeanette—Clare
Green, Josephine—Clare
Green, L. H.—Surrey, 1906
Green, L. W.—farmer, Summerfield
Green, M. E.—1907
Green, Martha—Harrison, 1903
Green, Raymond—farmer, Clare
Green, R. E.—businessman, Clare
Green, Samuel—farmer, Hatton
Green, Sarah—telephone operator
Green, Sidney—Leota, 1901
Green, Thomas—bookkeeper
Green, Willis—jewelry store
Greenaway, Harry—A.A.R.R.
Greene, Chester—lumberman
Greenfield, Richard—music teacher
Greenlee, Vivian—teacher, Clare
Greer, Burt—Clare, 1905
Greer, Bert—men's wear clerk
Greer, Frances—Clare
Greer, John—cement plant, Clare
Greer, M.—Hamilton, 1915
Gregg, Harry—farmer, Grant
Gregory, Edith—Farwell, 1908
Gregory, Elroy—Marion, 1917
Gregory, Frank—Clare, 1907
Gregory, F.—Farwell, 1909
Gregory, James—Gilmore, 1900
Gregory, O. F.—Garfield, 1905
Grewe, Henry—Hatton, 1915
Grewe, Victoria—Clare
Grieb, Wm.—Sheridan,1916
Grieber, Paul—tailor, Clare, 1903
Griesser, Paul—merchant, tailer
Griesser, Roy—Clare, 1900
Grieve, H.—farmer, Hatton, 1914
Griffen, George—Summerfield
Griffin, Albert, WWI, 1918
Griffin, D.—Farwell, 1914
Griffin, Frank—Grant, 1917
Griffin, John—Summerfield, 1903
Griffith, Emma—Temple, 1903
Griffith, Vesta—Temple, 1903

Griffin, Albert—Hayes, 1917
Griffin, Darius—Gilmore, 1903
Griffin, George—Harrison, 1918
Griffin, G. W.—Clare, 1904
Griffin, Wm.—Surrey, 1917
Griffin, Z. T.—Farwell, 1914
Griffon, John—Leota, 1909
Grigg, Harry—farmer, Sheridan
Grigg, James—farmer, Sheridan
Grigg, James—1918
Grigg, Nellie—Colonville, 1908
Grigsby, Faith—Garfield, 1911
Grigware, Clare—Clare, 1907
Grigware, Joseph—telephone op.
Grigware, Percy—Clare, 1905
Grill, Charles—jeweler, Clare, 1914
Grill, Pearl—Clare, 1915
Grillette, Dr. F. F.—physician
Grimason, Hiram—Clare
Grimason, Jessie—Clare
Grimm, Clarence—Harrison, 1917
Grimm, Wm.—Gilmore, 1914
Grimmason, John—R.F.D. carrier
Grimason, Joseph—pioneer, Vernon
Grimason, Joseph—Clare
Grimm, C. E.—Farwell
Grimm, Wm.—Gilmore, 1917
Grinn, Edwin—Hamilton, 1901
Grinnell, Rev. J.—Baptist minister
Griswold, Rev. J. B.—Free
   Methodist pastor, 1915
Griswold, Charles—Clare, 1901
Groeb, Wm.—Sheridan, 1917
Grogan, Charles—Farwell, 1904
Grogan, James—1902
Grogan, Thomas—Vernon, 1902
Gronda, Chas.—Frost, 1903
Gronda, Charles—farmer, Harrison
Gronda, Dortha—Clare, 1907
Grosvenor, Arthur—farmer, Clare
Grounds, Jeff—farmer, Sheridan
Grounds, Mae—Wise, 1909
Grove, Elizabeth—Clare, 1915
Grover, Annabelle—Clare
Grover, Frank—Clare, 1903
Grover, George—Clare
Grover, Henry—Clare, 1900
Grover, Henry—Clare, 1915
Grover, Wm.—1914
Groves, Bernice—Clare
Groves, Betty—Clare
Groves, Estella—teacher
Groves, Gwen—Clare, 1919
Groves, Henry—farmer, 1905
Groves, Milton—Redding, 1908
Groves, Thomas—farmer, Clare,
   Greenwood, b. 1841 - d. 1915
Groves, Thomas—auctioneer,
   restaurant, Clare, 1915
Grow, Howard—road builder
Gruett, Dan—Andersonville, 1909
Grunda, C. A.—Frost, 1904
Grunda, Fred—Long Lake, 1909
Grunda, Will—Frost, 1909
Grundler, Elizabeth—music teacher
Gruno, Charles—WWI, Harrison
Gruno, E.—Hatton, 1906
Gruno, Elsie—Hatton, 1916
Gruno, Hartley—Hayes
Gruno, Henry—Clare
Gruno, Herman—WWI, Hayes
Gruno, William—farmer, 1903

Gruno, Wm.—Hayes, 1917
Guenther, A.—Harrison
Guenther, Ed—Harrison
Guernsey, Allen—Temple
Guernsey, Jay—Redding, 1908
Guest, Calvin—WWI, Sheridan
Guest, Forest—WWI, 1918
Guiles, Alexander—Redding, 1903
Guiles, E. E.—Temple, 1903
Gullen, Floyd—Clare Supt.
Gumser, W. J.—Clare Supt.
Gunderman, George—Freeman
Gunderman, Theo—cook, Surrey
Gunn, Darius—Franklin, 1914
Guntheir, David—Loomis, 1909
Gurd, J.—8 Pointe Lake, 1904
Gurlitz, Paul—Hayes, 1917
Gustev, Yek—Harrison, 1908
Guthrie, Frank—Winterfield, 1914
Gutting, S.—Clare, 1906
Guyler, Alexander—Temple, 1903
Guyles, Earl—Temple, 1913
Guyles, Ed—Redding, 1906
Hackett, L. B.—movie theatre mgr.
Hackett, Lovina—teacher, Harrison
Hackett, Mae—teacher, Sheridan
Hackmuth, Nettie—Clare
Hackmuth, Ruby—Clare
Haddix, C. M.—farmer, Farwell
Hadley, Jane—Hatton
Hadsell, M. M.—Hamilton, 1906
Hafner, George—Clare
Hagen, A. A.—truant officer
Hagen, Andy—AEF, Harrison
Hagle, Gladys—teacher, Clare, 1903
Hagel, Kenneth—clerk, Clare, 1909
Hagle, Jonathan—Clare, 1908
Hagel, Kenneth—baseball player
Hagen, A. A.—Hayes, 1910
Hagen, Andrew—AEF, Harrison
Hagle, Roy—Clare, 1903
Haines, Edd—farmer, Eagle, 1918
Haines, Melvin—Arthur, 1917
Haines, Myrle—farmer, Sheridan
Hains, Adelbert—merchant, Dover
Hains, Alvera—Arthur, 1914
Hains, A.—1904
Hains, Henry, Jr.—Eagle, 1904
Hains, Murl—Clare, 1909
Hains, Robert—1903
Hains, Merle—Dover, 1904
Hains, Verne—Grant, 1884
Hale, Glen—Sheridan, 1912
Hale, Henry—farmer, Winterfield
Hale, Ora—Arthur, 1906
Hale, Pomeroy—Arthur, 1915
Hale, R. R.—farmer, Arthur, 1906
Hale, Simeon—farmer
Hale, Warren—WWI, Clare, 1917
Hales, Effie—teacher, Clare, 1909
Hales, Glen—farmer, Clare, 1894
Hales, Harry—Vernon, 1900
Hales, Henry—laborer, Clare
Hales, Henry—Clare
Hales, Lewis—Vernon, 1916
Hales, Ray—WWI, Vernon
Hales, Walter—Vernon, 1915
Hales, Wm.—Supervisor,
  Winterfield, 1904
Haley, Albert—Clare, 1910
Haley, Wm.—stock-buyer, Clare
Halford, James—farmer, Lincoln

Hall, Arthur—Redding, 1917
Hall, Edmund—lumberman,
  lawyer, Farwell, 1870
Hall, Eva—Harrison, 1906
Hall, George—R.R., Clare
Hall, Rev. H. C.—minister,
  auto mechanic, Sheridan, 1916
Hall, Henry—Redding, 1908
Hall, John—Surrey, 1916
Hall, Lee—decorator, Farwell
Hall, Louis—Lincoln, 1904
Hall, Perry—WWI, Franklin, 1917
Hall, Peter—Farwell, 1914
Haller, C. F.—Clare, 1912
Haller, Catherine—Clare
Haller, C. F.—drayman, Clare
Hallet, Frank—Harrison, 1918
Hallett, Glen—bartender, Harrison
Hallett, Harvey—Frost, 1906
Hallett, L. A.—Harrison, 1916
Hallett, Olive—Harrison
Hallett, S. C.—Winterfield, 1912
Halstead, Abel—Clare, 1910
Halstead, Chester—WWI,
  Canadian Army, Lake
Halstead, Edward—Clare, 1900
Halstead, Elmer—grocery, Clare
Halstead, George—restaurant, Clare
Halstead, Herschel—businessman,
  produce buyer, Clare, 1909
Halstead, John—farmer
Halstead, Lillian—teacher, Clare
Halstead, Mabel—1903
Halstead, Otis—Vernon, 1905
Ham, L.—Temple, 1909
Hamer, J. B.—Grandon, 1903
Hamer, K. Burr—Grandon, 1917
Hamilton, D. V.—teacher, Redding
Hamilton, Edna—teacher, Arthur
Hamilton, F. H.—Vernon, 1912
Hamilton, Gladys—Clare, 1910
Hamilton, J. J.—Hayes, 1906
Hamilton, John—Temple, 1909
Hamilton, P.—Harrison, 1913
Hamilton, Richard—farmer
Hamilton, Robert—Sheridan, 1900
Hamilton, Samuel—postmaster
Hamlin, Fred—rancher, Hatton
Hamlin, Hattie—Hatton, 1917
Hamlin, Lamont—Clare
Hamlin, St. Clair—rancher, Hatton
Hamlin, St. Claire, Jr.—WWI
Hamlin, W. R.—Hatton, 1907
Hammadier, Charles—merchant
Hammerberg, Dr. Kuno—physician
Hammersley, Charles—Franklin
Hammersley, Lyle—Hamilton, 1906
Hammon, Cyrus—jewelry, Clare
Hammon, W.—Surrey, 1906
Hammond, Archie—Redding, 1918
Hammond, Della—Temple, 1917
Hammond, Delos—Temple, 1917
Hammond, Lewis—Clare, 1917
Hammond, Sylvester—Coldwater
Hampton, A. D.—farmer, Grant
Hampton, Agnes—Clare
Hampton, Andrew—Grant, 1918
Hampton, Bernie—garage, Harrison
Hampton, Dusten—farmer, Grant
Hampton, Edna—teacher, Harrison
Hampton, Frank—teacher, Sheridan
Hampton, Fred—Clare, 1917

Hampton, I. E.—farmer, garage,
  Sheridan, 1900
Hampton, James—Sheridan, 1877
Hampton, Jesse—garage, Clare
Hampton, John W.—farmer
Hampton, Leo—Clare
Hampton, Tuff—teacher, Colonville
Hampton, Wm.—Grant, 1906
Hance, W. K.—Crooked Lake
Hanchett, A. C.—Civil War
  Vet, Clare, 1914
Hanchett, Earl—WWI
Hanchett, Harold—stockbuyer
Handy, John—farmer, Hatton, 1906
Hanes, Ed—farmer, Sheridan, 1900
Hanes, Henry—farmer, Sheridan
Hanes, Henry, Jr.—Eagle, 1904
Hanes, Mary
Hanes, Merl—Clare, 1908
Hanes, Raymond—Dover, 1913
Hanes, Wm. J.—farm hand, Grant
Hanley, Ed—Clare, 1910
Hanley, John—produce merchant
Hanley, Patrick—barber, WWI
Hanley, Thomas—engineer, Clare
Hansler, John—Hayes, 1906
Hansen, Jay—teacher, Clare, 1913
Hanson, Walter—Lincoln, 1917
Harder, Alvin—farmer, Garfield
Hardie, Ruth—teacher, Clare, 1929
Hardt, Phillip—Wise, 1917
Harding, John—AEF, Redding
Hardy, Charles—Clare
Hardy, Guy L.—carpenter, Clare
Hardy, Ray—businessman, Saginaw
Harger, David—farmer, Hatton
Harger, James—farmer, Hatton
Harger, Myrtle—Hatton, 1911
Harger, Riley—WWI, Clare
Haring, Carl—Sheridan, 1906
Haring, Chris—Wise, 1900
Haring, Dora—1909
Haring, George—farmer, Wise
Haring, John—farmer, Vernon
Haring, John, Jr.—Clare, 1917
Haring, John III—Wise, 1918
Haring, Karl—farmer, Sheridan
Harlin, George—threshing
  machine operator, W. Grant
Harmon, Thomas—farmer, Vernon
Harns, Thomas—Surrey, 1906
Harold, Tessie—teacher, Arthur
Harper, Ada—teacher, Harrison
Harper, D. E.—Grant, 1906
Harper, Edward—Temple, 1918
Harper, Gayla—Harrison, 1907
Harper, Ida—teacher, Harrison
Harper, J. A.—Clare, 1909
Harper, W. L.—Harrison, 1907
Harper, Wallace—county poor
  farm comm., Harrison, 1904
Harper, Wm. W.—postmaster
Harpster, John—Brown, 1909
Harpster, Willard—Grant, 1917
Harpster, Wm.—farmer, Grant
Harring, George—farmer, Clare
Harring, Marie—Clare, 1911
Harrington, A. L.—Grant, 1906
Harrington, C. S.—Harrison, 1902
Harrington, Clark—hotel, Grandon
Harrington, Ethel—Winterfield
Harrington, Helen—Clare

Harrington, H. L.—store, Farwell
Harrington, J. L.—blacksmith
Harrington, John—Dover, 1918
Harrington, Lew—pioneer
Harrington, Ralph—Temple, 1917
Harris, Al—farmer, Temple, 1907
Harris, Clyde—Racket Store, Clare
Harris, Clyde—Harris & Hirt
    Hardware, Clare, 1903
Harris, Frank—Clare
Harris, Fred—Clare, 1903
Harris, Grace—Temple, 1908
Harris, Isaac—carpenter, Civil
    War Vet, Clare, 1905
Harris, John B.—miller, Farwell
Harris, John W.—grocer, Clare
Harrison, Alfred—Frost, 1918
Harrison, Ellis—garage, Clare, 1920
Harrison, H. L.—farmer, Frost
Harrison, James—farmer, Arthur
Harrison, Rose—millinery, corsets
Harrison, Shirley—teacher, Clare
Harrison, Wm. Arthur—1911
Harrold, Arthur—Clare, 1917
Harrold, Herbert—businessman
Harrold, M. E.—farmer, Arthur
Harrold, Ray—farmer, Arthur
Harrold, Rollie—RFD carrier
Harsh, Ira—Wise, 1917
Harsh, Lucille—Clare
Harsh, Starrie—Wise, 1917
Harshman, Gertie—teacher, 1903
Hart, Cyrus—Summerfield, 1906
Hart, Orlean—Clare
Hartford, _____—farmer, Freeman
Hartman, Carrie—teacher, Hatton
Hartman, Claude—telephone mgr.
Hartman, Frank—salesman, Clare
Hartman, Glen—Grant, 1915
Hartman, Jeff—Arthur, 1900
Hartman, Jess—farmer, Arthur
Hartman, John—Arthur, 1900
Hartman, John—farmer, Sheridan
Hartman, Pearl—lumberman
Hartman, Wm.—Arthur, 1908
Hartsell, A.—Temple, 1900
Harvey, Calvin J.—Hatton, 1905
Harvey, Carson—auctioneer
Harvey, Cord—Elm Grove, 1918
Harvey, Eslie—WWI, Sheridan
Harvey, Frank—laborer, Leota
Harvey, Fred—Clare, 1907
Harvey, Horace—1903
Harvey, Leon—Clare, 1905
Harvey, Mildred—Clare
Harvey, Obadiah—carpenter, 1911
Harvey, Philip—farmer, Arthur
Harvey, Philo—Hamilton, 1906
Harvey, Ralph—WWI, Hayes
Harvey, Thomas—WWI, Harrison
Harvie, A. E.—Farwell, 1900
Harwood, Wm.—1914
Haskell, N. J.—Grant, 1906
Hastings, Frank—Harrison, 1917
Hatch, Clare—Harrison, 1915
Hatch, Claudia—Leota, 1910
Hatch, Donald—farmer, Surrey
Hatch, E. O.—Harrison, 1903
Hatch, Ena—teacher, Farwell, 1915
Hatch, Eula—teacher, Grant, 1913
Hatch, Frank—Leota, 1900
Hatch, Glenn—Leota, 1910

Hatch, Lester—Farwell, 1915
Hatehouse, James—Garfield, 1915
Hatfield, Charles—farmer, Isabella
Hatfield, George—Farwell, 1916
Hatfield, John—Harrison, 1902
Hatfield, John—WWI, Farwell
Hatfield, Julius—Hayes, 1903
Hatfield, Wm. F.—Redding, 1917
Hatfield, Wm. H.—farmer, Garfield
Hathaway, Grace—Clare, 1903
Hathaway, Ida—Temple, 1918
Hathaway, W. H.—Clare, 1903
Hathaway, Rev. W. J.—minister
Hathaway, Wm.—Redding, 1917
Haught, Russell—Temple
Haven, Elmer—hotel, Harrison
Haven, Eva—Harrison, 1917
Havens, Julia—teacher, Temple
Havens, Milo—Harrison, 1916
Haver, Harold—Clare, 1915
Hawes, Edward—Meredith, 1894
Hawk, Alonzo—Grant, 1918
Hawkins, Bernard—WWI, 1918
Hawkins, Ed—Clare, 1915
Hawkins, Edward T.—farmer
Hawkins, Olney—civil engineer
Hawkins, Pearl—teacher, Clare
Hawkins, Roy—AEF, 1918
Hawkins, Sylvin—Clare, 1903
Hawkins, Will—farmer, Clare, 1915
Hawkins, Wm.—farmer, Clare
Hawkinson, J. A.—Hatton, 1910
Hawley, Henry—Arthur, 1879
Hawley, James—Harrison, 1908
Hawley, Mable—Arthur, 1910
Haws, C. E.—Clare, 1915
Hay, Stuart—WWI, 1917
Hayden, Helen—teacher, 1909
Hayes, Clyde—mgr., Clare, 1909
Haynak, Frank—Temple, 1900
Haynak, Frank, Jr.—merchant
Haynak, Steve—Temple
Hayner, C. E.—farmer
Hayner, Clarence—Clare, 1915
Hayner, Isaac—Loomis, 1904
Hays, Clyde—businessman, Clare
Hayward, Marlon—Surrey, 1917
Hayward, Marvin—WWI, Farwell
Hayward, Martin—WWI, Surrey
Hayward, Richard C.—Surrey
Hayward, Richard O.—WWI
Hazelrod, W. A.—Freeman, 1913
Hearns, Curtice—Clare, 1909
Heartwell, Wm.—Franklin, 1917
Heath, A. E.—Clare, 1915
Heath, George—telephone operator
Heber, Charles—farmer, Harrison
Heber, Otto—lumberman, teacher,
    superintendent, Hatton, 1904
Heber, Robert—Harrison
Heckathorn, Cristel—teacher
Heckathorn, J.—farmer, Alward
Hecker, Roy—Harrison, 1916
Heibler, M.—Hatton, 1906
Heilman, I.—Harrison
Heilman, Wm.—farmer, Harrison
Hein, Anna—Grant, 1909
Hein, Augusta—Arthur, 1904
Hein, Martin, farmer—Randall
Hein, Pearl—1907
Heintz, George—Greenwood, 1917
Heintz, Henry—WWI, Greenwood

Heintz, Lee—WWI, 1918
Heintz, Marvin—Harrison, 1955
Heintzelman, Henry—Grant, 1917
Heirholzer, Adolph—Clare
Heirholzer, H. J.—farmer, Clare
Heiser, Charles—farmer, Alward
Heiser, Ivan—WWI, Brand, 1918
Heiser, J. R.—Arthur, 1913
Heiser, L. R.—farmer, Arthur
Heiser, Leland—Arthur, 1915
Heiser, Martha—1907
Heiser, Martin—WWI, Arthur
Heiser, Roscoe—Arthur, 1908
Heiser, Roy—Arthur, 1908
Heiser, Warren—Arthur, 1916
Heiser, Zorah—Eagle, 1909
Heisman, Henry—musician,
    lumber co., Harrison, 1881
Helke, August—Hamilton, 1906
Hellems, John—Loomis, 1900
Heller, Ralph—Arthur, 1914
Heller, Stephen—farmer, store
    mason, Arthur, 1917
Hellwig, John—Frost, 1906
Hellman, Charles—auctioneer
Helms, Warner—mill owner, Leota
Helper, Frank—Sheridan, 1917
Helstand, Mrs. P. J.—Freeman
Hempfinger, Jacob—1903
Hemstreet, George—Eagle, 1908
Hemstreet, Inez—Clare
Hemstreet, Nathan—WWI, Grant
Hemstreet, Nelson—Grant, 1906
Hemstreet, Scott—WWI, 1918
Henchback, Mrs.—Grant, 1906
Henderson, Bessie—Clare, 1910
Henderson, David—pioneer, Grant
Henderson, Earl—Grant, 1917
Henderson, Eliza—Clare, 1902
Henderson, Hugh—Grant, 1905
Henderson, James—farmer, Grant
Henderson, Maude—teacher, Clare
Henderson, Roy—Temple, 1906
Henderson, Samuel—farmer, Grant
Henderson, Wm.—Lake, 1913
Henderson, Wm. A.—Gd. Trunk
    R.R., Co. Clerk, Clare, 1907
Hendrie, Ben—farmer, Eagle, 1918
Hendrie, Florence—Grant, 1911
Hendrie, George—Grant, 1910
Hendrie, Hezekiah—farmer, Vernon
Hendrie, J. B.—farmer, Eagle, 1918
Hendrie, J. W.—Clare, 1912
Hendrie, Kenneth—Clare
Hendrie, Viola—Clare
Hendrie, Wm. A.—Vernon, 1917
Henry, Glen—WWI
Henry, G. H.—farmer, Vernon
Henry, John—elevator, meat
    market, Farwell, 1900
Henry, Joseph—farmer, Vernon
Henry, Samuel—brickyard, Farwell
Henry, Wm.—Winterfield, 1913
Henscheie, Christian, Clare, 1904
Hepbourn, Myrrha—teacher, Clare
Hepburn, Myhrra—teacher, Clare
Hepfinger, Jacob—farmer, Clare
Herman, E. H.—farmer, Lincoln
Herman, Edward F.—WWI, 1918
Herman, Ernest—Hatton, 1917
Herman, Henry—farmer, Hatton
Herman, Irwin—Freeman, 1918

Herman, Phillip—Loomis, 1900
Herrick, Alfred—clerk, Clare, 1909
Herrick, Bernice—Clare
Herrick, Edward—farmer, Sheridan
Herrick, J. R.—Sheridan, 1903
Herrick, M. A.—Farwell, 1904
Herrick, Marjorie—Clare, 1918
Herring, Karl—farmer, Sheridan
Herring, John—farmer, Vernon
Herrington, Arthur—laundry, Clare
Hermann, Lem—Wise, 1917
Herrmann, Peter—1918
Herron, Charles—Sheridan, 1903
Herron, Earl—laborer, Clare
Hersey, George—bowling alley,
    discount stamp co., Clare, 1903
Hersey, James—Sheridan, 1910
Hersey, Julius—farmer, 1904
Hersey, Mary—Loomis, 1914
Hess, F. L.—farmer, Sheridan
Hess, Dr. H. R.—osteopathic
    physician, Clare
Hess, Jacob—Lincoln, 1915
Hess, John—creamery, Clare, 1900
Hess, Walter—Sheridan, 1918
Hess, Warner—saw mill, Sheridan
Heter, Helen—teacher, Clare
Hetrick, Ervin—Clare, 1910
Heuschele, August—farmer, WWI
Heuschele, Chas—Grant, 1903
Heuschele, Christian—farmer
Heuschele, Paul—farmer, Grant
Hewer, Isaac—Farwell, 1907
Hewer, J.—Farwell, 1909
Hewer, L.—Surrey, 1906
Hewett, Edmond—farmer, Freeman
Hewett, Ella—chicken farm
Hewett, Elwood—Freeman, 1905
Hewlett, E. L.—mgr. Mich.
    Creamery Co., Clare, 1911
Hickey, Alfred—AEF, Clare
Hickey, Emerson—Clare, 1911
Hickey, George—Clare, 1914
Hickey, James—Clare, 1910
Henderson, Anna—Clare, 1913
Hickey, James G.—Clare, 1911
Hickey, J. Bennett—Clare, 1880
Hickey, Mildred—Clare, 1916
Hickok, Eljia—supervisor, Freeman
Hickok, Everett—AEF, 1918
Hickok, Guy—WWI, Freeman
Hickok, Wm. C.—Freeman, 1909
Hicks, N. A.—Clare, 1912
Hicks, T. W.—Clare, 1907
Hicks, Wm. T.—Clare, 1904
Hiestand, P. J.—Freeman, 1918
Higbee, James—Clare
Higgins, Charles—WWI, Farwell
Higgins, Charles—Surrey, 1917
Higgins, Frank—Harrison, 1900
Higgins, Harry—Surrey, 1917
High, John—fur buyer, Clare, 1903
Highlen, George—farmer, Clare
Higley, Wm. A.—Greenwood, 1912
Hilborn, Florence—Sheridan, 1914
Hilborn, George—farmer, Arthur
Hilborn, Mable—Arthur, 1912
Hilborn, W. A.—Arthur, 1900
Hilborn, Wm. R.—farmer, Arthur
Hildebrandt, Adolph—farmer
Hildebrandt, Albert—WWI, 1918
Hildebrandt, August—Arthur, 1919

Hildebrandt, Fred—WWI, Arthur
Hildebrandt, Robert—AEF, Arthur
Hildebrandt, Rudolph—farmer
Hildebrandt, Wm.—farmer, Arthur
Hileman, Charles—r.r. fireman
Hileman, I. A.—Mannsiding, 1916
Hileman, Isaac—farmer, Harrison
Hileman, John—Hatton, 1903
Hileman, Nannie—Clare, 1912
Hileman, O. A.—Mannsiding, 1917
Hileman, Wm.—WWI, Harrison
Hill, Fannie—Harrison, 1912
Hill, John—Harrison, 1910
Hill, John—Harrison, 1918
Hill, Wm.—Harrison, 1912
Hillabrandt, Clement—Harrison
Hillerger, Ben—Lake George, 1909
Hilliker, Ben—Freeman, 1916
Hilliker, Charles—Surrey, 1917
Hilliker, George—Freeman, 1916
Hilsennegan, George—1915
Hilson, Nellie—Farwell, 1900
Hilson, Thomas—Farwell, 1872
Hilson, Thomas—Farwell, 1900
Himes, Herbert—WWI, 1918
Hinch, George—Clare, 1905
Hinds, Ruth—Farwell, 1908
Hines, Edward—hardware,
    twp. clerk, Farwell
Hinkle, Fabian—farmer, Grant
Hinkle, John—Grant, 1906
Hinkle, Labian—Grant, 1907
Hintz, Henry—WWI, Arthur, 1918
Hirt, Charles—Ann Arbor
    conductor, Clare, 1892
Hirt, Tom—A.A.R.R.
    employer, Clare, 1900
Hirzel, Albert—Clare, 1906
Hirzel, Ellen—Clare, 1908
Hirzel, Wm.—Grant, 1903
Hiscock, Harry—Freeman, 1912
Hitchcock, Doris—Clare, 1900
Hitchcock, Ethelyn—Clare, 1913
Hitchcock, May—1907
Hitchcock, Wm. H.—grocery
    store, Grant, 1900
Hitts, A. A.—Hatton, 1906
Hitts, Frank—Harrison, 1913
Hitts, James—Hatton, 1917
Hitts, J. J.—Hatton, 1904
Hixon, Elizabeth—teacher
Hoag, Emma—teacher, Harrison
Hoag, Harold—Clare, 1910
Hoag, Joseph—barber, Harrison
Hobson, Watson—Vernon, 1911
Hochstetler, Alice—Clare
Hochstetler, Frank—Harrison
Hockstetler, Virgil—Clare
Hochstetler, Wm.—Clare
Hochstetler, Wilma—Clare
Hock, Vernon Z.—Temple
Hocking, Elizabeth—millinery
Hockstattler, Frank—Harrison
Hodges, Gerald—farmer, Grant
Hudgins, Florence—Temple, 1900
Hodgins, James—farmer, Vernon
Hodgins, James—Vernon
Hodgins, Ray—Vernon, 1895
Hodkinson, John—farmer
Hodkinson, Myra—teacher, Clare
Hodkinson, Rose—Clare
Hodkinson, Wm.—pioneer, Civil

War Vet, Vernon, 1871
Hodson, Eva—Clare
Hoefle, Gottfried—farmer, Grant
Hoeneke, Rev. H. H.—minister
Hoff, Otto—Hatton, 1915
Hoffman, Julius—jeweler, Clare
Hoffman, R.—Surrey, 1906
Hogan, Lodie—teacher, Frost, 1918
Hoisington, J.—Harrison, 1900
Holbrook, Alanson—Temple, 1909
Holbrook, Alfred—mail carrier
Holbrook, Carl—AEF, Clare
Holbrook, Donald—attorney, Clare
Holbrook, Florence—Clare, 1907
Holbrook, Frank—Clare
Holbrook, Henry—painter, Clare
Holbrook, Marie—Clare, 1907
Holbrook, Nina—teacher, Clare
Holbrook, Ray—Clare, 1900
Holbrook, Thomas Carl—attorney
Holbrook, Thomas, Sr.—1884
Holbrook, Thomas C.—businessman
Holbrook, Wm.—Clare, 1900
Holcomb, Beatrice—Sheridan, 1905
Holcomb, Daniel—pool room,
    WWI, Clare, 1917
Holcomb, Frank—farmer
Holcomb, Frank—telephone
    line man, Clare
Holcomb, Hazel—Sheridan, 1915
Holcomb, Howard—Clare
Holcomb, James—farmer, Sheridan
Holcomb, Ralph—Clare, 1917
Holden, Rev. C. W.—M-E, Farwell
Holden, Horace—Surrey
Holderman, Katie—Franklin, 1915
Holderman, Levi—Hamilton, 1913
Holderman, Mabel—Hamilton
Holderman, Monroe—farmer
Holderman, Pearl—Hamilton, 1917
Holderman, Pyrie—farmer
Holderman, Samuel—Franklin
Holderman, Wm. P.—farmer
Hole, H. F.—Temple, 1903
Holford, Leroy—Temple
Holiday, C. C.—Grant, 1915
Holiday, E. W.—Clare, 1915
Holland, Dan—stock farm, Freeman
Hollatz, Jullous—1922
Holley, M. R.—farmer, Greenwood
Hollritz, Julius—Arthur, 1914
Holly, Walter—Clare, 1913
Holmes, Emmett—Wise, 1917
Holmes, Eugene—restaurant, Clare
Holmes, Frank—teacher, Clare
Holmes, George—Gilmore, 1906
Holmes, Glenwood—Clare
Holmes, Harry—teacher, Clare
Holmes, Jennie—teacher, Farwell
Holmes, Rev. L. E.—M-E, Leaton
Holmes, L. G.—rancher, Garfield
Holmes, Ruth—teacher, Farwell
Holmes, Thomas—photographer
Holmes, Venie—Clare
Holmes, William—Clare, 1915
Holmes, Wm. J.—water
    works engineer, Greenwood
Holt, Burton—Clare
Holt, Thomas—auto salesman
Holtz, Rudolph—farmer, Grant
Holtz, Wm.—pioneer, Isabella
Homer, Perry—Mannsiding, 1919

Honey, Charles—ticket agent, Clare
Honeywell, Clayton—Farwell, 1900
Honeywell, J. M.—Farwell, 1903
Honeywell, Vee—teacher, Farwell
Honeywell, Warren—Farwell, 1903
Honeywell, Watson—farmer, Surrey
Hood, George—Clare, 1914
Hood, Georgia—Clare, 1913
Hood, R. E.—dairy, Clare, 1913
Hood, Sidney—Arthur, 1917
Hook, Stephen—blacksmith, Loomis
Hooker, Herbert F.—WWI, 1918
Hooker, Herbert K.—WWI, Clare
Hooker, Ray—Farwell, 1917
Hooker, Willis—Clare, 1907
Hoot, Clarence—A.A.R.R. agent
Hoover, Charles—farmer, Vernon
Hoover, Christopher—Harrison
Hoover, Dan—Temple, 1917
Hoover, D. E.—farmer, Dover
Hoover, Glen—1919
Hoover, Henry—Greenwood, 1900
Hoover, John—farmer, Hatton
Hoover, Leon—farmer, Greenwood
Hoover, Roy—Dover
Hoover, Saul—Temple, 1909
Hope, George—Freeman
Hopkins, A. J.—farmer, Winterfield
Hopkins, C. W.—Lincoln, 1917
Hopkins, James—farmer, Gilmore
Hopkins, Judson—Winterfield, 1912
Hopkins, Luther—Wise, 1917
Horan, John—farmer, Vernon, 1910
Horan, Mary—Vernon, 1906
Horan, Oswald—farmer, Vernon
Horan, Patrick—Vernon, 1912
Horan, Thomas—farmer, Isabella
Horgan, Frank—Clare
Horan, George—Arthur, 1908
Horn, J. W.—farmer, Arthur, 1905
Horn, Rosa—Clare, 1908
Horn, Scott—laborer, Clare, 1905
Hornberger, Donald—AEF, Clare
Hornberger, Harold—AEF, Clare
Hornberger, Helen—teacher, Clare
Hornberger, J. J.—supt. of
  schools, Clare, 1915
Horning, Adam—farmer, Clare
Horning, Ambrose—Clare, 1918
Horning, Arthur—carpenter
Horning, Mrs. _____—dressmaker
Horning, Clarence—Clare, 1910
Horning, E. B.—Clare, 1903
Horning, Floyd—AEF, 1918
Horning, Henry—Clare, 1900
Horning, Ida—1922
Horning, Jesse—Clare
Horning, J. T.—mill, Vernon, 1871
Horning, Oscar—Clare, 1903
Hornsby, Ethelbert—Harrison, 1913
Horning, Clyde—Clare, 1904
Horning, E. B.—Clare, 1900
Horton, Arthur—Clare, 1918
Horton, Audrey—Clare, 1918
Horton, Leon—Hamilton, 1909
Horton, Marion—Clare
Horton, Thomas—Clare
Horton, Zella—Hamilton, 1912
Hoskey, August—Harrison
Hoskey, John—Harrison
Hosler, Anna—Greenwood, 1903
Hosler, Elmer—Greenwood, 1906

Hosler, Wm. A.—farmer, pioneer
Hotchkin, George W.—lumberman
Hounson, Robert—pioneer
House, Alex J.—farmer
House, Chancellor—butcher, 1913
House, Edward—mechanic, Vernon
House, Emma—Clare
House, Eustace—Rosebush, 1915
House, Frederick—Clare
House, George—farmer, Rosebush
House, George—Rosebush, 1908
House, Helen—Clare
House, Henry—Farwell
House, Henry S.—Rosebush, 1906
House, Homer—Clare
House, Roger—Temple, 1909
House, William—Clare
Houser, John—Gilmore, 1917
Houtz, Bertha—Clare, 1903
Howard, Albert—Grandon, 1903
Howard, B. T.—Grandon, 1903
Howard, Bert—pioneer, Grandon
Howard, Bert—AEF, Winterfield
Howard, Bertha—Farwell, 1900
Howard, Mrs. C.—postmistress
Howard, Edna—Clare, 1917
Howard, Elmer—Grandon, 1903
Howard, Freeman—pioneer
Howard, Gilbert—Civil War
  Vet, Clare, 1880
Howard, Gilbert, Jr.—Grandon
Howard, Grace—teacher, Farwell
Howard, Grant—postmaster
Howard, Hazel—teacher, Surrey
Howard, Ina—teacher, 1909
Howard, J. H.—1912
Howard, J. W.—Frost, 1906
Howard, Marie—Clare
Howard, Nelson—Grant, 1906
Howard, Roy—WWI, Grant, 1918
Howard, R. V.—Farwell, 1903
Howe, Charles—mechanic, Clare
Howe, Fred—Winterfield, 1918
Howe, Merle—WWI, 1918
Howe, Ray M.—printer, Clare
Howe, W.—Frost, 1906
Howes, Miss _____—vocal teacher
Howes, Alvah—WWI, Winterfield
Howey, Bert—WWI, Freeman
Howick, John—farmer, Eagle, 1901
Howland, J. W.—farmer, Vernon
Howlett, John—plumber, Clare
Howlett, M. R.—Clare
Hoy, J.—Arthur, 1915
Hoyt, Thomas—mill, Leota, 1907
Hubbard, Harry—Loomis, 1900
Hubble, L. D.—dairy, Clare, 1914
Hubel, Alfred—Grant, 1906
Hubel, Charles—farmer, Sheridan
Hubel, Captain—Grant, 1918
Hubel, Eddie—Clare
Hubel, Elias—Clare, 1900
Hubel, Ensley—Clare, 1906
Hubel, Fred—farmer, Grant, 1906
Hubel, Harry—Grant, 1901
Hubel, John—Grant, 1903
Hubel, Lillie—teacher, Clare, 1905
Hubel, Lovange—Clare, 1908
Hubel, Mary Ann—Grant, 1909
Hubel, Nelson—Grant, 1905
Hubel, Ora—Clare, 1912
Hubel, Pearl—Clare, 1903

Hubel, Phoebe—Clare, 1904
Hubel, Roy—city employee, Clare
Hubel, Reuben—Clare, 1890
Hubel, Roy—1911
Hubel, Violet—Clare, 1916
Hubel, W. E.—farmer, Grant, 1906
Hubel, William—Grant, 1914
Huber, Charles G.—Harrison
Huber, Fred—Hamilton, 1913
Huber, Henry—farmer, Harrison
Huber, J. B.—Hamilton, 1910
Huber, John C.—Bunker Hill
  Ranch, Hamilton, 1906
Huber, S.—Bunker Hill
  Ranch, Hamilton, 1906
Huddleston, E.—farmer, Arthur
Hudson, Allie—school teacher
Hudson, Anthony—Harrison, 1912
Hudson, Benjamin—farmer, meat
  market, WWI, Clare, 1906
Hudson, D. D.—farmer, Grant
Hudson, Eugene—Surrey, 1917
Hudson, Fred—RFD carrier, Clare
Hudson, George—Surrey, 1906
Hudson, Guy—bank clerk, Clare
Hudson, Ira—Surrey, 1906
Hudson, John—farmer, Dover, 1905
Hudson, John, Jr.—Hatton, 1918
Hudson, Joseph—farmer,
  banker, Grant, 1900
Hudson, Leah—teacher, Clare
Hudson, Robert—farmer, Hatton
Hudson, Wm.—Dover, 1900
Huffman, C.—hustling farmer
Huffman, Florence—teacher, Clare
Huffman, Gilbert—Freeman, 1909
Huffman, Jule—Clare, 1915
Huffman, Chas—farmer, Farwell
Hughes, Bessie—teacher, Harrison
Hughes, Ellis G.—banker,
  merchant, Harrison, 1907
Hughes, E. J.—Harrison, 1900
Hughes, E.mer E.—Harrison, 1903
Hughes, Frank—Clare, 1908
Hughes, Harold—attorney, Clare
Hughes, H. W.—Harrison, 1903
Hughes, John E.—Clare, 1938
Hughes, Ralph E.—teacher
Hulbert, Lucius—photographer
Hulet, E. L.—cream buyer, Clare
Hulin, Earnest—WWI, 1918
Hulin, Lee W.—1908
Hulin, Lewellyn—1918
Hulling, M.—Clare, 1907
Hummon, Cyrus—jeweler, Clare
Humphrey, Arthur, Gilmore, 1917
Humphrey, Henry—farmer
Humphrey, James—planing mill,
  saw mill, Clare, 1903
Hunt, A.—Garfield, 1906
Hunt, Camilla—teacher
Hunt, Elmer—Sheridan, 1900
Hunt, George—Gilmore, 1917
Hunt, Gilbert—Garfield, 1911
Hunt, Iva—Winterfield, 1910
Hunt, James—postmaster, farmer
Hunt, Julius—sheep ranch, Clare
Hunt, Margaret—teacher
Hunt, Millie—teacher, Winterfield
Hunt, Samuel—Hatton, 1907
Hunter, David—Hatton, 1906
Hunter, Francis—teacher, Farwell

Hunter, Isaac—Farwell, 1915
Hunter, M. H.—Farwell, 1900
Hunter, Wm. C.—Freeman, 1909
Hunting, John—Hamilton, 1913
Huntington, John W.—Calkins
  Hotel, Clare, 1917
Huntley, A. P.—farmer, Sheridan
Huntley, Fred—laborer, Clare, 1917
Huntley, Fred, Jr.—Clare
Huntley, George—Farwell, 1900
Huntley, Orman—r.r. section hand
Huntley, Stuart—Harrison
Huntoon, Daniel—Frost, 1917
Hunwick, Rev. _____—Elm Grove
Hursh, Starrie—WWI, 1918
Hursh, Sterling—mechanic, Clare
Hursh, William—Clare, 1909
Husted, George—P.M.R.R.
  brakeman, Clare, 1914
Husted, Harry—glass manufacturer
Husted, Annie—Clare, 1911
Husted, Charles—Clare
Husted, George—Clare, 1900
Husted, Jay B.—Clare, 1918
Husted, Julius—blacksmith, saloon
Husted, J. C.—1915
Husted, J. G.—Clare, 1900
Husted, John—Clare, 1918
Husted, Roy—minister, Clare, 1900
Husted, S.—farmer, Franklin, 1906
Hutchens, Walter—Gilmore, 1917
Hutchins, Howard—telegraph op.,
  P.M. ticket agent, WWI, Clare
Hutchins, Lillian—Clare, 1914
Hutchins, Orange—farmer, Redner
Hutchinson, Algernon—Harrison
Hutchinson, F.—bakery, Harrison
Hutchinson, Iris—Clare
Hutchinson, George—farmer
Hutchinson, Robert—sheriff
Hutchinson, Thomas—Sheridan
Hutchinson, W. J.—supt. of schools
Hutchison, Albert—Clare, 1909
Hutchison, Frank E.—farmer
Hutchison, George—Harrison
Hutchison, Julia—Eagle, 1901
Hutchison, Marie—Clare
Hutchison, Robert, Jr.—Dover
Hutchison, Thomas—Sheridan
Hutchison, W. J.—Clare, 1905
Hyde, Frank D.—Civil War
  Vet, Winterfield, d. 1915
Hyde, John—Clare
Hyman, Frank—farmer, Garfield
Hyser, Fred—Temple, 1903
Hyser, Grace—Temple, 1903
Hyslop, Fred Jesse—Surrey, 1917
Ickes, Chalmers—Grant, 1916
Ickes, Charles—WWI, Grant, 1918
Ickes, George—Grant, 1918
Ickes, Russel—Grant, 1911
Immick, Ruben—Clare, 1904
Ingersol, Anna—Clare, 1906
Inks, Anthony—Summerfield, 1918
Ireland, Wilber—electrician, Clare
Irish, Fred—farmer, Clare, 1898
Irish, Mortie—Clare, 1893
Irish, Nelson—farmer, Vernon
Irish, Wm. Nelson, Jr.—AEF, Clare
Irish, William N.—clerk, Wise
Ironmonger, Belle—teacher, 1901
Irving, Andrew—Clare

Irving, Andrew—farmer, Clare
Irwin, Aaron—Farwell, 1915
Irwin, Andrew—Vernon, 1912
Irwin, E. E.—supt. of schools
  Lapeer, Clare, 1914
Irwin, Ena—Clare
Irwin, George—laborer, Clare, 1914
Irwin, Gertude—teacher, Farwell
Irwin, Homer—Clare
Irwin, James—farmer, Clare, 1900
Irwin, Leo—laborer, Clare
Irwin, Mary—Clare
Irwin, Robert—Gilmore
Irwin, Robert Wm.—Vernon, 1887
Irwin, Wm.—Vernon, 1913
Irwin, Rev. W. H.—M-E pastor
Isbell, Simon—1914
Isbister, Douglas—1917
Ishaway, _____—farmer, Grant
Iutzi, Crist—farmer, Hamilton
Iutzi, Elsie—Hamilton, 1915
Iutzi, Homer—farmer, Harrison
Iutzi, Rolla—Hamilton, 1915
Ives, Chauncey—Redding, 1912
Ives, John—Temple, 1905
Ives, John—Temple, 1905
Ives, Mrs. S. A.—Temple, 1910
Jackman, Wm.—Rosebush, 1908
Jackson, Castle—Clare, 1922
Jackson, C. H.—farmer, Greenwood
Jackson, Charles A.—WWI, Clare
Jackson, Charles A., Jr.,—r.r.
Jackson, Charles E.—Clare, 1894
Jackson, Cleaton—1927
Jackson, D. Lewis—Clare, 1910
Jackson, Dan—farmer, Grant
Jackson, David—Farwell, 1908
Jackson, Earl—pumper, Clare, 1907
Jackson, Edna—teacher, Clare
Jackson, Ethel—Clare, 1907
Jackson, Francis—butcher, Clare
Jackson, Fred—farmer, Gilmore
Jackson, Flossie—teacher
Jackson, George—Clare, 1915
Jackson, Guy—Gilmore, 1917
Jackson, Harold T.—stockbuyer
Jackson, Herbert J.—WWI, Clare
Jackson, John, Jr.—stockbuyer
Jackson, John A.—butcher, Clare
Jackson, John D.—Powell Ranch
  foreman, Hayes, 1906
Jackson, John I.—Carpenter
Jackson, John L.—laborer, Clare
Jackson, Lawrence—meat market
Jackson, Laura—Clare
Jackson, Marjorie—Clare, 1919
Jackson, Nelle—Clare, 1912
Jackson, Niel—Clare, 1912
Jackson, Robert—Clare
Jackson, Roy—Clare, 1909
Jackson, _____—Clare, 1915
Jackson, Thomas—P.R.R.R., Clare
Jackson, Wm. H.—auto mechanic
Jackson, Wm. Roy—WWI, Clare
Jacobs, Bert—Garfield, 1913
Jacobs, Earl—Garfield, 1915
Jacobs, John—A.A.R.R.
Jacobs, Noah—Garfield, 1914
Jacobs, Reva—Lake George, 1916
Jacobs, Warren—Vernon, 1916
Jakes, Joseph—hired hand,
  Squires Ranch, Franklin

James, Miss Clare—teacher
James, D.—Farwell Grocery, 1904
James, Edward—Clare, 1906
James, Joseph—Colonville, 1906
James, Thomas R.—farmer, Grant
Janes, J. J.—Sheridan, 1906
JaQuish, Ilo—Temple, 1909
JaQuish, L.—wagon maker, Temple
Jaquish, Vida—Temple, 1914
Jardin, Nelson—Harrison, 1909
Jarman, _____—farmer, Gilmore
Jarman, Glenn—WWI, Gilmore
Jarman, S.—farmer, Farwell
Jasmin, Fabian—1910
Jefferies, Frances—Garfield, 1908
Jefferies, "Rem" G.—Clare, 1900
Jefferson. E. M.—Central Gas Co.
Jehnsen, Henry—farmer, Mecosta
Jenks, Rev. _____—pastor Dover
  Church, Dover, 1918
Jenney, Gladys—1st woman
  diver in Mich., Clare, 1911
Jenney, R. H.—Clare, 1901
Jennings, Charles—Franklin, 1918
Jennings, David—Clare, 1903
Jennings, Emma—teacher, Clare
Jennings, Esta—Surrey, 1915
Jennings, Floyd—Wise, 1917
Jennings, Henry—8 Point Lake
Jennings, Herbert—WWI, Clare
Jennings, Leo M.—Wise, 1916
Jennings, Mildred—Clare, 1903
Jennings, Wm. J.—farmer, Wise
Jennings, Zella—Surrey, 1905
Jenny, E. Burt—Clare, 1900
Jenney, R. H.—lumberman, Clare
Jerome, _____—school
  moderator, Temple, 1903
Jerred, Jasper—Clare, 1908
Jerred, John—farmer, Arthur, 1906
Jerred, Joseph—Clare, 1915
Jerred, Walter—miller, Clare, 1924
Jerrett, Rev. M. P.—M-E, Farwell
Jesse, Lawton—farmer, Hamilton
Jesse, Margaret—Clare, 1903
Jesse, Marie—Hamilton, 1915
Jessett, George—Redding, 1903
Jessie, Frank—Hatton, 1906
Jewell, Eber—Loomis, 1900
Jewell, James W.—pioneer, Loomis
Jocking, Paul—poolroom, Farwell
Jockwig, Herman R.—Gilmore
Johnson, Arthur—farmer, county
  surveyor, Harrison, 1906
Johnson, Albert—Gilmore, 1904
Johnson, Arthur, L.—farmer, Clare
Johnson, Arthur D.—surveyor
Johnson, B.—farmer, Farwell
Johnson, Bert—WWI, W. Grant
Johnson, Bessie—Clare, 1919
Johnson, Beulah—Clare, 1912
Johnson. Bryon—pathmaster, Grant
Johnson. C.—Clare, 1903
Johnson. Carl—Winterfield, 1909
Johnson, Carl A.—WWI, Arthur
Johnson, Charles—Clare, 1908
Johnson, Charles—AEF, Clare
Johnson, David A.—AEF, Freeman
Johnson, Dorothy—Clare
Johnson, D. R.—Dray Service
Johnson, Earl—Clare, 1900
Johnson, Eber R.—WWI, Hayes

Keys, Ormel H.—Garfield, 1903
Keysor, Andrew—WWI, Hamilton
Keysor, F. B.—Hamilton, 1917
Keysor, Lloyd—WWI, Hamilton
Kibbie, David H.—lumberman
Kidder, Allen—Clare
Kidd, Albert H.—Farwell, 1908
Kidd, Lucy—Clare, 1904
Kidd, Philipp—Loomis, 1910
Kidd, Thomas—farmer, Vernon
Kidder, Altha—Clare
Kigar, H. W.—Sheridan, 1911
Kilbourn, John H.—Surrey, 1900
Kilbourn, Lydia A.—1909
Kilbourn, Pansie—teacher, Farwell
Kilbourn, Edward C.—Lincoln
Kilbourne, E. J.—Surrey, 1918
Kilbourne, V.—Winterfield, 1911
Kilburn, B.—Lincoln, 1906
Kilburn, J.—Lincoln, 1906
Kilburn, Pansie—teacher, Farwell
Kilburn, Theodore—Maple Grove
Kilner, C. H.—Clare, 1915
Kilpatrick, Ira—Long Lake, 1918
Kimball, Gladys—Farwell, 1917
Kimball, J. H.—Clare, 1912
Kimball, J. S.—livery barn, Farwell
King, Ed—Freeman, 1914
King, F.—Redding, 1906
King, Fred—Wise, 1912
King, Ida—accountant, Clare
King, James G.—farmer, Grant
King, John—Freeman, 1912
King, Napoleon—Redding, 1906
King, Thelma—principal, Farwell
Kingelhofer, John—farmer
Kinney, Bert—Eagle School, 1908
Kinney, David E.—Freeman, 1912
Kinney, G.—Hamilton, 1906
Kinney, Harry W.—Harrison, 1909
Kinney, Olive—Franklin, 1912
Kinney, W. L.—sheep rancher
Kinsey, Roy—lineman, Clare, 1904
Kinzel, Adolf—Hamilton
Kipfer, Wm.—WWI, Harrison
Kirby, C.—farmer, Winterfield
Kirby, Frank—Winterfield, 1910
Kirchmer, James—Temple
Kirkbride, Samuel—merchant,
   postmaster, Clare, 1900
Kirkpatrick, Clarence—mgr.
   lumber yard, 1903
Kirkpatrick, Dortha—Clare
Kirkpatrick, Floyd—drug store
Kirkpatrick, George H.—Clare
Kirkpatrick, John—pioneer,
   grocery store, 1903
Kirkpatrick, Robert—Clare, 1917
Kirkpatrick, Wm.—Clare
Kirshbaum, Harry—conductor
Kistler, William—Colonville, 1919
Kirtz, Charles—Clare, 1906
Kirvan, E. A.—Arthur, 1903
Kissick, George—Sheridan, 1900
Kissick, M.—Sheridan, 1906
Kissick, Perry—WWI, Sheridan
Kistler, A. J.—farmer, Clare
Kistler, Clyde—farmer, Clare, 1901
Klains, Otto—Hamilton
Klann, Gottfried—Arthur, 1917
Klann, John—WWI, Hamilton
Klann, Michael—Hamilton, 1909

Klein, Raymond—1915
Kleiner, A. G.—well driller, Clare
Kleiner, C. H.—meat market, Clare
Kleiner, C. M.—farmer, Arthur
Kleiner, Ernest—farmer, Clare
Kliner, Henry—farmer, Eagle, 1906
Kleiner, Henry, Jr.—farmer
Kleiner, Marie—Clare
Kleiner, Otto—AEF, Sheridan
Kleinfield, Benjamin—farmer
Kleinhardt, Benjamin—Hatton
Kleinhardt, Rev. Charles—Hatton
Kleinhardt, Charles—WWI, Hatton
Kleinhardt, Earnest—carpenter
Kleinhardt, Reuben—Hatton, 1917
Kleinhardt, Roger E.—press man
Kleman, C. H.—rancher, Hatton
Klengman, R.—Grant, 1906
Kliebler, Matthew—farmer
Kliewoneit, Ernest L.—Nester Dam
Kliewoneit, Fritz—Hamilton
Kliewoneit, Gustav—Hamilton
Kliewoneit, Karl—Hamilton
Kline, A. J.—Surrey, 1904
Kline, Lyn—Surrey, 1915
Kline, Thelma—teacher, Clare
Klinger, Harry O.—Frost, 1906
Klinglehofer, John—farmer, Grant
Kliewoneit, Daniel—Hamilton
Klong, _____—Arthur, 1914
Klute, Edward—Clare, 1914
Knapp, Charles C.—farmer
Knapp, Cora—Dover, 1906
Knapp, F. W.—Sheridan, 1918
Knapp, Eugene—farmer, Frost
Knapp, Fred—Frost, 1916
Knapp, Linton—WWI, U.S. Navy
Knepper, J. L.—farmer, Surrey
Knight, Asher—farmer, Clare, 1911
Knight, C. W.—P.M. agent
Knight, G. L.—meat market
Knight, Rev. I. W.—minister, Clare
Knispel, Rudolph—Arthur, 1917
Knowles, L. J.—Garfield, 1906
Knowles, Muriel—teacher, Clare
Koch, Charles—farmer, Long Lake
Koch, Frances—Clare
Koch, Frank—WWI, Winterfield
Koch, George—farmer, Clare
Koch, Max—Clare
Koch, Paul—Clare
Koch, Russell—Standard
   Oil agent, Clare, 1919
Koch, Virginia—Clare
Koch, Willard—Clare
Koecher, Catherine—Clare, 1907
Koeplinger, Frank—WWI, Grant
Koffman, Henry—farmer, Arthur
Kogan, M.—farmer, Arthur, 1986
Kogler, Anna—Temple, 1917
Koher, Denver—oil field worker
Komp, "Del"—barber, Clare
Komp, Hallie—Clare, 1914
Kool, Peter—1914
Koons, Kate—teacher, Clare, 1904
Koontz, Elizabeth—Clare, 1903
Koontz, J. W.—Grant, 1906
Koontz, Mamie—Vernon, 1900
Koontz, Robert—farmer, Clare
Koontz, R. B.—AEF, 1918
Koschick, Peter—killed, hit by auto
Kotek, Harry Joe—WWI, Redding

Krabill, David—Lake, 1917
Kramer, Sarah—teacher, Clare
Kramer, S. L.—mens clothing
Krampetz, Christian—Hamilton
Krantz, Mrs. A. S.—millinery
Krapole, Edward—hotel clerk
Kratz, H. D.—Dray & Delivery
   Service, Clare, 1915
Kratz, Ruth—Clare
Kraus, Matthew—farmer, Arthur
Krause, Herman—Lake George
Krause, Michael
Krchmar, Margaret—Temple
Krchmar, Paul—Temple
Kreger, Ira—Clare, 1918
Krell, Adolph—printer, Grant, 1900
Krell, Christian—Grant, 1900
Krell, Charles—farmer, Grant
Krell, Christian—farmer, Grant
Krell, Christian J.—Grant, 1891
Krell, Elfreda—Grant, 1911
Krell, Elizabeth—Clare
Krell, Fred J.—teacher, WWI
Krell, Freda—teacher, Clare, 1915
Krell, Gottlieb—lumber jack,
   r.r. engineer, Dover, 1900
Krell, Lida—Clare
Krell, Mary—Eagle, 1905
Krell, Pauline—nurse, Grant, 1904
Krell, Wm.—farmer, Grant, 1905
Kress, Alice—teacher, Temple, 1915
Kress, C. H.—A.A.R.R., Clare
Kress, Earl—teacher, Temple, 1917
Kress, Harry—Lake George, 1900
Kress, Harvey—Lincoln, 1910
Kress, Henry—Lake George, 1915
Kress, Lilah—Redding, 1910
Kress, Newton—store keeper
Kress, Russell G.—Lake George
Kress, Thompson—Civil War and
   Mexican War Vet, Lake
   George, 1906
Kress, Weton—Temple, 1912
Kretzer, John—WWI, 1918
Krider, David—Freeman, 1912
Krienke, Hattie—Clare
Krienke, Herman—Wise
Krompetz, Walter—trucker
Krug, A. J.—farmer, Clare
Krug, John E.—laborer, Clare
Krunke, Herman—Clare
Kube, Arthur G.—1918
Kube, Clara L.—Lake Geoge, 1911
Kube, Emma—1909
Kube, Frank—Winterfield, 1915
Kube, Irene—Lincoln, 1915
Kube, Paul—Lake George, 1914
Kube, Wm.—farmer, Lake George
Kube, Wm., Jr.—farmer, WWI,
   U.S. Army, Farwell, 1916
Kuepfer, Ezra—farmer, Harrison
Kuffler, John—well driller, Clare
Kump, Dell H.—barber, Clare
Kump, Will—Clare
Kump, Zachariah—
   gun smith, Civil War, Clare, 1901
Kurz, Charles—farmer, 1903
Kurz, John—farmer, 1903
Kuster, Deyo—farmer, Arthur, 1915
Kuster, John E.—Arthur, 1915
Kyes, Wm. B.—Clare, 1941
Lackie, Albert—Hatton, 1887
Lackie, Alex—prop. National
   Hotel, Clare, 1918

Leeth, Mack—Grant, 1904
Leggitt, James—Temple, 1914
Legrow, A.—Farwell, 1907
Lehman, Herman—Summerfield
Lehman, Inez—Clare
Leibrand, G. C.—attorney, Clare
Leichti, Herman—Wise, 1913
Leichti, Samuel—Wise, 1913
Leighton, A. J.—teacher,
    principal, Harrison, 1915
Leis, Albert—Clare
Leis, Anna—Clare
Leis, Herman—Clare
Leis, William—Grant, 1900
Liese, Godfrey—Hatton, 1900
Liese, Wm.—Harrison, 1903
Leitch, T. J.—Clare, 1910
Leitner, Ida—Arthur, 1911
Leitner, Lorin—WWI, Arthur, 1918
Leitner, Marcia—Arthur, 1909
Leitner, Mary E.—teacher, Arthur
Leitner, Milton—Arthur, 1917
Leitner, Orin—WWI, Arthur, 1918
Leitner, Sam A.—farmer, Arthur
Leitner, Samual A.—Arthur, 1909
Leitner, S. J.—Percheron
    Society, Clare, 1903
Lenninger, Calvin—Temple, 1906
Lennon, Nicholas—Sheridan, 1900
Lennox, Beulah—Clare
Lennox, Charles—Wise, 1917
Lennox, Claude—hotel cook, Clare
Lennox, Donald—Wise, 1912
Lennox, Lewis—Wise, 1917
Lennox, Otis—Wise, 1917
Lent, C. A.—Silverbrook Farm
Lent, Inez—Grant, 1904
Lent, Kate—Grant, 1903
Lent, Lewis—Grant, 1900
Leonard, Alice—Clare, 1900
Leonard, Asa—pioneer, Civil
    War Vet, d. 1921
Leonard, Catherine—Clare, d. 1925
Leonard, Dr. Edward—physician
Leonard, George—Temple, 1903
Leonard, Homer—Farwell, 1912
Leonard, L. F.—grocery store,
    hay-feed, Farwell, 1906
Leosch, Alvin J.—WWI, Wise, 1917
Leosh, John R.—Wise, 1917
Leosh, William—Wise, 1918
Leposky, Ralph L.—clerk, Clare
Leposky, Robert—gas station, Clare
Leston, Hamilton L.—1914
Lett, Arnold—livery, bootlegger,
    Farwell, 1909
Leusenkamp, _____—dry
    goods store, Clare, 1900
Leston, Hamilton—Garfield, 1914
Levington, Samuel J.—
    Superintendent, Harrison
    Branch R.R., d. 1900
Levinson, Henry—WWI, 1918
Levinson, Marion—Clare, 1917
Levison, Sara—Clare, 1917
Lew, Wm.—Harrison, 1912
Lewis, Bert S.—tinsmith, plumber
Lewis, Bessie—teacher, Clare, 1911
Lewis, C. H.—Harrison, 1900
Lewis, Rev. Christlieb—minister
Lewis, Frank—stave mill hand
Lewis, George—Redding, 1909

Lewis, Jasper—Loomis, 1878
Lewis, Lester—Hayes, 1906
Lewis, Myrtle—Temple, 1908
Lewis, Pauline—Clare
Lewis, W. P.—Clare Cigar Factory
Liddell, George W.—farmer, Grant
Liebrand, G. C.—mail carrier
Liechti, Helen—Clare
Liechti, Herman—Wise, 1917
Liechti, Maxine—Clare
Liechti, Samuel—farmer, Clare
Liechti, Samuel—Sheridan, 1917
Liese, A.—Clare, 1902
Liese, Godfried—1901
Light, Rev. A. F.—minister
Light, Guy—teacher, Greenwood
Likes, E. G.—farmer, Grant, 1909
Likes, Homer—farmer, Colonville
Lindemueller, Garrett—farmer
Lineberry, W. L.—Clare, 1853
Lingley, Lottie—bookkeeper, 1903
Lingreen, Ed—rancher, Hamilton
Liniger, Howard—Frost, 1909
Link, Walter F.—farmer, Grant
Linnger, Calvin—Temple, 1905
Linsea, E. D.—Grant, 1906
Lippold, Raymond—oil well driller
Liscomb, Wm. L.—farmer
List, John, Jr.—factory, Clare
Listenfeltz, Chester—Clare, 1904
Listenfeltz, Della—Vernon, 1915
Listenfeltz, Ralph—AEF, 1918
Lister, Mrs. A. B.—Clare, 1895
Lister, Fred—mill-man,
    banker, Clare, 1903
Lister, Grace—Clare
Lister, Mary—Clare
Lister, Viola—Clare
Little, Andrew—AEF, Vernon
Little, Burton—farmer, Vernon
Little, Beryl—farmer, Arthur, 1913
Little, Edward—Gleaner district
    mgr., Vernon, 1915
Little, Ernest—WWI, Vernon, 1918
Little, John—pioneer, Vernon, 1866
Littlefield, Franklin—Farwell, 1900
Littlefield, Josiah—businessman
Litwiller, John—farmer, Harrison
Livingston, Harry—WWI
Livingston, F. W.—Union
    Depot agent, Clare, 1900
Livingston, U.—pack peddler
Livingston, John—farmer, Sheridan
Lloyd, Arthur—telephone lineman
Lloyd, Bert—farmer, Clare, 1915
Lloyd, Chan—race horses, Harrison
Lloyd, Chauncey—livery, under
    sheriff, Clare, 1906
Lloyd, Don—Clare
Lloyd, Glen J.—Clare
Lloyd, James—Clare
Lloyd, John—lumberman, Clare
Loar, C.—Sheridan, 1906
Loar, John—Brush College, 1914
Loar, L.—Surrey, 1906
Locke, Ray—Farwell, 1919
Lockwood, _____—Canadian
    Army, WWI, 1918
Lockwood, Albert—ranch forman
Lockwood, D.—Harrison, 1900
Lockwood, _____—well-driller
Lockwood, Felix—farmer, Rosebush

Lockwood, Frank—miller, Harrison
Lockwood, George—farmer
Lockwood, Germain—Surrey, 1910
Lockwood, Eunice—Bell system
    operator, Farwell, 1918
Lockwood, Joanna—teacher
Lockwood, John—Hatton, 1910
Lockwood, Johnson—livery, AEF
Lockwood, Rev. J.—minister
Lockwood, Lewis—Winterfield
Lockwood, Margarite—teacher
Lockwood, Norman—stone mason
Lockwood, Raymond—farmer
Lockwood, Wallace—WWI
Loecy, Mrs.—Harrison, 1904
Loewenburg, R.—dry goods, Clare
Logan, Claude—Clare, 1907
Logan, Sherman—Civil War
    Vet, Gladwin
Logic, Mary—Clare
Lohrke, C. W.—grocer, Clare
Loman, Rev. John—Free Methodist
Lommis, Ruth—Clare
Long, Arthur—prop. Los Vegas
    Ranch, Supervisor, Dodge, 1906
Long, Nellie—musician, 1912
Long, Rev. S. A.—Cong. church
Looker, Arthur—WWI,
    U. S. Navy, Hamilton, 1918
Looker, Cora—teacher, Hamilton
Looker, James—Hamilton, 1900
Looker, Wm. R.—farmer, Dodge
Loomis, A. T.—farmer, Clare, 1905
Loomis, Benton—farmer, Clare
Loomis, Dora—teacher, Gilmore
Loomis, Evah—Clare
Loomis, Frank—woodsman, Vernon
Loomis, Fred—farmer,
    restaurant, Clare, 1900
Loomis, Homer—farmer, Wise
Loomis, Harold—barber, Clare
Loomis, Marjorie—Clare, 1916
Loomis, Martin—welder, AEF
Loomis, Mary—Clare, 1914
Loomis, Melvin—Vernon, 1900
Loomis, Miney—1909
Loomis, Myron—1916
Loomis, Philo M.—Vernon, 1900
Loomis, Sam—farmer, Vernon
Loomis, Wm.—Clare
Loose, Frank—farmer, Sheridan
Loose, Harold—Temple, 1918
Loose, Hazel—Harrison, 1910
Loose, St. Clair—Greenwood, 1917
Lorr, Herman—1936
Louch, Alfred—blacksmith,
    wagon-maker, Clare, 1874
Louch, Alfred, Jr.—Clare, 1898
Louch, C. P.—Clare, 1900
Louch, Ethel—Clare, 1917
Louch, Frank—Davy & Co.
    employee, Clare, 1900
Louch, G. T.—Clare, 1900
Louch, Harold—road worker, Clare
Louch, James—livery, blacksmith,
    shoemaker, Clare, 1900
Louch, Mrs. James—Clare, 1904
Louch, James—mechanic, Clare
Louch, Lena—Clare, 1919
Louch, Miss Louie—teacher, Clare
Louch, Tess—Clare, 1915
Louch, Ward—Clare, 1909

Louden, Elmer—farmer, twp. clerk, Franklin, 1903
Louer, Mrs. _____—Grandon, 1903
Loundra, Wm.—city marshal
Loveland, D. K.—lumberman
Loveland, Ralph—farmer, Sheridan
Lovinson, Harry—Wise, 1917
Low, Lewis—Leota, 1914
Lowe, Asa B.—teacher, Lake, 1919
Lowe, Rev. John—Baptist minister, Clare, 1905
Lowen, Rev.—minister—Eagle
Lower, Arthur—Fisher Body employee, Detroit
Lower, Mrs. B. M.—Dover, 1907
Lower, Edna—Clare
Lower, Glen—Arthur, 1917
Lower, Ira—farmer, Arthur, 1906
Lower, James—farmer, Arthur
Lower, Joseph—Eagle, 1909
Lower, Lowie—teacher, Clare, 1907
Lower, Mrs. M. B.—farmer
Lower, Wm.—Clare, 1900
Lowery, Alex—pioneer, Vernon
Lowry, Kathren—Grant, 1907
Lowery, Murney—photography
Lowery, Wm.—farmer, Clare
Lowns, Frank—lumberman, Hatton
Lowry, Archie—1903
Lowry, John—Vernon, 1917
Lowry, Lavell—Clare, 1915
Lowrey, Paul—art instructor, Clare
Lowrey, Wm.—Farwell, 1940
Lucas, Rev. Alto—pastor Cong. Church, Harrison, 1914
Lucas, George—Lake George stock farm, 1918
Luce, Andrew—Reed City, Lake George, 1911
Luce, Don—Lake George, 1918
Luce, Frank—merchant, Lake George, 1903
Luce, Vera—Lincoln, 1906
Lucre, James—farmer, Hamilton
Lukes, Joseph—Sheridan, 1906
Lumley, Eva—Clare, 1909
Lumley, E. B.—Lake George, 1902
Lumley, George—farmer, Colonville
Lund, Ernfrid—WWI, Arthur, 1918
Luther, George—Clare, 1912
Lydell, Bert—Farwell, 1903
Lydiatt, Ada—Hatton, 1909
Lydiatt, Henry—Grant, 1912
Lyford, Edyth—teacher, Clare, 1916
Lyford, Rev. George—Cong. minister, Clare, 1912
Lynch, Alfonzo—1918
Lynch, David—veterinarian, WWI
Lynch, Frank H.—WWI, Vernon
Lynch, Patrick J.—WWI, Grant
Lynch, Percy—WWI
Lynch, Thomas—restaurant, Clare
Lyon, August—Hamilton, 1906
Lyon, Cecil—Harrison, 1920
Lyon, Elmer—1903
Lyon, Norris—Harrison, 1917
Lyons, August—farmer, Hamilton
Lyons, Byron—Hamilton, 1917
Lyons, F. D.—Temple, 1903
Lyons, John—farmer, Wheatley
Lyons, John—farmer, Harrison
Lyons, Norris—Harrison, 1914

Lyons, Wallace—Dover merchant, Temple saloon, Clare, 1900
Lyons, Wm. R.—farmer, Grant
Lytle, Gertude—Clare
Lytle, Grover—farmer, Hamilton
McAllister, Rev. J. J.—Catholic priest, Clare, 1907
McAllister, Wm.—furniture merchant, Clare, 1923
McAlvey, M.—Coldwater, 1912
McAninch, David—Farwell, 1903
McAninch, John—lumberjack
McAninch, Julie—Lake, 1911
McAninch, S. M.—Surrey, 1906
McBride, Clyde—Clare, 1910
McBride, Retinald—farmer, Clare
McCall, R. J.—Harrison, 1906
McCambly, John—harness shop
McCann, Dr. Robert—dentist
McCarey, Freeman—farmer, highway comm., Grant, 1906
McCarey, Wm. Louis—1918
McCartney, Frank—Farwell, 1905
McCartney, Richard—Harrison
McCarthy, D.—Sheridan, 1903
McCarthy, Frank—Grant, 1917
McCartney, Alexander—Harrison
McCartney, Richard—Harrison
McCartney, Thomas—Harrison
McClellan, Frank—Farwell, 1900
McClellan, Frank—Clare, 1917
McClellan, Chester—engineer
McClellan, John—pioneer, Vernon
McClellan, Stanley—tailor, dry cleaning, Clare, 1913
McClellan, Wm.—grocery, Dover
McCloud, Angus—carpenter, Clare
McClung, Harold—AEF, Sheridan
McClung, Helen—Sheridan, 1911
McClung, Jennie—Sheridan, 1917
McClung, Jim—bridge builder
McClure, P. J.—Hamilton, 1906
McCollum, Inez—teacher, Arthur
McCollum, James—WWI
McComb, Wm.—Winterfield, 1908
McCombley, _____—harness maker
McCon—carpenter, Lake, 1913
McConnell, Catherine—teacher
McConnell, Francis—Clare
McConnell, Gertude—Clare
McConnell, Isabel—Clare
McConnell, James—farmer, Vernon
McConnell, John—Clare
McConnell, Mary—Clare, 1911
McConnell, Pat—Clare
McConnell, R.—Clare, 1915
McCormick, John—farmer, Farwell
McCormick, Sarah—Farwell, 1904
McCracken, Ward—WWI
McCrary, Wm.—Farwell, 1914
McCray, W. W.—Farwell, 1913
McCrea, Lotan—Clare
McCreary, George S.—farmer
McCrimmon, Donald—farmer
McCulloch, L. E.—Clare
McCullom, James—Garfield, 1917
McCurry, James—1904
McDermott, Howard—attorney
McDole, Wm.—pioneer, Winterfield
McDonald, Allen—Wise, 1905
McDonald, Rev. A. O.—minister
McDonald, Belle—Clare, 1913

McDonald, Charles—farmer
McDonald, Chrysta—teacher, Clare
McDonald, Clarence—WWI, 1918
McDonald, Colin—businessman
McDonald, Edd F.—Clare, 1917
McDonald, Frank—Vernon, 1918
McDonald, Francis—Vernon, 1917
McDonald, Helen—Clare
McDonald, Irene—nurse, WWI
McDonald, Rev. J. E.—minister
McDonald, J.—Temple, 1900
McDonald, John—farmer, Vernon
McDonald, John A.—farmer
McDonald, Josephine—Temple
McDonald, Kate—teacher, Clare
McDonald, K.—Harrison, 1918
McDonald, Kenneth—Clare, 1907
McDonald, Neil—1914
McDonald, Perry—Clare, 1910
McDonald, Ralph—Wise, 1917
McDonald, Reeta L.—Clare, 1910
McDonald, Ronald—Summerfield
McDonell, Angus—candidate for 28th Senate Dist., Mich., 1914
McElhaney, Charles—farmer
McElhaney, J. A.—Vernon, 1918
McFadden, Vincent—WWI
McFarlan, Wm. J.—farmer, Vernon
McFarland, Chester—Clare, 1907
McFarland, Ellen—Clare
McFarland, Eva Joy—Clare
McFarland, Frederick—Harrison
McFarland, John M.—saw mill
McFarland, John W.—teacher
McFarland, Joseph—1905
McFarlane, Chester—Vernon, 1900
McFarlane, Francis—Clare
McFarlane, Gerald—Clare
McGary, E. A.—Hayes, 1906
McGary, Freeman—Clare, 1903
McGary, G.—Hayes, 1906
McGarey—Harrison, 1904
McGillivary, C. B.—orchard ranch
McGinnis, Herbert—Farwell, 1917
McGinnis, Rev. J. B.—M-E pastor
McGinnis, James—farmer, Parkview Hotel owner, Surrey
McGivern, Herman—Hatton, 1914
McGivern, J.—farmer, Sheridan
McGivern, Joseph—Vernon, 1914
McGivern, Thomas—farmer
McGlone, Wm.—Farwell, 1904
McGoogan, Agnes—Farwell, 1910
McGoogan, David—Surrey, 1918
McGoogan, James—farmer, Farwell
McGoogan, Margaret—teacher
McGoogan, Marie—teacher, Farwell
McGoogan, Sam—farmer, Farwell
McGreaham, Harriet—teacher
McGuire, Burt—farmer, Farwell
McGuire, Carl—Vernon, 1917
McGuire, Dennis—farmer, WWI
McGuire, Dominic—farmer
McGuire, Ellen—teacher, Hamilton
McGuire, Francis—Vernon, 1917
McGuire, Fred—banker, Farwell
McGuire, Hazel—teacher, Hamilton
McGuire, James—farmer, Hamilton
McGuire, Jerome—Vernon, 1917
McGuire, Joseph—farmer, Clare
McGuire, Mamie—teacher
McGuire, Margaret—1918

McGuire, Russell—WWI, Vernon
McGuire, R. B.—village clerk, Farwell, 1911
McGuire, R. P.—Gilmore, 1918
McGuire, Thomas—Farwell, 1914
McIlhargie, Edith—teacher
McIntosh, Gordon—Clare
McIntosh, Herb—farmer, Franklin
McIntosh, Ivan—farmer, Clare
McIntosh, John—Grant, 1909
McIntosh, Kenneth, Jr.—Clare
McIntosh, Kenneth—Clare, 1880
McIntosh, Kenneth, Jr.—Clare
McIntosh, Llewellen—pharmacist
McIntosh, Wm. J.—P.M.R.R.
McIntosh, Wm.—Clare, 1881
McIntyre, A. S.—bank stockholder
McIntyre, A. W.—carpenter, Clare
McIntyre, Donald—Leota, 1896
McIntyre, G. W.—farmer, Redding
McIntyre, George—Civil War Vet, Gilmore, 1897
McIntyre, George—farmer, Temple
McIntyre, Iva—Temple, 1910
McIntyre, John—WWI, Clare, 1907
McIntyre, Kenneth—AEF
McIntyre, Loyal—Winterfield, 1917
McIntyre, Perry—Temple, 1919
McIntyre, Rory—Sheridan, 1914
McIntyre, Wm.—Temple, 1917
McJames, Nellie—teacher, Wise
McJames, Samuel—Herrick, 1885
McJames, Wm. H.—Clare, 1905
McJames, Wm.—1905
McKay, Andrew—Clare, Vernon
McKay, Anna—teacher, Clare
McKay, Edmond J.—Vernon, 1900
McKay, George W.—Dover, 1906
McKay, James A.—farmer, Dover
McKay, Joseph—Clare, 1913
McKeever, Florence—teacher, Clare
McKeever, George—merchant
McKeever, George H., Jr.—WWI
McKeever, Glenn—Clare, 1917
McKeever, Jim—P.M.R.R., Clare
McKeever, Peter—Farwell, 1915
McKeever, ____—W. Grant, 1900
McKeever, Thomas—Clare, 1904
McKeever, Wm.—pioneer
McKellar, Donald—Hamilton, 1912
McKenna, Edward—farmer, Farwell
McKenna, Francis—teacher
McKenna, John—Clare, 1915
McKenna, John—farmer, Hamilton
McKenna, Nellie—teacher
McKenna, Roseanna—teacher
McKenna, Wm.—WWI, AEF, 1918
McKenzie, Mrs. D. W.—millinery
McKernacher, Burt—Clare, 1904
McKerracher, John—harness maker
McKerring, H. G.—theatre mgr.
McKimmey, George—Harrison
McKimmey, Lloyd—Wise, 1917
McKinley, Allen—farmer, 1903
McKinley, Burt—farmer, Grant
McKinley, Edward—Civil War Vet, Sheridan
McKinley, Henry—WWI, Clare
McKinley, J. B.—WWI, Clare
McKinley, James—pioneer, Civil War Vet, Clare
McKinley, Kate—Eagle, 1901

McKinley, Matie B.—missionary to India, 1890
McKinley, John—Vernon, 1900
McKinley, John—WWI, Sheridan
McKinley, Katherine—1906
McKinley, Wm.—farmer, Arthur
McKinnon, Albert—Clare, 1913
McKinnon, Alexander—Vernon
McKinnon, Alex—city clerk, Clare
McKinnon, Archie—blacksmith
McKinnon, Bernice—Clare
McKinnon, Bruce—1903
McKinnon, Charles—lumberman, farmer, Vernon, 1900
McKinnon, D. J.—Grant
McKinnon, Donald—Clare
McKinnon, Fred—farmer, Vernon
McKinnon, Frederick, Jr.—Vernon
McKinnon, Hector—Clare
McKinnon, Hugh—farmer
McKinnon, James—Clare
McKinnon, Kyle—AEF, Clare
McKinnon, Martha—Clare, 1915
McKinnon, Robert—farmer
McKinnon, Roy—teacher, garage
McKinnon, Stella—teacher, Clare
McKinzie, J. M.—farmer, Sheridan
McKnight, Dr. Francis—dentist
McKnight, James—Clare, 1912
McKnight, Velma—Clare
McKnight, W. F.—dentist, Clare
McKnight, Wm.—well driller
McLain, E. E.—Clare, 1918
McLain, John—Franklin, 1906
McLain, Wm.—Franklin, 1915
McLaren, J. D.—hay barn, Clare
McLaughlin, Chas—driller, Clare
McLaughlin, Emery—teacher, Clare
McLaughlin, Jennie—grocery, Clare
McLaughlin, John—farmer, Vernon
McLaughlin, Joe—Clare
McLean, Laughlin—pioneer
McLellan, Frank—undertaker, merchant, Farwell, 1900
McLellan, John—farmer, pioneer
McLeod, Angus—contractor, carpenter, Farwell, 1904
Hickey, Elsie—Clare, 1914
McLeod, Jessie—teacher, Farwell
McLeod, Katherine—Farwell, 1909
McLouth, Albert—farmer, Arthur
McLouth, Fred—Arthur, 1917
McManaman, Agnes—teacher
McManaman, James—Vernon
McManaman, Margaret—Clare
McManaman, Thomas—Clare
McMaster, Daniel—farm mgr.
McMichaels, J. W.—store, Farwell
McMillan, Miss ____—teacher
McMillan, Archie—farmer, Grant
McMillan, Charlotte—Farwell, 1895
McMillen, Ervin—farmer, Farwell
McMillen, Fern—Temple, 1909
McMullen, Al—Temple, 1909
McMullen, Ferna—Redding, 1911
McMullen, P. O.—Farwell
McNamara, J. F.—teacher
McNeil, Rev. F.—Catholic priest
McNeil, Alex—Grant, 1906
McNeill, Andrew—WWI, Hatton
McNeill, Cecil—WWI, 1918
McNeil, Delby—Gilmore, 1904

McNeil, Dorothy—Clare
McNeil, Elmer F.—Dover, 1913
McNeill, Herbert—blacksmith, AEF, Farwell
McNeill, Joseph—Hatton, 1917
McNeil, John—meat market
McNeil, Leon—W. Grant, 1918
McNeil, Martha—teacher, Clare
McNeill, Faye—Clare
McNeill, George—Clare, 1915
McNeill, Herbert—Farwell, 1908
McNeill, James—WWI, 1918
McNeill, John—farmer, Hatton
McNeill, Russell—WWI, Hatton
McNeill, Stella—Greenwood
McNeill, W. L.—blacksmith, Clare
McNeil, Wallace—farmer, Arthur
McNeil, Wm.—Gilmore, 1904
McNerney, Pauline—1913
McNicoll, George
McNicoll, Mabel—Vernon, 1911
McNutt, S. L.—1903
McNutt, Walter—Clare, 1904
McPhall, Clayton—plumber, Clare
McPhall, David—hdwe dealer
McPhall, Otis—truck driver, Clare
McPhall, Winifred—Clare, 1905
McQuade, R.—Loomis, 1900
McQuire, Fred—assistant cashier, bank, Clare, 1892
McQuiston, Ed—Lincoln, 1918
McQuiston, Lester H.—Lincoln
McQuiston, Merrill—Harrison
McQuiston, William—Clare, 1904
McRae, Charles—Loomis, 1900
McRae, Olive—Loomis, 1900
McReynolds, J.—hotel, Farwell
McShea, Allen, Isabella
McTavish, Rev. D. J.—Sheridan
McVay, George—Harrison
McWalty, Jno—Harrison, 1903
McWatty, Mrs. Sarah—Greenwood
McWatty, John—farmer
McWatty, W. A.—lumber scaler
MacDonald, Sarah—Clare, 1913
MacGregor, Douglas—attorney
Mack, Mrs. A. E.—Clare, 1907
Mack, A. R.—Clare, 1909
Mack, Symphony—Harrison, 1914
Macklem, Anne—Clare, 1914
Macklem, Gerald—Sheridan, 1918
Macklem, Harrison—cook, Surrey
Macklem, Martin—1914
Macklem, S.—farmer, Loomis, 1916
Mackley, John—Temple, 1909
MacKinnon, Alexander—Vernon
MacKinnon, Cecelia—Clare
MacKinnon, Dan—miller, Vernon
MacLane, ____—U. S. Army, 1915
MacLane, George—Civil War Vet, Confederate, Grant, 1915
MacLane, Grant—WWI, Garfield
MacLen, S.—farmer, Sheridan
Madden, Carrie—teacher, Sheridan
Madison, Albert—Grant, 1914
Madison, Frank—Summerfield
Madison, Glenn—farmer, Grant
Madison, John—farmer, Grant
Maelege, George—Temple, 1918
Magnus, Edward—farmer, Clare
Magnus, Wm.—farmer, Hatton
Mahan, Fred—WWI, 1918

Mahan, James—farmer, Garfield
Mahan, James—1918
Mahan, John—Crooked Lake, 1904
Mahan, John F.—WWI, Garfield
Mahan, Joseph—Garfield, 1917
Mahan, Patrick—Vernon, 1911
Mahar, John—Vernon, 1900
Mahar, Wm.—Vernon, 1900
Mahoney, John—grocery, Garfield
Mahoney, Marie—Clare, 1914
Mahoney, Pearl—millinery, Clare
Mailson, Wm.—farmer
Maken, Alta—Sheridan, 1903
Makin, Charles—WWI, 1918
Makin, Young—Surrey, 1918
Maklem, Anna—Clare, 1910
Makley, Jackson—Redding, 1908
Malburg, Nicholas—Frost, 1910
Malcolm, D. A.—1903
Malconson, Donald—farmer
Malcomson, Leo—AEF, 1918
Malcomson, Robert—farmer
Malison, W. M.—Farwell, 1907
Mallery, George—Farwell, 1908
Mallory, Sam—farmer, Sheridan
Malone, Rev. D. E.—Catholic
  priest, Midland, 1903
Malone, Edna—teacher, Clare, 1905
Malone, John—pioneer, Winterfield
Maloney, Agnes—teacher, Clare
Maloney, Ella—teacher, Clare, 1903
Maloney, Etta—teacher, 1906
Maloney, James—oil worker, Clare
Malosh, Clifford—teacher, mgr.
  Lake store, AEF, Lake
Malosh, Peter—Garfield, 1906
Maltby, A.—Maltby Lumber Co.,
  Garfield, 1904
Maltby, Florence—teacher
Maltby, Frank—Garfield, 1915
Maltby, Harry—Lake, 1900
Maltby, Thomas—merchant,
  postmaster, Crooked Lake, 1900
Maltby, Thomas, Jr.—WWI
Maltby, Walter—U. S. Navy, 1900
Manaming, J.—Hamilton, 1906
Manee, C. F.—meat market, Clare
Manee, Paul—Standard Oil
  agent, AEF, Clare, 1916
Mangle, Harley—farmer, Sheridan
Manlay, Joseph—state hwy foreman
Manley, Archie—P.M.R.R.
  conductor, Clare, 1903
Manna, N.—road bldr., Surrey
Mannaman, Leo—Vernon, 1917
Manning, W. C.—Temple, 1917
Mansell, Edith—Clare, 1914
Manwaring, Charles—1918
Manwaring, Joseph—WWI, 1918
Mapes, John W.—rural mail carrier
Mapes, Willis—Loomis, 1909
Mapp, Violet—Harrison, 1902
Marble, George—farmer, Loomis
March, Stephen—WWI, Hayes
Maricelles, Frederick—WWI
Maricelles, Wm.—restaurant, Clare
Mark, Eleanor—teacher
Mark, John—farmer, preacher,
  Civil War Vet, Alward, 1905
Mark, Noah—farmer, Arthur, 1914
Markert, Johnston—welder, Clare
Markey, Wm.—farmer, Grant, 1917

Marks, William—Freeman, 1919
Marlin, Blake—AEF
Marlin, David—farmer, Wise
Marlin, George—Herrick, 1900
Marlin, James—farmer, Wise, 1882
Marlin, James, Jr.—Wise, 1910
Marlin, J. W.—farmer, Surrey
Marlin, John—farmer, Vernon
Marlin, William—Wise, 1910
Marr, E. H.—Sheridan, 1906
Marr, Fred J.—farmer, Greenwood
Marr, John—farmer, Clare, 1902
Marseilles, Andrew—Vernon, 1900
Marseilles, Anthony—Vernon, 1900
Marsceills, John—Clare, 1900
Marsh, John—WWI, Farwell, 1911
Marshall, Arthur—Vernon, 1917
Marshall, Clifford—Surrey, 1918
Marshall, Frederick—Vernon, 1917
Marshall, Jason S.—farmer
Marshall, John—truck driver, 1906
Marshall, Kenneth—Wise, 1917
Marshall, Leon—WWI, Wise, 1918
Marshall, Thomas—farmer, Vernon
Martell, Gregory—Lake George
Martin, Bertha—Harrison, 1907
Martin, Blake—Sheridan, 1919
Martin, Charles—Clare, 1909
Martin, Elvin—Temple, 1900
Martin, Eliza—Grant, 1903
Martin, Francis—Garfield, 1906
Martin, Fred—Garfield, 1906
Martin, Grover—Clare, 1908
Martin, James—Freeman, 1909
Martin, John H.—threshing
  machine man, 1899
Martin, John H., Jr.—farmer, Clare
Martin, Lorenzo D.—Garfield, 1918
Martin, Lorenzo—R.R., farming
Martin, M. A.—Clare, 1912
Martin, Perry E.—Clare, 1909
Martin, R. J.—farmer, pioneer
Martin, Robert—Freeman, 1903
Martin, Russell—Clare, 1907
Martin, Stephen—WWI, Garfield
Martin, Verne—Clare, 1908
Martin, Walter S.—Grant, 1901
Martin, Wesley—thresher, Sheridan
Martin, Wm.—cobbler, Clare, 1912
Martin, Wm. H.—Surrey, 1900
Martindale, Dr. Earl—veterinarian
Marvin, Bert—Garfield, 1918
Maseline, Fred—policeman, Clare
Mason, George—Clare, 1908
Mason, Harry—Redding, 1911
Mason, Jacob—merchant, Clare
Mason, Jacob, Jr.—barber, Clare
Mason, Morris—1914
Mason, Orin—WWI, Garfield, 1917
Mason, Wm.—farmer, Garfield
Masten, Clyde—Farwell, 1909
Masten, Dietrich—teacher, Farwell
Masten, Mrs. Hattie—teacher
Masten, Stanley—Borden Co.
  employee
Masten, Thomas—farmer, Vernon
Masten, Wm.—Farwell, 1904
Mater, Daniel—farmer, Clare, 1903
Mater, Doris—Clare
Mater, George—carpenter, Clare
Mater, Hazel—teacher, Hatton
Mater, Peter—farmer, Mannsiding

Mater, S. B.—Clare, 1903
Mater, Vaughn—Wise, 1917
Matier, Wm.—twp. supervisor, Wise
Mathis, C.—Clare, 1901
Mathews, Fred—AEF, 1918
Matthews, Iola—teacher, Clare
Matthews, Walter—WWI, Hamilton
Mattison, Albert—Grant, 1900
Mattison, John—Grant, 1906
Maung, John—WWI
Maurer, C. I.—grocer, Farwell
Maver, John—businessman, Clare
Mavis, Carl—Arthur, 1915
Mavis, Laura—teacher, 1914
Mavis, Lena—teacher, Harrison
Maxwell, Anna—Vernon, 1900
Maxwell, Bert—farmer, Herrick
Maxwell, Edna—Clare, 1909
Maxwell, Francis—pioneer, farmer
Maxwell, Rev. G. W.—M-E
  minister, Farwell, 1903
Maxwell, George W.—Grant, 1914
Maxwell, Nellie—Clare, 1914
Maxwell, Norman—Clare
Maxwell, Oscar—Sheridan, 1917
Maxwell, Wm. B.—farmer, Grant
Maxwell, W. G.—M-E, Farwell
Maxwell, Wm. J.—farmer, Wise
Maxwell, Wm. Walter, Mt. P.
May, Charles H.—Garfield, 1909
May, John—pioneer, 1880
May, Lee B.—Greenwood, 1906
May, Wm.—farmer
Maybee, Harry—farmer, Isabella
Maybe, Mynard—Harrison
Mayer, Austin E.—hatchery owner
Mayer, Basil—poultry raiser, Clare
Mayes, T.—Farwell, 1908
Mayhew, Arthur—WWI, Sheridan
Mayhew, Eliheu—Isabella, 1889
Mayhew, Lawrence—farmer
Mayhew, Stewart—U.S. Army
Mayhew, Wm.—Hamilton, 1917
Maynard, Albert—insurance, Clare
Maynard, Emerson—Frost, 1903
Maynard, Dr. F. H.—Clare, 1918
Maynard, Perry—WWI, 1914
Maynard, Dr. Thomas H.—
  pioneer, physician, Clare
Maynard, Thomas H., Jr.—Clare
Maynard, Thomas—Clare, 1911
Mayor, August—farmer, 1916
Mayor, W. H.—Lake George, 1917
Mead, Amber—Frost, 1911
Mead, Clara—Frost, 1911
Mead, Harry—barber, Clare
Mead, L.—Long Lake, 1904
Mead, Richard—Clare, 1911
Meade, _____—pharmacy, Clare
Meade, Harry—farmer, Harrison
Medcalf, Fred B.—Winterfield
Medcoff, Frank—farmer, Farwell
Mede, Richard—Farwell, 1900
Melville, George—water works
  engineer, Farwell, 1903
Melvin, A. A.—Farwell, 1909
Melvin, Francis—Surrey, 1917
Melvin, George—Farwell, 1900
Menerey, David—editor, Coleman
Menerey, Jacob—Andersonville
Menery, Matt—Isabella, 1908
Menerey, Wallace—farmer, Wise

Mercer, Benjamin N.—Clare
Mercer, Mrs. B. N.—Clare, 1929
Mercer, Victoria—Clare
Merchant, Watson—Leota, 1904
Merrill, Carl—WWI, 1918
Merrill, Charles—farmer, Arthur
Merrill, Charles E.—Harrison, 1917
Merrill, John—P.M.R.R., Harrison
Merrill, Joseph—Mt. Pleasant, 1916
Merrill, Wm.—Temple, 1917
Merritt, Mrs. C.—farmer, Hamilton
Merritt, Doris—teacher, Clare
Merritt, S. R.—Harrison, 1913
Merton, Oliver—foreman, ship
    yard, Bay City, Sheridan, 1918
Mertz, Ed—farmer, Harrison
Mershon, Wm. B.—farmer, Clare
Messenger, Clare—Sheridan, 1917
Metcalf, George—Freeman, 1906
Methner, Fritz—Wise, 1917
Methner, Edd—Wise, 1917
Methner, Hulda—Clare
Methner, John—Clare
Methner, Joseph—Wise, 1917
Methner, Wm.—Wise, 1917
Metner, August—Wise, 1917
Metzen, Edward—Vernon, 1914
Meyers, Jacob—farmer, Arthur
Meyers, F. P.—farmer, Sheridan
Michael, T. W.—editor,
    COURIER, Clare Granger
    organizer, Vernon
Michand, Louis—Clare
Michner, Sherd—merchant
Mickins, Arthur—A.A.R.R. agent
Mickle, Amos—WWI, Arthur
Mickle, H. C.—farmer, Arthur
Mickle, Vere—Arthur, 1891
Mickle, Wm.—farmer, Clare, 1905
Middleton, Herbert—Farwell, 1903
Middleton, Jay—Farwell, 1911
Mielke, Albert—Harrison
Mielke, Carl
Mielke, Rudolph—Hamilton
Mielke, Samuel—Harrison
Milam, Courtney—AEF, Redner
Milam, J. B.—ranch foreman
Milan, Chester—Clare
Miles, Arthur—farmer, Farwell
Milkie, Enoch E.—WWI, Arthur
Milkie, Natalie—E. Hamilton, 1917
Milkie, Samuel—Bingham's Corner
Milkie, Wm.—farmer, Arthur, 1906
Milks, M.—Farwell, 1914
Milks, W. J.—Farwell, 1914
Mill, Earl—Frost, 1916
Miller, Albert H.—undertaker
Miller, Anna—Hamilton
Miller, Archie—farmer, Vernon
Miller, Archie, Jr.—state hwy dept.
Miller, Archibault—farmer, Clare
Miller, Bert—Dray Service, Farwell
Miller, Charles S.—WWI, Clare
Miller, Cina—Tonkin, 1908
Miller, Clarence—Surrey, 1916
Miller, C. W.—Garfield, 1909
Miller, David—Clare, 1917
Miller, David, Jr.—AEF, Wise
Miller, David—oil field worker
Miller, Donald—Sheridan, 1911
Miller, Ed—A.A.R.R., Clare, 1905
Miller, Elmer—farmer, Sheridan

Miller, Frank—AEF, Clare, 1908
Miller, George—farmer, Arthur
Miller, Glenn—Wise, 1917
Miller, Harrison—Wise, 1917
Miller, Ira—store, Clare
Miller, John J.—Vernon, 1913
Miller, John T.—Temple, 1915
Miller, John—AEF, W. Wise, 1918
Miller, Kate—teacher, Clare, 1906
Miller, Marie—Clare, 1917
Miller, Mary Ann—Grant, 1908
Miller, Milo—Greenwood, 1906
Miller, Nettie—teacher, Clare, 1905
Miller, Noah—Arthur, 1911
Miller, Paul—twp. clerk, Vernon
Miller, Samuel—Hatton, 1900
Miller, Samuel L.—Civil War
    Vet, Clare, 1911
Miller, Sarah—Clare, 1917
Miller, Soloman—Winterfield, 1914
Miller, Truie L.—salesman, Clare
Miller, Velma—Clare
Miller, Warren—Grant, 1900
Miller, "Will"—Farwell, 1918
Miller, Wm.—night operator,
    Union Station, Clare, 1900
Miller, William E.—Wise, 1917
Milliken, Carl J.—r.r. telegraph op.
Mills, A. E.—Frost, 1906
Mills, Arthur—farmer, Harrison
Mills, E. D.—mgr. Mich.
    Creamery Co., Clare, 1910
Mills, Earl H.—Frost, 1903
Mills, Earl S.—Frost, 1917
Mills, Elvin H.—Frost, 1915
Mills, George—carpenter, AEF
Mills, Hazel—Farwell, 1908
Mills, H. C.—Summerfield, 1903
Mills, L. D.—1914
Mills, Lawrence M.—Frost, 1918
Mills, Morey S.—Farwell, 1912
Mills, Orton—farmer, Elm Grove
Minacka, Jack—Hatton, 1909
Minar, George S.—Gilmore, 1915
Minner, Bert—farmer, Freeman
Minnier, Wm.—farmer, Freeman
Miser, Earl—Hatton, 1915
Miser, George—pioneer, Grant
Miser, Henry—Dover, 1914
Miser, Irvin—Dover, 1909
Miser, James—Dover, 1903
Miser, John—Dover, 1915
Miser, Jousha—Grant, 1903
Mitchell, Andrew—farmer, Vernon
Mitchell, Ansylm—Hamilton, 1917
Mitchell, Basil Owen—1918
Mitchell, Charles—farmer, Vernon
Mitchell, Frank—Wise
Mitchell, Frank—electrician, Wise
Mitchell, Freeman—Vernon, 1918
Mitchell, Helena—teacher
Mitchell, I. V.—musician, Harrison
Mitchell, Jacob—Clare
Mitchell, James—Hamilton, 1909
Mitchell, John—Wise, 1917
Mitchell, John L.—Harrison, 1900
Mitchell, Levi—Harrison, 1907
Mitchell, Loretta—teacher, Hayes
Mitchell, Neill J.—WWI, Wise
Mitchell, Stanley—Harrison
Mitchell, Wm.—pioneer, farmer
Mitchell, Wm.—Harrison, 1910

Mitchener, Angela—teacher, Arthur
Mitchner, Guy Everett—Franklin
Mix, George—Clare, 1900
Mixter, Herbert L.—1918
Mixter, Solomon—Harrison, 1907
Moarey, Harry—Lake George, 1908
Mock, Claude—1911
Moden, Austin E.—supt., Clare
Moder, Albert—Hatton, 1917
Moder, Edwin—farmer, Harrison
Moffatt, ____—pioneer, Winterfield
Moffet, Rev. J. E.—minister
Mogg, Ernest—farmer, Clare, 1914
Mogg, Reuben—farmer, Loomis
Molda, Oscar—8 Point Lake, 1904
Moline, Harold—Clare
Moline, Illa—Farwell, 1909
Moline, Martha—Clare, 1900
Moline, Verne—Hinkleville, 1917
Moline, Wm.—watchman,
    r.r. roundhouse, Harrison
Moll, ____—r.r. section forman
Monday, Carlton—farmer,
    AEF, Hatton, 1918
Monday, Mack—Hatton, 1905
Monday, Wm.—WWI, 1918
Monroe, E. L.—Harrison
Monroe, George—Winterfield, 1911
Monroe, Lulu—piano teacher, Clare
Monroe, M. Linus—Lincoln, 1917
Monroe, Walter—Vernon, 1906
Montney, Clayton L.—Grant, 1916
Montney, Floyd—creamery route
Montney, Levi—Civil War
    Vet, Clare, 1904
Montney, Lizzie—clerk, Clare, 1903
Montney, Mildred—Clare
Montney, Ray—Clare, 1916
Mooney, Almer—drayman, Clare
Mooney, Blanche—Clare, 1900
Mooney, Douglas—star football
    player, WWI, Clare
Mooney, Frank—baggage master
Mooney, Henry—WWI, Clare
Moore, Adeline—teacher, Farwell
Moore, Alvin—teacher, Lake Geo.
Moore, Baldwin—WWI, 1918
Moore, Bernise—Clare
Moore, Berthel—Grandon, 1904
Moore, Clyde—lumberman, Eagle
Moore, Edgar—Temple, 1903
Moore, H. C.—farmer, Garfield
Moore, John—farmer, Surrey, 1910
Moore, John B.—farmer, WWI
Moore, Judson
Moore, James—Temple, 1903
Moore, Louis—WWI, Freeman
Moore, Marvin—AEF, 1918
Moore, Mercedes—Clare
Moore, Paul—market, Harrison
Moore, Pearl—Clarence, 1914
Moore, Rhoda—Dover, 1907
Moore, Robert—Temple, 1917
Moore, Sam W.—Maple Grove
Moore, Tilden—Grant, 1903
Moore, Walter—WWI, 1918
Moran, Walter H.—WWI, Clare
Morden, Jemima—Clare, 1911
Morden, John S.—Vernon, 1917
Morden, Wesley—farmer, Vernon
Morgan, Earl—Garfield, 1913
Morgan, Frederick—grocery
    store, teacher, Clare, 1905

Morgan, Harry—Vernon, 1914
Morgan, John—farmer, Clare, 1922
Morgan, Lewis—Vernon, 1917
Morgan, Rolland—Vernon, 1900
Morgan, W. H.—farmer, Vernon
Morris, Rev. A. J.—M-E pastor
Morrison, Bruce—Loomis, 1913
Morrison, Dora—Clare, 1916
Morrison, Frank E.—supt.
    Weidman Schools, Clare, 1915
Morrison, Rev. F. J.—priest, Clare
Morrison, James—teacher, Surrey
Morrison, Wm.—Sheridan, 1914
Morrison, Wm., Jr.—Clare
Morrissey, Burke—U.S.
    Navy, WWI, Hayes
Morrissey, Francis—county clerk
Morrissey, Frank—Harrison, 1904
Morrison, Annie—Sheridan, 1903
Morrison, Bruce—Wise, 1918
Morrison, John—Clare, 1903
Morrison, Max G.—Clare
Morrissey, S. A.—mail clerk, Clare
Morrissey, W. Everrett—1918
Morrison, Wm.—farmer, Sheridan
Morrison, Wm. Earl—farmer
Morrow, Elizabeth—Harrison
Morrow, Gideon—carpenter, Hayes
Morrow, Loren—Hamilton, 1916
Morrow, Ruth—Harrison, 1903
Morrow, S.—twp. supervisor, Hayes
Morse, J. P.—Sheridan, 1903
Morse, Berthyl—Grandon, 1903
Morse, H. C.—Farwell, 1908
Morse, John—farmer, Winterfield
Morse, R.—Loomis, 1900
Morse, S. H.—harness maker, Clare
Morton, Earl—WWI, 1918
Morton, Ernest J.—Hamilton, 1917
Morton, Mabel—teacher, Hamilton
Morton, Samuel—pioneer, farmer
Mosehouse, W. G.—Garfield, 1906
Mosher, Emma—Clare, 1913
Mosley, Rev. Henry—Cong.
    minister, Farwell, 1914
Mott, Royal—Hayes
Mott, Sanford—farmer, Vernon
Mott, Wm.—farmer, grocery,
    Surrey, 1917
Moulton, DeForest—Harrison, 1938
Mount, June—Clare
Mowatt, Robert—Redding, 1903
Mowl, Ettie—Farwell, 1915
Moyer, Albert—lumber business
Moyer, Dorothy—Clare
Muir, George—Lake, 1908
Muir, Sam
Mulder, A. E.—dentist, Clare, 1903
Mulder, Louis—Clare
Mull, B. F.—farmer, Arthur, 1906
Mull, Claude—P.M.R.R., Clare
Mull, Edward—farmer, Clare, 1911
Mull, Glen—Arthur, 1908
Mull, Herbert—Grant, 1917
Mull, Wm.—1919
Mullen, _____—hotel man, Clare
Mullen, John M.—sawmill, Frost
Muma, James—livery, Clare
Muma, Opal—Clare
Muma, T.—Hamilton, 1906
Munger, Fannie—Farwell, 1909
Munger, Miles—Civil War

Vet, Clare, 1911
Munger, Miles, Jr.—Clare, 1914
Munger, Seth—Civil War
    Vet, Farwell, 1910
Munsell, Aseneth—Hayes, 1911
Murdock, Duncan—Grant, 1917
Muringer, Louis—WWI, Surrey
Muringer, Walter—1915
Murphy, Andrew—pioneer,
    Civil War Vet, Hayes, 1906
Murphy, Francis—Sheridan, 1917
Murphy, Frank—farmer, Clare
Murphy, Ida—Harrison, 1912
Murphy, James—farmer, Sheridan
Murphy, John—Sheridan
Murphy, Joseph—Vernon, Grant
Murphy, Joseph, Jr.—Clare
Murphy, Mary—farm, Clare
Murphy, Nancy—Hayes, 1906
Murphy, Pat—Harrison, 1913
Murphy, Peter—farmer, pioneer
Murphy, Peter, Jr.—Clare
Murphy, Richard—Brinton, 1916
Murphy, Wm.—1903
Murphy, Wm.—general
    merchandise, Mayor, Harrison
Murray, Frank—Lincoln, 1919
Murray, Friend—farmer, Gilmore
Murray, Guy—farmer, Garfield
Muscott, Ralph—wooden ware
    manufacturer, Civil War
    Vet, Clare, 1880
Mussell, A. E.—drug store, Clare
Mussell, Dr. Arthur—pharmacist,
    physician, AEF, Clare
Mussell, David E.—Clare, 1938
Mussell, Dorsey—Clare
Mussell, Edward—Clare, 1900
Mussell, Robert—druggist, Clare
Mussell, Theo.—Clare, 1912
Mutton, David—Sheridan
Myers, Beatrice—Clare
Myers, E. E.—ranch, Arthur, 1906
Myers, Edith—nurse, Arthur, 1918
Myers, Frank M.—rancher, Arthur
Myers, George—farmer, Temple
Myers, G. W.—Mich. Produce
    Co. employee, Clare, 1911
Myers, Howard E.—Wise, 1917
Myers, Jacob P.—rancher, Arthur
Myers, John—farmer, Hamilton
Myers, John H.—farmer, Arthur
Myers, Mildred—Clare
Myers, Milo—Grant, 1909
Myers, Rev. N. J.—Cong. minister
Myers, Peter—Hayes, 1918
Myers, Robert—Grant, 1909
Myers, Ralph—Farwell, 1910
Myers, Roy—Temple
Myers, Ruth—Clare, 1920
Myers, W. E.—farmer, rancher
Neagle, Dewey—WWI, 1918
Neagle, George—Redding, 1917
Naldrett, Hugh—1917
Naldrett, I.—movie theatre owner
Naldrett, Job—Lincoln, 1916
Nash, Philip—Greenwood, 1903
Nash, Wm.—farmer, Hamilton
Nass, Anna—1911
Nass, August—farmer, Grant, 1906
Nass, Chris—well driller, Grant
Nass, Jacob—farmer, Grant, 1900

Nass, Emma—Grant, 1892
Nass, Emma—Clare
Nass, Gottlob—farmer, Grant
Nass, Jacob—Grant, 1914
Nass, Paul C.—farmer, Grant, 1900
Nass, Paul, Jr.—thresher, carpenter
Nass, Will—Grant, 1909
Naumes, Joseph—attorney, Clare
Naylor, Thomas—Clare, 1903
Neagle, George—WWI, 1918
Neal, Laura—Clare, 1900
Neal, Thomas—Harrison, 1903
Nederhood, Mrs. A.—farmer
Nederhoed, Jasper—Greenwood
Nederhoed, Wm. A.—Winterfield
Neelands, Dr. Hugh—dentist, Clare
Neeley, Ralph—farmer, Clare, 1894
Neeper, John—Garfield, 1906
Neeper, Roy—farmer, teacher, Lake
Neff, C. B.—dentist, Clare
Nehls, Fred—machinist, 1917
Neiderhoed, Albert—pioneer
Neidholt, Sgt. Claude B.—1914
Neigle, J. George—sawmill
Neimeyer, Charles—Clare
Neithercut, Charles—Colonville
Neithercut, Charles—Clare, 1917
Neithercut, John—farmer, Sheridan
Neithercut, Wm. A.—attorney
Nellis, Herbert—1918
Nelson, A.—Surrey, 1906
Nelson, Benjamin—clerk, 1903
Nelson, Charles—saloon, 1903
Nelson, E.—Temple, 1914
Nelson, George—Garfield, 1919
Nelson, Lester—Redding, 1908
Nelson, Tony—pioneer, Winterfield
Nevill, James—farmer, Vernon
Nevill, James, Jr.—Vernon
Nevill, John—farmer, Vernon, 1900
Nevill, Loran—farmer, Grant
Nevill, Thomas—farmer, Vernon
Nevins, Thelma—Clare, 1916
Nevins, Wm. F.—Wise, 1917
Newberry, Al E.—farmer, Hamilton
Newberry, Truman—candidate
    for senate, 1918
Newbound, Harold—Harrison, 1916
Newbound, Joseph—P.M.R.R.
    conductor, Harrison, 1917
Newcomer, Wm.—farmer, Arthur
Newkirk, Henry—judge, legislator,
    banker, Ann Arbor, 1913
Newman, Arnold—Clare, 1911
Newman, B. S.—farmer, Dover
Newman, Donna—Arthur, 1915
Newman, Frank—Arthur, 1915
Newman, Jessie—farmer, Arthur
Newman, Raleigh—WWI, Clare
Newman, Vesta—Brush College
Newson, Fred—mechanic, 1932
Newth, Jacob—Civil War
    Vet, Grant, 1873
Newton, Rev. O. E.—Episcopal
    rector, Clare, 1913
Newville, James—Franklin, 1917
Newville, Wm.—Leota, 1918
Nichols, Clarence—Winterfield
Nichols, Harley—Lincoln
Nicholis, Henry—Clare, 1929
Nicholls, A.—Loomis, 1900
Nicholls, Emmett—WWI, 1918

Nicholls, James—pioneer, Loomis
Nicholls, James—Grant, 1912
Nicholls, Sam—Farwell, 1908
Nichols, Emmett—Gilmore, 1917
Nichols, Samuel—Gilmore, 1917
Nickels, Leonard—merchant
Nickerson, Bonnie—WWI, Clare
Nickerson, E. A.—Clare, 1918
Nieler, Mrs. S. C.—Loomis, 1909
Niemeyer, Charles—P.M.R.R.
Niemeyer, Roy—Valley
    Telephone Co. employee, Clare
Nivison, Gerald—Clare, 1911
Nivison, Gladys—teacher, Clare
Nivison, Guy—Clare, 1909
Nix, Sarah—Clare, 1902
Nixon, Andrew—Vernon, 1900
Nixon, Charles—head sawyer
Nixon, Ford—teacher, Clare, 1912
Nixon, Jacob—pioneer, Winterfield
Nixon, Kenneth—tool dresser, Clare
Nixon, John—Clare, 1906
Nixon, Mabel—teacher, Clare, 1910
Nixon, Maggie—teacher, Temple
Nixon, Manley—barber, Temple
Nixon, Pioyne—Temple, 1903
Nixon, Robert—twp. treasurer,
    Redding, 1906
Nixon, W.—Greenwood, 1908
Noack, Rev. Ernest—minister
Noflizge, Russell—clerk, Clare
Nolin, Harry—Clare, 1909
Norman, Archie—Frost, 1914
Norman, J. H.—1909
Norris, Burt—gambler, Harrison
Norris, Byron—Arthur, 1913
Northen, Oscar—Clare, 1900
Norris, Rev. A. H.—Cong. minister
Northey, Dr. F. O.—physician
Northey, Richard—Clare, 1908
Northey, S.—carraige painter, Clare
Northon, Agnes—Farwell, 1908
Northon, Charles—pioneer, Vernon
Northon, C. E.—1914
Northon, Charlotte—Vernon
Northon, Edward—Clare, 1908
Northon, Esther—Clare
Northon, Jarvis—farmer, Vernon
Northon, John—Clare, 1911
Northon, Joseph T.—supt. of
    Farwell Schools, Farwell, 1905
Northon, Mabel—Clare, 1900
Northon, Marion—Clare
Northon, Oscar—farmer, Vernon
Northon, Otix—Clare
Northon, Sam—Clare, 1915
Northon, Wm.—Clare
Northon, Wm., Jr.—Clare, 1908
Northrop, Henry C.—Farwell, 1907
Northrup, Ruie—WWI, Farwell
Norton, A. B.—1903
Nowlen, Harry—Clare, 1937
Nowlan, Henry—1916
Nowlen, Wellington—well driller
Nowlen, Wellington, Jr.—WWI
Nowlin, Henry T.—Clare, 1901
Nye, Frank—interior decorator
Oakley, Mrs. ____—Lake George
Obenover, Robert—Freeman, 1912
Oberholtzer, E. G.—Freeman, 1918
Oberholtzer, Earl—WWI, Freeman
Oberholtzer, Edward—farmer

Oberholtzer, Oliver—1918
O'Brien, F. L.—Clare, 1910
O'Callaghan, John—M-E, Clare
Ochert, Joseph—farmer, Farwell
O'Conner, Amanda—Clare
O'Conner, Ray—student, 1904
O'Conner, Clair—Clare
O'Conner, George—Harrison
O'Connor, James J.—grocery
O'Connor, James—Civil
    War Vet, Clare, 1880
O'Connor, J. H.—prop. Lewis
    House, Harrison, 1906
O'Connor, Jerry—Surrey, 1912
O'Connor, Nina—teacher, Clare
Odell, Frank—WWI, Garfield, 1918
Odell, Henry—Garfield, 1917
Oden, Leo—mail carrier, WWI
O'Dette, Charles—farmer, Grant
Odette, Raymond—WWI, Grant
O'Donald, Charles—banker,
    businessman, Clare, 1886
O'Donald, J. J.—Clare, 1903
Ogden, Flora—teacher, Farwell
O'Grady, James—Vernon, 1900
O'Grady, John—pioneer, Vernon
O'Grady, John R.—Vernon, 1900
O'Grady, Wm.—Grant, 1904
Ohman, Gust—1907
O'Kain, Barney—farmer
Olden, P. O.—Eagle, 1909
Oldenhouse, Herman—Winterfield
Older, Rev. P. C.—minister, Eagle
Olds, A. W.—Grant, 1906
Olds, Carrie—Clare, 1903
Olds, Frank—Surrey, 1912
Olds, L. T.—War of 1846 Vet.
Olds, Sherman—Clare, 1903
Olds, Thomas—Loomis, 1907
Oles, Frederick—Clare, 1916
Oles, Harry B.—WWI, Clare, 1916
O'Leary, Ed—Hamilton, 1906
Oleson, James—Lincoln, 1906
Oliver, A.—Grant, 1986
Oliver, Clare—Clare
Oliver, Florence—Harrison
Oliver, Floyd—cashier, Farwell
Oliver, John J.—Clare, 1879
Oliver, John L., Jr.—banker,
    Farwell, produce buyer, Clare
Olsen, Arthur—Lake George, 1912
Olsen, Axel—Harrison
Olson, Arthur—farmer, Lake Geo.
Olson, John—R.F.D. carrier, WWI
Olson, Jonas—farmer, Lincoln
Olson, Jonas A.—Lake George
Olson, Ove—teacher, WWI, 1918
O'Malley, Joseph—Farwell
Oman, Anna—Lake, 1900
Oman, Carrie—Lake, 1910
Oman, Charles—WWI, Lake, 1917
Oman, John—Garfield, 1900
Oman, Lars—Garfield, 1914
Oman, Louis—cook, Garfield, 1905
Oman, Marcus—Garfield, 1900
Oman, Mary—Lake, 1900
Oman, Peter—teacher, postmaster,
    county official, twp. treasurer,
    Crooked Lake, 1900
O'Mealey, Anthony—farmer
O'Neil, John—Garfield, 1903
O'Neil, Mary—1903

O'Neil, Wm.—farmer, Vernon
Ordeway, L.—Franklin, 1906
O'Reilly, T. W.—Grant, 1906
Orr, George—Vernon, 1918
Ort, Florence—teacher, Clare
Ort, Henry—businessman, Clare
Ort, Lydia—teacher, Clare, 1903
Orth, Barbara—1911
Orth, Emerson—Clare, 1903
Orth, Dr. G. E.—physician, Clare
Orth, Henry—auctioneer,
    Central Hotel, Clare, 1882
Orth, Sarah—bookkeeper, Clare
Orvis, Bert—farmer, Sheridan
Orvis, Erwin—farmer, Clare, 1915
Orvis, Eugene—Clare
Orvis, Forest—farmer, Arthur
Orvis, James
Orvis, L.—farmer, Sheridan, 1906
Orvis. Mary—Eagle, 1908
Orvis, Rex E.—Arthur
Osborn, Audrey—Clare
Osborn, Delbert W.—Clare
Osborn, Elmer—butcher, Clare
Osborn, Kathleen—Clare
Osborne, Leslie—Clare
Oseson, Mrs. ____—Long Lake
Osgerby, Nellie—teacher, Clare
Osgood, Sarah—Maple Grove, 1909
Osterout, Bert J.—R.R., Farwell
Osterrout, John—farmer, Grant
Osterhout, Lodine—Clare, 1907
Ostrander, James—businessman
O'Sullivan, Cornelius—bookkeeper
Ott, Albert—Hatton, 1908
Ott, Arnold—Arthur, 1917
Ott, Bertha—Hatton, 1908
Ott, Charles—Arthur, 1915
Ott, Chris—lumberjack, Hatton
Ott, Clara—Hatton, 1908
Ott, Clarence—Hatton, 1908
Ott, David—Hatton, 1908
Ott, Emma—farm, Hatton, 1906
Ott, Fred Wm.—1918
Ott, Fritz—Hatton, 1908
Ott, George A.—Hatton, 1917
Ott, George L.—farmer, Hatton
Ott, Henry—Hatton, 1900
Ott, Herman—Hatton
Ott, Jacob—Hatton, 1906
Ott, Joanna—Hatton, 1908
Ott, John—farmer, Hatton, 1880
Ott, John, Jr.—farmer, Hatton
Ott, Louis—Hatton, 1908
Ott, Louisa—teacher, Hatton, 1906
Ott, Martha—Hatton, 1908
Ott, Mary—Hatton, 1908
Ott, Nora—Arthur, 1900
Ott, Rosa—Hatton, 1908
Ott, Robert—WWI, 1918
Ott, Selma—Hatton, 1910
Ott, Thelma—Hatton, 1908
Otto, Lewis—farmer, WWI, Temple
Ouderkirk, Alice—Clare, 1912
Ouderkirk, Archie—Clare, 1901
Oudekirk, Charles W.—Loomis
Ouderkirk, Edna—Clare
Ouderkirk, John H.—Vernon, 1908
Ouderkirk, Ray Nathan—Vernon
Ouderkirk, Wm. H.—Vernon, 1908
Ousterout, Bert—P.M. freight
    conductor, Farwell, 1911

Ousterout, James—Farwell
Ousterrout, George—farmer, Grant
Overmyer, Alford—Winterfield
Overton, Alonzo—Surrey, 1910
Overton, E. F.—Clare, 1900
Overton, Ernest A.—Maple Grove
Owen, G. E.—shingle dealer, 1912
Owen, Jason—dairy, Lake, 1914
Owen, "Will", Long Lake, 1916
Owens, Earl—farmer, Vernon, 1897
Owens, Jason T.—Surrey, 1906
Owens, Phillip—farmer, Gilmore
Packard, Lillian—teacher, 1900
Packard, Wm. E.—ranch foreman,
   Lake George, 1903
Paddock, George—pioneer
Page, ____—WWI, Frost, 1916
Page, Charles H.—farmer, Frost
Page, Harry—farmer, Harrison
Page, Henry—Harrison, 1908
Page, Wm.—farmer, Vernon, 1904
Palmatier, Marvin—Sheridan, 1900
Palmer, A. E.—farmer, 1900
Palmer, Almer—Temple, 1903
Palmer, Carl—mill hand, Temple
Palmer, Charles—Surrey, 1903
Palmer, Curtis, Colonville
   merchant, postmaster, 1900
Palmer, E. D.—supt. of schools,
   Clare Co. School Comm.,
   ex-editor, Sentinel, Clare, 1905
Palmer, George W.—mail carrier
Palmer, George—Garfield
Palmer, Jess T.—store, Farwell
Palmer, Jesse—Farwell, 1913
Palmer, Nellie—teacher, Farwell
Palmer, O. M.—Farwell, 1910
Palmer, T. W.—Winterfield, 1908
Palmer, Veryl—Farwell, 1908
Palmer, Will—Temple, 1912
Palmer, Winifrede—teacher, Farwell
Parcell, W. D.—Clare, 1909
Parent, Omer A.—merchant, WWI
Paridic, George—Clare, 1901
Parish, Ernie—Clare, 1914
Parish, Ray—Vernon, 1917
Parish, Riley B.
Park, Bernard—WWI, Frost, 1917
Park, Edmond D.—twp. hwy
   commissioner, Frost, 1915
Park, Harry—farmer, Greenwood
Park, W. L.—ranch, Clare
Parker, Acey—Clare
Parker, Amos—feed barn, Clare
Parker, Caroline—1913
Parker, Fremont—Harrison, 1908
Parker, F. W.—Clare, 1907
Parker, Hattie—Clare
Parker, James—Grandon, 1917
Parker, Ray—Temple, 1916
Parks, Archie—WWI, Clare, 1917
Parks, Edmond—twp. supervisor,
   Frost, 1917
Parks, George—Wise, 1917
Parks, John—WWI, Clare, 1917
Parks, John W.—laborer, Grant
Parks, Eugene—Frost, 1906
Parks, John—Clare, 1909
Parks, O.—Frost, 1906
Parmelee, C. W.—sawmill
Parmelee, Phillip—Winterfield, 1903
Parmerclingle, ____—Sheridan

Parmeter, Walter—butcher, Clare
Parrish, Art—gas station, Clare
Parrish, Benjamin B.—Clare, 1934
Parrish, C. H.—farmer, Civil
   War Vet, Arthur, 1903
Parrish, Dale—Clare
Parrish, Frank—lumberman, Clare
Parrish, Jerry—farmer, Hatton
Parrish, John—Grant, 1915
Parrish, M. E.—Clare, 1902
Parrish, M. T.—millinery, Clare
Parrish, Ora—farmer, Arthur, 1906
Parrish, Ray—farmer, WWI
Parrish, Riley—Clare, 1905
Parrish, Stanley—Clare, 1919
Parrish, Wm. L.—Clare
Parrish, Wm.—marshal, Clare
Parsell, Florence—Herrick
Parsell, W. D.—farmer, Clare
Parsell, Warren—Wise, 1917
Parsonage, W.—Lake George, 1904
Parsons, Rev. Carsen E.—
   missionary to China, Clare, 1905
Passimore, R. B.—Lincoln, 1906
Pastorino, A. G.—merchant, Clare
Patience, Benjamin—Clare, 1882
Patnode, H. P.—Crooked Lake
Patrick, C. H.—hardware, Clare
Patrick, Lewis—Clare, 1911
Patrick, Howard—Clare
Patrick, U. H.—Clare, 1909
Patrick, Willard—Clare, 1911
Patten, Mart—Dover, 1903
Pattengill, H. R.—state supt.
   of schools, Farwell, 1900
Patterson, Tom—W. Grant, 1915
Patti, D. D.—supt. Harrison
   Schools, 1903
Paul, Arthur—farmer, Redding
Paxton, Dewey—auto mechanic
Payne, Clara—Greenwood, 1909
Payne, Floyd—Slabtown, 1900
Payne, George E.—Hatton, 1908
Pearl, Josephine—Clare, 1900
Payne, O. D.—Grandon, 1903
Pearl, Josephine—Clare, 1900
Pearson, Adla—Grant, 1906
Pearson, George—AEF
Pearson, George M.—Sheridan
Pearson, Earnest—WWI
Pease, Charles—farmer, truant
   officer, Hayes, 1906
Pease, Charles—Clare, 1897
Pease, F. E.—Grant, 1900
Pease, George B.—farmer, Grant
Pease, Harry—Hayes, 1906
Pease, Winnifred—Grant, 1916
Peck, Charles—farmer, 1905
Peck, Dr. H. B.—itinerent dentist,
   Clare, 1918
Pedgrift, Flora—Clare
Peek, Chas—farmer, Hatton, 1906
Pelch, Anna—Farwell, 1918
Pelch, Ben—Farwell, 1907
Pelch, Bruce—WWI, Farwell, 1917
Pelch, Venus—Farwell, 1897
Pelcher, Thomas—WWI, Wise
Pell, James—Grant, 1903
Pelton, C. B.—farmer, Civil
   War Vet, Clare, 1913
Pelton, Fred O.—Express officer
Pelton, Max—Clare, 1908

Pemberton, George—Farwell, 1905
Pendell, C.—Elm Grove, 1917
Pendell, Delbert—farmer, Sheridan
Pendell, Leonard—Sheridan, 1917
Pennock, Peter—Temple, 1911
Pennock, Phil—Pennock, 1913
Pennock, Ross R.—1909
Penny, L. L.—Arthur, 1903
Penny, Wm. J.—oil tool dresser
Penrose, Earnest—farmer, Grant
Penrose, Ethel—Clare, 1924
Penrose, Howard—farmer, Sheridan
Penrose, Ina—Sheridan, 1911
Penrose, Lowell—farmer, Clare
Penrose, Orin—Eagle, 1904
Penrose, Orris—farmer, Clare, 1886
Penrose, Pearl—Eagle, 1903
Penrose, Willard—Sheridan, 1910
Pepka, Charles—Clare, 1885
Perron, Frank—Grant, 1940
Perry, A.—farmer, Gilmore, 1915
Perry, Adna—Temple, 1918
Perry, Alpheus—mail carrier,
   AEF, wounded, Clare
Perry, C. H.—farmer, Grant, 1900
Perry, C. W.—lawyer, Clare, 1900
Perry, Guy—AEF, POW, Gilmore
Perry, Heeson—farmer, Farwell
Perry, Laverne S.—Gilmore, 1917
Perry, Orville—Gilmore, 1917
Perry, Phebe—Clare, 1917
Perry, R. K.—Hatton, 1906
Pervorse, Frank—farmer, Hatton
Petchnik, Frank—Clare
Pete, Della—Sheridan, 1903
Peter, Wm.—farmer, Sheridan
Peters, Alpha—farmer, Hamilton
Peters, Chas—laborer, Grant, 1900
Peters, Nelson—laborer, Clare, 1908
Peters, Sarah—Grant, 1909
Peters, Walter—Wise, 1917
Petershans, Rev. C. D.—missionary
   on the field, Leota, 1907
Peterson, Alfred—Garfield, 1918
Peterson, Carl—WWI, Garfield
Peterson, Charles—Lake, 1916
Peterson, C. F.—farmer, Hatton
Peterson, Dale—Clare, 1918
Peterson, Edgar S.—music
   professor, violin, piano, Clare
Peterson, Richard V.—WWI,
Peterson, Wm..—1909
Pettibone, Frank—farmer, Grant
Pettibone, Nathan—Hatton, 1904
Petit, Carl E.—P.M. ticket
   clerk, game warden, Clare, 1905
Pettit, Carl, Jr.—truck driver, Clare
Pettit, Edward—champion
   wrestler, WWI, Clare, 1903
Pettit, Fred D.—Frost, 1909
Pettit, Gene—deputy game
   warden, Clare, 1910
Pettit, Robert—Clare
Pettit, Walter—carpenter, Clare
Pettit, Walter D., Jr.—carpenter
Pettitbone, John P.—pioneer
Peuson, George—1918
Pfannes, A.—farmer, Hatton, 1906
Pfannes, Frank—Hatton, 1880
Pfannes, John—farmer, Harrison
Pfannes, Joseph W.—1906
Pfannes, Sebastian—farmer, Hatton

Pfannes, Vess—farmer, Harrison
Pfetsch, Chas—farmer, Hatton
Pfetsch, George—Hatton, 1917
Pfetsch, Henry—farmer, Hatton
Pfetsch, Jacob—farmer, Hatton
Pfetsch, John—farmer, Hatton
Phares, W. H.—Grandon, 1918
Phelps, Alvin L.—Lincoln, 1916
Phelps, Edwin—farmer, Arthur
Phelps, George—hotel man, Clare
Phelps, Levi—Lincoln, 1906
Phelps, Ruth—principal, Farwell
Phelps, W.—Lincoln, 1906
Phillips, A. A.—farmer, Arthur
Phillips, Andrew—Holiness
  movement Church, Clare, 1887
Phillips, Asahel—Maple Grove
Phillips, Charles—WWI, Arthur
Phillips, Edward—Farwell, 1914
Phillips, Erney—Garfield, 1917
Phillips, Fred—farmer, Wise, 1910
Phillips, Fred, Jr.—Clare, 1910
Phillips, George—Freeman, 1918
Phillips, James—Vernon, 1900
Phillips, James—farmer, Vernon
Phillips, Lester—Clare, 1887
Phillips, Ralph—laborer, Clare
Phillips, Samuel—farmer, Grant
Phillips, Thresea—Lake, 1919
Phillips, Wm.—lumberman
Phillips, Zoe—teacher, Garfield
Phinisey, Earl—farmer, Vernon
Phinisey, John B.—farm mgr. for
  C. W. Perry, Vernon, 1903
Phinisey, Thelma—Clare
Phinisey, Theodore
Phipps, Anna May—Farwell, 1911
Phipps, David—Civil War
  Vet, Gilmore, 1865
Phipps, Francis—farmer, Gilmore
Pickard, Charles—lumberman, 1904
Pickard, Lilly—Clare, 1906
Pickel, Chas L.—druggist
Pickering, George—Clare, 1900
Pickering, Wm.—farmer, Arthur
Pickett, Gladys—teacher, Farwell
Pierle, D. D.—Farwell, 1900
Pierre, Grovenor—businessman
Pierce, H. W.—merchant,
  contractor, Clare, 1900
Pierce, Lodaska—1909
Pierce, S. E.—Harrison, 1905
Pierce, W. H.—livery, Clare, 1903
Pierson, Sanford—oil station, Clare
Pietsch, Otto—Lincoln, 1918
Pifer, Albert—general laborer, Clare
Pifer, Clyde—Frost, 1917
Pifer, Iva—teacher, Summerfield
Pike, Ed—Greenwood, 1909
Pike, Seer—Aero Sqdn, AEF, 1918
Pinnock, Joseph—Clare
Piper, George—Clare, 1911
Pires, Fred—grocery, Farwell, 1904
Pitcher, Henry—Temple
Pitsch, Otto—Lincoln, 1906
Pitts, Albert—farmer, Gilmore
Pitts, Albert L.—Gilmore, 1908
Pitts, G. A.—Gilmore, 1918
Pitts, George E.—farm, butcher
Pitts, James, Jr.—farmer, WWI
Pitts, Milard—farmer, Farwell
Pitts, Walter—Gilmore, 1917

Pitts, Wm.—Gilmore, 1908
Pixley, Byron B.—farmer, Hayes
Pixley, Earl—Hayes, 1900
Pixley, Eddie—Hayes
Pixley, George—Hayes, 1900
Pixley, John—Hayes, 1906
Pixley, Judson—Greenwood, 1909
Pixley, Lonnie—Hayes
Pixley, Orville—Hayes
Pizer, Samuel—dry goods, Farwell
Platt, Callie—Tonkin, 1908
Platt, Calvin—house painter, Clare
Platten, John—farmer, Vernon
Plitz, Segmong—Farwell, 1914
Plude, John—Clare, 1912
Poe, ____—WWI, Harrison, 1917
Poet, E.—farmer, Sheridan, 1906
Poet, Frank—farmer, Sheridan, 1906
Poet, Glen—Brand, 1914
Poling, N.—Clare, 1905
Pollard, August—farmer, Gilmore
Pollard, Daniel—Gilmore, 1900
Pollard, Gus—Isabella
Pollard, James—farmer, Vernon
Pollard, John—Isabella
Pollard, Mary—Clare
Polson, Harold—Clare, 1914
Pomeroy, Anson—Hamilton, 1914
Pomeroy, E. H.—Hamilton, 1906
Pomeroy, G. H.—farmer, Hamilton
Pomeroy, George H.—farmer
Pomeroy, H. W.—farmer, Hamilton
Pomeroy, Hazel—teacher, Clare
Pomeroy, M. C.—farmer, Hamilton
Pontius, Harry—Temple, 1909
Pontius, Vern—P.M.R.R. agent
Pontius, Wm.—Temple, 1909
Pope, George—farmer, Wise, 1910
Pople, Porter—Harrison, 1904
Popple, Wm.—Harrison, 1900
Porcher, Elizabeth—Clare, 1898
Porges, Sam—Farwell, Iron &
  Metal Co., 1918
Post, Edith P.—Temple, 1908
Post, Floyd—Clare, 1906
Post, John—millman, Clare, 1900
Postema, John—Winterfield, 1906
Postema, Jacob—Grandon, 1903
Potter, A. E.—Grandon, 1917
Potter, Bessie—Clare, 1911
Potter, E. L.—farmer, Clare, 1904
Potter, Dr. K. B.—veterinarian
Potter, Rev. N. D.—Baptist
Potter, N. V.—Clare, 1902
Potter, Phoebe—Clare, 1907
Potter, Raymond—farmer, WWI,
  aero sqdn, Wise, 1917
Potter, Wm. B.—supt. of schools,
  Harrison, 1900
Poulson, Kenneth—farmer, Clare
Poulson, O. L.—supt. of
  schools, Clare, 1912
Poulson, Harold—WWI, 1917
Pound, Ernest E.—Clare, 1938
Pound, Lizzie—Clare, 1911
Powell, Alice—teacher, Clare, 19198
Powell, Almond—farmer, Farwell
Powell, Elizah—pioneer, Harrison
Powell, John—Farwell, 1917
Powell, Lucy—Farwell, 1914
Powell, Rufus—creamery, Farwell
Powers, Alvy—grocery, Clare, 1907

Powers, Ed—Farwell, 1907
Powers, Fred—Vernon. 1917
Powers, Geneva—Clare, 1940
Powers, Josephine—Clare
Powers, Roy—WWI
Powlison, Clifford—mail carrier,
  farmer, Garfield, 1914
Powlison, Cornelius—RFD carrier,
  farmer, Garfield, 1909
Powlison, E.—Crooked Lake, 1906
Powlison, Nealy—farmer
Pratt, Arthur—lumberman, Clare
Pratt, Charles—Lincoln, 1912
Pratt, Edward—lumberman, Dover
Pratt, M. Ethyl—teacher, Clare
Pratt, Melissa—Grant, 1902
Prentis, Will—Freeman, 1915
Prentiss, Henry—Clare
Presley, Bell—nursing home, Clare
Presley, E. W.—1900
Presley, George—Loomis, 1900
Presley, Joel I.—farmer, Sheridan
Presley, John—farmer, Sheridan
Presley, John, Jr.—farmer, Sheridan
Presley, Joseph—nursing home,
  farmer, Clare, 1870
Presley, Joseph—Herrick, 1900
Presley, Lewis—Clare, 1911
Presley, Mary—Clare
Presley, Minnie—teacher, Clare
Presley, Oran—Grant, 1918
Presley, Orin—farmer, Herrick
Presley, Thomas—farmer, Grant
Presley, Walter—Sheridan, 1917
Price, Brian—Hamilton, 1917
Price, Clifford—WWI, Hamilton
Price, Dan—Hamilton, 1906
Price, Earl—WWI, Hamilton, 1918
Price, E. J.—Hamilton, 1906
Price, Elroy—Hamilton, 1917
Price, Fird—WWI, Hamilton, 1918
Price, Gerald—barber, Clare, 1914
Price, Jesse—Clare, 1903
Price, Roy—Hamilton, 1906
Price, Wm. S.—Hamilton, 1906
Prielipp, Fred—Greenwood, 1917
Priest, Levi—farmer, Sheridan
Priest, Noah—Farwell, 1903
Prine, George—farmer, Greenwood
Pringle, Frank—Surrey, 1900
Pringle, Lorenzo—Gilmore, 1917
Pringle, U. S.—saloon, Surrey
Pringle, Wm. S.—farmer, Gilmore
Pritchard, Rev. ____—pastor
Printchard, Daphne—teacher
Probasco, Frank—Temple, 1903
Protzer, John—Hamilton, 1917
Prosser, Mary—Sheridan, 1908
Prosser, Thomas—Sheridan, 1908
Proudfoot, C. M.—Clare, 1915
Prover, Felix—Clare, 1936
Prover, Julian—farmer, Clare, 1935
Pruden, Frank—Temple, 1916
Pruden, Fred—Temple
Pruden, Theo.—Temple
Pudvay, A.—sheep farmer, Sheridan
Pudvay, Floren—farmer, Sheridan
Pudvay, Joseph—Sheridan, 1900
Pudvay, Liseam—farmer, Sheridan
Pudvay, Liseam, Jr.—Sheridan
Puffer, Wm.—Farwell, 1914
Pullen, Dr.—physician, Mt. P.

Purcell, Paul—barber, Clare, 1917
Purdy, A.—Clare, 1912
Purdue, Wm.—Clare, 1900
Purdy, Al—Clare, 1903
Purdy, Frank—burglar, Clare
Purdy, Wm. F.—farmer, Arthur
Purnstrum, B.—farmer, Vernon
Pursell, James—Clare, 1917
Putnam, Bert—Gilmore, 1906
Pyers, Fred—Dray business, Farwell
Pyers, S. L.—farmer, Farwell, 1906
Quackenbush, Alverdo—Civil
    War Vet, Vernon, 1910
Quehl, Rev. E. F.—Lutheran
Quick, James—farmer, Hatton
Quinlan, Thomas—Summerfield
Quinn, Dores—Harrison, 1906
Quinn, John—attorney, Harrison
Quinn, Stanley—attorney, Harrison
Quinn, Wm.—Harrison
Quist, Anthony—Winterfield, 1912
Race, Francis—Franklin, 1900
Radabough, ____—Winterfield
Radford, ____—Temple, 1900
Radway, Warren—Clare, 1901
Rady, Bryan—farmer, Vernon
Raleigh, Albert—Clare, 1903
Ramage, Cyrilla—teacher, Clare
Ramer, C.—Redding, 1906
Ramey, Clarence—Vernon, 1900
Ramey, Clarence, Jr.—Vernon
Ramey, Eli—restaurant, Clare
Ramey, Ernest—farmer, Vernon
Ramey, Ernest—meat market, Clare
Ramey, Flossie—Vernon, 1916
Ramey, George—Vernon, 1912
Ramey, George, Jr.—Clare
Ramey, John—Sheridan, 1910
Ramey, Joseph—farmer, Vernon
Ramey, Katie—Vernon, 1900
Ramey, Maria—housewife
Ramey, Mildred—Clare
Ramey, Phoebe—1914
Ramey, Samuel—Vernon, 1916
Ramey, Stanley—Vernon, 1900
Ramey, Thomas—Vernon, 1900
Ramey, Thomas, Jr.—mechanic
Ramsey, George—mgr. Leota
    Telephone Co., 1915
Ramsey, John—farmer, Sheridan
Ramsey, James—Farwell, 1914
Ramsey, Maud—Sheridan, 1900
Ramsey, Wm.—farmer, WWI
Ranck, D. J.—farmer, Wise, 1916
Ranck, George—barber—Clare
Ranck, Harry J.—Wise, 1917
Randall, Ada—Sheridan, 1903
Randall, Arthur—Arthur, 1909
Randall, Clifford—WWI, Sheridan
Randall, Dale—Clare
Randall, Hazen—1918
Randall, Herbert Wm.—Clare
Randall, J.—farmer, Sheridan
Randall, James—1904
Randall, John T.—WWI, Sheridan
Randall, Porter—Civil War
    Vet, Clare, 1905
Randall, S. LeGraw—pastor,
    Gilmore Church, 1916
Randall, Thomas—Clare, 1904
Randall, William—Sheridan, 1909
Randle, Floyd—oil field, Clare

Randolph, Ezra—Gilmore, 1917
Rankin, Albert—Harrison
Ransom, Henry—farmer, Gilmore
Rapson, R. A.—laundry, Clare
Rassat, Alice—Loomis, 1900
Rassatt, Dolores—Clare, 1918
Rasset, F. F.—Loomis, 1910
Rassat, James—Loomis, 1900
Rassat, Ruth—Clare
Rauch, Joseph—Hamilton, 1917
Raught, E. B.—pioneer, Leota
Raudpath, Dell—1907
Rawley, Niel—Winterfield, 1912
Rawson, Charles—farmer, Surrey
Rawson, Ed—WWI, 1918
Rawson, Frank—Gilmore, 1905
Rawson, James—farmer, Farwell
Rawson, John H.—Dray, oil
    ice, gasoline, Farwell, 1917
Rawson, Joseph A.—Gilmore, 1917
Rawson, Joseph H.—farmer
Rawson, Lewis—farmer, Gilmore
Ray, H. P.—Lake George, 1917
Ray, James L.—Lincoln, 1909
Raymer, Howard—Clare, 1916
Raymer, Marvel—farmer, Temple
Raymond, Alfred—Clare, 1910
Raymond, Charlotte—Clare
Raymond, Guy—Clare, 1911
Raymond, Helen—Clare
Raymond, John—farmer, Sheridan
Raymond, Rosanna—Clare
Rayner, Rev. E. A.—missionary
    to Philippine Islands, Farwell
Reading, Carlos—lawyer,
    teacher, Clare, 1903
Reaker, Claude—Hatton, 1903
Reakes, Edward—farmer, Vernon
Reamer, H.—Lake George, 1903
Reaves, J. A.—Hayes, 1906
Reams, Wm. Henry—Civil
    War Vet, Lake George, 1918
Reams, W. R.—Lake George, 1914
Reber, Charles—Justice of
    the Peace, Redding, 1914
Reber, Louis—Winterfield, 1912
Redford, Alice—Norway Lake, 1900
Redford, Gertude—teacher, Clare
Redmond, T.—farmer, Arthur
Redner, Uriah—city constable
Reed, Charles—Loomis, 1906
Reed, C. E.—Sheridan, 1906
Reed, Elston—Sheridan, 1862
Reed, Grace—hotel clerk, Clare
Reed, Irving—U.S. Army,
    WWI, Hamilton, 1895
Reed, John—WWI, Hamilton, 1918
Reed, John—Wise, 1909
Reed, Joseph—farmer, Civil
    War Vet, Farwell, 1927
Reed, Leslie—Harrison, 1900
Reed, Margaret—1916
Reed, Stephen—Civil War
    Vet, Grant, 1906
Reed, Wm.—farmer, Grant, 1918
Reeder, Dr. J. A.—physician, Clare
Reeder, Vernell—Clare
Reef, Lillian—Vernon City, 1918
Reemer, Gus—Hamilton, 1915
Reeves, E. C.—Lincoln, 1904
Reeves, Ella—Clare, 1911
Reeves, Ernest—chiropractor, Clare

Reeves, W. B.—Lincoln, 1906
Regan, Patrick—farmer, Vernon
Regan, Tim—farmer, Vernon, 1911
Reger, Adam—WWI, Sheridan
Reger, Carl—farmer, Sheridan
Reger, Charles—1909
Reger, Chris—1918
Reger, Rosa—1909
Reger, Roy—r.r. section hand
Reichelt, Elfreda—1903
Reid, Floyd—general produce
    business, Clare, 1900
Reid, George—Hamilton, 1912
Reid, Herbert—Clare, 1903
Reid, Wm. D.—farmer, Sheridan
Reid, Wm. H.—Colonville, 1905
Reid, Wm. H., Jr.—Sheridan, 1903
Reigle, Effie—teacher, Clare, 1906
Reigle, Elias—farmer, Civil
    War Vet, Grant, 1938
Reigle, Gerald—Harrison, 1917
Reigle, Gertude—Grant, 1907
Reinhart, Werner—Sheridan, 1906
Reis, John J.—Garfield, 1917
Reiss, Hershel—farmer, Farwell
Reithmeier, Rev. H. J.—Lutheran
    minister, Sheridan, 1907
Reitz, Thomas—Frost, 1917
Reker, Claud—moonshiner, Arthur
Remer, Emma—Grant, 1907
Remer, Fred—farmer, Grant, 1900
Remer, Helen—Grant, 1908
Remer, John—Grant, 1900
Remer, Martin—Clare, 1900
Remer, Rudy—Eagle, 1908
Renner, J. F.—Grant, 1906
Renner, John—farmer, Brinton
Renner, Robert G.—Gilmore, 1917
Renner, Ross—farmer, Farwell
Renner, Sam—Farwell, 1909
Renner, Valmo J.—Gilmore, 1917
Retan, A. S.—Garfield, 1906
Retan, Aden S.—Lake Side
    Dairy, Crooked Lake, 1908
Rexroth, Charles—farmer, Vernon
Rexroth, Elliott—feed barn, Clare
Reynolds, Charles—farmer
Reynolds, Dale—Farwell
Reynolds, Grover—Grant, 1917
Reynolds, Henry—lumberman
Reynolds, James—Civil War
    Vet, Winterfield, 1917
Reynolds, John—Farwell, 1914
Reynolds, L. A.—Grant, 1912
Reynolds, Leila—Clare
Reynolds, Orin—Surrey
Reynolds, Scott—farmer, Grant
Reynolds, Stella—Grant, 1919
Reynolds, W.—farmer, Arthur
Rhoades, Andrew E.—businessman
Rhoades, A. S.—grocery store,
    stave mill, Clare, 1903
Rhoades, Maude—Clare, 1903
Rhoades, Raymond—Clare, 1903
Rhoades, Mrs. S. A.—Clare, 1911
Rhoades, Walter—WWI, Harrison
Rhoades, Wm.—Tonkin, 1900
Rhodes, Adah—Arthur, 1903
Rhodes, George—1918
Rhodes, J.—farmer, Arthur, 1906
Rhodes, James—Arthur, 1911
Rhodes, Johanna—Leota, 1912

Rhodes, Leota—Harrison, 1919
Rhodes, Reuben—WWI, 1918
Rhodes, Roy—Harrison, 1903
Rhodes, Walter—Summerfield
Rhodes, Wm.—Arthur, 1917
Rhodes, Wm. P.—acted as agent
  for John F. Brand of Saginaw
Rhyder, Emiline—Harrison
Rile, Leo E.—printer, Clare, 1903
Richard, S.—Hamilton, 1906
Richards, Arthur—Garfield, 1917
Richards, Earl—Temple, 1914
Richards, Ed—Pennock, 1906
Richards, L. G.—Civil War
  Vet, Farwell, 1909
Richards, Rev. L.—Cong., Farwell
Richards, Lewis—Garfield, 1917
Richards, Rebecca—Clare, 1903
Richards, William J.—Vernon
Richardson, Arla—Temple, 1914
Richardson, Bonnie—teacher
Richardson, C. J.—Hayes, 1912
Richardson, Charles—Harrison
Richardson, E. H.—Hamilton, 1914
Richardson, Edward—Clare, 1908
Richardson, Ernest—Hamilton
Richardson, George—Clare, 1910
Richardson, Grace—teacher, Hatton
Richardson, Lewis—Arthur, 1919
Richardson, Lilah—teacher, Temple
Richardson, Wm. H.—merchant,
  farmer, Harrison, 1903
Riches, Stanley—1910
Richison, Audie—Lake George
Richmond, Alfred—farmer, Farwell
Richmond, ____—pioneer, Farwell
Richmond, Alfred—livery, Farwell
Richmond, Arthur E.—WWI, 1918
Richmond, Arthur E.—1918
Richmond, Cyrus—WWI, Farwell
Richmond, Fleda—teacher, Farwell
Richmond, Ira—farmer, Arthur
Richmond, Isabell—teacher
Richmond, James—Farwell, 1900
Richmond, John H.—merchant,
  pioneer, county treasurer,
  Harrison, 1905
Richmond, Minerva—teacher
Richmond, Olive—Hamilton, 1909
Richmond, ____—Harrison, 1905
Richmond, Norman—Harrison
Richmond, Wm.—A.A.R.R.
  section foreman, Farwell, 1917
Richter, Bernard—Harrison, 1910
Richter, Henry J.—Grant, 1908
Richter, Wm.—Garfield
Rick, Forrest—Clare, 1917
Rickles, R. W.—blacksmith,
  farmer, Garfield, 1900
Rider, Henry—Harrison, 1907
Rider, Len—Harrison, 1909
Ried, Bill
Riegel, Elias—Dover, 1900
Riemer, A. C.—Hamilton, 1915
Riggles, Gerald—Harrison
Riggs, Andrew J.—Harrison
Riggs, D. J.—Hayes, 1906
Riggs, John P.—farmer, Harrison
Riggs, Walter—supt., Clare, 1902
Riker, George—Wise, 1909
Rilett, Arthur, 1913
Rilett, Elizabeth—teacher, Clare

Rilett, Frank—1913
Rilett, George—1913
Rilett, George R.—Beaverton
Rilett, Henry—1913
Rilett, J. W.—farmer, Coleman
Rilett, Wm.—farmer
Riley, Hugh—Farwell, 1914
Rinkey, J.—Freeman, 1914
Ripenbarg, Estella—Clare
Ripenberg, George W.—seed man
Ripenberg, Gordon—bicycle
  mechanic, Clare
Ripenberg, Phillip—Clare, 1904
Ripple, Lynn M.—A.A.R.R., Clare
Ritchie, George—Farwell, 1909
Ritchie, John—mail carrier, Farwell
Ritchie, Wm.—pioneer, Farwell
Ritter, Clark A.—teacher, Clare
Ritter, Claude—Greenwood, 1910
Ritchie, Clyde—teacher, Eagle
Ritter, Edna—Clare
Ritter, Florence—Temple, 1900
Ritter, Gerald—Grant, 1917
Ritter, Grace—Temple, 1909
Ritter, H.—Grant, 1906
Ritter, Illa—teacher, Redding, 1910
Ritter, Kenneth—dry cleaners
Ritter, Martin—A.A.R.R., Temple
Ritter, Murl—AEF, Harrison
Ritter, Ora—Grant, 1903
Ritter, Orin—Greenwood, 1916
Ritter, Thomas—Greenwood, 1906
Roach, D. N.—farmer, Clare
Roache, Robert—Farwell, 1903
Roash, Joseph E.—mgr. gas station
Robart, Bessie—Clare, 1910
Robart, David—Sheridan, 1917
Robart, Ella—Clare, 1910
Robbins, Charles—Gilmore, 1909
Robbins, Coral—Clare
Robbins, Elizabeth—post mistress
Robbins, Stephen—1903
Robbins, Wm.—farmer, Greenwood
Roberts, Alex—Grant, 1906
Roberts, Asa—Clare, 1914
Roberts, C. R.—Vernon, 1912
Roberts, Dale—farmer
Roberts, S. A.—Grant, 1906
Roberts, S. H.—farmer, Grant
Robertson, John—sheep ranch
Robinette, Clarence—Sheridan
Robinett, Coe—1912
Robinett, Della—Clare, 1907
Robinette, Emmette—laborer, WWI
Robinett, Eula—Clare
Robinette, James—Clare, 1911
Robinett, Joseph—1912
Robinett, Laurence—Arthur, 1907
Robinett, Matilda—Arthur, 1906
Robinett, May—1908
Robinett, Menzo—farmer, Arthur
Robinett, Milo—farmer, Arthur
Robinett, Misco—farmer, Arthur
Robinett, Rex—farmer, Clare
Robinett, Theron—WWI, 1918
Robinett, Thurman—Arthur, 1917
Robins, Rev. ____—Freeman, 1915
Robinson, Capt. ____—Temple
Robinson, Arlington—Greenwood
Robinson, Durwood—farmer
Robinson, Edith—teacher, Clare
Robinson, Ernest—Vernon, 1917

Robinson, Faith—teacher, Clare
Robinson, Frederick—lab
  mechanic, oil field—Clare
Robinson, George—Vernon, 1916
Robinson, George—Grant, 1912
Robinson, James—Winterfield, 1904
Robinson, Joseph H.—farmer
Robinson, Millard—mill owner,
  Garfield, 1903
Robinson, Oscar—farmer, Sheridan
Robinson, Perl—Clare, 1904
Robinson, R.—farmer, Farwell
Robinson, Roy—Vernon, 1917
Robinson, Rev. Sullivan—Clare
Robinson, Dr. Thomas—eye
  specialist, Wise, Loomis 1870
Robinson, William—Clare
Robinson, Willard—Farwell, Lake
Robinson, Wm.—Sheridan, 1900
Robison, Earl—Sheridan, 1917
Robison, Faith—teacher, Clare
Robison, O. D.—Sheridan, 1901
Robison, Sherm—Clare, 1909
Rockafellow, Arthur—accountant
Rockafellow, John—businessman,
  Clare, 1900
Rockwell, Claude—racket store
  owner, Clare, 1903
Rockwell, Charles H.—Clare, 1900
Rockwell, Walton B.—Hamilton
Rodabaugh, Bertha—Clare
Rodabaugh, Daniel—Sheridan
Rodabaugh, John—laborer, Clare
Rodapaugh, John—bootlegger,
  tailor, dry cleaning, 1913
Rodabaugh, Maud—Clare, 1903
Rodebaugh, J.—Hatton, 1906
Rodebaugh, Peter—Sheridan, 1907
Rodgers, A. N.—Farwell, 1919
Rodgers, Delbert J.—Temple
Rodgers, James R.—Farwell, 1918
Rodgers, Milford—Temple, 1905
Rodgers, Maude—Clare
Rodgers, Muriel—teacher, Clare
Rodrick, Irene—Farwell, 1909
Rodwell, Alfred—farmer, Sheridan
Roe, Alfred—garage, Colonville
Roe, Alice—Sheridan, 1909
Roe, Arthur E.—1908
Roe, Bernice—Clare, 1912
Roe, Blanche—Clare, 1919
Roe, Charles A.—Harrison, 1915
Roe, Charles H.—AEF, Harrison
Roe, Duncan—auto sales, Sheridan
Roe, Edgar—Grant, 1903
Roe, George—Arthur
Roe, Dr. J. B.—dentist, Clare, 1908
Roe, John—farmer, Wise, 1907
Roe, Junius—Colonville store, 1915
Roe, Lois—Greenwood, 1911
Roe, Louise—trained nurse, Clare
Roe, Mildred I.—Harrison, 1910
Roe, Minnie—Clare, 1915
Roe, P.—Summerfield, 1906
Roe, William—Sheridan, d. 1901
Roe, William—Sheridan, 1910
Rogers, A. L.—Clare
Rogers, Adda—teacher,
  Lake George, 1903
Rogers, Anthony—keeper of poor
  farm, Harrison, 1912
Rogers, Atherton—barber, Clare

Rogers, Barney—Farwell, 1919
Rogers, Charles—Harrison, 1913
Rogers, B.—Farwell
Rogers, Bessie—Grandon, 1903
Rogers, C. F.—farmer, twp.
   treasurer, Grandon, 1903
Rogers, Dalton—WWI, Aero
   squadron, 1918
Rogers, Emma—Clare
Rogers, Glen—bus driver, Clare
Rogers, Gordon—Clare
Rogers, Herman—Clare Hdwe
   employee, Clare, 1900
Rogers, Homer M.—Gilmore, 1917
Rogers, Ira—Farwell, 1916
Rogers, Jay—drayman, Clare, 1907
Rogers, Joy—Harrison, 1913
Rogers, Louisa—teacher, Clare
Rogers, Milward—AEF, Farwell
Rogers, Nelson S.—Vernon, 1916
Rogers, Romano S.—Clare, 1910
Rohr, Henry—prop. Calkins
   House, Clare, 1918
Roland, C. E.—farmer, Greenwood
Roland, Rev. Henry—E.U.B.,
Rolland, Fay—carpenter, Harrison
Roller, John M.—farmer, Arthur
Roller, Russell—Arthur, 1915
Rondot, Dr.—medical doctor
Rood, F. C.—farmer, Garfield
Roode, J. Q.—school supt., Clare
Roof, Wm.—Clare, 1910
Root, Alvin—G.A.R. Vet, farmer
Root, Bert—farmer, Grant, 1903
Root, Bienna—Franklin, 1912
Root, Calista—Franklin, 1912
Root, Chancy—depot agent, Hatton
Root, E. H.—Garfield, 1906
Root, Frank—Surrey, 1917
Root, Ira—Hatton, 1917
Root, Raymond—farmer, Garfield
Root, Roy—farmer, Maple Grove
Root, Samuel—R.R., Lake, 1911
Root, Solista—Hatton, 1909
Rose, L. J.—Hamilton, 1906
Rose, G. A.—Clare, 1903
Rose, John Wm.—Hamilton, 1917
Rose, June W.—Harrison
Rose, Procter—Harrison, 1909

Rose, Reuben—Hamilton, 1917
Rose, W. A.—Colonville, 1908
Rose, William J.—WWI 1918
Rosenburg, Sam—dry goods, Clare
Rosendall, Joseph—Clare
Rosevear, Alma Elroy—electrician
Ross, Angus—Grant, 1903
Ross, Charles—farmer, Grant. 1904
Ross, D.—sawmill, Franklin, 1906
Ross, Donald—lumberman,
   Beaverton, 1907
Ross, Durwood—Clare, 1917
Ross, Frank I.—printer, Grant
Ross, Giles A.—Clare, 1901
Ross, Herman—farmer, section
   forman, Harrison branch, Hatton
Ross, Junius—clerk, 1900
Ross, Laura—hay and feed store

Ross, Maude—Clare, 1903
Ross, Walter—Grant, 1903
Ross, William—merchant, hay,

feed store, road contractor
Ross, W.—sawmill, Franklin, 1906
Roth, Charles L.—Hayes
Roth, Daniel—Temple, 1917
Roth, David—Harrison, 1917
Roth, Gleason—AEF, 1918
Roth, Opal—Temple, 1917
Roth, Robert—Harrison, 1907
Rought, E. B.—mill, Summerfield
Rought, Steve—Leota, 1908
Rounds, J. D.—postmaster, Farwell
Rounds, Walter—Franklin, 1917
Roundtree, Frank—Hamilton, 1900
Rouse, John S.—Redding, 1913
Rouse, Julius W.—harness maker
Rouse, Willis—Redding, 1914
Rousch, James A.—Grandon, 1918
Roux, Oscar—farmer, Freeman
Rowe, Asa B.—Clare, 1916
Rowe, A. J.—farmer, Surrey, 1906
Rowe, Dan—farmer, ice harvester
Rowe, Eva—teacher, Grant, 1918
Rowe, James—Clare, 1900
Rowe, Ira V.—Clare, 1910
Rowe, Leone—teacher, Farwell
Rowland, Carrie—teacher, Clare
Rowland, Martin—teacher, Wise
Roxburgh, James G.—Clare, 1903
Royal, Edward—farmer, Arthur
Royce, Mrs. Philomela—Clare
Roys, A. H.—ice cream parlor
Roys, H. M.—Farwell, 1900
Roys, Nina—Farwell, 1900
Roys, Spencer—insurance agent
Ruble, Kenneth—W.P.A. worker
Ruby, Harley—farmer, Brush
   College, 1914
Ruby, J. V.—Brush College, 1915
Ruby, Ray—Brush College, 1915
Ruby, Wm.—Brush College, 1915
Rudapaugh, James—Farwell, 1904
Rudapaugh, Mark—Hamilton, 1909
Ruegsegger, Loyd F.—Gilmore
Ruh, John—carpenter, Clare, 1910
Rulapaugh, Alfred—farmer, Surrey
Rulapaugh, Dale—WWI, Arthur
Rulapaugh, DeLos—Eagle, 1918
Rulapaugh, John—farmer, Eagle
Rulapaugh, Leon—WWI, Sheridan
Rulapaugh, Nellie—Clare, 1910
Rulapaugh, Oscar—Sheridan, 1900
Rulapaugh, Peter—farmer
Rulapaugh, T.—Grant, 1906
Rule, R. V.—store, teacher,
   photographer, Clare, 1912
Rule, Roy—1916
Rumley, Olive—Harrison
Rummer, Edwin—Greenwood, 1913
Rummer, James—Redding, 1906
Runge, Frederick—Clare
Runyan, Courtes S.—farmer
Runyan, Duard—Eagle, 1905
Runyan, Edwin—farmer, Sheridan
Runyan, Fannie—Grant, 1911
Runyan, George—WWI, Farwell
Runyan, John—farmer, Grant, 1906
Runyan, J. W.—Grant, 1906
Runyan, Mayme—Eagle, 1901
Runyan, Myra—Eagle, 1905
Runyan, Wm.—farmer, Eagle, 1901
Rush, Wm.—Maple Grove, 1909
Russ, C.—farmer, Grant, 1917

Russ, Elsie—teacher, nurse, Farwell
Russ, Fred—WWI, 1918
Russ, John—farmer, Grant, 1906
Russ, Myron—lumber camp cook
Russeau, Alexander—farmer, 1903
Russell, Ben—Clare, 1903
Russell, Bernice—Temple, 1909
Russell, Bruce—Leota, 1917
Russell, Charles—farmer, Colonville
Russell, E. L.—Vernon, 1918
Russell, Earnest—Grant, 1918
Russell, Edward—Clare, 1915
Russell, Edward E.—Clare, 1915
Russell, Edwin—farmer, Clare
Russell, Emily—housewife, 1924
Russell, Henry—farmer, Wise, 1903
Russell, I. H.—r.r. depot, Temple
Russell, J. H.—store, Temple, 1907
Russell, Joe—Leota, 1917
Russell, Joseph A.—Temple, 1903
Russell, Leo—mgr. Farmers
   Produce Co., Wise
Russell, Nellie—Clare, 1918
Russell, Mrs. Rachel—farmer
Russell, Ralph—Franklin, 1917
Russell, Wm.—Grant, 1906
Russell, W. A.—racket store, Clare
Russell, Wm. H.—farmer, Clare
Rust, Welthena—Hatton
Ruth, Belle—beauty shop, Clare
Ruthven, Alex—r.r., Hatton, 1905
Ruthven, E.—Arthur, 1906
Rutledge, Edith—teacher, Harrison
Rutter, Alfred—farmer, Sheridan
Rutter, Alfred—foundry laborer
Rutter, Bert—farmer, Sheridan
Rutter, Chas—farmer, Clare, 1907
Rutter, Edward—Sheridan, 1890
Rutter, Henry—WWI, 1918
Rutter, Louis—WWI
Rutter, W. C.—Surrey, 1903
Ryan, Ada—registered nurse, Clare
Ryan, Floyd—Harrison, 1914
Ryan, Ruth—teacher, Clare, 1910
Ryan, Wm.—grocery—Clare, 1909
Ryder, A. C.—Harrison, 1914
Ryder, Harold—Harrison, 1916
Ryerson, Ivan—teacher, Coldwater
Sabin, John—Redding, 1908
Sabin, Oliver—Clarence, 1918
Sable, Louis—businessman, Clare
Sabothie, Joseph—farmer, Arthur
Saffell, John—farmer, Farwell, 1916
Sage, Ella Mae—Clare
Sage, George—Clare
Sage, Ronald—carpenter, 1880
Salisbury, Florence—teacher
Salisbury, John—baker, Clare
Salisbury, Stella—teacher, Leota
Samborn, Wilson—plumber, Clare
Sample, Hugh—Winterfield, 1909
Sampson, George—Crooked Lake
Sanborn, Charles—Maple Grove
Sanborn, Charles H.—farmer
Sanborn, Clark—Surrey, 1917
Sanborn, Everett—Wise, 1917
Sanborn, Henry—storekeeper, Lake
Sanborn, Lalla—1914
Sanborn, Velva—Farwell, 1906
Sanburn, Clark—Clare
Sanburn, Fred—WWI
Sanden, Orville—Sheridan, 1907

Sanders, Birtie—Sheridan, 1907
Sanders, Cecil—1910
Sanders, Charles—WWI, Sheridan
Sanders, Charles—Sheridan, 1917
Sanders, Delbert—Arthur, 1917
Sanders, Earl—farmer, Arthur
Sanders, Evart—Arthur, 1915
Sanders, Frank—farmer, Arthur
Sanders, Hazel—Sheridan, 1912
Sanders, Henry—Sheridan, 1903
Sanders, Joseph—Harrison, 1912
Sanders, Leo—salesman, Clare
Sanders, Lewis—Arthur, 1911
Sanders, Nelson—farmer, Sheridan
Sanders, Orval—Sheridan, 1911
Sanderson, George—WWI, AEF
Sanderson, Otis—AEF, Farwell
Sanderson, Roa—teacher, Farwell
Sanford, Dr. Burton--physician,
   AEF, Clare, 1900
Sanford, Charles—WWI
Sanford, Clarence—Clare, 1916
Sanford, E.—Grant, 1906
Sanford, Dr. F. C.—physician
Sanford, George—farmer, 1900
Sanford, George—pioneer, Lincoln
Sanford, James—Garfield, 1915
Sanford, William M.—Freeman
Sanford, Wilson—Lincoln, 1905
Saperstone, E.—Farwell, 1900
Sarringer, Dr. Albert M.—
   pioneer, dentist, Farwell, 1878
Sarver, A. R.—Clare
Satison, A.—farmer, Arthur, 1906
Satison, Alma—Clare
Satison, Hiram—real estate sales
Satison, Homer—farmer, Hatton
Satison, Nannie—Harrison
Saull, Dewey—Farwell, 1915
Saul, E.—Arthur, 1906
Saul, Frank—Dover, 1904
Saul, Garfield—Dover, 1903
Saul, James—pioneer, Civil War,
   P.O.W., Dover, 1874
Saul, Jay—Clare, 1906
Saul, Mertie—Grant, 1903
Saul, Samuel—Grant
Saull, C.—Grant, 1906
Saunders, L. H.—farmer, Sheridan
Saunders, Earl—Arthur, 1915
Saunders, Joseph—farmer, Hayes
Saunders, Mary—teacher
Saviers, Col. L.—banker, Harrison
Sawtell, Dr. Benjamin—physician
Saxton, Ethel—Farwell, 1909
Saxton, George—r.r. interlocker
Saxton, John J.—postmaster
Saxton, Milton—1903
Saxton, Percy—banker, AEF
Sayer, _____—Temple, 1911
Schaaf, Bernice—teacher, Harrison
Schaaf, Carl—Greenwood, 1914
Schaaf, Clair—Clare, 1907
Schaaf, Don—Greenwood, 1917
Schaaf, F. D.—farmer, 1918
Schaaf, Franklin—chemist, Clare
Schaaf, Fred—farmer, Harrison
Schaaf, T. D.—Hayes, 1918
Schaaf, Warren—laborer, 1903
Schaar, Charles—Grant, 1917
Schaar, Hershel—mechanic, Lake
Schaeffer, Alice—Clare

Schaefer, Cora—Clare, 1913
Schaeffer, Harold—bank clerk,
   post office, Clare
Schaeffer, Julius—farmer, Clare
Schaeffer, Lowell—Clare
Schaeffer, Rudolph—teacher, WWI
Schaeffer, Viola—Clare
Schaeffer, Von Henry—WWI
Schaff, Fred—1909
Schaff, Iva—Clare
Schaffer, Cora—teacher, Clare
Schaffer, Peter—AEF, 1918
Schaffer, W. H.—Hayes, 1906
Schellas, John—creamery, Clare
Schelter, Ernest—farmer, Sheridan
Scherlitz, Louis G.—twp. clerk
Schermerhorn, L. F.—Crooked Lk.
Schermerhorn, Lola—Crooked Lake
Schermerhorn, Loren—Crooked Lk.
Schermerhorn, Oscar—teacher
Schermerhorn, Paul—Crooked Lake
Schermerhorn, Samuel—farmer
Scherving, Charles—Freeman, 1915
Schieber, William V.—farmer
Schieber, Ruby—Arthur, 1915
Schieman, Fred—farmer, Arthur
Schilling, Henry—farmer, tannery
   in Clare, 1904
Schilling, John—farmer, WWI
Schillings, George—farmer, Farwell
Schlegel, Irwin—clerk, Clare Hdwe
Schlegel, John—Farwell, 1917
Schleman, Earnest—Hamilton, 1917
Schmemann, Gustav—farmer
Schmit, Mathias—Surrey, 1917
Schoar, Sadie—Farwell, 1907
Schofield, Elmer—Maple, 1915
Schofield, Francis—Grant, 1914
Schofield, Elmer—farmer, Farwell
Schofield, Ira—farmer, Gilmore
Schofield, Miles—farmer, Gilmore
Schoonmaker, Bern—Summit, 1914
Schoonmaker, George—Summit
Schoonmaker, Vern—Summit, 1914
Schoonover, Clinton—farmer, Clare
Schoonover, Clinton, Jr.—Clare
Schoonover, Devere—C.P.A., Clare
Schoonover, Frank—1904
Schoonover, Franklin—supt. oil
   field, Harrison, 1905
Schoonover, Glen—Clare, 1914
Schoonover, Guy—Clare, 1903
Schoonover, Ida—Clare, 1903
Schoonover, Orson—Harrison, 1906
Schneider, Alfred—Clare
Schrader, John S.—farmer, Clare
Schram, Peter—bootlegger, Temple
Schroeder, Amanda—1909
Schroeder, Anna—farm, Clare
Schroeder, Herbert—Grant, 1917
Schroeder, John H.—farmer, Grant
Schroeder, Walter—carpenter, Clare
Schuett, Eugene—owned a steam
   traction engine, 1914
Schuett, Fred—Harrison, 1938
Schug, Albert—Vernon, 1917
Schup, Fred—farmer, WWI, Clare
Schugg, Albert—farmer, Clare
Schugg, Julius—farmer, Vernon
Schultz, Albert—WWI, Clare
Schultz, August—farmer, Sheridan
Schultz, Ernest—Clare, 1891

Schultz, Gottlieb—Harrison, 1925
Schultz, John—WWI, Clare, 1907
Schultz, John—sailor, Clare, 1918
Schulz, Leo—farmer, Harrison
Schumaker, John—WWI
Schunk, Augusta—Sheridan
Schunk, George—farmer, twp.
   official, Sheridan, 1900
Schunk, Stanley—Sheridan, 1917
Schunk, Grace—Sheridan, 1900
Schunk, Joseph—Sheridan, 1904
Schunk, Stanley—Sheridan, 1900
Schunk, Tudor—pioneer, Sheridan
Schutt, Dr. Christina—osteopath
Schutt, Eugene—Clare
Schutt, Erwin—Vernon, 1915
Schutt, Lawrence
Schwanz, Edward—Hayes, 1927
Schwanz, Fred—WWI, Summerfield
Schwanz, Hance H.—Hayes, 1920
Schwanz, Harry H.—Hayes
Scisco, Effie—1919
Scofield, Arthur—farmer, Hayes
Scofield, James—farmer, Garfield
Scott, Bert—farmer, Garfield, 1906
Scott, Charles W.—Harrison, 1904
Scott, Clair—Lake, 1917
Scott, Clarence—Clare, 1922
Scott, Darius—supervisor, Garfield
Scott, Frank—Hayes
Scott, George—store, Lake, 1917
Scott, Jack—Lake, 1914
Scott, Jack, Jr.—Lake, 1917
Scott, Julie—Hayes, 1923
Scott, Meryl E.—AEF, Garfield
Scott, Robert—farmer, Garfield
Scott, Wm.—farmer, Crooked Lake
Scott, Wm., Jr.—laborer, 1897
Scowley, Andrew—Frost, 1914
Scrimger, A. J.—Frost, 1906
Scrimger, A. W.—Frost, 1900
Scrogle, B.—farmer, Grant, 1903
Seaman, Albert—WWI, Sheridan
Seaman, Grant—farmer, twp.
   supervisor, Greenwood, 1906
Seaman, Margaret—Elm Grove
Seaferson, S.—farmer, Sheridan
Seal, Henry—farmer, Vernon, 1918
Searle, A. J.—Surrey, 1903
Sears, Ethel—teacher, Harrison
Sears, George—farmer, Franklin
Sears, Harold—Franklin, 1914
Sears, Mrs. K.—farmer, Franklin
Sears, Lyman—Harrison, 1908
Searsaw, Charles—WWI, Hamilton
Searsaw, Geoerge—WWI, Hamilton
Searsaw, Wm.—WWI, Harrison
Seastrum, Rev. Frank—M-E
Seaver, Berley—WWI, 1918
Sebert, Albert—WWI, Winterfield
Seeley, Alfred J.—1903
Seeley, Arlie—chiropractor, Clare
Seeley, A. L.—Civil War
   Vet, Farwell, 1911
Seeley, Floyd—farmer, Vernon
Seeley, F.—Garfield, 1906
Seeley, J. H.—farmer, Vernon
Seeley, Milo—Farwell
Seeley, Orletta—teacher, Clare
Seeley, Ruth—Clare, 1908
Seferson, Sefas—Sheridan, 1918
Seilinger, Elizabeth—1909

Steelinger, Jacob—Hayes, 1918
Sellinger, Frank—Hayes
Sellinger, Margaret—Harrison
Seelock, Peter—Frost, 1903
Seidel, John
Seil, George—farmer, 1903
Seil, Howard—Lake
Seiter, David—Vernon
Seiter, Wm.—Clare
Seitz, P. B.—Hayes, 1906
Sempowski, Henri—pharmacist
Sersaw, Lorenzo—1914
Sersaw, Robert—1914
Sersaw, "Will"—1914
Servis, Alvah—farmer, Wise, 1903
Servis, George—Clare
Severson, Alex—farmer, Clare
Severson, Arlington—WWI
Severson, George—Sheridan, 1901
Severson, Henry—Sheridan, 1901
Severson, Severt—farmer, Sheridan
Sexsmith, Ed—Farwell, 1904
Sexsmith, Emma—Clare, 1884
Sexsmith, Herb—Clare, 1903
Sexsmith, Jennie—clerk, Clare
Sexsmith, John H.—lumber
  inspector, Clare, 1902
Sexsmith, M.—Clare, 1900
Sexsmith, ____—Clare, 1882
Sexton, Fred—Clare, 1918
Seymore, Chas—Temple, 1903
Seymour, David—Hatton, 1912
Seymour, Edith—teacher, Farwell
Seymour, Elam—WWI, Gilmore
Seymour, William—WWI, Hatton
Shafer, Cora—teacher, Clare, 1900
Shafer. Levi—Clare, 1903
Shafer, Sadie—teacher, Greenwood
Shafer, Wm.—Harrison, 1914
Shaff, Ruth—Clare
Shaffer, Arlan—Hayes, 1917
Shaffer, Clarence—Freeman, 1909
Shaffer, Clayton—teacher, Harrison
Shaffer, Edith—teacher, Harrison
Shaffer, J. W.—farmer, Greenwood
Shaffer, Mary—Freeman, 1909
Shaffer, Orlando—WWI, 1918
Shaffer, Von Henry—teacher
Shaffer, Rev. Wm.—Harrison, 1915
Shaffer, Wm. H.—farmer, barber
Shamel, Clark I.—Hamilton, 1914
Shamel, George—Harrison, 1914
Shamel, Otis—Hamilton, 1917
Shamel, Roy—Hamilton, 1917
Shaner, Isaac—Gilmore, 1917
Shank, George—Farwell, 1910
Shannon, Mrs. ____—Clare, 1904
Sharland, Arthur—Hatton, 1906
Sharland, Florence—Clare
Sharp, Anna—Sheridan, 1900
Sharp, Clarice—Sheridan, 1903
Sharp, George—livery, Farwell
Sharp, Hazel—Sheridan, 1903
Sharp, J. E.—Arthur, 1906
Sharp, John-Franklin, 1918
Sharp, Ralph S.—AEF, Vernon
Sharp, Reginald—farmer, twp.
  supervisor, Franklin, 1906
Sharp, Walter—Franklin
Sharp, Wesley—Sheridan, 1900
Sharp, Wilson—Clare
Sharpe, Reg—farmer, Harrison

Shaver, Albert A.—painter, Clare
Shaver, Albert, Jr.—Arthur, 1917
Shaver, Burley—1918
Shaver, Hugh—farmer, Eagle, 1917
Shaver, "Will"—Sheridan, 1918
Shaver, William—farmer, Arthur
Shaver, Willard—Brinton, 1906
Shaw, ____—Parkview Hotel
  owner, Farwell, 1911
Shaw, Andy—A.A.R.R., Lake Geo.
Shaw, Dr. B. Corning—physician,
  surgeon, Clare, 1903
Shaw, Dr. C. F.—physician, Clare
Shaw, Charles—Surrey, 1917
Shaw, Clarence—AEF, aero sqdn
Shaw, Edward—Clare, 1909
Shaw, Irene—Clare, 1903
Shaw, John P.—1903
Shaw, John W.—sold patent
  medicine door to door, Clare
Shaw, Orrin—gasoline attendant
Shaw, Wm. K.—Temple, 1917
Shea, John—farmer, lumberman,
  Hamilton, 1882
Shea, Joseph—Hamilton, 1917
Shea, Lizzie—Hamilton, 1903
Shea, Michael—pioneer, Hamilton
Shea, Mortimer F.—Hamilton, 1915
Shea, Mortimer, Jr.—farmer
Shea, Nellie—teacher, Hamilton
Shea, Patrick—farmer, Hamilton
Sheahan, Albert—Vernon, 1917
Shear, Harmon—1918
Shear, Lesley Roy—Farwell, 1910
Shear, Roy—Farwell
Sheardy, M.—farmer, Garfield
Sheckell, A. C.—Farwell, 1906
Sheffield, Arthur—WWI, Frost
Sheffield, George—WWI, 1917
Sheiley, Margaret—Clare
Shekell, Alonzo—constable, Surrey
Shelber, Wm.—farmer, Arthur
Sheldon, Allan—Grant, 1906
Sheldon, Anson H.—Freeman, 1914
Sheldon, Bessie—teacher, Frost
Sheldon, Charles—Surrey, 1917
Sheldon, Harry—Hayes, 1906
Sheldon, J. B.—Hayes, 1906
Sheldon, J. H.—Hayes, 1906
Shelly, Edna—Clare
Shelley, Margaret—Clare, 1909
Shelter, George—farmer, Sheridan
Sheneman, George—WWI
Shepard, Fred—farmer, Farwell
Shepard, Marion—Greenwood
Shepard, Susan—teacher, Farwell
Shepherd, Fred—Farwell, 1907
Shepherd, Susan—teacher, Farwell
Shepherd, W. H.—sheep ranch
Sheppard, Foster—Wise, 1917
Sherman, Rev. ____—Grandon
Sherman, Anna—teacher
Sherman, C. M.—Garfield, 1916
Sherman, C. S.—Grant, 1906
Sherman, Earl—WWI, Surrey, 1918
Sherman, Elton—mechanic, Clare
Sherman, Frank—Garfield, 1906
Sherman, Georgia—teacher, Clare
Sherman, James—WWI, Freeman
Sherman, Martin N.—pioneer
Sherman, Mary—Farwell, 1908
Sherman, Milton—WWI, 1918

Sherman, Orval—garage, WWI
Sherman, Sidney—farmer, Vernon
Sherman, Thomas—Vernon, 1914
Sherman, William—farmer, WWI
Sherrick, Frank—farmer, Clare
Sherwood, David—farmer
Sherwood, Earl—Harrison, 1907
Shilling, George—Gilmore, 1917
Shilling, Harvey—Gilmore, 1917
Shilling, John—Gilmore, 1917
Shillinger, Gaius—WWI, Arthur
Shimmell, Alta—teacher, Clare
Shimmons, ____—Temple, 1918
Shimmons, ____—WWI
Shimmons, ____—WWI
Shimmons, Leonard—WWI
Shinabarger, Roy Phillip—Freeman
Shinabarger, S. E.—Freeman, 1914
Shinabarger, Stanley—Freeman
Shipp, Wm.—r.r. worker
Shippey, Charles—lumberman
Shippey, Earl—WWI, Lake, 1917
Shippey, "Track"—farmer
Shipway, Rev. W. A.—Cong.
  pastor, Clare, 1910
Shoecraft, Miss ____—teacher
Shoesmith, John—Temple, 1907
Shook, J.—Farwell
Shorey, James H.—Farwell, 1900
Short, ____—Short & Gardner
  Store, Harrison
Short, Wilma—Hatton
Shorts, A.—Hamilton, 1914
Shorts, Wm. H.—WWI, Hamilton
Shoup, Elmo—Clare
Shufelt, Blair—Franklin, 1915
Shug, Harry—Clare
Shull, Alice—teacher, Long Lake
Shull, Clarence—farmer, Arthur
Shull, Elsie—Clare
Shull, Lowell—Clare
Shull, Marguerite—teacher, Arthur
Shull, Ralph—farmer, Clare, 1911
Shull, Robert—farmer, Clare
Shull, Rollin—Clare
Shull, Ruth—Clare
Shumway, Durias—1936
Shumway, Forest—barber, Farwell
Shumway, Lillian—Farwell
Shumway, L. M.—Hatton, 1906
Shumway, Maud—Farwell, 1903
Shumway, Milo—Farwell, 1909
Shumway, Roy—WWI, Harrison
Shumway, S. F.—Farwell, 1904
Shurfelt, Wesley—Greenwood, 1917
Sias, Elias—farmer, Surrey, 1906
Sible, Burt—Clare, 1913
Sickles, Charles—Temple, 1918
Sickles, Webster—Farwell, 1919
Siebert, Benjamin—merchant, 1917
Siel, ____—Garfield, 1919
Siel, David—baker, Clare
Siel, Henry—Civil War Vet,
  Vernon, 1905
Siel, Thomas—Vernon, 1917
Siel, Wm. L.—laborer, Clare
Siemantel, John—farmer, Sheridan
Sifton, Emma—teacher, Rosebush
Sifton, Mabel—teacher, Clare, 1912
Sifton, Myrtle—millinery, teacher
Silloway, L. D.—hotel, livery,
  saloon, Crooked Lake, 1906

Snyder, Walter—teacher, Clare
Solar, Lewis—farmer, WWI, Arthur
Solridge, Charles—Temple, 1915
Somers, Mr. O. M.—Grant, 1915
Sotham, Thomas F., Jr.—cattleman
Southwick, D. A.—auctioneer
Sova, Louie—Harrison, 1907
Sowle, Harley—mail carrier, WWI
Sowle, Mark P.—farmer, Sheridan
Sowle, Scott—Brinton, 1917
Sowle, Vivian—Clare
Sowle, William—Lake
Spangler, Lewis—farmer
Sparbel, John K.—surveyor, Clare
Sparks, Albert—Grant, 1915
Sparks, Burton—Lincoln, 1915
Sparks, Emelined—Lincoln, 1906
Sparks, Frank—Lincoln, 1917
Sparkers, Bert—Grant, 1918
Spaulding, Charles E.—Lincoln
Speck, Fred—Hamilton, 1913
Speer, Rev. Gordon—Cong.
    minister, WWI, Clare, 1918
Speer, J. H.—farmer, Redding
Spence, Harry—Lake, 1886
Spence, James—labor agitator
Spence, Orrie—mechanic, Clare
Spence, Thomas—Clare, 1903
Spencer, Goerge—Summerfield
Spencer, George A.—Clare, 1914
Spencer, Hazel—Temple, 1907
Spencer, Hiram—Herrick, 1904
Spencer, Irvin—Winterfield, 1908
Spencer, Isaac—WWI, Gilmore
Spencer, Louis—Hayes, 1906
Spencer, Martha—teacher, Harrison
Spencer, Verne—hotel chef, Clare
Spicer, Carl—WWI, 1918
Spicer, Elymas E.—Arthur, 1910
Spicer, Floyd—carpenter, farmer
Spicer, Ira—Arthur, 1910
Spicer, Ivan—WWI, 1918
Spickerman, Curt—farmer, Denver
Spigelmire, Amos—farmer, Dover
Spiglemire, Mary—Eagle, 1901
Spiglemire, Nina—Dover, 1904
Spink, Douglas—Frost, 1918
Spink, Edith—Temple, 1903
Spink, Franklin—farmer, Alward
Spink, Owen—farmer, 1904
Spink, O. B.—Temple, 1903
Spitalsky, Alois—Redding, 1912
Spohn, Charles—chairman of
    Twp. War Prep. Comm., Hayes
Spohn, Rachel—Hayes, 1906
Spohn, Ray—Harrison, 1909
Spohn, B. L.—1903
Spohn, Charles—Harrison, 1906
Spohn, Ernest—1903
Spohn, Rachel—Hayes, 1918
Sprague, Adella—Greenwood, 1915
Sprague, Arthur—Greenwood, 1906
Sprague, Chester—Lincoln, 1901
Sprague, D. C.—Harrison, 1910
Sprague, Earl—farmer, Greenwood
Sprague, Ernest—Clare
Sprague, Ila—teacher, Greenwood
Sprague, Meta—Greenwood, 1909
Sprague, Ralph—farmer
Sprague, W.—farmer, Greenwood
Sprague, Wm.—laborer, Clare
Spring, Boyd—Surrey, 1906

Spring, George—Clare, 1915
Spring, Ralph—merchant, Farwell
Springer, Leona—Clare
Sprunger, _____—horse breeder
Spurrier, Wm.—Garfield, 1906
Spurter, Wm.—Garfield, 1906
Squires, Amos—Grant, 1904
Squires, E.—Surrey, 1906
Squires, Emma—Clare, 1889
Squires, Fred—Grant, 1918
Squires, H. O.—restaurant,
    Dray Service, Clare, 1903
Squires, Joseph—Grant, 1917
Squires, Ray—Grant, 1917
Squires, Roy—1910
Squires, V.—Grant, 1906
Squires, Walter—Grant, 1917
Staffield, Charles C.—Hamilton
Stahl, Charles—teacher, Harrison
Stahl, Frank C.—Freeman, 1914
Stahl, George—Hayes, 1902
Stanchfield, Chas—Hamilton, 1904
Stanley, Clair—Surrey, 1916
Stanley, Eugene—farmer, Grant
Stanley, F. H.—farmer, Garfield
Stanley, Fern—teacher, Clare, 1913
Stanley, Fred—ashery, Clare, 1903
Stanley, James A.—Farwell, 1918
Stanley, James W.—Sheridan, 1917
Stanley, Jennie—1903
Stanley, Leon—Clare
Stanley, Leonard—Clare
Stanley, Otis—Clare
Stanley, Rose—Clare, 1911
Stanton, Hazel M.—teacher, Clare
Stanton, LeRoy—hotel man, WWI
Stanton, Wm.—1904
Starkey, Addie—Harrison, 1904
Starkey, James W.—Greenwood
Starkey, Thomas W.—farmer
Starkey, Stella—teacher, Greenwood
Starkey, Thomas—Greenwood
Starns, Orrin E.—Redding, 1913
Stauffer, D. M.—Farwell, 1908
Stauffer, George—Farwell, 1908
Stayler, August—Vernon, 1917
Stead, Judd—Farwell, 1917
Stearns, Edw.—bldg. mover, Clare
Steed, Judd—Farwell, 1916
Steele, Rev. Newland—minister
Steele, Ralph—Arthur, 1917
Stehle, George—farmer, Sheridan
Stein, Ellen—Vernon, 1903
Stein, George—Vernon, 1903
Stephens, Andrew L.—Clare, 1915
Stephens, Earl—Clare, 1910
Stephenson, Wm. J.—mechanic
Sternaman, E. H.—photographer
Sternaman, Earl—photographer
Sterns, P. D.—Grant, 1906
Stetson, F. R.—Clare, 1900
Steurmer, Herman—Greenwood
Steurmer, Rudolph—Harrison, 1914
Stevens, Arthur T.—asst cashier
Stevens, Bernice—Clare, 1919
Stevens, Bert—1914
Stevens, Bruce—farmer, Garfield
Stevens, E. A.—heading mill,
    Civil War Vet, Clare, 1906
Stevens, E. J.—pool room, Farwell
Stevens, Elton—heading mill
Stevens, Ernest—farmer, Clare

Stevens, Ethel—Clare, 1901
Stevens, Etta—Temple. 1903
Stevens, Eva—Lake, 1910
Stevens, Henry—Civil
    War Vet, Clare, 1908
Stevens, Henry C., Jr.—Clare, 1909
Stevens, Jerome—r.r., treasurer,
    Garfield twp., Crooked Lk.
Stevens, Joseph J.—Wise, 1917
Stevens, Lewis C.—foreman
Stevens, Lizzie—Crooked Lake
Stevens, Mayme—Clare
Stevens, Melvin—Clare
Stevens, Milton—Farwell, 1917
Stevens, Ralph—barber in Farwell,
    owned restaurant in Clare,
    WWI, U.S. Navy, Clare
Stevens, Verne—Clare
Stevens, Walter—Clare, 1918
Stevens, Dr. William—physician
Stevenson, D. S.—attorney
Stevenson, Earnest—Clare, 1911
Stephenson, Faye—teacher
Stevenson, Thomas A.—law violator
Stevens, Elton—Farwell, 1916
Stewart, James—Vernon. 1910
Stewart, Harry—glass blower, Clare
Stickland, Ida—Farwell, 1908
Stid, Owen—Winterfield, 1917
Stillwell, Charles—farmer, WWI
Stinchcombe, Arthur—teacher,
    WWI, U.S. Navy, Farwell, 1917
Stinchcombe, Charles—Lake George
Stinchcombe, Frank—teacher
Stinchcombe, Miss _____—teacher
Stinchcombe, Homer—Farwell
Stinchcombe, James H.—grocery,
    meatmarket, Farwell, 1905
Stinchcombe, James—Farwell, 1918
Stinchcombe, Lester—teacher, 1918
Stinchfield, Charles—Hamilton
Stine, George W.—farmer, 1908
Stirling, Dr. Charles—veterinarian
Stirling, Mildred—Clare
Stirling, Naomi—Clare, 1907
Stirling, Dr. Neil—veterinarian
Stockwell, C.—Hayes, 1906
Stockton, George—farmer
Stockton, Wm. D.—Lincoln, 1912
Stockwell, Orley—farmer, Harrison
Stoddard, George—1903
Stoddard, Henry—Clare, 1885
Stoll, Carl—farmer, Grant, 1906
Stoll, F. W.—Grant, 1906
Stoll, Rose—Dover, 1900
Stoll, Sophie—waitress, Clare, 1900
Stone, C. J.—laundry, Clare, 1905
Stone, Charles—dairy, Sheridan
Stone, Charles Selden—Grant, 1917
Stone, Fred—engineer grad,
    WWI, AEF, Clare
Stone, Lulu—teacher, Clare
Stone, Olive—Clare, 1914
Stone, Selden—Grant, 1916
Storey, Clyde—farmer, Vernon
Storms, A.—Nester Dam, 1908
Storms, Frederick—farmer, Arthur
Storms, James—Clare, 1910
Stottlemeyer, Robert—Clare, 1885
Stough, Annie—Vernon, 1904
Stough, Dale—Clare
Stough, Ernest—Vernon, 1917

Stough, Florence—Clare, 1920
Stough, George—Vernon, 1915
Stough, George—Vernon, 1917
Stough, James—1911
Stough, John—Vernon
Stough, Percy Wm.—teacher, Clare
Stout, Harvey—farmer, Lake Geo.
Stowe, Miss ____—principal
Stoy, A. C.—farmer, Wise, 1911
Stoy, Clyde—farmer, Vernon, 1911
Stoy, Ellsworth—Vernon, 1917
Stoy, Eslie—Wise
Stoy, Freeman—farmer, Vernon
Stoy, Wm.—Clare, 1916
Strait, Arnold—Clare, 1922
Strait, Harry—teacher, Clare, 1914
Strange, Charles—petroleum, Clare
Stratton, Al—Crooked Lake, 1904
Stratton, E. A.—lumbermill
Stratton, Fred—Harrison, 1919
Stratton, Hilda—Greenwood, 1904
Stratton, Odell—WWI, 1918
Strauch, Charles—WWI, Wise
Strauch, D. E.—farmer, Wise, 1917
Strauch, Ray D.—oil fields, Clare
Straugh, Raymond D.—Wise, 1917
Strauss, Louis—WWI, Hatton, 1918
Strauss, Ralph—WWI, Hatton
Stredley, John—farmer, Lake Geo.
Stringham, Ada—teacher, 1911
Stroup, Mrs. C. L.—Clare, 1914
Stroupe, H. A.—A.A.R.R., Clare
Stroupe, Helen—Clare
Strouse, Charles E.—farmer, Clare
Strouse, Clair—WWI, 1918
Strouse, Glenn—Sheridan, 1909
Strouse, J. W.—Sheridan, 1906
Strouse, Ray—farmer, Clare
Strubble, Edna—teacher, 1909
Struble, Nila—Clare
Stuber, Frank W.—Wise, 1917
Stuhle, Ralph—WWI, 1918
Stump, Frank—Redding, 1904
Stump, Homer—post office
Stuart, John—Surrey
Sturgis, J.—Frost, 1906
Sturgis, Mary—Frost, 1906
Sugar, Henry—WWI, Grant, 1918
Sullivan, Agnes—teacher, Hamilton
Sullivan, Anna—teacher, Hamilton
Sullivan, Frances—teacher
Sullivan, Jerry—farmer, Hamilton
Sullivan, Joseph—farmer, Hamilton
Sullivan, Thomas—WWI, Vernon
Sullivan, Wm.—farmer, Hamilton
Summerville, Kirk—Lake, 1917
Sunday, Carrie—Grant, 1900
Sunday, Daniel—farmer, Grant
Sunday, "Icy"—Grant, 1900
Sunday, Harold—farmer, Clare
Sunday, Lewis—stock buyer,
  farmer, sheriff, Arthur, 1900
Sunday, Walter—Harrison, 1908
Sunday, Wm.—Brown, 1915
Surfeit, Blair—Franklin, 1917
Sursaw, George—Clare, 1903
Sutherland, C. E.—tailor, Clare
Sutherland, Clark H.—Clare, 1900
Sutherland, Kirk—banker, Clare
Sutherland, O. M.—engineer, Clare
Sutherland, Rev. Samuel—M-E
  minister, blacksmith, Civil

War Vet, Clare, 1916
Sutherland, Ted—merchant, Clare
Sutton, Belle—teacher, Clare, 1912
Sutton, Dan—Clare, 1911
Sutton, Emmett F.—Grant, 1917
Sutton, Ernest—Clare, 1909
Sutton, Florence—Clare, 1900
Sutton, Frank—Grant, 1898
Sutton, George—Grant, 1907
Sutton, Henry—Grant, 1880
Sutton, Hiram—pioneer, 5 Lakes
Sutton, Hugh—Grant, 1906
Sutton, James—teacher, farmer,
  WWI, Clare, 1917
Sutton, Jay F.—barber, Clare, 1909
Sutton, John H.—Winterfield, 1906
Sutton, J. W.—farmer, Windover
Sutton, Mabel—Grant, 1905
Sutton, Manuel—contractor, Clare
Sutton, Thomas, Jr.—farmer, Grant
Sutton, Thomas A.—Grant, 1900
Swales, ____—Lake, 1915
Swan, Avis—teacher, Wheatley
Swanson, Frank—Lake George
Swanton, Floyd—drug store
Swanton, Miss ____—durggist
Swarts, John L.—Harrison, 1917
Swartz, Andre—Redding, 1910
Swartz, Herb—WWI, 1918
Swartz, John—Harrison
Swartz, Thurman—Temple, 1917
Sweeney, Dr. ____—physician
Sweet, Charles—heading mill
  operator, Harrison, 1921
Sweetman, James—saloon, Clare
Sweetman, John—Clare, 1915
Sweeney, Dr. ____—physician
Swigart, R. G.—teacher, Clare
Swindlehurst, Philemon—Grandon
Swinehart, Edward—Lake, 1915
Swinehart, Mabel—teacher, Arthur
Swinson, James—laborer, Clare
Swisher, D. S.—Summerfield, 1916
Swisher, Perry—WWI, Freeman
Switzer, Berten E.—Temple
Switzer, Edgerton—fruit farmer,
  butter factory, creamery, Clare
Switzer, G. H.—Hamilton, 1918
Switzer, Dr. John—physician
Swoveland, J. A.—Clare, 1916
Syckle, W.—Surrey, 1906
Symons, Henry—Harrison, 1929
Taggart, Adele—Five Lakes, 1909
Taggart, Florence—Grant, 1909
Taggart, James—Grant, d. 1905
Taggart, Marie—teacher, 1912
Taggart, Mary—teacher, Grant
Taggart, Sadie—teacher, 1912
Taggart, Ogle—Grant, d. 1906
Tait, Hugh—farmer, Surrey
Tasker, Will J.—P.M.R.R., Clare
Tatman, Alina—teacher, Clare
Tatman, Alma—Clare, 1900
Tatman, Christine—teacher, Clare
Tatman, Rev. Elijah—minister,
  Eagle, 1900
Tatman, Elva—Clare, 1903
Tatman, I. F.—Clare, 1908
Tatman, James A.—Clare, 1900
Tatman, James A.—clerk, Clare
Tatman, James F.—grocery, Clare
Tatman, John, Jr.—Clare, 1904

Tatman, Marie—teacher, Clare
Tatman, Marv—Clare, 1900
Tatman, Mary—Clare, 1903
Tatman, Pearl—Clare, 1903
Tatman, Roy Alonzo—AEF, Clare
Taylor, A. E.—farmer, Grant, 1914
Taylor, Cara W.—teacher, 1909
Taylor, David—1909
Taylor, Dillon—farmer, d. 1929
Taylor, Edith—teacher, Harrison
Taylor, Harry G.—Vernon, 1917
Taylor, Joseph—r.r. contractor,
  built A.A.R.R. through Clare
Taylor, O. C.—night operator,
  Union depot, Clare, 1903
Taylor, Ray—Hamilton, 1917
Taube, Gustave—Lincoln, 1912
Teachout, Adell—farm, Farwell
Teachout, Frank E.—lumberman,
  farmer, Gilmore, d. 1914
Teachout, Hortense—Vernon Hill
Teachout, M.—Farwell, 1908
Teachout, Phillip—WWI, 1918
Teagarden, Reuben—Greenwood
Teale, Alfred—Eagle, 1908
Teale, Burt—Arthur, 1908
Teale, David—farmer, Sheridan
Teale, George—farmer, Sheridan
Teale, James W.—farmer, Clare
Teale, John W.—Sheridan, 1918
Teale, Ralph E.—Sheridan, 1909
Teale, Wesley—Sheridan, 1915
Teale, Wm. A.—farmer, Sheridan
Teall, Allen—painter, d. 1911
Teall, Asher M.—farmer, Sheridan
Teall, Henry—Brinton, d. 1917
Teaman, Herman—Grant, 1918
Tedeman, John—Surrey, 1906
Teed, Rev. J. L.—Church of
  God, Elm Grove, 1913
Teeter, Carl—laborer, Clare, 1901
Teeter, Earl G.—1907
Teeter, Ira—mechanic, Clare, 1926
Teeters, George—mechanic, Clare
Teeter, Wm.—farmer, Vernon
Temby, Howard E.—WWI, Clare
Tempe, J. E.—farmer, Farwell
Temple, Mary—Temple, 1909
Temple, Wm. Martin—farmer,
  postmaster, real estate dealer,
  Civil War Vet, Temple, 1869
Tenant, George A.—teacher, 1906
Tennant, Glen—WWI, 1918
Tenant, Leroy—Clare, 1910
Tenant, S. W.—Garfield, 1906
Tenant, Leroy—Clare, d. 1906
Tennant, George—teacher, Garfield
Tenniswood, Irva—Clare
Teppler, Allen—telephone
  operator, Farwell, 1910
Terry, ____—Farwell, 1919
Terry, Harry A.—farmer, ranch
Terry, Josephine—piano player
  for Princess Theatre, Clare, 1915
Terry, Maud—Clare, 1913
Terry, Owen I.—Sheridan, 1900
Terry, Thomas—farmer, 1903
Terwilliger, Bernice—teacher, Clare
Terwilliger, Calvin—bookkeeper,
  teacher, Clare, 1909
Terwilliger, Grant—harness
  maker, auto dealer, Clare, 1913

Terwilliger, Ivan—Standard Oil Station, Clare, 1900
Tessman, A.—Harrison, 1914
Tessman, Lewis—farmer, Harrison
Tessman, Otto—farmer, Harrison
Tew, Lorne S.—1918
Tew, Pearl—teacher, Harrison
Tew, Wm.—Hayes, 1903
Thayer, Arthur C.—Clare
Thayer, Chester—farmer, Vernon
Thayer, Clarence—farmer, Vernon
Thayer, Clarence, Jr.—farmer
Thayer, Clifford—farmer, Farwell
Thayer, Delmar—farmer, Gilmore
Thayer, Dorothy—Clare
Thayer, Earl—WWI, Farwell, 1917
Thayer, Edward—farmer
Thayer, Fraulien—Clare
Thayer, Gerald—Clare
Thayer, Goldie—Clare
Thayer, Julia—Vernon, d. 1916
Thayer, Lanson—creamery, Clare
Thayer, Louis—Wise, 1912
Thayer, Marguerite—Clare, 1922
Thayer, Melissa—widow, Vernon
Thayer, Orlando B.—feed barn
Thayer, Orlando B., Jr.—Clare
Thayer, Rennie—Clare, 1903
Thayer, Rollin
Therring, Wm.—farmer, Clare
Thomas, E. S.—Surrey, 1906
Thomas, Fred—Indian, 1908
Thomas, Lawrence—tool dresser
Thomas, Roy—tool dresser, Clare
Thompson, Archie—Wise, 1917
Thompson, Arnold—Clare
Thompson, C. A.—Clare, 1903
Thompson, Rev. E. A.—Cong. minister, Farwell, 1912
Thompson, Edna—Arthur, 1903
Thompson, Edward C.—Winterfield
Thompson, Eliga—Wise, 1917
Thompson, Elisha S.—farmer
Thompson, Ervin—Temple, 1915
Thompson, Faye—Clare, 1910
Thompson, Floyd—Clare, 1913
Thompson, Frank—Clare
Thompson, Fred—Clare, 1890
Thompson, Fred, Jr.—Clare, 1914
Thompson, George E.—teacher
Thompson, Grace—Clare, 1901
Thompson, Harold—farmer, Grant
Thompson, Ida—Sheridan, 1910
Thompson, Isaac J.—bartender
Thompson, J. F.—P.M.R.R. agent
Thompson, J. M.—farmer, Sheridan
Thompson, James—miller, Grant
Thompson, James—Vernon, 1908
Thompson, James—Temple
Thompson, James, Jr.—farmer
Thompson, James A.—Farwell
Thompson, James L.—Clare, 1912
Thompson, L. G.—Clare
Thompson, L. J.—Clare
Thompson, Laura—teacher, Harrison, 1903
Thompson, Leila—Dover, 1909
Thompson, Lewis H.—Clare Implement dealer, Sheridan
Thompson, Lindsey H.—farmer
Thompson, Louis H.—Clare
Thompson, Mathew—Temple

Thompson, Maud—Clare, 1903
Thompson, Morgan—farmer
Thompson, Nettie—Sheridan, 1906
Thompson, Ora—Clare, 1907
Thompson, Philip—Sheridan, 1900
Thompson, Ralph—clerk, Clare
Thompson, Robert—farmer
Thompson, Robert G.—farmer
Thompson, Robert—Clare, 1912
Thompson, Robert C.—ticket agent
Thompson, Ross D.—attorney
Thompson, Sarah—Redding, 1909
Thompson, Sidney—Harrison, 1906
Thompson, Truman—Clare, 1917
Thompson, Warren—Clare, 1912
Thompson,, Wesley—Wise, 1917
Thompson, William—Clare, 1912
Thompson, Wm. H.—farmer
Thompson, Wm. T.—Clare
Thorburn, Myrtle—teacher, Clare
Thorburn, Rose—teacher, Clare
Thorne, John—Loomis, 1909
Thorpe, A. H.—Clare, 1915
Thorpe, A. W.—grocery, Clare
Throop, Eugene—Clare
Thurston, Albert—undertaker
Thurston, Allen W.—Harrison
Thurston, Carolyn—teacher, 1909
Thurston, Charles A.—funeral director, Clare, 1903
Thurston, Russell—Clare
Tibbals, Elmer—dog trainer
Tibbets, A. B.—Harrison, 1903
Tibbetts, Chas A.—d. 1939
Tibbils, N. L.—jeweler, Clare
Tibbits, A. Wallace—Harrison
Tibbles, Jennie—night telephone operator, Clare, 1909
Tibido, E. S.—Cornwell Ranch, Arthur, 1913
Tice, Clarence—Vernon
Tice, Elrey—Clare
Tice, John C.—Clare, 1916
Tice, Morton—Vernon, 1911
Tichenor, W. E.—principal, Clare, 1929
Tiedeman, Alma—Surrey, 1915
Tiedeman, Denzil—WWI, Surrey
Tiedeman, George W.—Grant
Tiedeman, John—Maple Grove
Tiedeman, Nelson—farmer, Grant
Tiedt, Ernest F.—Clare, 1905
Tillotson, Fred—Clare, 1914
Tillotson, George D.—Temple, 1904
Tilletson, Myrtle—Clare, 1900
Timm, Fred—farmer, Grant, 1906
Timm, Gertude—Clare
Timm, Lena—Clare.
Timm, Ludwig—farmer, Grant
Timm, Wm.—Grant, 1904
Tingley, Henry—Grist miller, Clare
Timpee, Roy—1916
Tingley, Earl J.—1918
Tingley, H. B.—Clare, 1914
Tingley, John—Freeman, 1914
Tinker, Ash M.—d. 1900
Tinklepaugh, B. Waite—publisher, Kalkaska Leader, Temple
Tipton, A. R.—carpenter, Grandon
Titus, Wm. H.—Express messenger
Tobias, Max—Clare, 1908
Todd, Dr. J. F.—Clare, 1890

Todd, F. J.—Claare, 1900
Todd, James—Clare, 1908
Toland, Herb—Vernon, 1900
Toland, Ross—1904
Tolley, James—brick mason
Tolly, J. W.—teacher, Hamilton
Tolson, Norman—commercial artist
Toman, A. B.—Harrison, d. 1907
Toman, Amos W.—1893
Toman, George—Harrison, d. 1924
Toman, Pearl—teacher, Harrison
Toman, Mrs. V. E.—photographer
Tomasek, Peter—Clare
Tomaski, Albert—laborer, Farwell
Tomaski, Joseph—butcher, Clare
Tomiazwcki, Joseph—Vernon, 1917
Tomlinson, Will—Harrison, 1906
Tompkins, P.—Surrey, 1906
Tooley, Arthur T.—Greenwood
Tooley, Erie—Hayes, 1906
Tooley, John M.—Harrison
Topham, Joseph—farmer, Sheridan
Topps, Beulah—Clare
Topps, Charles—salesman, Farwell
Topps, Louise—Clare
Toten, Frank—Harrison, 1915
Touroo, James—cooper, Clare, 1914
Tover, F.—Grant, 1906
Tow, Merle—pumper, Temple
Tower, C. W.—bank clerk, Clare
Tower, Ellen—nurse, Spanish American War, Clare
Tower, Elmer—Sheridan, 1914
Tower, Leon—1903
Tower, Theodore—Sheridan, 1915
Tower, Thomas—Garfield, 1904
Tower, T. L.—farmer, Sheridan
Tower, William—Lake
Towers, Isaac—Brinton, 1914
Towler, H. L.—1917
Town, Frank—pioneer, Harrison
Towne, Earl W.—Farwell, 1913
Towns, ____—teacher, Hatton
Towns, Earl—Lincoln, 1915
Townsend, Earl—Hamilton, 1917
Townsend, Mrs. G.—1911
Townsend, Harold—Clare, 1908
Townsend, John—Hamilton, 1904
Tracey, Delilia—pioneer, Vernon
Tracey, Mary—Clare, 1909
Trafford, Miss E.—Clare, 1908
Trainer, Thomas—Harrison, 1903
Trauman, ____—Crooked Lake
Travis, Gertude—telephone office
Travis, Vincent J.—Vernon, 1917
Treanor, Leo J.—banker, teacher, WWI, aero squadron, Harrison
Trevidick, Henry—druggist, Clare
Trietch, Frederick—farmer
Trietch, Kenneth—truck driver
Trietch, Wm.—farmer, Hatton
Trofford, Emmogene—teacher
Troumble, Nate—Harrison, 1913
Trowbridge, Ira J.—WWI, Harrison
Trucks, Ford—fieldman, Clare
Truman, W.—Crooked lake, 1906
Trumble, Austin—grocer, printer, Hatton, Summerfield, 1903
Trumble, Henry O.—restaurant
Trumble, ____—Brand farm, 1909
Trumble, Nate—RFD carrier
Trumbolt, Cynthia—Clare, 1907

Tryon, Alfred—stock raising
Tryon, Alfred, Jr.—farmer,
supervisor, Garfield, 1897
Tryon, Archie—WWI, 1918
Tryon, Calvin—Garfield, 1930
Tryon, Calvin, Jr.—Garfield
Tryon, Henry—Garfield
Tryon, Henry, Jr.—cheese factory
Tryon, Leonard—Lake, 1900
Tryon, Lucy—Arthur, 1908
Tryon, Perl—twp. supervisor,
hwy comm., farmer, Garfield
Tryon, Volney—farmer, Arthur
Tryon, Wolley—Garfield, 1904
Tryon, Zella—Arthur, 1908
Tubbs, Floyd M.—farmer, Wise
Tubbs, James—WWI, Wise, 1909
Tucker, Melvin—businessman,
Civil War Vet, Loomis
Tupper, Vera—Clare
Turbock, George—farmer, Surrey
Turbush, Carl—Vernon, 1917
Turbush, Fred—telephone co.
repairman, Vernon, 1911
Turbush, George A.—farmer
Turbush, Jesse—Vernon, 1909
Turley, Dallas—Winterfield, 1917
Turner, Bertha—Sheridan, d. 1912
Turner, Burt—farmer, Arthur, 1901
Turner, Charles—Franklin, 1909
Turner, Claude—Hatton, 1903
Turner, Mrs. Claude—dress maker
Turner, Frank—Harrison, 1909
Turner, H. T.—Harrison, 1918
Turner, Hazel—teacher, Harrison
Turner, J. L.—D. & M. R.R.
mail clerk, Harrison, 1903
Turner, Kelley—farmer, Brand
Turner, L.—Harrison, 1903
Tuxbury, Georgia—teacher, Clare
Tyler, Tim—Clare, 1907
Tyndall, R. F.—Farwell
Tyron, Mrs. Mary—Clare
Ulch, Frank—RFD carrier, Lincoln
Ulis, Fretta—Summerfield, 1910
Ulrich, Arthur C.—Clare
Ulrich, August—Sheridan, 1917
Ulrich, Lila—Clare
Ulsh, Harry—farmer, Freeman
Updegraff, Blanche—Farwell, 1914
Updegraff, Carl—Farwell Village
president, WWI, Harrison
Updegraff, J. D.—Harrison, 1903
Updegraff, J. W.—sheriff, Harrison
Updegraff, Maude—telephone
operator, Harrison, 1903
Updike, L. B.—farmer, Windover
Upthegrove, Alfred—laborer, 1911
Upthegrove, Arthur—Clare, 1924
Upthegrove, Christy—Clare, 1900
Upthegrove, Richard—Clare
Upthegrove, Walter—Clare
Upthegrove, William—d. 1927
Urschel, E. D.—restaurant, Clare
Utley, Gladys—Farwell, 1915
Utley, Lee—Surrey, 1907
Utley, Maud—Farwell, 1915
Utley, Ray—WWI, Farwell, 1910
Utley, Roy—Surrey, 1917
Utley, Simon—Surrey, 1906
Utley, Wm.—Garfield, 1906
Valley, George—restaurant, Clare

Van Alstine, Charles—Vernon
Van Blarcum, Charles—farmer
Vanbonschoten, Fred—farmer,
twp. supervisor, Summerfield
Van Brunt—merchant, Civil
War Vet, Clare, 1876
Van Brunt, C. H.—grocer, baker
Van Buskirk, Fanchon—1918
Vanbuskirk, Gabriel—farmer
Van Buskirk, George—Greenwood
Van Buskirk, Jennie—Clare, 1900
Van Buskirk, John—Dray, Farwell
Vance, Beulah—Clare, 1914
Vance, Velma—Clare, 1916
Vance, W. E.—mgr. Farmers
Ind. Prod. Co., Clare, 1916
Van Conant, Ed C.—farmer
Van Conant, Harvey—Garfield
Van Conant, John—farmer, Dover
Van Conant, L.—Farwell, 1900
Van Conant, Milo—Garfield, 1915
Van Conant, Philip—farmer, Grant
Van Conant, Wm. A.—Clare, 1900
Van Debogart, George—
Maple Grove, 1909
Vanderhoof, W. A.—farmer
Vandelinder, Wm.—Wise
Vandeman, Herbert A.—Farwell
Van Deusen, J. M.—secretary,
Clare Co. Fair Board, 1918
Vandewarker, George—grocery
store, twp. supervisor, Sheridan
VandeWarker, Leona—Clare
Vandewarker, Neil—Clare
Vandewarker, Rev. Nicholas—
Colonville store, Sheridan, 1914
Vandewarker, Orville—mechanic
Van Deusen, James—Hayes, 1912
Van Dyne, Evelyn—Clare
Vanderwarker, Orval—store
Vandusen, J. M.—real estate
Van Fleet, Lelah—teacher, Clare
Van Horn, Charles—Franklin, 1916
Van Horn, George—farmer
Van Horn, Dr. W. H.—veterinarian
Van Leuven, Ruth—teacher, Clare
Vannater, Ben—farmer, Arthur
Vansicklen, Edgar C.—Vernon
Van Sicklen, Florence—telephone
operator, Clare, 1915
Van Sicklen, Mrs. F.—Clare, 1911
Vansicklen, Jack—Clare
Van Sicklen, Llewellyn—Clare
Van Sicklen, W.—fruit farm
Vansicklen, Wilmot—farmer
Van Swerington, T.—horse trader
Van Ulerah, F. E.—Temple, 1900
Van Valkenburg, D.—farmer
Van Valkenburg, David—WWI
Van Valkenburg, Ina—teacher
Van Valkenburg, Raymond—WWI
Van Vleet, Wm.—race horses
Van Vorst, A.—Harrison, 1917
Van Wagoner, Dan—bunco artist
Van Wormer, Bert—1903
Van Wormer, Frank—Vernon, 1914
Van Wormer, Lyman—P.M.R.R.
Varney, Albert—Franklin, 1905
Varney, Arthur—Wise, 1917
Varney, S.—Hatton, 1906
Varty, John—Clare, 1887
Veale, Edgar—farmer, Vernon

Veeder, Alethea—Clare
Veeder, Doris—Clare
Veeder, Eva—Clare
Veeder, W. A.—baker, Clare, 1915
Velie, Lou J.—pioneer, Grandon
Venner, Agnes—d. 1927
Venner, L.—farmer, Vernon, 1918
Verrette, Joseph—farmer, Vernon
Verrette, Pierce—Clare, 1922
Vetr, Henry—Temple, 1936
Vetr, Jerry—Temple
Vick, ____—arsonist, Summerfield
Virtue, Wm. H.—farmer, Grant
Visnaw, Lloyd—WWI, Grant, 1918
Vittler, Joseph—Hamilton, 1903
Vollans, Wm.—Arthur, d. 1888
Vollmer, Eugene—Hayes
Vollmer, George—Hayes, 1917
Vollmer, Robert L.—Hayes
Von Dusko, W. H.—Civil War
Vet, Clare, 1910
Von Leuven—teacher, Clare, 1915
Von Linsowe, Henry—Hamilton
Von Linsowe, Rev. John—Lutheran
pastor, Hamilton, 1917
Von Linsowe, John, Jr.—Hamilton
Vontross, Martha—Temple, 1909
Vosburg, Harry—printer, Clare
Vosburgh, John A.—farmer
Vosburgh, Keith—Greenwood, 1911
Vosburgh, Louis—WWI,
Greenwood, 1911
Voss, George Herman—Greenwood
Voss, Herman—Greenwood, 1916
Vreeland, Bert—AEF, Surrey, 1918
Vreeland, Iva—teacher, Surrey
Vreeland, S.—Farwell, 1906
Vreeland, Wm.—P.M.R.R.
engineer, Hatton
Vrooman, J.—Sheridan, 1903
Vrooman, Nellie—Sheridan, 1903
Vrooman, Samuel—farmer
Waddell, Guy A.—Surrey, 1918
Waddington, Gilbert—farmer
Waddington, Henry—farmer
Waddington, John—Gilmore, 1909
Waddington, Milessa—Clare
Waddington, Gilbert—d. 1910
Waddington, H.—farm implements
Waddington, Rosella—Clare
Wager, Lillie—Clare, 1901
Wager, J.—farmer, 1903
Wager, Norman—minister, Clare
Wager, Willie—1906
Waggoner, Charles—Clare, 1913
Wagner, E.—Surrey, 1906
Wagner, P.—Surrey, 1906
Wagner, Ruth—Harrison, 1903
Wagner, W. H.—hoop dealer
Wagoner, Stella—Harrison, 1906
Wagoner, Henry—Hamilton, 1904
Wahl, Frank—laborer, worked
on Panama Canal, Herrick, 1909
Wahl, Fred—Clare, 1923
Wahl, James—Wise, 1917
Wahl, Wm. Grant—AEF, 1918
Waidlich, Rev. Care—Lutheran
minister, Clare, 1907
Waidelich, Gertude—Clare, 1918
Wait, A. P.—Farwell, 1906
Wait, C. B.—teacher, Farwell, 1903
Wait, D. R.—Justice of the

Peace, Farwell, 1903
Wait, Earl—telephone lineman
Wait, Fred S.—lumberman, Temple
Wait, Holly—Farwell, 1900
Wait, Lawrence—Clare
Wait, Leo—Farwell, 1907
Wait, Lyle E.—WWI, Grant, 1918
Wait, R. A.—salesman for
  Haish Wire & Implement Co.
Wait, Stanley—attorney, Farwell
Wait, Wm. D.—Farwell Livery,
  WWI, Surrey, 1917
Wait, Wm. J.—carpenter, Clare
Waite, Bert J.—Grant Twp.
  Clerk, Clare, 1916
Waite, D. W.—Freeman, 1915
Walcott, M. J.—Freeman, 1906
Waldron, Edd—Temple
Waldron, Francis E.—Temple
Walker, Albert—farmer, Greenwood
Walker, Bessie—teacher, Harrison
Walker, Bruce—farmer, Gilmore
Walker, D. J.—farmer, Greenwood
Walker, E. F.—merchant, Harrison
Walker, H. C.—Gilmore, 1912
Walker, Henry Oral—Vernon, 1917
Walker, Jacob—Clare
Walker, John—Greenwood, 1914
Walker, John D.—Freeman, 1906
Walker, John J.—Clare, 1911
Walker, Louisa—Clare, 1917
Walker, Olin—farmer, Gilmore
Walker, Paul D.—Farwell, 1912
Walker, Rev. Quinton—M-E
  minister, Clare, 1908
Walker, Quinton, Jr.—teacher
Walker, Thomas—Clare, Leota
Walker, Ulysses—drowned, Leota
Wall, Florence—teacher, Clare
Wallace, Earnest—farmer, Arthur
Wallace, Everett—farmer, Franklin
Wallace, Glenn—Arthur, 1917
Wallace, Henry—farmer, Arthur
Wallace, J. E.—Grant, 1906
Wallace, Wm.—Franklin, 1917
Wallace, Wm. D.—farmer
Wallen, J.—Hamilton, 1906
Waller, Don—Clare, 1917
Waller, E. A.—Clare, 1904
Waller, Ed H.—shoe store, Clare
Waller, Ward—produce house,
  WWI, Clare
Waller, Will H.—dentist, Clare
Walling, Darwin U.—Harrison
Walling, D. W.—farmer, Harrison
Walling, J.—Clare, 1903
Walling, Ray—teacher, Harrison
Walsh, Frank—steam shovel sales
Walsh, Harper—Vernon, 1900
Walsh, James—pioneer, farmer
Walsh, James, Jr.—Vernon, 1900
Walsh, James C.—Vernon, 1917
Walsh, John—farmer, Vernon, 1900
Walter, Chester D.—Grant, 1906
Walter, Erwin C.—mechanic, Clare
Walter, Gottlob—Grant, 1918
Walter, Herman K.—farmer, Clare
Walter, Henry R.—Clare, 1917
Walter, William H.—physician
Walters, Albert—farmer, Arthur
Walters, Andrew—supervisor, 1938

Walters, Beulah—Clare, 1910
Walters, Charles—farmer, Clare
Walters, Ezra—Arthur, 1914
Walters, Frank—farmer, Clare
Walters, Fred—Clare
Walters, George—farmer, Arthur
Walters, Guy—Loomis, 1914
Walters, John—Arthur, 1906
Walters, Kenneth W.—Clare
Walters, Lee—farmer, Arthur, 1906
Walters, Oma—Arthur, 1913
Walters, Roy—Arthur, 1912
Walters, "Von"—Eagle, 1915
Walters, Wm.—farmer, Arthur
Walton, Herbert—Clare, 1913
Walton, James P.—farmer, Wise
Walton, Lemon E.—Vernon, 1917
Walton, Nicholas—Isabella, d. 1915
Walton, Thomas A.—Wise, 1912
Walton, Thomas W.—blacksmith,
  farmer, hotel, Loomis, d. 1913
Walton, Vesta—Clare
Waltz, Fred—Clare, 1910
Walven, W.—farmer, Sheridan
Ward, Absalom—Clare, 1900
Ward, A.—Harrison, 1916
Ward, Clare—Clare
Ward, Clara—d. 1911
Ward, David—hardware, farm
  implements, auctioneer, mayor,
  sheriff, bootlegger, Clare, 1900
Ward, Delos—AEF, Clare, 1900
Ward, Harold—Clare, 1910
Ward, Mabeele—Clare
Ward, Marjorie—Clare
Ward, Richard—Clare, 1916
Ward, Winifred—teacher, Clare
Wardell, C.—Surrey, 1906
Wardell, Joe—Clare
Wardell, William—WWI, 1918
Wardon, Bert—farmer Summerfield
Ware, Alva M.—Arthur, 1912
Warner, Alvin—farmer, Arthur
Warner, Harold E.—Gilmore, 1917
Warner, Henry—farmer, Sheridan
Warner, John D.—Farwell, 1914
Warner, R. M.—Winterfield, 1912
Warner, Walter—stationary
  engineer, Clare, 1914
Warren, Vance—livery barn, Grant
Warson, Benjamin F.—farmer
Warson, Frank—Winterfield
Warson, James—Winterfield, 1900
Waters, Arthur—Vernon, 1914
Watkins, Clara J.—Lake, 1918
Watkins, Frank—farmer, Garfield
Watkins, John—Garfield, 1918
Watkins, N. D.—photographer,
  Civil War Vet, Farwell, 1900
Watson, Dan—telephone company
  worker, Clare, 1915
Watson, Rev. J. A.—Free
  Methodist minister, Clare, 1900
Watt, Ray—WWI, Greenwood
Watzel, Louis—machinist, Harrison
Wayman, Clarence—Garfield, 1917
Weage, Paul D.—Grant, 1917
Weatherhead, Fred W.—Harrison
Weatherhead, Nellie—Harrison
Weatherhead, Nettie—Harrison
Weatherhead, Paul—Harrison, 1918

Weatherwax, W. W.—businessman
Weaver, A. J.—Frost, 1906
Weaver, Arthur—truck driver
Weaver, Barton—farmer, 1912
Weaver, Earl—Farwell, 1918
Weaver, Edith—Brown School, 1909
Weaver, Fred A.—Surrey, 1917
Weaver, F. S.—Arthur, 1914
Weaver, Fred A.—WWI, 1918
Weaver, Irvin—foreman on
  Page Ranch, Frost, 1915
Weaver, W. E.—Frost, 1916
Weaver, W. W.—Crooked Lake
Webb, Vernon—Loomis, 1900
Webb, W. B.—Clare, 1915
Webb, Wm. M.—Civil War
  Vet, Vernon, 1908
Webber, Esther—Greenwood, 1917
Webber, Thomas—bridge builder
Webber, Thomas K.—Greenwood
Webber, William—Greenwood
Weber, Chris—Arthur
Webster, E. E.—farmer, Hatton
Webster, Perry—WWI, 1918
Weckersley, Wm.—pioneer
Wedel, Lewis—Wise, 1917
Weeks, Franklin—Frost, 1909
Weeks, Hazel—Frost, 1911
Weeks, John W.—farmer, Frost
Weeks, Miss Pearl—Frost, 1906
Weiber, H.—farmer, Harrison
Weible, Orlie—bookkeeper,
  Irelands Garage, AEF, Farwell
Weible, R. H.—Farwell, 1914
Weidman, Rev. G. W.—Free
  Methodist minister, Clare, 1910
Weidner, Charles—Harrison, 1912
Weihl, George L.—Wise, 1917
Weihl, Archibal O.—Wise, 1917
Weir, Earl—rancher, Clare
Weir, W. T.—Hamilton, 1906
Weisman, Bert—Farwell, 1907
Weisman, Bernard—Farwell, 1907
Weisman, Bernice—Clare, 1909
Weisman, Edith—Farwell, 1910
Weisman, Libbie—Farwell, 1907
Weisman, Louis—merchant, Farwell
Welch, Annie—Clare, d. 1908
Welch, Ben—Clare, 1903
Welch, Charles—Farwell, 1890
Welch, E. A.—Farwell, 1919
Welch, Edgar—teacher, publisher
Welch, Edward B.—Farwell, 1912
Welch, Emma—teacher, Clare, 1903
Welch, Frank—soldier, Clare, 1900
Welch, Fred A.—Clare, d. 1903
Welch, Harley—Lincoln, 1917
Welch, Henry—Clare, 1903
Welch, James—grocer, butcher
Welch, Johanna—Temple, 1909
Welch, L. E.—r.r., Farwell, 1909
Welch, Leo B.—WWI, U.S. Navy
Welch, Sam—farmer, Gilmore, 1918
Welch, "Tess"—mail carrier
Welch, W. H.—Clare, 1915
Weliden, ____—1915
Wellert, Charles F.—Lincoln, 1917
Wellert, Frederick—Lincoln, 1917
Welling, Jack—Clare, 1903
Wellman, A. M.—Harrison
Wellman, C. A.—Clare

Wellman, Henry, Sr.—Lake George
Wellman, Henry—Lincoln, 1916
Wellman, J. L.—twp. supervisor
Wellman, J. M.—Lincoln, 1906
Wellman, Lela—Lake George, 1903
Wellman, Vira—Lake George, 1903
Wells, Dr. _____—physician, Evart
Wells, Aletha—teacher, Harrison
Wells, George—Clare Furnace Co.
Wells, H. B.—Clare Furnace Co.
Wells, Hazel—Temple, 1909
Wells, J.—Temple, 1903
Wells, John—Temple, 1903
Wells, Rosemary—Temple, 1900
Wells, Sarah—Temple, 1911
Wells, Steve—Temple, 1911
Wells, W. A.—meat market, Clare
Wells, Ward Mason—Clare, 1917
Wells, Willard—Harrison
Wentworth, Anias H.—Grant, 1909
Wentworth, Mary—Clare, 1909
Wentz, Robert—engineer, Farwell
Wesch, Johanna—Temple, 1909
Westfall, Anna—teacher, Clare
Whaley, Grace—Long Lake, 1906
Whaley, R. T.—farmer, postmaster,
  Frost twp. supervisor, Long Lake
Wheaton, Claude—Garfield, 1914
Wheaton, Wallace—farmer, Lincoln
Wheeler, Charles E.—Temple, 1913
Wheeler, C. M.—groceries, Alward
Wheeler, E. B.—farmer, Winterfield
Wheeler, George—farmer, Lincoln
Wheeler, J. B.—Grandon, 1903
Wheeler, M. W.—farmer, Temple
Wheeler, Willard—Winterfield
Wheeler, William—Lincoln, 1908
White, Carl E.—jeweler, Clare
White, Charles—Windover Lake
White, Clyde—Dover, 1903
White, Daniel—Freeman, 1918
White, Earl M.—Clare, 1909
White, Ed. A.—jeweler, Grant
White, Edward—florist, Clare, 1910
White, Edward E.—Clare, 1912
White, Edward J.—Clare
White, Elisha—Farwell, 1918
White, Elizabeth—1915
White, Emmet—pioneer, Farwell
White, Ethel—Clare
White, F. M.—farmer, Freeman
White, Florence M.—Clare, 1915
White, Frank—teacher, Surrey
White, George J.—jeweler, Clare
White, Harold A.—Vernon, 1917
White, Howard—Clare
White, John—engineer, Clare, 1900
White, Julia—teacher, Farwell, 1903
White, O. D.—Freeman, 1914
White, Ruby—Clare, 1910
White, Thomas—Leota, 1912
White, Thomas R.—oil pumper
White, Vernon E.—Wise, d. 1918
White, Walter—farmer, horse trader
Whiteky, Harry—rail clerk, 1905
Witeside, Arthur—Clare, 1901
Whiteside, George W.—farmer
Whiteside, Ola—Clare, 1910
Whitford, E.—farmer, Grandon
Whitford, Tecumseh—Grandon
Whiting, John—Civil War
  Vet, 1912

Whitlock, A. N.—Dover, 1906
Whitlock, Charles—farm machinery
Whitlock, N.—variety Store, Clare
Whitman, Sherman E.—Garfield
Whitney, Alanson—Civil War
  Vet, Clare
Whitney, E. N.—movie house, Clare
Whitney, Edwin—Civil War, Clare
Whitney, M. E.—poolroom, Clare
Whitney, Melanthon—blacksmith,
  Civil War Vet, Clare, 1882
Whitney, Willis L.—Clare, 1912
Whitside, Mabel—Clare
Whittmore, James—farmer
Wicklund, J. V.—Clare
Wickwire, John—coal miner, Clare
Wickman, _____—farmer, Grant
Widener, Charles—Harrison, 1907
Wiebel, Lois—Farwell, 1908
Wier, Earl—Clare, 1913
Wier, Mable—teacher, Clare, 1903
Wier, Wallace T.—pool hall, Clare
Wiggins, Ben—Temple, 1904
Wiggins, David—farmer, Farwell
Wiggins, Edmon—farmer, Farwell
Wiggins, Flavilla—Lincoln, 1909
Wiggins, Isaac—Gilmore, 1914
Wiggins, Richard—Gilmore, 1910
Wiggins, Robert—Surrey, 1906
Wiggins, Wm. I.—Gilmore, 1917
Wilber, Chalres A.—Winterfield
Wilbert, Wm.—Lincoln, 1918
Wilcox, Edson—Summerfield, 1909
Wilcox, George W.—Sheridan, 1917
Wilcox, Sam—Dover, 1903
Wilcox, Dr. Wilford—veterinarian
Wild, Harry—WWI, Vernon, 1916
Wild, Henry—farmer, Vernon, 1889
Wild, Herman—plumber, Clare
Wild, Wilma—Clare
Wild, William—laborer, Clare, 1917
Wilde, Harry—farmer, Clare
Wildman, Elizabeth—Clare
Wildman, G.—1906
Wildman, James—Grant, 1906
Wildman, Hugh—Grant, 1906
Wildman, Samuel—Grant, 1906
Wilds, James—woodsman, Grant
Wiles, Rev. Daniel—minister, Eagle
Wiles, Ross—Winterfield, 1911
Wiley, Aleck—WWI
Wiley, Charles—Clare, 1903
Wiley, Eugene—salesman, Clare
Wiley, Oscar—Clare, 1914
Wilkie, George—butcher, Clare
Wilkins, A. H.—farmer, Farwell
Wilkins, George H.—farmer
Wilkins, L.—Farwell, 1900
Wilkinson, S. A.—implement store
Wille, C.—Grant, 1906
Willit, Edward—automobile
  business, Detroit, 1915
Willey, Albert—1911
Willey, Andrew—WWI, 1918
Willey, Charles F.—P.M.R.R.
Willey, Earl Wm.—Vernon, 1917
Willey, Henry D.—Vernon, 1917
Willey, S. E.—Vernon, 1900
Williams, Rev. _____—minister
Williams, A.—Temple, 1915
Williams, A. F.
Williams, Bart—Sheridan, 1918

Williams, Bert—ship yard, Farwell
Williams, R. Bruce—teacher
Williams, Burt—WWI, 1918
Williams, Charles D.—merchant
Williams, C. F.—heading mill
Williams, Carmen—Clare
Williams, E. L.—Harrison, d. 1909
Williams, Floyd—1903
Williams, Frank—farmer
Williams, Fred H.—Garfield, 1915
Williams, G. A.—Clare, 1903
Williams, Grant—Clare
Williams, Henry—farmer, Hatton
Williams, Kathleen—Clare
Williams, John—P.M.R.R., Farwell
Williams, Joh—WWI, 1918
Williams, Lester—Lake, 1914
Williams, Lyman—Harrison, 1903
Williams, Leota—Clare
Williams, Mary H.—Hayes, d. 1909
Williams, Maud—teacher, Arthur
Williams, Noal—Clare, 1926
Williams, Paul—Arthur
Williams, Pauline—Farwell, 1915
Williams, Philip—Hatton
Williams, R. B.—twp. clerk,
  Sheridan, 1906
Williams, Reynard—lumberjack
Williams, Russell—Arthur
Williams, Spraye—teacher, Harrison
Williams, Varmen—Clare, 1907
Williams, Verlin—auto salesman
Williams, Verne—Harrison, 1903
Williams, Wm.—farmer, Winterfield
Willis, Dennison—mgr. McLaren
  Elevator, Clare, 1915
Willis, John H.—Clare, 1915
Williston, Mary—Clare
Willoughby, R. J.—photographer
Wilson, "Abe", farmer, Greenwood
Wilson, Albert—WWI, Clare, 1917
Wilson, Alex—farmer, Arthur, 1909
Wilson, Allen—WWI, Clare
Wilson, Asa—Wise, 1918
Wilson, Cecil—Vernon, 1917
Wilson, Dan C.—Vernon, 1914
Wilson, Delbert—Clare, 1901
Wilson, Demorest—mechanic, Clare
Wilson, Dr. Earl C.—Harrison
Wilson, Edna—Clare
Wilson, E. F.—real estate, Harrison
Wilson, Ed—Temple, 1909
Wilson, Ethel—Clare
Wilson, Etta—teacher, Clare, 1906
Wilson, Floyd—Vernon, 1893
Wilson, Frank—WWI, Redding
Wilson, George—farmer, Grant
Wilson, George A.—Arthur, 1917
Wilson, George—Leota, 1915
Wilson, George—Temple, 1909
Wilson, G. S.—Harrison, 1916
Wilson, Harvey—Sheridan, 1918
Wilson, Henry—Farwell, 1900
Wilson, J. W.—Freeman, 1918
Wilson, Jacob—Clare, 1918
Wilson, James—farmer, Sheridan
Wilson, James—Freeman, 1914
Wilson, John A.—woodsman
Wilson, John—farmer, Vernon
Wilson, John H.—tailor, Clare
Wilson, John H.—farmer, Clare
Wilson, Joseph—farmer, WWI

Young, Angus—Isabella, 1910
Young, A. S.—postmaster, Harrison
Young, Cecil—Harrison, 1903
Young, Eleanor—Harrison, d. 1907
Young, Electa M.—Hayes, 1912
Young, Holly—farmer, Arthur
Young, Rev. J.—Baptist preacher
Young, Mary E.—d. 1915
Young, Nellie—teacher, Harrison
Young, Samuel—farmer, Grant
Younglove, Rev. W. N.—minister,
    Civil War, Farwell, Clare, d. 1938

Youngs, Mrs. F. O.—Freeman
Zeiter, Samuel—lumberman
Zelinski, Joseph—Grant
Zeller, Audrey—Sheridan, 1907
Zemmer, Edward—auto dealer
Zerbey, Walter—farm laborer, 1914
Zielke, Emil—farmer, Hamilton
Zilka, Adolph—Hamilton
Zilka, Delia—Hamilton, 1917
Zilka, Walter—Hamilton, 1917
Zilky, A.—Hamilton, 1915
Zimmermann, Bertha—Sheridan

Zimmermann, Earl—Arthur, 1910
Zimmerman, Minnie—Clare
Zimmerman, Paul—farmer
Zink, Fred—Redding, 1917
Zink, John—Temple, d. 1937
Zinn, Roger—superintendent, Clare
Zinser, Erwin—laborer, Clare, 1926
Zinser, ____—Clare
Zinser, Katherine—Clare, 1919
Zuschnitt, Verda—teacher, Clare

Index